DISCARDED

DIPLOMAT OF THE AMERICAS

WILLIAM I. BUCHANAN IN 1901

DIPLOMAT OF THE AMERICAS: A BIOGRAPHY OF WILLIAM I. BUCHANAN
(1852-1909)

Harold F. Peterson

State University of New York Press
Albany 1977

Published with assistance from
the Buffalo State College Foundation, Inc.
and
the University Awards Committee
of State University of New York

First Published in 1977 by
State University of New York Press
99 Washington Avenue, Albany, New York 12246

© 1977 State University of New York
All rights reserved

Composed by
Typography Services
Loudonville, New York 12211

Printed in the United States of America

Library of Congress Cataloging in Publication Data

Peterson, Harold F.
Diplomat of the Americas.

Bibliography: p.
Includes index.
1. Buchanan, William I., 1852-1909.
2. United States—Foreign Relations—Argentine Republic.
3. Argentine Republic—Foreign Relations—United States.
I. Title
E664.B885P47   327'.2'0924 [B]   76-22652
ISBN 0-87395-346-0

To
Mary Williams Avery
Hoyt Insco Williams
and
William Grey Williams
who generously granted unrestricted use
of their
grandfather's papers and memorabilia

CONTENTS

List of Illustrations.............................. ix
Preface... xi
Acknowledgments................................ xv

1. Diplomat of the Americas..................... 3
   Prologue
2. Beginnings of Career and Family............... 7
   Ohio, 1852-1882
3. Crocks, Choruses, and Corn Palaces............ 22
   Iowa, 1882-1891
4. Homage to America's Discoverer............... 46
   Chicago, 1890-1894
5. Diplomat in the Making....................... 73
   Argentina, 1894-1895
6. Diplomat in Action........................... 92
   Argentina, 1894-1898
7. Diplomat's Routine........................... 113
   Argentina, 1898-1899
8. Building a World Exposition................... 140
   Buffalo, 1899-1901
9. Homage to a Hemisphere...................... 163
   Buffalo, 1901-1902
10. Promoting the Pan American Spirit............ 192
    Mexico, 1901-1902

11. Diplomat of American Business.................. 211
    Europe and South America, 1902-1903
12. Nursemaid to an Infant Nation.................. 238
    Panama, 1903-1904
13. Back to the World of Business.................. 261
    England and Europe, 1904-1906
14. From Hemisphere Stage to World Arena.......... 278
    Rio de Janeiro and The Hague, 1906-1907
15. Promoting Stability in Unstable Nations.......... 303
    Central America, 1907-1909
16. Claims, Counter Claims, and Arbitration.......... 326
    Venezuela, 1908-1909
17. Pioneer Good Neighbor........................ 346
    Epilogue

Notes.. 356
Bibliography... 407
Index.. 423

ILLUSTRATIONS

William I. Buchanan in 1901   Frontispiece
The Buchanan Papers

ILLUSTRATION SECTION FOLLOWING PAGE 270

Sioux City Corn Palaces, 1887, 1888, 1889, 1890
The Buchanan Papers

World's Columbian Exposition—Ground plan
The Chicago Historical Society

World's Columbian Exposition—Court of Honor
The Art Institute of Chicago

World's Columbian Exposition—Replicas of Columbus's caravels
The Chicago Historical Society

Pan-American Exposition—Ground plan
The Buffalo and Erie County Historical Society

Pan-American Exposition—The Electric Tower
The Buffalo and Erie County Historical Society

Pan-American Exposition—President McKinley addressing audience
The Buffalo and Erie County Historical Society

Pan-American Exposition—The Beck design
The Buffalo and Erie County Historical Society

Elihu Root—Secretary of War and Secretary of State
Pan American Union, Organization of American States

In Argentina with Friends—Buchanan, Mrs. Buchanan,
  Donald, Florence
  The Buchanan Papers

At an Argentine Estancia—Florence Buchanan with her father
  The Buchanan Papers

Second Conference of the International Bureau of American
  Republics, Mexico, 1901-1902—United States delegation
  The Buchanan Papers

Third Conference of the International Bureau of American
  Republics, Rio de Janeiro, 1906—United States delegation
  The Buchanan Papers

Central American Peace Conference, Washington, 1907—
  Buchanan, Enrique Creel, and delegates
  The Buchanan Papers

Inauguration of the Central American Court of Justice,
  Cartago, Costa Rica, 1908—Buchanan, Creel, and judges
  The Buchanan Papers

PREFACE

It was some years ago, while working on Argentine-American diplomatic relations, that I first came across the name of William I. Buchanan, American minister to Buenos Aires in the 1890s. It seemed natural to me at that time to assume that he was just another run-of-the-mill political appointee in the succession of quite undistinguished representatives the Department of State had sent to that emerging South American nation in the nineteenth century. I soon discovered, however, that he was shaped in a different mold.

Exceptional among noncareer diplomats in the American foreign service, Buchanan served under presidents of both major political parties. His three-year record in Argentina during the Democratic administration of President Cleveland persuaded President McKinley to retain him in the post another two years—longer than any other envoy of Democratic persuasion. His demonstrated interests in Argentina's countryside and its pastoral economy, as well as his devotion to literature and the arts, won him the genuine respect of the country's leaders. Their decision to entrust to his mediation a century-old Andean boundary dispute with Chile revealed the confidence he had inspired.

During the following decade, as an emissary-on-call for Secretaries John Hay, Elihu Root, and Philander C. Knox, Buchanan fulfilled sensitive missions for the Roosevelt and Taft administrations. Frequently he was called upon to represent

American interests in Hemisphere trouble spots. Without flourish or acclaim he demonstrated that a nation's foreign policy does not consist solely of presidential pronouncements and foreign office directives. There is also the envoy in the field, who day after day must confront the issues and attempt to resolve apparently unyielding problems. In these years when the inter-American movement was young, Buchanan, as a trusted negotiator who knew the Latin American leaders and appreciated their problems and predilections, made an indelible contribution to the improvement of political and economic relations among Western Hemisphere nations.

As I sought to understand Buchanan's success in inter-American diplomacy, I came to realize how many sided his career had been and how faithfully it mirrored distinctive interests and ambitions of American society in the late nineteenth and early twentieth centuries. As a traveling salesman for cigar and chinaware companies he was among the pioneer drummers who blazed trails to the cities, towns, and whistle-stops of the Middle Western and Plains states. As theater manager he brought good music and Broadway entertainment to the culture-starved people of the Missouri Valley. Through a series of executive positions with local fairs and world expositions, he accentuated their educational value and helped encourage the breeding of thoroughbred livestock and the improvement of agricultural techniques.

Later, in his affiliation with two early transnational corporations, Buchanan participated in the nation's mounting drive to export its ideas of social progress, industrial growth, and commercial development. Notably in the field of life insurance he carried abroad the American doctrine of periodic savings to fulfill the growing quest for personal security. Through continuing advocacy—both in official reports and in personal statements—of an interoceanic canal, a Pan American railroad, American-owned shipping, and branch banks overseas, he epitomized the nation's emerging role as a world power.

By the time I had finished my research and preliminary composition a salient fact about Buchanan's life impressed me: in the shaping of his career all these diverse currents gradually merged to establish him an as integral link in the deepening collaboration between American business and the Department of State. As a diplomat of business he espoused America's overseas commercial expansionism during the Progressive Era. As a State Department representative under four presidents and eight secretaries of state he provided greater continuity than any other Hemisphere diplomat to the early evolution of the inter-American organization.

During his lifetime Buchanan lived and worked in many American cities, and he served his government and his business employers in many Latin American and European countries. I have tried to visit by car and plane all the cities and countries he reached by ship and train. Specifically, I found pertinent data in the collections of the following libraries and archives: Archivo Nacional (Santiago, Chile), Biblioteca Nacional (Buenos Aires, Argentina), British Museum (London), Buffalo and Erie County Historical Society, Buffalo and Erie County Public Library, Butler Library of Columbia University, Chicago Historical Society, Columbus Library of the Pan American Union (Washington), Companies Registration Office (London), Dayton and Montgomery County (Ohio) Public Library, Library of Congress (Washington), National Archives and Records Service (Washington), New York Public Library, Ohio Historical Society (Columbus), *Piqua Daily Call* (Piqua, Ohio), Piqua Public Library, Registry of Business Names (London), Sioux City (Iowa) Public Library, State University College at Buffalo, State University of New York at Buffalo, and Westinghouse Electric Corporation Central Library (East Pittsburgh).

In each of these institutions willing staff personnel responded unfailingly to my requests for data or counsel. Most essential for my purposes were the manuscript collections in the Diplomatic Branch of the National Archives and Records Service (Washington) and the Buffalo and Erie County Historical Society. In Washington two veteran archivists—Mrs. Kieran Carroll and Milton O. Gustafson—protected me from the risk of overlooking documents pertaining to Buchanan's fifteen-year diplomatic service. In Buffalo many staff members, but especially Director Walter S. Dunn, Jr., and Associate Director Lester W. Smith, provided indispensable assistance in facilitating my use of the Buchanan family papers and the Society's extensive records of the Pan-American Exposition.

To verify the accuracy of my information and test the soundness of my interpretations I was fortunate to find four qualified persons willing to assist me. In addition to reading the Ohio chapter, the late A. E. Buchanan of Piqua, Ohio, a distant cousin of William I., guided me through the complicated genealogy of the Buchanan clan. My former collaborator, Watt Stewart, reviewed several chapters with the discerning eye of a Latin American specialist. Through his kindness in locating relevant sources and reading the entire manuscript Lester Smith improved my portrayal of Buchanan's Buffalo connection. From his breadth of interests in American social and intellectual history my colleague Eric Brunger gave me chapter-by-chapter encouragement that served to lift my horizons and sharpen my analysis.

Financial grants from two institutions—the Research Foundation of the State University of New York and the Buffalo State College Foundation, Inc.—assisted me through the various stages of research and publication. I hope the appearance of this volume will adequately express my thanks to the University Awards Committee of the former and to E. K. Fretwell, Jr., College president, Leonard J. Poleszak, chairman, Earle Y. Hannel, director, and other members of the Board of Trustees of the latter.

Throughout my association with the State University of New York Press I received only the most generous consideration from its Editorial Board, its director, Norman Mangouni, and its professional staff members, Mrs. Margaret A. Mirabelli and Mrs. Elnora D. Carrino. For their graciousness and perception I must acknowledge my appreciation.

In typing a final manuscript draft that was almost flawless, as she had done for me on a previous occasion, Mrs. Muriel Kam made more pleasant the work of copy readers and typesetters. With steadfast patience and encouragement, as well as by practical assistance in the humdrum phases of research and proofreading, my wife, Lucille, kept the lengthy project moving comfortably over a steady course.

Buffalo, New York HAROLD F. PETERSON
May 1976

ACKNOWLEDGMENTS

The author is grateful for permission to quote from the following authors and publishers:

Dodd, Mead & Company, New York, for Tyler Dennett, *John Hay: From Poetry to Politics* (1933), by permission of the author's son, Tyler E. Dennett, New Haven, Conn.; Philip Caryl Jessup, *Elihu Root* (1938); and Allan Nevins, *Grover Cleveland: A Study in Courage* (1932).

Harcourt Brace Jovanovich, Inc., New York, for Lloyd Lewis and Henry Justin Smith, *Oscar Wilde Discovers America* [1936], and Henry Fowles Pringle, *Theodore Roosevelt, A Biography* [1931].

Harvard University Press, Cambridge, Mass., for Morton Keller, *The Life Insurance Enterprise, 1885-1910: A Study in the Limits of Corporate Power* (1963); Theodore Roosevelt, *The Letters of Theodore Roosevelt,* sel. and ed. by Elting E. Morison (1951-1954); and Elihu Root, *Latin America and the United States: Addresses by Elihu Root,* ed. by Robert Bacon and James Brown Scott (1917).

Houghton Mifflin Company, Boston, for Henry Adams, *The Education of Henry Adams; An Autobiography* (1918).

The New York Life Insurance Company, New York, for Lawrence Fraser Abbott, *The Story of NYLIC: A History of the Origin and Development of the New York Life Insurance Company from 1845 to 1929* (1930).

Stanford University Press, Stanford, Calif., for Carolina Nabuco, *The Life of Joaquim Nabuco,* trans. and ed. by Ronald Hilton [1950].

University of Alabama Press, University, Ala., Salvatore Prisco III, *John Barrett, Progressive Era Diplomat: A Study of a Commercial Expansionist, 1887-1920* (1973).

DIPLOMAT OF THE AMERICAS

Chapter 1
DIPLOMAT OF THE AMERICAS
Prologue

Next to ELIHU ROOT, he has done more than any North American to develop true Pan-American good will and friendship."[1] With this terse judgment a director general of the International Bureau of the American Republics once epitomized the diplomatic career of William Insco Buchanan.[2]

In large part, Secretary of State Root's image as "the first good neighbor"[3] reflects Buchanan's adept services as roving envoy for the second administration of President Theodore Roosevelt. Between 1906 and 1909, at Root's urgings, Buchanan undertook no less than eight special assignments related to Washington's growing interest in Latin American affairs. He headed the United States delegation to the 1906 Rio Conference of the American States and chaired an American committee to implement its decisions while preparing plans for the Buenos Aires Conference of 1910. As a North American delegate to the Second Hague Peace Conference, he helped introduce the Latin American diplomats to their first world assembly.[4] He represented his government at the 1907 Central American Peace Conference and, as High Commissioner, travelled to Costa Rica for the inauguration of the Central American Court of Justice.[5]

As Root's personal representative, Buchanan negotiated with diplomats of Colombia and Panama to find a tripartite solution of their long-strained relations.[6] To resolve pending claims and restore severed relations with Venezuela in 1909 he labored for two months in Caracas and later prepared an American claims case against Venezuela for presentation at The Hague.[7]

Long before Root's secretaryship, however, Buchanan had established his place as an American diplomat and businessman specializing in Hemisphere affairs. As early as 1894 President Cleveland had appointed him minister to Buenos Aires to invigorate commercial relations with the burgeoning economy of Argentina. Disregarding Buchanan's Democratic leanings, President McKinley retained him in the post two more years. As a climax to this five-year mission, both Argentina and its neighbor Chile accepted his decisive conciliation of a century-old Andean boundary dispute.[8]

Just before and immediately after his assignment in Argentina Buchanan was intimately associated with two world expositions emphasizing the progress and growing interdependence of Western Hemisphere nations. At Chicago's World's Columbian Exposition in 1893 he served as chief of agriculture and of three other key departments.[9] As director general of Buffalo's Pan-American Exposition a few years later, he oversaw its construction and operation from beginning to end.[10] In paying homage, first, to the discoverer of America, then to the Western Hemisphere, he came to know scores of Latin American leaders, grew familiar with their problems, and made himself available to assist their aspirations.[11]

In 1901, as President McKinley and Secretary of State John Hay moved to convene the Second International Conference of the American States in Mexico City, they invited Buchanan's return to the diplomatic service as a key member of the United States delegation.[12] Two years later, when Roosevelt determined to take advantage of revolutionary change in Panama, he unhesitatingly turned to Buchanan as the most qualified diplomat available to establish appropriate contacts with the infant republic and assure American canal-building rights across the Isthmus.[13]

But Buchanan's alternating services to expositions and the Department of State represented only part of his enduring involvement in Latin American affairs. Combining his experience in the dissimilar worlds of business and diplomacy, he developed still a third career; he became what a journalist termed a "diplomat of business."[14] From 1900 until his death he served continuously as full-time or part-time consultant and overseas representative for the New York Life Insurance Company. His primary function in foreign countries was to secure legislation favorable to the investment or underwriting activities of nonnational insurance companies. In visiting Mexico, Brazil, Uruguay, and Argentina, as well as nations of Western Europe, he made full use of his State Department connections to approach presidents, cabinet ministers, and legislative leaders. From time to time Department officials assisted his efforts to expand overseas markets for the American insurance enterprise.[15]

Buchanan's career of service to the cause of inter-American friendship was three-dimensional.

On his last day in office (25 January 1909), while his right-hand man was still on active duty in Caracas, Secretary Root recorded his appreciation of Buchanan. "I leave behind me this letter," he wrote, "for the purpose of saying how highly I have valued your great and effective service for the Government in the numerous questions relating to our Latin American neighbors in regard to which I have called upon you during the past three or four years."[16] In other times and other places diverse Pan American leaders volunteered their own testimonials. A Mexican ambassador to Washington accentuated the American's "great and important services to the noble cause of Pan American unity, friendship, and fraternity to which he is dedicating his energies and talents."[17] A Costa Rican foreign minister lauded him for "his noble and luminous cooperation for the harmony of [the Spanish-American] nationalities."[18] An Argentine minister in Washington reported to Secretary Hay that Buchanan enjoyed "the greatest esteem of the Argentine government for his high intellectual endowments and the precision and uniform tact of his official and private actions."[19] An Argentine president wrote to Buchanan that "all here recognize your rectitude, your honorable character, and your high ideals of intelligent civilized progress."[20] A Washington journalist placed his estimate in global terms: "Probably no diplomat in the world enjoys in so large a measure the confidence of the governments of the large South American states."[21] Clearly these and other Western Hemisphere spokesmen viewed Buchanan as a "diplomat of the Americas."[22]

In view of these contemporary encomiums, William I. Buchanan's career has remained strangely obscure. Yet, few, if any, noncareer diplomats have equalled his record for length of service or number of special assignments. During a period of fifteen years he responded unfailingly to the invitations of four presidents to undertake special missions involving inter-American affairs. As diplomat-on-call, he fulfilled the instructions of eight secretaries of state.[23] Plunged into the vortex of one crisis situation after another, he became an early prototype of Washington's mid-twentieth-century trouble-shooting emissaries.

In a variety of ways Buchanan represents an unlikely figure in the annals of American and Pan American diplomacy. Almost without formal education or training for the foreign service, he rose from an Ohio farm background to the highest councils of the Hemisphere. Though he grew to maturity in the raw frontier of the Middle West, he managed to replace provincial biases with cosmopolitan tastes and points of view. Soon after he abandoned early careers as farm hand and commercial salesman, he achieved a regional reputation as an impresario of public entertainment and, later, Hemisphere fame as division chief or director of world expositions. Through assiduous self-discipline he learned to negotiate in the Latin American languages with foreign diplomats and heads of state. Until he reached the age of thirty-seven he had scarcely heard of Latin America, yet he devoted the rest of his life to the improvement of inter-American relations.

The making of Buchanan's career—from Ohio farm boy to Pan American statesman—is a story uniquely American.

Chapter 2
BEGINNINGS OF CAREER AND FAMILY
Ohio, 1852-1882

It was in the bountiful countryside of Miami County, Ohio, that Buchanan spent the years of his youth and early manhood. Born on 10 September 1852,[1] he joined a plethora of cousins to form the fourth generation of the propagative Buchanan clan to live along the valley of the Great Miami River. There, among gently rolling hills between the villages of Piqua and Covington, he enjoyed the advantages and endured the hardships of any American farm boy growing up in the mid-nineteenth-century Middle West. He inherited the worthy traits of his sturdy Scottish ancestry but not the advantages of wealth, social status, or extended formal education.

The western Ohio region in which the young Buchanan's forebears had settled was rich in historic lore and replete with manifestations of America expanding westward. The area had long been a favorite retreat of Chief Cornstalk's tribe of Shawnee Indians and had known the wandering feet of Miamis, Wyandots, Ottawas, and Delawares. It had been the site of both French and English frontier posts and the scene of one of their last battles for control of interior North America. In his campaigns against the English in 1780 George Rogers Clark had marched across these lands, and at Fort Recovery, only a few miles to the northwest, General St. Clair in 1794 had suffered his defeat by the Indians. General Anthony Wayne, seeking revenge for St. Clair's disaster, had based his campaigns at an outpost on the future site of Covington.[2] Twenty years later, during the War of 1812, General William Henry Harrison had established his headquarters near the settlement soon to be called Piqua. And as the Indians continued to menace frontier settlements, the governor of Ohio had appointed George Buchanan as captain of a volunteer militia company to protect the area. The blockhouse they built near General Wayne's old stockade on the Stillwater River came to be known as Fort Buchanan. George Buchanan was William's great grandfather.[3]

The story of the boy's forebears in the early and middle decades of the nineteenth century blends inseparably with the evolution of the state of Ohio.[4] Within months of its admission to the Union in 1803 George Buchanan had determined to abandon his birthplace near Natural Bridge, Virginia, and join the expanding migration of Scotch-Irish and Germans to the waiting American Eden. Placing his new bride on horseback, he escorted her across the mountains of western Virgina, settled her for a short time in the burgeoning Ohio River port of Marietta, and hurried on to Deerfield, a few miles north of Cincinnati. Stopping barely long enough to attend the birth of their first child—William Insco's grandfather, James Harvey—they soon moved up the valley of the Great Miami River to West Milton in southern Miami County. There, after 1805, as George carved out a career in the wilderness and served as officer in the frontier militia, they raised their growing family.[5]

The land to which this Scottish family[6] had come was destined by nature and man's initiative to become a principal crossroads of Ohio's developing transportation system. Only a few miles to the south the lengthening Cumberland Road would bring wave after wave of pioneers heading westward from Wheeling and the seaboard states.[7] At the same time the configuration of rivers in western Ohio made Miami County a focal spot in the north-south transportation system the state would develop between Lake Erie and the Ohio River. The contiguity of river sources—the Maumee flowing northeastward to Toledo and the Great Miami running southward to Cincinnati—originally assured a short, low portage and then fairly easy canalization. By 1837 Ohio's massive canal-building program enabled packet boats to reach Piqua from Cincinnati. Eight years later the waterway was opened to Lake Erie, and

Piqua prepared to become the principal canal port between Toledo and Dayton.[8]

Meanwhile, in the late 1820s George Buchanan and his eldest son, James Harvey, had established homesteads on the watershed between the Great Miami and Stillwater Rivers seven miles to the west of Piqua and three miles north of Covington.[9] Year by year, as the river valleys filled and roads replaced bear paths and Indian trails, they and the other pioneer families shared in transforming a recent fur-producing forest land into a thriving agricultural region. Soon they began to see Miami County's corn, flour, bacon, linseed oil, lumber, and furniture move out by flatboat and barge to the Ohio River and Lake Erie waterways. By midcentury Piqua had grown into a bustling commercial and manufacturing center with a population of more than three thousand. Its strategic location made it a natural transshipment point for heavy goods from eastern cities and local produce destined for distant markets. Its port facilities often "teemed with canal boatmen and travelers." The town now boasted waterpower for its new mills and factories and telegraphic connections with the outside world. Soon street lights, express services, and railway transport were available as well.[10]

But seven miles to the west, amid the verdant groves along Trotter's Creek, these developments in Piqua had little immediate effect upon the lives of James Harvey Buchanan and his wife Joanna, or upon their children and grandchildren. Like his father and other pioneer settlers, James Harvey had cleared a few acres, fitted the logs for a one-room cabin, and made most of the furniture to render it livable. Then, to accommodate his wife's needs and provide living space for their growing brood, he added one room after another, built a second story, and surrounded the rambling structure with spacious porches. Here in the 1830s and 1840s, close to the soil and the out-of-doors, the Buchanans raised their six children. Their second born was George Preston, whose marriage to Mary Eliza Gibson would soon add another grandchild—William Insco—to the proliferating George Buchanan clan in Ohio.[11]

Long before William's birth in 1852 his grandparents had established a firm place in the farmland community between

Piqua and Covington. Through acts of hospitality and neighborliness to fellow settlers they had demonstrated their devotion to friends and fondness for children. James Harvey's commitment at age seventeen to the Christian faith led him to support any public enterprise that might promote the spiritual, as well as the educational and financial, welfare of his community.[12]

For James Harvey's offspring the big house he had built with his own hands became the focal point of their work, play, and family loyalty. But especially for grandson William the Trotter's Creek farm place became a true home during most of his childhood and adolescent years. Orphaned at age eight, the boy grew up under the stern but enlightened tutelage of his grandparents.[13] However close to the raw wilderness they had entered or to the brash civilization relentlessly replacing it, the Buchanan household developed and maintained an aura of gentility and self-respect. This was the ambience in which the orphaned William spent most of his early years: guided by a grandfather who personified traits of courage, industry, piety, and dignity; indulged and cherished by a grandmother who managed the affairs of a home often filled with relatives, friends, and guests; and stimulated by a social atmosphere that emphasized learning, aesthetic appreciation, artistic expression, and good breeding.[14]

Unfortunately, contemporary family records do not exist to depict the day-to-day, or even the year-to-year, growth of George Preston's eldest child. In later years, however, as exposition manager and diplomat, he developed the habit of using family letters and public speeches to reminisce about his early experiences on the Trotter's Creek farm. In these he presented a plausible picture of his youthful years of work, play, and education, both formal and informal.

Early in his youth William began to experience the trials and woes of life on the farm. Like his contemporaries, sometimes cajoled into disagreeable jobs by "big, lazy men," he felt he always received the most irksome of the work crew tasks. At threshing times, placed behind the big machine to put away the straw, he found his eyes filled with dust and his perspiring flesh irritated by blowing chaff. In haying season, assigned to tramp the fodder in the suffocating mow, his bare feet "found all the thorns" and his bare head "all the nails in the roof." When log-rolling operations got under way, he "always got the short end of the handspike." On frosty mornings he was first out to rout up the cows for milking. Between these team jobs there was always wood to chop, fruit to pick, or a garden to weed.[15]

At the same time, while displaying youthful distaste with these daily and seasonal chores, he fell back upon his own resourcefulness to discover the joys of his rural environment. By day he wandered in the woods with dog and gun; by night he joined coon hunts. In summer he revelled in the Trotter's Creek swimming hole a few yards from the big house; in winter he enjoyed sleigh rides to distant spelling contests. At the appropriate season he found special delight in sugar-making and in corn huskings and apple peelings, with their opportunities to sit near one's favorite girl. And each summer, as if to remind the young boy of encroaching civilization, his grandparents took him to Piqua for circus day.[16]

Besides his familiarity with the routine operations of a frontier farm, Buchanan developed skills in identifying the local trees and flowers, fish and fowl, animals and insects. He could sympathize, he once said, with a popular poet of the 1890s, Eugene Field, when he wrote

> I once knew all the birds that came
>   And nested in our orchard trees;
> For every flower I had a name—
>   My friends were woodchucks, toads, and bees; . . .
> I knew the spot upon the hill
>   Where checkerberries could be found,
> I knew the rushes near the mill
>   Where pickerel lay that weighed a pound![17]

But, whatever his woes or joys in these early years, an older Buchanan would come to place a high value on what he called his outdoor training in Miami County. Speaking to a Chicago assembly of farmers in 1893, he assured them that "I would not trade the outside education I picked up in the country for all the college lore you could pile before me."[18] In similar vein he would tell a New York audience, "I would not exchange the recollections of that time for the boyhood of any city bred youngster."[19]

The rugged outdoor life to which his grandfather had introduced him, Buchanan came to feel, helped to account for his health in youth and contributed to the unflagging industry and inexhaustible energy of his mature years.[20] At the same time, he would one day remind his son, once the day's work was over, however begrimed and disheveled, he bowed to his grandmother's insistence on a clean body and tidy grooming. "I know it always made me feel much greater self confidence as a boy when I had my boots blackened and a clean rig on my back."[21]

But James Harvey Buchanan believed in indoor education and self-instruction as well as outdoor training and by his own example provided intellectual stimulation to his children and grandchildren. Around the family fireside he gave them the benefit of his varied interests. Here he entertained itinerant preachers, conducted prayer meetings, and indulged his lifelong habit of reading and writing. Fostering his curiosity about the literature of the day, he read and reread his favorite authors. He developed a strong love of poetry and his conversation sparkled with his selections of favorite lines. Sometimes perhaps the quotations were his own, for, one descendant remembered, he could compose verse while "pushing the plane, following the plow, or garnering the ripened grain."[22] From these sessions in the home William absorbed his grandfather's ardor for quoting poetry, telling stories, and commenting on favorite topics.

Whether at family prayer meetings or regular church services, visiting preachers brought in news of the outside world as well as familiar religious messages. On occasion, however, during long sermons, young Buchanan's thoughts would stray to the pleasures awaiting him beyond church walls. He would long remember the "delightful sensation [he] used to feel as a boy when a tiresome Trotter's Creek preacher would reach that part of his inflictions on the delights to be had outside in the drowsy summer sunshine, when he said, 'and now, lastly brethern [sic]!'"[3]

For his more formal indoor education Buchanan had access only to the traditional country school of the mid-nineteenth-century West. Along the dusty roads of autumn and through the snows of winter and mud of spring he tramped a mile and a half each morning in search of whatever instruction awaited him. Stimulated during these years both by his grandfather's example and by his school experience, he developed a deep enthusiasm for books and magazines. He became enamored with *Ivanhoe, Kenilworth,* and other Scott novels, but, grudging the need to read every line to follow the plot, he balked at too much of Dickens. Early in his youth he cultivated the habit of reading himself to sleep at night, a practice he would continue throughout his life.[24]

Sometime in the late 1860s or early 1870s Buchanan determined to forsake his grandparents' benevolent paternalism. Impelled perhaps by growing dissatisfaction with the farmer's life or perhaps by some inner compulsion to make his own way, he set out to try his hand at other careers. Wandering westward into Indiana, he took up the craft of edge-tool making and settled for a time at Delphi to work at the blacksmithing trade. By 1874, evidently attracted by the possibility of a career in government, he had made his way to Indianapolis. There for some months he served as engrossing clerk of the Indiana State Legislature.[25]

In late 1875 attachment to his native state or perhaps the vagaries of Indiana patronage politics led Buchanan to return to Ohio. Settling now in Dayton, thirty miles south of his former home, he found a city rapidly establishing itself as a manufacturing and distributing center. Its canal facilities and nine railroads attracted a steady flow of both capital and enterprise for the establishment of a wide variety of factories, mills, machine shops, and foundries. With its population approaching forty thousand, and these largely of the working class, Dayton offered solidity and stability to a young man seeking employment opportunities.[26] Buchanan took a job as sales representative for a rising young Dayton firm, Miller Brothers, manufacturers of cigars and wholesale dealers in plug, fine cut, and smoking tobaccos.[27]

In his first years as salesman Buchanan carried his sample cases to regions within comfortable reach of Dayton—northwestern Ohio, central and northern Indiana, southern Michigan. Later, however, as the company expanded its production, he travelled as far as Pittsburgh and western Pennsylvania, northern and central Illinois, and even to the remote Lake Huron shores of Michigan. Often his field trips would last three or four weeks, with visits to at least one, sometimes two or three, cities or towns each day.

Even as his market horizons continued to expand, Buchanan preferred to keep Dayton as the base of his operations. After the early months of 1876, however, it was more than location of the Miller Brothers factory that drew him back. The added allurement was the attractive daughter of a widely known artist, John Insco Williams. A pioneer in panoramic painting, Williams had conceived an imaginative tableau of Biblical history, with scenes from the creation to the fall of Babylon. When in 1850 it was destroyed by fire in Independence Hall, Philadelphia, he executed another that covered four thousand yards of canvas and arranged to exhibit it throughout the country.[28]

Williams's wife, too, was an artist of more than local repute and his eldest daughter, Mrs. Eva Best, was a composer, dramatist, illustrator, and, as story teller, a writer for national publications. She contributed articles to the *Dayton Journal,* the *Cincinnati Times-Star,* and the *Detroit Free Press* and stories to such prestigious magazines as *Frank Leslie's, Godey's,* and *Peterson's.*[29] But it was a younger daughter, Lulu, her reputation as an artist still to make, who captured the twenty-four-year-old Buchanan's attention. After two years of courtship they were married on 16 April 1878.[30]

During the next four years Buchanan tried to make the best of a job that did not please him or offer sufficient challenge to his intellectual and aesthetic inclinations. In frequent letters to his young bride he tried to portray the troubles and discomforts of his life as commercial traveller as well as the interests and hobbies he was seeking to nurture. He also revealed his evolving views of politics, his concept of proper family relations, and the character of his personal development.

Even in the late 1870s, Buchanan learned, transportation schedules and small-town hotel accommodations in the states of the Old Northwest Territory were not geared to oblige the travelling man. Meeting the scheduled stops of his town-by-town itineraries often meant arrival after midnight or departure before sunrise. The hotels were usually primitive, the food indifferent. When utilizing boat travel, as he sometimes did from Toledo to Detroit or from Bay City to the northern Michigan logging town of Alpena, hail, snow, or wind storms might delay his movements.[31] Even southern Michigan, to Buchanan's surprise, had not yet been wholly civilized. On one trip to Grand Rapids he reported sighting bears at the edge of settlement and enjoyed good deer and wildcat hunting in the adjacent woods. But not all layovers in small towns were as satisfactory and the recent bridegroom complained to his wife of empty Sundays that stimulated sulky moods.[32]

In the larger cities, however, Buchanan gave free play to his unslaked interest in literature and the performing arts. Regularly while on the road he purchased new books, both contemporary and classic, read them quickly, and sent them on to Mrs. Buchanan. On one occasion in a small Michigan town he paid forty-six cents for a copy of Dante so that he could get his "mind down to read something that will benefit a mortal a little."[33] "Books are my delight and hobby," he confided to his wife, "I think . . . that the only real ambition of my life is to have an elegant library. . . . I should like to be able when I grow older to recall with pleasure the things I have read and to be able to converse intelligently on general topics."[34]

Like his grandfather in Miami County, Buchanan let his literary tastes range widely—historical themes, current topics, fiction, sometimes even whimsey. Because he had always wished to know more of England and its history, he read George Otto Trevelyan's *Early History of Charles James Fox* and Justin McCarthy's *Short History of Our Own Times.* Because he wanted to learn the facts about modern Spiritualism rather than accept the "popular superstitions" about it, he bought a copy of W. D. Howells's *The Undiscovered Country.* He enjoyed Henry James's *A Bundle of Letters* and Richard D. Blackmore's *Christowell.* He thought Sir Edwin Arnold's *The Light of Asia* "the finest thing I have read." When books were not available, he resorted to his favorite periodicals—*Harper's, Scribner's, Century,* and *St. Nicholas.* Occasionally he enjoyed an issue of *Puck.*[35]

Buchanan's thirst for music and drama was less easily gratified. Yet each business trip to Detroit, Chicago, or Toledo assured his attendance at a symphony concert or an operetta performance. He became an early enthusiast for Gilbert and Sullivan and only months after their English premières he saw English casts in performances of *The Sorcerer, H. M. S. Pinafore,* and *Pirates of Penzance.* Though *Pirates* became his favorite, he bought the score of *The Sorcerer* and alerted his wife to prepare for "some jolly music" upon his next homecoming. He trained himself to evaluate operatic voices, recognize symphonic movements, and follow the themes carried by orchestral instruments. While less fortunate in his chances to enjoy serious drama, he often expressed his eagerness to see Sarah Bernhardt, Edwin Booth, and other leading stage figures of the day.[36]

His repeated one-night stops and weekend layovers gave Buchanan the time to satisfy another evolving urge—to sample the religious, historical, and intellectual resources of the cities and towns of the Middle West. In a serious effort to clarify his own theology, he attended Sunday services of different denominations and endeavored to inform himself about Unitarianism, Buddhism, Spiritualism, the Shakers, and the activities of the Jesuits. Once, however, he declared that he had no desire to go to church unless "the music is exceptionally fine or better yet the minister an able one." His interest in history kindled by his grandfather, Buchanan made special efforts to visit Lincoln's tomb in Springfield, Illinois, Grant's home in Galena, and other local or national shrines. He attended lectures by Robert Ingersoll and other famed speakers as well as numerous political rallies for the 1880 presidential candidates.[37]

In his many letters to his wife, no topic so absorbed Buchanan as did the 1880 presidential campaign. His travels from town to town gave him opportunity to measure the appeal of the candidates and the pulse of the voters. In periodically detailing his findings, he also revealed the metamorphosis of his own political inclinations.

When in early June the Republicans nominated James Garfield, Buchanan was sure that the candidate would not "stand the scorching criticism he will get as his record is not invulnerable [and] if the Democrats are prudent and use good careful judgment they can name the next President." Clearly

Buchanan approved the Democrats' judgment, for he thought General Winfield S. Hancock "without spot or blemish and the one man against whom the arrows of calumny will fall helpless from the bow." Without reservation he predicted that the Democrats would carry New York and Indiana, along with the Solid South, to win the presidency.[38]

But very soon, as newspapers began their partisan attacks, he deplored the "low filthy spirit" to which they appealed. "In either party," he wrote, "[I] despise the paper that has the guttersnipes' appetite for a diseased lying imagination." By election eve, "heartily sick of this political caldron," he expressed the wish that "a new party would spring up with new thoughts . . . a party that has progressive ideas." He believed that such a party should stand for lower tariffs, the free ballot, no employer coercion of employees, nonimportation of Chinese laborers, and support of younger candidates, "whose ideas are of the present and future and not fossilized things [like] the Dred Scott Decision . . . and all such old time graveyard issues."[39]

Once the election results became clear, Buchanan could only acknowledge that "the majority rules in this country and if they want Garfield why they can have him and be blowed." In a more temperate post-mortem comment, however, he spelled out one of the special benefits he had envisioned in Hancock's election—what he termed "the disintegration of the Southern States on local matters." Could that be brought about, he argued, "the Negro would become a factor in politics and not a cipher and then he would get his rights and be treated more considerately. I feel that is the only solution of the Southern question."[40]

Even in his disappointment with Hancock's defeat and while acknowledging "our worst party corruption," Buchanan retained his confidence in the American political system. From his current reading of eighteenth-century English politics, he concluded that "public life now is simply perfection . . . Elysium compared to those times when even Lord Chesterfield went to a broker and offered 2800 pounds for a seat in Parliament for his son."[41]

But pursuit of these diverse interests, hobbies, and ideas was peripheral to the main purposes of Buchanan's six years of travelling. Day after day he called upon wholesalers and retailers to market his cigars and tobacco products. On a good business day he might sell 6,000 cigars and net $20-$30. Once he reported exceptional daily sales of 20,000 and a weekly total of 52,000, but a daily order for 2,000, with commission of $10, was far more usual.[42]

Supporting his wife and Dayton household on his salesman's commissions was never easy. "Hope to get out of debt some time on Earth" was his frequent plaint. When he forwarded funds for living expenses, he usually accompanied them with detailed suggestions on which debts should be paid. "I enclose you P.O. order for 6.00. You can pay your mamma 5.00 on board and pay the washing and you will have 50 cts to spend." At another time a money order for $12 was intended to cover an even greater variety of obligations: sewing machine repairs, $1.50; butter, $1.12; steak, $.30; building association, $.75; and the balance for board, washing, and personal expenses.[43] By switching his wares from tobacco to whisky, he once acknowledged to his wife, "I could get a very considerable larger salary but I dont want to ever get to that point."[44]

Coping with family finances was only one of the problems Buchanan faced in trying to create a happy marital relationship while pursuing a drummer's career. Occasionally during their first year of marriage Mrs. Buchanan accompanied her husband on one or another of his regular beats. She learned to share and appreciate the frustrations as well as the pleasures of his peripatetic occupation. With the coming of their first child, however, on 23 September 1879, these joint expeditions ceased.[45]

In a variety of ways during the next two and a half years, especially through his frequent letters and acts of thoughtfulness, Buchanan tried to bridge the geographic gap. Aware of his wife's loneliness, he encouraged her to travel to Cincinnati or other cities and consciously to cultivate new friendships. "I believe one can become so neglectful of society," he mused, "as to finally drop out of sight and then time passes rather slowly I should think."[46] From time to time he bought her new hats, one "at the toniest place in Detroit," and repeatedly urged her to decide on new dresses. "I want you to be as handsomely dressed as anyone [because] you were born for a modiste."[47] To animate her artistic talents, he sent her easels, painting materials, and instruction books, as well as operetta scores and piano sheet music.[48]

It was to ways of assuring the compatibility of their minds, however, that Buchanan devoted his primary thoughts. Besides sending her the books and magazines he had read, he forwarded a steady stream of newspaper clippings, especially editorials, poems, and reviews.[49] Through his commentaries and recommendations he revealed the maturing of his own mind as well as the directions he hoped hers would take. For his own intellectual standards, he wrote, he had gradually arrived at certain guiding principles:

> I am willing to investigate anything that has for a foundation an inherent look of reason and common sense.
>
> An atom of fact, an item of positive science, is worth a ton of theory and speculation.
>
> I expect to devote the balance of my life to more general study that will benefit me and to live for my wife and baby.[50]

His sermonets for Mrs. Buchanan were permeated with the nineteenth-century ideal of mutual improvement:

> What improves one of us ought to improve the other. Our letters, our conversation, and our readings are all we have and I hope we will be able to make more of them.
>
> Give me your ideas of men and matters on which you read. Thus we gain an insight into each other's thoughts more than any other way.
>
> Let us draw each other out and make our selves keener and sharper for the contact of our minds.[51]

In focusing upon his wife's welfare and happiness Buchanan did not neglect thoughts for their young daughter, Florence, or "Binnie" as they came affectionately to call her.[52] Even more now than in the past he longed for employment that would end his perpetual travelling and permit permanent reunion with his family. In imaginative moments he dreamed of their moving to New York, where he could appease his own growing ardor for music and drama and where his wife could study in a school of design and their daughter receive the best education. His earlier visits to Philadelphia for the Centennial Exposition and to New York for Broadway plays had stimulated his interest in the advantages of metropolitan residence.[53] But in a more realistic mood, reflecting his background of twenty-eight years, he wished he might enter some retail business in Dayton so that they could begin to consider plans for building their own home.[54]

When the opportunity for change appeared, however, it came from a source he had not anticipated and involved adjustments he had not foreseen. To improve the family's income, they would go, not east as he had fantasied, but west, where he knew they would find "the hospitality and charm of the Western people."[55] It was his brother-in-law, J. K. Prugh, husband of Mrs. Buchanan's sister Mamie, who persuaded the younger man to join his mercantile venture in the growing West. In his youth Prugh had moved with his parents from Cincinnati to Burlington, Iowa, then to Ottumwa, where as an errand boy he had developed an interest in the chinaware business.[56] Early in 1881 he had shifted to Sioux City to set up a dealership in crockery, china, glassware, and queensware. By buying his stock direct from manufacturers and avoiding middlemen, Prugh hoped that his firm's reduced prices would attract purchasers of hotel and bar goods from Sioux City's expanding market area. Buchanan could soon turn his experience in selling cigars in the Old West of Ohio, Indiana, Illinois, and Michigan to the selling of crockery in the New West of Iowa, Nebraska, and Dakota.[57]

By the time the Buchanans had determined to abandon their native state and test their fortune in western Iowa, Will was approaching his thirtieth year. Though his experience as commercial traveller had often left him frustrated and dissatisfied, still unsettled on a permanent career, he had developed aptitudes and cultivated tastes that would be of indispensable service in future undertakings. In tracing and retracing his circuits through the heartland of the Middle West he had come to know the region. He had learned to deal with people of diverse religions and national origins and to diagnose the factors that shaped popular reactions. Through endless discussions with merchants and frequent attendance at public lectures and political rallies he had increased his understanding of local and national issues.

His lonesome evenings and weekends in dreary hotel rooms, especially after his marriage, had fostered in him the practice of self-examination. He sought to improve the orderliness and acuteness of his mental powers. Through study and observation he tried to develop his "capacity for detail" and to improve his abilities to distinguish fact from phantasm, "to dissect character," and to exercise "a cool critical judgment."[58] Through diversified reading he taught himself to recognize writings that were "scholarly and polished," that marshalled "adroit and powerful argument," and that embodied an "inherent look of reason and common sense." While admitting his own "glaring inconsistencies [and] imperfect and lame ideas," he deplored what he called the "impolitic ideas and reasonings" of some candidates for public office and the "arrant humbug" and "twaddle" of certain religious teachings.[59]

Important to him as was this self-disciplining of the mind—for his wife as well as for himself—he never minimized the essential contribution to well-rounded personalities of properly developed aesthetic tastes. Yet, however skeptical of the cultural opportunities they might find in Sioux City, they had made the decision to risk the gamble. Clearly, dispensing chinaware in the Missouri Valley would satisfy neither his aesthetic nor his professional ambitions, but established residence in a frontier boom town, both the Buchanans soon came to realize, held latent opportunities they had not even envisioned.

Chapter 3
CROCKS, CHORUSES, AND CORN PALACES
Iowa, 1882-1891

The northwestern corner of Iowa to which the Buchanans transferred their home in the early 1880s was barely a generation removed from raw wilderness. Only in the 1840s had the last of the Sacs, Foxes, and other Siouan tribes moved beyond the Missouri River to new hunting grounds on the Great Plains. At midcentury, buffalo, elk, and deer still roamed the unplowed prairies, bear and wolf prowled the unexploited woodlands, and beaver and otter swam the unbridged rivers. Chokeberries and wild pears continued to thrive.[1]

Along most of Iowa's western boundary the mighty Missouri drained virgin soil of almost inexhaustible fertility. Within fifty miles of the river no plowshare had yet turned sod in the rich earth that would shortly begin to produce fantastic yields of Indian corn. As the Missouri flows from the northwest to form the Iowa-Nebraska boundary, roughly halfway between southern Minnesota and Omaha, it veers directly eastward for several miles. Here, on the northern or Iowa shore, between the mouths of the Big Sioux and Floyd Rivers, the land rises sharply from the water's edge, the only point in Iowa where bluffs contain the channel of the Missouri. As much by chance probably as by plan, this short river escarpment with a southern exposure became the site of western Iowa's first important settlement, Sioux City.

Beyond its choice elevated position, an unusual coalescence

of natural advantages ensured Sioux City's emergence as one of the early boom towns of the Missouri Valley. In the heart of corn country, half way between Chicago and Denver and on direct route between the Twin Cities and Omaha, it became a logical gateway to the Great Plains and a jumping-off point for the Black Hills and the still-untamed Northwest. Its river location gave it access to Omaha, Kansas City, St. Louis, and the Mississippi. In these circumstances the inevitable growth of corn-hogs and plains-cattle economies would exalt Sioux City to what its loyal boosters in the 1880s chose to call the "Peerless Princess of the Plains."[2]

Its nascent years foretold something of the boom decades that would follow. Though in 1855 it contained but a few log cabins and a tent store, a village population of a hundred or so was on hand the following June to welcome the first steamboat bearing needed supplies. Before the end of 1856 Sioux City had been designated county seat of Woodbury County, a land office had been opened, and the first sermon preached. Within another year enterprising citizens, now numbering more than five hundred, had created a board of education, started a school, founded a newspaper, organized two churches, and taken steps to incorporate their village. The inauguration in 1857 of horse-powered ferry service across the Missouri and the early development of fur trade with the Indians suggested the eagerness and resourcefulness with which citizens moved into the jobbing and mercantile trade — a preliminary focus of Sioux City's growing prestige throughout the Missouri Valley.

Early in its history the area's natural advantages were seen to be as ideal for rail connections as for water transport. When the village was first plotted in 1854, not a single steel rail existed in the state of Iowa, yet within less than two decades, in spite of the Civil War, Sioux City gained access to the direct rail service from Duluth on the Great Lakes to Galveston on the Gulf of Mexico and by varied outlets to both the Atlantic and Pacific coasts. Before 1880 Sioux City would become the railroad center of northwestern Iowa.[3]

From the very outset the settlement reflected both the religiosity and the ethnic diversity of its pioneer citizens. Its 3,000 residents of 1870, or 7,500 of 1880, found little difficulty in organizing or affiliating with churches of their traditional faiths. In the 1880s diverse ethnic colonies—Danes, Norwegians, Swedes, Africans, Germans, and French—established congregations for their numbers. But, like any frontier or river town experiencing the fever of bustling growth, Sioux City also attracted its share of rowdy and bawdy elements. River boats and trains brought a steady stream of adventurers, goldseekers, and gamblers headed for Dakota and Montana and military men detailed for action against the Indians. Already by 1871 its citizens could boast of or regret two beer gardens, nine liquor stores, and thirty-four saloons (one for each ninety inhabitants).

This was the Sioux City to which Buchanan chose to move in February 1882 and to which he brought his wife and young daughter three months later[4]—a growing, wide-open town preparing to take off on a decade of fabulous growth that would quintuple its population to 40,000 by 1890. This was the frontier community to which he also brought his experience as commercial salesman, his developing sense of the importance of human relations, and his self-taught interest in the arts and civic affairs. As he took advantage of his new opportunities, the maturing of the man would parallel the flowering of the city.

The Ohioan's first impressions of the swelling Iowa town were, at best, decidedly mixed. Though pleased with its business prospects, he wrote to his wife, it is "a beastly place in every other sense . . . one big black mudhole."[5] While approving the general surroundings of the residential area, he despised the monotonous types of houses available for rental. After sampling Sunday services at Congregational, Catholic, and other churches, he "was not too impressed too profoundly with the people" he saw, though he confessed his ideals might be too high. He found his boarding house unclean, its "hash foundry" offerings cheerless, and its blustery proprietress a woman who talked with a "roar like the echoes of eternal thunder." On the other hand, he was enthusiastic about the town's clear air and magnificent vistas, especially those from Prospect Hill westward up the Missouri River—scenes appropriate, he recommended to his wife, for her sketching.

But however stimulating he found the surrounding atmosphere and panoramas, Buchanan quickly formed a low estimate of Sioux City's level of aesthetic sensitivity. "I am somewhat impressed with the belief from what I see," he confided to Mrs. Buchanan, "that this place has less culture than any place of the size I can remember of seeing in my natural life." At the time of his arrival, the city's only theater—the Academy of Music, opened in 1870—was featuring a touring stock company whose repertoire included such dramas as *Bertha, the Sewing Machine Girl, Honeymoon, or How to Rule a Wife,* and *Peril, or Love at Long Branch.* Yet had he looked forward to the theater's listing of "coming attractions," he might have anticipated the prospect of hearing the Holman English and the Fay Templeton Star Opera Companies and of seeing Lawrence Barrett in *Hamlet* and *Richelieu.*[6]

In any case, within a month of his arrival in Sioux City Buchanan made the most of his opportunity to hear Oscar Wilde's celebrated lecture on "The English Renaissance." In planning his extensive cross-country lecture tour from New York and Boston to Denver, Leadville, and the Pacific Coast, the D'Oyly Carte Company booked the English aesthete for a one-night stand in Sioux City. Strangely, perhaps, Wilde greatly enjoyed the Iowa countryside's "brown prairies so somber and lovely" and warmly praised the intelligence of Sioux City's audience of "working people."[7] On the other hand, in reviewing Wilde's performance, the *Sioux City Journal* was blatantly derisive. To its critic, "the apostle of aestheticism [was] a spiritless namby-pamby nondescript [and] a caricature on robust manhood. . . . We have seen Oscar, and if art is responsible for the like of him, we want no art in ours."[8]

Once he heard of the Englishman's approaching visit, the Ohio newcomer determined to hear him. Immediately after the lecture he penned a detailed report to his Dayton family. "I must not allow myself to go to bed until I tell you of Oscar Wilde. I have just come home from hearing him, and I was well paid for going. His lecture was real good and was a practical plea for the beautiful in Life." Buchanan was undisturbed by the speaker's ineffective voice ("just about such a one as mine"), his poor enunciation, his queer delivery, or his Cockney "wail." Nor was his sensitivity offended by the velvet cutaway, the knee breeches, the lace ruffles, and the white kid gloves. "After a short while listening you become used to his appearance and it doesn't bother." Moreover, the evening's experience seemed to vindicate Buchanan's earlier judgment of Sioux City's cultural tone, for "the audience numbered about 150," he wrote, "and was just as I had expected a fair sample of what the town as a place of culture is."[9]

But during his first months of Iowa residence enjoyment of what he felt to be Sioux City's meager cultural attractions and concern for its aesthetic tastes were quite peripheral to Buchanan's daily routine. In seeking to consolidate his place with J. K. Prugh & Company, he worked long hours to master the diverse aspects of the wholesaling business in a booming frontier community: unpacking shipping crates, checking invoices, attending correspondence, meeting the trade, learning the qualities of fine wares like Haviland and Limoges china, painting signs for posting the country roads, and making preparation for the selling trips he would soon be taking to distant parts of Nebraska and Dakota. Equally pressing was the problem of selecting living quarters for his family. In a steady stream of letters to Dayton, he advised Mrs. Buchanan of the alternatives, consulted her wishes, and reported developments.[10]

With the reuniting of their family in late May and first settling into a home with the Prughs, the Buchanans could move into their new world, with its new way of life, and, to some degree, a new kind of people. In spite of his earlier reservation about the gentility of Sioux City people, William, and his wife as well, promptly established happy contacts; townspeople acknowledged and gratefully utilized their artistic talents in community activities. Almost at once the Ohioans became an integral part of the Iowa city's commercial and recreational growth and remained so throughout the booming eighties.

Though choosing membership in the First Baptist Church and sharing fully in its activities, the family displayed a kind of nineteenth-century ecumenical spirit. Will's "fine tenor voice," as the local music critics recurrently described it, quickly won him a steady role in the church's mixed quartet, which over the years appeared at diverse religious and civic functions. He became the leader of the Baptist Church Music Club and frequently served as soloist and music consultant for the choir of the St. Mary's Catholic Church. When groups like the GAR or the Knights Templar gathered in formal or informal assembly, he usually received the call to lead the group singing. From time to time Lulu contributed her soprano voice to her husband's choral direction and often donated hand-painted art objects to the fairs and bazaars of the Methodist Episcopal and other churches. When in 1885 Sioux City leaders planned memorial services for General Grant, it was Buchanan who chaired the committee on music, speedily organized a chorus of 125 voices, and directed the singing of such appropriate selections as "He Watching Over Israel" from *Elijah* and Julius Eichberg's national hymn "To Thee, O Country." It was "the largest and finest chorus ever organized in the state," editorialized the *Journal,* "a revelation of the musical resources of Sioux City."[11]

With his home established, his family made comfortable, and his social contacts secured, Buchanan could turn to what was probably his most essential contribution to the commercial success of J. K. Prugh & Company—bringing its wares to the attention of prospective customers throughout Sioux City's potential market area. Intermittently during the next half dozen years he carried his catalogs and his samples to the developing towns of western Iowa, northern Nebraska, and southern Dakota. His normal routine consisted of town-by-town stops along the main routes and feeder lines of the new transcontinental roads, the Northwestern and the Chicago, Milwaukee, and St. Paul. As in his earlier selling years, he fretted at times over frequent nighttime travel or a succession of 2:00 or 3:00 A. M. departures from wayside stations. Once, to make a connection, he pumped a hand car eleven miles. Even more exhausting were his travels by horse or horse-drawn conveyance, sometimes up to thirty miles a day, to reach towns not served by rail.

Despite the fatigue and loneliness his travels invariably produced, Buchanan had long since learned to squeeze personal benefit from new contacts and fresh experiences. In visits to frontier towns of ethnic individuality, he sought to understand and adjust to the distinctive traits of Scottish, Russian, German, Scandinavian, and other immigrant colonies. From time to time, as opportunity presented, he attended a church service, enjoyed a travelling circus, or patronized home-talent entertainment. Once again he began reading regularly, a habit he had somewhat neglected since his cigar-selling days.[12]

Long evenings in small-town hotels gave the Sioux City drummer opportunity to renew a penchant developed in the first years of his marriage—what he described as his "profession of writing long love letters." "I can I think make the lead pencil talk," he once wrote from Sioux Falls, Dakota Territory, "(something would break if I could not talk somehow)." At the same time, not forgetting their growing daughter, he more often wrote to "My Little Darlings" than to "Dear Lulu" or "Dear Laurie," as he sometimes affectionately addressed his wife.

Buchanan's literary ruminations reveal his growing awareness of the importance of personality. On one occasion, after conversing at length with a young Congregationalist minister, whose sermon he had just heard, he confided to his wife that

> I somehow seldom want to get personaly [sic] in any sense acquainted with those whose words or writing has made any impression on me as I always feel an indefineable [sic] something like fear that they will tear down the little castle I have built with themselves as Sir Knight. Only those whom nature and a divine light have molded in the crucible of intellectual worth can stand a close inspection. Poor weak human passions and blemishes stand out so prominent on close acquaintance that the real worth in them is so much more infinitissimal [sic] than you think seeing them at long range that you somehow learn to criticize men too quick and naturally grow selfish and cynical.[13]

This growing interest in personality revived his introspective habits. In one instance of intensive self-analysis, he acknowledged his long-standing habit of creating fancies and building castles. He was considering at the moment, he wrote, a plan of writing out his dreams and laying the sketches aside to reread when his thought had matured and his life's experiences lay behind him. "Would not a person," he queried Lulu, "be almost able to see the chrysalis of their mind changing into the mature intellect if they did that way?"[14]

Back in Sioux City between these taxing but enlightening field trips, Buchanan, with his wife's assistance, found time to expand participation in the community's cultural life, especially in the realm of the musical theater. Before the end of their first year in Iowa, both found themselves deeply enmeshed in a local production of *The Pirates of Penzance.* Under the auspices of the Young Ladies Society of the St. Thomas Episcopal Church, Will managed the entire production, drilled and directed the choruses, and through three performances sang the role of Major General Stanley. His solos, like the scenery and costumes designed by Lulu, received enthusiastic reviews from the *Journal.* With the assistance of two professional soloists from St. Paul and Boston, Sioux City was treated to the Gilbert and Sullivan "hit" barely three years after its world premiére.[15]

This first success led to the presentation a year later of *Iolanthe,* this time (May 1884) only eighteen months after the operetta's first performance in London. Again the Buchanans displayed their respective talents to packed houses. As Lord Tolloller, Will rendered the tenor solos "Of All the Young Ladies I Know" and "Spurn Not the Nobly Born." While chiding him a bit for his dancing routine, the local press lauded his overall contributions to the production of the local Choral Union—"his experience, familiarity with all necessary details, and good capacity for organization, to say nothing of the invariable good humor and patience under circumstances that would cause a less even-tempered person to lose control of himself as well as of his pupils."[16] By 1884, therefore, amateur impresario Buchanan was grooming himself, unwittingly perhaps, to become professional theater manager Buchanan.

Typical of many burgeoning communities on the mining and cattle frontiers, Sioux City achieved spectacular growth during the 1880s. Hometown boosters of 1890 claimed for it the greatest ten-year population rise of any United States city except Superior, Wisconsin—more than 500 percent. Its 1880 figure of 7,365 doubled by 1884, redoubled in the next three years, and soared to nearly 40,000 in the 1890 census. With delight its residents extolled their Missouri River bluffs as the best site from British Columbia to the Gulf of Mexico for building a great metropolis.[17]

Like the builders of most American cities, however, Sioux City leaders failed to recognize the need for long-range planning. Instead, they improvised to meet the needs of the average monthly influx of some three hundred new residents. Somehow they shaped an economy to employ, feed, clothe, and house them. Before the end of the decade some forty-five firms were sending out several hundred travelling men to promote their wares—farm goods like implements, hardware, and oils, routine necessities like clothing, boots, and drugs, and luxuries like fine china. Six years after the organization of a stockyards company in 1884, three meat-packing plants were slaughtering nearly 15,000 head of livestock each day and their owners dreamed of rivaling the production of Omaha, Kansas City, and Chicago.[18] Along with wholesaling and meat-packing, small manufacturing establishments, especially of agricultural implements, stoves, linseed oil, bricks, and tiles, were expanding employment possibilities.

All of these mercantile and industrial activities depended heavily on the railroad. In 1889 eight trunk and five branch lines hauled 52,910 carloads of freight into the city, while moving out 24,095 carloads. At the same time, townspeople and visitors could utilize the services of sixty daily passenger trains.[19]

As the city spread out along the river shores and up the Iowa bluffs, increased public transit became essential to its routine functioning. Its five horse-drawn cars of 1884 could no longer meet growing needs. By 1890, however, soon after the most progressive of American cities, energetic leadership gave Sioux City a planned transit system of electric and cable lines—some twenty miles of routes served by eighty-two cars. They took special pride in an elevated line connecting the stockyards with the central business district.[20] Meanwhile, the inauguration of other public services—telephone, electric lights, city water, and a pontoon bridge across the Missouri—contributed to the city's surging growth.

While private business and public utilities were making these indispensible contributions to Sioux City's economic expansion, its citizens were actively promoting civic and associational activities of every sort. By 1890 interested persons could choose among thirty-seven churches, fifteen or more fraternal bodies, and associations concentrating on such varied interests as literature, scientific developments, cooking, boating, and tennis. A college, a YMCA, and a professional baseball team added to the community's cultural, recreational, and athletic opportunities. Meanwhile, with upward of seventy saloons and many licensed gambling places and houses of prostitution, Sioux City perpetuated its early reputation as a lusty exponent of the frontier spirit.[21]

All these developments the Buchanans viewed with interest or concern. But as a civic-minded family they were never content merely to observe. Once they determined the activities they wished to support, they plunged in, got involved, and committed their talents. For Will it was public entertainment and the professional theater that most attracted him. Unimpressed upon his arrival by the general tone of Sioux City's aesthetic expression, he later devoted his efforts to lifting its cultural horizons. Repeatedly during his decade of residence in Sioux City, he demonstrated his conviction that in a frontier community refinement of intellectual and aesthetic tastes must keep pace with material expansion.

Following his successes with amateur productions of Gilbert and Sullivan, Buchanan moved first to the sponsorship of nationally known platform speakers, then to the promotion of professional stage presentations. After collaborating for a season in what the local press termed a "first-class" lecture series, he soon accepted the managership of Sioux City's only truly legitimate theater and community meeting place, the Academy of Music. On the upper floor of a downtown business block, like so many nineteenth-century opera houses in small midwestern towns, the 800-seat theater had provided since 1870 a stage for whatever touring companies, music groups, and lecturers could be persuaded to endure its cramped quarters. For more than three years the Academy gave Buchanan the opportunity to gain experience as promoter of professional entertainment.[22] Here he first established the connections with actors, musicians, public lecturers, political speakers, and booking agencies that would serve him so effectively in later assignments.

During his tenure at the Academy, Manager Buchanan revealed his own catholic tastes as well as his eagerness to broaden Sioux City's cultural opportunities. He booked such currently popular lecturers as Robert Ingersoll, Henry Ward Beecher, and the nationally syndicated cartoonist of *Harper's Weekly,* Thomas Nast. He introduced his fellow citizens to the Redpath Concert Company of Boston and gave them a performance of *Faust* by the Milan Grand Opera Company.[23] None of these presentations, however, aroused local excitement to match that stirred by the popular idol, Lawrence Barrett, when he appeared in the Dante classic, *Francesca da Rimini,* years before Eleanora Duse popularized it on Broadway. Buchanan's successful advertising brought patrons from a number of towns in northwestern Iowa and even from Mitchell, Dakota Territory, eighty miles away. Not to be outdone by the fashions of theater-goers along the Eastern seaboard, a few ladies in Barrett's audience, including Mrs. Buchanan and her sister, Mrs. Prugh, dared to attend the performance without the customary bonnets.[24]

After his years as manager of the Academy of Music, now well respected for his artistic standards, Buchanan was prepared to join in fostering a new and quite different kind of community entertainment. This was the harvest celebration known as the Corn Palace, soon to become the hallmark of Sioux City's claim to recognition as "The Corn Palace City of the World." In October 1887 and the four succeeding autumns public-spirited citizens collaborated in massive community efforts to extol the productivity of Iowa soil.[25] From what was first planned as a purely local jubilee, the Corn Palace idea grew into an annual festival that attracted national, even international, attention. Of the merchants, industrial men, and political leaders who conceived and promoted the project, Buchanan was a key figure. Among the Sioux City ladies who contributed their artistic skills to the motifs and details of decoration, Mrs. Buchanan was invariably prominent.

From the birth of the idea to its realization required barely six weeks. On 20 August a group of businessmen gathered, more or less spontaneously, to consider the possibility of a civic celebration to express their thanks for the year's promising harvests. Word had come to them of widespread drought and serious crop failures in other sections of the nation. Yet Sioux City and the corn empire which surrounded it were enjoying a lush growing season. In the typical frontier spirit of gratitude for well-being, they felt, it was a time for a special demonstration of thanksgiving. One citizen proposed a "harvest home," with mounds of corn displayed at each downtown street intersection. Another suggested that the Court House be decorated with corn stalks and sheaves of grain. Other ideas were presented and discarded until a more imaginative concept came forth: "Saint Paul has her Ice Palace, why not Sioux City have a Corn Palace?"[26] Immediately the idea took hold and enthusiasm began to mount:

> There will be a grand palace of corn, unique and suggestive of the cereal; the arches will be decorated with corn, as will also be the principal streets of the city and our large business houses. St. Paul and Montreal can have their ice palaces, which melt at the first approach of spring, but Sioux City is going to build a palace of the product of the soil that is making it the great pork-packing center of the northwest.[27]

Within a week planning and organizational wheels were beginning to turn. A local architect sketched preliminary plans for construction of the palace. A downtown site was selected. Such features as indoor exhibits and outdoor sports events, daily parades and horse races, and evening displays of flambeaux and fireworks were projected. A finance committee was enjoying unexpected ease in raising funds. Ten other committees were at work on such essentials as decorations, advertising, transportation, program, and music. Already an old hand at the management and promotion of public entertainment, Buchanan was a natural choice to serve as one of the principal fund raisers and chairman of the music committee.[28]

Within another ten days a large force of workmen began construction of the palace, a skeleton frame structure designed to be sheathed with corn and cereals in all their forms. As the palace walls and towers quickly took shape, more than three hundred volunteers, including Mrs. Buchanan as superintendent of one of eleven ladies' subcommittees, prepared to undertake the task of decoration. On 15 September the first load of corn arrived, soon to be followed by another 20,000 bushels. Each day masses of other grains and grasses reached the palace site. Tradesmen who had spent their lives decorating walls with paint, wallpaper, or clay quickly developed new techniques for embellishing a building with the unprocessed products of the soil.[29]

With the festival's opening less than a week away, however, civic officials suddenly realized that the project had grown to proportions they had not foreseen. Countless arrangements sorely needed integration. On 27 September, therefore, they resolved to create a five-member Board of Control "to have entire charge of everything pertaining to the Palace." For its chairman they turned to Buchanan.[30]

Under the chairman's firm guidance, the Board of Control successfully rounded up all details for the dedication ceremonies scheduled for 3 October. Occupying the greater portion of a downtown city block, the Corn Palace itself was the central attraction. Its 100-foot spire, braced by mock flying buttresses, rose above a mélange of towers, minarets, balconies, and arched entrances. Every exposed surface had received its veneer of corn—crosswise and lengthwise sections of the ears, laboriously split, then nailed piece by piece to the bare boards. From varicolored species—golden yellow, blood red, snow white, violet, etc.—resourceful designers had created murals or simulated frescoes of appropriate scenes and themes. To provide borders and to frame openings, they used sheaves of wheat and oats and tufts of millet and sorghum. They thatched the roof with green cornstalks and from many flagpoles floated pennons of native grasses. Atop the central spire they contrived an allegorical representation of Mondamin, the Indian god of corn, flanked by Ceres and Demeter. "Tall and beautiful he stood there, in his garments green and yellow," a local newspaper appropriately quoted from Longfellow's *Hiawatha*. The three deities appeared to embrace a large cornucopia filled to overflowing with the season's harvest. Symbolically, from this Iowa focus, the agricultural bounty fell upon three large square towers representing its neighbors, Nebraska, Minnesota, and Dakota Territory.[31]

To a nineteenth-century purist, perhaps, the edifice that had mushroomed from idea to reality in forty-five days may have represented no architectural style purer than "Iowa Gothic." But to loyal Sioux Cityans, basking in the joy of their own creative and cooperative endeavor, the palace was "a melody of form, ... one grand harmonious whole, ... made of a myriad of beautiful and fantastic details, as if wrought out by the magic of some modern Merlin." On the more material side, as they had envisioned, it was "a stately witness of the bursting bounty of the Northwest, the realm of King Corn."[32]

The interior of the palace received even more meticulous treatment. Like exhibit buildings at any county fair, it abounded in elaborate displays of farm and garden produce. Beyond these, however, it also featured two- and three-dimensional mosaic designs, emblems, and tableaux completely fashioned from multicolored kernels of corn and other seeds. Reproductions of Millet's *Angelus* and a United States map revealed the feminine touch in creative designs. When night fell over the palace and adjacent streets, thousands of gas jets, set in colored globes and affixed to festooned arches, cast a festive glow over a city not yet generally equipped with electricity.[33]

Beyond supervision of the palace's completion and decoration, Chairman Buchanan and his Board of Control were also responsible for coordinating the week's schedule of outdoor events. Each morning the program opened with a parade organized around a distinctive local theme. Especially appropriate was the "pioneer procession"—stage coach, pack train of ponies, emigrant train of pioneer wagons, and several hundred Omaha and Winnebago Indians, many of them mounted and fully adorned in war paint and feathers. On another day a civic and military parade attracted labor organizations, bands, and National Guard units from a score of cities in Iowa, Nebraska, and Dakota Territory. Each evening the festivities closed with a drill and fireworks display by the Sioux City Flambeau Club.[34]

During these busy weeks if the Buchanans followed the extensive local newspaper coverage of the Corn Palace preparations, they received their introduction to the Latin American world they would come to know so well. The *Journal* recalled the early development of corn culture in Mexico and around Lake Titicaca and recounted the significance of maize in the religious rituals of the Mayas. It concluded that "the American Ceres" must surely be Centeotl, the Aztec goddess of Indian corn.[35]

However rewarding to him the Corn Palace experience may

have been, it was from a sequel to the festival week that Buchanan received his most propitious windfall, one that would shape the directions of his future career. This was the opportunity to serve as official host to a number of distinguished national figures who visited Sioux City for the express purpose of viewing its unique tribute to "King Corn." Among these were Chauncey M. Depew, president of the New York Central Railroad, Cornelius Vanderbilt, other railroad executives, and, during a brief stopover on their "swing-around-the-circle" honeymoon, President and Mrs. Grover Cleveland.[36]

Immediately upon learning in late August of White House plans for a social trip through the Middle West and South, the Corn Palace authorities resolved to invite the president to visit Sioux City.[37] That acceptance of the invitation would require a slight change in the announced itinerary did not cool their enthusiasm. Anticipating a favorable response, they decided that the formal invitation should be both elegant and distinctive; they invited Mrs. Buchanan to prepare it. For elegance she chose corn-colored silk plush and white satin; for distinctiveness she settled on water color paintings of local scenes. On the cover she portrayed the Corn Palace, with pumpkin vines in the foreground and a cornfield in the background. To depict Sioux City's dramatic growth, she used inside pages for contrasting views of its "skyline" from the Nebraska shore of the Missouri—one in 1854, the other in 1887. The text of the invitation breathed the eagerness of the community's citizens to entertain the president and his young bride.[38]

At 5:00 A. M. on 12 October the city's firebells rang out to awaken people for the presidential visit an hour later. Thousands from the city and surrounding countryside turned out to witness the "meeting of royalty—the president of the United States . . . welcomed by King Corn to the capital city of his kingdom." At the Corn Palace, where the Clevelands spent most of their half-hour stopover, Buchanan and his colleague, W. H. Beck, served as the official reception committee and personal escort for the quick tour. Fresh from the countryside of western New York, Mrs. Cleveland was enthusiastic about all the displays, but intrigued by the unique creations from corn, whether in the form of kernels, ears, husks, or stalks.

She responded warmly when Mrs. Buchanan and other ladies presented her a bouquet of flowers they had selected from the decorations.[39]

Though he greeted his early morning hosts and their special pride with obvious good humor, the president was less ebullient than his wife. His most genial comment appears to have been, "Well, here is something new at last."[40] On the other hand, his true feeling may have been more candidly expressed several weeks later in a letter he was purported to have written about his journey for the Cincinnati *Commercial Gazette.* It represented him as recalling that

> from Minneapolis we went a whooping down by night through Minnesota and Iowa, which did not vote for me, to Omaha, stopping at breakfast time at "a considerable town," called Sioux City. The city had used up all the corn which the surrounding country had produced to build a tremendous house, which they took us out to see. While I bowed and smiled, and said "yes" to countless things the reception committee said about it, I reserved my real opinion for the book, which is that I know a better use to put corn to than building houses.[41]

To the civic leaders and home-town boosters of Sioux City, however, the Corn Palace project was a triumph. They were gratified that their innovative creation had attracted visits from the Clevelands and other notables. They enjoyed the national press coverage they had received. They estimated that nearly 100,000 persons had visited their city during festival week. At the same time, they realized that some crudities and incongruities had marred their grand design and that only the immense effort and enthusiasm of the community had overcome mistakes caused by haste and uncertainty. To repeat their success in 1888, the festival's sponsors fully understood, would require greater foresight, tighter organization, and more imagination.[42]

In early March, then, a group of community leaders took the first organizational steps to assure a second fall festival. Deciding to formalize their project as "The Sioux City Corn Palace Exposition Company," they promptly drafted articles of incorporation, fixed capital stock at $100,000, adopted by-laws, and carefully defined the duties of officers and directors. As one of the principal moving spirits, Buchanan was a logical appointee to several key positions: member of the original Board of Directors, chairman of the committee on advertising, and member of committees on plans and finances. By early June it became apparent, as it had at a critical moment in 1887, that central management was needed to coordinate the work of a dozen committees. Again the task fell to a five-man group and again it was Buchanan who headed it.[43]

The advertising coup of the 1888 celebration took the form of a special Corn Palace train to Chicago—a practical demonstration of Sioux City's hopes of rivalling Kansas City, Omaha, and St. Paul in commercial importance. Banded with streamers proclaiming "Corn is King!" and festooned with bunting and cornstalks, the train rolled across the prairies to Chicago. Arrayed in white pearl plug hats and linen dusters, each sporting a cornstalk cane, Buchanan and his fellow citizens paraded behind their band to acquaint Chicagoans with "the Corn Palace city of the world." Back home on the Missouri, the heartiest enthusiasts could cry, "Why not send one to Washington!"[44]

Meanwhile, Buchanan and his committees proceeded with plans to enlarge and improve their tribute to bountiful harvests. The new building, a fortress-like structure dominated by a lofty octagonal tower, surpassed the first palace in both size and design. Its external decorations were more complete, more elaborate, and more imaginative. Its 148 display booths, many decorated by Mrs. Buchanan and her colleagues, featured replicas of a Grecian temple, an Egyptian shrine, a Chinese pagoda, and an Indian village—all, as before, executed in local seeds, grains, and grasses. To emphasize good music, while continuing outdoor sports and amusements, Buchanan engaged the well-known Elgin, Illinois, concert band and himself found time to sing in a specially assembled Corn Palace chorus of 150 voices. Open twice as long as its predecessor, the 1888 edifice attracted triple the number of visitors.[45] Sioux Cityans could agree that their annual festival had come to stay.

Yet overseeing the Corn Palaces represented but one phase of Buchanan's continuing efforts to improve the quality of Sioux City entertainment. As first manager of the Peavey Grand Opera House, he timed its dedication and première performance to coincide with the harvest celebration of 1888. For opening week, he engaged the Heinrich Conried English Opera Company, direct from New York and Chicago, to present Strauss's *The Gypsy Baron* and other popular operettas of the day.[46] To deliver announcements of the grand opening, Buchanan employed special messenger boys clad in blue costumes with white neckties and gloves; a fresh pansy garnished each announcement. As he personally greeted patrons of the theater's première, ushers distributed programs printed on yellow silk.[47]

Buchanan's active promotion of a new opera house for Sioux City had paralleled his tenure as manager of the aging Academy of Music. Its inadequate stage, he quickly learned, could not accommodate, nor its small seating capacity support, the kind of theatrical attractions he wished to schedule. As early as July 1884 he had travelled to Minneapolis to inspect its new opera house and had collected ground plans for theaters recently erected in other cities.[48] But four years went by before Buchanan's urgings culminated in the Peavey's gala opening.

With its gilded boxes, ornate decor, modern stage appointments, and 1440-seat capacity, the Peavey Grand Opera House quickly gained fame in theatrical circles as "the finest theater between Sioux City and San Francisco." Focus of main-line railroads and center of an agrarian heartland, the city became a natural stopover point for road companies travelling from Chicago to Denver and the west coast. Long before dramatic producers Marc Klaw and Abraham Erlanger formed their powerful syndicate, Manager Buchanan engaged them as the Peavey's New York representatives.[49] Through this association Sioux City theatergoers were able to enjoy Edwin Booth in *Hamlet,* Lawrence Barrett in *Othello,* Joseph Jefferson in *Rip Van Winkle,* the Drews in *The Rivals,* and a host of other Broadway stars.[50]

To increase and maintain the Peavey's patronage innovations became an essential part of Buchanan's entrepreneurship. When celebrities trod the stage, he activated a searchlight atop the theater to beam the news forty miles over nearby villages and surrounding farmlands. During a performance of *The Bohemian Girl* in 1887 he permitted a "talking machine" company to make a "phonographic impression" of the operetta. He made opera glasses available to any patron willing to insert a ten-cent piece in the slot of a box attached to his seat. But no innovation better revealed his resourcefulness than the production of an aquatic drama entitled *A Dark Secret*. This specialty presentation required a full stage covered to a depth of eight feet with 3,000 cubic feet of water and featured a drowning scene, a contest of racing sculls, and a small steamboat carrying passengers.[51]

During the three years of Buchanan's managership the Peavey Grand became the center of Sioux City's cultural life. To diversify its offerings from time to time he scheduled big-name lecturers, opera companies, the Boston Symphony and other orchestras, and such lighter entertainment as magicians and minstrels. When not fulfilling its primary purpose as professional theater, the Peavey served as the city's principal assembly hall—for amateur dramatics, school exercises, lodge meetings, conventions, and political rallies.[52] It attracted state conventions of both the Democratic and Republican parties— the first time any Iowa city had wooed the GOP away from Des Moines. Time after time for these assemblies Buchanan received the nod to serve as chairman of a committee "on hall and decorations."[53] Thus, while the Peavey stage was growing rich in theatrical lore, its manager faithfully pursued his hope that Sioux City's progress in the arts would parallel its growth in population and economic stature.

Despite his fulltime managership of the Peavey Opera House and his continuing commitment to J. K. Prugh & Company, Buchanan assumed again in 1889 his usual responsibilities for the annual Corn Palace celebration. As chairman of an enlarged Executive Committee, he insisted upon expansion and improvement of old patterns. In every dimension the third palace exceeded its predecessors, its floor space greater, central tower more lofty, secondary spires and pinnacles more numerous, balconies and terraces more spacious, exterior and interior decorations more artistic. As in 1888, a Corn Palace train travelled eastward to advertise the jubilee, this time to Washington and New York. A special train from Boston brought eastern businessmen interested in Iowa real estate investments. The 71st New York Regiment Band provided the principal musical entertainment. Assisting in the project as before, Mrs. Buchanan served as chairman of the Women's

Committee and president of the Ladies Corn Palace Decorating Association.[54]

But, as happened two years earlier, it was a post-festival visit of notables that brought the richest satisfaction to both Buchanan and Sioux City. As early as July the Corn Palace authorities had learned that representatives of the Latin American republics were assembling in Washington in October for a special conference on such common Western Hemisphere problems as arbitration and tariff schedules.[55] This first of the many Pan American (later Inter-American) Conferences would create the International Bureau of American Republics, one day to evolve as the Pan American Union and later to flower as the Organization of American States.[56] Before settling down to cope with difficult agenda items, Department of State officials reasoned, the Latin Americans should see something of the United States, especially its commercial advantages and growing economic power. A railroad excursion along the Atlantic seaboard and through the Mississippi midlands would accomplish this purpose and at the same time stimulate popular interest in the Conference.[57]

To cover the planned itinerary of 6,000 miles, the Pennsylvania Railroad made available its most modern train. Equipped with the latest safety improvements, it provided the delegates with every convenience and comfort of a metropolitian hotel —five sleepers, a diner, and a composite car (appropriately named *Esperanza*) with library, smoking room, barber shop, and bathroom. For six weeks the elegant train would carry the guests to dozens of towns in New England, along the Great Lakes, through the upper Mississippi and Lower Missouri Valleys, then eastward up the Ohio Valley and on to Philadelphia, New York, and Washington. They would visit mills, factories, museums, and universities.[58] The Corn Palace executives speculated that the Latin Americans might find welcome a chance to view Sioux City's novel tribute to maize, the cereal first domesticated, then solemnly worshipped, by the Aztecs, Mayas, and Incas. Accordingly, through the efforts of Iowa Senator William B. Allison, Sioux City became the tour's only stopover between St. Paul and Omaha.[59]

During the morning hours of 26 October Iowa notables and

townspeople extended their warmest hospitality to the visiting dignitaries. Buchanan made essential contributions at each stage of the proceedings. He was a member of the official reception committee which greeted the diplomats upon their arrival. At the Peavey Opera House, to which mounted troops and a local band escorted them, he assigned the guests to special ushers for the procession to the theater stage. As a local newspaper put it, he had arranged appropriate decorations with "admirable discrimination and good taste"—on the stage, flags and emblems of all the nations and throughout the theater, more than a thousand plants, among them South American rubber trees. A packed house awaited the ceremonies, while hundreds gathered about the entrance. To greetings addressed to their "Brother Americans" by the mayor, the governor, and a United States senator, the Colombian delegate, Carlos Martínez Silva, responded for the visitors. At the Corn Palace each guest received a solid gold Corn Palace medal. The Ecuadorian Juan F. Velarde was heard to remark, "your beautiful and wonderful Corn Palace will remain in our memories forever."[60]

Clearly, for a small midwestern city, the opportunity to entertain diplomats from nearly every Western Hemisphere nation was an unique experience. But a local newspaper editor effectively placed the episode in an even broader context. The Latin American nations, he wrote,

> have grown amazingly in wealth and in social advancement. They have built great cities; cities which in population, business and modern facilities rival the miracles of city-building in the United States. In many respects [they] distance the people of this country. . . . The time is ripe for the drawing together of the American nations along the lines of their common interests. . . . This was the dream of Simon Bolivar and Henry Clay, and the time has come to begin to realize what they longed to bring about.[61]

No spokesman could more faithfully have mirrored Washington's rationale for convening the First International Conference of the American States.

Deeply involved as he was in winding up affairs of the third Corn Palace and in inaugurating his second season as manager of the Peavey Opera House, Buchanan may or may not have read this perceptive editorial. In any case, he probably did not envision the future import for himself of the developing Pan Americanism which he and Sioux City had helped to foster.

Certainly he could not have foreseen that, twelve years hence, he would be a full-fledged delegate to the Second Conference of the American States in Mexico City and, five years later, chairman of his country's delegation to the Third Conference in Rio de Janeiro.[62] In view of these and other developments in his later career, Buchanan's management of the receptions at the Peavey Theater and the Corn Palace must have come under the observation of William E. Curtis, special State Department agent in charge of the excursion.[63]

Their success in attracting and entertaining the Latin American diplomats convinced Sioux Cityans once again of the merit of their Corn Palace idea. Their exuberance led logically to an early decision, this time by action of a "town meeting," to sponsor a fourth annual festival in 1890. Arriving late for the session, Buchanan expressed some surprise at the result of the vote just taken. In what his fellow townsmen had long since learned was a characteristic gesture of their "Buck" in a contemplative mood, he inserted his thumbs in the armholes of his vest and said, "Well, that settles it." But, he then admonished them, "a Corn Palace this year means work and expense. A novelty must be produced that will be as different and as much better than the former palaces as money and ingenuity can make it. It must be on a much broader and more comprehensive scale than ever before." Within a week the Corn Palace officers invited him once again to oversee the exposition, this time with the encompassing authority of general manager.[64]

In a variety of ways Buchanan and his aides proceeded to search for the novelty and the broader scale he had recommended. To supplement the traditional displays of grains and grasses they sought industrial and railroad exhibits and invited southern states to send samples of their typical semitropical products. They engaged the French designer, François Dubois, who had served New Orleans as consulting artist, to provide "the most unique, novel and dazzling street pageant ever seen outside of the Mardi Gras City." They invited P. T. Barnum to plan a special parade.[65] To assure the attendance of notables—by now a featured Corn Palace attraction—they expanded the official invitation list to include President Harrison, former President Cleveland, Secretary of State James G.

Blaine, Secretary of Agriculture Jeremiah H. Rusk, the Comte de Paris, who was then touring the United States, the governors of Iowa and nearby states, and all members of the recently appointed National Commission for the World's Columbian Exposition.[66]

From a stately throne King Mondamin would rule over a Corn Palace larger and more exotic than its predecessors. It would simulate an Islamic Mosque with multiple domes and a variety of arabesque features, all, as usual, veneered in products of Iowa soil. It would house an illuminated waterfall, thirty-two feet high and twenty feet wide, its waters gushing from an artificial woodland setting. To expand publicity Manager Buchanan contracted with a Chicago firm to print colorful lithographs—one designed by Mrs. Buchanan—and invited townspeople to affix a million small stickers to their out-of-town mailings.[67]

Except that many of the invited dignitaries were unable to attend, most of the projected features came to fruition. For its creative aspects and its widened geographic base, the 1890 Corn Palace festival must have seemed to Buchanan the most successful of the four he had directed.[68] Certainly this was the judgment of the local press. Yet, as so often happened in his entrepreneurial and managerial career, his influence was largely a behind-the-scenes one. Honors usually went to mayors and other elected officials, but without the manager's drive and resourcefulness there would have been fewer honors for those he served.

From another direction, however, came unexpected recognition. In May 1890 President Harrison invited Buchanan to serve as one of two Iowa representatives on the National Commission for the World's Columbian Exposition, planned by the city of Chicago to honor the quadricentennial of the discovery of America.[69] Though already committed to his managerships of the Corn Palace celebration and the Peavey Grand Opera House and still affiliated with J. K. Prugh & Company, he could not refuse an appointment offered by the president of the United States. It was an assignment that would soon lead the Iowan into new and absorbing experiences.

In the meantime, if he chose to ruminate about his connection with four Corn Palaces, Buchanan could justifiably view as integral the role he had played in each. Curiously and fortuitously, each one either coincided with a significant new appointment or afforded new contacts that would shape his future career. In 1887, as a principal host to the presidential party, he had come to the attention of President Cleveland, who seven years later would appoint him minister to Argentina. Managing the Peavey Opera House after 1888 had gained Buchanan familiarity with the essential techniques of public relations and established solid contacts with national figures of the entertainment world—experiences which helped prepare him for the managerial positions he would assume with Chicago's Columbian and Buffalo's Pan-American Expositions. The visit of the Pan American delegates in 1889 had introduced him personally to some of the distinguished leaders of Latin American nations that he would come to know during his years as director of expositions, State Department envoy, and overseas representative for two American corporations. The somewhat honorary post as Iowa member of the National Commission for the Columbian Exposition in 1890 placed him in a strategic position to take over full-time direction of several key exposition departments.

As he neared the end of his Sioux City decade, therefore, the transplanted Ohioan could count the fruits of his Iowa experiences. He had worked hard, contributed his enthusiasm to diverse nonremunerative activities, and demonstrated his solid citizenship. He had won popular confidence as a sound businessman and expanded his competence in handling both human and public relations. He had gained esteem as a patron of agriculture and as an impresario of public entertainment. He had established more than passing acquaintance with state governors, national senators, two presidents of the United States, and a score of Latin American diplomats. In a throbbing frontier community he had grown in acumen, urbanity, and self-confidence. At every turn Mrs. Buchanan had abetted her husband's career while contributing her own artistic spirit to offset a boom town's earthiness. Chicago would find them prepared for the challenges of an established metropolis.

Chapter 4
HOMAGE TO AMERICA'S DISCOVERER
Chicago, 1890-1894

In moving from Sioux City to Chicago in 1891, the Buchanans transplanted themselves from a bustling town of 40,000, wrought in the spirit of the expanding American West, to a bristling city of over a million, dedicated to relentless competition with older municipalities in the East. Leaving behind a community which still betrayed its pioneer origins and frontier brashness, they found themselves in an aspiring metropolis which itself had only recently shed frontierlike qualities and begun to assume airs of urban sophistication. Yet far more rapidly than he had risen from obscurity to leadership in Sioux City, Buchanan would establish himself in Chicago as a successful administrator in the world of exposition education and entertainment.

The Buchanans' arrival in Chicago roughly coincided with the city's emergence as the nation's second largest metropolitan area.[1] Chicagoans had utilized the two decades since their great fire of 1871 not only to build a new city on the ashes of the old but also to solidify it as the seat of the Middle West's greatest economic empire. Aggressive entrepreneurs who had already established themselves as the region's leading dealers in lumber, grain, livestock, and meat-packing turned to mergers, pools, and other monopolistic practices to widen their business domains. By founding new industries to satisfy popular wants other promoters speedily reduced the city's former dependence upon the output of eastern cities. By 1890 they had elevated

Chicago to second place behind New York in gross value of manufactured products and were providing wholesale supply to the new middlemen of hinterland cities. Relentless exploitation of its lakeside site, an unsurpassed network of rail connections, and easy access to sources of supplies and raw materials assured the maturing of this dynamic economic base.

Just as the rapid peopling of the Upper Mississippi and Missouri valleys provided an expanding market for Chicago's industrial production, so its teeming industry and commerce attracted laborers and their families from these areas as well as from Europe and the Far East. Between 1871 and 1890 the reciprocal effects of economic growth and population influx combined to push census figures from approximately 298,000 to more than a million. Supplementing the Germans and Irish of earlier migrations, increasing numbers of Scandinavians, Central Europeans, and Asiatics served to perpetuate Chicago's cosmopolitan life and culture. Though growing proportions of the citizenry could claim the United States as their birthplace, the large majority were of foreign parentage. As social patterns grew more complex, they also grew more fluid and amorphous. To enterprising citizens of all ethnic groups unlimited opportunities for new businesses afforded the chance for quick wealth. New fortunes pushed new men, whether native or foreign born, into positions of civic leadership. Their wealth, their tastes, and their ambitions became the model for Chicago's thousands and the touchstone of the city's future.

The problem of housing this burgeoning population, as well as the new factories and mercantile concerns, forced the city's extension. Hemmed in on the east by Lake Michigan, the boundaries pushed in all other directions. By the time of the Columbian Exposition in 1893 Chicago had engulfed most of the 185 square miles that would comprise the twentieth-century corporate entity. At the same time soaring land values in the old inner city stimulated revision of construction techniques and development of skyscraper architecture. Little-known architects—Daniel H. Burnham, William LeBaron Jenney, John W. Root, and Louis Sullivan—became the precursors of a global revolution in the adaptation of building methods to urban housing needs.[2]

The qualities of determination, civic pride, and frontier boastfulness that had produced Chicago's resurgence after the 1871 disaster motivated its leaders to seek some distinctive medium that would dramatize its achievement before the world. As early as 1885 they began to consider the possibility of a world's fair to commemorate the quadricentennial of Columbus's first voyage to the Western Hemisphere. Such a tribute, civic-minded boosters must have reasoned, could serve as an appropriate testimonial to the rise and maturing of the new Chicago. For the next five years they worked to organize, finance, and secure congressional approval for their plans. Confidently they countered fervid and sometimes ruthless competition from New York, Washington, and St. Louis.[3] Finally, however, on 25 April 1890, they could rejoice over the official designation of Chicago as the site of the World's Exposition of 1892.[4] Second thoughts soon changed the name to the more appropriate World's Columbian Exposition and the opening date to the less precise 1893.

Even before Chicago won the battle to secure congressional endorsement of its proposal, the name of William I. Buchanan had become associated with the Columbian Exposition. After the House of Representatives had passed the necessary enabling bill but while the Senate was still considering it, business friends of the Sioux Cityan were urging Iowa's Governor Boies to nominate him as the state's Democratic member of the proposed National Commission for the Exposition.[5] In urging Buchanan's appointment, a Sioux City newspaper publisher characterized him as "one of the LORDS ANNOINTED [sic]." More worldly in his estimate, another journalist saw him as a "business man of ability and shrewdness," who would discharge his duties "in a manner creditable to him and to the exposition city that he represents." Before the end of May Governor Boies and President Harrison had acted favorably on these recommendations.[6]

For whatever duties this new appointment might entail Buchanan realized that he would have to squeeze time from his already engrossing commitments to the Corn Palace, the Peavey Opera House, and his business firm. Fortunately, until after the Corn Palace celebration and the opening of the Peavey's fall season, he was able to restrict his new duties to attendance at the Chicago meetings of the National Commission and its subcommittees. Yet, the limited nature of his early activities did not inhibit his enthusiasm for the new post and the opportunities it offered the state of Iowa. Even before the Commission held its first session in late June Buchanan collected his drawings of the 1890 Corn Palace and hurried off to Chicago. "We intend to have it here," he told a reporter of the *Chicago Tribune,* "and it will be a novelty." When asked about the Commission, he responded that, though "its powers are mostly advisory, . . . we are all working for the best interests of the fair, and wish to do all that we can to make it a success."[7]

Already by the first and second meetings of the Commission the Iowan found himself deeply involved in a dispute over the sites originally selected for the exposition. Upon the advice of landscape artist Frederick Law Olmsted and architectural supervisor Daniel H. Burnham, the local organizers had selected Jackson Park on Chicago's south side. Though still largely undeveloped, its lakefront location and abundance of dunes and marshes suggested the potentialities for waterway construction and landscape beautification.[8] Moreover, superior transportation facilities—the Illinois Central Railroad, cable and electric surface lines, a new elevated railway—promised rapid transit from the inner city. As the representative of a farm state, however, Buchanan firmly opposed the plan to locate the agricultural exhibits on grounds seven miles west of Jackson Park. Such an arrangement, he protested, would discourage visitors from the western states and might even cause legislative reluctance to subsidize state exhibits. Yet back home in Sioux City he maintained a much more buoyant tone about the exposition's prospects:

> Again, I say, the fair is going to be a success anyway. . . . And another thing: Iowa is going to be in it in 1892, whether the fair is held at Jackson Park, or Pullman, or Kankakee, or wherever it is. Iowa will be there with the greatest agricultural exhibit ever made by any state in any exposition.[9]

Urged by Buchanan and his farm state colleagues, the authorities soon found a way to relieve the developing impasse. They determined to utilize the grounds of Washington Park, located only a mile west of Jackson Park and connected to it by the

Midway Plaisance, a planned, but as yet undeveloped, green belt 400 yards wide. The *Sioux City Journal* hailed the decision as a great victory for the West and agriculture and a worthy recognition of Iowa and its representative.[10]

At the second meeting of the National Committee in late September additional responsibilities fell to Buchanan. His years of experience with the Sioux City Corn Palaces made him a natural appointee to the chairmanship of the important Committee on Agriculture, while his even longer service as manager of theaters suggested his appointment to the Committee on Fine Arts. Assuming the chairmanship without delay, he began to solicit the active participation of all the states and territories. Not forgetting his home state, he made early application for Iowa's exhibit space, especially for two acres of ground for its state building.[11] At a joint session of the Committees on Fine Arts and Foreign Affairs he successfully urged the desirability of separate display facilities for the performing arts like music and drama and for works of art in the more traditional sense. On this and other matters he strongly recommended committee consultation with Chicago's most prominent artists.[12]

Toward the end of November the administrative organization of the exposition underwent a metamorphosis that not only altered Buchanan's status but also pointed the way to his continued career in public life. As plans were developing too slowly, key authorities gradually had come to recognize the cumbersomeness of their executive structure. The federal statute had left unclear the respective functions and jurisdictions of the two governing bodies, the National Commission and the local Board of Directors of the Exposition Company. Their parallel arrangement of committees was causing unnecessary expense and duplication of effort. Without greater centralization of control, it became clear, the organization and building of the fair could not possibly be completed within the designated twenty-nine months. The reorganization plan agreed upon at this juncture provided for the creation of more than a dozen "great departments," each to be headed by a chief officer with his own bureau of clerks. Appointed by the director general, each chief would have charge of securing exhibits for his department and of all negotiations with the exhibitors. At the outset several departments might be placed under the control of a single chief.¹³

From his position as member of a purely advisory commission Buchanan suddenly found himself thrust into an executive post integral to the success of a great world's fair. On 12 December 1890 Director General George R. Davis appointed the Iowan chief of the Department of Agriculture and at the same time placed him in charge of the Departments of Live Stock and Forestry. Subsequently he received responsibility for the Department of Dairying as well. His annual salary, like those of all department chiefs, was fixed at $5,000. Prior to his appointment, Buchanan had indicated the need for five months to wind up his affairs in Sioux City. In the meantime, he suggested, before moving to Chicago he would be willing to direct the preliminary organization of his departments without salary.¹⁴ With this understanding, he resigned his position as Iowa member of the National Commission and inaugurated the work that would absorb him for the next three years. Understandably enthusiastic over this recognition of their state, Governor Boies and various Iowa newspapers saluted "Farmer Buchanan" as "a man of magnificent ability, [who] possesses in full measure the various elements and qualifications requisite for one to successfully manage such an interest as that of the agriculture of this country."¹⁵

Even before his appointment, Buchanan had outlined to Davis his concept of a plan of operations for the Department of Agriculture. At the very outset, he would invite the sympathetic cooperation of all state boards of agriculture and county agricultural societies as well as the active participation of the National Grange, the Farmers' Alliances, and kindred organizations. Through these diverse agencies he hoped to stimulate in individual agriculturists a "feeling of personal interest in the success of the Exposition."¹⁶ To Buchanan, as to the Congress, it seemed "fit and appropriate that the four hundredth anniversary of the discovery of America be commemorated by an exhibition of the resources of the United States of America, their development, and of the progress of civilization in the New World."¹⁷ Consistent with both his suggested *modus operandi* and his philosophical understanding, he set out to win for agriculture what he regarded as its proper educational role in a world exposition.

From his home base in Sioux City, while continuing to function as businessman and theater manager, Buchanan began his public relations campaign almost within hours of his appointment as department chief: First, recalling a friendship developed at the recent Corn Palace celebration, he requested and secured the advice and assistance of Secretary of Agriculture Jeremiah H. Rusk and his department.[18] In writing to state boards of agriculture, he urged that they support legislative appropriations for official exhibits and invited their suggestions and counsel on all matters. He addressed similar appeals to members of the National Commission and to officers of the Grange, the Alliances, and many state and county fairs. To increase and diversify the educational exhibits he wrote to scores of associations of beekeepers, dairymen, livestockmen, and the like. From Jacob Ruppert of New York he sought to learn how much exhibit space the brewing industry would require and from Charles H. Deere of Moline, Illinois, the requirements of farm implement manufacturers. At the same time he developed a comparable program to foment interest in his plans for forestry and forest products.[19] His records reveal the mailing of hundreds of letters, thousands of circulars, and tens of thousands of labels and other promotional materials.[20]

During the first five months of his tenure Buchanan travelled to Chicago at least once each fortnight to appraise the needs and plans for the buildings to house his departments.[21] At an early stage, after touring the grounds with official sculptor Augustus Saint-Gaudens and other professional consultants, he revealed his growing exuberance about the exposition's promise. "To see ... the stakes that mark off the ground, stretching away like endless rows of young cornblades," he commented, "is to get a new realization of what an immense affair this is to be." His enthusiasm mounted as he envisioned the immense agricultural building designed by McKim, Meade & White, leading architects of New York City. He admired its classic style and its proposed setting amid artificial "lagoons, fringed with beautiful growing plants and flowers."[22]

Despite his satisfaction with the aesthetic surroundings, however, the veteran of four Sioux City Corn Palaces was less than content with the space allotments for his various departments. He reported to Chief of Construction Burnham and Director General Davis the wide response his preliminary promotional campaign had stimulated among potential exhibitors. Ever alert to the Hemisphere and global appeal of the exposition theme, he emphasized the interest developing among foreign producers. Fortified with comparative statistics from Philadelphia's Centennial Exposition, Buchanan presented to his superiors a well-documented plea for additional exhibit facilities. He argued for larger or separate buildings for agricultural implements, forest products, and the dairying and brewing industries. And when he learned that only twenty acres had been reserved for livestock exhibits, he secured another sixty.[23]

By the spring of 1891, therefore, while commuting between Sioux City and Chicago, Buchanan had firmly established his relationship with the exposition's managers and completed organizational groundwork for the functioning of his departments. With the winter season of the Peavey Opera House drawing to a close, he could now wind up his business affairs in Sioux City and undertake the move to full-time residence in Chicago.[24] For himself and his family alike the shift would not be easy. Throughout a satisfying decade the Iowa city had been their home, with relatives, friends, valued social relationships, and solid business interests close at hand. They had helped it grow from a crude river town on the cattle frontier to the thriving business center of a broad agrarian heartland. They could feel that they had contributed generously to the improvement of its aesthetic and spiritual tone. Though, in contrast, boisterous, pulsating Chicago must have seemed alien land, Buchanan's affiliation with the Columbian Exposition promised fresh stimulation both to himself and his family.

When in early June they reached Chicago's south side, they were in time to see hundreds of horse teams and drivers beginning to break ground at the exposition site in Jackson Park. From this first scooping of earth for the lagoons to the last closing of an exhibition hall, their nearby home gave the family opportunity to witness the entire physical evolution of a world exposition. To them, as to millions of others, the speed of construction, like the finished product itself, appeared an architectural miracle. Unlike its predecessors, the Centennial Exposition of 1876 and the Paris Exposition of 1889, the Columbian was planned and designed around a central unifying theme. That the motif was Greco-Roman rather than late nineteenth century American may have offended some innovative architects, but it did not diminish the satisfaction of the millions of average Americans who came to learn and enjoy.[25]

As construction proceeded and opening day approached, the Buchanans could begin to appreciate the exposition's grand design. The thematic heart of the exhibition expanse was the Columbian Court of Honor. Perpendicular to the shore of Lake Michigan a grand esplanade ran westward, along both sides of a large basin, to the Administration Building. At the lake or east end of the basin stood the immense statue of "The Republic" by Daniel Chester French and at the west rose the ornate Columbian Fountain by Frederick MacMonnies. Connected by a complex of canals and inlets to ponds and lagoons north and south, the basin provided a decorative focus as well as passage for sightseeing boats. Exhibition buildings in classic style lined both its flanks. Satellite to this artistic core, other essential exposition areas ranged northward along the lake shore. Attractively sited around the system of waterways and islands were other exhibition buildings, including those of state, national, and foreign governments. Jutting a mile northwestward from the main grounds, the Midway Plaisance accommodated scores of amusement and educational attractions, many of them exotic importations from round the world. A "Street in Cairo," Hagenbeck's Animal Show, reproductions of foreign villages, and models of St. Peter's and the Eiffel Tower typified the midway offerings.[26]

Remembering his earlier struggle against a separate locale for the agricultural and livestock exhibits, Buchanan had good reason to exult over the locations finally assigned to them. An essential component of the Court of Honor, the Roman-styled Agriculture Building graced almost the entire south front of the basin and lay immediately adjacent to the site of most of the exposition's ceremonial functions. To the rear, but within easy walking range, visitors could reach the Dairy and Forestry

Buildings, the Stock Pavilion, a saw mill, and the sprawling livestock exhibits. For these separate buildings and compact arrangements agriculturists and lumbermen could thank the foresight and persistence of "Farmer Buchanan." In acknowledging his assistance to the lumbering industry, for example, the *Northwest Lumberman* described him "as a typical Western man . . . as restless as an engine with steam on, [who] appears to have about the same push. . . . In manners he is brusque, but courteous, and can talk straight to the point, or diplomatically, as may best meet his purpose."[27]

Yet, securing appropriate buildings and adequate exhibit space was only the most conspicuous of Buchanan's varied administrative functions. If his four departments were to be fully operative by the exposition's scheduled opening date, 1 May 1893, he would have to oversee the emplacement of hundreds of exhibits, some live, some inanimate, not to mention the promotional and clerical work involved in their recruitment and assembly. In directing the Sioux City Corn Palaces, his constituency had consisted of parts of three states; now, in potential at least, it embraced the world.

Almost at once the transplanted Iowan realized the need for incessant follow-up to the preliminary promotional campaign he had initiated from Sioux City. This he sought to accomplish through extensive travelling, frequent speechmaking, even writing for the press. He went to Washington to determine the national government's plans for his departments. He attended a kennel club show in New York to line up dog exhibits. He travelled to Nebraska to arrange a display of the beet sugar manufacturing process.[28] His speechmaking took him to various cities and towns in the Middle West, especially to state capitals to plead for official support.[29] Regularly in these presentations he underscored the educational values of the exposition, always emphatic about how "the exhibits of the several countries would show the inter-dependence of one nation upon the others, thus helping to promote universal brotherhood of man."[30] Nor did he neglect the artistic aspects. In one of his press articles he described the transformation of "a section of swampy, sandy land, sparsely covered with a growth of scrub oak, . . . Aladdin-like [into] 120 acres of palaces, Venetian waterways, islands of roses, acres of flower beds, and hundreds of groups of statuary, fountains, monuments, and commemorative columns."[31]

At his desk in Chicago, Buchanan faced administrative chores as essential if not as stimulating as his promotional excursions. In the Agriculture Department, for example, plans to compartmentalize exhibits and grant awards demanded a system of classification that was simple, logical, and scientifically sound. Guided by the recommendations of the National Commission, he adopted a scheme of eighteen groups, embracing more than a hundred classes—from cereals to confectionary and from paste to potatoes.[32] Numerous regulations handed down by the director general had to be adapted to departmental realities; other rules had to be conceived at the local level. When should the buildings be open? Who should receive passes? How should quarantine regulations on livestock, especially that from foreign countries, be enforced? Should the Thomas I. Lipton Company be granted permission to sell cups of tea? What giveaways should be authorized: Heinz pickles—small cakes—tins of meat? Or samples of liquor?[23]

As the variety and scope of these questions increased, Buchanan gradually expanded the size and capabilities of his departmental staffs. Though in the early months clerks and stenographers were able to perform all essential tasks, the diversification of functions soon brought the need for messengers, cashiers, draughtsmen, engineers, and for each department a superintendent and an assistant superintendent. As exhibits began to arrive, he recruited a veterinary surgeon, chemists for the dairy tests, and analysts of varied specialties. Throughout the period of the exposition security for the displays was provided by 104 members of the Columbian Guard.[34] But the serious business of recruiting responsible personnel also had its sportive side. When Buchanan announced that he was seeking good-looking dairy maids, a Chicago newspaperman waggishly reported that several hundred red-headed girls were to be engaged. The yarn quickly spread across the country and when applications, some containing samples of auburn locks, began to arrive, another journalist suggested that "the good humored Chief would walk around the biggest block in

Chicago half a dozen times to escape a red-headed girl with possible aspirations to be a dairy maid."[35]

With all these administrative arrangements perfected, or at least well in hand, Buchanan and his staff could look forward to the receipt of exhibit materials. In January 1893 a trickle of shipments began to arrive; within weeks it had swelled to a flood. From some thirty-four foreign countries and colonies came more than 19,000 packages: sacks of coffee from Brazil and tea from Japan—iron-covered crates of German products and willow-sheathed boxes from Ceylon—rare wines from France and well-aged Scotch and Irish whiskies—bales of wool from New South Wales—national specialties and exotic items from every continent. From domestic farms, fields, and factories the volume and variety were even greater: farming tools and implements—windmills of a diversity that would have complicated Don Quixote's choice—dairy equipment and distilling machinery—fertilizers and forestry products—livestock of every species—a colossal statue of Columbus in chocolate—food articles and manufactured goods of infinite variety. Altogether, it was estimated, the equivalent of some 609 carloads of freight were unloaded, uncrated, then catalogued and positioned in interior booths or open air displays. By the eve of the exposition's opening 85 percent of the exhibits were in place and all was ready for what Buchanan confidently described as "one of the most complete agricultural shows ever planned."[36] Meanwhile, other departments attained a similar state of readiness.

Authorized as it was by federal statute and dedicated by its promoters to the discoverer of the New World, the Columbian Exposition appropriately opened its gates on an international keynote sounded by President Cleveland. "We stand today in the presence of the oldest nations of the world," said the chief executive, "and point to the great achievements here exhibited, asking no allowance on the score of youth." "It is an exalted mission in which we and our guests from other lands are engaged," he continued, "as we co-operate in the inauguration of an enterprise devoted to human enlightenment; and, in the undertaking we here enter upon, we exemplify in the noblest sense the brotherhood of nations."[37]

Fresh from his own recent inauguration and responsive to the tumultuous greeting of his audience, the president blithely pressed the gold and ivory button that activated all the exposition machinery. By this simple gesture he caused whistles to blow, chimes to ring, fountains to play, guns to belch, engines to revolve, and snow-white doves to fly. But more significantly, the electric impulse unfurled some 800 flags, with the banners of Castile and Aragón on flagstaffs of special honor to symbolize the Spanish royal union which sponsored Columbus's voyage of discovery.[38]

Buchanan has left no record of his part in these colorful opening-day ceremonies nor of his reactions to them. Yet, in view of his earlier associations with President Cleveland, it seems safe to assume that he was at least an attentive listener. As former director of the Corn Palaces, he could well remember the guide service he had rendered the Clevelands during their brief 1887 visit to Sioux City. Five years later, on presidential election day, he had made a special twenty-four-hour round-trip to his Iowa home to cast his ballot. "I don't know much about politics," he confessed to a reporter, "but you know where my heart is when I come 500 miles to vote for Cleveland."[39] Moreover, the inaugural activities of 1 May centered in the Court of Honor only a few steps from Buchanan's offices in the Agriculture Building.

Between this opening day and late autumn the World's Columbian Exposition attracted nearly 28,000,000 visitors—more even than attended the Paris Exposition four years before and almost triple the admissions to the Centennial Exposition at Philadelphia. On the day of greatest attendance a multitude of 716,881 thronged the spacious grounds.[40] Many of these came to view the exhibits of man's creativity in all forms of artistic expression; others came to marvel at his inventiveness in promoting industrial progress or his resourcefulness in improving products of the soil and field. They enjoyed daily concerts by nationally known artists or world-renowned composers. They attended congresses or symposia on a variety of nonindustrial themes, such as women's progress, suffrage reform, arbitration and world peace, problems of labor, and problems of religion. They were taught by the educational exhibits along the midway or entertained by its exotic attractions. Even in the midst of deepening economic depression in the nation, perhaps to seek temporary escape from their despair, crowds came just to admire the grandeur or the glitter of Chicago's "White City."

Buchanan spent the summer and fall performing the administrative routine of his multiple positions while enjoying the prestige and social glamour which accompanied it. As the only exposition chief responsible for four departments, he was called upon to supervise the functions and activities of hundreds of exhibitors, judges, and employees and to oversee the operation, maintenance, and security of scores of buildings and outside exhibits. His tours of inspection took him to every nook and corner of the exhibit areas, even to the recesses of the numerous livestock barns. As the summer progressed, he gave increasing attention to the planning of livestock displays in the open air pavilion, to the judging of entries in all competitive classes, and to the announcement of award winners.[41] Late in September, for example, he arranged a gala exhibition of prize-winning horses from all parts of the world: Shetland ponies, French trotters, German coach horses, Arabian steeds, Russian work horses, Clydesdales, and Percherons. Serving as parade marshal, while himself driving a spirited animal, he led the procession through the principal avenues of Jackson Park.[42]

Consistent with the educational emphasis projected by the exposition managers, Buchanan planned a continuing series of congresses on problems related to the jurisdiction of his departments. Whether dealing with agriculture, horticulture, livestock, or forestry, these conferences attracted such speakers as the new secretary of agriculture, J. Sterling Morton, as well as specialists from Australia, Ceylon, Siberia, and other world areas. Even more innovative were the symposia he scheduled on "good roads" and "patents, trademarks, and inventions." Often he addressed the opening sessions of these convocations.[43]

Like other American fairs and expositions before and since, the World's Columbian set aside special days to honor particular persons, events, states, or nations—and, of course, to increase the turnstile count. When these had a pertinence to Buchanan's departments, he was invariably on hand to welcome and entertain his guests. Yet, no opportunity to serve as host pleased him as much as that provided on 21 September, Iowa Day. Special arrangements for the occasion called for the Iowa governor and his party to be escorted through the midway, and northward along the lakefront esplanade to the Iowa State Building, designed, as Buchanan had promised three years before, to simulate a Sioux City Corn Palace.

Perhaps by coincidence but certainly through good fortune, the subsequent welcoming ceremonies brought together two Iowa friends of long standing: Agricultural Chief Buchanan, who substituted for the director general, and Governor Horace Boies, who in 1890 had recommended the Sioux Cityan's appointment to the National Commission. On behalf of his chief Buchanan extended to the governor and people of Iowa the exposition's thanks and congratulations for their support and contributions. Appropriately, he used the occasion to recall that exactly "100 years ago last Monday" President Washington had laid the cornerstone for the national capitol. During that century, he then reminded his Iowa friends, "Americans had conquered a wilderness, established in that wilderness a granary, built mighty cities, laid a lacework of railroads and telegraph wires—built this White City and supported it with over a million a week even during financial troubles. Iowa has stood in the forefront of this growth."[44]

For both the Buchanans the social whirl to which they were exposed by virtue of his administrative posts went far beyond the simple conviviality they had enjoyed in Sioux City. As the summer wore on, they found both stimulating and demanding the crowded schedule of official receptions, dinners, dedications, and testimonial functions. They received invitations to banquets in honor of Queen Victoria, the Emperor Francis Joseph, the czar of Russia, the king of Spain, and the sultan of Johore—to dinners given by the Imperial German, the Imperial Japanese, the Royal Korean Commissioners—to Latin American fiestas, receptions, and concerts, often featuring native musicians playing indigenous music. Not to be outdone by their overseas visitors, the exposition management sponsored or encouraged a similar variety of extracurricular social affairs. To the hundreds of invitations they received—many ex officio to be sure—the Buchanans must occasionally have felt obliged to send regrets.[45]

Though not an active worker in exposition affairs as she had been for the Corn Palaces, Mrs. Buchanan still managed to complement her husband in his social responsibilities. A journalist described her as "one of the liveliest women that have been seen in Jackson Park . . . a stately blonde with big, handsome blue eyes and a fine complexion. She dresses with rare taste and often so designs her dinner gowns that the costumes present a felicitous combination of dress and natural flowers."[46]

But for Will Buchanan the unquestioned high light of the exposition social season was the complimentary banquet given him on 21 July by several hundred gentlemen connected with his departments—exhibitors, judges, commissioners, other officials. The Grand Pacific Hotel's six-course dinner with as many wines, an elaborate ten-page menu-program, and the gift of a large gold-lined silver loving cup symbolized the respect and appreciation of guests who represented nearly every country of the world and many of its colonies.

After the customary toasts to the president of the United States, rulers of foreign nations, and even to Columbus, Toastmaster Henry W. Pearson, British superintendent of agriculture, called upon citizens of six different countries to pay honor to Chief Buchanan. A Russian judge of awards, E. T. Mitcherlich, while praising "the warm friendly relations" existing between Russia and the United States, extended thanks to the American people as well as to Buchanan. Cyrus H. McCormick, of Chicago, referred to him as "so genial, so worthy, and so eminent a man." The spokesman for Liberia suggested the possibility of starting a presidential boom.[47]

Even though he fully sensed the hyperbole in these encomiums, Buchanan could not have misconstrued the sincerity his hosts sought to convey. His response to the toasts was modest and brief. Recalling the roofs crushed in by ice, the exhibits damaged by snow, rain, and heat, and "a thousand small, irritating things," he wondered at their patience and kindness. Then, reiterating the international theme to which he was becoming increasingly dedicated, he declared that "if the friendships and acquaintances made among us shall broaden our knowledge of the interests and countries represented here, as I know they will, we shall have been repaid for all our labor."[48]

But however multifarious their social functions and routine duties, neither the fair's directors nor department chiefs could afford to neglect the central theme around which they had promoted and developed the Columbian Exposition—homage to America's discoverer and the modern lands of Iberian heritage. Actually, as early as mid-1890 the management began to search for distinctive means to illuminate this feature. And in a number of ways Buchanan found himself drawn closer to the Latin America he had first come to know during the visit of its diplomats to Sioux City in 1889.

To consolidate its activities in this direction the exposition's executive committee, in August 1891, activated a Latin American Bureau by appointing as its chief William E. Curtis, a long-time enthusiast for Pan Americanism.[49] In 1884-1885, as a member of President Arthur's special commission on trade with Latin America, Curtis had toured a number of the countries. Envisioning bright commercial potentialities, he mobilized all his efforts to promote improved relations among the American nations. By 1889 he had published two books of a descriptive nature designed to stimulate the interest of United States manufacturers and exporters.[50] As Secretary of State Blaine's right-hand man during the First Pan American Conference of 1889-1890, he had served as official escort of the Latin American diplomats on their extended railroad excursion. Thus it was, on the delegates' Sioux City stopover, that Buchanan first came in contact with the promoter and his ardor for the Pan American idea.[51] A year later he was not surprised to learn of Curtis's appointment as first director of the International Bureau of American Republics.

But months before the exposition authorities had formally engaged Curtis to head its own Latin American Bureau, he had been advising them from Washington on the solicitation of exhibits from Latin America.[52] Consistent with his suggestions, a dozen young men were commissioned to visit Hemisphere nations with the express mission of awakening interest in the exposition. Most of these were young army and navy officers detailed as legation attachés. All were familiar with the languages and customs of the countries to which they travelled and had received appropriate orientation on the plans and purposes of the exposition. In recruiting exhibits for his departments Chief Buchanan worked closely with these young agents.[53]

Once he assumed active direction of the exposition's Latin American Bureau, Curtis revealed his resourcefulness in realizing plans to dramatize the Columbus theme. Conceiving the Convent of La Rábida in Spain as "the cornerstone of American history," he secured authorization to build a replica at the exposition.[54] Authorized by joint resolution of Congress and subsidized by the Department of State, Curtis travelled to Spain and elsewhere to collect nearly a thousand items of Columbian memorabilia for display in the building.[55] With the La Rábida project under way, the authorities turned to the possibility of persuading Spanish notables to visit the exposition. They were able to secure from Congress another joint resolution, which requested President Harrison to invite the Spanish rulers and descendants of Columbus to attend the opening ceremonies.[56] Escort for the dignitaries was the Spanish ambassador, Enrique Dupuy de Lôme, whose name would become better known to Americans at the time of the Spanish-American War. All reached Chicago in time for the inaugural ceremonies; most remained until early June.[57]

Curtis then planned a still more exciting coup. This was the reproduction in Spain of Columbus's three caravels, their tracing of the discoverer's route to the Indies, and subsequent transit to Chicago. It was a heady dream, to be realized only after months of delays, confusion, and diplomatic maneuvering.[58] By arrangements with the Madrid government the construction of the replicas—*Santa María, Pinta, Niña*—took place in Spanish shipyards under joint Spanish-American direction. For the United States all construction and executive details were placed in the hands of Lt. W. McCarty Little, a retired navy officer whose patience, forbearance, and admiration for Spain eventually overcame all his frustrations. On one festering question, for example—which nation's crews should man the vessels—he irrevocably settled the matter when he wrote, "the 'Santa Maria' in Chicago with an American Crew would be Hamlet left out with a vengeance!"[59]

When the caravels had finally passed inspection as seaworthy, they rendezvoused for Spain's Columbian quadricentennial celebration at the port of Huelva[60] and moved out to sea past the Convent of La Rábida. After impressive international naval reviews at Hampton Roads, Virginia, and New York harbor, the little fleet edged northward for the two-month voyage through the St. Lawrence and the heart of the continent.

The arrival of the fleet in Chicago on 7 July marked the historic climax of the Columbian Exposition. Still flying the emblem of Castile and greeted by booming guns and a huge flotilla of yachts, the caravels cast anchor just offshore from the exposition's replica of La Rábida. Gaily decorated cutters promptly transported the fleet officers, Ambassador Dupuy de Lôme, and American dignitaries to the reviewing area before the Administration and Agriculture Buildings. Here a singular escort of honor awaited the Spaniards: English grenadiers and French marines; Eskimos in furs and Scotch Highlanders in kilts; Sioux Indians in war paint and Arab Bedouins with scimitars. In all, the colorfully garbed representatives of fifty nations then passed in review.

Following more traditional patterns of welcome, President Thomas W. Palmer of the Exposition Board called upon Senator John Sherman of Ohio and Secretary of the Navy Hilary H. Herbert for the formal speeches of salutation. In responding for his officers and men, Captain Victor M. Concas happily noted that, in sailing from Spain's La Rábida to Chicago's, his flotilla had travelled much farther than that of Admiral Columbus.

At this point, except for the balls and receptions to follow, the official welcoming ritual was about to end. Yet, two incidents, as curious as they were unexpected, preceded the final cheers. In what he fully expected to be the terminal remarks, Chairman Palmer reiterated his respect for Spain and commended its post-Columbian policies toward the Indians of the Americas:

> Senator Sherman has spoken of the difference with which the natives of the continent have been treated by the Spaniards and by the Anglo-Saxons. The English speaking people have not only stolen this country of the aborigines, but have nearly killed all those aborigines. The Spaniards deserved very much credit for preserving the aborigines of the continent

> wherever they located. But there is one man who is hardly ever spoken of at these festive gatherings, who 400 years ago was a philanthropist in the highest sense of the term, who was born a fighter, who was born a wealthy man, and who was a gentleman in the sense of the gentleman of that day, and yet who gave up all his prospects to devote himself to the amelioration of the condition of the Indians 400 years ago. That was Las Casas. He was a Spaniard. . . . I wish, in conclusion, to propose three cheers for Spain, the Spanish people, the Spanish Navy, and Las Casas.

When he added, "Now, give it with a tiger!" the multitude lustily complied.[61] Yet, it seems likely that few in that day's audience had ever heard of Bartolomé de las Casas, the Dominican friar whom many Latin Americans still revere as the "Apostle to the Indians." And probably many had been brought up on the so-called "Black Legend"—so patently indicted by Palmer—of Spain's career in the Americas.

There remained, however, still another unplanned episode—the lone disharmonious note in the day's festivities. Chicagoans in the crowd refused to disperse until they had heard from their long-time mayor, Carter Harrison. Picking up his cue from previous speakers, the mayor left his hearers in no doubt about his views on the white man's treatment of the Indians. "Senator Sherman thanked the Spaniards," he recalled,

> that they had not killed out the Indians. We thank the Anglo Saxons that they did kill out the Indians and gave America really to the white race—not that we love the Indians less, but we love civilization and the white men more.[62]

When shouts of "No! No!" rose from a group of Indians and others nearby, Chairman Palmer faced a tense moment.

Fortuitously in this taut situation another insistent demand from the crowd relieved the chairman's plight: "Why doesn't Fred Douglass speak to us?" They were calling for a platform guest, who, like Mayor Harrison, had not been scheduled to speak. Frederick Douglass was now an aging white-haired man—former slave, active abolitionist, confidant of John Brown, recently United States minister to Haiti, and currently serving as Haitian commissioner to the exposition. With obvious reluctance he quietly responded to the appeal:

> If I say anything it will be this: I think it a great thing to be a Spaniard; I think it a great thing to be an Englishman and a very great thing to be an American; I think it more than all to be a man; to be a member of the

human family; to be a part of the whole rather than the whole of a part.⁶³

A wild yell from the Indians led the cheers which followed, a band struck up "Hail Columbia!" and, as tensions eased, the throng slowly moved away.

For all these variations on the Columbian theme Buchanan had no direct responsibility. Yet, with the Agriculture Building fronting on the Court of Honor, he had a virtual ringside seat from which to observe each feature as it developed. Even without his evolving interest in Latin America, he could not have missed the excitement these commemorative displays produced nor the import they conveyed.

At the same time, far more productive for Buchanan's continuing orientation to the Hispanic world were the friendships that developed from the routine administration of his departments. Few of the Latin American nations had ever participated in a world's fair. The essential character of the Columbian Exposition, however, attracted exhibits from nearly every one of the republics as well as from several colonial lands, Cuba, British Guiana, and British Honduras. Most of these, like the nations of Europe and Asia, delegated national commissioners to remain in Chicago for the duration of the exhibition. In addition, many of the hundreds of Latin American exhibitors were on hand for part or all of the fair's duration. By the very nature of his duties Buchanan came in direct contact with all of these persons, and he made the most of these opportunities to broaden his understanding of other cultures. Gradually he became more sensitive to the interests and problems of these people as well as to their customs, temperament, and social values, even the rudiments of their languages. From this orientation at Chicago, therefore, Buchanan had learned how to make himself *simpático* to the Latin Americans.

With the approach of the exposition's closing date, Buchanan faced his most frustrating assignment—overseeing the dismantlement of the sprawling establishment he had assembled. The display materials and livestock had to be moved out—sold, given away, destroyed, or returned to their point of shipment. Protests from disgruntled entrants in award classes had to be adjudicated. Personnel services had to be terminated, financial accounts balanced, and the official records of four departments assembled and appropriately secured. All of these things were to be completed and the buildings cleared by 1 January 1894, when they would be turned over to Chicago's South Park commissioners.[64]

These onerous duties fulfilled, Buchanan could turn to the preparation of the final reports required for his departments. In each of these he incorporated a comprehensive chronological accounting of his activities, a topical resumé of the agency's operations over the three years of his administration, and a series of recommendations for future international expositions. Six years hence, Buffalo's Pan-American Exposition would give him the chance to test his own recommendations. The Department of Agriculture report, dated 26 March 1894, to which he appended a brief statement of appreciation to Director General Davis and other exposition officials, terminated his exposition obligations.[65]

In the midst of preparing these departmental reports, an opportunity came Buchanan's way to crystallize his thoughts about the place of agriculture in American life. The opportunity stemmed from invitations to address audiences in two eastern cities in mid-January: in Trenton before the New Jersey State Agricultural Society and in New York as part of a special lecture series at Cooper Union. Preparation of papers for these events forced him to synthesize ideas that had been germinating during his seven years as director of corn palaces and chief of exposition departments.[66]

"I firmly believe that what is most required by the farmers of the United States," he asserted to his Trenton audience, "is a more thorough understanding of the conditions existing throughout the world as they affect agricultural products." Farmers should be familiar with the operations of supply and demand, with the market they trade on, and with world market conditions. They "must use the same willingness to profit by close study, the same skill, the same shrewdness, and the same good management displayed by the banker or manufacturer."

Agriculture would not attain its rightful place in American society, Buchanan further argued, without a broadened emphasis upon agricultural education in all its forms. In agricultural colleges, to be sure, but also in the normal schools, in all public schools, even in the country schoolhouse! He saw no paternalism in government support for these programs. He strongly approved farmers' institutes, experiment stations, and county and state fairs. "There is nothing in education like observation."

In his Cooper Union talk two nights later Buchanan used the Columbian Exposition as his point of departure. He focused on the diversified benefits to be gleaned from world's fairs, especially for farmers, stockmen, and manufacturers. By viewing exhibits and chatting with specialists, farmers at Chicago learned of new seeds, new methods of cultivation, and new techniques for treating the soil. Stockmen were able to sell breeding animals to Latin American buyers who had previously relied solely upon English and Scottish breeders. Manufacturers of agricultural implements took orders from Latin American and other countries where their products had previously been unknown. He then turned to forestry, which, he said, his department had hoped to present as a science. But, after scouring the country, they could find only one forester qualified to demonstrate scientific methods of forest preservation. This was Gifford Pinchot, whom they engaged to display the methods he was developing for George W. Vanderbilt at Biltmore, North Carolina. Buchanan went on to deplore his country's lag behind European nations in forest development and preservation.

Through these public presentations Buchanan revealed much of the practical wisdom he had distilled from his years of experience as farmer, travelling salesman, businessman, impresario of popular entertainment, and director of agricultural expositions. He had come to recognize the interdependence of American agriculture and world markets—to acknowledge the achievements of alien cultures—to appreciate the indispensable role of education, both formal and informal, in American life—to sense the utility of both the business world's practicality and the scientific world's theories—and always to emphasize the aesthetic as counterweight to the mundane.

Long before he composed these public lectures, however, Buchanan had begun to consider a more personal matter—his own future career and the welfare of his family. Though they had left Sioux City with every expectation of returning and continued to regard it as their real home, three years in Chicago had greatly altered their outlook. The children—Florence, now fourteen, and Donald, six—were growing up; absence had weakened their ties with Sioux City.[67] However strong the yearning to return to her relatives and friends in familiar surroundings, Mrs. Buchanan could appreciate her husband's dilemma. His years at the exposition had brought him new contacts, broadened his interests, and lifted his horizons. It was doubtful that Sioux City could now offer him a career that he would find adequately challenging or even satisfying, one that would let him take full advantage of his Chicago experience. Fortunately, new opportunities became available.

In view of his successful record of public service in Sioux City and Chicago, it was natural that Iowa Democrats should see in their colleague a possible candidate for political office. Accordingly, soon after Cleveland's election, they had lost little time in urging the president-elect to appoint him secretary of agriculture. When asked by a reporter if he would accept the position, the Iowan replied, "I never refuse or accept anything until it has been offered to me. Until such time I have nothing to say." Again in August 1893, he was mentioned as one of the several possibilities to oppose Governor Boies's bid for renomination.[68] And there were isolated suggestions that he was presidential timber.[69] Although Buchanan has left no further record of his reaction to these boomlets, it is doubtful if he took them very seriously.

A more realistic possibility for his future employment was the opportunity to serve as managing director of a large commercial company seeking to encourage inter-American trade. Early in 1892 a group of New York importers and bankers had approached Buchanan about their plans for a "Pan American company." Their proposals were impressive: a bureau of information to be maintained in New York City; a commerical museum for the display of both American and Latin American products; the issuance of a weekly foreign trade bulletin for manufacturers and investors; and the publication of a monthly foreign trade review. William E. Curtis would become editor of these publications. At the close of the Columbian Exposition the company would take over many of the exhibits for the New York museums and would send Buchanan to Latin America for a study of its resources. Clearly the proposition appealed to the agriculture chief, though he refused to commit himself until the close of the exposition in late 1893.[70]

However, on 9 October the *Chicago Tribune* and other newspapers carried detailed stories of the entire project. Their source was a prospectus issued by its promoters; it announced the affiliation of both Buchanan and Curtis. For the Iowan the announcement was unfortunately premature; by this time an even more attractive possibility was dangling before him.

In early September key leaders of the Iowa Democratic Party, strongly supported by powerful agricultural and commercial interests, had initiated a drive to persuade President Cleveland to appoint Buchanan minister to the Argentine Republic.[71] Lamenting the frequent appointment of diplomatic officers for reasons of "social prestige, wealth, party service," *The Breeders Gazette* declared, "we believe him to be one of the most completely equipped men in America to-day for the Argentine mission."[72] Scores of letters in the appointment files of the Department of State disclose the strength and diversity of the backing which promoted his appointment.

Leadership of the campaign on Buchanan's behalf apparently centered in an Iowa Democrat, J. J. Richardson, publisher of the *Davenport Democrat* and member of the executive board of the party's national committee. Periodically between September and January he wrote or forwarded messages to the White House and the Department of State.[73] At the same time a stream of endorsements flowed to Washington: from the executives of half-a-dozen stockgrowers associations and from the presidents of nationally known industries, such as Swift and Company, John Deere and Company, Studebaker Brothers, and the Pabst Brewing Company; from public officials (an Iowa senator, the Iowa governor, the mayor of Chicago) and from other prominent Chicagoans (Cyrus H. McCormick, Potter Palmer, Director General George H. Davis and other exposition officials); from the Association of American Agricultural Colleges and Experiment Stations and from the New Jersey State Board of Agriculture; from Democrats and from Republicans who were eager to support even a "pronounced Democrat."[74] Clearly, this pressure to send Buchanan to Argentina stemmed largely, though not exclusively, from the actions of vested interests, political and economic.

Nevertheless, even if the endorsements are derogated somewhat as overblown references, they reveal understandable reasons for the selection of Buchanan for the Argentine post. In a sense, the Columbian Exposition had symbolized the post-Civil War maturation of American industry and agriculture. By the 1890s, seeking new markets for increased productive capacity, manufacturers of agricultural machinery and implements eyed the surplus food-producing economy of the pampas. Similarly expansive, livestockmen were eager to challenge the monopoly English breeders had long enjoyed in supplying pure-bred animals to improve Argentine native stock. Conjecturing that a qualified American diplomat in Buenos Aires could help penetrate that market, Buchanan's sponsors spelled out the reasons for believing him to be the man.[75] He had studied the resources of the Latin American countries, come to know their leading agricultural men, and acquired practical knowledge of the market conditions governing inter-American trade. Besides his discriminating judgment and demonstrated executive ability, he was resourceful, tactful in dealing with people, impressive and dignified on public occasions. And as Cyrus H. McCormick wrote to Secretary of State Walter Q. Gresham, the Iowan was "fully imbued with the importance of the Pan-American idea."[76]

Aware of the influence being exerted on his behalf, Buchanan felt constrained to remind the president of his total inexperience in a diplomatic post and of his conviction that his friends had overrated his abilities. He also wrote that "under no circumstances could I afford to accept any position under the Government except with the knowledge that my services and abilities were believed of value to Americans."[77]

While on his speaking trip to Trenton and New York in mid-January, Buchanan learned that President Cleveland had transmitted his nomination to the Senate. By the end of the month he received official notification of the Senate's confirmation.[78] For the entire Buchanan family Will's prompt acceptance initiated six weeks of hasty preparations for another shift in their life pattern.[79] There was still a final exposition report or two to be completed. There were friends and relatives to be visited in Chicago and Dayton. There were homes to be closed in Chicago and Sioux City. Nevertheless, they found time at their Iowa home to relax among friends at diverse functions arranged in their honor.[80] Once these duties and amenities had been met, they could move on to Washington. Several days of briefing at the Department of State, a family call at the White House, and a dinner with Argentine Minister Estanislao S. Zeballos and Washington notables gave all the Buchanans a running introduction to one facet of a diplomat's world. On 21 March, aboard the *City of Berlin,* Buchanan and his family embarked from New York on his mission as envoy extraordinary and minister plenipotentiary to the Argentine Republic.[81] Departure might have been more difficult for all of them had they known his tour of duty would stretch out to more than five years. Yet, unlike Columbus at La Rábida, they could be sure their first voyage across the Atlantic would lead them to a new world.

Chapter 5
DIPLOMAT IN THE MAKING
Argentina, 1894-1895

William Buchanan began his diplomatic career in the Argentine Republic. His abrupt shift from the world of expositions to the arena of diplomacy took him to the country considered by many to be the most stable and progressive in Latin America—to a country already highly geared to the commercial production of livestock and grains, yet confidently preparing to augment the productive capacity of its ranches and fields. In the Argentine cities and countryside, as he sought to cultivate new markets for the United States and its citizens, he could put to effective use the agricultural knowledge he had gained in Ohio, Iowa, and Chicago. But first the neophyte minister needed to learn the procedures and protocol of the diplomatic game while at the same time acquainting himself with the land and its people. Thanks to two presidents—one Democratic, the other Republican—he would have more than five years to accomplish his mission.

Next to the United States, Buchanan was aware, Argentina was the oldest nation on the American mainland. Six years before declaring their independence from Spain in 1816, Argentine creole leaders had begun to replace the royal establishment with their own governmental institutions. A half century of internal schisms and political experimentation then preceded gradual stabilization, but through it all the Argentine people successfully defended their sovereign independence. From the very outset they regarded Buenos Aires as their capital city and all the lands of the former Spanish Viceroyalty of the Rio de la Plata as their rightful territorial heritage. But the Bolivians and Paraguayans to the north and the Uruguayans to the east had no more desire to be ruled from Buenos Aires than from Madrid and determined to follow their own paths to independence.

Even without these coveted borderlands, postindependence Argentina embraced a vast territory in the heart of South America's most habitable region. Stretching from the tropical scrub forests of the Chaco to the windswept tablelands of Patagonia and from the 1600-mile Atlantic coastline to the even longer mountain wall of the Andes, it was one of the half dozen largest countries in the world. Superimposed upside down on a map of eastern North America in comparable latitudes, it would reach from Hudson Bay to well south of Key West, its total area roughly equivalent to the United States east of the Mississippi.

At the core of this elongated domain lie the pampas, incredibly flat, generally treeless, reasonably well watered, and incomparably fertile. From the estuary of the Río de la Plata, the pampas extend north, west, and south to encompass a region as big as Texas. Here, in early colonial days, Spanish settlers had begun to congregate, then to generate a lucrative traffic in the hides of wild cattle. On this economic base, after independence, their Argentine successors had developed one of the world's great cattle- and grain-producing centers. By amassing vast expanses of the rich pampas, a new class of wealthy landowners was able to create a string of sprawling *estancias,* each adorned by a chateau-like manor house. From these rural mansions in the 1890s they continued to oversee their herds of thoroughbred livestock and their bands of gaucho tenants.[1]

Inevitably, the export of bulky foodstuffs demanded a central point of transshipment with adequate rail and port facilities. And naturally, the influential *estancieros* required an urban base in which to exert their economic and political power and to enhance their social prestige. Hard by the shores of the La Plata, yet easily accessible from all parts of the pampas, Buenos Aires had long since established itself as that port and seat of power. By the 1890s it had become a clamorous railroad center and world port and a burgeoning metropolis of well over half a million *porteños*. This was the exotic new world into which the four Buchanans moved late in the fall afternoon of 7 May 1894. "Tomorrow we begin a new experience," Will had confided to his diary the previous evening, "hope we will like it."[2]

Yet during the seven weeks of their tiring passage from New York, there must have been times when the Buchanans wondered if they would ever reach their destination—the safe haven early Spanish mariners had termed the place of "good airs." Even as late as the last decade of the nineteenth century no passenger-carrying boats sailed regularly from New York to the east coast ports of South America. Like every Argentine-bound American diplomat since Joel Roberts Poinsett in 1810, Buchanan was forced to reach his post by the circuitous route via Southampton. Leaving New York on 21 March, the family spent ten days on the *City of Berlin* to the English port and another twenty-seven on the *Elbe* to Argentina. Rarely in his life did Buchanan keep a diary, but these days of shipboard leisure gave him time to record daily activities.[3]

On the North Atlantic crossing—their first trip by sea—foul weather compelled them to endure successive days of fog, cold, snow, freezing rain, gale-force winds, and rough seas. One day an alarming combustion in a cargo of hay forced temporary stoppage of the ship's engines. Only a final spell of smooth sailing and Will's selection to preside at a benefit concert brightened an otherwise cheerless voyage.[4]

Their six days in England were a welcome respite from ship travel for all the family. They rode through Trafalgar Square, Hyde Park, and Regent's Park. They drove past Buckingham Palace and toured St. Paul's Cathedral. At Westminster Abbey, they stood in the Poets' Corner through a Sunday service, and in the House of Commons they heard Lord Arthur Balfour debate the Scotland Home Rule question. Sometimes leaving the family to enjoy shopping sprees or ride the omnibuses, Will conferred with Ambassador Thomas F. Bayard, lunched with London's Lord Mayor at the Oxford and Cambridge Club, and under the guidance of the queen's farmer inspected the dairy, stock, and poultry yards at Windsor Castle.[5]

Their London business and sightseeing finished, the Buchanans departed Southampton on 6 April for the long voyage to Argentina. They caught their first glimpses of the European mainland at Vigo, Spain, "a quaint white place," and at Oporto, Portugal, where Will bought gloves and a cane for the 5900 reis he exchanged for his American gold piece. Then sailing toward the South Atlantic, they began to enjoy days of "tropical sunshine . . . water blue as indigo [and] great number of nautilus sailing the wind"—sometimes interrupted by days of fog, seasickness, and "state rooms hot as smoke." Still recalling his farmboy life, Will occasionally visualized the Ohio countryside in the changing ocean scene: "schools of flying fish scud out of the water and fly like a covey of quail . . . in a grain field and skimming and settling down just as they do." Church services, a special luncheon on their wedding anniversay, and another master of ceremonies assignment—this time for a circus performance—helped them all to pass the time.[6]

Fourteen days out of Southampton the *Elbe* made its first landfall on the South American mainland at Pernambuco, Brazil. Then came Maceio, where it took on a number of deputies bound for the national congress in Rio de Janerio—Bahía, where the Buchanans admired the well-preserved colonial buildings—Rio, where the beautiful bay, a severe epidemic of yellow fever, and evidences of a recent revolution left them with mixed impressions—and Montevideo, where "it looked good to see the Stars and Stripes flying over ships of the Navy's South Atlantic Squadron." One more leg and their "outward bound" passage brought them to Argentine waters.[7]

Then came five days of almost unrelieved monotony while the ship lay in quarantine in the middle of the La Plata within binocular site of Buenos Aires. On the first day the Buchanans received a spirited marine salute as George W. Fishback, secretary of the United States Legation, and a number of Americans circled the *Elbe* on a harbor tug. On each of the following days the doctor's boat brought them mail and newspapers from Chicago or Sioux City. In the meantime the family could do little but contemplate the brown surface of the La Plata, which they likened to the muddy waters of their familiar Missouri, or gaze across the Argentine shoreline to fields that reminded them of Iowa. More important for Will, he could prepare for his first official act as the new United States minister—the address he would give upon his presentation to the president of Argentina.[8]

On 7 May the family disembarked at Ensenada, there to be greeted by Secretary Fishback, Consul Edward L. Baker, and a representative of the Argentine Foreign Office. By special railroad car the party moved in style to Buenos Aires. That evening Minister Buchanan composed his first dispatch to Washington from Buenos Aires, a report of his arrival and a chronological statement of his itinerary.[9] The onetime Ohio farmboy had learned another reality of becoming a United States diplomat in the late nineteenth century—reaching one's post might take a long time.

Two weeks later the minister presented his letter of credence to President Luis Saenz Peña. Though the ceremony may have lacked some of the pomp and circumstance of similar occasions in Madrid or Rome, it was by Buchanan's Iowa and Chicago standards an event of considerable pageantry. Escorted by the subsecretary of foreign affairs, a high-ranking general, and a detachment of cavalry, he was driven to and from the Casa Rosada in the state coach. In the presence of cabinet members, a representative of the archbishop, and a number of military and naval officers and prominent citizens —all in full dress—he read his long presentation address to the president. After the customary salutations and congratulations, the minister thanked the Argentine government for its generous and well-planned participation in the Columbian Exposition and expressed his hopes for beneficial results to the nation's business enterprises.[10] In reproducing the entire address the following day, an English-language newspaper frankly characterized Buchanan as an exponent of "true Americanism," one who would not "occupy himself in stirring up the great American eagle and making the bird of freedom scream."[11] To some Argentine critics, at least, the minister appeared to have passed his first test. Within another forty-eight hours, he made the expected round of personal calls—on the president, all cabinet members, and the chiefs of most diplomatic missions in the capital.[12]

Even before fulfilling these matters of protocol, Buchanan had begun to cope with both the routine and the challenge of his new position. With but two days of predeparture briefing at the Department of State, he now had no choice but to acquire the essential knowledge and skills through self-arranged, on-the-job training. First of all, he faced the mundane problems of adequate quarters for the legation and comfortable housing for his family.

When the minister first entered his mission headquarters, he could feel only dismay and shock. Its total space comprised two small office-building rooms—and these without a semblance of artificial heating. As he promptly reported to Washington, furnishings were extremely sparse: two small writing desks, three bookcases, four chairs, a table, a sofa, one pair of curtains, three "North American" flags, and two legation shields. The bookcases contained some four hundred volumes, but these were mostly sets of United States government documents. There was no typewriter, no press for copying letters, and no security or letter files of any sort. It had not been a rule, he discovered, to provide the State Department with copies of all correspondence to the Argentine Foreign Office, nor even to maintain a complete set among legation records.[13]

Putting to good use his long managerial experience, Buchanan at once undertook to rectify these housekeeping defects. It was his wish, he wrote, "to make the Legation as effective and as creditable in every way as possible within economical and reasonable limits." From personal funds he bought a small gas stove to heat the two rooms. He persuaded the State Department to let him spend $148.50 for a letter press and other office needs. He instituted a system for recording, filing, indexing, and securing all correspondence and transactions. For three months he accommodated himself to this austere working space, then moved the legation to more commodious quarters. In the meantime, after much searching for a comfortable home for his family, he rented for six months the furnished residence of the German consul general.[14]

Almost at once after his arrival Buchanan began to compile and send off to Washington the kind of despatches he knew the State Department desired. With the aid of Secretary Fishback he prepared reports on such varied topics as the annual message of President Saenz Peña, the season's phenomenal wheat harvest, the generally unsatisfactory business outlook, and official 1893 figures on immigration and emigration. He prepared to comply with the Department of Agriculture's request for monthly reports on volume and prices of Argentina's cereal and beef exports. During his first six weeks, even in the midst of preliminary routine and establishing initial contacts, he averaged nearly a report a day.[15]

With 4 July coming so soon after their arrival, the Buchanans were forced quickly to absorb the significance of a quite different responsibility of the diplomat's life—the social and ceremonial side. Barely settled in their new home, they had little time in which to prepare the customary open house to honor Independence Day. Nevertheless, with the aplomb they had developed through their exposition experience and with the assistance of Consul Baker and Secretary Fishback, they successfully entertained more than three hundred guests at a reception and buffet. In addition, the occasion provided an opportunity to introduce all the Buchanans to the capital's notables.[16] As reported by the press, Mrs. Buchanan entertained "with that grace and distinction characteristic of North American ladies," and both the children fulfilled their minor social responsibilities.[17]

Only five days later came Argentina's Independence Day, commemorated by a *Te Deum* in the National Cathedral. At the reception which followed Buchanan was pleased to hear Saenz Peña express his admiration for President Cleveland and the United States and his conviction that "arbitration is the proper and right solution of all international questions."[18] At about the same time the minister received invitations to a banquet in honor of the diplomatic corps and to a memorial funeral service for President Sadi Carnot of France. Thus the steady round of receptions, fiestas, and ceremonials began quickly to build up.[19]

His preliminary housekeeping chores and social and ceremonial obligations adequately attended, Minister Buchanan could turn to an essential objective of his mission—to know and understand Argentina and the Argentines. Until he learned their language, familiarized himself with their capital city, and visited the provinces, he knew he could not fully satisfy either himself or those responsible for his appointment. His family too, though accustomed by this time to meeting new situations, faced special problems in orienting themselves to life in a foreign land, especially one in the Southern Hemisphere.

Having left their homeland in the fading days of winter, the Buchanans endured a long voyage, only to find another winter season awaiting them. And a Buenos Aires winter, they soon discovered, was not like Iowa's, with frequent crisp, snowy spells, but rather it was a succession of cold, disagreeably rainy days. They quickly experienced as well the reality of inadequate heating in homes, stores, offices, and public places.[20] As an added problem, each faced the language barrier. Promptly placed in a school with instruction in both Spanish and English, the children learned readily. By December they had gained enough competence to appear publicly in a school program; Florence recited a Spanish declamation entitled "No me olvides," Donald, "La perla y el diamante."[21] For Mrs. Buchanan the solution was not so easy. Will, of course, had picked up a few expressions from his summer-long contacts with the Latin Americans at the exposition. Moreover, his daily contacts and his own determination enabled him to progress adequately, and long before the end of his five-year tour he would become relatively fluent.

As they began their trips about Buenos Aires, the former Chicagoans found many things to remind them of the metropolis they had left. Both cities had been plotted in traditional checkerboard pattern, with many of the narrow streets traversed by noisy car lines or intersected by railroad tracks. Since neither city had zoning restrictions, both contained conglomerates of factories, meat-packing establishments, stockyards, railroad terminals, bakeries, and stores. Both were expanding their open-space areas, with Buenos Aires well ahead in plazas and Chicago in spacious parks, though beautiful Palermo was probably superior to the Illinois city's Jackson or Lincoln. The fabulous new townhouses going up along the Avenida Alvear near the Buchanans' home were a reminder of the elegant mansions they had seen on Chicago's south side. Both cities enjoyed and exploited the large body of water beside which it had grown up.[22]

Yet, essential differences in architectural styles rendered these similarities decidedly less significant. The Buchanans were quick to observe that the new skyscraper-type buildings they remembered from Chicago's inner city had no counterpart in the Argentine capital. Its growth was not upward, but outward into the limitless pampas. And on most residential streets the plaster or stucco walls of one- and two-story houses came flush to the sidewalks, their patios or gardens closed to the passerby. The Iowans missed the well-groomed front lawns of Sioux City or even the fenced-in flower gardens of Chicago.

With its 1895 population surpassing 600,000 Buenos Aires like Chicago was trying to assimilate a never-ending stream of immigrants. Well over half of the city's residents had been born in Europe, the majority in Italy or Spain. A few of the new arrivals ventured to the pampas to become tenant farmers or sharecroppers, but most remained in the city to seek employment in the factories, mills, stockyards, and railroad shops. Denied by law or practice the rights to acquire land or exercise suffrage, they faced little prospect of gaining an influential place in the socioeconomic or political systems. Under Argentine traditions of constitutional democracy, political power rested securely in the hands of a ruling few, principally the estancieros. Eventually, as their numbers increased and their fortune slowly improved, the immigrant groups would coalesce with the voteless creoles to demand an equitable share in the governing process.[23] But the class structure Minister Buchanan had to try to understand and interpret in his time was a typical pyramid of social strata—the creole-immigrants as the broad base, the small oligarchic group at the apex, and a rudimentary middle class between.

In still broader perspective, like Chicago Buenos Aires served as the throbbing focus of a vast agrarian heartland and its principal transfer point in the shipment of foodstuffs and manufactured goods. Yet again, it was like New York as the nation's greatest port and principal avenue to the outside world. It also resembled Washington—even in the design of its prospective capitol—as the seat of a national political system, though Argentina's administrations dominated the provinces and municipalities to an extent Potomac leaders would not have considered.[24] Above all, porteño leaders like Chicago's promoters were entertaining visions of future greatness, but with a difference. The Argentines were dreaming of a greater nation, while the Chicagoans were thinking first and foremost of a greater city.[25] In any case, with his Chicago years behind him, Buchanan was advantageously prepared to record the growing pains of the southern metropolis.

However engrossed the ex-Chicagoan became in the growth problems of Buenos Aires and the operation of its institutions, his true interests lay in the fabulous agricultural and pastoral hinterland beyond the port city. Barely two months after arrival his enthusiasm led him to advise Washington that he planned to make two extended trips before the end of the year—in August to the provinces north and northwest of the capital as far as Tucumán and in October or November to the southern provinces.[26] In announcing the minister's journeys *La Prensa* reported that he wished to assess the true economic complexion of Argentina, especially its agricultural population, industries, lines of communication, and future course of development.[27]

Apprised of Buchanan's travel plans, the National Railway Board of Commissioners made available to him an official government car. A friend from Columbian Exposition days—member of the Argentine National Commission for the Fair and one of the international panel of judges—served as his host and guide. Their sixteen-day journey took them 2600 miles through six provinces: up the Río Paraná valley through Santa Fé, where the wheat and flax fields reminded the minister of Nebraska; to Santiago del Estero with its hot winds and arid lands; to the elevated sugar cane oasis of Tucumán; southward through the sierras, hilly uplands, and grain and alfalfa fields of Córdoba; thence to the Andean foothills of San Luis; and back to the capital through the wheat and pasture lands of northern Buenos Aires province.[28]

Alerted by national officials, the governors in every provincial capital had prepared elaborate hospitality. At theater performances in Santa Fé and Córdoba the American flag was displayed with the Argentine and audiences applauded the playing of the national anthems. At each principal stop newsmen interviewed the minister, and the big dailies of Buenos Aires recorded his movements through the provinces.[29] All reported the contagiousness of his enthusiasm for their countryside.

Because of his longtime association with agriculture, but also because of the special mission assigned him, Buchanan focused his observations on the production methods of the grain *haciendas* and sugar plantations and on the breeding techniques of the cattle and sheep estancias. But he also visited a variety of schools and, when opportunity presented, ventured to suggest to his hosts that Argentina might profitably create additional agricultural schools and experimental farms. Beyond his attention to these matters of farm and field, the North American made a special effort to observe the operations of the British-owned railroads and the functioning of municipal reservoirs and other public utilities. Throughout the trip he was given every opportunity to see exactly what he desired. His copious notes, he wrote to Washington, would provide substance for future reporting and for the magazine articles he contemplated.[30]

When in late 1894 circumstances prevented his projected tour of the southern provinces, Buchanan decided to postpone it until the following spring. In the meantime he secured State Department approval to visit neighboring Paraguay and Chile, with which Argentina had pending border and boundary problems. Accompanied by his family, in July-August 1895 he made the four-day voyage up the Rivers Paraná and Paraguay to Asunción. Frequent stops at river ports, especially Rosario, Paraná, and Santa Fé, gave him the opportunity to observe the extent to which Argentina utilized its internal waterways for the movement of people and cargo. Upon arrival in the Paraguayan capital he left his family to enjoy its exotic sights while he made excursions into the Chaco and other remote sections of the country seldom seen by alien visitors.[31]

In each of his remaining years in Buenos Aires Buchanan renewed his travels into the countryside. Before the end of his five-year residence he had visited every region of Argentina —from the Chaco to Patagonia, from the Atlantic to the foot of Mt. Aconcagua. Well before the end of his mission a porteño newspaper could assert that

> there was never a Foreign Minister [sic] to this Republic who knew the Country so well as Minister Buchanan, and there are few Argentines who know it so well as he does. Not only has he travelled all over it, but he has done so with both eyes open and has given no end of labour to the thorough examination of its resources. He is to-day probably the best authority as to its possibilities, either native or foreign.[32]

But Buchanan's skill as an observer of Argentina's potentiality developed only gradually. At the time of his first travels to Tucumán and Asunción in 1894-1895 he was still serving his diplomatic novitiate in Buenos Aires. Though from the moment of his arrival he had found himself heavily occupied with official obligations, he quickly became aware that he could not ignore still another phase of a diplomat's life—his personal relationships with individuals and groups. Apart from routine attendance at the neverending succession of social and ceremonial affairs, he discovered, Argentines and aliens alike expected a newly arrived minister "to make use of the word," as the porteños expressed their propensity for public speaking. Frequent invitations to offer a toast, introduce a speaker, or deliver an address left him little choice but to accept. Moreover, his decade of association with theaters, Corn Palaces, and the exposition had taught him to value the spoken word and he had learned to enjoy opportunities for public address. However handicapped at the outset by his inadequate Spanish and ignorance of local lore, he could count on his sense of humor, touch of humanity, and growing urbanity to ingratiate himself with whatever audience. Within a few months, while still not conversing fluently in the Argentine idiom, he was venturing public statements in Spanish. His manuscripts and notes for speeches, many in his own handwriting, reveal broad understanding of his own country's history and culture as well as growing appreciation for Argentina's.

Though their numbers were still relatively small, the minister's fellow Americans were the first to call upon his services as speaker. Among these was the friendly pastor of the American Methodist Episcopal Church, the Reverend W. P. McLaughlin, who had assisted the Buchanans in their search for family housing and in their orientation to Argentine life.[33] By

Thanksgiving time he evidently felt that the newly accredited diplomat should be ready to make his Argentine debut as speaker. The diplomat cheerfully complied.

Recalling his recent visit to Tucumán's historic "independence hall," Buchanan chose for his Thanksgiving talk the simple theme that "every nation has its holidays." First, for the Argentines he cited the significance of 25 May and 9 July as symbolic of their early progress toward self-government and independence. Then, for the North Americans he epitomized what he termed "a great thought, purpose or principle," for each of their national days: Washington's birthday, Lincoln's, Arbor day, Flag day, July 4th, Labor day, and Thanksgiving. These two strands he then sought to intertwine when he concluded that Thanksgiving

> is distinctly American in its origin, customs, and observance and illustrating its lessons we can have no higher compliment paid us by the people among whom we live than to have them say that we are good citizens and that our lives and actions reflect credit upon our home, our friends and our country.[34]

On a later occasion at the Methodist Church Buchanan was invited to introduce a speaker on "Abraham Lincoln." Again, as in his Thanksgiving day remarks, he pinpointed a link between Argentine and American attitudes, this time through their concepts of national leadership. "The deeds of great men are the common heritage of the world," he said, "and thus the valor of a San Martin, the nobleness of a Lafayette, the wisdom of a Franklin, the heroism of a Grace Darling, and the unselfish life of a Pasteur become guidons for us to follow."[35] He introduced appropriate quotations not only from North Americans Horace Greeley and George Bancroft but also from Argentina's former president, Bartolomé Mitre. Even more exceptional perhaps, in his view of the time and place, was his reference to the black orator and patriot, Frederick Douglass. Buchanan credited Douglass with having said that "Lincoln was the only white man with whom he had ever talked, or in whose presence he had ever been, who had not, consciously or unconsciously, betrayed the fact that he recognized his color."[36]

Buchanan's Scottish ancestry inescapably brought him an early invitation to speak to The St. Andrew's Society of the

River Plate, whose members or whose members' forebears had been among the first non-Spanish immigrants to the Argentine Republic. On each St. Andrew's day (30 November) during his residence the Society invited the minister, usually along with distinguished Argentines, to offer or respond to appropriate toasts. In spirit of camaraderie, he never failed to entertain them with a touch of sentiment and a sizeable ration of the Scottish brand of ethnocentrism. Sometimes with humor, sometimes with irony, but always to the delight of his hosts, he chaffed the "quiet and lowly Yankee" and the "lamb-like Englishman." Delicately skirting the risk of lampoon or satire, he referred to the "bashful and unobtrusive Republic" from which he came, to his "modest countrymen," and to their "childlike faith in humanity."[37]

At one of these annual meetings, while responding to a toast to "The United States," he offered some evidences of North American "backwardness in adopting many of the simon pure customs of the mother country;—our unorthodox gastronomic taste; and our deplorable intellectual warp in preferring base ball to cricket [and] thinking it more comfortable to ride at a canter than to be shot into the air, piston like, by the trot." "I am possessed by a suspicion," he went on,

> that National prejudices are everywhere so rugged and healthy that I have no doubt the venturesome Englishman who should attempt to break down the custom his countrymen have immortalized of using whisky to sterilize and flavor soda water, by introducing American homeopathic habit of "taking a bit straight" would quickly find himself above the line of perpetual snow.[38]

But however closely he approached the use of burlesque or travesty in characterizing Englishmen or his own countrymen, he studiedly avoided any allusion that might have been offensive to Argentina or its officials. In lauding the activities of Scottish pioneers in Argentina, he always judiciously subordinated their contributions to the overall progress of the young republic. When referring on one occasion to the enormous migration of Scots to the United States and Canada, he said, "the story of a smaller part of this Scotch outpouring is bound up with that of the Aladdin like progress that has been made in the River Plate country during the past 50 years." Or again,

"Seated about this table to-night are many who are the children or descendants of Scots who formed part of the leaven by which this great city and Republic have been raised to their present proportions."[39]

Meanwhile in Argentine circles, while struggling to cope with the conjugations of irregular verbs, the minister freely confessed his "excessive lack of knowledge" of the Spanish language. At one gathering of diplomats and public officials not long after his arrival, he acknowledged the great difficulty he was having with the past tense of the verbs "haber" and "tener." He then continued in simple Spanish: "Nunca me gustó el 'tiempo pasado' en cosa alguna. Prefiero el futuro con sus esperanzas, sus posibilidades, y su encantamiento." On strictly formal occasions during these first months he followed the practice, student fashion, of writing out his proposed remarks in English, then laboriously translating them. This was the technique he used when he and Mrs. Buchanan gave their first reception for the Argentine president, members of the Cabinet and Supreme Court, colleagues of the diplomatic corps, and other distinguished guests. In offering a lengthy toast to the president, he began with the usual witty sally, then quickly apologized to all his guests for what he called his "most imperfect semblance of Spanish."[40] In his later Argentine years, however, he made sure that such apologies were unnecessary.

Most surprising perhaps of Buchanan's public speaking appearances were his presentations on diverse aspects of American literature. Years before, in his travelling days, he had utilized his long evenings to develop a working acquaintanceship with nineteenth-century American writers. Now, in Buenos Aires, he found a certain diversion in selecting favorite passages from a representative author, piecing them together with his own interpretive commentary, and presenting the resultant mosaic as a form of intellectual divertissement for English-speaking groups. Without pretense of expertise or of elocutionary skill, he entertained one audience with extracts from Washington Irving's *Tales of the Alhambra, Legend of Sleepy Hollow,* and *The Sketch-Book;* another with excerpts from Henry Thoreau's *Walden, A Week on the Concord and Merrimack Rivers,* and several essays.[41]

Ranging far beyond these programs of readings, however, and indeed far more creative, was a formal lecture the minister prepared for the English Literary Society in October 1895 on "An Hour with American Writers."[42] His none-too-modest theme was the past, present, and future of American literature; his thesis, that writers in his country had laid the foundation for a literature that was "distinctly American in its coloring and setting" and not merely an offshoot of the English model. In his view, environment was a far stronger influence in molding an author's work than early training, education, sympathies, or any other factor. It is environment, he contended, that enables him to present "with correctness, the manners, the language and the lights and shadowes [sic] common to the life about him." As evidence he offered the works of Cooper, Irving, Whittier, Longfellow, Harte, Howells, Cable, Eggleston, and Wister. Driving home his point, he deprecated the growing tendency among writers to spend a few months in a country other than their own, the language of which they often do not speak, then "with their provincialism, and national ideas and prejudices as a yard stick, ask readers to accept the measurements they give of the morals, habits, religious instincts, home life, culture, and character of the people they have been among."

Early in his presentation the speaker made it clear that he was analyzing literature in the broadest sense, not merely fiction and verse. To illustrate the wide range of thought that interested American writers he mentioned historians Prescott, Motley, Bancroft, and Mahan, botanist Asa Gray, philologist William Dwight Whitney, geologist James Dwight Dana, statesman John Jay, and lawyer Justice Story. Whatever the preoccupation of most Americans with "light [and] clean healthy literature," as they consumed it in such magazines as *The Century, Harper's, The Atlantic, Scribner's,* and *St. Nicholas,* they were deeply concerned with topics involving the world's progress.

Then, warming to his theme, Buchanan undertook to refute the critics of American literature, or, as he styled them, "alleged critics." He singled out three of their allegations. First, he dissected the criticism that the United States had been underproductive in literary creativity. "There is no average of a man of genius to so many thousand or million of persons," he submitted. "No one can tell why, . . . in the 200 years between Chaucer and Shakespeare, England produced no poet of importance, nor again, in the 150 years between Milton and Wordsworth."

In defense of American literary productivity, the minister than marshalled a lengthy roster of writers, both past and contemporary. Among poets he emphasized Whitman, Poe, and the New England group, but listed Sidney Lanier, Joaquin Miller, Eugene Field, and James Whitcomb Riley. Among fiction writers he mentioned not only Cooper and Irving, but also Howells, James, Cable, Twain, Lew Wallace, Frank R. Stockton, and many others. Among women he cited Louisa May Alcott and Harriet Beecher Stowe but did not overlook Helen Hunt Jackson, Julia Ward Howe, and Ella Wheeler Wilcox. And so he continued for other forms of literary expression. Altogether his list of exhibits numbered more than eighty.

Next, Buchanan took up the plaint of the critics that American literature contained too much of the commonplace. Again he submitted a roll of authors, living and dead, whose output would "substantiate the claim that in every quality—merit, good English, earnestness of purpose, and purity of thought —they rank as high as do those of any other nation." The trouble with critics, the speaker interpolated at this point, is that "they glide on through their picturesque and erratic lives serene in the belief that they are in some way guiding the reading world."

The minister's third quarrel with the critics, both English and American, stemmed from their indictment that an overabundance of dialect and slang in American writings was polluting and injuring the English language. "These distinguished and worthy gentlemen overlook the fact," he argued,

> that in his gradual extension over the face of the earth the Anglo-Saxon . . . whether in India, or the Australian bush, or in Africa, as a cowboy or miner in the West, as a farmer in Indiana or New York, as a planter in the South, as a stock-broker, as a society swell in London or Newport, or as a denison [sic] of this southern land has not failed to produce from his fertile brain or his surroundings the terse word or phrase he needed to express what he meant.

If readers do not object to the use of dialect or slang in Burns,

Hardy, or George Eliot, he queried, why should they object to it in Cable, Wister, or Riley?

For any American diplomat in any country in whatever era, the minister's presentation would have been notable. But for William Buchanan—completely lacking formal instruction in American literature, laboriously preparing his manuscript while still adjusting to a new career, and composing it in the Buenos Aires of the 1890s without access to an extensive English language literary collection—it was a singular performance. Some in his audience, composed largely of British residents, may have questioned his optimism or disagreed with his sallies against British literary critics; they could hardly have doubted his sincerity or failed to appreciate the effort he had put forth.

No one can say how much, if at all, the minister's literary discourses before English-speaking groups enhanced his effectiveness at the diplomatic bargaining table. Yet the Argentine elite, like that in many Latin American countries, has always admired in its own public officials the marriage of intellectual interests and leadership vigor. It has not been above rewarding its literary lights with election or appointment to high diplomatic and political office. To the extent, therefore, that Argentine officialdom became aware of Buchanan's literary concerns, it is safe to assume that his prestige mounted in their eyes. Certainly his wide reading and evaluative efforts contributed to his own growing savoir-faire as an American diplomat in Buenos Aires.

In these ways during the first year of his Argentine assignment Buchanan served his diplomatic apprenticeship. For the forty-two-year-old Ohioan, who had spent most of his adult years in the world of business and entertainment, the functions and responsibilities of an American envoy represented a completely new departure. The procedures and protocol of diplomacy required him, while serving as chief of mission, to develop new talents. Calling upon the same resourcefulness and joy with which he had met previous challenges, he bent to the task.

Both in Buenos Aires and in provincial capitals the minister had met the leading political figures, with several of whom he would gradually develop close friendship. He and his family quickly fell into the pattern of observing the appropriate social amenities—of entertaining, being entertained, attending ceremonial and fiesta occasions, accepting invitations to speak publicly. From the start he worked assiduously to learn the Spanish language, first to make himself intelligible, then to do it with some correctness and grace. As head of the legation, he began on his first day ashore to transmit intelligence reports to the Department of State and other Washington agencies. With the assistance of his small staff, he learned to collect information on assigned or volunteered subjects and to evaluate the reliability of the data and the credibility of his sources. Above all, perhaps, in his own scale of priorities he sought to know and understand the Argentine Republic as a nation and the Argentines as a people. Only with this knowledge and understanding, he seemed to feel, would he be able to negotiate competently on the major diplomatic issues in Argentine-American relations. Even during his months of apprenticeship, however, circumstances forced him to undertake these negotiations.

Chapter 6
DIPLOMAT IN ACTION
Argentina, 1894-1898

Minister Buchanan's arrival in Argentina in May 1894 brought him almost at once into an arena of active policy negotiations. However much he may have longed for a period of self-educating apprenticeship, free from major decision-making, he faced the necessity of prompt diplomatic action. With the Cleveland administration's new tariff bill moving through its final stages in Congress, legislative and diplomatic jockeying prevailed in both Washington and Buenos Aires. Other problems pressed for attention. His specific charge to improve the climate of trade relations, coupled with Argentina's long-standing dissatisfaction with Washington's tariff policies, gave the fledgling diplomat a rare opportunity. At the same time, the situation demanded background knowledge he had not yet accumulated and negotiating skills he had not yet developed. His briefing at the State Department had been superficial. The correspondence files of the legation archives were woefully inadequate.

Yet among the diverse factors which had conditioned these relations throughout most of the century several must have been self-evident to the newly arrived envoy.[1] From first-hand experience he could appreciate the reality of geographic separation and the obstacles it presented to the growth of a genuine community of interests. The lack of regular, direct shipping lines between ports and the consequent slowness of correspondence hampered efforts of American exporters to compete with Europeans for Argentine markets. Moreover, the British enjoyed near monopolistic control of cable traffic to the countries of the South Atlantic.

Like the United States, Buchanan knew full well, Argentina was endowed with a temperate climate and unlimited agricultural potential. Their economies had long been essentially competitive. After the 1860s American flour shipped to La Plata was forced to compete with the local product; Argentine wool could enter the United States only over the handicap of protective tariffs. In contrast, Argentine producers readily exchanged their exports for the manufactured goods of England and Western Europe.

Following the commercial pattern, Argentine leaders looked to London for loans and investment capital, to Paris and Madrid for cultural contacts, and to Rome for religious inspiration. In the main, they found little to attract them in America, while Washington officials responded with apathy or disregard of Argentine interests. On the surface there appeared to be little natural basis for the growth of mutual interest between the Argentine and American peoples.

Even if these realities of the Argentine-American relationship were apparent to Buchanan, there were some subtleties of the southern republic's posture that may have been less transparent. Until he had lived and travelled in the country for some time, Buchanan could not have sensed, for example, the strength of Argentina's drive to establish some form of hegemony in southern South America. Its insistence on control of the Río de la Plata estuary, its competition with Brazil for supremacy in the buffer states of Uruguay and Paraguay, and its boundary disputes with all its neighbors had recurrently involved the diplomacy of the United States. Particularly over the matter of national boundaries, like other American representatives before him, Buchanan would be drawn into Argentina's disputes with its neighbors.[2]

The minister may not have realized at once the symbolic importance to Argentines of the British-controlled Falkland Islands, bleak sentinels guarding the Atlantic entrance to the Strait of Magellan. Soon after independence they had been successfully incorporated into the young nation's domain only to fall into British hands in 1832. Incensed that the USS *Lexington* only a year earlier had disarmed the islands and removed a number of its residents, Argentine leaders blamed the United States for loss of this strategic possession. On various occasions for half a century Buenos Aires fruitlessly petitioned Washington for some form of redress. The rebuffs were not quickly forgotten by articulate publicists or nationalist spokesmen.[3]

From the earliest years of independence Argentine statesmen had developed other tenets of foreign policy to which their successors into the 1890s steadfastly adhered. Conspicuous among these was devotion to their special brand of isolationism and forthright avoidance of multilateral diplomacy in any form. In 1826 they had spurned Simón Bolívar's invitation to the Panama Congress of Latin American states. They ignored subsequent conferences planned by Mexico and Peru. And in 1889-1890, at the First International Conference of the American States, held in Washington, their able spokesmen throttled James G. Blaine's hopes both for an inter-American customs union and for a Hemisphere arbitration agreement. In the middle and late 1890s Buchanan would find their stance only slightly less resolute.[4]

Rarely since the opening of official contacts in 1810 had the Argentines been impressed with the caliber of envoys sent by the United States. Until midcentury, while intercourse remained minimal, Washington had been content to entrust its representation to consuls, special agents, and chargés d'affaires. A number of these had proved to be incapable or overzealous; several had committed indiscretions. Though in 1853 the two countries had agreed to exchange ministers resident, most of the Americans subsequently designated were political appointees who failed to distinguish themselves. In contrast, the roster of nineteenth-century Argentine ministers to the United States included a future president, a future minister of foreign relations, and other prominent citizens. Sensitive porteño leaders could only assume that Washington's failure to select more able men revealed its comparative lack of interest in their country.

By 1887, as bilateral relations gradually widened, Washington and Buenos Aires had finally raised their missions to full legation status. It was as envoy extraordinary and minister plenipotentiary, therefore, that Buchanan undertook the responsibility of reversing his country's record of unimpressive diplomatic representation in Buenos Aires.[5] But Buchanan had never been one to let obstacles stand in the way of his natural bouyance or needlessly frustrate the attainment of his objectives. In his determination to improve the Argentine image of the United States he could emphasize significant similarities between the two nations without ignoring troubling differences. He could see that they had followed roughly comparable paths of independence, federalization, and constitutional practice. He could sense in each the capacity to assimilate universal culture patterns without sacrificing national sovereignty. On the soil of both countries there was occurring the "miracle of America," as a twentieth-century Argentine president would delineate to the United States Congress the mingling of people from diverse latitudes, languages, and creeds.[6] Buchanan's experiences and contacts in the American West and Chicago's south side had helped prepare him to recognize and appreciate such realities.

During his five years in Buenos Aires, four paramount areas of concern occupied Buchanan's attention. These were the promotion of improved trade relations, the modernization of treaty arrangements, the protection of American interests during the Spanish-American War, and assistance to Argentina in defining its boundaries.[7] Mindful of the influences which had persuaded President Cleveland to give him the Argentine assignment, Buchanan concentrated first on the cultivation of new markets for American exports.

At the outset, like each of his predecessors in the post, Buchanan faced the hard fact that the volume of Argentine-American trade had never reached impressive figures. Even in the last quarter century before his arrival, American sales to Argentina averaged less than four million dollars a year. At the same time, Argentina's exports to the United States consistently gave the South American nation a favorable balance of trade, sometimes two or three to one.[8]

Though Yankee trading vessels had begun to call at the port of Buenos Aires long before Argentina became independent, they confronted from the start the strong British drive for South American markets and porteño preference for British-made goods. Even after recognizing Argentina in 1824 the United States had been forced to wait thirty years to secure a commercial treaty that would place it on an equal footing with Britain and France. Under the Treaty of 1853 then, for the first time, the most-favored-nation clause assured American exporters equitable treatment for their manufactures, lumber, tobacco, and other goods. Yet during the next forty years British and French sales far exceeded the American, while the Germans and Belgians, too, usually outsold the Yankees.[9]

Among factors militating against healthy Argentine-American trading, none was more damaging than Washington's tariffs on raw wool, pivot of Argentina's foreign commerce. With its wool clip mounting fifteenfold between 1860 and 1900, exportation was indispensable to Argentine prosperity. More or less regularly in these years wool exports accounted for more than half its earnings from overseas sales. Yet in Washington after the Civil War, with protectionist doctrines dominating congressional thought, a powerful combination of wool-growers and manufacturers in 1867 secured a prohibitive duty on wool. Over the repetitive protests of Argentine diplomats in Washington, succeeding tariff laws perpetuated the high rates.[10] By 1883, according to one minister, American annual purchases of Argentine wool had plummeted from 37,000,000 pounds to 2,000,000—less than 1 percent of Argentina's total wool exports and a fraction of American total imports of 64,000,000 pounds.[11] Wool became the perennial Argentine whipping boy; the 1867 tariff still shadowed Argentine-American economic diplomacy when Buchanan arrived in Buenos Aires.

This festering issue had reached one of its several climaxes with the enactment of the McKinley Tariff Act of 1890. The measure provided not only still higher duties on wool but also retaliatory action against any nation refusing to sign a reciprocal treaty. For more than a year in 1891-1892 Minister John R. G. Pitkin in Buenos Aires pressed Argentina for action. His principal adversary was Foreign Minister Estanislao S. Zeballos, the fiery jurist who would soon become minister to Washington.[12] Each of the disputants called upon both reason and threat to win over the other, but neither was in a position to concede free entry of imports in volume. After months of debate in Buenos Aires and Washington the tariff and treaty situations remained unchanged. The United States would admit hides and skins free of duty; Argentina would not tax farm machinery or unworked pine; no new convention would be signed.[13] But Washington's refusal to recede from its adamant position on wool only thickened the accumulating veneer of resentment that had long stunted the growth of harmonious commercial relations.

This was the uncomfortable climate that greeted Minister Buchanan in May 1894, as he undertook to broaden the market for American goods. As chance would have it, his counterpart in Washington was now his predecessor's recent adversary, the redoubtable Zeballos. Moreover, the former Iowan approached his task with an economic philosophy almost antithetical to that his government had long practiced. He believed that international trade must be seen as a two-way street, that favors are won only in return for favors granted, and that underselling competitors is a more effective means to increased markets than seeking tariff concessions or reciprocity treaties.

Writing candidly to a Chicago newspaper soon after his arrival in Buenos Aires he elaborated these views:

> We need simply the same energy we display at home and the desire and ability to compete with other countries. The first two cannot be created by legislation nor by treaty; . . . If we are not clever enough, as a people, to sell our goods here . . . in fair competition with those of other countries without placing ourselves in the humiliating position of asking tariff concessions from other countries we do practically nothing for, it would seem to be proper for us to either correct our own business system or retire from international business.[14]

By way of contrast he stressed the assistance given to the South American countries by England, France, Italy, and Germany as they poured in investment capital, opened banks, built railroads, and provided ocean carriers.

The minister then proposed alternatives to traditional American protectionist policies. "More can be done," he argued,

> toward developing our foreign trade with South American countries by sticking to a rational tariff, made in our best interests as a people, one that will yield simply the revenue we need, and . . . by making our currency,

as a whole, good over any bank counter in the world, and by establishing an American bank here and in other South American cities, than can be done by all the legislation and all the reciprocity treaties that can be enacted or made in the next fifty years.[15]

Though clearly not the Democratic "free trader" he was sometimes labelled, he was staunch in his opposition to unwarranted protection for vested interests.[16]

In the first weeks of his residence Buchanan could envision some hopes for a more rational tariff and an improved commercial outlook. His hopes rested on Argentina's encouraging response to Democratic proposals that would place wool on the free list and terminate McKinley reciprocity. When during the previous January the bill had been reported out of the House Ways and Means Committee, Minister Zeballos in Washington had expressed Argentine satisfaction. He assured Secretary of State Walter Q. Gresham that the Argentine Congress would reciprocally exempt American lumber, lubricating and fuel oils, and refined petroleum.[17] In June, after the United States Senate had passed its version of the bill, Foreign Minister Eduardo Costa called in person at Buchanan's home to report Argentine willingness to grant concessions on American goods. For the American minister, only six weeks resident in his post, it was a crucial moment. Promptly he requested and received State Department authorization to seek tariff modifications on specific items he believed would sell in Argentina.[18]

Final enactment of the Wilson-Gorman Tariff Act, however, suddenly pricked Buchanan's bubble of hope. Both the Congress and the White House had approved the measure without consideration of his recommendations or of Argentine overtures. They had removed the duty on wool before the minister could seek prior concessions for American products. They had not even acknowledged the apparent willingness of porteño diplomats to reduce discriminating rates. The Argentines, assessing the removal of the wool tariff as purely an expediency to satisfy domestic demands, felt no obligation to grant corresponding concessions. They professed to see in the American action only indifference toward their markets.[19]

Despite this initial setback, Buchanan wrote to Gresham, he was still determined to direct his efforts toward "attracting in every way the products of as many of our factories as possible to this market."[20] Given time to study Argentine trade reports, he tactfully pointed out erroneous and misleading conclusions of official statisticians. By incorporating imports from Canada with United States figures, they created the impression that American trade was much greater than it was. After analyzing Argentine consumption habits, he came to realize the hollowness of Zeballos's offer to place crude petroleum on the free list. For its imports of fuel the nation had long depended solely upon coal; Buchanan saw no prospect of a shift to oil. He emphasized that his government admitted 73 percent of Argentine goods without duty, while Buenos Aires permitted only 6 percent of American items to enter without tax.[21]

As the Argentine tariff bill came up in late 1894 for its annual renewal, the minister held a number of conferences with Foreign Minister Costa, who only a few months before had volunteered his government's readiness to assist United States commercial interests. In particular, Buchanan protested the proposed tariff increases on farm machinery and lumber, the principal American exports. But the conferences availed little. The new tariff act carried some slight reductions on petroleum, farm wagons, carriages, harness, and other items of small export volume, but raised or left untouched the duties on such key items as lumber and iron and steel products.[22]

As the Wilson-Gorman Tariff Act went into effect, Argentine exports to the United States reached the highest value in history. At the same time, under Argentina's 1895 tariff law, its purchases of American goods represented less than 6 percent of its total imports.[23] By lifting the barrier against Argentine wool the Democratic Congress had reversed a trend of twenty-seven years, but by taking the action in a diplomatic vacuum it had failed to capitalize on its break with Republican tradition. Whether from lack of foresight or ignorance of the situation, Buchanan's own party had cut the ground from under what should have been a strong bargaining position.

However dismayed by the plight in which these tariff developments had placed him, Buchanan resourcefully turned to other methods of promoting better trade relations. In October 1895 he broached to Secretary of State Richard Olney a plan for bringing to Argentina a group of prominent American manufacturers and representatives of leading commercial associations. Such a visit would help to fulfill his "desire to see everything done that can be to extend our trade and widen the knowledge, among our people, of these Southern Republics."[24]

Buchanan had already secured the approval of the new Argentine foreign minister, Amancio Alcorta, and gained assurance that his government would welcome the visitors and assist them to examine the nation's progress. He had also asked Secretary Fishback—about to return to the United States on leave—to confer with American ministers in Montevideo and Rio de Janeiro on the possibilities of extending the proposed itinerary to other South Atlantic nations.[25] Once Secretary Olney had approved the scheme and invitations were forthcoming from Argentina, Uruguay, and Brazil, Fishback became a kind of unofficial State Department adviser to the expedition and accompanied it to South America. All twenty members of the party were selected by a committee of the National Association of Manufacturers, which had received the original invitations from the Latin American governments.[26]

In Argentina, thanks to Buchanan's contacts and prearrangements, the group enjoyed warm hospitality. They met the president and the ministers of foreign affairs and finance, as well as the heads of boards of trade and leading commercial houses. Special express trains whisked them about the countryside. They saw agricultural and industrial facilities and resources of all kinds, especially those that would assume greater importance if commercial relations with the United States were to improve. To provide whatever data they requested, a high official of the Ministry of Finance, Dr. Francisco Latzina, accompanied the visitors throughout their stay. As chief of the Bureau of Statistics, Dr. Latzina supplied each guest with a specially prepared printed report of geographical and statistical data.[27]

Minister Buchanan felt reasonably reassured with the results of his project. During their July-August visit he had enabled his countrymen to inspect actual conditions and to meet appropriate leaders in both government and business. He was delighted with the prime realization to which they had come: that American exporters could not compete with European suppliers unless they had access to the same kind of facilities. This meant American banks, branch distributing houses, systems of long credits, and better steamship services. These ideas, of course, conformed essentially to Buchanan's beliefs, and, as he had learned, to recommendations his predecessors had been sending Washington for several decades. In only one respect was the minister less than satisfied. Except for J. M. Studebaker and one or two others, the delegation had not included the men of broad experience and national reputation he and his legation colleagues had expected to attract.[28]

In promoting the visit of American businessmen, Buchanan had hoped to divert attention from continuing tariff controversies and to encourage more imaginative actions to improve the climate of trade. But the experiment proved to be no more than a diversionary interlude. Even while the expedition was in the planning stage, Argentine diplomats were beginning to show concern over the possible outcome of the 1896 presidential and congressional elections. They realized that Cleveland was not likely to receive a third term and they could discern that the tide was running against the Democrats. Once the Republicans nominated William McKinley, the Argentines foresaw the probable return of the wool tariff and the reciprocity approach of his 1890 statute.[29] For Buchanan, certainly not attracted by the Democratic party's stand on the silver issue, the prospect of a return to Republican protectionism contravened his economic philosophy and dampened his hopes.

After McKinley's election, however, personal considerations intruded to divert the minister's attention from matters of high policy. For nearly three years he and his family had lived in a foreign land, separated from their Sioux City home and friends. For more than a year he had struggled along without a secretary of legation, while the State Department sought a suitable replacement for the dependable Fishback. A lengthy leave of absence to visit the United States had been out of the question. Now, with political change in the White House imminent, Buchanan knew that protocol required his resignation; however, he learned that friends and admirers in both countries were preparing to petition President-elect McKinley to retain him in his post. Nevertheless, four weeks after the election he composed a formal request for leave and sent it off to Washington. Thanks to irregular mail service, he waited more than six weeks only to learn that Department rules precluded a leave that would extend beyond the date of a new president's inauguration.[30]

Meanwhile, eager to retain the minister's "especial fitness... to stimulate commercial interests between the two countries," seventy-one American firms and individuals in Buenos Aires had formalized their petition to the president-elect. Even one so accustomed to public acknowledgment as Buchanan must have been surprised, certainly gratified, when the text of the document appeared on the front page of a porteño newspaper. "You may go North, South, West," the petition declared,

> and everywhere the American Minister is known, esteemed, and liked. We need not refer to our social midst, where a diplomatist is always eagerly sought; but take the politician, the army man, the naval officer—take the banker, the merchant, the capitalist, the broker—go lower, take the haberdasher, the small trader, take the very masses—sound them, ask them their views, present the petition, and all will wish to sign it. Why? Therein lies the magnetism of this quiet American gentleman. We think that under such circumstances even a Republican Government can afford to retain him as Minister in our midst.[31]

Even with these unsought compliments before him, Buchanan felt constrained to submit his resignation to the new president, its effective date to follow his long-anticipated and hard-won leave of absence. He despatched the letter on 11 March.[32] Meanwhile, as the weeks went by without reply by mail or cable, Argentine indignation over the new Republican tariff bill began to mount. By 22 April, with the Congress preparing to open its sessions, Buchanan suspected the possibility of retaliatory tariff action. Still without a legation secretary to serve as chargé d'affaires *ad interim*, the minister felt a duty, he wrote to Washington, to postpone his family's planned visit to Sioux City. June came before he received the State Department's reply. It appreciated his disposition and invited him to remain in Buenos Aires until the arrival of his still-unnamed successor.[33]

This combination of developments left Buchanan to fight the continuing battle of the tariffs. In contrast to the Wilson-Gorman Act, the new Dingley Act (24 July 1897) incorporated both the higher protectionism and the reciprocity he opposed. Obviously he lacked the advantage he had enjoyed in 1894 of recent first-hand contacts with State Department officials and members of Congress. Serving now under a Republican administration in Washington, he was virtually a lame-duck diplomat, his future status undetermined. Moreover, even though Fishback's replacement, François S. Jones, arrived in July, he needed time to acquire the necessary orientation to Argentina. On the other hand, the minister was no longer a freshman diplomat.

The most forceful pressures against the new measure came from the Sociedad Rural Argentina, since 1866 a powerful organization of livestock breeders, and the Unión Azucarera, a younger body representing the sugar producers. Through the press and the Congress they concentrated their principal criticisms on wool and sugar. In countering each stricture the Democratic minister attempted to represent the policy interpretations laid down by Republican Secretary of State John Sherman.

Accustomed since 1867 to criticizing American tariff policy, the sheep-raisers now found new grounds for protest. They professed to regard the reimposition of duty on wool as a direct attack on the Argentine product and on Argentine commercial interests. Buchanan explained that immense American imports of wool made it a logical field for raising revenue and that the law applied uniformly to similar grades regardless of source.[34]

Even before enactment of the Dingley Act, the sugar-growers began to voice their concern. Seeking new markets for their rising production in Tucumán province, they asked exemption from the legal clause that imposed additional duty on sugar from countries granting export bounties. Skirting the legalistic question of whether or not Argentina granted such bounties, Buchanan suggested that its best hopes for increased sugar sales in the United States lay in liberalization of its own tariff rates.[35] Moreover, in cases of alleged hardship for individual nations, Sherman directed him to point out, President McKinley had appointed a special commissioner to adjudicate grievances. Beyond this, a reciprocity treaty, as authorized by law, might alleviate points of discord.[36]

But Buchanan was not content to rest his case merely with

defense of the Republican tariff law nor to bide his time until the arrival of his successor. Receiving no word about the appointment of his replacement, he spent the remaining months of 1897 in trying to minimize tariff retaliation by the Argentine Congress. Throughout the weeks of debate, he conferred repeatedly, at times almost daily, with friends in the Congress as well as with the ministers of finance and foreign affairs. He believed that these efforts had helped to forestall tariff increases recommended by the president, especially on such key American exports as agricultural implements and machinery, farm wagons, and yellow pine lumber.[37]

With the conclusion of these negotiations in January 1898, Buchanan prepared for Secretary Sherman a comprehensive review of his actions.[38] To it he appended some of the conclusions he had reached after nearly four years of struggle to improve the climate of Argentine-American trade. In his view, the principal barrier to improved commerce continued to be the unfriendliness generated by the wool tariffs. Only special effort, he declared, could erase the widely held conviction that American policy was designed specifically to discriminate against Argentine wool.

The minister felt similar concern about what he called the "reprisal" idea expressed by some American journalists—that Argentines would have to buy from the United States, whatever its attitude toward their needs or complaints. If this view became prevalent, he asserted, American manufacturers would never capture Argentine markets from current European suppliers.

On still another tack, the American minister noted the growing pressure on the Argentine government for increased protectionism in trade policy. Elements of the press and the still small industrial community were clamoring for modification of the traditional free trade policy long supported by the powerful stockgrowers and rural associations. As this pressure grew, he predicted, American efforts to secure lower duties would be correspondingly frustrated. In view of all these considerations, he recommended prompt attempts to negotiate the type of commercial treaty authorized in the Dingley Act.[39]

The former businessman and exposition chief apparently composed this lengthy analysis as a kind of valedictory to his diplomatic mission under two presidents. Although, even ten months after the Republican president's inauguration, he had still not received his recall, he wrote to Secretary Sherman that "the work done by the Legation during my residence here is now nearly closed." He expressed his gratitude for the opportunity he had had "to be of some possible service to our commercial interests"—interests he had tried "to faithfully and constantly uphold and assist in every proper way."[40] This statement, coupled with his earlier recommendation that treaty negotiations be initiated, may have been the key to President McKinley's continued delay in naming a new minister. Though he did not know it at the time, Buchanan's mission to Argentina was not finished.

Some weeks before composing these observations the minister had renewed his request for the long-postponed leave of absence to return home. Unwilling this time to brook the interminable delays of sea mail, he sent his message by cable. Within twenty-four hours Secretary Sherman had granted the request, but, to the dismay of all the Buchanans, "SUBJECT TO APPOINTMENT SUCCESSOR."[41] Nevertheless the family moved ahead with plans for departure soon after adjournment of the Argentine Congress in January. For reasons not apparent in the official correspondence, of which growing somewhat tired of "foreign life" was admittedly one, Buchanan determined at this time to submit his resignation.[42] In another laconic cable, dated 8 January, Sherman replied, "RESIGNATION ACCEPTED TO TAKE EFFECT ON APRIL FIRST."[43]

Excited now at the prospect of return to Chicago and Sioux City, each of the Buchanans set about preparation for departure. While winding up pending legation business, Will tended to such personal matters as terminating their house lease and booking passage for New York, fortuitously by a steamer scheduled to follow the direct route so infrequently used. Mrs. Buchanan and the children tended to the packing of personal effects and the shipping of household goods.[44]

Even in their joy over going home, leavetaking was difficult for each of them. At the same time, they must have found satisfaction in the warm thoughts that accompanied the farewells of their porteño friends. François Jones, taking over as chargé d'affaires *ad interim*, epitomized "the general regret prevailing in the city," when he reported to Secretary Sherman that "this sentiment has not been restricted to American residents, but is entertained by many of the most influential professional and business men of other nationalities as well as by the representative Argentines with whom he [Buchanan] has come in contact, officially and socially."[45]

Among the press commentaries, one journalist was much more literal, though no less laudatory, than the chargé, when he described the American minister as one who "knows as much about the wool business now as the hoariest exporter or most veteran consignee: he has been to the Central Market to see the wool sold, and to the barracas to see it skirted, pressed, and baled." Beyond this, the writer went on, "he has studied the trade statistics at the expense of midnight oil, and traveled the interior to gauge attentively the country's capabilities."[46]

The Buchanans' good fortune in securing direct passage limited their homeward voyage to five weeks instead of the seven they had endured on their outward journey. They reached New York on 2 March. Anticipating his debriefing at the State Department and eager to place before Republican officials his views of the Argentine situation, Will immediately hastened to Washington. If his nomination to the diplomatic service four years before had caught him without warning, an equally great surprise awaited him now. As a Cleveland appointee, avowedly opposed to tariff protection for vested interests, he had for more than a year expected his recall. But at an unexpected White House conference, in the presence of the Iowa senators, President McKinley advised the returning minister that he had no intention of accepting his resignation. However deeply Buchanan wished to leave the government service and renew contacts with the business world, he could do no less than request time to consider.[47]

Yearning, as they all acknowledged, for return to customary American living, the Buchanans had reached their country at an unpropitious moment. During these early March days Washington was tense with the developing impasse over the Cuban situation. Only two weeks before, the *Maine* had blown up in Havana harbor. The American naval court of inquiry was still conducting its investigation. On 6 March the president asked Congress for $50,000,000 to strengthen the nation's defenses. With strong popular support the administration was edging toward war with Spain. Under these circumstances Buchanan was not one to meditate long over personal preferences. His sense of duty to country, along with his appreciation of the president's graciousness, stimulated a prompt decision. He would return to Argentina.[48]

The Buchanan family then travelled to Chicago, where on 11 April the former department chiefs of the Columbian Exposition held a dinner reunion to honor their onetime colleague.[49] That same day President McKinley had recommended armed intervention in Cuba. Two days later, when he learned of the congressional resolution to recognize Cuban independence, the minister advised Secretary Sherman of his readiness to leave for Buenos Aires within twenty-four hours of telegraphic notice. He was deeply concerned about the possible anti-American activities of some 200,000 Spanish citizens resident in Argentina.[50] As the Congress prepared to comply with the president's recommendation, the four Buchanans pondered their family's future. First, at any rate, they would move on to Sioux City to fulfill their long-anticipated return to relatives and friends. They arrived on the day Congress declared war. So for Will, after travelling nearly three months and over seven thousand miles, the homecoming lasted just one day. Taking time only to greet the Prughs, a few friends, and a journalist or two, he was off again—this time without his family—for Washington, New York, London, and Buenos Aires. Florence would soon enroll in preparatory school. Mrs. Buchanan and Donald would divide their time between Sioux City and Chicago, and possibly join Will later.[51]

As he rode the trains toward the capital, Buchanan viewed with disheartenment the prospect of prolonged separation from his wife and children. Repeatedly during the coming months he would search for ways to bridge the miles. At the very outset he hit upon the scheme of numbering his letters so that the family would know if any failed to arrive.[52] During the sixteen months of separation Will sent seventy-six numbered letters and numerous incidental notes and cablegrams. Collectively they constitute not only a kind of diary of his movements and activities but also a journal of his innermost thoughts about the Spanish war and other matters that concerned him. Often they contained observations that did not appear in his official despatches. Invariably they included special greetings or messages for the children, even an offer of fifty centavos for each letter written in Spanish, five dollars per month pin money, and double to Florence if she would take her piano lessons seriously.[53]

While admiring the April blossoms of cherry, pear, and haw trees from the Baltimore and Ohio train to Washington, he composed letters number 1 and 2 in his planned series. But even the springtime freshness could not obscure his misgivings about the war with Spain. He found humiliating for the United States what he called "Minister Woodford's fizzle." In Washington, where Spanish Minister Dupuy de Lôme had first received the American ultimatum, he immediately *asked* for his passports; in Madrid, by contrast, before he could present the proposition, Woodford has been *handed* his. Moreover, as the war progressed, Buchanan feared, the intervention of a European power or some catastrophe to the armed forces would produce chilling effects on American public opinion. Though he patently disagreed with the course his government had been following, he now had no other thought than to support wholeheartedly its war efforts.[54]

In Washington the minister had to forgo buying much needed new clothes; instead he spent a day in conference with State Department officials and with his Iowa friend, Senator Allison. He took advantage of the opportunity to tell the senator that he was returning to Buenos Aires at "considerable sacrifice" and wished to be "retired (?) gracefully" whenever the McKinley administration desired. Allison told him that he was not likely to be shifted but that, if he were, it would be done to his "credit and liking" or there would be "the biggest row the White House had seen in years."[55] With this reassuring confidence, Buchanan headed for New York to board the *Winifreda*, a new 7,000-ton ship carrying 700 cattle and 120 horses as well as first-class passengers.[56]

On the ten-day crossing to England Buchanan found himself still preoccupied with considerations of the war. Between blasts of howling winds and a gramophone playing Sousa marches, he read the complete testimony taken by the naval court of inquiry on the *Maine's* explosion. He placed little credence, he confided to Mrs. Buchanan, in "more guess work and 'impressions' and contradictory testimony and 'I think sos' than I would ever have believed possible." Shipboard reports on the capture of Manila greatly surprised him. "I thought we were after Cuba—but let her go Gallagher I suppose."[57] Looking ahead to his voyage from England to Argentina, he determined to shift his reservation from a ship scheduled to call at Coruña, Spain. He suspected that the authorities there might regard him, along with army and navy officers and mules, as "contraband of war" and cause unpleasantness to both him and the ship.[58]

The minister's change of ship reservations forced him to spend three impatient weeks in London. Fortunately, however, the delay gave him opportunity to meet with Argentine Minister Martín García Mérou, returning through London to his post in Washington. Through their harmonious conversations Buchanan felt that they had laid the groundwork for the kind of commercial agreement authorized in the Dingley Act. Earlier he had conferred with Ambassador John Hay on the latest diplomatic and military developments in the war with Spain.[59]

The Iowan's weeks of waiting also provided the chance to indulge personal fancies. He visited the Tower of London, the National Gallery, and city parks aglow with spring blossoms. Discarding the temptation to make a side excursion to Paris, he substituted a trip to Warwick and Kenilworth castles. In one letter to his family he described at length his view of Queen Victoria and her entourage moving out to Windsor Castle: the embellished royal carriages, the mounted guards, the liveried servants, and the royal luggage wagons bearing the royal galoshes, hat boxes, and trunks. "The queen looked tired, blasé, and as though she was sick of the thing." She had ruled for sixty-one years, he recalled, as he wrote of England's mourning over the death of William Gladstone, who as a young member of Parliament had witnessed the queen's coronation.[60]

Often lamenting his separation from the family, he searched for gifts he thought might please them. He found special joy in sending them the *Book of the Tartan* and two bolts of Buchanan plaid with its brilliant oranges and yellows and muted blues and greens. He closely observed shop windows and women's fashions, clipped advertisements to send home, and urged both Lulu and Binnie "to keep up with the procession . . . dressed like you know I love to see you—nicely and smartly." But fashions aside, he was far more concerned with his daughter's developing personality. He urged his wife to help her "keep that poise and balance she has and develop into what I know she will be—a most delightful, brilliant, and accomplished woman with her mother's character, and grace, and charms." Anticipating lonely hours on the passage to Buenos Aires, Will purchased a number of books—among them recent works by William Dean Howells, Joel Chandler Harris, Frank Stockton, and Brander Matthews.[61]

Unable to communicate with his family during the twenty-day voyage, Buchanan substituted daily entries in what he called "The Log of the 'Royston Grange'—England to Buenos Aires," to be mailed home upon arrival.[62] Out of touch as well with world news developments, he rarely referred to the war. Once, however, after sailing past the Canary and Madeira Islands, he wrote of the zest added to the trip by not knowing at what moment a man-of-war might "rise up from the Horizon." Otherwise, travelling at sea for the first time without his family, he found shipboard life singularly dull, with little to comment upon except ship movements, land sightings, and other passengers. Nevertheless, he managed to extend his log to sixty-two closely written sheets.

In addition, also to be posted upon landing, Buchanan prepared for his family a fatherly letter of instruction and requests. In their hasty visits to Chicago and Sioux City, they had found no time to plan their separate lives. Now, belatedly, he spelled out suggestions for Lulu on how to endorse drafts, keep bank books, and set up a simple bookkeeping system. He listed some of the personal needs he had been unable to purchase at home: six units of underwear ("size 44 for short and fat people"), two dozen pairs of black hose, two pairs of shoes, white silk shirts, neckties of black and white, pajamas, a soft leather case to hold his five razors, and a supply of Cuticura soap. Not forgetting the children, he reiterated some of his favorite ideas about their education and home training. Finally, upon the shoulders of his "young Prince 'Donnekins'" he placed the responsibility for looking after their ladies. Counselling his ten-year old son in Spanish, the father commended him to "write me often and always work for and take care of your very distinguished mother and sister, and I do not forget that I owe you a salary of five pesos per month."[63]

On 15 June, more than seven weeks after sailing from New York, Minister Buchanan returned to Buenos Aires. Of the 140 days he had been absent from his post, he had spent 88 in travelling to and from the United States. Though in many ways he had experienced a most unsatisfying leave of absence, the warm greetings of both Argentine and American friends now brightened his horizon. Even before he unpacked bags in his hotel room, Foreign Minister Alcorta climbed three flights of stairs to say that "the President and all the cabinet and the whole of the Argentines were jubilant" at his return. Day after day friends called to greet the returned diplomat.[64] The climax of the welcomes came on 4 July, when some five hundred persons—none of them specifically invited—crowded the legation to pay their respects. Among the guests he was especially delighted to see General Julio A. Roca, soon to become Argentina's president, Alcorta again, and the ministers from Britain, France, Russia, and many other countries. This warming salute was wholly spontaneous. With his nation at war and his hostess wife in Sioux City, the minister had deemed it inappropriate to offer the customary Independence Day open house.[65]

In several ways Buchanan's second stretch of duty in Argentina began under circumstances strikingly different from those that had attended his first arrival. In May 1894 he had been a tyro in the world of diplomacy, lacking command of the tools of the trade as well as intimate knowledge of the country to which he was assigned. By June 1898 he had risen to the top of the list of envoys extraordinary and ministers plenipotentiary in Buenos Aires. He would soon become dean of the diplomatic corps.[66] During these four years he had travelled Argentina's countryside, met its people, and learned to speak their language. He had accumulated knowledge of its resources and appreciation of its potential. He had gained an understanding of the crosscurrents of Argentine life. He was confident that he had come to know the Spanish character and how best to win the respect and approval of the Argentine people. Most important, perhaps, he had developed satisfying working relationships with cabinet ministers, congressional leaders, and prominent members of the business community. On his first tour the minister had been the appointee of a Democratic president, free to support tariff principles in which he genuinely believed. Now he was the designated representative of a Republican administration, expected to justify protectionist policies and negotiate the kind of a reciprocal treaty he had once criticized.

As Buchanan had written to his family during his three weeks of waiting in London, he was "extremely and wildly anxious to get to Buenos Aires and to work." He was eager, he said, to make a better record than his previous one.[67] Clearly his departure the previous January had left him with a feeling of incompleteness. He had diagnosed troublesome barriers to improved commerce but failed to secure their elimination. He had initiated conversations for a commercial treaty but not brought it to the point of negotiation. He had concluded an extradition treaty and discussed several other bilateral agreements but lacked the time to consummate them.[68] Though he had secured settlement of several long-standing claims that American citizens had against the Argentine government, others required solution.

Still, tying up these ends was not his only concern. As long as the war with Spain continued, he would have to watch over his country's image and protect its interests in a neutral land with many Spanish inhabitants. Moreover, the inauguration of a new Argentine president would soon necessitate the establishment of contacts with a new administration.

Chapter 7
DIPLOMAT'S ROUTINE
Argentina, 1898-1899

Buchanan's return to Buenos Aires in June 1898 coincided with a change in the Argentine government. Just three days before his return members of the electoral college had gathered in the provincial capitals to cast their ballots in presidential elections. Within two months the Congress would proclaim a new chief executive for the term 1898-1904. Within four months he would be inaugurated. The successful candidate was General Julio A. Roca, Indian fighter, former president, and perennial leader of the political conservatives.[1] At the end of a decade of economic collapse, fitful recovery, and indecisive administration, Roca represented the stabilizing influence that would reinvigorate Argentina's drive for economic greatness.

Though now fifty-five, General Roca was no latecomer to the Argentine presidency. In 1880, following his conquest of the Indians on the Patagonian frontier, the nation had rewarded him with election to the Casa Rosada. By securing foreign loans to build railroads, telegraph lines, public buildings, and enlarged port facilities, he had immensely quickened Argentina's march to become the world's principal supplier of surplus foodstuffs. At the same time, by opening up vast sections of the liberated Indian lands to friends and speculators he had accelerated the concentration of natural wealth in the hands of a select few. Through the personal fortunes he helped to create or enlarge, Roca had solidified the estanciero class that would govern the nation for the next half century. Thus he became its recognized leader.

But, unfortunately for Argentina, the speculative impulse which Roca had stimulated led to unbounded waste and corruption under his chosen successor, his brother-in-law Miguel Juárez Celman. By 1890 overborrowing, depletion of gold reserves, unrestrained inflation, and soaring prices had transformed Roca's boom into Juárez Celman's political and economic collapse. Out of this national disaster was born a movement and a political party, one that would spend the next forty years in bitter challenge to the entrenched aristocracy that had modernized Argentina while submerging the great amorphous mass of creoles and recently arrived immigrants. Seeking honest government, civil rights, and widened suffrage, the *Unión Cívica Radical* became the organization and voice of an incipient middle class. The Radicals, as they came to be called, girded for relentless struggle with the ruling minority.

Shaken by both the economic crash and the determination of the new party, the Conservative leadership struggled through the nineties to maintain its traditional preeminence in public life. The Radicals forced from office two successive presidents and rendered uneasy the position of the vice-presidents who succeeded them. Only by political maneuvering, control of election machinery, and occasional resort to force was the old regime able to parry the growing opposition.[2]

During his first four years of residence in Buenos Aires Buchanan had witnessed several rounds in this developing struggle and become closely acquainted with its principals. Now, freshly returned from Washington, he could sense the significance of Julio Roca's return to the presidency.[3] To regain their hold on the government and to revivify their economic expansionism the Conservatives had called again upon the tested leader they called "The Fox." Whatever may have been the minister's personal reaction to their goals and tactics, he would find President Roca's administration more amenable than its predecessors to the consummation of his unfinished business. The retention of the friendly Amancio Alcorta as minister of foreign affairs would prove additionally reassuring.

In the beginning, however, Buchanan had difficulty in picking up the loose ends of his mission. Roca's more approachable administration did not take office until October. In the meantime, a lame-duck chief executive, himself a vice-president elevated to the Casa Rosada, and a lame-duck Congress still occupied the seats of power. Their primary foreign policy concern at the moment was a new and touchy phase of the perennial boundary dispute with Chile, a dispute soon to involve United States diplomats in Buenos Aires and Santiago. Moreover, Buchanan could not overlook the paramount reason he had cut short his leave at home and hastened his return to Argentina—the war with Spain and his compulsion that American interests in the South Atlantic might need the protection of a fully accredited minister. A Spanish gunboat was threatening United States shipping in Argentine waters. Prompted by pro-Spanish newspapers, increasing numbers of the 80,000 Spaniards in the capital were growing more wrathful toward Washington.[4]

As a matter of fact, this was not Buchanan's first experience in evaluating Argentine reactions to American pretensions in the Hemisphere. Three years before, at the peak of the long-simmering Anglo-Venezuelan dispute over the boundary of British Guiana, President Cleveland's evocation of the Monroe Doctrine had prompted quick response in Buenos Aires. Seconded by most porteño newspapers, leaders like Roca and Zeballos had supported the American position. An articulate segment of the press and leadership, however, held that no European power, certainly not England, posed a territorial threat to the Hemisphere nations; Washington's action was no more than subterfuge to conceal its commercial ambitions in Latin America.[5] With this precedent to guide him, Buchanan was prepared for the wider and far more heated polarity kindled in Argentina by his country's war with Spain.

The American minister's anxieties throughout the period of the war stemmed from the militant elements of the Spanish colony, their Argentine sympathizers, and the unrestrained pro-Spanish press which incited them. Receipt of an anonymous threatening letter soon after his arrival alerted him to the need for prudence. When he learned that only police action had saved the United States Consulate in Rosario from a surging mob of over 6,000 Spanish partisans, he anticipated the possibility of a demonstration against the legation. Normally cautious and reserved, he bristled over the malicious and scurrilous attacks of such weekly caricature sheets as *Don Quijote* and *El Guerrillero Español,* especially when they called the United States a "rabid beast" and referred to its citizens as an "immense horde of robbers and assassins" or "the degenerate descendants of puritans kicked out of England."[6]

Recalling General San Martín's historic campaigns to end Spanish colonial rule in South America, Buchanan sought to understand official indifference toward Cuban independence and popular sympathy for the Spanish cause. He found the explanation in local political and economic conditions. Argentina's uncultivated lands needed settlers; fifteen-sixteenths of its current immigrant tide came from Spain and Italy. The nation's population included more Spaniards than any country except Spain itself; through intermarriage and penetration of the export-import business, they exerted a powerful influence upon foreign commerce. The possibility of war with Chile over the boundary question was in the air; Argentina could not afford to alienate its large Spanish majority. Normally powerful in shaping public opinion, the great porteño dailies, *La Nación* and *La Prensa,* had at first approved the American intervention; sharp drops in circulation had forced them to a more neutral position.[7]

Behind all these realities the minister sensed a deep distrust of United States motives in initiating action against Spain. Even while approving Cuban independence, public officials saw the war as the beginning of eventual American expansion into South America. Professing to regard it as a negation of the Monroe Doctrine, they pressed Buchanan for his views on the future of Hemisphere policy of the United States. With his usual directness he responded that his country's sole aim had been to end the lamentable conditions that had long existed in Cuba and that talk of expansion into South America was "trifling" and "valueless." Washington hoped, he explained, that its action might assist the Cuban people to create a respectable government, but, if this did not happen, then and then only might it consider annexation. But even this eventuality implied no territorial threat to the other nations of Latin America. However, in unusual candor, he went on to express what some analysts might regard as an antecedent to President Roosevelt's "Corollary" to the Monroe Doctrine. "In the end," he ventured,

> there will probably be a new precept added to international law, as a result of this war, whereby the right of a nation to stop the suffering and injury done its citizens, its moral sense, and its commerce, by revolutions and uprisings in a neighboring country, will be admitted, when brought about and kept in existence by the impotence and inability of the Government of such country.[8]

In these words the minister related to the secretary of state his rationalizations of American policy for his Argentine interrogators.

At the same time, in regular letters to his Sioux City family, he expressed himself with more feeling. While reiterating ideas from his official despatches, he bared a genuine skepticism of Washington's wisdom in undertaking the war and a deep concern for the grief his countrymen might still have to endure. "We will probably many times wish we had never heard of Cuba or the Cubans."[9] Once the American people began to count the millions spent and the lives lost, he was convinced, they would demand some recompense. In spite of presidential and congressional avowals to the world, they would not let their government "leave Cuba and the Philippines free and independent." "It makes no difference," he contended, "what we say nor how hard we may work toward that end I feel that the cold fate of things will take us on the annexationist road . . . we will find that we can do nothing but take the land we have fought for."[10]

Throughout the weeks of the "Ninety-Day War" the American minister sought to conduct himself with his normal calmness and dignity. In the realization that his every word or movement incited the emotions of Spanish elements, he avoided public appearances and all but the most essential visits to government ministries. When pushed into discussion of the war or war news, he responded only along the lines of argument he had meticulously prepared. Continuously stressing Argentina's neutrality, he urged his countrymen to temper their enthusiasm over American victories.[11]

With the termination of hostilities in August, Buchanan observed closely the fluctuating attitudes of the Argentines, Spaniards, and Cubans in Buenos Aires. The Argentine people, he reported, regarded the armistice terms as "magnanimous." While the Spanish population remained as bitter toward the United States as before, its indignation was now tempered by denunciations of Madrid for agreeing to humiliating terms of peace. As for the few Cuban residents, they began to denounce American newspapers for their unwarranted criticism of the island's insurgent leaders and their expanding sentiment for annexation.[12] Again, as during the war, the minister wrote to his family with less reserve. He had no more sympathy for "professional revolutionists" of Cuba than for their former Spanish oppressors. He feared that this faction would quickly dominate the island's "people," on whose behalf the United States had intervened. He apparently felt deeply that the revolutionary government

> must not expect that . . . we will turn over the island to them after the effort it has cost, until we can show to the world that they can not only govern it, but, most important and problematic of all, that they can govern themselves. In the end the Island will be ours and it will never amount to anything until then nor will we be free from a huge unpalateable [sic] difficulty until then.[13]

During these weeks of self-imposed abstention from public affairs Buchanan found himself with time for more personal matters. He accelerated the pace of his numbered letters to Mrs. Buchanan in Sioux City and sent her a number of guanaco rugs and other reminders of their years in Argentina. On occasion he wrote to son Donald, as he began to get his first taste of an elementary schoolroom at home, and to daughter Florence, as she left her family for the first time to attend St. Mary's Episcopal School for Girls in Knoxville, Illinois. To each of them he sent copies of Spanish books, with the promise of $5.00 for each one they would read. "The problems the future will bring to us in Spanish America—commercial and administrative—" he wrote to their mother, "will make the knowledge of Spanish an acquisition of the greatest value to a young man." But, happily for the children, their father sent along other items he thought would please them: for Donald, a bag of yerba mate with the customary gourd cups and *bombillas* for drinking it, and for Florence, music from *La Boheme* and *La Giaconda,* as well as a number of *habaneras.* When she began to show an interest in current world affairs, he promised to keep her supplied with clippings from Argentine newspapers and excerpts from Foreign Office publications."[14]

Taking further advantage of this respite in pressing official business, the minister resumed his travels into the Argentine countryside. In August, at an estancia 180 miles west of Buenos Aires, he tramped a hundred miles in two days while hunting ducks and other wild life. In September he accompanied President-elect Roca and his party to an estancia near La Plata. In October, shortly after Roca's inauguration, Buchanan accepted an invitation to use the presidential car for a trip to Mendoza, then up into the high Andes. Later he crossed the La Plata to visit friends in Montevideo.[15]

But this interlude of relative calm in the minister's official routine was only a lull preceding the flurry of diplomatic activities that marked the last months of his mission. None of these brought him greater personal satisfaction or more favorable attention in Buenos Aires than his role in adjudicating one of Argentina's perennial boundary disputes with neighboring Chile—this one over the Puna de Atacama.[16] His indispensible contributions to the 1898-1899 settlement represented both a sequel to an 1881 agreement facilitated by American diplomats and a prelude to the 1902 King's Award that led to the erection of the "Christ of the Andes" on the long-disputed border.

When in 1881 border violations had brought the two nations to the verge of war, American ministers in Buenos Aires and Santiago had offered their services as intermediaries to effect a settlement. Their efforts made possible the negotiation of "The Wire Treaty," an agreement concluded exclusively by telegraphic exchanges between American diplomats in the estranged capitals. After decades of mutual recriminations over Andean frontiers, the neighboring republics agreed that their mountain boundary should follow a line connecting the highest peaks "which divide the waters."[17] This was the ancient principle of *divortia aquarum,* or watershed, which reappeared in 1899 to challenge the mediatory skills of Minister Buchanan.

As the American diplomat had reported during the first year

of his mission, the 1881 settlement had not brought an end to Argentine-Chilean boundary troubles.[18] Demarcation experts over the years had become impaled on divergent interpretations of the treaty phrase "the most lofty peaks of the Cordillera which divide the waters." Argentina persisted for the chain of highest peaks; Chile claimed the line of the watershed. The implementing conventions of 1888 and 1895 and a clarifying protocol in 1893 failed to allay popular animosities or the recurrent threat of war.[19]

In a new convention signed on 17 April 1896 the nations sought to narrow the area of their disagreement. Any differences which arose over the mountain frontier south of latitude 26° 52' 45" were to be submitted to the British government for arbitration. North of that point to the 23° parallel, a distance of about three hundred miles, the boundary was to be worked out in conjunction with Bolivia.[20] The region between 23° and 26° 52' 45" was the bleak, uninhabited plateau, the Puna de Atacama. Though it was one of the few parts of Argentina he had not visited, Buchanan knew the Puna to be a kind of South American Tibet, a vast, forbidding wasteland lying at the northwest angle of Argentina's frontiers with Chile and Bolivia. Scanty in water, sparse of vegetation, poor in resources, even today it offers no attractions to man or beast. In 1898 fewer than a thousand primitive Indians braved alternate frigid blasts and scorching sun to eke out a wretched existence.

The twelve-thousand-foot floor of the Puna is dissected by a maze of lofty ridges and pierced by snow-capped peaks reaching more than sixteen thousand feet. Surrounded by two great spinal columns of the Andean Cordillera, the Puna's drainage system is independent of the continental divide. Since its waters drain into neither the Atlantic nor the Pacific, the 1881 principle of the *divortia aquarum* offered no solution to the boundary question.[21]

Argentina, Bolivia, and Chile had laid claim to the Puna de Atacama since the expulsion of Spain. After decades of negotiation, Bolivia in 1889 ceded its rights to Argentina. But Chile, whose troops had occupied the area during the War of the Pacific, was not a party to that treaty and refused to recognize the validity of Argentina's title.[22] Thus, its disposition unresolved by the 1881 treaty, the Puna became the symbol of Argentine-Chilean national fervors and the subject of separate diplomatic settlement.

Just before Buchanan returned to Buenos Aires from his trip to the United States, the controversy began to reach a more ominous phase. In a recent report to the Chilean Congress Foreign Minister J. J. Latorre had produced the impression that Argentina was responsible for the delay in boundary demarcation. When the Argentine minister in Santiago took umbrage, several exchanges of sharp notes followed.[23] To calm the troubled atmosphere the foreign minister decided to solicit the assistance of Washington. Directing the Chilean minister to suggest discreetly that the United States might find it opportune to repeat its 1881 tender of good offices, he insisted that such an offer must appear spontaneous and not the result of Chilean solicitation.[24]

The State Department, however, was reluctant to trespass upon the prerogatives of Great Britain, already designated as arbiter of the long boundary south of the Puna de Atacama. Moreover, it did not wish to intervene in any controversy unless the situation were extremely grave, nor to join Germany or any other power in seeking to settle problems of third parties.[25] Nevertheless, on 29 July Secretary of State William R. Day directed Buchanan and his counterpart in Santiago, Henry L. Wilson, to urge speedy arbitration. He also advised them confidentially of American willingness to respond to an invitation for specific assistance.[26]

In relaying Washington's hopes for settlement by arbitration, the ministers found both governments eager to avoid hostilities. At the same time, they observed that passions continued to rise and relations to deteriorate. Beyond this, however, the two diplomats differed sharply in their estimates of the situation. Wilson in Santiago suspected Argentine intransigence; Buchanan in Buenos Aires believed that Chile was seeking to bring about arbitration of the entire frontier rather than of specific differences.[27] Wilson persistently reported that war was "most probable"; Buchanan said he had "never believed the two countries would fight."[28]

Even in a steady exchange of friendly personal missives

across the Andes the Americans were unable to reconcile their divergent interpretations. In one of these letters the Iowan detailed the rationale for his evaluations. "Organically, the Latin Races love anything martial;" he wrote,

> they have had inbred in their bones for one hundred years hereabouts, for instance, a belief in and a passion for the argument of arms. They will decry it, and do, but a cold blooded outsider sees that they take to schemes for national guards, mobilizations, and the exhilarating talk of buying and equipping [sic] war ships as a duck does to water, and with a hundred times the zest they do to the every day, plain clothes, humdrum of the daily "grind" for bread. . . . I have felt sure that when the moment arrived when a solution of the Limits controversy had to be reached they would find a way to arbitrate it that would be supremely pleasing to both peoples.[29]

Meanwhile, as the State Department ascertained that Britain had no objections to American interposition, Buchanan met frequently with the Chilean minister in Buenos Aires and kept in almost daily touch with Foreign Minister Alcorta.[30] In September the center of diplomatic jockeying returned to Santiago, where the limits commissioners labored day by day to find the key that would halt troop movements and naval preparations. A ray of hope flickered on 15 September, when the Chilean foreign minister tentatively acceded to Argentine insistence upon separate treatment of the Puna de Atacama. But the nations endured another six weeks of tension before the diplomats succeeded in framing a specific plan.[31]

During the last week in October, while enjoying his excursion to Mendoza, Buchanan received an urgent request from the foreign minister to return at once to Buenos Aires. Already the American diplomat suspected, as he confided in a letter to his wife, that he was to be invited to "take a prominent part in the settlement of the most vexatious end [of the] endless Chilian question."[32] Within a few days the governments of Argentina and Chile revealed a new plan for resolving the Puna matter. An international conference of ten delegates, five from each nation, would meet in Buenos Aires to trace the Atacama line. If not successful after ten days of study, its task would be turned over to a demarcation commission with definitive powers. The commission would be composed of one Argentine, one Chilean, and the minister of the United States to the Argentine Republic, William I. Buchanan.[33]

By naming an American as the third commissioner the rival nations recognized the United States contribution to the settlement of 1881.[34] At the same time, they also paid tribute to Buchanan's long and respected career in southern South America. Even before the agreement of 2 November, the Chilean minister in Washington had expressed his government's eagerness to secure the American's services.[35] The Argentine minister, in his message to the State Department, was even more explicit. His government had selected Buchanan, he wrote, because of the "impartiality of his judgment" and "his high spirit of justice."[36] Although President McKinley chose to announce the "selection" in his December message to Congress, official invitations were delayed until late February.[37]

The joint conference authorized in the 2 November agreement met in Buenos Aires in early March 1899. When each proposal for tracing the line from 23° to 26° 52' 45" resulted in a vote of five to five, the demarcation commission of three was convened. Thus, Buchanan received the opportunity to play his decisive role. He freely admitted his lack of scientific knowledge about the principles of *divortia aquarum* and the "mountain chain." But, once appointed to the commission, he read and reread, he said, "every book, pamphlet, report, study, and prominent newspaper or magazine article written on the subject."[38]

The commission held four sessions, on 21, 22, 23, and 24 March. The Argentine and Chilean delegates, José E. Uriburu, former president, and Enrique MacIver, presented proposals for marking the Atacama boundary. Both plans were rejected, with Buchanan casting each deciding vote. The minister then submitted his proposal—a division of the line into seven sections, with a separate vote on each. Four times Buchanan voted with the Argentine representative, twice with the Chilean. On one section, with the terminal points fixed, the vote was unanimous.[39] In this simple and expeditious fashion the respected American minister resolved the troublesome question of the relatively worthless Puna de Atacama.

Again, as in 1881, the American minister in Buenos Aires received official acclaim for removing grounds of misunderstanding between two American peoples. Popular approval of the commission's actions, however, was by no means unanimous, either in Argentina or Chile. Though *La Nación* in Buenos Aires editorialized that the results had been "received by Argentine public opinion with perfect equanimity, without rejoicing and without discontent," the ultra press in both countries was less decorous.[40] Closely following this journalistic debate, Buchanan acknowledged to his wife that "both sides are dissatisfied so I know I am right as right can be. . . . The agony is over. The Puna question is settled. My mind is easy."[41] Then, seeking relief from his months of reading and pressure, he joined the minister of agriculture and an official party in a thousand-mile, six-day railroad trip to southern Argentina. In a special train, "with all the comforts of home," they journeyed across the pampas to Bahía Blanca, the valley of the Río Colorado, and the northern reaches of Patagonia.[42]

Back in the capital from this southern excursion, the minister confronted several matters to be tidied up before he could regard the Puna affair as closed. First, there was the preparation of his official report for Secretary Hay. Incorporating extensive translations from the Spanish documents and a review of the commission's deliberations, it turned out to be a voluminous forty-three-page despatch.[43]

The other matter, however, was less routine and, for Buchanan, somewhat seriocomic. Embellished by the press, a rumor had sprung up that the Argentine and Chilean governments were preparing to reward him for his services as demarcation commissioner with an "honorarium" of £20,000 sterling. At first, he inclined to regard the yarn with the levity he thought it deserved. " 'Such is fame,' " he wrote to Sioux City. "In the meantime I closely scour my hotel bill for 'Milk with biscuits—20 centavos.' 'Such is real life.' "[44] But the rumor persisted. The figure escalated to £30,000, then £50,000. Hearing the story in Santiago, Minister Wilson wired Buchanan for the facts, then reported to Washington Chile's hostility toward the idea. Eventually the Department of State gave assurance that neither Argentina nor Chile had offered the American minister an honorarium in any amount.[45] "This story is the nearest I shall ever approach that sum of lucre," Buchanan confessed to his wife and children.[46]

However thorough his self-preparation for the Puna boundary settlement or zealous his earlier watchfulness over American interests during the war with Spain, these assignments were clearly peripheral to Buchanan's primary goal in Argentina. At the core of support for his original appointment in 1894 had been confidence in his ability to improve the climate of bilateral trade with the fast-growing pampas economy. Stimulated by his experience at the Columbian Exposition, the Iowan had shared the enthusiasm for South American markets generated by manufacturers of agricultural equipment and their colleagues in the export trade. When he departed Buenos Aires in early 1898, he regretted the meager results of his four-year effort to improve trading relations. Later, when President McKinley insisted that he return to his post, he was persuaded in considerable part by his eagerness to consummate the reciprocal agreement the administration desired.

Upon the Iowan's return to Buenos Aires in late June, two encouraging developments awaited him. The first of these was his secretary's interim report to Washington that Argentine opinion seemed to be growing more favorable to a commercial agreement. The other was a State Department directive that advised him to initiate "informal conversations." If Argentina's leaders responded favorably, the department would conduct the negotiations with the minister in Washington, Martín García Mérou.[47] Buchanan's long-established friendship with Foreign Minister Alcorta quickly opened the door for the proposed talks—and kept it open for his suggestions and recommendations.[48] Moreover, remembering his exchange of views with the friendly García during his recent London stopover, Buchanan saw in these plans real hope for a satisfactory arrangement.[49] The department also requested the minister to submit a comprehensive analysis of recent Argentine-American trade, current rates of duty, and negotiable tariff reductions. It especially desired his observations on what Argentina would accept as equivalent concessions up to the 20 percent permitted under the Dingley Act.[50]

At the time they made their pledge to talk, neither Buchanan nor Alcorta could have foreseen that their serial conversations would stretch out over a year. In both Buenos Aires and

Washington unexpected obstacles arose to cause delay. At the outset the American encountered difficulty in securing essential data from various government ministries. The report he began to prepare in July did not reach appropriate State Department desks until November. Once completed, however, it was a comprehensive document containing critical commentaries and forthright recommendations as well as the statistical tables the secretary of state had requested.[51]

In comparing the United States with Argentina's five other principal trading partners over a six-year period (1892-1897), the minister found its showing to be "trifling, unimportant, and most unsatisfactory." American exports to Argentina consistently lagged behind those of Britain, Germany, and France and frequently behind Italy and Belgium as well. Each year the United States purchased less from Argentina than any of its trading rivals except Italy. This situation, Buchanan lamented, "can only be considered a reflection upon our productive and business ability, enterprise, and energy." On many occasions he had reported the barriers to improved trade. Now, he reemphasized two: alleged discrimination against Argentine wools and high freight rates resulting from inadequate direct steamship service.[52]

When he came to the point of suggesting a basis for negotiation, the minister ventured specific recommendations. The United States should offer the full 20 percent reduction of Dingley rates on wool, hides, and sugar. In return, it should seek from Argentina rate modifications on as many items as possible from a long list he appended, principally lumber, canned fruits and seafoods, and manufactured articles. He also passed along Foreign Minister Alcorta's expressed desire that the negotiations be transferred from Washington to Buenos Aires.[53] Subject to several reservations and the general requirement that all rate schedules be subject to departmental sanction, Secretary Hay promptly granted Alcorta's request.[54] Upon the Argentine's initiative, therefore, Buchanan's role advanced from mere relayer of messages to principal negotiator. "I will now dream," he wrote to his wife, "of wool, sugar, hides, furniture, canned fruit, lumber, carriages, and heaven knows how many other things."[55]

Much to the discomfiture of both Buchañan and Alcorta, the negotiations dragged on for another six months. Though they themselves had little difficulty in reaching agreement on key issues, each was hemmed in by the objections or reservations of his colleagues. The American, of course, was inhibited by the necessity of clearing every concession with his superiors in Washington. The Argentine was inhibited by legal restrictions that demanded concurrence of the minister of agriculture on all commercial arrangements.

Even after the negotiators had reached a tentative basis of agreement, the agriculture minister continued to hammer at traditional Argentine concerns. The new reciprocity proposals would antagonize European countries. They would endanger the welfare of domestic manufacturers. They would reduce customs revenues, from which the government derived 75 percent of its income. Behind all these arguments lay the perennial criticism of the wool-classification standards used by the United States and its suspected discrimination against foreign, especially Argentine, wools.[56]

From Secretary Hay Buchanan received continuing instructions on the limits of his authority as well as reminders of what was politically possible in the Congress. If the United States granted Argentina the suggested 20 percent tariff reductions on wool, hides, and sugar, it expected liberal concessions in return, with rates at least as low as those granted any other country. Repeatedly he asked the minister to secure for American goods some stabilization or regulation of *aforo* rates, a peculiar system of customs valuation that fluctuated with selling prices. Acknowledging the power of American woolgrowers, the secretary reminded Buchanan that "our protective duty on wool is a point on which a large portion of our people, as you are aware, are very sensitive."[57] Moreover, as barriers erected by both parties seemed to balk compromise, the Dingley Act deadline of 24 July threatened to frustrate the diplomat's determination to conclude the agreement.

Five weeks before this terminal date Buchanan cabled Washington that he had "EXHAUSTED THE SUBJECT AND ARGENTINE GOVERNMENT HAS SHOWN EVERY DISPOSITION TO MEET US." In return for the projected tariff reductions of 20 percent on wools, hides, and sugar, Argentina would lower duties as much as 50 percent on several dozen enumerated exports and fix aforos on most of them. "CONSIDERING ITS DIFFICULTIES WITH REGARD TO REVENUE, MANUFACTURING INTERESTS AND EUROPEAN TRADE," he declared, "THE ABOVE . . . IS THE ONLY BASIS PRACTICABLE OR OBTAINABLE. I BELIEVE IT FAIR AND ADVANTAGEOUS. RECOMMEND OUR ACCEPTANCE." While urging the minister to seek further concessions, Hay promptly authorized him to conclude and sign the convention. On 10 July Buchanan and Alcorta affixed signatures to the first Argentine-American commercial accord since 1853.[58]

Though Buchanan acknowledged to his family that he felt "very proud and cocky . . . over the satisfactory ending . . . of the long tussle," he tempered his enthusiasm with an unpunctuated reservation that foreshadowed the treaty's ultimate fate in Washington. His work, he felt, had been of "some good even though nothing shall come of the thing in the end since I have demonstrated that I could get a basis here for a Reciprocity Convention nevertheless it may not be considered sufficiently good by the Department to justify us concluding it."[59]

Consistent with his long-standing belief in reciprocity treaties, President McKinley soon transmitted Buchanan's convention—the first under the Dingley Act to be negotiated with a Latin American country—to the United States Senate. There for several years, in the files of the Committee on Foreign Relations, it languished until quietly forgotten.[60] Some months after Buchanan's return to the United States Hay confidentially explained to the Iowan's successor in Buenos Aires that influential American woolgrowers deemed "the present protection duty essential" to their prosperity.[61] The Democratic minister's months of efforts to fulfill the mandate of a Republican president had foundered before the staunch protectionism of a special interest group. The Senate's failure to act punctured Buchanan's hopes of reversing the country's thirty-year aversion to Argentine wool and of increasing Argentine-American trade.

The minister's struggle to consummate the trade agreement was only one of his attempts to modernize treaty relations with

Argentina. In scanning legation records shortly after he first arrived in Buenos Aires, he had found evidences of several uncompleted moves to amend or supplement the partially outmoded 1853 Treaty of Friendship, Commerce, and Navigation. As part of his mission to improve the climate for American products, he sought to tie up these loose ends as well as undertake new directions.

Next to the trade agreement Buchanan's principal treaty concern was an extradition convention his predecessors since 1887 had failed to effect. He requested authorization to renew negotiations. Though the wheels of diplomatic intercourse began at once to roll, for Buchanan they revolved with distressing slowness. To his dismay the time span from the day of his request in 1894 to the day of the treaty's official proclamation stretched out to nearly six years.[62]

Two years went by as Buchanan and Alcorta sought to hammer out an agreement that would satisfy both foreign offices. Washington desired a treaty similar to those recently concluded with Sweden and other countries; Buenos Aires insisted on terms that were compatible with domestic laws. They disagreed on a clause that would authorize the signatories to surrender their own citizens. The necessity of drafting and redrafting compromise clauses postponed signature of the convention until September 1896.[63]

Though the United States Senate then approved the treaty with unexpected promptness (January 1897), the State Department failed for seventeen months to notify Buchanan. Explaining merely that the document had been "accidentally overlooked . . . through a pressure of official duties," Secretary Day belatedly directed the minister to seek Argentine approval of the convention as amended by the Senate.[64] By the end of December 1898, Buchanan could report favorable action by the Argentine Congress. Only routine steps then remained—agreement on translation, ratification by each nation, exchange of ratifications, and official proclamation in each capital. Yet even this routine required another year and a half. Not until June 1900 did the extradition treaty become effective.[65] Perhaps because of his initiative in sponsoring it, or perhaps because he had persistently promoted it, Buchanan in later years recalled the convention as "one of the best things I did when I was in the Argentine."⁶⁶

In his other attempts to broaden the base of Argentine-American treaty relations, Buchanan was less successful. When he sought to revive a proposed protocol to the 1853 treaty that authorized the arrest and detention of deserters from merchant and war vessels, the Argentine Senate refused to confirm the American version.⁶⁷ When he urged American adherence to a multilateral agreement to protect copyrights, trademarks, patents, and university diplomas, the State Department ignored him.⁶⁸ Five times between 1895 and 1898 he requested authority to negotiate a parcel post and money order convention; he received no encouragement.⁶⁹ At the end of his mission, therefore, the minister could claim for all his treaty-making efforts only the hard-won extradition convention.

While striving in these ways to stabilize Washington's diplomatic relationships with Buenos Aires, Buchanan worked with equal zeal to increase Argentina's involvement in the nascent Hemisphere organization known as the Bureau of American Republics. Since 1889, when he had served as Corn Palace host to members of the First International Conference of the American States, his own interest in the Western Hemisphere idea had been growing. His recurring contacts with William E. Curtis, first director of the Bureau, and his experiences at the Columbian Exposition had made plain to him the inescapable relationship between inter-American comity and his country's drive to expand its overseas markets. In 1894 his assignment to Buenos Aires gave him the opportunity to work at first hand with the Latin American nation most reluctant to support the fledgling international body.

Since 1892 Argentina had neither participated in the work of the Bureau nor even remitted its modest share of the $36,000 budget advanced annually by the United States. Soon after his first arrival in Buenos Aires Buchanan had received instructions to remind Argentine officials of their 1893 obligation to the United States—$1,063.⁷⁰ In 1895 and 1896 he relayed similar reminders to the Foreign Office. In reply to the last of these Foreign Minister Alcorta spelled out Argentina's position. The Congress had never authorized the annual payments.

Government officials did not regard the agreements of the Washington Conference as obligatory. They looked upon some of the Bureau's publications as prejudicial to the interests of member nations. They felt that the Latin American republics were powerless to influence the Bureau's policies and operations.[71]

In spite of Alcorta's categoric explanation of his government's views, neither the State Department nor the American minister interpreted Argentina's refusal to pay its dues as tantamount to withdrawal from the Bureau. Moreover, Buchanan continued to believe that its active participation in the Bureau's activities would "do much toward bringing us closer to the Argentine people."[72] Some months earlier, as he was about to embark for his new post in Washington, Minister García Mérou had responded warmly to Buchanan's appeal for his aid in restoring Argentina's full membership. He promised to speak to both the Argentine president and the American secretary of state.[73] Matters then moved with the customary slowness of Argentine-American diplomatic intercourse.

In Washington the State Department initiated a reorganization of the Bureau that gave the Latin American states a larger voice in its operations. Agreeing to serve as a member of the newly created governing board, García Mérou became increasingly appreciative of the Bureau's purposes and functions. By the end of 1898, after a series of conferences with Secretary Hay, he recommended that Argentina resume its support of the Bureau. Meanwhile in Buenos Aires, with the Roca administration now in the saddle, Buchanan was able to convince Alcorta that, under its recent reorganization plan, the Bureau was no longer "seemingly but an adjunct of the State Department." Within a matter of hours President Roca cabled Washington that Argentina would resume payment of dues. As to his country's unpaid obligations to the United States, García Mérou told Hay that Buchanan was in a better position than he to arrange a satisfactory settlement.[74]

The combination of special assignments which came Buchanan's way in 1898-1899 was clearly the most engrossing of his five-year mission in Argentina. In these, as in many other activities of a United States diplomat, he found much to stimulate his interests and challenge his skills. Moreover, he could find satisfaction in the acclaim he received for his conduct as minister and the prestige he enjoyed as dean of the diplomatic corps. Yet his Iowan realism made him sense something unreal and illusory about the world of diplomacy. When these thoughts struck him, he sometimes set down his meditations in letters to his wife.

On occasion Buchanan felt that the chief of a diplomatic mission operated behind a kind of façade that he would like to dismantle. He sensed this particularly during the exasperating struggle to reconcile discordant national postures on the commercial treaty. "Once in a great while," he wrote to Mrs. Buchanan, "after the fashion of atmospheric and cyclonic forces you do actually rise up and assert all and severally the rights, privileges, immunities, and what not that appertain to the genus homo by birth." "It must be a great satisfaction," he went on, "to be able to do and say just what one pleases. I have not for years had a chance to try the thing but I imagine the sensation would be novel." Then, as the diplomat in him took over, he quickly added, "I expect . . . that if we could all do just as we pleased and say what we wanted to we would find ourselves dining quite alone in a short time."[75]

At other times, however, to seek relief from official pressures, the minister ruminated on themes of more personal implication. Spending his birthday for the first time apart from his wife and children, his thoughts turned to the importance of family harmony. "There is some profit in growing old," he mused, "one learns to appreciate the relative value of things," especially the mutual "formative power" exerted by family members. Then, calling up similes from his musical background, he suggested that

> we all stand for something—have some harmonic quality of usefulness in life and, if we are fortunate enough to be thrown into groups harmonically correct—well and good—we each add our individuality . . . and can feel satisfied. If, however, we get jumbled up, in life, into discordant groups, then the whole value of each individuality is lost and we struggle along without accomplishing our best—a sort of intellectual chromatic exercise, indifferently played.[76]

From time to time the minister's correspondence reflected the more commonplace aspects of the diplomatic life, especially one spent in an understaffed legation in a less than glamorous post in the late nineteenth century. Behind the prestige and the public esteem, there was always the routine and the humdrum. Occasionally without a legation secretary for extended periods, always without a research assistant, he frequently found himself performing everyday office chores as well as representing his country in high-level policy decisions. Even in negotiating the commercial treaty and adjudicating the boundary dispute, he tramped from ministry to ministry to collect the data he needed.

The archives of the Buenos Aires post reveal the diversity of the minister's more mundane duties. He answered letters from American businessmen inquiring about the market potential for typewriters, mattresses, carriages, and all manner of manufactured goods—and from engineers and other compatriots seeking job opportunities. He handled requests for United States naval vessels to enter ports or take target practice. He counselled Americans travelling or left stranded in Argentina. He shopped for essential office furnishings and supplies.[77]

Of all his routine responsibilities Buchanan found most annoying the handling of private claims against the Argentine government. American citizens seeking redress for alleged losses did not hesitate to ask State Department assistance on their behalf. Though none of the claims was large in amount, several had dragged on for more than twenty-five years. Meanwhile, hundreds of documents had accumulated in official files. In each instance the United States minister was caught in the middle. When Buchanan arrived in 1894, he inherited five unsettled cases. By the end of 1898 he had arranged settlement of each of these.[78]

Most vexing and discomforting was the case of Thomas Jefferson Page, an aged officer retired from the United States Navy. In 1853 Lieutenant Page had commanded the USS *Water Witch* on an official exploratory expedition to the principal tributaries of the Río de la Plata. Following his official report to the secretary of the navy he had published privately an informative but somewhat exaggerated account of the region's economic potential. Later, upon his retirement from the navy, he had established himself as an estanciero in the province of

Entre Rios. Always ambitious and aggressive, Page had promptly ingratiated himself with high Argentine officials. Observing the weakness of the nation's naval defenses and calling upon his own experience, he had submitted specifications for four war vessels and secured a contract to oversee their construction in English shipyards.

During Page's three-year absence in England the Argentine army, while suppressing a revolutionary outbreak, had confiscated valuable livestock from his estancia. Upon his submission of claims for compensation, he found the Congress unwilling to meet his full demands. Moreover he felt that he had received inadequate remuneration for his supervision of the warship construction, especially after a former president had told him that he had done more for Argentina "than any living man." Unable year after year to secure a settlement he believed just, the navy veteran had eventually moved to Rome to spend his declining years.[79]

All these details of an octogenarian's obvious hardship, together with myriad pleas for assistance from Page's son and from Thomas Nelson Page in Washington, came to Buchanan's attention soon after his first arrival in Buenos Aires. Secretary Olney's instruction to seek a settlement soon followed.[80] Recurrently, then, for the next three years the minister presented the claim to the Argentine government. Ultimately, he could write his wife, *"as a courtesy* to me" the Congress appropriated $4242.35 for Captain Page. "I am thankful the claim is settled. It completes my claim record."[81] Six weeks later President McKinley thought the Page settlement important enough to mention in his annual message to Congress.[82]

In pressing the cases of these individual claimants, Buchanan acted under explicit authorization of the secretary of state and did not hesitate to put the prestige of his own office behind his actions. With American financiers, however, operating under loan contracts with Argentine national and provincial governments, his authority was less clear-cut. A difficult assignment awaited him, therefore, in 1898-1899, when he was confronted by a case of defaulted interest payments owed by the province of Santa Fé to Morton, Rose & Company of New York.

During Argentina's economic boom of the 1880s the New

York firm and its London affiliates had secured Santa Fé loans totaling some $15,000,000. When financial crisis later forced the province to suspend interest payments, the firm's head, former Vice-President Levi Morton, approached the State Department for assistance. To avert any possible charge of exerting official pressure on behalf of American bondholders, Secretary Day directed Buchanan to "exercise merely good offices."[83] In collaboration with the British minister, then, but carefully avoiding any formal overture or written communication, the American broached the matter to President Roca and his finance minister. After working for some months "as stealthily and persistently as a terrier," he was able to effect a refunding arrangement that appeared to satisfy both American and English bondholders. The settlement he helped to catalyze gave Buchanan deep satisfaction and also stimulated his sense of humor. Returning to his hotel after the three-hour "fencing and parrying" session that brought final agreement, he chanced to receive his personal financial statement, a modest account of $60.00. When he found that he had been charged $1.00 for a "whiskey and soda" he had not ordered, he promptly queried his wife, "Isn't the human intellect elastic and adaptable that can get from $500,000−$15,000,000−$180,000 to $1.00 paper during the same afternoon?"[84]

Though he made effective use of his "good offices" in the case of the bondholders, Buchanan met less success when he tried similarly to assist the New York Life Insurance Company. In late 1898 the American corporation encountered difficulties with the Argentine government over new regulations affecting foreign life insurance companies. When the two parties disagreed on the nature of a required license tax, the company appealed to the State Department. In the interest of continued harmonious relations between the two governments, Secretary Hay directed him to "continue the strenuous exercise" of his good offices.[85] The controversy had reached this apparent stalemate in July 1899, when the Iowan embarked on leave to the United States. Official resolution of the case, therefore, would rest with his successors, though he himself, once returned to private life, would maintain a prominent role in the settlement. More important for Buchanan, his familiarity with the case would lead to his later affiliation with the New York Life Insurance Company—and to a new, quite different mission in Latin America.[86]

As early as January 1899 Buchanan had begun to make specific plans for return to Sioux City. After months of absence he increasingly felt the need to attend private business matters and to renew family ties. Moreover, he realized that his agenda of pending assignments—the commercial and extradition treaties, the Puna mediation, the bondholders and New York Life cases—would keep him deeply involved for four to five months. For these reasons he requested and received permission to take extended leave beginning between late May and early July.[87]

Though Buchanan scheduled his departure for mid-June, the pressure of winding up legation affairs postponed his sailing date to 11 July.[88] Whether or not at this juncture he was still contemplating return to Argentina is unclear; probably he had not made up his own mind. He must have known, however, that he was the last Democratic appointee still serving the McKinley administration as chief of a foreign mission. Moreover he had received an unexpected cablegram from the authorities of Buffalo's Pan-American Exposition, already scheduled for 1901, which flatly inquired, "FOR WHAT AMOUNT WILL YOU ACCEPT DIRECTOR-GENERAL PAN-AMERICAN?"[89] Intriguing as he found this terse query, he determined to make no decision until he had had the opportunity to talk with both the White House and the exposition officials.[90]

In Argentine circles, however, the opinion seemed to prevail that Buchanan would not return to Buenos Aires, for his friends in Argentine officialdom regaled him with a series of creole *despedidas*. To repay the many courtesies he in turn gave dinners for those who had honored him. During one ten-day period, he wrote his wife, he took only one meal in his hotel.[91] On the day of his sailing dockside well-wishers included the entire diplomatic corps, the ministers of foreign affairs and marine, a presidential aide, and a number of prominent citizens.[92] The porteño press reflected the sentiments of Argentine officials. "The noble Minister was bid affectionate farewell by his many friends and acquaintances," commented *La Pren-*

sa, "and many of them accompanied him to the steamer." An English-language newspaper described him as "by far the most satisfactory Minister that has represented the United States here, of whom the present generation has any knowledge."[93]

Scheduled to reach New York on 6 August, Buchanan's ship, the *Wordsworth,* experienced serious engine difficulties en route from Rio de Janeiro. For ten days it lay adrift in open seas, then, after temporary repairs, crawled to Barbados. Eventually transferred to another ship, the passengers reached New York only on 3 September.[94]

However frustrating to his hopes for early conferences at the White House and in Buffalo, the two-month passage gave Buchanan ample time for rest and relaxation. Though he apparently kept no log of this voyage, he must have given some hours to reminiscing of his mission to Argentina. Without prior training or extensive briefing he had served for more than five years as United States diplomat under two presidents. Under a Republican administration during two of those years the Iowa Democrat had apparently satisfied the expectations of the White House. Without jeopardizing the interests of the country he represented, he had established warm relations with the political and business leaders of the nation to which he was accredited. In turn, their confidence in his judgment and sense of justice had ripened.

Availing himself of the trust he had stimulated in his hosts, Buchanan had been able to deal successfully with most of the concerns that had confronted him. He had submitted to Washington a variety of proposals for the improvement of trade relations. He had negotiated and signed two treaties long desired by the State Department. He had zealously looked after his country's interests in wartime. Beyond all this, upon the invitation of Argentina and Chile, he had contributed indispensably to settlement of the long-festering Puna de Atacama boundary dispute.

In fulfilling the essential intelligence coverage of his mission, the minister had transmitted more than six hundred despatches to Washington, many of them based on his own leg work, some of them written or typed by his own hand.[95] In addition, he had composed innumerable other communications—cables to the

State Department, notes to the Ministry of Foreign Affairs, memos to diplomatic colleagues in nearby capitals, and letters to business firms in the United States.

Buchanan's reporting on the economic situation in developing Argentina extended to periodic estimates published in *U. S. Consular Reports*. His travels had enabled him to report on such diverse topics as immigration, census returns, powers of attorney, mining methods, sugar production, tariff changes, and export bounties.[96] Several of these articles so impressed former Foreign Minister Zeballos that he translated and published them in his prestigious review, *La Revista de Derecho, Historia y Letras*.[97] Remembering his friends from Corn Palace and Columbian Exposition days, the Iowan had even described "Life on the Estancias of Argentina" for *The Breeder's Gazette*.[98]

But if the Cleveland appointee found a certain shipboard satisfaction in these positive aspects of his five-year service in Argentina, he must also have given some thought to his principal disappointment. Sent to Buenos Aires primarily to cultivate the Argentine market, he was fully aware that he had not brought about the trade increases expected. Like his predecessors, he had reiterated in vain the obstacles to improved American markets in Latin America. Though export volume was growing, it had by no means reached the levels he had envisioned. Even the commercial treaty he had so laboriously negotiated—which would never become operative—did not achieve the "rational, broad, common sense application on our part of the principle of commercial Reciprocal Conventions" he believed essential.[99]

During these weeks at sea Buchanan must also have found particularly "alluring" the prospect of serving as director general of the Pan-American Exposition. It would allow him to capitalize on the understanding he had gained of the Latin American world and the status he had attained in southern South America. It would enable him to apply the recommendations he had made at the close of the Columbian Exposition. He could settle down with his family "at home."[100] But, however enamored of these prospects, he would adhere to the course of action upon which he had determined in June. He would delay decision on resignation from his diplomatic post until he had conferred, first, with President McKinley, then with the exposition officials.

Chapter 8
BUILDING A WORLD EXPOSITION
Buffalo, 1899-1901

On 2 November 1899 Buchanan arrived in Buffalo to assume his mantle as director general of the Pan-American Exposition.[1] However new to him the western New York metropolis and its civic leaders, successive experiences had thoroughly acquainted him with the energy and dynamism of ambitious urban communities. Whether in Sioux City, Chicago, or Buenos Aires, he had witnessed or shared in the efforts of an enterprising citizenry to widen its influence and enlarge its economic domain. In the 1880s he had helped to build Sioux City's reputation as the Peerless Princess of the Plains and the Corn Palace City of the World. In the early 1890s he had contributed to the planning, construction, and administration of Chicago's renowned White City. During five years in Buenos Aires he had observed the relentless porteño drive to make Argentina the world's leading breadbasket for surplus foodstuffs. Now, in western New York, Buchanan was moving into a position to reinforce Buffalo's claim to be the "Queen City of the Lakes."

The former diplomat would soon find that, like the other flourishing cities in which he had lived and worked, Buffalo was swelling with local pride. After half a century of continuous growth, its progress toward urban maturity had faltered in the depressions of the seventies and early nineties. Now, however, at century's end, it was economically as well as psychologically ready to seek new outlets for its rejuvenated civic spirit.[2]

The city's readiness to take its place in the firmament of great American urban centers was made apparent in April 1897 by the appearance of an energetic new promotional medium called *Greater Buffalo*. Its expansive title intimated a regional concept, one that would eventually embrace both sides of the Niagara River from Lake Erie to Lake Ontario, an area soon to be popularized as the Niagara Frontier. In its first and subsequent monthly issues, continuing through the days of the Pan-American Exposition, the journal trumpeted in superlatives Buffalo's emergence as a great commercial city.

It acclaimed the Queen City of the Lakes as the nation's leading market for flour and sheep and second only to Chicago in handling traffic in grain, lumber, and livestock. Reaching for global comparisons, it heralded Buffalo as the world's largest coal-distributing center and its harbor the world's fourth busiest, with annual waterborne commerce quintupling the volume of the Suez Canal.[3]

Even without these comparisons, citizens of rival Great Lakes cities could envy Buffalo's strategic location. As the western terminus of the Erie Canal and the easternmost terminal for lake traffic, it had long been a natural transshipment point for goods to and from the growing Middle West. Freighters bringing grain from the plains states, lumber from Lake Superior's shores, and iron ore from Minnesota reloaded with coal from Pennsylvania and manufactured goods from seaboard cities. Moreover, as *Greater Buffalo* drummed month by month, the city lay within a night's railroad ride of 162 large cities and 38,000,000 people in the United States and Canada.[4]

To handle this ceaseless flow of cargo scores of corporations had provided facilities for transportation, storage, and transfer. Twelve steamship lines made Buffalo a regular port of call and twenty-six railroads entered the city. Along nineteen miles of waterfront—lake, river, and canal—more than fifty elevators could store 20,000,000 bushels of grain. Within a space of twenty-four hours, during the navigation season, docks could unload 2,000,000 bushels of grain and reload with coal. At the same time city and state authorities were cooperating to improve the harbor and deepen the Erie Canal.[5]

But financial interests in Buffalo in the late nineties were not content that its growing influence should be restricted to commercial preeminence. They knew that balanced urban development demanded industrial growth to complement the commercial. For too long the city's manufacturing establishments had limited their production to diversified small-scale products. Now, reasoned enterprising financiers, they could compete with other lake cities only by attracting heavy industry, particularly iron and steel.[6]

Three fortuitous circumstances then played into the hands of Buffalo's promoters. The opening of Minnesota's Mesabi Range meant that iron ore could be brought in by inexpensive lake transport. The election of President McKinley seemed to assure recovery from the 1893 depression and presage more prosperous times; his campaign manager, the ironmaster Mark Hanna, might prove "a friend at court" for producers of steel.[7] Capping these developments, the Lackawanna Iron and Steel Company in early 1899 determined to move from Scranton, Pennsylvania, to western New York. Its recapitalization at $60,000,000 and purchase of lakefront property brought local leaders the heavy industry they had sought to round out the Queen City's economic versatility.[8]

But undergirding all Buffalo's growth as the end of the century approached was one salient development—the arrival on 15-16 November 1896 of cheap hydroelectric power from Niagara Falls, more than twenty miles away. Never before had electric energy been transmitted such a distance.[9] At a great banquet two months later civic leaders savored the prophetic words of inventor Nikola Tesla: "Niagara Power will make Buffalo the greatest city in the world!"[10] Less encompassing, though more eloquent, was the commentary of a local writer: "We are at the threshhold of the temple of electric wonders. . . . Buffalo stands in the full glow of the electrical sunrise."[11] Dreams of a great exposition to symbolize these poetic thoughts were already forming.

To man this expanding commercial-industrial complex, as well as its supporting public services, employers could reach into a labor reservoir that was constantly being replenished from Europe. From 1880 to 1900 Buffalo's population more than doubled to 352,387. Two-thirds of these were native-born, though only a fourth were offspring of two American-born parents.[12] As earlier immigrants from Germany, Ireland, and Britain gradually climbed the socioeconomic ladder, even larger numbers from eastern and southern Europe moved in to replace or supplement them in the labor force. Though these included sizeable colonies of Jews and Hungarians and smaller contingents of diverse Slavic peoples, the Poles and Italians far outnumbered other newcomers. Among American cities in 1900 Buffalo was second only to Chicago in size of its Polish population.[13] Settling inexorably into their respective ethnic neighborhoods, these various groups would present to Buchanan the same jigsaw puzzle pattern of residence he had come to know during the Columbian Exposition. More important for him, however, they would provide an indispensable supply of artisans and laborers for the Pan-American and an essential part of its patronage.

In economic terms, as in social, these ethnic clusters revolved much like satellites around the sun of "old Buffalo"—the coterie of upper-middle-class families whose founders had bequeathed wealth, fine homes, and social status to their descendants. Yet, as in most American cities of the Gilded Age, no social stratum was impenetrable; industry, thrift, and perseverance might bring wealth and economic power to bridge social chasms.[14]

In any case, the publicists who in the late nineties began to extol Buffalo's bright future sought to speak for all residents of the Queen City. They described it as "the best city in the world to live in ... most healthful ... most beautiful ... coolest in the summer." They claimed for it more beautiful trees than in Paris or Washington and more paved streets than London.[15] However extravagant these claims may have been, Buffalonians could safely point with pride to the refurbishing of their inner city with new construction: a bank that resembled an imposing French chateau, an office building designed by Louis Sullivan, a modish hotel, and a postoffice that towered over them. The architectural gem of all the new structures may have been the Ellicott Square Building, designed by Buchanan's colleague of Columbian Exposition days, Daniel H. Burnham, and, in the eyes of one historian, reminiscent of Cosimo de

Medici's palace in Florence. It already housed the innovative 500-seat restaurant of E. M. Statler and would soon become the headquarters of the Pan-America Exposition Company and the seat of Buchanan's operations until 1901.[16]

Out of this combination of circumstances—geographic good fortune, accumulated wealth, ethnic diversity—Buffalo generated the local pride and enterprising civic leadership to conceive, finance, and produce a distinctive world exposition. A group of business and political leaders successfully fused their ideals and economic motives to push the project to completion. As Buchanan would write in his final report, for a city of barely one-third million inhabitants it was a courageous but hazardous undertaking. No city so small had attempted a world's fair so pretentious.[17]

As early as 1895 the idea of a civic-sponsored world exhibition had begun to intrigue Buffalo's promoters. While representing their city on "Buffalo Day" at the Cotton States and International Exposition in Atlanta, several Buffalonians began to dream of a comparable festival for the Niagara Frontier. A year later a Niagara Falls newspaper cited a rumor that somewhere along the Niagara River in 1899 an exposition would be held to dramatize the progress of the New World during the nineteenth century—an early, if not the first, mention of the Pan American theme.[18]

Rumor soon began to approach reality. Supported by Niagara Falls electric power interests and the American Exhibitors Association, Buffalo businessmen formally incorporated the Pan-American Exposition Company and began to draft preliminary plans for the enterprise. By August 1897 company officials had selected a site on Cayuga Island near Niagara Falls, persuaded President McKinley to drive a memorial stake, and initiated a public relations campaign by entertaining some fifty Latin American commercial representatives. Within the next six months they secured assurances of cooperation from Latin American diplomats in Washington, negotiated with Buffalo bankers the terms of a bond issue, and solicited recognition and aid from both state and national governments.[19]

By the early weeks of 1898, therefore, Buffalo's plans for its ambitious civic project were proceeding smoothly. Until mid-

February its launching on schedule seemed assured. Then, abruptly, destruction of the battleship *Maine* in Havana harbor shattered hopes for the immediate future of Pan American comity. Buffalo could scarcely offer homage to Western Hemisphere progress, much less invite sixteen Spanish-American nations to share its celebration, while the United States waged war against their Iberian motherland. Fully aware of these realities the company's board of directors advanced the exposition date to 1901.[20]

In many ways this sudden shift in timetable brought unexpected benefits to the Pan-American venture. The landing of American troops in Cuba and Puerto Rico focused the nation's attention on the Latin America it had long ignored. Liberation of Spain's last Western Hemisphere possessions stressed again the economic opportunities awaiting American enterprise on its Caribbean doorstep and beyond in South America. In Buffalo, as elsewhere in the nation, the earlier Pan American ideas of James G. Blaine had not been forgotten. "The time is ripe," editorialized a new Buffalo monthly publication, *The Pan-American,* "for new movements to bring about more intimate relations between the countries of North and South America."[21] Shortly after the war's conclusion an enlarged group of businessmen and public officials moved to grasp the city's opportunity.

Though hundreds of citizens shared in this reawakening, it was Buffalo's energetic mayor, Conrad Diehl, who officially breathed new life into the dormant project. Three days after peace was signed with Spain he appointed a committee to plan the formation of a new, greatly augmented Pan-American Exposition Company. At the same time, already apprised of Detroit's efforts to win Washington's approval for a world exposition, he named a special delegation to visit the White House.[22] "You can rely on me to do anything in my power for this enterprise," President McKinley assured the mayor and his colleagues, "I shall be very glad to do anything I can for Buffalo." A similar delegation to Albany won equally enthusiastic support from Governor Theodore Roosevelt. By early March both national and state governments had authorized funds for the erection of their exhibit buildings.[23]

Meanwhile, in Buffalo an expanded board of directors moved swiftly to capitalize on the regenerated community "spirit of energy, confidence, and progress." They secured a new charter, adopted new by-laws, and elected new officers. To broaden the scope of the exposition, they increased capitalization from $1,000,000 to $2,500,000; to enlarge its potential patronage, they shifted the site from an island in the Niagara River to a park area on Buffalo's north side.[24] The public-spirited citizens chosen to oversee these expansion moves were John G. Milburn, president, Edwin Fleming, secretary, George L. Williams, treasurer, and John N. Scatcherd, chairman of the executive committee. A typical cross section of the leadership which conceived and administered the exposition, these men represented law, journalism, the leather business, and the lumber industry.[25]

Their absorption with decisions regarding organization, financing, and site did not blind the directors to another overriding consideration—the need to select and appoint a qualified professional as the exposition's director general. Understandably, they gave special attention to the unsolicited recommendations of former officials of the recent World's Columbian Exposition. Without exception the Chicagoans nominated a single candidate—William I. Buchanan. In the view of Daniel H. Burnham, architectural supervisor at Chicago, he was the one ideal man for the Pan-American post. Among others urging Buchanan's appointment was William E. Curtis, former director of the Bureau of American Republics, who had already been engaged to publicize the exposition in South America.[26]

The Buffalo directors evidently saw in the Iowa diplomat the precise combination of qualifications they sought, for they gave scant consideration to other candidates.[27] His experiences with local exhibitions like Sioux City's Corn Palaces and a world's fair like Chicago's Columbian assured them of his executive capacity. His five years as a diplomat in Argentina, together with his fluency in Spanish and his understanding of Spanish character, left no doubt that he could translate the Pan American theme into reality. His intimate connections with the White House seemed to guarantee President McKinley's promised support. His contacts at the Department of State would facilitate efforts to secure active participation of the Latin American governments.[28] Moreover, his earlier association with leading figures in agricultural societies, import-export organizations, and the entertainment world would ease the task of securing exhibitors and concessionaires. Above all, perhaps, the Buffalo directors must have been impressed by Buchanan's probity, his enthusiasm for any assignment he undertook, and his demonstrated belief that expositions should be educational as well as recreational. Early in June they directed Secretary Fleming to send the laconic cablegram: "FOR WHAT AMOUNT WILL YOU ACCEPT DIRECTOR-GENERAL PAN-AMERICAN?"[29]

As he had arranged with the Buffalo authorities before leaving Argentina on 11 July, Buchanan postponed decision on Fleming's query until after his return to the United States.[30] En route, however, as requested, he consulted with public officials in Uruguay and Brazil to urge their participation in the exposition.[31] Meanwhile, Curtis had been performing a similar function in Ecuador, Peru, Bolivia, and Chile.[32] Arriving in New York on 3 September, Buchanan went immediately to Washington to confer with President McKinley and to report to the State Department on his Argentine mission. Five days later he reached Buffalo, there to meet with President Milburn and other exposition heads but also to enjoy reunion with his family after seventeen months of enforced separation.[33]

A series of conferences and inspection trips with his hosts convinced Buchanan that the Buffalo project was viable. He understood and appreciated their businessmen's approach. He approved the organizational and promotional steps already taken. With the landscaping and beautification possibilities that its position next to a public park system provided the exposition site whetted his imagination. Clearly if an offer followed the interviews and contractual terms satisfied him, he was inclined to accept the appointment.[34]

As a veteran of exposition management, however, the Iowan was frankly insistent about several considerations. To maintain efficiency and coherence, the director general of the exposition must be manager in fact as well as in title. Since at best the position would be temporary but would require him to resign from his government post, he would expect a contract for two-and-a-half years, with appropriate safeguards to each signatory in case of disagreement. He asked an annual salary of $12,000. Finally, since he would plan to visit Mexico, Cuba, and other countries, he also requested reimbursement for all travelling expenses.[35]

To these terms the exposition directors raised no objections. Meanwhile, returning to New York and Washington, then travelling homeward to Chicago and Sioux City, Buchanan consulted friends about the wisdom of accepting the appointment. Everywhere, even in Washington, they encouraged him. From his Iowa home on 18 October he communicated his acceptance and signified his intention to assume his duties on 1 November.[36] He then promptly resigned his diplomatic post and headed for Buffalo and new challenge—the opportunity to interweave the management of a world exposition with his deep interest in Latin America.

The director general utilized his first days in Buffalo to assess the status of the enterprise now entrusted to his stewardship. He fully realized that he had just eighteen months, embracing two western New York winters, to build and ready the exposition for its opening on 1 May 1901. Yet before attempting to formulate a plan of operations, he needed to understand the goals envisioned by the directors, to clarify the channels of administrative responsibility, and to examine the extent and details of actions already taken. "I want to get all the strings in my grasp first," he told an inquiring journalist, "I want to find out where things are at and where I am at. . . . I shall look into the farthest nooks and crannies of the whole affair."[37]

His first tour of inspection left Buchanan with a comprehensive inventory of the strings he would have to grasp. A complex of committees had been at work since the previous spring and their reports used as bases for policy formation; he planned to continue the committee system. The officers had already organized most of the key departments and appointed their directors. They had named a board of architects, whose plans for a dozen buildings were already on the drawing boards. They had agreed on a ground plan and completed fencing of the entire exposition site. Groundbreaking was under way.[38]

Most surprising to Buchanan of all the preparatory work was the effectiveness with which the exposition authorities had initiated their promotional campaign.[39] As early as May they had given Hemisphere-wide circulation to a comprehensive "Preliminary Prospectus," with Spanish and Portuguese versions prepared by William E. Curtis. Through both personal representatives and official State Department communications, they had solicited the participation of the Latin American governments.[40]

As a device to stimulate public interest, the management had invited artists to submit designs for an official exposition emblem. From over 400 suggestions received they had chosen one they thought distinctively symbolic of inter-American friendship. It depicted two nymphlike figures superimposed on a map of the Western Hemisphere. Each clad in flowing diaphanous gown, the North American maiden appeared to be reaching southward across Central America—in obviously friendly, if slightly uncomfortable, posture—to grasp the extended hand of the South American señorita. Known as the Beck design, it would become increasingly familiar during the next two years, as manufacturers eagerly sought to use it on stationary, playing cards, napkin rings, glass and porcelain articles, and dozens of other souvenir items.[41]

From the very outset Buchanan insisted upon delineating his management principles. Though he believed in the committee system, he saw it as a source of well-threshed ideas, not as the instrument for decision-making or executive direction. He felt that all rules and regulations should receive his approval, that all bureaus and agencies should report only to him, and that all concessions contracts and material requisitions should flow through his office. Subject in these matters to the direction of the Executive Committee, the director general should have the power to take definite action between sessions of that body. These were the procedures of sound corporation management, Buchanan believed, by which Buffalo businessmen would wish to see their exposition directed. Properly administered, they should cause no friction or disharmony. To his satisfaction the exposition's Board of Directors promptly incorporated all of them in the company's by-laws.[42]

Reassured by this legalization of the authority he had requested, the director general could systematize plans for permanent organization. Meeting at frequent intervals with department heads and committee chairmen, he sought to establish procedures that would liquidate overlapping jurisdictions, prevent delays, and streamline the interplay between recommendations and executive decisions. Once his machinery began to function, he was able to present an almost daily batch of propositions to the Executive Committee for enabling authorization.[43] By the end of the year, Buchanan had established the pattern of operations he deemed workable, one that would permit consummation of original plans with adequate allowances for essential modifications and unforeseen delays.

During these same months the former diplomat faced another, much more personal, organization problem—the reassembly of his family under one roof. For more than a year and a half, while he was rounding out his diplomatic mission to Buenos Aires, his wife and son had maintained their family home in Sioux City and his daughter had sampled boarding school in Knoxville, Illinois. Their strong family ties demanded early reunion around a common hearth. Without delay they moved into a large comfortable home, located conveniently midway between the exposition headquarters in downtown Buffalo and the exposition site on the north side.

Interviewed in the new home only hours after her arrival, Mrs. Buchanan frankly expressed her ignorance about the exposition. Immediately, however, she inquired about plans for women's activities. Recalling her active participation in Sioux City's Corn Palaces and civic carnivals, the journalist sensed her willingness to contribute "her experience, skill and artistic taste" to the exposition. His introductory characterization of Mrs. Buchanan presented her to Buffalo readers as "very pleasing in appearance . . . gracious and courteous in manner . . . a woman of culture, refinement, simplicity and rare good sense."[44] By New Year's Day 1900, all the Buchanans were ready to cope with their new city of residence, the fourth in nine years.

His usual buoyancy restored by daily family contact, Buchanan could attack with new vigor the complex and formidable assignment he had accepted. With one eye on opening day, the other on budgetary limitations, he would have to push construction and accelerate publicity while planning a diversified program. As the need developed, he had to broaden his organizational base. To none of these tasks could he give his undivided attention; all he must pursue simultaneously, at the same time keeping sight of the goals and ideals of the Buffalo promoters and his own beliefs in the educational value of expositions and the importance of Latin America. Labor problems, freakish weather, and shortage of funds would recurrently upset his delicate timetable.

With dozens of buildings to be built, service facilities to be constructed, lakes and canals to be dug, roads to be paved, and sidewalks to be laid, the work of construction usually headed the director general's agenda. As in any major building project, each unit required the successive steps of notification to architects, preparation of drawings, drafting of specifications, advertising of bids for construction, awarding of contracts, and inspection of progress. During all the months of preparation Buchanan was the overseer of this assembly-line process and the middleman between the Executive Committee and the department chiefs who fulfilled his directives.[45]

By midsummer 1900 he could report that contracts for all major exhibition buildings had been awarded, with construction under way on most of them, and excavation for lakes and canals virtually completed. He had arranged for increased use of Niagara electric power, laying of fire and water lines, preparation of special railroad sidings to bring in mountains of building materials, and installation of new traction facilities to transport expected crowds of patrons.[46] To permit daily inspection of these widespread activities he had secured two horses and two wagons for the use of himself and his director of works.[47] As he had demonstrated at the Chicago exposition, no detail of his vast jurisdiction was too small to demand his attention.

Though Buchanan had had no voice in the selection of the exposition site, theme, basic ground plan, or original building design,[48] virtually every subsequent action bore the stamp of his initiative or supervision. As the "controlling spirit" of the entire undertaking, he could cast the exposition in a pattern he believed appropriate—could give it both the unity and variety he felt its theme demanded.[49] For him the key to this end lay in rigorous and vigilant attention to matters of educational appeal and of refinement.

Unlike Henry Adams at one stage of his development, Buchanan never overtly "professed the religion of World's Fairs," without which education would be "a blind possibility." Yet, he might well have supported a less encompassing view, that in expositions "education found new forage . . . ; one seemed to see almost an adequate motive for power; almost a scheme for progress."[50]

Buchanan's experiences in Sioux City and Chicago, together with the aesthetic sensitivities of his wife, had also convinced him that public exhibitions should be

> a source of gladness and delight, and a pride as well. . . . [They should] bring together about these central salient points, those finishing, connecting links of fountains, of brilliant lighting effects, of music, of gardens, of entertainments, and of novelty, which go far toward making up the real life of a great Exposition.[51]

Moreover, in his view, the enormous expense of majestic physical structures was justifiable only if they elevated art, stimulated good taste, and brought a sense of "uplift" to millions of people.[52] Fortunately, within the limits of their budgetary operations, the Buffalo authorities supported this philosophy.

To implement his beliefs Buchanan had urged from the beginning the use of color and widespread display of decorative sculpture. Once he had persuaded the Executive Committee to authorize the appointment of directors of color and sculpture, he was able to secure two nationally known artists, C. Y. Turner and Karl Bitter, to fill the positions. Uniquely, in the building of world expositions, architects, contractors, painters, and sculptors worked together to achieve harmony in a general scheme of ornamentation.[53]

With equal zeal the director general supported his staff and committees in other matters of artistic expression and adornment. By this time, for example, access to Niagara electric power offered them limitless possibilities. The power lines built only a few months before to service Buffalo's street railways were now adequate to provide the entire city with light, heat, and energy. This availability of cheap Niagara power made possible the world's first use of artistic electric lighting for illumination of an entire exposition. Early in their planning the exposition authorities determined that, like the symbolic Electric Tower itself, all principal exhibition buildings and walkways should receive this decorative treatment.[54]

To provide a natural scenic backdrop for all these manmade features, no part of the exposition ground would lack the landscaping and beautification upon which Buchanan and his sponsors insisted. As early as November 1899 search had begun for several hundred monumental cedar trees and for a thousand Lombardy poplars at least twenty-five feet high. Greenhouses were erected to propagate roses, lilies, and other flowers for the gardens and conservatories.[55]

Though pleased with the public relations activities begun before his arrival, Buchanan knew from experience that advertising an exhibition was a many-phased proposition, one that demanded specialized techniques and constant reinforcement as well as imagination and resourcefulness. It must begin early, utilize diversified approaches, and exert wide appeal. It must reach, first, public officials and the press, then potential exhibitors of all kinds, producers of midway attractions, and other concessionaires, and finally, the public.[56] Alert to these realities, the director general and the Executive Committee mounted their campaign.

Seeking to enlist the interest and support of state and territorial governments, they invited each governor to appoint two citizens to serve as honorary vice-presidents of the exposition and two women to become honorary members of the Board of Women Managers. As a follow-up they sent copies of a twenty-four-page booklet to thousands of legislators and other state officials. Similar invitations and publications in appropriate languages went to governments of the Latin American republics. To appeal to the general public the Publicity Bureau prepared a variety of brochures—in quantities up to 100,000—with maps, photos of buildings, and descriptions of the grounds. These were sent to people on mailing lists purchased from more than 20,000 manufacturing concerns.[57]

At the same time, Buchanan and his staff were utilizing other propaganda approaches. To encourage and assist exhibitors they printed 10,000 forms for space applications. For the Post Office Department they prepared designs for a series of Pan-American commemorative stamps. They authorized the *New York Times* to publish a special exposition edition and maintained a steady flow of press releases to newspapers around the nation. Hoping to improve the literary output of his Publicity Bureau, Buchanan sought to recruit writers with some background knowledge of Latin America.[58] By midsummer 1900 exposition officials were speaking here and there, but as with their other publicity programs, they would hold their heaviest salvos until the late winter and spring of 1901.

The Pan-American's program was to comprise a diversity of exhibitions, demonstrations, concerts, sports, and amusements. In the early months Buchanan devoted only intermittent attention to programming details, yet from time to time his recommendations to the Executive Committee revealed the directions his interests would follow. He would emphasize music: a pipe organ must grace the Temple of Music and bands like Sousa's must entertain. He would feature livestock showings: premium lists must be prepared and promptly circulated among breeders. Underscoring his belief in the educational benefits of expositions, the director general would have such live exhibits as a model dairy, a graphic arts workshop, and a functioning Iroquoian village.[59] Continuously he urged his staff to accelerate recruitment of displays for the many exhibition halls, especially those of state, national, and foreign governments.

The midway, on the other hand, gave the management no such problem of recruitment. More than a year in advance impresarios began to reserve space for their productions: exotic imports like the "African Village," "Arabian Nights," "Beautiful Orient," and "Temple of Isis" and familiar domestic attractions like the "Scenic Railway," "Old Plantation," and "Mirror Maze." "Moving Pictures" and "A Trip to the Moon" were harbingers of twentieth-century technical advances.[60]

The acceleration of all these activities during the early

months of 1900 called for periodic additions to both administrative and labor personnel. As construction material began to arrive in quantity (more than 400 carloads monthly by July) and buildings began to take shape, Buchanan urged attention to security in all its aspects. For police protection he recommended the formation of a uniformed and well-drilled guard unit; eventually it became a force of 164 officers, patrolmen, and detectives. In return for the loan of Buffalo firemen and their equipment he secured exposition funds to build new engine houses that would eventually become city property. He also insisted upon the creation of a Medical Bureau, a service to be of such indispensible assistance during President McKinley's visit to the exposition.[61]

Of all the auxiliary agencies constituted under Buchanan's direction, none occupied a more focal position than the Labor Bureau. Long dissatisfied with working conditions in their area, Buffalo's labor organizations sought to utilize the exposition to bring about general wage increases and wider unionization. This situation confronted Buchanan and his Labor Bureau with a genuine dilemma. On the one hand, the exposition could be completed on time only with the cooperation of Buffalo labor elements, both union and nonunion, or through the importation of workers from other cities. Recourse to importation would inevitably alienate potential patrons in western New York, and, at the exposition's end, leave Buffalo with a surplus of skilled labor. On the other hand, acceding to labor's demands, especially the closed shop, would jeopardize the position of those Exposition Company directors and stockholders who did not recognize union labor in their private business operations.[62]

The Labor Bureau worked out a compromise arrangement. The bureau would provide free registration for all Buffalo laborers and require contractors to give preference to registrants who could claim one year's residence in Buffalo. The exposition would recognize the eight-hour day and pay prevailing wage rates, with time and a half for overtime and double time for Sundays. The labor organizations would recognize the exposition's open-shop policy and do all in their power to fulfill the agreement and prevent strikes. Long aware that exposition building required tight deadlines and short construction schedules, Buchanan in later months was satisfied that the agreement was restricting labor problems to a minimum.[63]

Like the Labor Bureau and other service agencies, the Board of Women Managers occupied an essential place in the director general's planning. Mindful of what a similar board had done at the Columbian Exposition and still recalling the support given the Corn Palaces by Mrs. Buchanan and her coworkers, he determined to utilize the assistance of Buffalo women.[64] At the outset, while preparing their own publicity brochures, the Board of Women Managers sought the active aid of their honorary members in other states and arranged speaking engagements before women's clubs, college alumnae, and school groups. As exposition time approached, they travelled widely to recruit conventions of women's groups for Buffalo; they secured such organizations as the National League of Women Voters, the National Household Economics Association, the International Council of Nurses, and many state bodies. During the months of the exposition, they would arrange teas, luncheons, or receptions for women journalists and visiting dignitaries, notably Mrs. McKinley and Mrs. Theodore Roosevelt.[65]

By early summer administrative additions had pushed the exposition payroll list to more than seven hundred, while construction projects engaged nearly fifteen hundred more. At the same time Buchanan was directing the entire operation with a minimum headquarters staff of seven: two stenographers, one copyist, three clerks, and one special assistant. Because much of his correspondence required it, he had insisted on one stenographer who could read, write, and speak Spanish and make use of a Spanish-language typewriter. For these special qualifications she received a salary of $50.00 per month.[66]

The end of July 1900 marked the midpoint of Buchanan's eighteen-month drive to prepare the exposition for its May Day opening. During his first nine months he had laid the administrative and procedural foundations he believed essential to fulfill his commitment. He had established harmonious working relationships with the exposition officers and committee chairmen, with many of whom he maintained daily contacts.[67]

He had guided the negotiation of scores of contracts with builders, exhibitors, concessionaires, artists, and performers. Relentlessly he had stressed the indispensability of imaginative and continuing publicity.[68] Meticulously he had respected the budgetary limitations of the company as well as its ideals and goals.[69] Though the Executive Committee had already designated seven gateway entrances to the grounds, another nine months remained until the gates would open.[70] Outwardly, at least, the director general and the exposition seemed to be meeting their timetables.

Yet however widespread the surface optimism, Buchanan could foresee that his second nine months would be far more fraught with crises and emergency actions than the first. His general stocktaking at this juncture revealed his special concerns: civic apathy, the city's failure to anticipate housing needs, inadequacies of advertising, lags in construction, and financial stringencies. As the responsible administrator, he regularly felt called upon to remind the Executive Committee of critical situations and the need for decisive measures and increased powers.

Seasoned to the civic drive of Sioux City in the eighties and of Chicago in the early nineties, the director general could not understand Buffalo's apathy about its exposition. "I am very much concerned," he told the Executive Committee in June, "at the absolute absence in this City—outside the Exposition grounds—of any evidence tending to demonstrate to a visitor here that an Exposition—even of the most ordinary dimension—was to open here within the next-eleven months."[71] In this view he gave official endorsement to the chiding exhortations of *The Pan-American Herald*: "It's high time to wake up! It's high time to get some Chicago into Buffalo. . . . The planned Exposition of next year will be one of the most comprehensive, far-reaching and beautiful that the world has ever seen, [but] Buffalo is in danger of remaining too long beneath the counterpane."[72] Concerned especially about the city's ability to house, entertain, and transport its visitors, Buchanan recommended measures to stimulate active civic interest and confidence in the exposition's success. His remedies involved reorganization of the Publicity Bureau.[73]

Far exceeding all his other concerns, however, was the status of building construction and grounds preparation. He knew that progress on the principal exhibition halls, the stadium, and the midway was far too slow. Work on the Electric Tower—to be the theme symbol for the exposition—was just getting started and only the ground preparation had been completed for the New York State and United States government buildings. Contracts had not yet been let for the important Temple of Music, nor for the stock barns and numerous lesser structures. Plans and specifications had still not been completed for the building of canal bridges, construction of decorative features, and paving of roads and walks.[74] Moreover, while the Labor Bureau had registered nearly eleven thousand skilled and unskilled workmen, it had found a critical shortage of lathers, steamfitters, and stucco workers.[75]

Crises, of course, were not new to Buchanan and he responded with the decisiveness he had learned at Sioux City and rehearsed at Chicago. First he secured authority to offer a financial premium for each day gained by contractors in completing their projects. Then, to free the director of works for additional supervision at the grounds Buchanan discontinued his required weekly written reports. Later he asked and received the widest latitude in making on-the-spot decisions and reporting them afterwards. Ultimately, when drastic action seemed indicated, he ordered night shifts and offered special bonuses to exceptional workmen.[76]

Perpetually shadowing the construction program, moreover, and often hampering the director general's freedom of action, was the exposition company's precarious financial structure. Despite repeated petitions, the authorities were unable to secure monetary assistance from city, state, or national governments.[77] Left to their own resources, the Board of Directors in May had fixed a ceiling of $4,250,000 as the total cost of the exposition.[78] Considerably less than half this amount came from stock subscriptions, the remainder from the sale of first and second mortgage bonds. Income, when it began, would flow directly to a committee of bankers.[79] Consistent with these arrangements Buchanan volunteered on the first of August to give the Executive Committee weekly budgetary accountings.

In each of these he incorporated a summary of all monies entailed to date along with estimates of the amounts still required to open, operate, and close the exposition. Though his first statement revealed that the allotted funds were almost exhausted, the company officials remained undaunted. They continued to float loans to expand their building program and beautification plans. By November Buchanan's estimates of total costs had risen to well over five million dollars and by January to almost seven million.[80] As these figures mounted, prospects for avoiding a deficit depended increasingly on the management's ability to develop and advertise attractions that would bolster attendance. With this in mind, Buchanan accelerated plans for both publicity and programming.

Sound as were the early publicity steps, they were only a prelude to the massive operations carried out through the fall and winter of 1900-1901. Through emphasis on originality, variety, and scope it would make the Pan-American the best advertised exposition in history.

Believing in the value of the personal touch, the management authorized wide use of special representatives. To supplement the preliminary work he and William Curtis had accomplished in South America, Buchanan sent agents to Mexico, Central America, the Caribbean islands, and Canada. The assistance of Secretary Hay and other officials of the State Department smoothed the entree of these agents to appropriate government officials.[81] Special committees visited state capitals to solicit aid of legislators in securing government exhibits. Other representatives journeyed to every village and town of a thousand or more within 175 miles of Buffalo, to every city of 15,000 in the quadrilateral embraced by Portland, Richmond, Milwaukee, and St. Louis, and to every winter resort along the South Atlantic coast. In each of these localities they placed framed notices and brochures in hotel lobbies and provided cuts to newspapers.[82]

Meanwhile, making generous use of the Beck design, the expanded Publicity Bureau was preparing some ninety-five different forms of printed material—brochures, booklets, and programs. Packets of these they sent to over four hundred colleges, to all libraries and YMCA's within five hundred miles, and to all clubs in cities over 75,000. With the assistance of railways and express companies they distributed another twelve million pieces of literature. For display in 35,000 post offices across the country they prepared posters embellished with reproductions of an original painting, "The Spirit of Niagara." They persuaded Buffalo business houses to utilize Pan-American stamps on their mail. To supplement the printed literature, the Bureau created diverse forms of audio and visual advertisements: programs of music for organists and musical societies; lantern slides of the exposition for lecturers; banners strung across the streets of twenty-six large cities; and a searchlight to ply the skies at Atlantic City.[83]

Perpetually inhibited by his tight budget, Buchanan relished the volume of free advertising secured by his Press Department in newspapers with total circulation of over 30,000,000. By January 1901 clerks had already mounted a hundred thousand columns of clippings, then felt compelled to discontinue their scrapbooks.[84] At a cost of less than $12,000 to the exposition company, the nation's newspaper readers had been given the message the director general most wanted to convey—that "the Exposition was not a circus for the amusement of children but an international event marking a momentous period in Western Continental history."[85]

While the Publicity Bureau maintained its steady pace of press releases and advertising innovations, Buchanan devoted whatever time he could spare for personal appearances and preparation of magazine articles. He accepted numerous speaking engagements, including important ones in Chautauqua, Rochester, and Brooklyn, and fulfilled public relations assignments in various Canadian cities.[86] In a long article in *Collier's Weekly* he effectively tied the Pan-American Exposition to the current status of inter-American relations.[87]

But, no matter how brilliant or pervasive, the Pan-American's public relations campaign needed more than elegant buildings and beautiful landscaping to advertise. As Buchanan and his businessmen colleagues well knew, they needed products to sell. More and more intensively, therefore, as opening day approached, they sought to assemble the diversified attractions they hoped would draw the necessary millions through the turnstiles: exhibitions of agricultural and industrial progress—demonstrations of the latest advances in electricity and transportation—exhibits as varied as forestry, horticulture, fisheries, mineralogy, and ethnology—displays of the graphic arts and productions of the performing arts—athletic contests and other performances of recreational and entertainment merit. Above all, to fulfill the exposition theme and demonstrate the Hemisphere's advance into the twentieth century, they continued to solicit distinctive contributions from twenty nations, numerous colonies, and all the states and territories.[88] By the time all was in place, they would have received, unloaded, and installed 1045 railroad carloads of exhibit materials with a weight of over 12,000 tons.[89]

By January 1901, despite progress in all areas, it was evident to Buchanan and his chiefs of construction that the exposition's buildings and grounds could not be completely ready for the May first opening. A protracted spell of foul weather—gale winds in early autumn, heavy rains in November, snow in December and January—had damaged half-completed structures and turned unpaved roadways into quagmires. Several months of western New York winter lay ahead. Moreover, the Labor Bureau had not been able to forestall strikes among key groups of skilled workmen.[90] Nevertheless when the Board of Directors refused to shift the opening date, the director general and his staff had no choice but to plunge ahead regardless of cost. From January to May they unloaded and transported to the grounds a daily average of eighteen freight carloads of building materials. Week by week, to cope with this flow, they enlarged the labor force.[91]

Meanwhile, as builders battled the snow and mud, Buchanan and the exposition officers suffered additional setbacks. Gradually they came to realize that exhibits from the other American nations would be far more limited than they had hoped. The relative scarcity of manufacturing establishments in both Canada and Latin America would reduce the international character of the industrial displays. Federal sanitary regulations forbade the entry of foreign livestock, even for exhibition purposes.[92] As exhibits began to arrive, Buchanan learned that structures designed for architectural beauty were not necessarily well suited to classification of displays.[93] Failure to complete the elegant new Albright Art Gallery, under construction on adjacent grounds as the gift of a Buffalo philanthropist, John J. Albright, necessitated the planning and construction of a building for the fine arts.[94]

As May Day approached, Buchanan moved between Executive Committee and department chiefs to fit in place a myriad of administrative details. At what hour should exhibition buildings open? When should midway attractions close? Should the exposition shut down on Sundays? How many tickets should be printed? Who should receive free passes? When and how should garbage be collected?[95] And, though peripheral to the exposition itself, there was the vexing housing problem—the need to counteract a rumor that Buffalo could not accommodate its guests. To canvass the situation, the management hastily created a Bureau of Information. When it found that the city and suburbs could house 260,000 guests per day, it promptly deluged the country with printed lists of available accommodations.[96] However, quartering the thirty or forty thousand blacks reportedly coming from the South was another story. Buchanan himself took the matter in hand. Suspecting that Buffalo's three hundred black families alone could not entertain these guests—and that the city's hotels might not do so—he invited a prominent member of the black community to assist the Bureau of Information in solving the problem.[97]

Throughout his eighteen months of preparation for opening day, Director General Buchanan had never lost sight of the hazards in the venture he was directing. Like his sponsors, he knew that any one of "the many elements of chance present in such great enterprises" could bring not only financial hardship to company stockholders but also disheartenment to the city and to the thousands of public-spirited citizens who had supported the project.[98] Yet, bolstered by the determination of his Executive Committee and Board of Directors, he continued to anticipate fulfillment of the Pan-American's primary goals: to improve Buffalo's image as a rising commercial-industrial center while pointing the way to better inter-American relations.

Chapter 9
HOMAGE TO A HEMISPHERE
Buffalo, 1900-1902

In Chicago and Buenos Aires Buchanan had enjoyed superior vantage points from which to observe the rapidly changing international posture of his country. From his post at the Columbian Exposition he had sensed the gathering thrust of American industrialists to find new world markets. During his diplomatic mission to Argentina he had sought to implement both Democratic and Republican party programs for the improvement of reciprocal trade with Latin America. When the United States was at war with Spain, he had experienced unexpectedly bitter manifestations of anti-Americanism from Spaniards and Cubans. Though personally deploring the trend, he had witnessed his country's entry into the international race for overseas possessions and the resultant extension of its administrative responsibilities to alien peoples in the Caribbean and far Pacific. In successfully restoring Argentina to good financial standing in the Commercial Bureau of American Republics, he had reinforced Washington's resolve to perpetuate that nascent inter-American organization. Overall, his five years of service under two presidents and five secretaries of state had made him acutely aware that the nation was moving inexorably toward world power status; this was especially clear from its new ambitions in the Western Hemisphere.

Throughout his administration of the Pan-American Exposition, therefore, Director General Buchanan was ever aware of the goals set by its businessmen promoters. Even before laying out his plan of operations in November 1899, he had sought clear understanding of their objectives. At the end of his first year of preparations he had utilized the columns of a nationally circulated periodical to set forth his interpretation of these purposes.[1] In his voluminous final report he reviewed the aims and ideals of the exposition's directors.[2] In each of these statements he incorporated his explanations of Pan Americanism and the Western Hemisphere idea.[3]

Since the Buffalo authorities had sought him and him alone to direct their exposition, Buchanan could only assume that they intended the Pan American theme to dominate the economic and educational, as well as the artistic, aspects of their project. Without depreciating Buffalo's desire to advertise itself as an advantageous field for new industrial enterprises, he felt that urban ambitions could be satisfactorily interlaced with appropriate homage to the Hemisphere. The exposition was not, he wrote, "either entirely or largely born of a selfish desire on the part of the people of the State of New York, and of Buffalo primarily, to draw attention to anything they possess, nor to acquire, wholly, local prestige and benefit from the undertaking."[4] Rather, he added, it was conceived by its founders as a fitting way to open the new century—to provide the people of the Hemisphere an opportunity to "show each other the advantages possessed by each, stimulating thus a common interest, a solidarity of purpose in all that tends to unify, elevate, develop and Americanize the Americas."[5]

Whether through speeches, press conferences, or published articles, the director general missed no opportunity to elaborate his convictions about the Hemisphere's economic and intercultural potentialities. By increasing governmental stability, he argued, improving living conditions, fostering better use of natural resources, and building up permanent national wealth, the Latin American nations had achieved greater progress in the 1890s than in the preceding half century. But now, to augment the production of their mines, fields, ranches, and tropical lands, they needed investment capital from the United States and Canada.[6]

Calling upon his experience in Argentina, Buchanan suggested other remedies for the improvement of commercial and cultural interchange. He recommended expansion of the United States shipping industry and establishment of branch banks in Latin America. Without pulling punches he criticized the United States Senate for its failure to ratify the McKinley reciprocity treaties. All the Hemisphere nations, he ventured, would profit from the building of a canal across the Isthmus of Panama and the construction of a continental railway. Moreover, United States citizens should cultivate greater use of the Spanish language.[7]

In appraising both the spurs and barriers to improved Hemisphere intercourse, Buchanan effectively tied the aims of the exposition management to the larger Pan American policy Washington was seeking to develop. With the changed relations brought about by the Spanish-American War, he suggested, the moment had come to wipe out for all time "the suspicion concerning the attitude of the United States toward them that has lain not wholly or always dormant in the Latin American republics."[8] In short, he conceived the Pan-American Exposition as a vast international "Information Clearing House."[9] The fulfillment of these major goals demanded the broadest possible participation of the other American republics, as well as of Canada and the Caribbean dependencies of European colonial powers. Even Cuba, Puerto Rico, and new American acquisitions in the Pacific—the Hawaiian Islands, the Philippines, and Samoa—were not overlooked.

But when the Buffalo officials projected the first international exposition restricted to the Hemisphere, they had failed to anticipate many of the hurdles they would confront in recruiting the active participation of governments and peoples. Even Buchanan was sometimes daunted by the obstacles that arose. Some nations pleaded lack of funds; others, lack of appropriate products for exhibit or experience in preparing their displays. Several countries were inhibited by internal political crises.[10]

From time to time unfamiliarity with diplomatic protocol or with national sensitivities embarrassed the exposition authorities. Their preliminary Spanish language invitations, prepared in August 1899, received serious criticism for lapses in form and phraseology.[11] Canadian officials took offense when their invitation arrived long after those to the Latin American republics. To smooth ruffled feathers and assure fullest Canadian participation, Buchanan made three trips to Ottawa and other Canadian cities.[12]

After sending an unusually warm personal invitation to his friend Argentine President Julio Roca, Buchanan learned that Washington's red tape would preclude the chief executive's reception as official guest of the nation.[13] Only act of Congress, supported by adequate financial appropriation, would enable the president to invite a head of state to visit the United States. Instead, after conferences with Secretary Hay and the Argentine minister in Washington, Buchanan recommended an alternative plan to the Executive Committee. The mayor and Common Council of Buffalo would be asked to send an invitation to General, not President, Roca. It would be transmitted to the Argentine executive through the United States minister in Buenos Aires, but only after prior endorsement by the governor and by the mayor and City Council of New York City, as the chief port of entry for South American products. This was the cumbersome alternative approved by Secretary Hay and the procedure to be followed in invitations to Roca, President Porfirio Díaz of Mexico, and other heads of state.[14]

Several fortunate circumstances minimized other false steps. Since the United States Congress had officially endorsed the exposition through appropriate enabling legislation, the Department of State made itself available to assist the Buffalo sponsors in all matters of protocol. Its chief clerk, Colonel William H. Michael, became the man in the middle. After Buchanan assumed the director generalship, he was able to make full use of this channel and his other Washington connections. At times he was in almost daily mail contact with Michael; not infrequently he journeyed to the capital to confer with him or with Secretary Hay. Once these channels were clarified, exposition communications to foreign governments were routinely cleared with the State Department, some of them despatched to United States diplomats with the secretary's directives.[15]

By the end of 1900 the director general and his colleagues had persuaded Canada and every Latin American republic to participate in the exposition. Eight nations had arranged to finance their own exhibit buildings.[16] Most of the others reserved space in one or more of the general exhibition halls. Several of the smaller countries limited their participation to exhibits by individual citizens or to appointment of resident commissioners.[17] To supplement its displays Mexico agreed to send a sixty-piece artillery band, along with a detachment of mounted rural troops.[18]

In none of these negotitations did Buchanan move more determinedly than in his efforts to secure exhibits from Cuba and the new dependencies acquired in 1898-1899. During his first months in Buffalo he accompanied exposition officials to Washington to discuss the possibilities with President McKinley and Secretary of War Elihu Root.[19] To secure the participation of Cuba and Puerto Rico he invited Governor General Leonard Wood and Governor Charles H. Allen to visit Buffalo for an inspection of the exposition grounds; when they declined, he substituted a conference with General Wood in New York City.[20] Only his preoccupations in Buffalo, Buchanan told the Executive Committee, prevented his undertaking a recruitment trip to both the islands.[21] To obtain exhibits from the Hawaiian Islands, the Philippines, and Samoa, the director general corresponded with Governor Sanford B. Dole of Hawaii and conferred in Washington with his Iowa friend, Senator Allison.[22]

While working in these ways to assure representation of all the Hemisphere's political entities, the exposition authorities had realized from the outset the importance of depicting the Pan American theme in all phases of their ambitious project. Even before the appointment of Buchanan, for example, they had resolved that the exposition's architectural setting should be one singularly complimentary to the Latin American republics, as well as aesthetically appealing to all people. Accordingly, the Board of Architects had wasted little time in recommending Spanish Renaissance as the general style for buildings and decorations. The director general staunchly supported this decision. "There will be placed before the visitors," he wrote for a national audience, "the most perfect, the most beautiful, and the most enchanting picture of Spanish architectural memories that has ever been presented in any country or place."[23]

From both historic and symbolic points of view art critics who visited the exposition generally applauded both the decision to adopt the Spanish style and the faithfulness with which architects and artists represented it. "No style of architecture is better adapted to the purposes of an Exposition," wrote one enthusiast, "than this, which emphasizes lightness and gaiety rather than massiveness or forbidding grandeur." For him the Spanish theme appropriately portrayed "that tide of Saracenic richness which swept from the Orient, bedizened Spain and trickled across to Latin America."[24]

On the other hand, as both the Buchanans had learned from prior experience, artistic displays arouse disfavor as well. Some exposition visitors would feel that too much of the French, Italian, or even German, Renaissance had crept in to dilute the purity of the Spanish. Others, while admitting the air of reality and permanence created by the buildings, would think them too flimsy and ephemeral. And there were devout Buffalonians who could see little relevance in the Spanish theme for an American city aspiring to industrial greatness.[25]

The architects' original ground plan suggested an urban, or Roman forum, pattern rather than the sylvan setting of the Columbian Exposition.[26] Bordered by gardens and sculptural ornamentation, the large Court of the Fountains served as the nucleus for the principal exhibition halls. Just to the south stretched the vast Esplanade, capable of accommodating 250,000 people for concerts and outdoor assemblies. Fronting this great plaza were the several United States government buildings and the soon-to-be-famous Temple of Music.

Designed as the heart of the exposition grounds, this inner core of decorative buildings and landscaped courts was appropriately encircled by a system of small lakes, basins, and connecting canals. At its southern extremity the Triumphal Bridge would bear the welcoming processions for President McKinley, Vice-President Roosevelt, the Latin American delegates, and other dignitaries. At the northern end the 410-foot Electric Tower, its 40,000 bulbs proclaiming Buffalo's recent acquisition of Niagara power, presided over the entire domain.

By moving north, east, and west from this central forum across the peripheral canals, patrons could visit the 12,000-seat stadium, the livestock exhibits, and the multiple attractions of the expansive midway. To the south they could inspect the exhibit buildings of individual states, as well as those of Canada and the Latin American republics.

Among all these architectural features none were as uniquely symbolic of the Pan American theme as the Propylaea. Erected at the extreme northern end of the exposition's central axis, they served as the main gateway for patrons arriving by railway or travelling to and from Niagara Falls by electric line. Along this lengthy succession of archways panelled inscriptions testified to the meaning of Pan Americanism,[27] notably

Panel I:
HERE BY THE WATERS OF THE NORTH, ARE BROUGHT TOGETHER THE PEOPLES OF THE TWO AMERICAS, IN EXPOSITION OF THEIR RESOURCES, INDUSTRIES, PRODUCTS, INVENTIONS, ARTS AND IDEAS.

Panel II:
THAT THE CENTURY NOW BEGUN MAY UNITE IN THE BONDS OF PEACE, KNOWLEDGE, GOOD-WILL, FRIENDSHIP, AND NOBLE EMULATION ALL THE DWELLERS OF THE CONTINENTS AND ISLANDS OF THE NEW WORLD.

Buchanan's insistence upon widespread use of color and generous display of decorative sculpture had given an aura of unity and symmetry to the exposition's grand design. In contrast with the pallidness of Chicago's White City or the visual heterogeneity of Philadelphia's Centennial, Buffalo's colorists added a schematic "afterglow" to the Spanish-style architecture.[28] Under the direction of sculptor Karl Bitter, forty-one artists and a hundred artisans had created sixty-five carloads of sculptured pieces for the Pan-American's buildings and grounds.[29]

Yet, bright as were these plans and prospects for the exposition's physical setting, they did little to allay the management's concern about readying all details for the scheduled inauguration date. Heavy snows in April, with cold winds whipping across Lake Erie, prevented virtually all outside work at the exposition grounds. Finishing touches on construction could not be completed. Scores of statuary pieces could not be moved into place. Flower beds could not be planted. Carloads of display materials remained to be unloaded and moved to appropriate exhibition halls; the halls themselves presented a face of disorder. Incompleteness reigned in every sphere. A last-minute round of actions, including additions to the labor force, placed new strains on the company's already overtaxed budget.[30]

In spite of all these adversities, however, the Board of Directors refused to hedge on its January commitment to open the exposition on May Day. Rather, they decided to issue a public announcement that, though incomplete, it would open as scheduled, but with formal inauguration ceremonies postponed to 20 May, to be known as Dedication Day.[31]

Under these circumstances, therefore, making no effort to draw crowds, Buchanan and his coworkers determined to keep the May Day activities simple and informal. The army of laborers striving to complete buildings, grounds, and walkways seemed almost to outnumber the 20,000 curiosity-seekers who passed through the turnstiles. They could hear bands blaring, watch air bombs bursting, and see swarms of pigeons released. They could visit some of the exhibit buildings, though with displays still moving into place. They could patronize the midway, though with many concessions still not open for business.[32] But there were no parades, no invocations, no dedicatory speeches, no distinguished visitors from Washington or other Hemisphere capitals, little to suggest that the Pan-American was to be an international exposition and not just another state or county fair.

All these traditional exposition rites the management postponed until Dedication Day. By then the public was ready to turn out. Beginning at 5:00 A. M. excursion trains began disgorging crowds that would swell the day's attendance to more than 100,000. By late morning, like Buffalonians along the line of march, they could witness the lengthy inaugural parade that began at City Hall. Headed by bands and military units and trailed by floats and midway performers, 104 numbered carriages bore distinguished guests and exposition officials to the long-beleaguered grounds. In each of the first three vehicles one of the featured speakers rode with his Buffalo escort: Vice-President Theodore Roosevelt with Exposition President Milburn, Massachusetts Senator Henry Cabot Lodge with Secretary George N. Williams, and New York's Lieutenant Governor Timothy L. Woodruff with Mayor Diehl. In the following carriages, their protocol order designated by Buchanan and his aides, came high-ranking military officers, foreign and state commissioners, exposition chiefs and judges, and journalists.[33]

On the platform at the ensuing Temple of Music ceremonies, the director general listened to the reading of greetings he had received from President McKinley and other Hemisphere chief executives. "I earnestly hope," the president had wired from California, "that this great exhibition may prove a blessing to every country of this hemisphere."[34] Buchanan also heard the clarion pronouncements of Vice-President Roosevelt and other spokesmen that the exposition represented a signal Buffalo tribute to Hemisphere comity and that the Monroe Doctrine was still a cornerstone of early twentieth-century American foreign policy.

"I believe with all my heart in the Monroe Doctrine," the Vice-President proclaimed in one of his climactic passages. "It should be regarded simply as a great Pan American policy vital to the interests of all of us." Senator Lodge was equally emphatic, as he exhorted the Latin Americans: "If you will put your faith in it and be true to it, we will defend it." But, if at this moment Buchanan happened to recall a familiar Argentine doctrine, he must have quailed a bit when he heard the senator challenge, "The motto of every American state should be not as a mere empty cry but as the utterance of a profound principle, 'America for the Americans.'"[35] The doctrine for which the former minister had gained profound respect during his Argentine years was that uttered by Roque Saenz Peña at the first Conference of the American States in Washington a decade before: "Let America be for humanity."[36] Beyond this, however, Buchanan must have been pleased to hear repeated calls for policies he had emphasized from Buenos Aires: the fostering of freer trade, the building of an isthmian canal, and the construction of an inter-American railway. Anticipating the night illuminations and gala fireworks displays to follow, one other feature of the inaugural ceremonies must also have been personally satisfying to the director general. As the audience filed from the Temple of Music, Buchanan heard dedicated to him the organist's own composition, "The Electric March."[37]

With these belated inaugural events auspiciously concluded, Buchanan and all of Buffalo could feel that their exposition was at last happily launched. Coupled with the magnetism of Vice-President Roosevelt and the colorful ceremonies of Dedication Day, the end of the hard winter's siege should have the attendance-priming effects on which the directors had counted. Yet hostile weather continued to betray them. Instead of the bright days they expected, May and June proved to be the wettest early summer months in seven years and June the coldest June in thirty years of Weather Bureau records.[38]

The weather's effects upon anticipated exposition patronage were even more devastating than the director general had foreseen. Early visitors were unimpressed by uncompleted construction, unfinished landscaping, and exhibit buildings in disarray. Dissatisfied patrons became biased advertisers and newspapers gave wide currency to their unfavorable reports.[39] As a result, daily paid attendance during the first two months averaged less than 11,000 and gate receipts for paid admissions barely $5,600. Against a capital outlay of nearly $7,000,000, the first third of the exposition's season netted from its principal source of revenue a return of only $354,000.[40] The Pan-American Company was moving closer to financial insolvency. "The month of May," Buchanan would write in his final report, was "one of lasting unpleasant memory for everyone connected with the management of the Exposition."[41]

In this situation the director general's primary responsibility after 20 May was to step up promotional activities in every direction that might stimulate attendance. He turned first to transportation. Fully aware that Buffalo's population alone could provide but a small portion of essential patronage, he regarded the cooperation of American railroads as indispensable to the exposition's financial success. In the hope that railway conductors and ticket agents would become "talking advertisements," he invited groups of them, sometimes with their wives and families, to visit the exposition. In the certainty that increased travel to Buffalo would benefit the railroads as well as the exposition, he went to New York City to present his case to the general passenger agents of all lines serving western New York. He invited their collaboration in offering for 15 June a round-trip excursion fare of $6.00 per person, with exposition admission included. The large crowds attracted by this bargain rate, he urged, would become "living witnesses" to the exposition's merit and provide impetus to the travel of others.[42]

Buchanan also made the fullest possible use of other publicity devices. Consistent with new powers granted by the Board of Directors, he adopted a more liberal policy on the issuance of passes. Consuls general of the Latin American countries and general passenger agents of all American railroads were among the recipients. He arranged for the location of new information booths at Chautauqua and other summer resort cities.[43] When distinguished visitors praised the exposition, his Publicity Bureau gave wide press circulation to their comments. They found especially newsworthy such reactions as those of Secretary Hay, who spoke of "the courts and palaces of this incomparable exhibition; this grand and beautiful spectacle never to be forgotten; a delight to the eye, a comfort to every patriot heart that during the summer shall make the joyous pilgrimage to this enchanted scene."[44] To the press release containing Hay's commentary, the Board of Directors attached the announcement that, as of 5 July, the exposition was complete.[45]

In relying on two other promotional techniques traditionally used for stimulating exposition attendance—the celebration of special "days" and the hosting of conventions—Buchanan now reinforced and expanded the vast amount of preparatory work which he and his staff had undertaken prior to Dedication Day. For the six months of the exposition they designated 111 such days to honor specific organizations or ideas. There were days for fraternal societies—Elks and Eagles, Redmen and Knights of Columbus, and others. There were days for colleges and days for nationalities. There was a Liederkrantz Day, a Saengerfest Day, and a Spielers Day. They honored Old Folks, the GAR, and the National Grange. Every holiday, even Bunker Hill Day, received its due.[46]

Most successful, however, in attracting large numbers of spectators, were the days designated for various governmental entities: cities from Detroit to Brooklyn and Toronto to Philadelphia; most of the states from New England to the Mississippi and a few in the South and Far West; and, of course, Canada and several Latin American republics.[47] It was Ecuador Day, featuring the dedication and gift of its building, that brought out the summer's largest assembly of Hemisphere diplomats. With characteristic Latin ardor, the special commissioners of Mexico and Nicaragua joined the Ecuadorian minister to Washington, Luis F. Carbo, in lauding the exposition as a symbol of Pan American interdependence. It is destined, said Carbo, "to make closer the ties of union and confraternity between the nations of the continent." When Buchanan was called upon to translate for several of the orators, he confessed his eagerness to convey their thoughts but his inability to transmit their eloquence.[48]

Knowing the importance of conventions for American commercial and professional life, the Pan-American's management invited or attracted 121 associations and societies to schedule their annual meetings for Buffalo during the period of the exposition. They entertained such national groups as the Spanish-American War Veterans and the National Education Association and such New York State societies as the Bankers' Association and the Medical Association. They welcomed the Roentgen Ray Society, the American Philatelic Association, and the International Cremation Congress. They saluted assemblies representative of brewers and blacksmiths, canoeists and cotton manufacturers, plumbers and yachting enthusiasts.[49]

On most of the special days and at the opening sessions of many of the conventions, Buchanan's schedule called for his participation. Whenever he was available, at any rate, and protocol did not call for the presence of President Milburn, it was the director general who formally greeted each of these groups and assemblies. Through scores of such appearances during the long trying summer, thousands of visitors came to enjoy his warmth, his resourceful touches of humor, and his sense of the appropriate.

Happily for Buchanan and fortunately for the company's

solvency, the combination of augmented promotion and summer's more accommodating weather contributed to sharply rising patronage. In July the average daily paid attendance more than doubled the May-June figure. In August it rose to nearly 41,000.[50] But this upsurge in the exposition's appeal did not result from resourceful promotion alone, nor even from the salutary accompaniment of fair weather. Without solid educational, aesthetic, and recreational offerings, Buchanan had learned as a Sioux City impresario, no publicly authorized exhibition could generate the volume of word-of-mouth advertising essential to its success. From the beginning, therefore, and throughout the exposition's season, he called upon his staff and committees to solicit appropriate exhibits and to recruit representative artists and performers. In all this, while emphasizing the Pan American motif, he knew it was a North American clientele they must please.

By design the exposition's chief educational thrust centered in the large exhibition halls erected at the core of the grounds and in the smaller structures built by state, national, and foreign governments. The five principal buildings revealed the essential phases of Western Hemisphere progress the sponsors sought to illuminate: Electricity; Agriculture; Machinery and Transportation; Manufactures and Liberal Arts; and Horticulture, Graphic Arts and Mines. Here, as in the various government buildings, hundreds of exhibitors used permanent displays and special demonstrations to illustrate the Hemisphere's twentieth-century prospects.

As Buchanan and his sponsors had already foreseen, however, the participation of foreign exhibitors fell far below their original expectations. Though eight nations had erected their own exhibit buildings, Argentina, Brazil, and several key countries were not among them. And in the main exposition halls they occupied less than 15 percent of available space. On the other hand, a full complement of resident commissioners was on hand to oversee and explain the imported displays and accept the more than three thousand special awards they won.[51] Overall, the entries of the Canadians and Latin Americans were representative if not all-inclusive.

For interior displays of the graphic arts the management

borrowed *objets d'art* from galleries and museums in New York and other cities. For the performing arts Buchanan's Music Committee insisted on a distinctive building that would be symbolic of the exposition's scope and worthy of the program they planned. In securing construction of the ornate Temple of Music they assured an appropriate assembly hall for a long succession of the summer's events. Twenty-five instrumental organizations, including Sousa's Band, the Mexican Artillery Band, and Victor Herbert's orchestra, would grace its stage. Seventy-one artists would test its custom-built organ. Dozens of nationally known speakers and lecturers would use its rostrum. Six hundred different audiences would pass through its doors.[52] And on President's Day in September it would become the focus of McKinley's visit.

Purposely isolated from the beauty and dignity of the exposition's central courts and plazas, the recreational attractions were concentrated in outlying areas—the midway, the stadium, and Camp Millard Fillmore. Though the Executive Committee searched for an innovative title to designate the amusements sector, it could not escape the traditional characterization, "midway." Yet, in Buchanan's view, the large majority of the three hundred concessions conducted their attractions in "honorable, straight-forward and satisfactory manner." No entertainment enterprise received approval until its proposal had passed the inspection of the Concessions Committee, the Executive Committee, and the director general.[53]

Attendance figures told something about American tastes in midway entertainment at the turn of the century. More than a million "tourists" rode the "Scenic Railway" and nearly as many visited "Beautiful Orient." Comparable numbers flocked to the "Johnstown Flood," "Indian Village," "Bostock Animal Show," and "Venice in America."[54] Mexican bullfights were less popular. To authenticate its personnel, one of the features, the "Japanese Village," required four months of international correspondence, even a touch of high-level diplomacy. Only Buchanan's personal appeal to John Hay and the secretary's direct intercession with the Japanese government brought the eight geisha girls deemed essential to give the village its proper atmosphere.[55]

By day and by night throughout the season the stadium featured programs for sports fans and circus enthusiasts: track meets, baseball games, bicycle races, sham battles, Indian riding, parades of midway performers, and fireworks displays.[56] And at Camp Fillmore forty-eight different military groups and drill teams succeeded each other in presenting their routine: Scots Highlanders from Toronto vied with drill teams from fraternal societies and cadet companies from West Point and Virginia Polytechnic Institute with guard units from a dozen states.[57]

While the director general devoted his major energies during the exposition season to these priority matters of promotion and programming, he could not escape the details of management routine nor the pressures of emergency situations.[58] In spite of the comprehensive executive authority granted him, Buchanan almost daily felt the need to consult with the company's officers or the Executive Committee. Weather conditions, fluctuating attendance, and retrenchment in the late summer contributed to a constantly shifting payroll. Staff changes, building alterations, or adjudication of disputes with concessionaires usually involved budgetary considerations. The wide ranging system of awards, requiring lengthy panels of judges and the presence of officials at award ceremonies, called for close planning and supervision. Routine rules and regulations sometimes needed modification.

Hardly a week passed without the necessity of overseeing the entertainment of distinguished guests—Washington officials, governors, foreign diplomats. There were accommodations to be arranged, protocol to be observed, and luncheons and dinners to be given, or at least attended. Many of these affairs, like the special days, demanded participation in official processions to and through the grounds. For both Buchanan and his wife, as at the Columbian Exposition, the social calendar included pleasant, though cumulatively onerous, responsibilities.

No phase of their summer's responsibilities, however, was as grievous to the exposition's officials as the exigencies created by the deaths of two distinguished visitors—the Chilean minister to Washington and the president of the United States. In these emergencies, affecting both personal and national sensitivities, good taste and appropriate ceremony were not easy to determine. As the chief administrative officer, Buchanan became a key figure in each instance.

The Chilean minister was Carlos Morla Vicuña, who had come to Buffalo to dedicate his country's building at the exposition. His association with the United States reached back to 1870, when as a young secretary in the Chilean Legation he had found a deep interest in American literature. He had translated Poe's *Raven* and Longfellow's *Evangeline* for his countrymen and praised the New Englander's interest in the Spanish language. During the thirty years between his Washington assignments he had represented Chile in London, Paris, Madrid, and other capitals and served a term as minister of foreign affairs. As minister to Argentina in the late nineties he had developed a warm friendship with Buchanan.[59] Now his visit to Buffalo promised a happy reunion in the interests of Pan Americanism.

Taken seriously ill upon his arrival in Buffalo, however, Minister Morla Vicuña was unable to participate in the dedicatory exercises. Instead, his secretary presented and Buchanan translated an appropriate statement. Upon the minister's death a month later the director general was again called upon, this time to send a cable of regret to the Foreign Ministry in Santiago and to serve as official State Department representative at the memorial services in Buffalo.[60]

William McKinley's visit to the Pan-American Exposition in September 1901 climaxed a determined courtship on the part of the Buffalo authorities. Three times between October 1899 and April 1901 the director general and his colleagues had conferred with the president about special occasions they wished to arrange in his honor.[61] Between these formal conferences Buchanan had made several calls at the White House to renew the invitations.[62] First they had invited him to attend a pre-exposition "Foundation Day." When the closing weeks of Congress and the Republican National Convention of 1900 made this impossible, they suggested successively "Opening Day," the improvised "Dedication Day," and a specially designated "President's Day."[63] All these plans withered, however, when the chief executive's spring railroad excursion to the Pacific coast culminated in Mrs. McKinley's worsening illness.[64]

At no time during these protracted negotiations did Buchanan sense presidential disinterest in the exposition nor disinclination to visit it. Repeatedly McKinley had assured the Buffalonians of his faith in what he once called "my Exposition" and his hopes for its impact on inter-American trade and cordiality.[65] Equally reassuring were the frequent communications received from his secretary, George B. Cortelyou. Moreover, the president had already shared in the groundbreaking ceremonies at the original Cayuga Island site, signed the bill authorizing the exposition, and boosted the project in two annual state-of-the-union messages.[66] Even as the summer progressed, therefore, Buchanan remained confident that the White House would eventually overcome scheduling conflicts to permit the president's exposition visit.

Once they learned that the McKinleys had moved to their home in Canton, Ohio, for a quiet three-month summer stay, the exposition officials determined to renew their efforts to bring them to Buffalo. Through Cortelyou Buchanan promptly arranged another conference—the fourth—for his Committee on Ceremonies.[67] During a pleasant afternoon drive through Ohio's country lanes Mayor Diehl presented once again Buffalo's invitation. When the president promptly accepted and agreed to arrive in the Queen City on the evening of 4 September, the Buffalonians urged the desirability of an address appropriate to the theme of Pan Americanism. President Milburn promised a stadium audience of 25,000 to hear the speech and a welcoming crowd of 250,000. The diplomatic corps, Supreme Court justices, Cabinet officers, and the United States Marine Band would also be invited.[68]

Returning to Buffalo by boat, after a brief conference with Mark Hanna in Cleveland,[69] Buchanan and his associates could settle down at last to prepare for the "President's Day" that had long eluded them. With just twenty-four days remaining, the director general now faced the most exacting responsibilities of his exposition administration. He must oversee preparation of a detailed timetable of all events and ceremonies related to the president's two-day stay. State Department officers must agree to transportation arrangements from Washington and accommodations in Buffalo for foreign diplomats and government officials.[70] Buchanan would have to clear all these plans with the meticulous Cortelyou, as well as those for the reception, hospitality, and security of the presidential party of a dozen or more. Streams of letters and telegrams then began to course the Buffalo-Canton and Buffalo-Washington channels.

No phase of these multifarious arrangements received more scrupulous attention than the safety of the president and the personal comfort of the recuperating Mrs. McKinley. By 3 September Buchanan was able to advise Cortelyou that all his recommended precautionary measures had been taken. The security of the president, as requested by his advisors, would be the exclusive jurisdiction of Secret Service officers; crowd control, discreetly exercised, would be the responsibility of the city and exposition police forces. Through conferences with the local police commandants and the exposition Executive Committee, the director general made sure these spheres of authority were clearly understood.[71] Buchanan himself, Director Scatcherd, and Mrs. Buchanan would give their personal attention to Mrs. McKinley's convenience and entertainment.[72] He also arranged appropriate hospitality for three McKinley nieces, the White House physician, Dr. P.M. Rixey, and other members of the presidential party.[73]

For the exposition managers and sponsors, of course, this special occasion involved plans of a commercial tone as well as those for hospitality and protocol. With its attendant pomp and splendor, the visit of a popular American president offered the possibility of recouping some of the early season's financial losses. In Canton McKinley himself hoped for this result. To swell attendance, therefore, Buchanan authorized last-minute advertising in more than eight hundred newspapers and the distribution of several hundred thousand bills and programs. Numerous special features, including five hundred dynamite air bombs and a gigantic fireworks piece called "The Power of the American Navy" were widely publicized.[74]

From its auspicious beginning to its tragic climax the story of President McKinley's participation in the Pan-American Exposition has been told in exhaustive detail.[75] Quite properly, the narrative has usually focused on the central figure and the chain of events which led to his assassination. Rarely has the spotlight singled out the workers behind the scenes, those who planned, coordinated, and administered the program of events and who, overtaken by unplanned developments, sought to cope with crisis. Foremost among these, of course—at first aglow over the president's generous patronage of the exposition, then overwhelmed by the tragedy to which it led—was Director General Buchanan. He had plotted every movement of the official party and throughout its visit would never be far from the center of action.[76]

With the arrival of the presidential special from Canton in the late afternoon of 4 September, Buchanan could begin his on-the-spot stewardship of the McKinleys' timetable. When the train stopped for a moment at the downtown station to permit Buffalo's first welcoming salute, he quickly climbed aboard to greet the city's guests and join fellow citizens who had already welcomed the party at Dunkirk, fifty miles west along the Lake Erie shore. Amid the constant din of guns, horns, and whistles the train then rolled on to the exposition terminal.

There, led appropriately by the director general, exposition officials escorted President and Mrs. McKinley to waiting carriages. With bands blaring, bells tolling, locomotive whistles blowing, and 40,000 people cheering, the procession pushed its way past the Electric Tower and Court of the Fountains to the Esplanade and across the Triumphal Bridge. As the president bowed and waved to the enthusiastic crowds, he was also stealing his first glimpses of "my Exposition." Leaving the grounds by way of the Lincoln Parkway gate, with Buchanan and the omnipresent Cortelyou close behind, the presidential carriage moved along elm-lined Delaware Avenue to the home of the Milburns, hosts to the McKinley party during his Buffalo stay. That evening the president and his secretary met briefly with Buchanan and the local Committee on Ceremonies. President's Day was now only hours away.

From Buchanan's point of view, as from McKinley's, the high point of the two-day program would be the president's single formal address. Since his second inaugural six months before the president had made no major statement on the new directions American foreign policy seemed to be taking. Clearly his victory over William Jennings Bryan in the election of 1900 had indicated widespread approval for the administration's promotion of imperialist expansion and a larger role in world affairs. Its eager acquisition of far-flung territories, its participation in the Hague Conference, its open-door notes on China, and its reorientation of relations with England were only partial evidence of the new manifest destiny. Perhaps by plan, more likely by chance, the exposition authorities had already presented among the summer's featured speakers three powerful contributors to these McKinley policies—Roosevelt, Hay, and Lodge.

Related more specifically to Buchanan's concerns for Western Hemisphere affairs, the recent enactment of the Platt Amendment, the developing plans for an American-controlled canal, and the accelerating search for foreign markets seemed to assure continuing administration attention toward Latin America. Though for the most part he had suppressed his reservations about Washington's policy toward Cuba, he had repeatedly endorsed the project for a canal. As minister to Argentina he had negotiated a reciprocal trade agreement that still languished in a committee of the United States Senate.[77] Moreover, he had already accepted appointment as delegate to the Second International Conference of the American States, scheduled for Mexico later in the year.[78] Buchanan's interests in the president's speech, therefore, were those of concerned citizen and involved diplomat as well as of responsible exposition administrator.

Like the director general, the distinguished gathering of diplomats was also alert to possible presidential pronouncements. By 10:00 on the hot morning of 5 September they began to reach the flag-draped rostrum near the Triumphal Bridge. Here their official attire offered colorful complement to the uniforms of the military and semiformal dress of the public officials. But in the vast Esplanade before them the fashionable dress of women offered sharp contrast to the rustic garb of farm dwellers.

Meanwhile, at the Milburn home, Buchanan and his aides had been lining up the McKinleys' second exposition procession. They sent two carriages as the vanguard, one bearing the McKinley nieces, the second, Mrs. Buchanan and other hostesses. Then, in open carriage drawn by four spirited horses at trotting pace, came President and Mrs. McKinley. As usual, Buchanan followed closely, this time with Dr. Rixey. A few minutes ride and the cavalcade reached the Triumphal Bridge. Here, between rows of troops, with presidential salute booming, Marine Band playing, and crowd roaring, the party approached and mounted the rostrum.

Like the thousands sweltering in the packed Esplanade, the director general from his first-row vantage point eagerly anticipated Chairman Milburn's formal preliminaries. The presiding officer did not keep them waiting. "Ladies and gentlemen, the President!" was his terse introduction. Buchanan then heard the president's comparably crisp salutation, "President Milburn, Director General Buchanan, Commissioners, Ladies and Gentlemen."

Buchanan has left no record of his reactions to the president's fifteen-minute speech. Yet he could hardly have felt disappointment in its salient passages. As chief administrator of the Pan-American he could agree that it had "done its work thoroughly, . . . illustrating the progress of the human family in the western hemisphere." From his foreign residence and frequent travel he must long since have convinced himself that national "isolation is no longer possible or desirable." Through his contacts at two world expositions he was aware that American industrialists were seeking new outlets for their surplus productive capacity. From his experiences in Argentina he knew that "the expansion of our trade and commerce is the pressing problem" and that "reciprocity treaties are in harmony with the spirit of the times, measures of retaliation are not." And he must have been overjoyed to hear presidential endorsement of his own recommendations for more adequate steamship service, the isthmian canal, and a direct cable to Pacific South America.[79]

After the president had acknowledged the lengthy ovation, he spoke for a moment with Mrs. McKinley, then passed her along to Dr. Rixey and Buchanan. Unobtrusively the two men escorted her to the Milburn home for a period of rest. Later in the afternoon they would return to take her for a drive along Buffalo's tree-shaded streets, far from the clamor and stress of the exposition grounds.

Meanwhile McKinley undertook to fulfill his lengthy schedule of complimentary visits and reviews. Accompanied by the diplomatic corps he went to the stadium to inspect troops. To meet foreign commissioners and view their principal exhibits he toured a dozen buildings. Everywhere throngs of the curious and the well-wishing surrounded him. By early afternoon he had reached the New York State Building for luncheon with the commissioners. Buchanan had already returned to verify the seating protocol.

Later in the afternoon the president willingly resumed the wearying agenda Buchanan and Cortelyou had arranged for him. At the United States government building he received a number of invited guests, Mrs. Buchanan among them. Allowing only time for a brief rest and early dinner, the director general and other officials escorted the entire presidential party back to the grounds for nighttime views. In the fading twilight they saw the gradual illumination of the Electric Tower and the buildings and walkways it seemed to dominate. In full darkness, from a flotilla of boats on Park Lake, they viewed the power of the United States Navy, with presidential salutes from fireworks battleships. At last the President's Day of official responsibilities was over. The morrow was to be his day for relaxation.

Accompanied by the Buchanans, exposition officials, diplomats, and commissioners—107 in all—the McKinleys set out the following morning on their excursion to Niagara Falls. There all transferred to trolleys for the scenic ride along the Great Gorge route. While Mrs. McKinley rested, the president undertook the Cataract City's package tour—a walk on the International Bridge, carriage ride around Goat Island, complimentary luncheon, and inspection of a power plant. By 3:30 their special train returned them to the exposition, the president to prepare for his public reception at the Temple of Music, his wife to return to the Milburn home.

Promptly at 4:00 o'clock, after McKinley, Milburn, Cortelyou, and the various security officers had taken their places, Buchanan signalled the organist to play a quiet overture. As the president spoke his approval, the doors were opened and the massed crowds began to move through the receiving line. Seven minutes later Leon F. Czolgosz fired the shots that would end

William McKinley's life.[80] Even in the pain and confusion of the following moments, the president urged Cortelyou to be careful in telling his wife and apologized to Buchanan that "this should have happened here."[81]

While exposition officials and doctors were attending the stricken president, Buchanan was hurrying to the Milburn house to look after Mrs. McKinley. It was now 4:45. Jumping from the carriage and rushing to the door, he explained to the McKinley nieces that they should "on no account allow Mrs. McKinley to hear of this." At once, then, he took charge of the house. He directed servants to admit no one, disconnected the telephone, and went to the house next door to summon additional police officers. "Post your men on each side of Delaware Avenue and allow no one to stop in front of the house or in the vicinity," he commanded. "I don't want Mrs. McKinley to notice anything unusual in the neighborhood when she awakens."[82]

A few minutes after five Dr. Rixey hurried into the house. Hastily approving Buchanan's actions and authorizing him, when he deemed it necessary, to break the news to Mrs. McKinley, the White House physician returned at once to the exposition hospital. Meanwhile, dignitaries began to arrive to convey their condolences. First to appear was the dean of the diplomats visiting Buffalo, Mexican Ambassador Manuel de Aspiroz. Diplomats from Peru, Colombia, Costa Rica, Spain, Japan, and other countries soon followed. As they approached the lawn or even nearby streets, Buchanan sought to intercept them with assurances that he would convey their messages later.

By 6:45, with darkness approaching and street crowds pressing against police barriers, he felt he could no longer postpone his visit to Mrs. McKinley. Just at this point, however, Dr. Rixey returned to assume the responsibility. To inquiring newsmen the director general announced, "He has gone in to break the news." An hour later a well-guarded ambulance brought the president to the Milburn home.

During the next twenty-four hours Buchanan joined Cortelyou and Milburn in an almost ceaseless vigil. They snatched moments of sleep when they could. Upstairs Dr. Rixey and the exposition's medical director, Dr. Roswell Park, watched over the president. By 6:00 o'clock the next morning, United States military authorities had taken charge of the house; sentries patrolled the entrances.

In response to Secretary Cortelyou's long-distance calls of the previous evening, national leaders soon began to converge on Buffalo and the Milburn house: Vice-President Roosevelt, Senator Hanna, Secretary of War Root and other members of the Cabinet. Milburn and Buchanan received them as they came. Inside and outside the house the flow of dignitaries, physicians, relatives, and reporters continued throughout the day. Late in the afternoon, with the arrival of secretaries and clerks from Washington, Cortelyou was able to improvise an executive office and release Buchanan and his colleagues for their other duties.

During the week that followed, as Buffalo and the nation awaited physicians' bulletins from the president's bedside, the director general tried to cope with the inescapable burden the assassination attempt had placed upon him. As loyal citizen and friend of the McKinleys, his first thought must be the president's health. Yet, as chief administrative officer of a huge business enterprise, he could not relax responsibility for the exposition's future welfare. In many ways the loyalty and the responsibility were interrelated. He would try to do justice to both.

On the 8th, for example, Buchanan arranged a conference with Vice-President Roosevelt, Secretary of War Root, and the local district attorney to consider the handling of publicity releases on Czolgosz's confession. Upon the suggestion of Secretary Root, they recommended the avoidance of any publicity that might disturb public calm or contribute to the martyrization of the prisoner.

With encouraging reports issuing from McKinley's physicians, exposition officials seemed justified in renewing their promotional efforts. On the 9th Buchanan recommended contingent plans for a "day" to express gratification over the president's recovery.[83] At the same time he conferred with Cortelyou about the text of a news release that would say, "all those about him [the President] are a unit in believing what they know to be his wish, that the closing months of the Pan-American Exposition should be a great and overwhelming success."[84]

But all these plans were founded on illusive hopes. The president's life soon ebbed. On the 13th, even before his death, the Executive Committee had directed Buchanan to close the exposition on the following Saturday and Sunday. A day later the Board of Directors appointed five of its members to accompany the funeral train to Washington and Canton.[85]

As his last formal act related to President McKinley's long-sought but ill-fated visit, Buchanan arranged a suitable marker at the spot of the assassination. The Executive Committee accepted his recommendation that no admission should be charged to future events in the Temple of Music.[86] His first official contact with the administration of Theodore Roosevelt came when he conferred with the new president only a few hours after he had taken the oath of office on the 14th. They "discussed matters of interest to them both," reported a local newspaper. Neither man revealed the nature of these matters.[87]

Following the president's death, Buchanan and his colleagues moved in a direction they thought consistent with McKinley's expressed hopes for the success of the Pan-American. Seeking ways to reduce impending financial losses, they took immediate steps to sustain the exposition's appeal. By paring general admission prices and diversifying program offerings they were able to counteract the pall thrown over the grounds by the presidential tragedy.[88] In spite of the shutdown for three days in September, average daily patronage for the month fell off only slightly from the August figure. October brought the season's highest monthly total of visitors.[89] At the same time by instituting a policy of gradual retrenchment—scaling down publicity, closing several gateways, reducing the number of employees—the management effected new economies of operation.[90]

When the final turnstile readings were in, Buchanan could report that more than 8,000,000 persons had visited the exposition, a respectable total, he thought, for a city of 350,000, even when compared with the attendance at expositions in such metropolises as Chicago, Philadelphia, and Paris.[91] The late summer's upsurge in patronage and gate receipts did not balance the Pan-American Company's ledgers; it did relieve some of the gloom that had hovered over its hazardous project in May.

Step by step through these final weeks the director general fulfilled his timetable for closing the exposition. Administrative officers operated with skeleton staffs. Individual exhibits shut down. Buildings closed. Band concerts became less frequent. Midway concessions reduced their performances. Fireworks displays ended. The stadium was empty. In brief ceremonies on 2 November—just two years after Buchanan had assumed executive leadership—Buffalo's contribution to the lengthening succession of world expositions ground to a halt.[92] Only clean-up crews, demolition squads, curiosity-seekers, youthful scavengers, mischief hunters, and a few security guards would now enter the Pan-American's once-proud estate.

Buchanan was not on hand to share in the formal closing. Instead, with his family, he was en route to Mexico to attend the Second International Conference of American States. Seven months earlier he had accepted appointment from President McKinley as member of the United States delegation. Prior to his departure on 25 October, however, he had advised the Executive Committee that he "was making all arrangements . . . so that there will be no phase left un-attended . . . my absence will in no wise embarrass the orderly working of the Exposition during its closing week." He also assured them that upon his return he would conclude all his exposition business and prepare a complete record of his two-year administration.[93]

Adjourning its sessions only at the end of January, the conference in Mexico proved far lengthier than Buchanan had foreseen. With stopovers en route, the long train ride home delayed his return to Buffalo until the middle of February. Several official trips to Washington and absorption with the delegation's plenary report then kept him occupied during the following weeks. It was well into March before he could seriously attack the detailed account he had promised the exposition Executive Committee five months before.[94]

Meanwhile a Buffalo newspaper had become openly critical of the director general. It chided him for failing to complete his report and for neglecting other obligations to the exposition

—in effect, for not earning the salary he was still receiving. It also suggested that his statement would contain "prods" against certain exposition officials, who were already anticipating the opportunity to retaliate.[95]

What the press apparently did not know at this time, however, was the nature of his salary renegotiations with President Milburn. In October 1901 Buchanan had been fully aware that his thirty-month contract (at $1,000 per month) still had six months to run. Contemplating his absence for the mission to Mexico, he had arranged that his last six-months salary be reduced to $4,000. And in February 1902, following the unanticipated length of that mission, he had requested a further reduction to $2,500. In addition, he volunteered to underwrite a considerable portion of the cost of preparing his final report.[96] As to the press rumors of his intended prods against colleagues, the prelude to his document seemed to prove them groundless. There were no reproofs, only his acknowledgment to all officers, committees, and employees of his "most sincere expression of gratitude for the constant and kindly courtesy, aid and encouragement they at all times so generously extended" to him.[97]

Buchanan's report was a comprehensive accounting of his tenure as director general. Besides his 107-page covering analysis, it comprised numerous annexes and supplementary exhibits — reports of all divisions and copies of catalogs, daily programs, and publicity brochures. Though he incorporated no description of the origin of the exposition, he urged that some competent person be engaged to prepare one. No future history of world expositions would be complete, he alleged, that ignored the Pan-American's origin, development, and achievements.[98]

Without minimizing the financial losses of the Pan-American Company's sponsors and investors, Buchanan was lavish in his appraisal of the exposition's general benefits to Buffalo, the nation, and the Hemisphere. He emphasized the new prestige it had given Buffalo as a "city of enterprise, stability, business energy," and capacity for industrial development. He pointed out the increase it had brought to the city's general wealth, as revealed by growth in bank deposits and trust accounts. To all kinds of business enterprise it had given new impetus and to labor it had brought steady employment and rising wage scales.[99]

In considering the exposition's contributions to the nation and Hemisphere, the director general was equally sanguine. It had fulfilled the mission, he wrote, for which its sponsors projected it—the "extension of social and economic fellowship" and the promotion of "commercial well being and good understanding among the American republics and dependencies."[100] From his recent experience at the Mexico Conference, Buchanan had collected some evidence that his evaluations were more than platitudes. Voicing complete satisfaction with their participation in the Pan-American, many of his Latin American colleagues assured him that it had contributed more to the growth of their commerce than the Columbian or any other exposition. Some even speculated that it had helped to assure the calling of the Mexico assembly.[101] In any case, it was this general feeling that led to the Conference resolution congratulating Buchanan, his exposition colleagues, and the city of Buffalo.[102]

By the spring of 1901 Buchanan had begun to ponder his family's fortunes once his exposition contract expired. Surely he realized that his experiences with two world expositions and a diplomatic post in Latin America had helped him acquire a unique combination of capabilities as well as a widening circle of personal contacts throughout the Hemisphere. At any rate, other agencies besides the Pan-American Exposition Company and the United States government were becoming interested in recruiting his services. As early as June he knew he would not lack for lucrative and satisfying career opportunities.

Rumors about his opportunities, however, had long plagued Buchanan. He had not forgotten the persistent gossip about an honorarium he was to receive for his successful mediation of the Argentine-Chilean boundary dispute.[103] In the spring of 1901, after enactment of the Platt Amendment, speculation took him to Cuba on one mission or another. At the same time reports circulated of his refusing a $25,000 annual salary, then asking $50,000, to direct the Louisiana Purchase Exposition St. Louis was planning for 1903. Buchanan did become a consultant to the St. Louis promoters; they sought especially to plumb his expertise on matters related to publicity, education, agriculture, and electricity.[104] Three times during the Pan-American season and intermittently thereafter he journeyed to the Missouri metropolis for conferences.[105]

But neither the special diplomatic mission to Mexico nor the part-time advisory post in St. Louis offered Buchanan the job security he sought after a decade of shifting professional orientation. Moreover his health dictated that he avoid both the exacting accountability of the career diplomat and the unceasing demands upon the exposition manager. In the end he chose the world of private business; he accepted the offer of the New York Life Insurance Company to undertake an assignment peculiarly suited to his special abilities and experience. It would involve the adjudication of differences that might arise over the company's expanding operations in Latin America. The position would entail annual trips to the West Indies and South America yet permit him to base his activities in New York.[106] Though he agreed to New York Life's proposal in July 1901, Buchanan did not assume the position until he had completed his duties at the Pan-American[107] and fulfilled his mission to Mexico.

Chapter 10
PROMOTING THE PAN AMERICAN SPIRIT
Mexico, 1901-1902

When Buchanan resigned his post as minister to Argentina in 1899 to undertake management of the Pan-American Exposition, he had no way of knowing that the directorship would be but an interlude in his diplomatic career. And in 1901, when he accepted a position with the New York Life Insurance Company, he could not have foreseen that special State Department assignments would recurrently interrupt the continuity of his business affiliations. But for high Washington officials the Iowan's two years of experience with the Buffalo exposition, combined with his deep personal commitment to the Pan American idea, constituted a human resource too valuable to ignore. Repeatedly the Roosevelt administration, like the McKinley before it, would call upon his expertise.

The first of these special appointments, made by President McKinley and continued by his successor, involved membership in the United States delegation to the Second International Conference of the American States in Mexico City.[1] For Buchanan the nomination represented an appropriate climax to twelve years of frequent association with Latin American leaders and intermittent connection with the embryonic inter-American organization. At Sioux City in 1889 he had served as host to the delegates who would later found the Commercial Bureau of the American Republics. As minister to Buenos Aires he had labored to overcome Argentina's reluctance to join its sister nations. At both the Chicago and Buffalo expositions he had collaborated with William E. Curtis, first director of the Bureau and vigorous advocate of closer relations among the Hemisphere republics. In addition, Buchanan continued to enjoy the confidence of Secretary Hay and other State Department officials. Few, if any, Americans of the moment could match his credentials for breathing life into the inchoate Pan American movement.

The Western Hemisphere organization James G. Blaine had so eagerly projected at the Washington Conference in 1889-1890 experienced no spectacular success in the decade that followed. Many of the Latin American republics were reluctant to follow Washington's bid for Pan American leadership. Argentina had consistently been wary of multilateral commitments of whatever sort. Colombia, Mexico, and Peru over the years had demonstrated their preference for a league of Spanish American states. Brazil, as the sole American offspring of Portugal, was hesitant to align itself with either the United States or the Spanish republics. Several of the smaller nations, anxious about pressures from their more powerful neighbors as well as from the United States, were too unstable to contemplate enduring international commitments.

Moreover, Washington's increased aggressiveness in the Hemisphere—economic, diplomatic, military—served only to intensify the Latin American irritation and distrust which Buchanan had frequently reported from Buenos Aires. In 1891 Chileans had resented what they regarded as United States overzealousness in handling the *Itata* and *Baltimore* incidents.[2] Four years later, when the Anglo-Venezuelan boundary dispute flared, Secretary of State Richard Olney had shocked the Latin American community with his arrogant dictum that "the United States is practically sovereign on this continent."[3] And as Buchanan had learned from first-hand experience, his country's quick defeat of Spain and projected suzerainty over the Caribbean islands had aroused Latin American suspicion of Washington's expansionist intentions.[4]

Consistently throughout his campaign on behalf of the Pan-American Exposition, Buchanan had revealed his awareness of this developing anti-Americanism. Tactfully but forcefully he had set forth the reasons "why a broader, more rational, better understood and more common-sense Pan-American sentiment should exist between the people of the three Americas than is now apparent." Often sustaining him through his two years of anxieties for the financial and educational success of the exposition was his conviction that its promotion of "better acquaintance" would minimize prevailing suspicions among Hemisphere nations.[5]

From the moment he arrived in Buffalo the director general had followed closely the McKinley administration's efforts to rejuvenate the inter-American movement. In his state-of-the-union message on 5 December 1899, the president had suggested the expediency of a new conference of the American states.[6] By early March the *Pan-American Herald* began to proclaim Buffalo, during the life of the exposition, as the ideal place for the proposed assembly. "By all means," its editor exhorted, "let the Pan-American Congress be one of the educational features of the Pan-American Fair."[7] Whatever his personal feelings about the proposal, Buchanan could offer no encouragement to the local enthusiasts. Through his contacts in the State Department he knew that Secretary Hay was urging Mexico as the conference site and that it would probably convene just before or just after the exposition.[8]

For himself, however, Buchanan saw wider options. In late April he wrote a long letter to Hay in which he offered to serve the conference cause "in any manner, or, to any degree" he could. He suggested that, in his private correspondence with President Roca of Argentina and public men of other republics, he might contribute to the administration's purposes. He felt that the conference would be of "the greatest value to our people if we are properly represented therein by those who know something of the questions which will be unquestionably brought up; and, have the ability and breadth of view sufficient to handle them in the proper and just spirit and manner." He hoped the secretary would keep him supplied with all available information.[9]

Just a year later, on the eve of the Pan-American Exposition's opening, President McKinley named Buchanan to the five-man delegation to the Mexico Conference. The group's senior member was Henry Gassaway Davis, railroad-builder, former United States senator from West Virginia, delegate to the Washington Conference, and long-time promoter of a Pan American railway. The youngest delegate was John Barrett, a foreign service officer who would one day follow Buchanan's footsteps as minister to Argentina and Panama, then enjoy a long tenure as director general of the Pan American Union. The other members were Volney Foster, a Wisconsin lumberman and Republican Party leader, and Charles M. Pepper, a Washington, D.C., journalist, who some years later would write a biography of his colleague, former Senator Davis.[10] Though Davis became the delegation's chairman, Buchanan would prove its key member.

Despite his deep involvement in exposition affairs all through the summer, Buchanan began at once his preparation for what he presumed would be the conference agenda. Faithful to his suggestion to Hay that the American people could be "properly represented" only by an adequately briefed delegation, he invited his colleagues to Buffalo to organize their mission while enjoying the exposition's attractions. In the absence of their senior member, former Senator Davis, the delegates agreed to ask his appointment as their permanent chairman. Meanwhile, designated acting chairman, Buchanan promptly advised Hay that each delegation member had accepted one probable agenda item for personal consideration: Barrett, an International Court of Claims; Pepper, promotion of agriculture, industry, and commerce; and Foster, transportation and patent laws. For Davis they reserved his pet project, the Pan American railway. By this allocation of responsibilities the delegates entrusted to Buchanan the most controversial question left unresolved by the Washington Conference—international arbitration.[11] It would become the pivotal issue at Mexico City.

Early in October, with Buchanan still serving as acting chairman, the delegates reconvened in Washington to formalize their organization. In sessions with Assistant Secretary of State Alvey A. Adee and President Roosevelt they heard at first hand the administration's aspirations for the conference.[12] A few days later, as they prepared for their October departure, they received the president's formal instructions on the principles which should guide their deliberations and parliamentary tactics. The document was a considered and statesmanlike affirmation of what Roosevelt and Hay thought United States policy toward Latin America should be.[13]

For all the delegates, but especially for the former minister to Argentina, the president's guidelines must have been singularly pleasing. Running through the lengthy statement was an unexpected tone of circumspection which seemed to take into account the spreading anti-Americanism of which Buchanan had frequently warned. The delegates should "impress upon the representatives of our sister republics of Central and South America," the president instructed, "that we . . . entertain toward them no sentiments but those of friendship and fraternity." They should seek to cultivate "relations of mutual good will and helpfulness" and give assurance that the United States wished to be "the friend of all the Latin-American republics."[14]

Beyond this general counsel on matters of attitude and deportment, Roosevelt detailed the administration's position on such agenda items as pacific settlement of disputes, adjustment of pecuniary claims, and improvement of inter-American commercial relations. Buchanan could find special satisfaction in the White House endorsement of specific means he had repeatedly recommended for the stimulation of American exports: reciprocal trade arrangements, better steamship services, an isthmian canal, participation in the banking business. In view of what he knew about Latin American suspicion of Washington's growing hegemony in the Caribbean area, he must have been heartened by the president's emphasis upon prudence and reserve. Temperamentally and ideologically the Buffalo Pan Americanist would have no difficulty in complying with these principles in Mexico City.

By the time Buchanan returned to Buffalo from the presidential briefing, the United States delegates had completed their travel plans. Accompanied by several Latin American diplomats stationed in Washington, they would depart by special train on 12 October.[15] This arrangement would enable them to reach Mexico City in time to reacclimate themselves after the six-day train trip and to orient themselves for the conference opening on the 22nd. Buchanan, however, would not be able to accompany the group. As he had advised both his fellow delegates and the exposition Executive Committee, he felt compelled to postpone his departure until he had completed all arrangements for closing down the exposition.[16] Moreover he had already agreed to visit St. Louis en route for another consultative session with the promoters of the Louisiana Purchase Exposition. Long before these official travel arrangements became fixed, Buchanan had arranged for his family to accompany him. Here was a chance for daughter Florence, now twenty-two, and son Donald, approaching fourteen, to see Mexico, renew their contacts with the Latin American way of life, and practice their Spanish. Like the children, Mrs. Buchanan did not want so soon another separation of the family.

But their belated departure, followed by the stopover in St. Louis, delayed their arrival until 4 November. With the conference already two weeks old, Buchanan's colleagues were delighted to welcome him. "Our Delegation will be materially strengthened by his presence," John Barrett reported to his mother in one of a series of letters on the social aspects of the conference. Nor did he neglect to observe that "his wife is a charming woman and his daughter a bright, attractive girl."[17]

The late arrivals were at once plunged into the social whirl that had surrounded the conference from the beginning and would attend it to its adjournment. Already high Mexican officials had repeatedly entertained their diplomatic guests at gala affairs. President and Señora Porfirio Díaz had opened the social season with a grand reception for the delegates, their families, the diplomatic corps, and leaders of Mexican society. From the balconies of the National Palace the visitors had received the welcome of thirty thousand Mexicans gathered in the Zócalo of the ancient Aztec capital. As fireworks boomed overhead and music by a 250-piece band filled the plaza, the delegates had admired the colored electric lights outlining the National Cathedral and nearby public buildings. When Foreign Minister Ignacio Mariscal and the governor of the Federal District followed with equally generous fetes, Barrett could comment that "we are working by day and feasting by night."[18]

Though the Buchanan family had missed these initial festivities, they did arrive in time for an even more elaborate function. This was a late afternoon garden party given by the president and his wife at their hilltop residence, historic Chapultepec Castle. Here, in the great salons and amid interior gardens, where the Emperor Maximilian had once paced and the Empress Carlota once fretted, the Buchanans met for the first time the assembled representatives of the Hemisphere nations and Mexican officialdom. And here, as twilight came, they could observe the shadows slowly lengthening from surrounding mountains and the lights gradually illuminating the capital city. Like the observant Barrett, they must have been impressed with the magnificence, as well as the dignity and graciousness, of Mexican hospitality.[19]

Between conference sessions during the following three months all the visitors had ample time to acquaint themselves with Mexico City and its nearby hinterland. In 1901 the capital may have lacked some of the éclat it had once enjoyed as the first viceregal center in Spain's great American empire or as the royal seat of Maximilian's ill-fated monarchy. But from the National Palace to Chapultepec Castle, the city was beginning to exhibit Parisian elegance and distinction. By the introduction of electric street cars, the erection of impressive public buildings, and the laying out of broad boulevards, President Díaz had set the tone for municipal modernization.[20] Invited to share in the president's developing design, Buchanan and his fellow delegates attended the cornerstone-laying for the new Independence monument soon to grace one of the spacious *glorietas* intersecting the grand Paseo de la Reforma.[21]

In this beautification of Mexico City President Díaz had created a display case for the order, stability, and economic advancement he had brought to the entire nation. Chief executive during twenty-one of the previous twenty-five years, he had overcome dissidents and courted power groups to keep himself in office. Through expansive invitations to foreign capital, he had built railroads, revived the mining industry, begun the exploitation of petroleum resources, initiated new industries, and expanded public utilities.[22]

To the domestic critics of the president's authoritarian methods, however, his program of urban beautification, political stabilization, and economic development was but a façade. In their view these signs of progress effectively masked the still prevalent poverty, illiteracy, and political impotence of urban workers and rural Indian peons. Within a decade the abused masses would find leaders to ignite their crusade for general reform.[23] But in 1901-1902 the conference delegates were unable, or perhaps disinclined, to analyze these human realities. Instead, they could only inspect and enjoy their host's visible achievements.

During the two weeks before Buchanan's arrival in Mexico City his colleagues had completed organizational preliminaries for dealing with their diversified agenda. Consistent with the code of behavior prescribed by President Roosevelt, the American delegates had refrained at every turn from assuming "the part of leadership." When a caucus of delegates urged Davis to make the official response to Foreign Minister Mariscal's address of welcome, the former senator insisted that the honor belonged to a Latin American. When a Colombian delegate nominated Davis for the conference presidency, he respectfully declined. And when an Ecuadorian representative suggested the designation of John Hay as honorary president, the American delegates took no action until they felt assured the decision would be unanimous. This premeditated posture of modesty and reserve contrasted sharply with the demeanor of the American delegation at the Washington Conference. Sole veteran of that earlier meeting, Davis seemed pleased to report to Hay that the revised American approach was gaining respect from the Latin Americans.[24]

Buchanan's arrival in Mexico City on 4 November did nothing to diminish this good feeling. Already he had come to know many of the diplomats with whom he would now be working. Along with several other distinguished Mexican officials, Foreign Minister Mariscal had visited Buffalo prior to the opening of the Pan-American Exposition. Luis F. Carbo of the Ecuadorian delegation had delivered the principal speech for the dedication of his country's building at the exposition.[25] During one of Buchanan's trips to Buenos Aires he had crossed paths in London with Martín García Mérou, current Argentine minister to Washington and articulate member of his country's mission to the conference. The American had formed a high opinion of his Argentine counterpart.[26] García Mérou, in turn, had written favorably of Buchanan in his commentary on life in the United States, *Estudios americanos*.[27] Tempered somewhat by their friendship and moderation, the two men would be able to minimize the kind of Argentine-American verbal fireworks that had marked the Washington Conference.

However willing to concede Mexico the primary role in the conference it entertained, the Americans did not refuse all appointments or honors offered them. Nor did they eschew leadership when national interests seemed involved or Hemisphere welfare at issue. When Davis suggested the creation of a committee on committees, he was immediately chosen to chair it. Each of the Americans then received appointment to at least two of the nineteen committees, with Buchanan designated to represent the United States on the pivotal matter of arbitration. He was also named to the Committee on Future Pan American Conferences and, along with his Argentine friend García Mérou, to that on General Welfare.[28]

Buchanan's appointment to the Committee on Arbitration represented recognition, by both delegation colleagues and Latin American diplomats, of his decisive role in the settlement of the 1899 Argentine-Chilean boundary dispute. In no other committee of the conference would the United States be able to utilize more effectively his understanding of the Spanish-American character, his familiarity with Latin American problems, and his command of the Spanish language. Moreover, his first-hand knowledge of Argentina would facilitate cooperation with another influential committee member, Antonio Bermejo, professor of international law at the University of Buenos Aires and former minister of justice.[29]

Every nation represented at Mexico City, it quickly became apparent, favored some form of conference action that would recognize the principle of peaceful settlement. Conflicting national interests, however, obstructed agreement on the direction that action should take. At issue were three basic questions. Should arbitration be voluntary or obligatory? Should pending as well as future controversies be covered? What categories of disputes should be excepted as nonarbitrable?[30]

As the sole Western Hemisphere participants in the Hague Peace Conference of 1899, Mexico and the United States had signed its Convention on Pacific Settlement of Disputes. At Mexico City, therefore, they might be expected to adhere to the Hague principle of voluntary arbitration, though Buchanan was specifically bound by President Roosevelt's admonition to avoid any pressure on the Latin Americans for acceptance of the Hague Convention.[31]

In contrast with the Mexicans and Americans, the Argentines were expected to move strongly for obligatory arbitration, even of pending disputes. This would align them with the Peruvians, who hoped for conference assistance in securing return of territories (Tacna and Arica) lost to Chile, Argentina's transmontane rival. Many of the smaller states would support Argentina's lead. But, like the Chileans, with unresolved boundary disputes, the Brazilians would support only the voluntary principle.[32] As United States representative on the Arbitration Committee, Buchanan was forced to plot his way warily among these shoals of strong national convictions. Fortunately for his tactical efforts his own delegation had not divulged the nature of its initial instructions.[33] This gave him room for maneuver among the proponents of various arbitration schemes.

At the outset of committee deliberations, however, Buchanan's position was unexpectedly complicated when the Mexican delegation introduced its version of a treaty project. This proposal cited the Hague Convention as a possible model but watered it down with permissible reservations for cases involving national independence or national honor. Buchanan quickly learned that the Argentines were completely dissatisfied with the Mexican project and that García Mérou was appealing directly to Secretary Hay to place the United States on the side of broad obligatory arbitration. Both the Argentine and American delegations at this time seemed to believe that only Washington's strong stand on peaceful settlement could prevent conference failure. Under these circumstances, Buchanan secured a ten-day committee recess for study of the proposals, during which time he began to press Hay for authorization to support the Hague principles.[34]

By the time the committee reconvened Buchanan had learned that Chile was ready to propose affirmation of the Hague Convention. Such an initiative by Chile, he was convinced, would precipitate the opposition of its rivals, Peru and Argentina, and reduce chances for the solution he thought most negotiable. To avoid hasty decision by the full committee, therefore, he moved the creation of a subcommittee of seven nations to consider all proposals.[35]

In its efforts to find a suitable draft to place before the full committee, the subcommittee met repeatedly during December and early January. As the host nation and sponsor of the first project introduced, Mexico became the prime mover in this group. Opinion gradually crystallized that no arbitration scheme could be successful without support of the United States, so Buchanan became the pivot around whom most of the negotiations revolved; his leadership was respected, his advice eagerly sought.

The American conferred frequently with the Mexican delegates and government officials. From time to time he met separately with Genaro Raigosa, president of the conference. At a key juncture he discussed possible Mexican-American strategy with José Ives Limantour, minister of hacienda and President Díaz's official liaison with his country's delegation. In addition, as he reported to his superiors, Buchanan consulted "cautiously and confidentially" with the Argentines, Chileans, and Peruvians.[36]

Through these conversations and negotiations Buchanan was able to win the support of both Hay and the Mexican leaders for a plan of action. The conference would be asked to urge Mexico and the United States to secure approval of the Hague signatories for Latin American adherence to the 1899 Convention. Beyond this the conference would authorize the drafting of a more general arbitration convention for consideration at a future inter-American assembly.[37] With the submission of this compromise proposal in late December and his timely divulgement of Washington's official position, Buchanan contributed indispensably to salvaging conference affirmation of the principles of peaceful settlement. However, the battle was still not completely over.

Acting outside the conference, Argentina and Mexico had already signed with eight other nations a project for compulsory arbitration. In another nonconference action the United States in mid-January joined fourteen nations in signing a protocol which supported adherence to the Hague arbitration principles. Excluded from both these deliberations, however, Chile and Ecuador threatened to bolt the conference.[38] Once again Buchanan acted to retain unanimity.

Aware that the two countries had already articulated their support for the Hague Convention, the American suggested that the appropriate minutes, as well as the approved protocol, be transmitted to official conference depositories. This would obviate the necessity of their signing an instrument they had had no share in negotiating. When Chile and Ecuador agreed, Buchanan delightedly reported to Secretary Hay that he "HAD CARRIED OUT SUGGESTION . . . AND ALL IS HAPPILY CONCLUDED WITHOUT THAT FRICTION WHICH HAS BEEN SO HARD TO AVOID."[39]

No sooner had Buchanan concluded his toilsome wrestling with the general arbitration protocol than he became deeply involved in the kindred debate over a pecuniary claims convention. This had been the province of John Barrett, but when he suddenly left for Washington in mid-December, it fell to the lot of his older colleague. Moreover the premature departure of Chairman Davis left Buchanan as acting delegation chief during the climactic closing weeks of the conference.[40]

Throughout the nineteenth century American citizens had importuned the State Department to press their claims for damages suffered under arbitrary or unresponsive Latin American governments. President Roosevelt's initial instructions, therefore, had strongly underscored the desirability of creating a Hemisphere tribunal to adjudicate such pecuniary claims, especially those involving individuals of one country against the government of another.[41] Like the president, Secretary Hay believed the time propitious for creating a court of international equity, but Washington would support such a proposition only if it were authorized for a tentative experimental period, if it involved nothing compulsory, and if individual claims were specifically limited in amount.[42]

Cooperating closely with the Mexican delegation, Buchanan successfully countered Argentina and other proponents of the compulsory principle. Though forced to compromise on a number of provisions, he persuaded Hay to authorize American endorsement of the convention. Exultant over its unanimous approval, the chairman advised Washington that "it will be considered by all of the Republics represented here as one of the chief benefits resulting from the Conference." Beyond this, he saw it as "a most excellent buffer between the Department and claimants whose cases are not believed by the Department of such moment as to warrant diplomatic intervention."[43]

An unexpected corollary of the general arbitration proposition also gave Buchanan special concern. This was the issue of the Monroe Doctrine. On two occasions he felt compelled to forestall its introduction at plenary conference sessions. Contrary to Hay's instructions and the counsel of his own colleagues, he thought it imprudent to seek recognition of the Doctrine in the arbitration protocol.[44] Later, when a Haitian delegate proposed to introduce a resolution on the Doctrine, the American took steps to have it killed. As he scrupulously explained in a "personal and unofficial" note to the secretary, Buchanan felt that the Doctrine was an American foreign policy that needed "no endorsement from anyone" and that its introduction on the conference floor would only open it to attack and possible amendment.[45]

Buchanan's almost continuous involvement in the deadlocked negotiation over the arbitration instruments pushed his other official assignments into a secondary position. Yet, as member of the Committee on Future Conferences, he found satisfaction in the approval of its recommendations that a third conference be held within five years and that each government report on its compliance with the recommendations of the second.[46]

Despite the implications of the title, the Committee on Welfare, his third assignment, restricted its agenda to a variety of noncontroversial topics. It recommended, for example, the creation of a commission to study means of protecting antiquities in the Hemisphere, including the possible establishment of a Pan American archaeological museum. The committee also proposed resolutions lauding the contributions of international exhibitions "to the improvement and fostering of the friendly relations between the different States of the New World." More specifically, the resolutions congratulated Buchanan and the citizens of Buffalo for their success with the Pan-American and expressed appreciation to St. Louis for the exposition it was planning. When the death of the Brazilian delegate, previously honored as first vice-president, caused possible complications for the delegates in the choice of a successor, Buchanan eased the situation by proposing that they select no substitute for the office.[47]

With the resolution of many other issues before the conference Buchanan had less intimate association. Yet either because of personal convictions or because of his position as acting delegation chairman, he frequently felt called upon to synthesize and cast United States votes. Consistent with his efforts to assure the convening of a third conference, for example, he supported plans for reorganizing the Bureau of the American Republics and broadening the scope of its powers. Still disturbed over the failure of the Senate to approve the commercial convention he had negotiated with Argentina in 1899, he heartily approved the conference decision to endorse the principle of bilateral tariff reciprocity. Remembering his varied efforts in Buenos Aires to reduce barriers obstructing the movement of Hemisphere commerce, he led his delegation in voting for a complex of measures aimed at the promotion of inter-American trade. Among these was a resolution applauding an American project he had often urged in speeches and articles—the construction of an interoceanic canal.[48]

This continuing round of official meetings—subcommittees, committees, caucuses, and plenary sessions—brought only slight contraction in the social life of the conference. In mid-November, a special train carried Buchanan and other representatives to Puebla, Orizaba, and Vera Cruz.[49] In early January President and Señora Díaz entertained all their guests at a ball in the National Palace. On other occasions smaller groups visited the Indian town of Xochimilco, attended special services at the Shrine of the Virgin of Guadalupe, and at the national mint received silver commemorative medals struck for the event.[50] Members of the various national delegations vied with each other in offering luncheons, dinners, and formal banquets. When families were invited, as they often were, all the Buchanans turned out to enjoy the festivities. Florence, easily winning popularity among her peers, received many invitations to teas and small luncheon parties.[51] Already schooled from his Buenos Aires years in the amenities of a diplomat's household, Donald had no trouble in holding his own.

As their part of the social season the Buchanans and other Americans concentrated most of their entertaining during Thanksgiving week. Highlight of the week was their formal dinner on Thanksgiving eve for conference delegates and prominent Mexican officials. Buchanan made all the arrangements. On the following evening the American colony in Mexico City presented its annual charity ball. Opened by President Díaz, the occasion seemed to John Barrett "gay and festive . . . but unusually decorous." Nor did the Americans overlook more intimate celebrations of their national holiday. At a midday dinner on Thanksgiving Day the Buchanans feted twenty-six of their countrymen—delegates, families, and secretaries. On the previous Tuesday the American contingent had enjoyed the hospitality of Ambassador and Mrs. Powell Clayton. For the Buchanans, Thanksgiving 1901 in Mexico City would be a holiday long remembered.[52] At year's end the Buchanans sought to repay some of their personal social obligations. Their guest list for a large luncheon included the United States ambassador, conference officers, and delegates from Argentina, Chile, Mexico, and Peru. Like many of the earlier affairs, the luncheon took place at the sumptuous Chapultepec Restaurant, only a stone's throw from the presidential residence.[53]

On 31 January 1902 the conference held its concluding assembly. Admitted to the Hall of Sessions for the first time during the conference, the Buchanans and other families occupied chairs crowded into the aisles and corners. In this festive atmosphere the delegates and guests heard Buchanan express thanks on behalf of his associates for Mexico's generous hospitality. Speaking in Spanish as well as English, he relayed Secretary Hay's telegraphic message of congratulations. Following the closing remarks of Chairman Raigosa and Foreign Minister Mariscal, the conferees said their farewells to President Díaz.[54]

While several of the American delegates tarried in Mexico to join an official excursion to Guadalajara and Monterrey, Buchanan and his family left at once for St. Louis. Following further consultations there with the sponsors of the Louisiana Purchase Exposition, Will would return to Buffalo, then move on to Washington to plan the delegation's definitive report on the conference.[55] The long homeward train journey gave him ample time to reflect upon his three months in Mexico.

Above all, perhaps, as de facto head of the American delegation, Buchanan could find satisfaction in the steps taken to perpetuate the Pan American organization he had fostered and to strengthen the Pan American idea in which he believed. On the statistical side, he could point to the arbitration protocol, the four treaties, and the five conventions the conference had enacted, to say nothing of the several dozen resolutions, propositions, and recommendations it had passed.[56]

In different vein, Buchanan and his colleagues could feel that they had faithfully followed the spirit and much of the letter of the Roosevelt-Hay instructions. Without retreating when United States interests seemed vitally involved, they had fulfilled the president's advice to treat the Latin Americans "with frankness, equity, and generosity." They had encouraged "a free expression of views among the delegates of the other powers" and supported "only such measures as have the weight of general acceptance."[57] Thus they had laid solid foundations for American recognition of the Latin American principle of the equality of states.[58]

If he were inclined to appraise his own role in the conference, Buchanan must have perceived that his experiences in Argentina and acquaintanceship with its leaders had minimized the kind of fervid Argentine-American interchange that had threatened to disrupt the Washington Conference. Particularly on the issue of arbitration he must have realized that he had contributed indispensably to the compromise and resolution of vexing international differences.[59] At any rate, with the advantage of hindsight he would write in 1903 that, largely because of the arbitration compromises, "a valuable and long-to-be-remembered conference of the western republics [had been] concluded in a spirit of confidence and good-will."[60] More immediately, however, an English-language newspaper in Mexico City accentuated his contribution: "To Buchanan, more than any single member, belong the laurels of the conference." It was his patience, tact, and perseverance, the journalist recorded, together with "his profound knowledge of the Spanish-American character and his familiarity with South-American questions," that catalyzed the arbitration agreement.[61]

But once Buchanan returned to the United States his timetable allowed few moments for further ruminations. After completing his consultations in St. Louis and arranging his family's visit to Sioux City, he hastened back to Buffalo. Already scheduled to leave for Brazil in late April on behalf of the New York Life Insurance Company, he had barely two months to consummate his obligations to the Department of State, to Buffalo's Pan-American Exposition Company, and to the St. Louis promoters of the Louisiana Purchase Exposition.[62] In addition, his personal agenda called for both speaking and writing commitments.

In spite of press criticism in Buffalo about his failure to produce his final exposition report,[63] Buchanan gave first priority to fulfillment of his State Department mission. In late February, therefore, he reassembled with his conference colleagues in Washington to plan their official statement. With little difficulty they agreed on the essential components of the instrument and directed John C. Williams, delegation secretary, to prepare a preliminary draft. It would include a lengthy account of their conduct of the mission followed by extensive appendices of conference minutes and documents.[64]

Recurrently, then, during the following weeks Buchanan received queries from Williams about the composition and organization of the report. When he reviewed a first draft of the arbitration section, he returned it with only a few editorial suggestions. When the secretary solicited advice on the proper sequence of subdivisions, Buchanan betrayed the philosophical approach he had developed through fifteen years of drafting business, diplomatic, and exposition reports. "I am inclined as I grow older," he mused, "to be less persistent with regard to a thing, and to see more humor in the persistence of others than I would have done a few years back. I am sorry I cannot see things always as others can, and this is peculiarly true in the matter of the work of the Conference." Though he felt that arbitration should be covered first, he doubted that different order would cause "any upheaval in the commercial world."[65]

When he read Williams's completed draft, the Buffalo diplomat urged the addition of several concluding paragraphs. These should express, he felt strongly, the delegates' convictions about the conference's contributions to international goodwill and their eagerness for congressional action on all recommendations. He also wished to convey the delegates' appreciation for Mexico's hospitality and their hopes for presidential and State Department approval of their work. As finally submitted, the delegation report incorporated all of Buchanan's suggestions.[66]

Meanwhile through March and April Buchanan was striving to cope with the other responsibilities that beset him. To polish off his varied tasks, he complained, "I could use with ease forty-eight hours a day for the number of days I have ahead of me previous to my sailing for London."[67] Trips to Washington, New York, St. Louis, and Boston interfered with the completion of his final Pan-American Exposition report. Testing his composure in early April, the press carried a story that President Roosevelt was preparing to appoint him minister to the infant Republic of Cuba. Consistent with his lifelong policy, Buchanan told an inquiring reporter that he could hardly accept a position he had not been offered.[68]

Yet when the American Peace Society of Boston invited him to speak on the Mexico Conference, he could not resist the opportunity to air his views about the developing Pan American movement. "We have certainly been remiss," he told his Boston audience, "in not having taken up years ago, as we are now doing, the endeavor to know the people and possibilities of these Republics better, and to have ourselves better known by them." He underscored the losses in commerce and prestige caused by United States negligence. Then, to buttress his thesis, Buchanan marshaled impressive statistics. Fewer than thirty-five Americans reside in all the nineteen republics, he alleged, and probably no more than a hundred are conversant with their laws and judicial procedures. Though the Latin Americans number forty-five millions who speak Spanish and ten millions Portuguese, not one in three thousand Americans can converse intelligently in either of these languages.[69] Moreover, he emphasized, "we have no ships or banks there." With this prologue before his audience, he proceeded to detail the contributions he thought the Mexico Conference had made to the improvement of Hemisphere relations. Printed in several journals,[70] Buchanan's speech gave some currency to the Pan American rationale that had become an integral part of his personality and that would guide him during the remainder of his career, both public and private.

Finally he endeavored to assemble the materials he needed for his exposition report. Determined that his statement and its supplementary exhibits should demonstrate the exposition to have been the success he thought it was, he methodically combed some ninety cabinets of correspondence and documentary evidence.[71] As his sailing date approached, however, Buchanan realized he could not complete the work by the late April deadline he had fixed. Accordingly, on 26 April, his thirty-month contract about to expire, he submitted his resignation to the exposition company, but with a promise to deliver the report upon completion.[72] Four days later, laden with essential exposition papers, he sailed for England. When the completed report reached Buffalo, it bore the date "May 22, 1902."[73]

In journeying to South America for the third time Buchanan was initiating another of the drastic shifts that characterized his ever-changing career. Since his Sioux City days he had tested his fortunes in such diversified worlds as those of business enterprise, public entertainment, exposition management, and diplomacy. Now for the New York Life Insurance Company he would try a new combination of his talents—the application of diplomatic skills to the business of promoting insurance sales. Happily for him, the arena of his new venture would be the Latin America he had come to know and understand.

Chapter 11
DIPLOMAT OF AMERICAN BUSINESS
South America and Europe, 1899-1904

Buchanan's decision in 1901 to accept full-time employment with the New York Life Insurance Company marked his reentry into the world of business he had abandoned a decade before. Eager for surcease from the bustle and pressures of exposition management and the deadlines and crises of the diplomatic service, he anticipated the more leisurely pace his new position promised and the larger income it assured. In addition, it provided him opportunity to merge his diplomatic skills and deep interest in Latin America with the worldwide operations of a powerful American corporation. With its overseas affiliations the New York Life in 1899 had become the nation's largest life insurance company.[1]

Though the company's records of its foreign agencies have been destroyed,[2] Buchanan's own papers and the official files of his diplomatic correspondence suggest the nature of his relationship with the giant corporation. Like his services to the Department of State, his association with NYLIC was enduring but intermittent. His first contacts with its activities in Latin America coincided with the last months of his mission to Buenos Aires. His use of a minister's good offices to represent the company's case against the Argentine government led upon his return to the United States, first, to appointment as paid consultant, then to engagement as full-time representative. Heavily preoccupied with his obligations to the Pan-American Exposition and his mission to Mexico, he postponed assuming his

NYLIC duties until 1 May 1902. During the next year, while travelling to the capitals of western Europe and eastern South America, he served as a roving agent to protect the company's interests. Then, as recurrent State Department assignments and other responsibilities interposed, he reverted to his status as part-time consultant for NYLIC's overseas business, a post he would occupy until his death.

Buchanan's episodic career with NYLIC coincided with a significant stage in the evolution of the life insurance business. In 1905-1906 New York State's Armstrong Committee investigations and resultant legislative restraints served as a genuine watershed, both at home and abroad, in the transformation of the venerable American enterprise. Buchanan's affiliation with NYLIC, therefore, spanned the decade of both its zenith as America's largest life insurance company and its enforced disengagement from the evils of overextended corporate power. The decade also bridged the period of NYLIC's widest overseas scope and its reluctant retreat from international insurance and investment activities.[3]

Founded in 1845, NYLIC was one of the pioneer companies which in the two decades before the Civil War helped to establish life insurance as an essential ingredient of American social and economic life. By the end of the 1860s, like most of the other companies, NYLIC had adopted standard rules and practices related to mutuality, tables of mortality, medical examinations, level premiums, dividend distributions, and agency market arrangements.[4]

During the next generation, as aggressive entrepreneurship swelled the productive capacity of American farms, forests, ranches, and mines, the insurance business experienced growth comparable to that of steel, oil, and railroads. High birth rates, increased longevity, and immigration combined to broaden the market for life insurance contracts. The ups and downs of the business cycle accentuated the popular quest for security.[5]

By 1890 three companies—New York Life Insurance Company, Mutual Life Insurance Company of New York, and Equitable Life Assurance Society—had outdistanced all rivals and were competing for primacy. By the end of the century NYLIC became the first American company to attain a billion dollars of insurance in force. This massive accumulation of capital forced the companies to search for new investment outlets to supplement their traditional reliance on mortgage loans. While concentrating on the purchase of corporation securities and affiliation with banks and trust companies, they also began to establish overseas branches and international syndicates.[6]

Like the other companies, NYLIC had initially entered foreign markets in the 1870s. With evangelistic fervor it exported the American gospel of life insurance's utility to Europe, Latin America, and more distant regions. It leased or constructed imposing office buildings in Paris, Amsterdam, Berlin, Vienna, and Budapest. It sought to influence the appointment of friendly American diplomats or, as in the case of Buchanan, employ former ones. By 1899 its letterhead boasted that it was "The Oldest International Life Insurance Company in the World. Supervised by 82 Governments."[7] NYLIC's overseas officers, wrote an admiring commentator, "were like the proconsuls of the ancient Roman Empire, separated from home but devoting themselves with loyalty to the great organization of which they were component parts."[8]

Yet already by 1900 currents were running that would soon restrict the uncurbed expansion of NYLIC and its competitors. The rise of pre-1914 nationalism in Europe and the increasing regulatory inclinations of the Latin American governments tended to decrease the profits and attractiveness of overseas operations. At the same time, prodded by legislative reforms resulting from the Armstrong Committee investigations, the companies were forced to exercise greater caution in investment policies and to begin retrenchment from foreign enterprises. NYLIC would be among the last to retire.[9]

As national mores evolved and ethical standards shifted, historians came to compose differing interpretations of the leaders and policies of these great insurance companies. Emphasizing its noble purposes in near-adulatory terms, Lawrence F. Abbott would write of NYLIC in 1930 that

> there is nothing more splendid and romantic in all the annals of business —not even in the records of the Venetian Doges of the Twelfth Century, or the great Fugger family of Germany in the Fifteenth and Sixteenth Centuries—than the spectacle of this unified, coherent organization with

one directing head carrying on a beneficent, upbuilding commerce in all parts of the earth.[10]

Three years later, in his study of Grover Cleveland's "courage," Allan Nevins would paint the "Big Three" in darker colors. "They were supposedly conducted," he wrote,

> with strict honesty and conservatism. Actually they were the arena of outrageous corruption and theft. . . . They used company funds to pay huge salaries, to meet personal expenses, to support nepotism; they took graft in the erection of enormous buildings; they protected themselves by giving company money to campaign funds and to powerful politicians employed as counsel at fat salaries. All this was done under a cloak of outward respectability.[11]

In describing for a later generation the entire life insurance enterprise, Morton Keller would take a slightly more restrained position. "The managers of these companies," he alleged,

> assumed more than strictly entrepreneurial roles. They defined themselves not only as sellers of insurance but as men of standing and power in the community; and they claimed for their corporations equally prestigious, quasi-public functions. In consequence, this self-contained society of companies took on an unusual ideology of corporate purpose and power.[12]

Buchanan, of course, lacked the advantages of the historians' perspective. Since he has left no statement concerning the revelations of the Armstrong investigation, his true feelings about NYLIC's policies and practices can only be surmised. Yet, as his correspondence reveals, though never privy to high-level decisions, he was in frequent communication with the hierarchy of company officials.

On occasion Buchanan conferred or corresponded with John A. McCall, NYLIC president from 1892 to 1906, who had risen from a background of Democratic politics in New York state to a position of distinction among the aggressive promoters of the life insurance enterprise. In fulfilling his various assignments, however, the former exposition director would deal more regularly with a trio of NYLIC vice-presidents: with David P. Kingsley, McCall's son-in-law and company president after 1907, with Thomas A. Buckner, like Kingsley a protegé of McCall's "right-hand man," George W. Perkins, and with Perkins himself.[13]

Because of his driving interests in foreign markets, it was Perkins who became Buchanan's principal NYLIC respondent and counsellor. Even after he became a partner in J. P. Morgan and Company in 1901 and achieved important roles in the genesis of the United States Steel and International Harvester Corporations, Perkins retained his vice-presidency in NYLIC.[14] Intermittently during these years, especially on matters of foreign insurance legislation and overseas company investments, Buchanan remained in touch with the powerful executive.

NYLIC's interest in Buchanan's services stemmed in part, obviously, from his knowledge of Latin America, his acquaintance with its public leaders, and his diplomatic experience. But, most of all perhaps, it stemmed from his continuing connections with the Department of State and the esteem in which he was held by its highest officials. During his decade with the company he was frequently in contact with the department about the problems of life insurance companies abroad. In diverse attempts to protect NYLIC's interests Buchanan responded to the instructions of Secretary Hay, requested the intercession of Secretary Elihu Root, and utilized the assistance of American diplomats in foreign capitals. He kept himself *au courant* on foreign insurance regulations through copies of appropriate correspondence supplied by the Department.[15] At no time did its officials refuse his requests, criticize his actions, or question their propriety. On the contrary, the White House repeatedly enlisted his services for official diplomatic missions.

It was Secretary Hay who first injected Buchanan into the troubled sphere of NYLIC's overseas business.[16] On 31 December 1898, six months before the end of Buchanan's mission to Argentina, Hay cabled him that "THE NEW YORK LIFE INSURANCE COMPANY REPORT THAT THEIR AGENTS IN ARGENTINA ARE THREATENED WITH IMPRISONMENT ON CHARGES OF NON-COMPLIANCE WITH CERTAIN NEW REGULATIONS IN VIOLATION OF EXISTING AGREEMENTS." "TRY TO HAVE PROCEEDINGS SUSPENDED," he instructed, "UNTIL COMPANY'S COMMISSIONER ARRIVES FROM NEW YORK WITH POWER TO ACT."[17]

Unaware of the need for haste, Buchanan prepared a lengthy estimate of the situation and sent it off to Washington by marine mail. In several respects, he alleged, the company had erred in its presentation of the pertinent facts. Since its agents on 30 December had already complied with the legal requirements, they were no longer in danger of imprisonment. Since they had cabled this information to New York on the same day, company officials were adequately informed. Since the officials had at once repudiated their agents' actions, they appeared to have determined on open defiance of the law.

Behind this immediate crisis lay NYLIC's confirmed opposition to Argentina's basic insurance law. However, Buchanan explained, the regulations in question were not new but had been in force throughout the year. The law required that foreign life insurance companies guarantee their operational rights by depositing $150,000 in government fixed-price bonds to be especially issued for the purpose. When the special bonds had not become immediately available, NYLIC and the other foreign companies had provisionally purchased treasury certificates in the required amounts. By offering these certificates on 30 December in lieu of the required bonds the company's agents felt they had complied with the legal regulations. However obnoxious or unjustifiable NYLIC regarded the law, Buchanan suggested to Hay, it was a regularly sanctioned statute and the company had no choice but to yield to it, refrain from business while putting it to legal test, or retire from the country.[18] Meanwhile, receiving no immediate response to his instructions, Hay cabled the minister to report at once.[19] This succession of directives alerted Buchanan to the importance the State Department attached to NYLIC's interests.

The negotiations which followed this preliminary incident were to be complicated and protracted. In complying with his instructions, Buchanan suddenly found himself beset by a complex of pressures and influences. Secretary Hay's continuing inquiries made clear the administration's determination to support NYLIC's allegations against the Argentine authorities. "It would be a matter of deep regret to this Government," Hay asserted, "if measures were now taken which would inflict injury upon the interests and prestige of this important business institution."[20] At the same time, the secretary's persistence in the matter gave Buchanan evidence of NYLIC's sustained efforts to gain State Department support.

Through conferences with the company's agents in Buenos Aires he learned of its prior struggles to establish a place in the Argentine market. From his own experience during the Spanish-American War, moreover, he knew of the anti-Americanism which had developed in Argentina. He could understand, if not fully endorse, the nationalistic intent to protect home companies against foreign competition. In addition, the veteran minister placed a high value on the cordiality of relations he had developed between his legation and Argentine leaders. He earnestly wished to take no action which might jeopardize his friendship with President Roca, Foreign Minister Alcorta, and other officials. While willing to do all he could to promote NYLIC's interests, Buchanan assured Hay, "I need not point out how desirous I am to be able to continue advantageously our *general* interest by utilizing in every proper way such agreeable conditions."[21]

Other factors complicated the minister's efforts. Hay had cautioned him to avoid invocation of the right of diplomatic intervention in the case; he should go no farther than the "strenuous exercise of . . . good offices."[22] Moreover, the NYLIC case evolved as he was deeply enmeshed in other absorbing matters: mediation of the Argentine-Chilean boundary dispute, efforts to conclude a commercial agreement, and preparation for closing out his mission to Argentina.

As the impasse developed during the following six months Buchanan responded to Hay's reminders with a series of cables and follow-up reports, several of them voluminous, one over a hundred pages. In compliance with his initial instructions, the minister had wired Washington that he would delay any request or protest until arrival of the company's commissioner. Meanwhile, in consultation with appropriate officials, he verified his understanding that NYLIC had done business during both 1898 and 1899 and was, therefore, liable for deposit of funds to guarantee its policies in force. As soon as the company representative, a former Chilean foreign minister, arrived in Buenos Aires, he concurred in the American minister's view that "opposition of the company [was] injudicious and fruitless." Nevertheless, when Hay reiterated his suggestion to solicit suspension of proceedings pending negotiation, the envoy reported that he had secured the acquiescence of the finance minister and vice-president.[23]

In April, as the stalemate persisted, NYLIC confronted Hay with an exhaustive memoir of its representations against the Argentine government. After analyzing the company's arguments the secretary saw the question as "simply one of the bare legal right of said Company to discontinue business in the Argentine and to withdraw the money which it has deposited." In transmitting the petition's details and his own analysis to Buenos Aires, he prodded Buchanan to effect a settlement satisfactory to both parties.[24]

At once the minister renewed his interviews with treasury officials and broached the question to his close friends, President Roca and Foreign Minister Alcorta. In the end, however, he could only report to Washington the helplessness of his situation. Resting upon its earlier decrees and decisions, the Argentine government would offer no new proposals. Assuming that the State Department had made the case a diplomatic question, the company would take no further action. Limited in his power to intervene diplomatically, Buchanan felt unauthorized to recommend a possible solution. On the eve of his departure for New York in early July, he assured Hay that the case would be left pending until they could confer in Washington.[25] In Buenos Aires he could do no more.

But Buchanan's return to the United States in early September did not terminate his involvement in NYLIC's case against the Argentine government. His various official connections at this time placed him in a strong tactical position to effect a compromise settlement. Until he submitted his formal resignation he would still have obligations to Secretary Hay and the Department of State. If opportunity presented, he could easily renew his warm relationship with Argentine officialdom. Moreover soon after his return he made his counsel available to officers of NYLIC; eventually he would become their salaried consultant.[26]

By early October—a month after his initial debriefing at the State Department and his Buffalo interviews on the Pan-American Exposition directorship—Buchanan had worked out his proposal for resolution of the NYLIC case. First, in conference with company officers President McCall and Vice-President Kingsley, he sought to convince them of "the friendship and high integrity of President Roca's administration" and the advantages of continuing company operations in Argentina. He also learned at first hand both the nature of the company's grievances and the conditions under which it would be willing to reopen its business.[27] Then, armed with knowledge of the company's position, Buchanan relayed the fresh information to Argentine Minister García Mérou in Washington. By detailing the weak points on both sides he endeavored to illustrate how misinformation and misunderstanding had permitted the case to escalate. The question of a monetary deposit would be unimportant if NYLIC officers could feel assured that "the decrees of the Argentine Government were to be relied upon and its policy dictated by the broadest and most friendly spirit toward all corporations."[28]

Winning García Mérou's approval of his assessment, Buchanan proposed that he incorporate these explanations in a letter to Foreign Minister Alcorta. In addition, he would suggest the simple formula he now believed would relieve the impasse: if the Argentine finance minister would offer to redeem the $120,000 in treasury certificates still held by NYLIC, the company would deposit the $150,000 for bonds stipulated by law and would renew its Argentine enterprise. To lend greater authenticity to his proposal he would first submit a draft to the scrutiny of both Secretary Hay and the company officers. He hoped the Argentine minister, in forwarding the letter to his superiors, would add his approving endorsement.[29] Once his draft letter had run the gauntlet of these invited critics,[30] Buchanan sent it to García Mérou for transmittal to Buenos Aires. Thoroughly convinced by this time of NYLIC's good intentions, he emphasized to the Argentine envoy his belief that it "is such a financial power here and can be of such inestimable advantage to a growing and prosperous country like your own, that I feel it to be of the greatest importance to your Government that the kindly and harmonious relations which will be brought about by the adoption of the course I suggested . . . should be secured."[31]

But Buchanan did not rest his case solely on his long communication to Foreign Minister Alcorta. Though just beginning to dig into his Pan-American Exposition responsibilities, he found the time to compose an even longer letter to President Roca. It was a warm, appreciative, and genuinely intimate communication. He advised the president that he was forwarding several *"recuerdos"* from all the Buchanans, a photograph of their new home in Buffalo, and four half-barrels of choice western New York apples. He invited Roca to attend the exposition and for his country's exhibits offered numerous suggestions on the kind of displays he thought would best typify for the American people the true nature of Argentine life and economy. The kernel of Buchanan's missive, of course, was his allusion to the NYLIC case and the compromise formula he had submitted to Alcorta. He left the president no room to doubt the advantages he believed a satisfactory settlement would bring about to both Argentina and the company. Nor did the Pan-American director general neglect to add that "a favorable solution in the manner I have indicated . . . means a great deal to me personally as regards my influence with the Company." "My relations with the President and Vice-President of the Company," he continued, "are very friendly and close and I am sanguine that I may, if the Company again takes up its work in the Argentine Republic, be enabled through it to be of much service to you and to your people."[32]

Like the NYLIC officials, Buchanan then anxiously waited two months to reap the fruit of his direct appeals to Alcorta and Roca. In mid-January the former envoy received the president's terse but welcome cable: "NEW YORK LIFE CASE ADJUSTED AS YOU DESIRED IT TO BE."[33]

A few days later the Argentine responded in detail to the more personal portions of Buchanan's friendly approach. Because of the long sea voyage, Roca lamented, most of the apples had arrived in a "bad state." Argentina would participate in the exposition but without the brilliancy it desired. Though he had long anticipated a trip to the United States, the realities of Argentine "political life" might prevent his leaving the country. "We have not yet arrived," he acknowledged, "at the point of reaching the stability of older nations." He also expressed special hopes for Buchanan's early return to Buenos Aires:

"You can be certain that you will always find here the decided co-operation of all the public authorities."[34]

But President Roca's warm salutation to the former American minister did not at once solve NYLIC's legal status in the Argentine Republic nor end Buchanan's services to the company. His intimate contacts with Argentine leaders and his indispensable role in the controversy led almost inevitably to his continuing affiliation with the company. At some time during these months he became a regular consultant for the company at an annual salary of $4,000.[35] For the next year, in spite of his absorbing obligations to the Pan-American Exposition, he would continue to be NYLIC's principal intermediary for dealing with its Argentine problem. In this role he began to work closely with NYLIC Vice-President George Perkins.

As the company's Argentine agents prepared to renew operations in the light of Buchanan's formula, they suddenly learned of a new, even more acceptable, alternative. Since the company was a purely mutual one, without capital stock and without shareholders, it might be entitled to recognition as a national company. Such a status, if granted, would exempt NYLIC from regulations affecting foreign corporations and place it on an equal footing with domestic companies.[36]

The possibility of embracing this new option appealed to company officials. Yet, in order to give them counsel on the obligations it would entail, Buchanan needed fuller information. Accordingly, after consultation with Perkins, he despatched a long letter of inquiry to the Argentine finance minister. Besides requesting copies of all pertinent laws, decrees, and regulations, he posed a series of questions regarding legal procedures and requirements.[37]

The resultant correspondence and clarification of NYLIC's special concerns required fourteen months. At each stage Buchanan served as the conduit of communication between Perkins and the Argentine authorities. Two salient questions prolonged the negotiations: the government's exclusive right to name a member of NYLIC's local board and the company's right to diversify its investment of assets in Argentine real estate, government bonds, and industrial securities. On the first point the porteño authorities remained adamant. On the second they would accede to NYLIC's insistence as long as the company maintained in Argentina adequate reserve funds to protect all policy holders. Buchanan had emphasized the indispensability to Argentine development of foreign capital investment.[38]

On 16 April 1901, even as he struggled to ready the Pan-American Exposition for its May Day opening, Buchanan reported to Perkins, "I think we are now in a position to go ahead with our plans in the Argentine with perfect safety and with confidence as to the future."[39] With this happy augury, he closed out his twenty-eight months of efforts to clarify NYLIC's legal status in Argentina. Three months later he could contract for full-time employment with the company.[40]

For nearly a year, however, Buchanan's diverse commitments permitted only passing thoughts to his future role in the insurance business. With its myriad responsibilities and unanticipated problems, the Pan-American Exposition absorbed his energies until late October. His service as a member of the United States delegation to the Mexico Conference kept him out of the country until early February. After his return he sought to clear away his unfinished business—preparation of the conference report to the president, assembly of materials for the final exposition report, and consultation in St. Louis with sponsors of the Louisiana Purchase Exposition. It was not until mid-March, therefore, that Buchanan could begin to make specific plans for his NYLIC mission to Europe and South America.

Even after setting his departure date for late April he found his travel plans subject to change. Upon the initiative of David R. Francis, president of the Louisiana Purchase Exposition, Buchanan received permission from NYLIC officials "to make a tour of some of the European Courts" on behalf of the St. Louis enterprise. His two- or three-month journey would take him to London, Berlin, St. Petersburg, Vienna, Paris, and Madrid, thence to Lisbon, where he would embark for Rio de Janeiro.[41] This accretion to the itinerary NYLIC had originally set for him also forced a change in Buchanan's plans for his family. Instead of travelling with him to London, as they had previously intended, Mrs. Buchanan and the children would now remain in Buffalo until Will's return from Rio. They would then decide whether to make their home in Buffalo, New York, or London.[42]

Buchanan arrived in London on 10 May.[43] During the next several weeks, even while fulfilling his secondary commitment to the Louisiana Purchase Exposition, he found ample time to lay the groundwork for his NYLIC mission to South America. Though Brazil was his principal objective, he would also visit Uruguay and Argentina to look after the company's interests.

NYLIC's primary motivation in sending Buchanan to Brazil at this time was its determination to reenter a market from which national legislation had excluded it since 1895. Thus, prior to his departure, company officials had armed him with essential credentials and background information. He carried an official statement, certified by the New York Commissioner of Insurance and the Brazilian consul general, that NYLIC was not a joint stock corporation but a mutual company in which all policyholders shared profits. He also bore a letter of introduction to company representatives in Rio which authorized his use of vouchers for obtaining expense funds.[44]

During his outbound voyage and his stay in London the agent reviewed the record of NYLIC's operations in Brazil and the local laws and decrees which had curbed its enterprise. The company had entered the Brazilian field back in 1885 and had soon placed its business under a Spanish American Department, headed by an agent, Joaquín Sánchez. When ten years later nationalistic winds forced foreign insurance companies from Brazil, the company had retired from the promotion of new sales and Sánchez had transferred his interests to a national insurance company, the Sul América (SALIC).[45] Buchanan also learned that NYLIC officials had developed an effective working relationship with the American Legation in Rio, headed by Charles Page Bryan, former colonel in the United States Army.

Buchanan's initial task in London was to draft an itinerary that would assure his timely arrival in Rio de Janeiro without undercutting his promotional visits for the St. Louis exposition. Forewarned that new insurance legislation was already before the Brazilian Congress, he realized the necessity of telescoping his visits to the European capitals. Once he had determined to sail from Lisbon about 1 July, he sought to verify his timetable with Colonel Bryan in Rio. To expedite and assure the secrecy of his cabled messages he secured permission to utilize State Department cipher books at the American Embassy.[46]

In a long sequel to these cables Buchanan spelled out the true nature of his mission to Brazil. "I know so well your relation to the Brazilian Government," he wrote to Bryan,

> and your appreciation of the importance of a just insurance law being passed by reason of the effect it will have upon those large and wide interests with us, and your personal friendship for myself that I feel sure I am not asking too much when I express the hope that you will be good enough to use your influence to have the subject held in abeyance until we can discuss it together.[47]

In the case of Uruguay, where new insurance legislation was reportedly in preparation, Buchanan resorted to a different avenue. By letter to a friend in the Uruguayan Legation in Washington he suggested the desirability of postponing action until his arrival in Montevideo. This would give him the opportunity, he added, to contribute to the drafting of a new law that would be "a model one, and thus tend to encourage the development of your country by means of the solidity and character it would give to the great financial factor in our modern civilization and business."[48] Patently, Buchanan was continuing to give NYLIC the benefit of his connection with the Department of State and his friendship with Latin American leaders.

Once he had initiated these advance arrangements for his NYLIC mission to South America, Buchanan could, for the six weeks after 26 May, carry the St. Louis message to Antwerp, The Hague, Hamburg, Berlin, Paris, Madrid, and Lisbon. Though his scanty account books do not confirm that he visited, as planned, either St. Petersburg or Vienna, the timetable for his other stops suggests that he may have done so.[49] In any case, he arrived in the Portuguese capital about 4 July prepared to embark for Rio de Janeiro.[50]

The agent's brief stopover in Lisbon gave him the opportunity to exchange cable messages with NYLIC officials in New York. He requested briefing on the latest insurance developments in Brazil and Argentina. Mindful of the rival company representatives he might encounter in the South American capitals, he advised his home office of the cipher system he would use to report his findings and recommendations.[51]

In the days immediately following his arrival in Rio Buchanan undertook to identify the roadblocks he would face in seeking legislation favorable to NYLIC's interests. In the first place, he would be dealing with a lame-duck administration. Incumbent President Manoel de Campos Salles was scheduled to leave office in November and personnel changes were already taking place in the key Ministry of Finance.

Second, Buchanan's arrival coincided with a rising jingoism in the Brazilian press over foreign exploitation of the Acre territory on the Bolivian frontier. Though its northern boundary with Brazil was still in litigation, the La Paz government had granted 80,000 square miles of Acre lands to a powerful consortium of Wall Street and European financiers. Carioca and other South American journalists professed to see in this enterprise a United States threat to outflank Brazil's patrimony on its western outposts. In their resentment they pictured Buchanan as the advance agent of Washington's imperialist intentions.[52] As a matter of fact, however, beyond his denial of official United States complicity in the enterprise, he considered the powers given the syndicate as "not unlike those granted to the old East India Company and similar to those which in South Africa, under the dominion of Cecil Rhodes, ripened into grave causes of controversy."[53]

Two other matters contributed to the discouraging milieu in which Buchanan found himself throughout his negotiations. With powerful connections in both the executive and legislative branches of government, SALIC and other local insurance companies strongly opposed any changes in the 1895 law, which placed few restraints upon their activities.[54] The envoy also encountered in official circles the lingering belief that NYLIC had initially approved the 1895 statute. Desirous itself of leaving Brazil, ran the argument, NYLIC had supported the legislation in order to force out its North American rival, the Equitable.[55]

Profiting by his earlier experience in the Argentine case, Buchanan now zealously solicited the assistance of influential persons, both inside and outside Brazilian officialdom. In his double role as former American diplomat and current petitioner for governmental favors, Buchanan first presented himself and the purpose of his mission to the minister for foreign affairs. In arguing his case he utilized the popular outcry against the Acre concession. If Brazil really wished to influence public opinion in the United States, he suggested, and thwart the growing consensus that American capital was not wanted, the government could do no better than modify its restrictions against foreign insurance companies. He received the minister's assurances of assistance.[56]

Before seeking audience with President Campos Salles, Buchanan enlisted the collaboration of three key individuals, each in a strategic position to assist his presentation. With the aid of the company's attorney, Dr. José Pires Brandão, he prepared an informal memorandum for advance submission to the president. To make personal delivery of the document, Buchanan secured the cooperation of an influential journalist, Dr. Carlos Rodrigues, editor of the *Jornal do Commercio,* friend of the president, and hearty supporter of NYLIC's quest to reenter the Brazilian market. And to sponsor his initial interview with the president, the agent prevailed upon United States Minister Bryan to accompany and support him.[57]

In a satisfying conference with Campos Salles Buchanan detected none of the anti-Americanism which pervaded the jingoistic press. Though already apprised of the case through a memorandum, the Brazilian executive listened attentively to the American's statement, then declared that his government bore no hostility toward foreign capital or enterprise. Buchanan responded that NYLIC was seeking guarantees on just three points: the right to establish an agency and direct it from New York; the right to invest reserves in Brazil in accord with company proposals; and equality with national companies in taxation and other matters. In concluding the interview the president expressed confidence that he could find a way, either by executive decree or legislative enactment, to facilitate NYLIC's return to Brazil.

But, with a new administration preparing to take office, Buchanan could foresee the possibility that outgoing President

Campos Salles might not be able to validate his proposed decree or persuade Congress to pass essential legislation. Relying again, therefore, upon Minister Bryan, the NYLIC agent laid his case before President-elect Francisco de Paula Rodrigues Alves, who, as finance minister, had sponsored the 1895 law. He now raised no objections to the NYLIC proposals.[58]

Of the American's planned roster of official Brazilian contacts, only the current minister of finance remained. Reacting favorably, like his colleagues, to NYLIC's proposals, he even solicited from Buchanan a draft project that would state the company's hopes. By 13 August, with all this groundwork sedulously laid, the agent felt that he could safely move on to Montevideo and Buenos Aires. At this time he planned to return to Rio within a month and confidently expected to sail for New York on 17 September with a satisfactory agreement in his brief case.[59]

Buchanan's arrival in Montevideo coincided with a recurrent phase of Uruguay's chronic political instability. The reform forces that would soon put José Batlle Ordóñez in the presidency were beginning to mobilize. Xenophobia was uncrystallized, but growing. The moment was not propitious for the representative of an American company to discuss insurance regulations with public officials. Under these circumstances the NYLIC agent could do no more than review the situation with the United States minister and the company representative. Asssured by both men that no adverse insurance legislation was pending, he persuaded them to keep him advised of developments.[60]

The way was now open for Buchanan's return to Buenos Aires, the scene of his first foreign service and his most satisfying diplomatic success. During the three years since his departure he had often reminisced about Argentina, and the Argentines had not forgotten his mediation of the Chilean boundary dispute. The *bienvenida* the porteños gave him was as warm as their *despedida* of the earlier year.

The former minister had barely unpacked his bags when friends crowded his hotel suite to greet him. Journalists interviewed him and their papers saluted him. "He is bound to Argentina by an affection which is sincere and mutual," said *La*

Tribuna.[61] The Argentine government owes him a debt which it ought to pay, *El Diario* declared.[62] "We would suggest a grant of land in the South," volunteered the *Standard*.[63] To all these salutations Buchanan responded in kind. "I came, in the first place," he said, ". . . to give myself the pleasure of greeting the many good friends I have here." From first-hand experiences, he reminded them, he knew of the nation's "colossal resources [and] prodigious energies." All over Europe, he continued, from London to Berlin and Antwerp to Madrid, he had heard favorable mention of the Argentine Republic.[64] In renewing his friendships with Argentine officials, the American found none more hospitable than President Julio Roca, in whose inauguration he had shared,[65] and Estanislao Zeballos, former minister to Washington. With the porteño government, of course, Buchanan had no specific NYLIC mission to fulfill. Eighteen months earlier, he had secured from Roca and his colleagues the principal objectives sought by the company. During his three week visit, therefore, the agent performed little company business except to inspect its Buenos Aires organization. It is a "most imperfect, . . . exceedingly loose and unbusinesslike one," he reported to Perkins, but recommended that action be suspended until his arrival in New York.[66]

Warmed anew by the dockside farewell of Argentine friends and foreign diplomats, Buchanan headed for Rio and the Brazilian problem he hoped soon to resolve. With the inauguration of a new administration only six weeks away, however, he knew his task would not be easy. Yet, he still planned to return to New York by mid-October.

Reassessment of Brazilian conditions upon his return quickly convinced Buchanan that the current administration could not pass the new insurance law for which he had hoped. The lame-duck Congress would soon adjourn. In the meantime, SALIC and other local companies might exert sufficient pressure to forestall prompt congressional action. Faced by this reality, the NYLIC representative determined to concentrate his efforts on securing an executive decree. Yet as a stratagem to checkmate the local companies, he would simultaneously maintain a smoke screen of approaches to Congress. Notifying New York of his decision, he postponed his departure by two weeks and focused his efforts on President Campos Salles.⁶⁷

As he had done before his La Plata interlude, Buchanan sought the guidance of his confidants, Editor Rodrígues and Minister Bryan. With their assistance he won the cooperation of Dr. J. da C. Barrados, eminent Brazilian jurist and occasional counsel of the president.⁶⁸ After Judge Barrados had prepared an opinion favorable to NYLIC's proposals, Buchanan presented it in person to the president and won his commitment to ask the jurist to draw up a suitable decree. Encouraged by these developments, the agent cabled NYLIC in New York to request "UNLIMITED AUTHORITY" to prepare and sign a formal petition to the government on behalf of the company. By eliminating local staff from these proceedings, he hoped to frustrate possible leaks to SALIC directors.⁶⁹

At this point, 13 October, Buchanan acknowledged that he had begun "to see some daylight" in the case; he thought a favorable decision possible within a week.⁷⁰ Other developments added to his new feeling of sanguineness. Through the intercession of Perkins in New York he had won Secretary Hay's approval of his recommendations that Minister Bryan postpone until December his departure for his new post in Lisbon and that his successor remain in New York until Buchanan could arrive to confer with him. Moreover, looking to the future, he had arranged with an attorney in each house of the Brazilian Congress to watch over NYLIC interests after his departure.⁷¹ Even in this moment of hopefulness, however, the agent frankly reported to Perkins that "this is about the most unsatisfactory mess of a thing I have ever had to tackle."⁷²

But in the midst of changing administrations the wheels of Brazilian government ground more slowly even than Buchanan anticipated. Six times between mid-September and mid-November he was forced to postpone his scheduled sailing dates. In renewing his complaints to Perkins, he wrote "I have had the toughest nut to crack here that I have met with and while I am bulldog enough to enjoy the 'hang-on' phase I am more than tired and glad to get away."⁷³

In the later stages of negotiation two new problems gave the NYLIC agent occasion for concern. Particularly troublesome was the phraseology and translation of the presidential decree.

To secure the exact terminology he thought would satisfy NYLIC's purposes, he conferred frequently with the outgoing president and his advisers and several times with the president-elect. Even more disconcerting was the escalated activity of SALIC officials. Once they learned the true nature of Buchanan's tactics, they marshaled their influence in the Congress and the Ministry of Finance to balk promulgation of the decree.[74]

During these final weeks of waiting Buchanan found time to deal with other NYLIC matters. One concerned company policy on investment in the bonds of individual Brazilian states. When NYLIC officials queried him about the advisability of a loan to the state of Rio de Janeiro, he tied his reply to the status of the insurance negotiations. If the company really wished to purchase state bonds, he submitted, it would do better to consider those offered by the larger state of Bahía, with its stronger delegation in Congress. Should the company one day wish to seek congressional approval for its Brazilian insurance operations, it could use "negotiation of the loan in question as a very effective club" to win Bahía's support. At the same time, however, he urged the company to assume no state loan without first securing the endorsement of the national government; this would not only improve NYLIC's guarantee but also "make unquestionable our right to diplomatic interference in case of necessity." But, above all, he suggested, the company should consider no Brazilian loans "until life insurance laws of the country [are] satisfactory."[75]

In similar vein Buchanan gave his attention to other investment possibilities. Often concerned about the counterlobbying activities of SALIC, he recommended at one point that NYLIC "absorb" its potential competitors in both Brazil and Argentina.[76] Although his company had no connection with the Acre Concession of the Bolivian Syndicate, the agent observed apprehensively the resentment it was arousing against the intrusion of American capital.[77]

It was not until 13 November that President Campos Salles finally issued the decree that guaranteed NYLIC's right to reenter the Brazilian insurance field.[78] By that time his administration was nearing its last hours in office and Buchanan's projected two-month itinerary in South America had stretched out to four. In his summary report of the prolonged siege, the agent made clear to NYLIC's officers that his "machine had been too carefully constructed" to permit denial of his petition. "My neck being quite short," he conceded, "and my ability to know when I am licked being about as sensitized as the poetic muse in a bull pup, I squirmed around seemingly impossible barriers." In further exposing his tactics, he wrote that he had "hung on to the President's and Minister of Hacienda's door knobs like grim death and in the end these came to the conclusion that they would either have to give me what I wanted or fix up a room in the Palace in which I might live or drown me, and as the first no doubt appeared to be the least troublesome and expensive they chose that horn of the dilemma."[79]

As his homeward-bound boat stopped over in Bahía, São Salvador, Pernambuco, Recife, and Barbados to pick up mail and cargo,[80] Buchanan must have entertained thoughts quite different from those of a similar voyage three years before. Then, as retiring minister to Argentina, he was preparing to leave the diplomatic service and assume direction of the Pan-American Exposition. Now, as part of a vast insurance enterprise, he had become a kind of roving evangelist for American business ideology.[81] The hard-won success of his mission to Brazil clearly confirmed the confidence placed in him by Vice-President Perkins and other NYLIC officials.

In a variety of ways Buchanan's recent experiences in South America represented in microcosm the practices employed by the big insurance companies in their salad days of overseas expansion—the practices so much analyzed by reform legislators in 1905 and by revisionist historians in later years. Through his experience, personality, and personal contacts he typified the companies' policy of engaging former United States diplomats as goodwill ambassadors or field representatives. He profited from the State Department's friendly response to NYLIC's entreaties and worked closely with its foreign service officers. In each country he utilized friendships formed as diplomat or exposition director to place his case before the highest public officials. Wherever possible, he engaged influential local lawyers and publicists to assist him.

Acutely aware of escalating Latin American nationalism and spreading anti-Americanism, Buchanan did what he could to wrap aggressive Yankee dynamism in a favorable aura. To his employers he emphasized the importance of public relations and to his Latin American hosts he stressed the indispensibility to their development of American enterprise and venture capital. As discreetly as he was able, he endeavored to counter local legislation that would constrain, unfairly regulate, or expel alien companies. Aware also of the problems created for his company by monetary instability, political corruption, and social unrest, he volunteered his advice about the character and timing of their investments in real estate, public bonds, and private business.[82] While representing in these ways the interests of his employers, the former minister to Argentina had tried to inject into his operations something of his own respect for Latin America and his hopes for greater Hemisphere interchange.

Back in New York after his seven-months absence, Buchanan tarried only long enough to report to NYLIC officials, then hurried on to Buffalo, where by this time the family had determined to make its permanent home. During the next five months he interspersed company business with his various other interests. After a quick trip to St. Louis in mid-December to report on his European activities for the Louisiana Purchase Exposition, he settled in to a regimen of almost weekly trips to New York and Washington.[83]

With his Buffalo residence as headquarters Buchanan gave continuing attention during these months to appropriate follow-up to his South American mission. Serving as the communications link between NYLIC officers in New York and their resident representatives in Rio, he became the source of recommendations on essential steps for reopening the Brazilian field. Warning of continued counteractivity by rival companies, he suggested a broad-based advertising campaign in carioca newspapers. He assisted in the translation to Portuguese of application blanks, report forms, and agents' contracts. And when he submitted a draft of his proposed scheme of organization for the Brazilian branch, he urged an early start to writing policies.[84]

For the NYLIC branch office in Argentina he recommended a comprehensive reorganization to correct abuses he had observed during his recent inspection.[85] In the case of Uruguay he received a far more onerous assignment—that of seeking justice in the incompetent courts of an unstable nation threatened by civil war. Though kept informed of the company's charges of fraud against an Uruguayan policyholder and the Uruguayan's countercharges of libel against the company, Buchanan in Buffalo could do little to protect the company's interests—or to prevent the case from dragging on for many months.[86]

But it was sudden crisis in Venezuela that became the real focus of Buchanan's concern. The event was the Anglo-German intervention against the government of Cipriano Castro to secure settlement of long-standing claims. While the Roosevelt administration debated, and American journalists alleged, infringement of the Monroe Doctrine, Buchanan and NYLIC Vice-President Perkins were prompted to consider financial proposals that might ease the situation.[87] As a significant development in inter-American and trans-Atlantic relations, this potential challenge to Hemisphere security has been frequently analyzed. Though marginal and tentative, Buchanan's involvement brought unexpected complications.

On 21 December, just two weeks after the allied ultimatum to Venezuela, Buchanan interrupted his exposition conference in St. Louis to send a surprising message to Perkins in New York. "YOU WILL RECALL," the agent wired him,

MY GOING OVER VENEZUELA LOAN MATTER TWO YEARS AGO FOR YOU WITH MAYOR [Charles R. Mayers] OF COLUMBUS[88] AND THAT I DRAFTED CONTRACT WHICH CASTROS PEOPLE THOUGHT IMPOSSIBLE CONSIDER AND THAT WE DROPPED MATTER. MAYOR NOW ANXIOUS RENEW NEGOTIATIONS AND HAS CABLED VENEZUELA THAT EFFECT AND HAD MY DRAFT CONTRACT BROUGHT ATTENTION STATE DEPARTMENT.... CASTRO WILL HAVE TO SECURE HIS MONEY THIS COUNTRY BUT SUCCESS SAFE SCHEME AND ADVANTAGEOUS CONDITIONS JEOPARDIZED IF HE FINDS MORE THAN ONE OPENING HERE FOR HIS NEGOTIATION. WHAT SUGGESTIONS HAVE YOU FOR MY GUIDANCE[?][89]

In reminding Perkins of his earlier mediation between Castro's representatives and American financiers, Buchanan was recalling the draft contract he had drawn for a multimillion dollar loan, at 5 percent, to be secured by customs collections. By late April 1901, however, when the Venezuelans had requested new revision of the proposed terms, he was deeply involved in last-minute preparations for the 1 May opening of the Pan-American Exposition and found himself unable to pursue the matter in depth.[90] Negotiations ultimately lapsed and the loan that might have forestalled the intervention of 1902 was not floated.

Now in the midst of the December crisis Buchanan was reminding Perkins that the loan project was again on his doorstep. As Venezuelan developments shifted toward the possibility of arbitration before the Hague Tribunal, Mayers was seeking to reenlist Buchanan's services in reviving the long-dormant loan negotiations.[91] Because of his diverse Latin American associations, his close ties with Washington, and his current NYLIC affiliation, Buchanan found himself pulled in various directions.

While conceding that the Anglo-German damage claims were probably justified, he had no doubt that, like most suits of private persons against governments, they were also exaggerated. In any case, he thought the coercive measures used were too drastic, almost like imprisonment for debt. No matter how indiscreet Venezuela may have been, he conjectured, its plight would have unsettling effects on other South American republics which might one day find themselves in similar position. "If the right of a foreign gunboat to collect civil debts is established," he declared to a newspaper reporter, "it will be a bit discouraging to all of them."[92] Most of all he was concerned about the setting of precedent in the case. Remembering his own arguments at the Mexico Conference just a year before, he urged that the case should not be settled in Washington, but should go to The Hague, where "some principles can be pretty well established."[93]

As Mayers stepped up his pressure to secure the Venezuelan loan, Buchanan grew wary of the situation he saw developing among American financiers. With the assistance of Ohio Senator Joseph B. Foraker in Washington, the Columbus banker was pushing for swift action and urging the Buffalonian to arrange an immediate trip to Caracas. When rumors reached Buffalo that other groups, including one headed by Chauncey Depew of New York, were seeking to move in on the prospective dollar market, the NYLIC agent argued that only an united front of American bankers, perhaps a syndicate, would secure a favorable loan contract from the Castro government.[94]

Meanwhile, resisting the pressure from Columbus and underscoring his own point of view, Buchanan sought information and counsel from his contacts in key positions. To presidential secretary Cortelyou he wired his theory of "TOO MANY COOKS, ETC." and asked for an early conference at the White House.[95] From a Venezuelan friend in the Bureau of American Republics, N. Veloz Goiticoa, he sought information on the situation in Caracas.[96] By telegram to Argentine Minister García Mérou he inquired about the "LATEST INSIDE DEVELOPMENTS IN VENEZUELAN MATTER."[97] And faithful to George Perkins he wired his Iowa friend, Senator Allison, to check on the possibility of "THE NEW YORK INTERESTS WITH WHICH I AM IN TOUCH HELPING OUT OR TAKING HOLD OF ANY PHASE OF A FINANCIAL SCHEME."[98]

By mid-February the blockading powers had effected agreement for adjudication of their claims—with several key questions to go before the Hague Tribunal—and lifted their sixty-day blockade. As the powers moderated their position during the extended negotiations, so Buchanan gradually shifted the focus of his involvement in the case—from that of assistance to American financiers to one of direct participation in the Hague procedures. His new interest developed as a result of invitations from several South American republics that he assist them in defending their general interests at The Hague.

As a former American diplomat, Buchanan found it natural to advise Hay of the complimentary invitations he had received. Through personal conference and formal letter he assured the secretary in early February of his eagerness to "do anything [to] benefit us first of all and then through us those to the south of us." He volunteered to serve as special agent at The Hague "without fee or expense of any kind to the Department." "It seems to me," he explained, "that the moment is one wherein we can do some advantageous missionary work among

South American Countries in our broader general interests, and if I can in any way add my mite toward that end I shall be only glad to be able to do so."⁹⁹

Buchanan's freedom to undertake a special State Department assignment at The Hague stemmed from plans for his second NYLIC mission to Europe. His itinerary called for a late April sailing from New York, then visits to Paris, Madrid, and Lisbon. By early June he hoped to be in London to await the arrival of Mrs. Buchanan and the children. Until his planned September return, he would make his NYLIC headquarters in Paris and time would be available for his projected mission to The Hague.¹⁰⁰

While awaiting reply from Secretary Hay and preparing for the NYLIC assignment in Europe, Buchanan filled the weeks with the diversified appointments of his social and professional calendars. In February he entertained a small group of Buffalo civic leaders to honor his friend, Enrique C. Creel, president of the Banco Central Mexicano and active proponent of a single monetary standard for the world's commercial nations.¹⁰¹ Still working with the Louisiana Exposition officials, he made another of his consultative visits to St. Louis. In mid-April, at the annual meeting of the American Academy of Political and Social Science, his address on "Latin America and the Mexican Conference" complemented the presentations of a distinguished array of diplomats and academic authorities on Latin America.¹⁰²

But Buchanan's offer to represent the United States at The Hague, twice repeated in later communications, reached Hay at a difficult time. The president was away from Washington and, under the pressure of added duties, Hay felt that "the whole world has broken loose." Only after reaching Paris did the part-time diplomat receive acknowledgment of his overture. Reporting that the president had already proposed other names for American representation at The Hague, Hay assured Buchanan that he still hoped to have "the benefit of your intelligent cooperation."¹⁰³ At the same time the secretary confidentially broached to Buchanan the possibility of a quite different diplomatic assignment, one that immediately appealed to him. This related to an imminent international conference in

Rio called to consider conflicting claims to the Acre territory. "It is more than possible," Hay suggested, "that I shall suggest your name to the President as the best informed jurist and diplomatist I know to act as our representative in the case."[104]

Buchanan's return from Europe in the early autumn of 1903 signalled another shift in the character of his affiliation with NYLIC. As so often in the past, new opportunities were awaiting him. Before the first of December he accepted an offer from George Westinghouse to take charge of his company's expanding interests in Europe.[105] And, while preparing to assume these duties, he received from Secretary Hay a completely unexpected invitation to undertake a special mission to the fledgling Republic of Panama.[106] Though the company records are incomplete, these developments appear to have terminated Buchanan's full-time relationship with NYLIC. Presumably, in view of his affiliation with Westinghouse, he reverted to his earlier status as sometime consultant on NYLIC's overseas business.[107] In any case, before returning to Europe for his Westinghouse assignment, he felt called upon to comply with President Roosevelt's emergency summons to duty in Panama.

Chapter 12
NURSEMAID TO AN INFANT NATION
Panama, 1903-1904

The Roosevelt administration's invitation to undertake a special State Department mission to Panama came to Buchanan as a complete surprise. Seven months before, Secretary Hay had suggested the possibility of his representing the United States at the Rio conference on the Acre dispute,[1] but fast-moving developments in Bogotá, Panama, and Washington during the late summer and autumn of 1903 forced the secretary's quick change of plans. Buchanan had been following the events which prompted this unexpected invitation. He knew that the government of Colombia in August had rejected the Hay-Herrán Treaty that would have given the United States exclusive rights to build a canal across the Isthmus of Panama. He had observed closely the startling sequence of actions that followed the Colombian refusal to bow to Washington's intentions: the 3 November revolt in the province of Panama; the proclamation of Panamanian independence; Washington's prompt recognition of the new republic; and Panama's swift ratification on 2 December of the Hay-Bunau-Varilla Treaty that guaranteed to the United States the canal rights Colombia had refused to cede.[2]

Moreover, Buchanan's close association with the McKinley and Roosevelt administrations had compelled him to keep abreast of the new Caribbean policy Republican expansionists were developing.[3] As a lifelong Democrat, he had from time to time been critical of Washington's imperialist tendencies. He had shown little enthusiasm for the annexation of Puerto Rico and other islands or the Platt Amendment's preemption of potential naval bases and coaling stations in Cuba. Yet the focal objective of this growing string of island sites—an isthmian canal and the traffic lanes serving it—had long been a favored subject of the Buffalo diplomat.

It was as minister to Argentina, while working to overcome the natural and political impediments to increased inter-American trade, that Buchanan had first become aware that the Hemisphere badly needed an interoceanic canal. Later, in his promotional writings and speeches for the Pan-American Exposition, he had invariably described the canal project as a signal key to the creation of a true Pan American neighborhood; he had applauded President McKinley's endorsement of the idea in his principal exposition address.[4] At Mexico City in 1901-1902 he had joined his colleagues in supporting a conference resolution calling for an American-constructed canal.[5] Beyond this, he had specifically discussed the Panamanian canal route with a Colombian delegate and future president, General Rafael Reyes, and recommended him to Secretary Hay as "an ideal man to cooperate with on that subject."[6] Though, like many Washington officials, he had initially favored the Nicaraguan route, Buchanan quickly fell in with the decision to build across Panama.[7] Once he learned that Hay had negotiated his treaty with Philippe Bunau-Varilla, he despatched an approving commentary to the secretary: "Our action has, I think, done much to rather settle doubts throughout South America as to just what we might, would, could, or should do."[8]

On the same day that Buchanan penned this endorsement, Hay was framing the offer that would send the special envoy to Panama within ten days. "We consider it very important," the secretary wrote, "that our Legation in Panama should start right. There will be in the next few weeks some rather important matters to settle between ourselves and Panama, and between Panama and Colombia and Costa Rica respectively. I know it is asking you to make a great sacrifice to go there as our first Envoy Extraordinary and Minister Plenipotentiary."

Then, aware of Buchanan's commitments to Westinghouse and NYLIC, Hay added that "the pittance which we are able to pay our ministers bears no relation to the value of the time of men like yourself; but I have thought it possible that you might arrange your present duties in such a way as to take a leave from them without giving them up, and so do a very important public service without too much damage to yourself."[9]

Buchanan promptly wired his acceptance of Hay's "command" invitation. "AM GREATLY SURPRISED AND COMPLIMENTED BY YOUR LETTER OF THE 5TH," he acknowledged, "I WILL GLADLY MAKE THE FINANCIAL SACRIFICE THE WORK WILL ENTAIL IF I CAN ARRANGE TO HOLD UP MY WORK AS YOU SUGGEST." Assuming the Panama mission could be completed by the following autumn, he volunteered to seek the necessary arrangements with his Westinghouse and NYLIC employers.[10]

Consistent with his impulsive actions in the whole Panama affair, President Roosevelt wasted no time in speeding Buchanan's appointment and hastening him off to the Isthmus. Determined to crystallize relations with the new republic at the earliest possible moment, he needed the services of an experienced diplomat who not only had knowledge of Latin America and its people, but who was immediately available for the mission.[11] Within a week of Hay's initial inquiry the president brought Buchanan to Washington for briefings.

In conferences with the president and, because of Hay's illness, with Secretary of War Elihu Root, Buchanan solicited suggestions on his first steps in Panama. He should "represent to the Panamans as strongly as possible," Root urged, "the importance of not delaying any further in the establishment of a constitutional government." The charter should incorporate the essential elements of the American bill of rights. While choosing delegates to a constitutional convention, the voters should also be asked to confirm such emergency actions of the revolutionary junta as the declaration of independence and the canal treaty.[12]

In corroboration of Buchanan's understanding with Hay, the president's official letter of appointment specified the assignment as that of "Envoy Extraordinary and Minister Plenipotentiary on Special Mission."[13] In a postappointment statement to the press, the envoy made clear his interpretation of "special mission." Without waiting for senatorial approval, he would leave for Panama on 15 December; because of his business commitments he could not accept regular appointment to the post and expected to return by 1 February.[14]

The administration's news release on Buchanan's appointment promptly stimulated widespread editorial approval and brought him a freshet of personal messages from friends in St. Louis, Sioux City, and other cities. From Mexico City the secretary general of the Mexico Conference of 1901-1902, Joaquín D. Casasús, wrote that the Washington government could not have appointed "a man more able nor more intelligent for an affair so delicate." A Peruvian newspaper, *El Comercio,* lauded the choice.[15]

Though the Republican-controlled Senate on 17 December routinely confirmed the president's nomination, the Democratic minority was unwilling to abide by the decision. Its spokesmen raised no objections to Buchanan personally nor to his qualifications for the special assignment. Rather, in a new manifestation of the historic constitutional struggle to direct American foreign policy, they questioned the legality and propriety of Roosevelt's hasty action. The president had no right, they contended, to send a minister to a country whose existence the Congress had not yet recognized. Moreover, they charged the administration with subverting Colombia's sovereignty in the Isthmus. On 19 December they moved to reconsider the confirmation motion.[16] Thus by despatching Buchanan to his post before senatorial confirmation of his appointment, the chief executive appeared for a time to have made the envoy the innocent victim of administrative impetuosity.

The resultant Senate debate on law and precedent in regard to the recognition of states dragged on for the next six weeks. Led by Henry Cabot Lodge and Buchanan's long-time Iowa friend, William B. Allison, the Republicans defended the administration's actions. They upheld the statutory rights of the executive to appoint envoys to governments with which the United States had not previously established relations. In any case, they argued, Buchanan was not a full-fledged minister but a special representative of the president. On 11 January the Republicans defeated the minority move to reconsider the confirmation.[17] Meanwhile, however, the State Department had assured Buchanan that the "ACTION TAKEN IN SENATE [IS] MERELY MOTION TO RECONSIDER.... YOUR AUTHORITY IS NOT DIMINISHED. YOU WILL CONTINUE TO ACT UNDER COMMISSION AND CREDENTIALS AS MINISTER ON SPECIAL MISSION."[18]

On 15 December, three days after his conference with President Roosevelt and Secretary Root, his appointment still unconfirmed, Buchanan had sailed from New York on his special assignment. Determined that Mrs. Buchanan and Donald should accompany him, he had joined them in hastily assembling wardrobes suitable for travelling from early Buffalo winter to the sultry tropics. Donald, now sixteen, was to serve as his father's "secretary." Once aboard their ship at New York, the envoy had held a last-minute conference with Bunau-Varilla, serving as temporary Panamanian minister to the United States. Earlier that morning Panama's copy of the treaty, already approved, had arrived in New York en route to Washington.[19]

Oppressed successively by cold winds, tropical heat, and seasickness, the Buchanans found what joy they could in their seven-day passage on the 3000-ton *Yucatán*. "The little tub rolls and rolls and it is so sweltering hot," Mrs. Buchanan confessed to her recently married daughter, left behind in Buffalo.[20] In more pleasant moments they caught glimpses of San Salvador Island, Columbus's first landfall in the Western Hemisphere, and, while crossing the Windward Passage, sailed close to the eastern shores of Cuba. But in fair weather or foul Will could not suppress the enthusiasm he felt for the objective of his special mission. "It seems quite like a dream," he mused, "to be going down to the Lesseps Canal country about which we have all read since I was old enough to know much."[21]

Relieved to abandon ship in Colón on 22 December, the Buchanans immediately boarded a Panama Railroad train to cross the Isthmus to Panama's Pacific shores.[22] For all of them, but especially for teenage Donald, travelling over the "Crossroads of the World" stimulated visions of earlier Isthmian visitors—Balboa and his conquistadores, Pizarro with Inca gold, Spanish galleons, English seadogs, Henry Morgan and Caribbean pirates, American "forty-niners" bound for California. Less romantically, the journey permitted Will to view first hand a potential route for the interoceanic canal he had long advocated. The hour-and-a-half transit brought them to Panama City, historic governmental seat of a Colombian province, now the capital of an independent nation.

But when Buchanan arrived the seven-week-old Republic of Panama still faced the necessity of consolidating its status as a nation. Though a dozen countries had already recognized its independence,[23] no one could ignore the possibility of a Colombian attempt to reoccupy the seceded province. Moreover the new nation was as yet only nominally a republic. Besides adequate security forces, it lacked a constitution, a legislature, and a popularly elected chief of state. A three-man junta, granted provisional authority at a mass meeting of Panama's leading citizens, would govern until the electorate could sanction a constitution and choose permanent leaders.[24] As these steps progressed, all Panamanians would anxiously await word that the United States had ratified the canal treaty and fulfilled its financial commitment of $10,000,000.

Though quite different in character, Buchanan's situation during these weeks was as amorphous as that of the young nation. As first United States minister to Panama, he had no established legation headquarters to which to report or from which to operate. He had no trained secretary and for some weeks not even a typewriter or dictionaries. He lacked access to official United States government publications he deemed indispensable, especially volumes on international law, treaties in force, the canal question, and past diplomatic correspondence with Colombia. More serious, State Department officials had failed to supply him with authentic maps or even a copy of the Hay-Bunau-Varilla Treaty.[25] Above all he regretted the absence of detailed written instructions from the secretary of state. In this formless situation he would try to serve as nursemaid to the infant nation. He would have six weeks to fulfill his special mission.

Buchanan waited less than twenty-four hours to advise the

governing junta of his readiness to present his credentials.[26] However inexperienced in diplomatic protocol, the Panamanian government missed no turn in welcoming the United States minister. On the day of his reception appropriate officials escorted him through troop-lined streets from his hotel residence to the executive mansion. There, in the presence of ranking political, military, and ecclesiastical leaders and members of small consular corps, as well as of Mrs. Buchanan and Donald, he exchanged messages with the junta spokesman, Colonel José Agustín Arango.[27]

As he reported to Washington that same day, Buchanan scrupulously avoided any allusion to the canal or American intentions to build it. Instead, referring to United States interest in Panama, he incorporated only the laconic understatement that "the advent and the future development of the new nation is a subject of keen and kindly interest to the American people." Equally circumspect in his reply, Colonel Arango assured the minister that his mission signified "that the oldest of the Republics of the American continent duly appreciates the youngest of the Republics, thereby placing it on the same terms as its sister Republics of the New World."[28]

Though inured to crisis situations since his Sioux City Corn Palace days, Buchanan now faced the most sensitive assignment of his public or private career. With only the sketchiest of verbal instructions from his own superiors, he must deal with the provisional authorities of a seceded state seeking legitimacy and status. At stake was Washington's determination, backed by the nation's rising zeal, to build an interoceanic canal. For six weeks at least Buchanan would be expected to serve as a kind of advance agent, commissioned ostensibly to assure the creation of a viable constitutional government that would safeguard American interests.[29]

Five days after Buchanan's arrival the Panamanian electorate went to the polls to select representatives to a constitutional convention. Despite the importance of this election to American interests, the minister made no attempt to define its nature or influence its outcome. He evidently deemed it premature at this point to inject the specific recommendations he had received from Secretary Root.

Meanwhile he and his family sought to adjust to both the tropical climate and the confused atmosphere of an emerging nation's capital. They missed features of the cities they had enjoyed on their former joint visits to Latin America—the urban elegance of Buenos Aires and the mountain setting of Mexico City. Though each of them succumbed to brief illnesses produced by the unfamiliar environment, they endeavored to make the most of the opportunities afforded them. In the capital city they attended official breakfasts and formal dinners and on both shores of the Isthmus enjoyed receptions on vessels of the United States Navy. On an offshore island picnic they caught their first views of coconut palms, orange groves, and fields of pineapples. Wishing for her artist's tools, Mrs. Buchanan admired "the colors of the trees . . . so rich, the leaves so large, the yellow sand and the purplish dark red rocks, the green and blue water and the soft lavender and blue distance and the beautiful clouds."[30] Clearly more utilitarian, Donald worked to earn the $25 weekly salary his father paid him for his secretarial duties. Still he found time to take geometry lessons, brush up his Spanish, experiment with tropical film, buy Panamanian stamps, win 80 cents in a lottery, and learn to waltz in accelerated Latin tempo.[31]

Once Buchanan had arranged the personal comforts of his family and analyzed the results of the preliminary election, he could concentrate on the major problems of his unique mission. During the next month four areas would command his vigilance: the need to assist the Panamanian leaders in drafting their first constitution; the timing of suggestions to Washington on possible amendments to the canal treaty and the urgency of early ratification; analysis of Panama's evolving relationship with Colombia; and attention to the health and sanitary conditions of the Isthmus.

By the end of December Buchanan began to meet on almost a daily basis with members of the junta and with Dr. Manuel Amador Guerrero, probable president-elect. Gradually and tactfully he sought at the outset to influence their thoughts on the broad format of the constitution. First of all he urged them to prepare a document that would be "simple and clear." Then, mindful at this time of Secretary Root's admonitions, he recommended that it should contain the specifics of a bill of rights and also, in appropriate form, confirmation of the junta's actions on independence and the canal treaty. Repeatedly he emphasized the need for completing a satisfactory draft prior to the assembling of convention delegates on 15 January.[32] In a summary despatch to Washington the minister reported that the Panamanian leaders were "willing to do anything we suggest, which they can harmonize with their own plans and purposes."[33]

Almost at once, however, Buchanan learned that the Panamanians did have "their own plans and purposes," esteemed legacies from the Colombian experience in constitution-making. Under the decree ordering election of delegates, they maintained, the convention would have authority to *"expedir"* a constitution. In accordance with this Colombian practice, the convention was empowered not only to draft, approve, and promulgate a constitution, but also to elect the first president and enact the first laws.[34] Under these circumstances the American minister could do no more than recommend popular referendum and election as more democratic procedures. But, his advice and American practice to the contrary, the local leaders had no intention of reversing Colombian precedent.

Though compelled to operate within these narrowed limits, Buchanan continued to work closely with Amador and the junta chiefs, always with the objective of assuring a stable government that could protect American canal-building rights. Both before and during the convention proceedings, he stressed the necessity of harmony in the drafting of a sound basic charter. To minimize interparty conflict between Conservatives and Liberals, he urged postponement of all lawmaking until the constitution was approved. He was insisting, he wrote to Hay at one stage, "that we would not have here any marks of the usual disorder, inconsistencies and irrational procedures which has been unfortunately the dominant characteristic hereabouts for many years."[35]

Buchanan's cardinal objective of securing safeguards for American canal-building rights led him to compose and support two specific articles in Panama's constitution. One of these he developed upon his own initiative, the other in response to overtures from junta leaders. The first article concerned American jurisdictional rights with respect to the building, control, and protection of the canal and the guarantee of Panamanian independence. The constitution, he reasoned, should authorize whatever present or future treaties might specify as the limits of American jurisdiction.[36] Accordingly, after consultation with Washington, he persuaded the convention to incorporate a generalized statement:

> under the jurisdictional limitations stipulated or hereafter to be stipulated in the treaties or conventions now concluded or hereafter to be concluded with the United States of America for the construction, maintenance, protection or sanitation of any mode whatsoever of interoceanic transit.[37]

A related proposition dealing with the United States right of intervention was more controversial and in future years would become the target of increasing anti-Americanism. Early in January, two weeks before the convening of the constitutional convention, several Panamanian spokesmen broached the matter to Buchanan. Both Amador and Tomás Arias, foreign minister-to-be, proposed the desirability of a constitutional clause "recognizing the right and obligations of the United States to intervene at all times, without reference to the limits of the canal zone."[38] Patently this proposal immensely broadened the intervention article in the canal treaty. It may even have reflected the annexationist sentiment the minister detected among elements seeking an end to the unrest they had known under Colombian rule.[39]

Buchanan was fully aware that he had no instructions on the possible use of intervention to insure public safety and orderly government. He could, however, envision the effects of political instability and internal disorders on the construction and protection of the canal. He sensed the rising Liberal Party opposition to the incumbent Conservative leaders with whom he was dealing. While assuring the Panamanians of his own indifference to the intervention accretions they proposed, the American cabled Washington for further instructions.[40]

Within a matter of hours Assistant Secretary of State Francis P. Loomis authorized Buchanan to use his discretion about the matter but without conceding the necessity of change in the canal treaty.[41] Two weeks later, however, after fuller analysis,

Secretary Hay advised the minister that "the Department thinks it preferable that the Panama constitution should contain nothing in conflict with the widest liberty of action on our part."[42] When Buchanan conveyed this view to the Panamanian authorities, he was informed that they had "served notice to all those who showed any opposition that on their least suggestion Amador himself will withdraw the article; but now, so far, they were unwilling to have it removed. 'Such is life among the tropics.' "[43] Though considerable opposition developed on the floor of the convention, the Conservative majority carried the vote for the broad intervention principle they had first suggested. Approved as Article 136, it read:

> The Government of the United States of America may intervene in any part of the Republic of Panama to reestablish public peace and constitutional order in the event of their being disturbed, provided that the nation shall, by public treaty, assume or have assumed the obligation of guaranteeing the independence and sovereignty of this Republic.[44]

In several subsequent communications, as if in anticipation of future criticism by Panamanian patriots, Buchanan explained in detail the origin of Article 136. Freely he admitted his endorsement of a constitutional provision authorizing United States intervention to protect Panamanian independence, but "whatever else may remain in the article," he wrote to his successor in office, "is purely the wish and good sense of the Panama people and has not had its origin with us."[45] At the end of a full explanation to Hay, he unswervingly asserted that "you will see from this the act was in reality one born here in the minds of the people themselves."[46] Yet his paper disavowals of United States initiative in the broadened intervention article would long remain hidden to critics of American policy.[47]

Even while assisting the Panamanians to draft their constitution, Buchanan was growing increasingly apprehensive about the Hay-Bunau-Varilla Treaty and the Senate's failure to expedite its ratification. Clearly he saw that early approval of both documents was indispensable to a young government seeking to insure internal order while securing external independence. Though the junta leaders had promptly sanctioned the treaty, opposition spokesmen were beginning to express anxiety about certain of its terms. And until Washington added its consent, Panama would be deprived of revenue desperately needed. It had already exhausted the $200,000 borrowed from J. P. Morgan and Company.[48]

In reporting this growing opposition Buchanan sought to mirror local fears that the nation would be deprived of customs revenues to which it was legitimately entitled. Like them, Buchanan believed that income from import duties was essential to adequate financing of government services. When Panamanian critics learned that Article IX would create "free ports" at Panama and Colón, they began to speculate about the customs liability of merchandise on ships touching the ports or transiting the canal. They anticipated possible abuses of Article X, which permitted canal "officers or employees" to import without taxation "property and effects" for their own use. And they were concerned that Article XIII on "access of employees" might result in the creation of a "canal commissary."[49] "This would be repugnant to commerce here," Buchanan reported, "and could hardly avoid being a serious expense to this country's customs revenue."[50] However unknowingly, he was fingering sensitive issues that would arouse the militancy of future nationalists.

Serious as he deemed the need for clarification of these points, Buchanan argued the inadvisability of Senate attempts to amend the treaty. Repeatedly after the middle of January he warned Washington of the possible consequences. Modification of specific clauses at this juncture would require reciprocal Panamanian action while the constitutional convention was still in session. Opposition delegates would have fresh opportunity to attack the clauses they opposed. Such an eventuality would be "a most unwise and risky step," Buchanan declared, and might cause prolonged delay in exchange of ratifications.[51]

Complementing his arguments for prompt Senate action, the minister offered an alternative solution for settlement of the disputed points. Panama's immediate need, he asserted, was concrete evidence of Washington's intentions. Only Senate approval of the basic treaty, with its commitment of the $10,000,000 payment for canal-building rights, would reassure them.[52] Once treaty ratifications were exchanged, clarifying and regulatory understandings could be worked out by executive agreement or supplemental convention.[53]

When Secretary Hay received these warnings in Washington, he confided to his diary that Buchanan was "protesting against amendment to treaty as vexatious and possibly disastrous." At once he relayed the message to President Roosevelt and, without much hope, to key Senate leaders. "The average Senator," he added, "delights to meddle."[54] As Hay anticipated, the Senate delayed its action; not until 23 February did it advise ratification.[55] By that time Buchanan had departed Panama, completed his debriefing at the State Department, and sailed for his Westinghouse assignment in England.

While counselling Panamanian leaders on constitution-making and Washington on treaty matters, Buchanan did not overlook a third critical area—Panama's relationships with Colombia. From day to day he tried to keep abreast of all aspects of the developing situation: the military problem of security against possible Colombian efforts to reconquer the revolted province; the financial question of Panama's responsibility to pay a share of Colombia's foreign debt; and such legal-political matters as Colombia's recognition of Panamanian independence and the fixing of international boundaries. On each of these issues the minister regularly reported to Washington.

In assessing Panama's overall security situation, the American's principal concern lay in the possibility of external instigation of internal unrest. He knew that American warships would interdict any major marine landing and that Colombian land forces in strength could not penetrate the tropical forests of the eastern Isthmus. But when he received reports that Colombia was inciting Indian uprisings, he kept in close touch with American naval commanders in both Caribbean and Pacific waters. As a long-range policy to forestall the threat of armed revolt, he recommended disbandment of the regular army, creation of a rural constabulary equipped only with revolvers, and storage of government arms and ammunition under United States control in the canal zone.[56]

On the matter of Colombia's foreign debt of some $12,000,000, junta officials had assured Buchanan that they were willing to assume Panama's fair share. Floated for the most part during the wars for independence, Colombian bond issues had been refunded and modified many times, but for thirty years had paid no interest to the English and Dutch bondholders. With the apparent approval of local lenders, the minister recommended to Washington that a portion of its $10,000,000 payment for canal rights be retained in the Treasury Department to guarantee Panama's commitments. He emphasized, however, that such an arrangement with Panama should be undertaken only in complete secrecy.[57] After consultation with Amador, Buchanan agreed to discuss the entire Colombian debt problem with bondholders in England. To provide him with essential background data Ricardo Arias, brother of the foreign minister-to-be, would collect the information and forward it to London.[58]

The final major concern of Buchanan's six-week mission involved the serious questions of public health and sanitation. His family's illnesses and his own brief bout with malaria alerted him to the hazards alien engineers, laborers, and soldiers would face during the long period of canal construction. No matter what sanitary measures were taken to minimize the risks of yellow fever and other tropical diseases, he reflected, "one thing will always stick—malaria. There are over 700 million tons of mosquitos born inland every day and all have the malaria from childhood to old age and I don't blame the brutes a bit for biting any one they can get at and saying, tag! you're it for a while."[59]

However unsophisticated himself in the techniques for protecting public health, the minister's correspondence with Panamanian leaders, United States Navy officers, and State Department officials reveals the breadth of his early attention to the problem. To prevent the introduction of contagious diseases he recommended the immediate stationing of United States medical officers in Colombia, Ecuador, Peru, Venezuela, and the Caribbean islands. He suggested the creation of a joint United States-Panamanian sanitary board to supervise the improvement of living conditions in Panama City and other communities. He urged the Panamanian government to tighten its quarantine regulations.[60]

Pertinent to the overall problem, too, was the desire of the

Pan American Medical Congress to hold its next assembly in Panama City. In exchanges with the American chairman of the Congress's executive committee, and with local officials, Buchanan ascertained Panama's willingness to host the meeting. "The only hotel worth consideration," he confided to the chairman, "is crude and you will all have to put up with considerable annoyance and discomfort but everything that can be done for you will be done and there is no place you could go where they would be more delighted to have you or where you could do as much good as here in Panama."[61]

As early as 7 January Buchanan began to plan his return to Washington. During the eighteen days since his arrival, he reported to Hay, he had "worked early and late" to accomplish the objectives assigned him. The draft constitution, soon to be in the hands of the convention delegates, would contain the essential features he had recommended. Because Panama's fiscal status was growing increasingly tenuous, only prompt Senate approval of the canal treaty would stabilize the situation. Effective dovetailing of the two documents to satisfy long-range national interests of both countries would require an extended period. Meanwhile, protection of American rights should be placed in the hands of "a strong tactful capable man," conversant with Spanish laws, habits, and languages, who would serve in a dual capacity as minister to Panama and civil administrator of the canal zone. Other problems concerning the Colombian debt, Panamanian security, the national budget, and public health he had discussed fully with Amador and other leaders. While summarizing these thoughts for Hay, the minister set 26 January as a tentative sailing date and formally requested a leave of absence.[62]

In anticipation of departure the Buchanans decided to transfer to Colón for the final weeks of their Panamanian visit. They hoped to find the Caribbean atmosphere more salubrious and a seaside house more pleasant than their Panama City hotel. Together they would sail from Colón. Unexpectedly, however, President Roosevelt scotched their sailing plans when he asked Will to remain at his post until 2 February. Mrs. Buchanan and Donald, therefore, departed on the 26th as planned; Will would follow a week later.[63]

Buchanan's final week in Colón proved the most trying of his brief tour, for he was suddenly struck by an attack of malaria. Instead of protocol farewell visits to his Panamanian hosts, he was forced into sending them notes from his sickbed. Less than seventy-two hours before his departure, he received a terse directive from Washington: "LEAVE COMPREHENSIVE LETTER OF INSTRUCTION . . . FOR RUSSELL, GIVING HIM COPIOUS INFORMATION ABOUT PERSONS AND THINGS."[64] Hastily transferred from Caracas to Panama, William W. Russell could not reach Colón before mid-February. While still abed, Buchanan began to assemble the "copious information."

Completed only hours before his sailing, Buchanan's letter to Russell was a many-paged document, replete with personality vignettes, situation estimates, and specific recommendations.[65] Among Americans who could prove helpful he mentioned top officials of the Panama Railroad Company, the Isthmian Canal Commission, the Marine Health Office, and the army and navy. Foremost among these was railroad superintendent Colonel J. R. Shaler, "whose judgment you can rely upon implicitly."

Among the Panamanian leaders the minister singled out three for distinctively favorable characterizations: the new president, Dr. Amador, who "can be treated by you with entire frankness and absolute confidence . . . unreservedly pro-American and would be an annexationist if that question should ever seriouly arise"; Tomás Arias, "a very clever and excellent man . . . openly American in sentiment and in favor of the United States intervention as a sure cure for the evils that may come to this Government"; and his brother, Ricardo, who "can reach every man from the President at any moment. . . . He has been of the greatest help to me." Buchanan also mentioned the favorable inclinations of other junta members and even of the bishop of Panama. But, in selecting these contacts for recommendation to his successor, the American acknowledged his comparative lack of acquaintance with elements opposed to the policies of incumbent officials.

In briefing Russell on the current situation, Buchanan took extreme pains to explain the origins of the controversial constitutional Article 136 and the misunderstandings of the equally controversial Article IX of the canal treaty. On other delicate issues he did not hesitate to give Russell specific bits of advice. On sanitary and health matters: "Do whatever you can to keep the Government screwed up to the proper pitch on this subject." On dissolution of the army: "Keep constantly before these people the necessity and wisdom of their deciding as quickly as the treaty is passed to get rid of their army and to try to have them create a constabulary throughout the country. . . . There are too many young officers strutting around Panama." Emphasizing Panama's need to establish cordial relations with Colombia, he hoped Russell would "have the subject kept constantly fresh and placed in the hands of some one person here to work out."

In addition to these basic issues, upon which he had freely advised the Panamanian leaders, Buchanan warned Russell that the new government must quickly deal with four other questions: settlement of a national monetary basis; preparation of laws and judicial procedures; framing of a budget and tax bills; and formulation with the United States of plans for immediate implementation of the Hay-Bunau-Varilla Treaty. Still recuperating from his own illness, the departing minister added one bit of personal counsel for his successor: "Try to keep well." This would be far easier, he granted, in a comfortable Colón cottage than in an irksome Panama City hotel.

Directly upon reaching New York Buchanan travelled to Washington to give Secretary Hay his personal report on the situation in Panama. He carried with him a copy of the second reading of the constitution project he had helped to draft as well as his continuing conviction that the United States Senate should promptly approve the canal treaty without amendment.[66] As he made clear to reporters, he felt confident that the Panamanians were making rational progress toward stable government, that the constitution would soon be approved, that relations with Colombia would be satisfactorily adjusted, and that internal reforms would proceed.[67]

On Capitol Hill, however, Buchanan's visit to Washington was received far less warmly than at the State Department. Almost at the hour of his conference with Hay, the minister's name and judgment were being ostentatiously besmirched on the floor of the United States Senate. In referring to an alleged Buchanan proposal for liquidating Panama's share of Colombia's foreign debt, Democratic Senator Henry M. Teller of Colorado proclaimed that "a more disgraceful and dishonorable proposition was never made by a person speaking for the American Government." The proposal attributed to the returned envoy was that Panama should secretly purchase Colombian securities from European bondholders at 5 percent and convert them at face value to discharge the former province's share of the Colombian debt. As an articulate opponent of administration policy toward Panama, Senator Teller charged that "no one would have dared to make such a proposal had not the actions of the administration in the whole Panama affair given our agents reason to believe that trickery and dishonor would be winked at, if it would result in advantage to the United States."[68]

By the time the minister returned to Buffalo he discovered the incident had ballooned into front-page headlines featuring "BUCHANAN'S SECRET LETTER." Reluctant, as a diplomat, to reveal the details of his confidential State Department correspondence, Buchanan, nevertheless, ridiculed the allegation that he had promoted such a scheme. "It is all moonshine," he told reporters.[69] Several weeks later, still dismayed by the incident, Buchanan brought the newspaper stories to Hay's attention.[70] In reply, while decrying leaks of confidential communications in official quarters, Hay assured the former minister that "there is not a shadow of foundation of my having disapproved anything which you did or which you approved. ... The fact that I have never heard of it until this day shows that it created no impression on the public mind, and was forgotten as soon as printed."[71]

Meanwhile, Buchanan had formalized his prearranged intention to resign as minister to Panama. In response to his letter, Hay conveyed President Roosevelt's "deep appreciation of the generous and unselfish spirit in which you accepted at such short notice a most important and difficult service."[72] Officially, the minister's special mission to Panama was concluded. Within a week of his return he embarked for England to assume his new duties with the Westinghouse Company and to resume his part-time advisory functions for the New York Life Insurance Company. For the next nine months, however, from his new base in London, he would keep in close touch with Panamanian developments through his old friends in Washington and new acquaintances in Panama City.

To keep his pledge to President Amador, Buchanan gave faithful assistance during these months to Panama's plans for adjusting its relations with Colombia. From the background information supplied by Ricardo Arias he learned that the Panamanian authorities had already notified the British ambassador in Washington of their intentions to pay their proper share of Colombia's foreign debt. He assumed that this action implied formal acknowledgment of Panama's obligation to pay.[73] Believing that he could effect an arrangement with the English holders of Colombian bonds, Buchanan scheduled a series of conferences with their agents in London, the Foreign Bond-holders Committee. From these conferences he developed a working proposal for submission to Amador. Through agreement with the Committee, Panama would seek tenders to purchase bonds equivalent in value to its estimated share of the Colombian foreign debt. Bondholders could offer to sell at prices they deemed proper; those unwilling to accept the market price could retain their bonds. At the current market price Panama could purchase about $5,000,000 in bonds, for, say, the $1,000,000 it might wish to appropriate for the purpose.[74] Thus, by discharging nearly one-half of Colombia's overseas obligation, thereby improving Bogotá's credit standing abroad, Panama would place itself in a favorable position to deal effectively on such issues as recognition and boundaries. Buchanan gave his assurance that, by working through Panama's fiscal agents in New York, he could carry out this scheme. In his view it would provide equity for all concerned parties.[75]

When in August Buchanan returned briefly to the United States for the Westinghouse Company, he sought to bring to fruition the plan he had proposed. In conferences with Panama's agents, J. P. Morgan and Company, and with George W. Perkins, he clarified the financial aspects. In meetings with a Panamanian representative, his friend Ricardo Arias, he reviewed the status of his negotiations in London and New York and received briefings on the current attitudes of Panamanian officials.⁷⁶

Gradually, however, Buchanan came to realize that President Amador was steadily hardening his posture toward Colombia. After advising the British ambassador of Panama's willingness to make payment on the Colombian debt, he had taken the position that Bogotá must first recognize Panamanian independence. Later, to promote that result, he had asked the Foreign Bond-holders Committee to use its influence with Colombia. When the committee refused to cooperate, Amador found new bases for delay. He feared that, without having improved its relationship with Colombia, Panama might be saddled with major holdings of valueless bonds. Moreover, he seemed now to be arguing that Panama admitted no financial obligation to Colombia.⁷⁷ By the time of Buchanan's return to England his scheme to improve Panama's relations with Colombia through voluntary sharing of the foreign debt had proved abortive.

But from his English vantage point Buchanan had already begun to explore other avenues for his mediation efforts. Even before leaving the United States in February he had written to a Colombian colleague of Mexico City days—General Rafael Reyes, temporarily residing in Paris while awaiting a call to his country's presidency—to suggest a possible conference.⁷⁸ In response to Buchanan's friendly approach, Reyes replied that "I think yet that you will be of great value to your country and to mine, and to Panama, in order that they settle in a fair and honourable way the pending questions about Panama." As a practical approach to ameliorating the troubled triangular relationship, he proposed that Colombia sell to the United States its little-used Caribbean possession, the Providencia Islands.⁷⁹ Located three hundred miles due north of Colón, the islands lay close to shipping lanes between the United States and Panama. As Buchanan suggested to Hay, they could have both economic and strategic value for the United States. More important, their purchase could provide "the key with which the whole Colombian-Panama affair can be finally closed," and "the means by which all phases of the Colombian question, both in the latter country and our own [,] could be disposed of."⁸⁰

Though nothing resulted from this particular proposal, both men sought to pave the way for eventual resolution of unsettled problems. The Colombian urged private action to effect a settlement along lines that are "equally honourable & just for all parties." Anticipating that "the moment may come when some advantage can be taken of this relation to the mutual benefit of everyone," the American recommended continuing contacts with Reyes.[81] Like the general, Buchanan would be involved in future efforts to unravel the issues caused by Panama's secession.[82]

Even though acting as a private citizen in all these overtures, the former minister regularly informed both Roosevelt and Hay of his activities. While advising preliminary consultations with the Panamanians, he urged the president to place "the administration of the strip in so far as its civil matters are concerned in the hands of one man,—preferably our minister to Panama, who should be made ex officio a member of the Canal Commission." Such an arrangement, he suggested, "would result in a perfectly smooth running self-adjusting piece of work that would be highly creditable to our administrative capacities as a people."[83]

Six months later, in reiterating this recommendation to Hay, Buchanan proposed that the American official be given the title of "civil administrator," not that of "governor." His long Latin American experience had taught him that to the Spanish mind the word "governor" carried an unfortunate connotation. "One cannot always avoid a certain partiality," he wrote in explanation of his sensitivity for the Panamanians, "toward children with which he has had to do in their infancy."[84]

His presence in London during the early summer of 1904 provided the Buffalonian still another occasion for expressing his views on the situation in Panama. In May he learned that his successor as minister to Panama would be John Barrett, delegation colleague at the Mexico Conference in 1901-1902, currently serving in the Argentine post Buchanan had once occupied. When Barrett reached London, en route to Washington and Panama City, he took advantage of the opportunity to solicit Buchanan's "complete and detailed account" of Panamanian affairs.[85]

These diverse unofficial activities during 1904 brought to a tentative conclusion Buchanan's association with Washington's Panama problem. Yet his brief mission had already given him opportunities to foster two long-cherished interests—the encouragement of inter-American comity and the promotion of an interoceanic canal. His efforts as a private citizen to reconcile the obvious differences between Panama and Colombia added to his growing recognition as a trustworthy mediator at the Hemisphere level. Though unsuccessful, his approaches to President Amador and General Reyes revealed the same harmonizing spirit he had displayed in his earlier State Department assignments—as an arbiter in adjudicating the Argentine-Chilean boundary dispute in 1899 and in resolving disagreements over mandatory arbitration at the Mexico Conference of 1901-1902. Like his friends in Washington, the Latin Americans had come to respect his conciliatory skills.

As the Roosevelt administration's special emissary to the young nation it had helped to create, Buchanan seems to have fulfilled the vaguely expressed duties expected of him. Working closely with Panamanian leaders, he had been able to assist them in creating a constitutional government that could maintain internal order while commanding international recognition. Though he had focused on American canal-building rights and the essential conditions for constructing and protecting the waterway, he had emphasized the need to assure democracy for the people of Panama and fairness for the government of Colombia. He had advised Panamanian officials on such diverse matters as public health, sanitation, public debt, and security. Again and again he had recommended to Washington the desirability of a civil administrator for the Canal Zone.

If the envoy had erred in any respect, it was on the side of minimal contact with minority Liberal elements in the constitutional convention. This he freely admitted. On the other hand, he had meticulously pointed out to Washington the nationalist concerns about the canal treaty that were already beginning to arise—questions about free ports, customs collections, United States rights to import, privileges of United States citizens in the Canal Zone, establishment of commissaries for

American personnel. These were the matters that would gradually crystallize into grievances and over the years embitter Panama's relations with the United States. If Buchanan at any time felt that Panama had by treaty or constitutional clause ceded too much of its sovereignty to the United States, he was hardly in a position to protest to President Roosevelt or Secretary Hay. Even before his appointment Panamanian officials had approved the Hay-Bunau-Varilla Treaty and it was they who insisted on Article 136 for their constitution.[86]

But deep as were his interests in Panama's future and that of the canal, Buchanan owed his primary responsibilities in England to the Westinghouse Company. Already late in reporting for his assignment, his new and unfamiliar duties consumed his attention. And he still retained his part-time commitment to the New York Life Insurance Company.

Chapter 13
BACK TO THE WORLD OF BUSINESS
England and Europe, 1904-1906

From the time Buchanan moved to Sioux City in 1882 he had never wanted for job opportunities, but before he embarked for England in February 1904, he had begun to follow a clear-cut, if unplanned, pattern of alternating public service with private employment. During the previous decade he had accepted invitations from three successive presidents to undertake State Department assignments in Latin America, and after each of these public missions he had found representatives of the private sector eager to contract for his particular combination of diplomatic and business skills. Now, upon completion of the mission to Panama, George Westinghouse eagerly awaited Buchanan's arrival in England to assume a new managerial position, this time in industry.

Long before Buchanan's affiliation with the company the name Westinghouse had attained widespread fame in the United States and Western Europe and was reaching to countries beyond. Through his manifold contributions to the improvement of railway transport and to the production and transmission of electric power Westinghouse had immensely accelerated the growth of industrial economies and the betterment of human living.[1]

In the United States as early as 1869 the inventive genius had organized the Westinghouse Air Brake Company to develop and market his device for stopping high-speed trains by a single action in the engineer's cab. Through a succession of patents leading to automatic controls and standardized and interchangeable parts he evolved braking equipment adaptable to all railroads and different types of rolling stock. A decade later he formed the Union Switch & Signal Company to produce apparatus, first for hydraulic, then for electropneumatic, control of signals and interlocking switch systems. Meanwhile, Westinghouse was broadening his interests in the harnessing of energy—especially natural gas and electric power—to meet the requirements of transport, industrial, and home users.[2]

By the mideighties the Westinghouse interests had become deeply involved in the alternating-current system of utilizing electric energy. They formed still another company to manufacture equipment for the generation and transmission of power transformed for industrial and lighting purposes. To assist in adapting alternating current for running motors, they engaged the brilliant young Croatian-American inventor, Nikola Tesla. The gradual perfection of the Westinghouse system led to contracts for lighting at the Columbian Exposition and for the first development of hydroelectric power at Niagara Falls, destined soon to service the Pan-American Exposition. Eventually, Westinghouse's inventions would lead to more than four hundred patents and his insatiable drive to the formation of scores of companies.[3]

After he had established the soundness of his air-brake venture in the United States, Westinghouse determined to claim overseas markets for his revolutionary inventions. Crossing the Atlantic repeatedly during the seventies, he spent half the decade in trying to convert reluctant English railroad men to the efficacy of his braking apparatus.[4] "I often wanted to sit down and cry," he told an English audience years later, "because I could not get anyone to believe in anything."[5] Finally, in 1881, he persuaded a group of English collaborators to form the Westinghouse Brake Company, Ltd. Similar companies, each granted broad territorial rights, soon followed in Germany, France, and Russia. Later, as the market for electricity developed, he established another network of companies across Europe to promote the installation of alternating-current systems.[6] As business expanded and companies proliferated from London to St. Petersburg, Westinghouse continued to use them primarily for marketing and construction purposes. Essential equipment—generators, stationary engines, rolling stock—was turned out in the laboratories, shops, and foundries at Pittsburgh. By 1899, however, he had determined that the European market should be supplied by equipment manufactured in England and on the continent. Through a new company, the British Westinghouse Electric & Manufacturing Company, he would build the largest and most modern industrial plant in Europe.[7]

Once he had purchased a tract of 130 acres outside Manchester, close to coalfields and accessible by canal to ocean shipping, Westinghouse imported American managers and workmen to spearhead the construction of his ambitious project. It would comprise more than thirty acres of covered foundries, machine shops, carpenter shops, and blacksmith sheds. Utilizing American design and construction techniques, three thousand men worked for some fifteen months to erect buildings, install twenty-seven miles of railroad tracks, and lay out a residential town nearby. By January 1902 they had completed basic construction. A year later most machinery, powerhouse equipment, and electric cranes, all brought from Pittsburgh, were in place. Employment rolls could eventually total five thousand. The entire project represented George Westinghouse in his boldest and most imaginative mood.[8]

As the culmination of his design to assure the success of this grandiose enterprise, Westinghouse made a special effort to court the leaders of Great Britain's financial and industrial communities. In early 1903 he arranged an elaborate banquet at Claridge's, then, as later, London's most prestigious hotel. To attract the attendance of desirable financiers, scientists, industrial managers, and railway executives, he arranged the participation, as toastmaster, of his friend Lord Kelvin, England's ranking scientist of the day. Clearly, Westinghouse hoped that Lord Kelvin's introduction, followed by his own remarks, would begin to thaw the English entrepreneurial conservatism he had tried for thirty years to break down.[9]

But Westinghouse's electrical "invasion of England" was not the triumph he had envisioned. He saw the English transportation system, with its suburban trains serving dense populations, as ideally suited to electrification. Large central power plants, fed by coal from nearby fields, would provide cheap energy. Alternating-current electricity, rather than coal, would be distributed. But English money managers and railway executives were not yet ready for these revolutionary changes. The anticipated demand for electrical equipment did not materialize. The colossal works at Manchester were larger than business justified. Almost from the start the British Westinghouse Electric & Manufacturing Company was in financial trouble, a burden to other Westinghouse interests at home and abroad.[10]

This was the deteriorating situation Westinghouse faced by the summer of 1903 and the inauspicious milieu Buchanan would enter early the following year. At the very moment when his complex of enterprises demanded his presence at home, the Pittsburgh promoter needed a managing director for his shaky Manchester venture and an overseer for his expanding operations elsewhere in Europe. His search for a deputy to assume these functions led him to the selection of William Buchanan.

Neither company archives nor personal papers offer clues to the origins of the Westinghouse interest in Buchanan's talents or to the time and circumstances of their contractual arrangements. In view of his company's contribution to the Colombian Exposition, however, Westinghouse must have known of Buchanan's successful management there. He must also have observed the Buffalonian's emphasis upon electric lighting at the Pan-American Exposition and his administrative ability in bringing that exposition to fruition. And considering his consuming interests in overseas expansion and the cultivation of foreign markets, Westinghouse must have been attracted by Buchanan's varied diplomatic experiences in Argentina, Mexico, and Panama and his recent European services for the New York Life Insurance Company.

At any rate, sometime during the fall of 1903, prior to his departure for Panama, Buchanan agreed to undertake the formidable assignment in England.[11] In commenting upon his European as well as English responsibilities, newspapers placed his annual salary as high as $30,000.[12] While President Roosevelt's envoy fulfilled his mission to Panama, Westinghouse persuaded the British company to accept his nominee as the corporation's managing director and deputy chairman. "William I. Buchanan . . . has had an exceptional experience in the management of important affairs," the chairman assured the company's directors, "and I am satisfied your business will have that constant supervision and direction which are so essential to complete success."[13] Eager though he was to return to Pittsburgh, Westinghouse would first see his surrogate properly introduced to English industrial and political leaders and adequately oriented to his prospective duties.

Buchanan's departure from New York in late February brought him face-to-face for the first time with the generosity and thoughtfulness of the Westinghouse family, as well as the extravagance and ostentation he would soon come to question. When he reached his cabin aboard the S. S. *Celtic,* he found an array of *bon voyage* gifts from Mrs. Westinghouse—boxes of South African peaches and hothouse grapes, a basket of oranges, tangerines, apples, and pears, and a bouquet of "the longest stemmed roses you can imagine." On his first day at sea still another present appeared—a dozen grouse and two dozen quail. Even amid the enjoyment of these luxuries, Buchanan's seven-day passage gave him the opportunity to renew the pattern of shipboard life he had now come to know so well—resting, reading, writing his family, catching up on business correspondence, analyzing his fellow passengers. "Same old sea," he assured Mrs. Buchanan, "same old cold air, same old rubber smell throughout the ship, same old crowd of people, who ride in streetcars at home and never by any chance stick their noses out of the house, walking the deck in the cold like mad." To free his mind for the onerous Westinghouse duties ahead he brought his New York Life responsibilities up to date by dictating letters to company representatives in Buenos Aires and Rio de Janeiro.[14]

When Buchanan reached the London headquarters of British Westinghouse, he found personal accommodations quite in contrast with those he had known as United States diplomat in Panama only two months before. Instead of a sparsely furnished hotel-room office, he would now enjoy a broad-windowed second-floor room overlooking the Strand just east of Trafalgar Square. Its appointments included a large red rug, mahogany desk, leather-covered chairs, and fireplace. The luxury of these amenities made him wonder how long he would need to get " the *feel* of the thing" into which Westinghouse had drawn him. "This thing of being the new dog in the yard is not to my liking," he wrote to Mrs. Buchanan, "but we may all be thankful I suppose that we are saved at least the other dogs comments."[15]

During the next ten weeks while Westinghouse remained in England, his newly arrived deputy did not lack for appropriate orientation, qualified counsel, or varied social life. Whenever in London they followed a routine of business appointments at breakfast or lunch and frequently at dinner. From time to time they entertained groups of cabinet officers, Westinghouse executives, railway managers, journalists, or United States Embassy officials. They were entertained by Lord and Lady Kelvin and once dined in a home that had belonged to Nell Gwynne. On rare occasions Buchanan found himself free to plan his own entertaining—to dine with former Argentine friends passing through London, indulge his long-standing love of the theater, or revel among the spring flowers on walks through Hyde and Regent's Park.[16]

From his earlier managerial experiences, however, Buchanan fully understood that "one can never know the innards of a thing until he gets into it."[17] Not until he had inspected the various Westinghouse works and talked to the men in charge did he realize the intricacies and immensity of the assignment he had undertaken. His first impressions did not leave him sanguine.

On their first trip to the provinces Westinghouse and Buchanan visited the sprawling new layout at Manchester and other installations at Liverpool. Reporting his preliminary reactions to Mrs. Buchanan, he wrote that "I am not at all happy over the inside business conditions I find here or over the outlook ahead for me. . . . Nothing thins out . . . and all the muggy ends of everything are coming to the surface for me to tackle." Later inspections only reinforced his initial impressions. "I seem to find one bad mess after another. . . . There are so many things to do that I am uncertain at times what to do first."[18] Visits to Newcastle-upon-Tyne and Glasgow did nothing to abate Buchanan's growing pessimism about prospects for company enterprises. At Newcastle Westinghouse had installed the power stations for a newly electrified railway, but lost the rest of the contract to lower bidders. In Glasgow Buchanan learned that two power plants under construction would probably become "White Elephants." The company had invested $2,000,000 without "a blooming contract made to use the power."[19]

Twice the two men travelled to Paris so that Buchanan could "have the troubles of the French Co poured over" him.[20] On one trip they stopped in Le Havre to inspect a Westinghouse automobile plant employing a thousand men. On another Buchanan insisted on motoring through Rouen to visit the memorials to Joan of Arc and Richard the Lion-Hearted. In Paris they booked in at a luxurious hotel on the Place Vendôme and, mixing pleasure with business, dined at the home of Baron Rothschild overlooking the Champs Elysées next to the British Embassy.[21] Even his burdensome responsibilities could not blind the onetime Ohio farm boy to the delights of Paris in April. Between polite dinners and endless conferences he managed to escape for the meditative walks he had long practiced. In one moment of reverie he wrote to Mrs. Buchanan that "the sunshine, the flowers, the trees in their new leaves, the bright *clean* looking people all nicely dressed with the livey [sic] sort of happy look every one wears is so lovely here that it is no wonder by comparison with other places that Paris grows on people."[22]

These visits to Paris in the springtime pushed Buchanan even further into the kind of contemplative mood his recent responsibilities had rarely permitted him. The weeks of intimate association with his new employer gave him opportunity to appraise the life pattern and personal character of an established American tycoon. "It makes me sick fairly to see the small fortune he daily spends everywhere": his private automobile costing $10,000 a year—three palatial homes in the United States—"secretaries galore and heaven knows what."[23] Though he found his employer to be "simply fine as a generous kindly loveable [sic] big man," Buchanan deemed him too splendid in his views and overoptimistic and careless in his business commitments. It was precisely this lack of care, Westinghouse made clear, that had led to his engagement of a deputy. At the same time, however deeply he longed for the liberty to move ahead on his own, Buchanan valued the resourcefulness and patience with which Westinghouse was overseeing his indoctrination.[24]

As he observed more and more of Westinghouse's labyrinthine involvements and manifestations of sheer extravagance, Buchanan began to reflect more frequently on his own future and his family's welfare. For fifteen years he had enjoyed each of eight different jobs and prospered satisfactorily, yet he had failed to settle into any specific career or business. Compellingly, however, his Westinghouse experience was pushing him toward one conclusion: "I don't think I ever want to be rich or at the head of any great enterprise where big sums of money are involved as they are in Mr. Ws things and in hundreds of others. The strain and risks and annoyances are so great that it would not attract me. The most medium road is more conducive to sleep and health and comfort." He was beginning to think in terms of "a business of some sort . . . in which Don could grow up."[25]

Uneasy about the uncertainties and complications of his new position and frustrated in his search for suitable housing, Buchanan gradually cooled on earlier thoughts of transplanting his household to London or Paris.[26] To complicate his problem he was finding transoceanic mail an unsatisfactory medium for counselling his family on their problems at home. Mrs. Buchanan was saddled with the management of houses they still owned in Dayton and Sioux City and of their residence in Buffalo. His daughter and son-in-law were contemplating the purchase of a lot and construction of a new home. Donald was pushing his father to select a Pierce as their first automobile.[27]

Even while meeting these responsibilities to company and family, Buchanan found time to attend the other obligations to which he had committed himself. Continuing his affiliation with the New York Life Insurance Company, he met from time to time with its resident agents and salesmen.[28] Still serving as consultant to St. Louis's Louisiana Purchase Exposition, he kept in touch with its administrators.[29] And with the newborn

Republic of Panama still very much on his mind, he found various ways to give its problems his continuing attention. In correspondence with Secretary of State Hay and General Rafael Reyes and in meetings with the Foreign Bond-holders Committee, he perpetuated his efforts to resolve Panama's relations with Colombia.[30]

His employer's departure for Pittsburgh at the beginning of May terminated Buchanan's ten-week personalized introduction to the complex of Westinghouse enterprises in England and France. More fully aware by this time of the thorny problems confronting him, he anticipated the greater liberty he would have to deal with them.[31] Yet his task during the next three months—until his first return to the United States— would prove more frustrating than any he had known.

With London as his base of operations, Buchanan travelled regularly to inspect Westinghouse plants and installations and confer with their directors and managers. He made frequent trips to the Manchester-Liverpool area, fairly commuted to Paris, visited various cities in Switzerland, and projected a trip to Lisbon. When problems became particularly acute, he exchanged cablegrams with Westinghouse in Pittsburgh, often two or three a day, sometimes more. His correspondence was heavy.[32]

The chief focus of Buchanan's concern was the giant new plant in Manchester, designed to turn out steam turbines, alternating-current motors, and other kinds of big electrical equipment. Examining more carefully now its operational details, he discovered that, with $15,000,000 invested and 5,000 men at work, the company's latest annual profit was less than $50,000. With such a complex outlay, he fully understood, an order of $100,000—and there were few of these—was but a drop in the bucket. The problem was clear-cut: how to pare expenses while increasing sales. But in view of English reluctance to electrify railroads and industries, an immediate solution was less apparent.[33]

As he came to closer grip with the other "muddles" he was expected to alleviate, Buchanan gradually developed the feeling that "all the mean things in business . . . in Mr. Ws basket appear . . . to have come together at one and the same time."[34] The electric railway under the Mersey River at Liverpool needed fresh capital. A railroad company was seeking $3,500,000 indemnity for alleged faulty work by Westinghouse employees. Other complaints and threats of legal suits had piled up. Outstanding accounts could not be settled.[35]

In France, though the Westinghouse interests were far less extensive, Buchanan encountered similar problems. Straightening out the affairs of the French Westinghouse company required six cross-channel trips, innumerable trans-Atlantic cables, and $2,000,000 in new capital.[36] Finally, by persuading six "big" French financiers to join its board of directors, he successfully reorganized the company. In the end, however, he had become "heartily sick of things and quite ready to swear just as hard as I can at the way in which Mr Westinghouse has been bled over here and has paid people to bleed him too."[37]

But as he had done regularly even before Westinghouse's departure, the deputy manager searched for ways to ease his self-confessed brain fatigue and growing disillusionment with big business and its multimillion dollar deals. In London he frequently strolled from his apartment at Claridge's to Green Park and Parliament Square or, farther afield, wandered through the East End markets. Eschewing the nightly entertaining he had endured with Westinghouse, he still managed to attend dinners honoring Andrew Carnegie, Sir George Trevelyan, and Gertrude Atherton. On one occasion he visited Salvation Hall on the Strand to hear the preaching of General Booth and enjoy the lusty singing of three thousand Salvation Army members.[38]

In Paris, where he had fewer social contacts, he sought solitary recreation even more frequently: daytime walks through the Bois de Boulogne—evenings at the Opera or Folies Bergère—a trip on the Seine—reading the latest essays of Maurice Maeterlinck. Here, too, he could devote more time to his New York Life responsibilities, whether conferring with the Paris manager or translating a new insurance law. On one weekend he joined NYLIC officials in a trip to Lucerne, Bern, Lausanne, and Geneva. And whether in London, Paris, or the provincial cities, he managed almost every day to compose a letter to his family.[39]

SIOUX CITY CORN PALACES, 1887, 1888, 1889, 1890

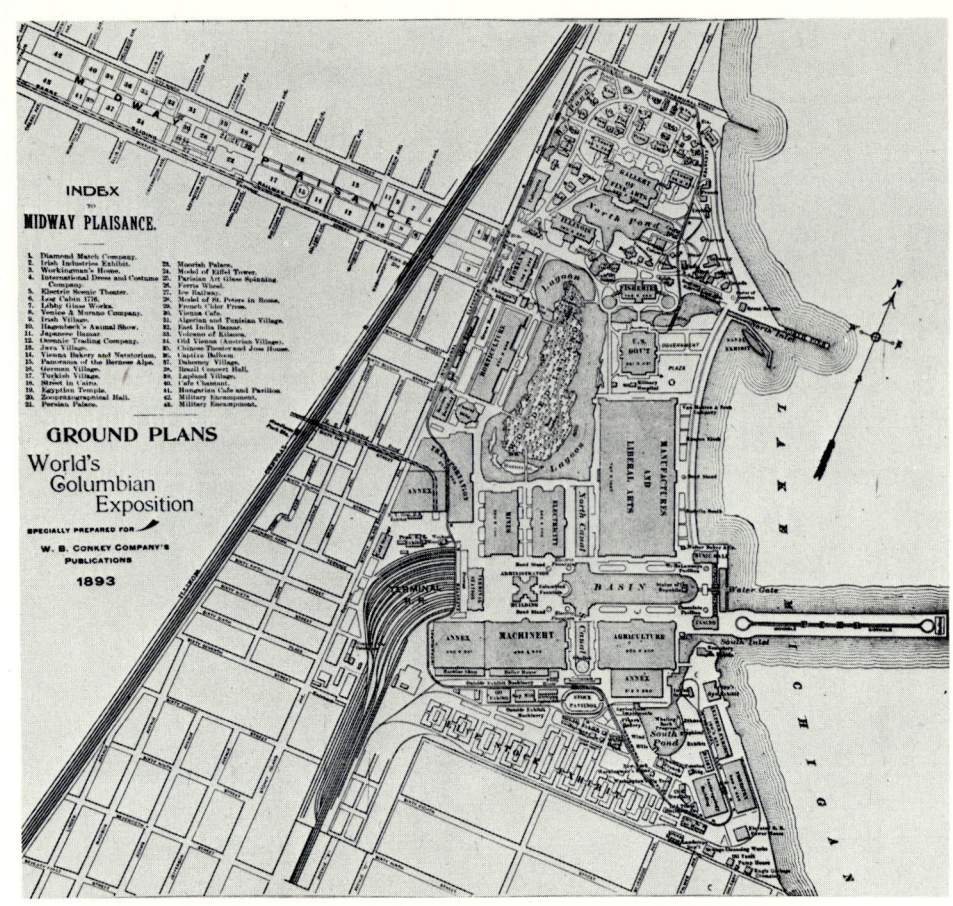

WORLD'S COLUMBIAN EXPOSITION, CHICAGO, 1893—Ground plan

WORLD'S COLUMBIAN EXPOSITION—Court of Honor facing west:
Agriculture Building (left), Daniel Chester French's statue of "The Republic"
(foreground), Columbian Fountain and Administration Building (rear),
Manufactures and Liberal Arts Building (right)

WORLD'S COLUMBIAN EXPOSITION—Replicas of Columbus's caravels at
anchor in Lake Michigan off exposition site

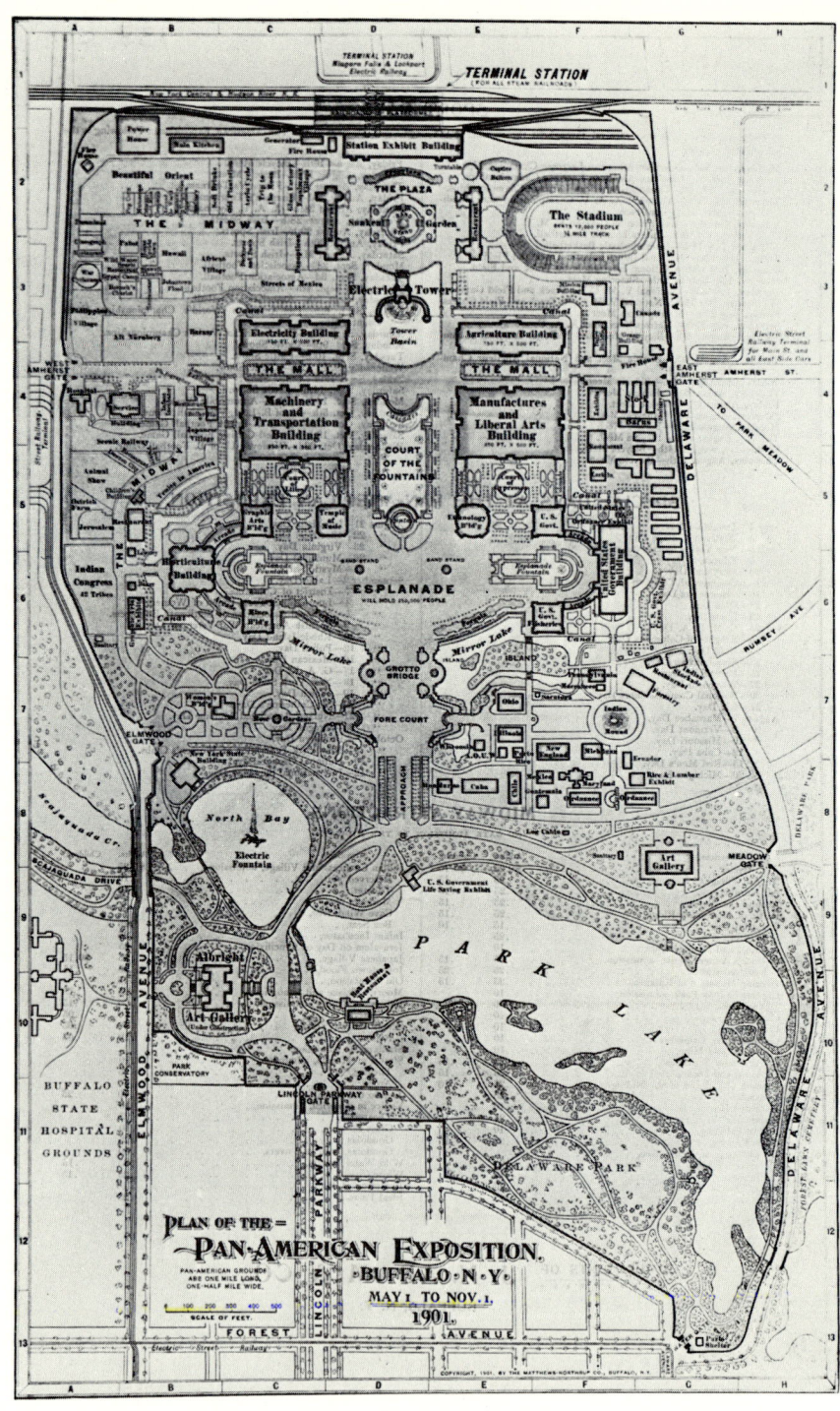

PAN-AMERICAN EXPOSITION, BUFFALO, 1903—Ground plan

PAN-AMERICAN EXPOSITION—The Electric Tower

PAN-AMERICAN EXPOSITION—President McKinley addressing audience in the Esplanade on September 5, the day before his assassination

IN ARGENTINA WITH FRIENDS—
Buchanan, Mrs. Buchanan, Donald (foreground), Florence (extreme right)

AT AN ARGENTINE ESTANCIA—
Florence Buchanan with her father

PAN-AMERICAN EXPOSITION—
Theme symbol known as Beck design

ELIHU ROOT—secretary of war, 1899-1904; secretary of state, 1905-1909

SECOND CONFERENCE OF THE INTERNATIONAL BUREAU OF AMERICAN REPUBLICS, MEXICO, 1901-1902—Sitting: U.S. delegates Volney Foster, Henry G. Davis, Buchanan; standing: Charles S. Pepper, John Barrett

THIRD CONFERENCE OF THE INTERNATIONAL BUREAU OF AMERICAN REPUBLICS, RIO DE JANEIRO, 1906—Sitting: U. S. delegates Paul S. Reinsch, Julio Larrinaga, Andrew J. Montague, Buchanan, Van Leer Polk (?), Leo S. Rowe; standing: aides, including Donald Buchanan (behind father)

CENTRAL AMERICAN PEACE CONFERENCE, Washington, 1907—
Delegates of the Central American Republics and (sitting center) Enrique
C. Creel, ambassador to the United States and representative of Mexico,
Luis Anderson, of Costa Rica, president of the conference, and Buchanan,
representative of the United States

INAUGURATION OF THE CENTRAL AMERICAN COURT OF JUSTICE,
CARTAGO, COSTA RICA, MAY, 1908—Judges representing the five
republics and (center) Luis Anderson, Costa Rican minister for foreign
affairs, flanked by Creel and Buchanan, high commissioners representing
Mexico and the United States

But nothing could diminish the enthusiasm with which Buchanan anticipated his return to the United States in early August. His home stay of two months reunited his family for the first time since their return from Panama in February. It also gave him the opportunity to try out the new family car, to assist his daughter's building plans, and to arrange his son's entry into the Mt. Pleasant Military Academy at Ossining on the Hudson.[40]

In addition Buchanan journeyed from one American city to another trying to disentangle his various business and diplomatic responsibilities. He met with Westinghouse for mutual briefings on the status of the enterprises in England and France and on the forthcoming annual meeting of British Westinghouse directors in London. He conferred with New York Life officials on their problems in Europe and South America. With New York bankers and a Panamanian representative he renewed negotiations on Panama's financial obligations to Colombia.[41]

In the midst of these diverse consultations Buchanan was happy to receive an October invitation to address the Thirteenth International Peace Congress in Boston. The expected participation of Secretary Hay, Samuel Gompers, Jane Addams, and more than a hundred European delegates excited his interest. At special sessions on "The Work and Influence of the Hague Tribunal," chaired by Andrew W. White, chairman of the United States delegation, the Buffalo diplomat was one of the principal speakers.[42]

Returning to London in mid-October, Buchanan undertook preparations for the scheduled British Westinghouse meeting. The still unsatisfactory performance of the Manchester plant presaged a confrontation. Prepared, however, to do little more than echo the reminders of his employer, the deputy chairman conducted a thrust-and-parry session on such matters as management economy, worker efficiency, pricing policy, and company plans.

When a shareholder asked, "Why should it be necessary to do so large a business to secure so small a profit?" Buchanan replied that "the works was evidently built . . . for the work that would one day come to it, be that day near or far."

"Why do expenditures continue to be abnormal? Have the works been planned on too large a scale?" Profiting from American experience, the management was seeking to perfect an establishment capable of satisfying the expected surge in use of electric generating equipment!

"What is the company's programme for the future?" In planning to maintain its branch offices and large selling force and to meet depreciation allowances, it would probably need to raise additional capital!

"Will the future bring greater profits?" In matters of business, prophecy has little value![43]

With these replies to shareholders' queries, Buchanan attempted to represent the management's point of view while casting the best possible light on a situation beset with difficulties. Yet, not even his diplomatic skills could parry one shareholder's gibe that "if we had known we were to build the works for posterity they would probably never have been built at all."[44]

Meanwhile, since his return from the United States, Buchanan had revived his activities on behalf of the New York Life Insurance Company. Following a request from Vice-President Perkins, he had begun to collect information on how the Russo-Japanese War had affected the economy of the imperial Russian government. In late November, working with London sources he believed credible, he had completed a lengthy estimate of the Russian financial situation.[45] And immediately after the British Westinghouse meeting in early December he made a special trip to St. Petersburg to gather first-hand intelligence for Perkins while at the same time inspecting the brake works of a Westinghouse subsidiary.

Perkins's interest in wartime Russia was a natural sequel to his earlier initiative in developing the tsarist nation as a market for both insurance policies and risk capital. In the late 1890s, while reorganizing NYLIC operations, he had worked closely with Finance Minister Sergei Witte on plans to secure American capital for Russian development. He had negotiated NYLIC purchase of bonds to expand the Trans-Siberian rail network and arranged flotation on the New York market of other Russian bond issues.[46] Now, in late 1904, he had a double purpose in utilizing Buchanan's services. Primarily, he desired immediate intelligence on the status of NYLIC's investment holdings and business operations. In addition, as an active power in the councils of Morgan and Company and the United States Steel Corporation, he was weighing the possibility of supplying Russia's wartime needs for loans, industrial equipment, and railroad rails and rolling stock.

During his December visit to St. Petersburg Buchanan attempted to fulfill Perkins's voracious appetite for timely information. After a private interview with Finance Minister Kokovsoff, the NYLIC representative reported the imperial official "ready and willing to give me any proper information that I might desire." Their conference ranged broadly over such topics as wartime budgets, gold reserves, monetary stability, and current status of NYLIC's railway securities. With officials of several railway companies he discussed plans for additional construction and potential demands for equipment.[47] From two United States military attachés, just returned from a twenty-six-day trip to the front in Manchuria, he learned of the condition and train-carrying capacity of the single-track Trans-Siberian Railroad.[48] Stopping in Paris on his return trip to London, Buchanan incorporated his findings in a series of lengthy situation estimates. With these he enclosed maps of the Russian railway system as well as copies of official government statements on annual revenue, tax policies, railroad earnings, and foreign trade.[49]

Buchanan's analyses led him to submit several conclusions. As to NYLIC's status, he found that "the general basic character of the railway securities held by the Company is excellent." As to the outlook for American sales, he saw a potential market for locomotives, ships, and shipbuilding equipment, if the orders were complemented by suitable bond sales in New York. As to the general outlook in Russia, he concluded that it is "one which need give no grave concern to us; but, on the contrary, . . . is one which, if we can take an intelligent advantage of conditions existing there, may be turned greatly to the advantage of our own people industrially, commercially and financially."[50]

But Buchanan was careful to temper his optimism with a

note of caution on Russia's developing domestic situation. In November 1904 the Zemstvo Congress had formulated its petition to Tsar Nicholas II for the establishment of representative government and the granting of political rights to all classes and nationalities. During Buchanan's visit to St. Petersburg the following month the tsar had issued his imperial ukase that he would consider the request for reforms.[51] "It can be taken for granted," the NYLIC representative wrote to Perkins, "that practically every intelligent person in Russia believes . . . that reforms in the interior administration of the Government are a necessity, the fulfillment of which must not be delayed"; yet they also doubted that the demands for peasant self-government would be granted.[52] Three weeks after he wrote, "Bloody Sunday" in St. Petersburg opened the door to Russia's 1905 revolution.

Upon returning to London, Buchanan renewed the Westinghouse duties that would principally occupy his attention for another year. Unfortunately neither company records, public archives, nor family papers reveal the precise nature of his activities during these months.[53] Yet he could hardly have ignored the insistent call he had heard at the annual meeting in December for "a little more common sense and economical management."[54] This could only have meant recommendations to Westinghouse on the need to improve labor efficiency, effect management economies, stimulate sales activities, and seek new capital.

Finally by November Westinghouse had determined to provide Buchanan the technical assistance he needed. He sent his first assistant, Newcomb Carlton, a vice-president of the American company, to join the English board as one of four managing directors. Though Carlton's investigations promptly led to recommendations for radical shifts in plant management and methods, they came too late to stifle the outcry Buchanan faced at the 1905 annual meeting. Again, as in 1904, he struggled to maintain shareholder confidence in his employer's plans and their company's future: "The fact that the works had not yet proved remunerative did not mean that they would not do so, should such strides take place in England as had recently been made in America."[55] But when he reported another disappointing year, without declaration of dividends, he heard only unreserved criticisms: "a huge shed at Manchester . . . , not there to face the music . . . , a sinking ship . . . , they had been trifled with."[56]

Director Buchanan's presence as presiding officer of the 1905 shareholders' session marked his last appearance at an annual company meeting. Two circumstances soon brought about his separation from the Westinghouse post. In early 1906 he accepted the State Department's invitation to undertake another special mission in Latin America—as chairman of the United States delegation to the Third International Conference of the American States.[57] And as Vice-President Carlton's recommendations brought in new American technicians to effect changes in the Manchester operations, the deputy chairman was gradually able to transfer his authority to colleagues.[58]

For the veteran of exposition management and sensitive diplomatic missions, the Westinghouse association had clearly not been the most satisfying or successful of his diverse undertakings. Yet, almost from the time of his arrival in London, as he repeatedly revealed in letters to his family, he sensed weaknesses in the overextension and faulty management of the far-flung Westinghouse empire. Clearly there were times when he felt both the helplessness and the hopelessness of his position. Without adequate authority or first-hand experience in industrial management, neither his diplomatic experience nor his *savoir faire* was able to overcome the twin obstacles that confronted him: the visionary plans of George Westinghouse and the conservatism of English railroad and industrial managers.[59]

During these months of heavy responsibilities to Westinghouse Buchanan gradually reduced his services to the New York Life Insurance Company, yet in his correspondence with Perkins he continued to manifest the loyalty he had developed through their years of intermittent association. When the Armstrong Committee investigations in late 1905 lowered a shadow over Perkins and precipitated his gradual withdrawal from NYLIC's management,[60] Buchanan's confidence in the vice-president's integrity never wavered.

Perkins's difficulties stemmed from his direct involvement in a $48,000 NYLIC contribution to the Republican National Committee during the 1904 presidential campaign. Though the gift was not illegal, his handling of the matter was looked upon as improper, and his subsequent indictment for larceny led to his resignation as NYLIC vice-president. "REGRET SEEING YOUR RESIGNATION REPORTED TODAY," Buchanan immediately cabled from London, "WILL CHANGE AFFECT OUR RELATIONS PLANNED?"[61] Five months later, when Perkins followed his acquittal of the larceny charge by resigning as NYLIC trustee, Buchanan wired again, "COURT CONCLUSION CONFIRMS WHAT EVERYONE KNEW WOULD BE RESULT. GLAD YOU ARE RELIEVED ANNOYANCE."[62]

Even the official end of Perkins's spectacular twenty-five-year career with NYLIC did not at once shut off his consultations with Buchanan about essential company business. When legislative reforms forced the great insurance companies to eliminate from their boards of trustees any members tainted by conflict-of-interest affiliations, the Buffalonian received the assignment of recruiting replacements. In close contact with the resigned vice-president, he sought to interest two former colleagues—John G. Milburn and Missouri Governor David R. Francis, one-time presidents of the Pan-American and Louisiana Purchase Expositions.[63] Before he could conclude these negotiations, however, Buchanan was called to Washington for presidential briefing on his new State Department assignment.[64]

Immediately following his conference at the White House he utilized a State Department letterhead to compose a "personal" note to Perkins. "I saw the President this morning," he wrote, "I gave him your message of thanks for his kindly reference to you during the past few months. He said many pleasant and kindly things of your good self which I know you would have greatly appreciated, and which you more than merit."[65] At that moment neither Buchanan nor Perkins could have foreseen an improbable sequel to President Roosevelt's approbation. During the 1912 presidential campaign he would endorse the one-time NYLIC vice-president as chairman of the nine-man Executive Committee of the Progressive National Committee.[66]

By June 1906 Buchanan was ready for another career shift.

Already he was heavily immersed in preparation for the Rio Conference, though he could also look forward to continuing indefinitely his unique consultant services for the New York Life. And looking back over his experience with Westinghouse, he could feel some solace that his two-year association was at an end. Separated as he had been from his family, the Buffalonian must have regarded these years as no better than an endurable interlude. Moreover, for the first time since his Columbian Exposition days, he had been almost completely cut off from the arena of his primary professional interest—Latin America and the improvement of inter-American relations. Now, however, as chairman of his country's delegation to the Rio Conference, he would have the opportunity to renew his association with Latin American leaders and the Pan American spirit he had sought to promote.

Chapter 14
FROM HEMISPHERE STAGE TO WORLD ARENA
Rio de Janeiro and The Hague, 1906-1907

Buchanan's two-year association with the Westinghouse Company was the last of his full-time commitments to private business. When he accepted the chairmanship of the United States delegation to the Third International Conference of the American States, he embarked upon a period of recurrent diplomatic duties that would make him virtually a career officer in the State Department's Foreign Service. As its principal envoy for crisis situations during the next three-and-a-half years, he would undertake no less than eight special assignments related to Latin American affairs. Between missions, and sometimes during them, he continued his occasional advisory consultations for the New York Life Insurance Company, but after 1906 he was regularly at the beck and call of President Roosevelt and Secretary of State Elihu Root.

From its first months in office the Roosevelt administration had faced problems created by the Spanish-American War and President McKinley's determination to establish a United States hegemony in the Caribbean. During Roosevelt's first term the actual shaping of policy toward the area had devolved mainly on John Hay and Elihu Root. As secretary of state, Hay had conducted all the essential treaty negotiations looking toward the construction of an isthmian canal,[1] while Secretary of War Root had contributed to the drafting of an organic law for Puerto Rico and the formulation of the Platt Amendment for Cuba.[2]

Except for the interest they had shown in the Mexico Conference of 1901-1902, Roosevelt and Hay had rarely looked southward beyond the Caribbean to project a larger Latin American policy. During the 1902 Anglo-German intervention in Venezuela, for example, they had spurned a friendly overture from Argentine Foreign Minister Luis Maria Drago that might greatly have altered the future complexion of the inter-American movement. Suggesting a kind of economic corollary to the Monroe Doctrine and a multilateral endorsement of its principles, Drago had declared "that the public debt can not occasion armed intervention nor even the actual occupation of the territory of American nations by a European power."[3] To perfect the machinery for American domination of the Caribbean and assure a protective screen for the future canal, President Roosevelt himself had overseen all action relating to those ends. In particular when he formulated his own corollary to the Monroe Doctrine in 1904, he had arrogated to the United States the international police power to arrest the chronic wrongdoing and impotence of weak Latin American states.

Meanwhile, as the Rooseveltian Caribbean policy expanded, the anti-Americanism which Buchanan had reported to Hay as early as 1898 continued to swell.[4] To make matters worse, Roosevelt, like Hay, held a low opinion of Latin American leaders and the governments they represented. Echoing the secretary's private estimate that their diplomats were "mostly dagoes & chargés," the president had once confided to Hay that American intervention in Venezuela would "show those Dagos that they will have to behave decently."[5] Though Root had contributed to both the Platt Amendment and the Roosevelt Corollary, he did not share his colleagues' disdain for the Latin Americans. "I really like them and intend to show it," he wrote to a senator, "I think their friendship is really important to the United States, and that the best way to secure it is by treating them like gentlemen."[6] This was the feeling he brought to the State Department in July 1905 and the conviction that would guide him throughout his tenure as secretary. It was a conviction that Buchanan could heartily endorse.

At no time in his career had Buchanan held the Latin American leaders in other than the highest esteem. From his first association with them during the Corn Palace and Columbian Exposition days he had liked and respected them. Through his long residence in Buenos Aires he had formed enduring friendships with distinguished Argentines. During the Pan-American Exposition he had worked intimately with delegates from all nations. Even while fulfilling missions for Roosevelt and Hay at Mexico City and Panama he had risen above what he must have sensed were their true feelings. On many occasions he had revealed his beliefs in the spirit of Pan Americanism.

Without reservation, therefore, Buchanan could support the "good neighbor" principles Secretary Root hoped to inject into Washington's relations with Hemisphere nations. In the view of one of Root's biographers, a leading historian of American foreign relations, the secretary undertook to infuse this new spirit by varied means: by developing friendships with certain Latin American diplomats; by cooperating with Mexico in efforts to keep peace in Central America; by arranging participation of the Latin American states in the Second Hague Conference; by attending the Rio Conference and touring South America; and by joining Mexico in sponsoring a Central American Peace Conference in Washington.[7] For all aspects of this program Buchanan would become Root's right-hand man.[8]

Upon returning from London in early 1906 the Buffalo diplomat immediately projected his plans for the Rio Conference. As delegation member at the Mexico Conference he had experienced the value of careful advance preparations. As chief of diplomatic missions to Argentina and Panama he had understood the necessity and utility of intimate interchange with the secretary of state. And as exposition manager he had mastered the administrative techniques for perfecting details without jeopardizing the grand design. Now, as the spearhead of Root's fresh approach to Hemisphere solidarity,[9] Buchanan would call upon this background of skills and experience.

Even before the administration had finally settled on delegation personnel, Buchanan was arranging ship schedules to Brazil and housing accommodations in its capital. He attended to matters of staff regulations and organization. Recalling his lack of documentary sources in Panama, he requested a lengthy list of books, pamphlets, and official records for delegation use.[10]

When he learned of a Senate proposal to increase United States representation from six to eight, he reminded Root that the Latin Americans would see this as "an attempt to rather crowd things a bit."[11] With these routine matters well in hand by mid-April Buchanan was able to revisit London and Paris to conclude his responsibilities to the British and French Westinghouse companies. Upon his return to Washington in early June, with delegation personnel now fixed, he could settle into final preparations for the Rio assembly.[12]

Almost at once the chairman called his five colleagues together for a preliminary planning session. Most widely known of the group was Andrew J. Montague, a former United States district attorney, who had just completed a four-year term as governor of Virginia. Van Leer Polk had been a member of the United States Consular Service. Tulio Larrinaga, a Puerto Rican civil engineer, was serving as the island's resident commissioner in Washington. Two professors of political science —Paul S. Reinsch of the University of Wisconsin and Leo S. Rowe of the University of Pennsylvania—completed the mission. Reinsch, onetime student in Berlin, Rome, and Paris, was the author of several distinguished legal and historical works. Rowe, who had worked on the codification of Puerto Rican laws, would later serve for many years as director of the Pan American Union.[13] The preliminary meeting left Buchanan and his colleagues no need to speculate on the nature of the Hemisphere problems they would face at Rio. The Governing Board of the Pan American Bureau had already prepared its official agenda and the State Department had compiled an extensive manual of background data.[14] Secretary Root was on hand to give them his personal briefing.[15]

As the only veteran of an earlier inter-American conference, Buchanan knew that arbitration, settlement of pecuniary claims, and reorganization of the Washington Bureau would be primary issues, but that several lesser problems might cause acrimonious debate. The political scientists were interested in the codification of international law, the unification of customs regulations, and the promotion of commerce.[16] But, mindful still of recent foreign threats against Venezuela and the Dominican Republic, all the delegates could anticipate that some action would be taken against forcible collection of public debts and that probably there would be a clash between the Monroe Doctrine, especially President Roosevelt's corollary, and the Argentine proposals of former Foreign Minister Drago.

In his written instructions to the delegates Root clearly revealed his desire to check mounting criticism from the Latin Americans and his determination to court their friendship. Though he paraphrased the conciliatory language of Roosevelt's instructions for the Mexico Conference, he went even further in seeking to forestall controversy in the Rio assembly. "Such a conference is not an agency for compulsion," he wrote, "or a tribunal for adjudication; . . . it should not sit in judgment upon the conduct of any State, or undertake to redress alleged wrongs, or to settle controverted questions of right." The true function of such a conference, he went on, "is to make such progress as may now be possible toward the acceptance of ideals the full realization of which may be postponed to a distant future."[17]

Though the secretary reflected this mollifying tone in his suggestions on specific agenda items, he did not overlook the tactical actions the delegates might need to call upon. As to the pecuniary claims convention, to which Buchanan had contributed so heavily at Mexico City, Root hoped that it might be extended for five years and urged efforts to secure the adherence of additional nations. On the matter of a general arbitration treaty, he directed the delegates to seek Latin American adherence to the Hague Convention, an option the United States had made possible by intercession with the original signatory powers.[18] Success in these directions might forestall expected Latin American pressure at Rio for compulsory arbitration of broad scope.

Similarly, on the delicate issue of Hemisphere policy toward the use of force in the collection of public debts, Root pressed the delegates to work for its transfer to the Second Hague Conference. Even while paying tribute to Drago's "excellent" 1902 suggestions, he argued against Pan American action on the subject. "Most of the American countries are still debtor nations," he alleged, "while the countries of Europe are the creditors. If the Rio Conference, therefore, were to take such action, it would have the appearance of a meeting of debtors resolving how their creditors should act, and this would not inspire respect."[19] At The Hague debtors could face their creditors in an open forum, to which, Buchanan and his colleagues remembered, Root had recently secured invitations for the Latin American states.

Clearly circumscribed by Root's instructions on these and other agenda items, yet buoyed by their conciliatory tone and reassured by his own experience at Mexico City, Buchanan could feel some confidence as he and his colleagues departed New York for Rio on 2 July. Accompanied by Mrs. Buchanan and Donald, now approaching eighteen, as personal secretary, Will at first felt disappointment that they were not retracing the usual itinerary to South America—via England by big trans-Atlantic steamship. The forty-passenger *Byron,* however, with lines more like a millionaire's yacht than a cargo ship, proved extremely comfortable, well suited to sociability among the American delegates, their counterparts from other nations, and the quartet of journalists who accompanied them.[20] Moreover, after four years of fairly constant overseas living without his family, Will could revel in this unusual opportunity to be together. Now, sailing southward on summer seas, they prepared to enjoy eighteen days of shipboard leisure, while anticipating the delights of Rio and a postconference side trip to visit friends and former haunts in Buenos Aires.[21]

The Brazilian capital at which the Buchanans and their shipmates arrived on 21 July was not yet "the most beautiful city in the world" enthusiasts would one day dub it. Choked with antiquated houses, narrow streets, winding alleys, and cobblestone pavements, the old city still retained much of its sleepy colonial character. Moreover, though renowned scientists were making headway in their fight against epidemic disease, Rio's 600,000 residents were not yet completely freed from the threats of smallpox, yellow fever, and bubonic plague. Nevertheless, Rio was not the same city Buchanan had known four years before. Ambitious carioca leaders had recently begun to realize an extensive program of modernization. By levelling blocks of old buildings they had driven a broad new avenue through the heart of the business district. Adorning it with flowerbeds, palm trees, new arc lights, and broad mosaic sidewalks, they had extended the mall-like artery several miles along the burgeoning water front. Beyond, for the new city as for the old, lay incomparable Guanabara Bay, with its green islands, unexcelled beaches, and scenic backdrop of palm-covered hills and thinly veiled mountain pinnacles.[22]

Conspicuous among the new structures along the Avenida Central was the edifice that would house all the conference sessions, a building Buchanan readily recognized as Brazil's contribution to St. Louis's Louisiana Purchase Exposition. After 1904 it had been dismantled, transported section by section from its Missouri setting, and reerected in the heart of Rio's parkway development. Only hours before the arrival of the American delegation workmen had completed their refurbishing of the "Monroe Palace," as it would come to be called, and the landscaping of its environs.[23]

All these sights of the old and the new Rio the Buchanans and other Americans began to enjoy as they rode from dockside through city streets, then up to the mountain retreat of Petropolis, residential annex for Rio's leaders. Here, above the disadvantages of the seaside capital, most of the delegates made their headquarters while commuting for conference sessions, social affairs, and sightseeing.

Whatever its blending of the colonial and the modern, Rio, the city, was not Brazil, the nation. And Brazil in 1906 was not so much a nation as a congeries of regions. Heavily settled in its coastal areas, its back country still largely unexploited, the sprawling giant was seeking to pull itself together and find its place in the Western Hemisphere. For a passing phase at least, the only Portuguese-speaking state in the inter-American organization had determined to align its foreign policy close to that of the United States, the only English-speaking one. Implementation of this decision rested largely upon the initiative and creativeness of a respected Brazilian statesman, Joaquim Nabuco, first to serve his country as ambassador to the United States. In the intimacy he developed with President Roosevelt and Secretary Root Brazilian-American friendship quickly flowered.[24]

Ambassador Nabuco had arrived in Washington to present

his credentials just six weeks before Root assumed the secretaryship of state. Veteran of Brazilian public life and prime mover in the emancipation of Brazilian slaves, he had served as minister to London since 1900. Long an advocate of shifting Brazil's foreign policy axis from London to Washington, he relished the opportunity to further his beliefs. "I am an ardent 'Monroist,' " he had written to Foreign Minister Rio Branco, "and for that reason a partisan of the ever increasing harmony between Brazil and the United States." In Nabuco's view, the great barriers to Brazilian-American friendship were American indifference to Brazil, Brazilian suspicion of the United States, and in each country a yawning ignorance of the other.[25]

Once Secretary Root had determined to improve Washington's relations with Latin America, it was natural that he respond to the warm overtures of Nabuco.[26] Had he not come to Washington, Roosevelt once told the ambassador, "Mr. Root would not be going to Brazil, because his decision to go was caused by the impressions which [you] made upon him."[27] By July 1906, after a year of diplomatic courtship, circumstances made the presence of the two men at the Rio Conference seem foreordained — Root to become an honorary president and Nabuco its presiding officer.

The Buchanans were old hands at experiencing the pomp and pageantry of an inter-American conference's formal inauguration; nevertheless they enjoyed Rio's exuberant welcome to its foreign guests — the troop-lined approaches to the Monroe Palace, the gaily illuminated grounds and adjacent parkways, and the demonstrations of eager crowds. Joining conference colleagues and Brazilian dignitaries in the opening session on 23 July, the Americans heard Foreign Minister Rio Branco's welcoming address and witnessed the election of Joaquim Nabuco as permanent president.[28] Like most of the audience probably, the Buffalonians were surprised and pleased at the first official action taken by the conference. An Argentine delegate proposed a special vote of thanks to the United States and Mexico for their success in conciliating a recent dispute among Guatemala, Honduras, and El Salvador. A few days later Buchanan would have the satisfaction of reporting President Roosevelt's cablegram of appreciation.[29]

With the conference decision to restrict controversy to committee rooms, President Nabuco's appointments became a matter of key import to Buchanan and his delegation colleagues.[30] As promptly as seemed appropriate, they advised Nabuco of the committee assignments for which they deemed themselves best qualified. In accordance with their own prior agreement, they proposed Buchanan for membership on three of the committees in which the United States had the most vital stake — those on a general arbitration treaty, arbitration of pecuniary claims, and forcible collection of public debts. In taking this action on behalf of their chairman, the Americans had recognized his tactful handling of the arbitration proposals at the Mexico Conference. Almost without exception Nabuco made the appointments requested. Buchanan would serve on the three for which his colleagues had named him, as well as on that for rules and credentials.[31]

While the conference was arranging these organizational details, the United States cruiser *Charleston* was steaming southward along the Brazilian coast with Secretary Root and his family. After stops at Pará (Belem), Nabuco's home town of Pernambuco (Recife), and Bahía (São Salvador), the American vessel entered Rio harbor in the early morning of 27 July to the salutes of a harbor fortress and the warships of several nations. Soon greeted on board by the American ambassador, Nabuco, and other Brazilians, the visitors were rowed ashore on the same sixty-four-oared barge that in 1808 had welcomed Dom João from Portugal. As hundreds of small craft plied the harbor and guns reiterated their welcome, the Roots began a two-hour triumphal drive through crowd-lined streets to their temporary Rio residence.[32]

For the next seven days, sometimes accompanied by his family and the other Americans, the secretary was all but engulfed in a ceaseless demonstration of carioca hospitality. Between formal affairs, the Roots enjoyed a steamer cruise around the bay and drives to Petropolis and up the jagged peak of Corcovado. They went to the theater and at the races watched a horse named E. Root finish out of the money.[33] Like the other Americans, the Buchanans did not participate in every phase of these festivities. Will was heavily saddled with preliminary work for his four committees as well as with the leadership of his delegation. Many of the functions were for men only. But when protocol required or invitation permitted, both the Buchanans were eager participants in Rio's effusive salutation to the secretary.[34]

Amid all the ceremony and regalement Root found time to meet informally with the United States Embassy staff and to confer at length with his conference delegates. Buchanan was especially eager that they learn the secretary's last-minute views on the Drago Doctrine and other salient matters.[35]

The culmination of Root's Rio week and the pivotal purpose of his visit was his formal appearance before the conference on 31 July. At the Monroe Palace his Brazilian hosts had arranged a brilliant setting. Thousands of marching students formed a torchlight parade before the building's entrance. Other thousands carried multicolored paper lanterns atop oscillating canelike poles. On the landing above the central stairway, awaiting the honored guests, were gathered the diplomatic corps, the conference delegates, and high Brazilian officials. At the center, as the principal host, stood the conference president, Joaquim Nabuco.[36]

To receive the Brazilian foreign minister and the American secretary of state—the honorary conference presidents—Nabuco had appointed two committees. Governor Montague and six Latin American delegates waited on the Baron of Rio Branco, while to welcome Secretary Root Buchanan headed a group of five Latin American ministers to the United States.[37] There followed two items of singular interest to the Americans. In his welcoming remarks Foreign Minister Rio Branco announced that, in Root's honor, the building in which they were meeting would henceforth be known as the Palácio Monroe. Later, in paying his own tribute to Root, Nabuco informed the assembly that the secretary's appearance in Rio marked the first time an American secretary of state had paid an official visit to a foreign country.[38]

Root's speech to the conference has become the most frequently quoted of his South American tour. Reflecting his long forethought, he intended it to be the touchstone of the "good neighbor" attitude he was trying to stimulate and the new Latin

American policy he was seeking to evolve. Recalling his Washington conversations with Nabuco, he stressed the necessity "of doing away with the misconceptions, the misunderstandings, and the resultant prejudices that are such fruitful sources of controversy."[39] Buchanan and his colleagues could remember the limitations of the secretary's confidential instructions when they heard him say that "no great and impressive single thing is to be done by you; no political questions are to be discussed; ... You labor more for the future than for the present." And to counter the antiimperialist invectives Latin American critics had been voicing since 1898, Root concentrated the essence of his message in the assurances that "we wish for no victories but those of peace; for no territory except our own; for no sovereignty except the sovereignty over ourselves."[40]

After several more days of carioca hospitality the Roots boarded the *Charleston* for their journey to southern Brazil, Uruguay, Argentina, and the west coast countries. Before leaving Rio the secretary had written to Roosevelt that he fully appreciated the evanescence of the demonstrations his visit had produced. "But I have no doubt," he added, "that there will be a residuum of friendly feelings and of confidence in our kindly feelings, left in place of the widespread distrust which seems to characterize South American opinion regarding the purposes and attitudes of the United States."[41] Already deeply involved in committee meetings and plenary sessions, the American representatives would soon be able to test his prophecy.

On the issue of a general arbitration treaty, Buchanan soon learned, several nations still adhered to the compulsory feature that had caused him so much difficulty five years before.[42] Now, however, along with the majority, he could argue that Latin American presence at the next Hague meeting placed the entire subject in new light. Without a Rio commitment to inhibit it, each nation would be able to propose and support the kind of world convention it wished. With this argument Buchanan was able to assure a unanimous committee report for conference consideration. The resolution as adopted proclaimed "adherence to the principle of arbitration" and recommended that each nation instruct its delegates to The Hague to work for a "general arbitration convention."[43]

The committee on arbitration of pecuniary claims experienced less difficulty. Buchanan realized that the compromise arrangement he had effected at Mexico City had been ratified by only nine nations. He was wholly satisfied, therefore, when the conference agreed to extend the treaty for five years in the hope of securing additional adherents.[44]

It was on forcible collection of public debts that Buchanan's diplomatic skills were most sternly tested. From the outset he faced a dual responsibility. Elected chairman of the committee and named to its subcommittee for drafting a resolution, he bore the charge of finding a formula that would produce committee unanimity.[45] Yet as chairman of the American delegation, duty required him to support Root's instructions to work for transfer of the question to The Hague.

Among the American nations there was no controversy in principle over a policy of proscribing European intervention to collect public debts. Disagreement arose only over the manner in which the policy should be presented to the nations of the world.[46] The Drago Doctrine had proposed an unconditional Western Hemisphere policy of resistance to any European intervention to collect debts. President Roosevelt's corollary to the Monroe Doctrine sought the same end, but in effect claimed for the United States the exclusive right to employ intervention, if necessary, to interdict European use of force.[47]

Other nations, however, questioned the wisdom of both the Argentine and American proposals. Some of the debtor countries, as Root had foreseen, wished to refrain from any action that might embarrass them with their creditors.[48] Eventually, however, two circumstances enabled Chairman Buchanan to find a compromise solution. Argentina's delegation, upon which Drago had refused to serve, now veered from the doctrine that bore his name. It took the position "that prohibition of force to collect public debts was properly a matter for jurisdiction of world law, not regional policy."[49] This shift opened the door for Buchanan. He could now argue more forcefully for Root's suggestion that the matter be transferred to The Hague. The Washington and Buenos Aires chanceleries had reached essential agreement: the conference should not proclaim a Hemisphere policy on the issue. It fell to Buchanan's lot, therefore, to frame a resolution with which no nation could disagree. His proposal went no further than to recommend to each American government that it invite the Hague Conference to consider the question. As committee chairman, he presented the resolution to a plenary conference session and moved its unanimous approval.[50]

With the other major actions of the conference Buchanan had less direct connection. Here his main responsibility was to round up the views of his American colleagues and cast delegation votes.[51] But to whatever degree these measures extended decisions he had supported at Mexico City, promoted the Pan American spirit, or strengthened inter-American solidarity, Buchanan found personal satisfaction. He was especially pleased, therefore, to register American votes in favor of resolutions that would make the Bureau of the American Republics more permanent, broaden its scope, and increase its efficiency.[52]

On a number of secondary matters Buchanan was able to contribute substantially. Two of these involved initiatives taken at the Mexico Conference. First, he presented the report of the Permanent Pan American Railway Committee, which had been chaired since the second conference by his colleague at Mexico City, Henry G. Davis. When the conference moved to continue the committee's work, Buchanan found himself appointed to its membership.[53] The other item related to the memorial voted to honor two Colombian explorers, Nestor and Enrique Reyes, who had died in the jungles of interior South America. Buchanan had been given the assignment of arranging a bronze tablet for their tomb in the National Cathedral in Bogotá. Upon receiving his report that he had fulfilled the mission in April 1905, his fellow delegates voted him their special thanks.[54]

When on 16 August multiple earthquake shocks shattered Valparaiso, Buchanan took the lead in sponsoring a conference resolution of condolence to the Chilean people. Recalling his own country's catastrophe at San Francisco a few months earlier, he could remark with feeling that

> the tremor of the earth sounds a responsive chord upon the better nature and sentiments of all people, so that today, not only in this assembly, but everywhere in the world the sympathy, the cordial feeling of brotherly good-will on the part of all is extended towards those, who in Valparaiso

are brought to suffer through the horrors of untimely death, the wreck of fortune and the destruction of years of patient and industrious effort.

Willingly he responded to the request of conference colleagues that he collect and transmit to Chile their personal contributions to a relief fund.[55]

By driving to complete their work within a month the delegates found less time for social activities than had their predecessors at Mexico City. Yet, when opportunity offered, the three Buchanans were happy to share Brazil's generous hospitality. Besides the usual round of dinners, balls, receptions, and concerts, they enjoyed a tour of Rio's famed Botanical Gardens, and, like the Roots before them, a cruise around the bay and excursions up the peak of Corcovado and to the mountains beyond.[56] For the Americans their own delegation dinner was the highlight of the social calendar. The guest list included Brazil's president, vice-president, and cabinet ministers, as well as state governors, city prefects, and local and foreign journalists. In advance of the dinner Buchanan felt obliged to cable Secretary Root that the affair's $3,700 cost would exceed their budgetary allowance by $1,200.[57] If this confession caused him some chargin, his discomfort must have been eased at the dinner when Nabuco paid him unexpected tribute. Buchanan's tact during the conference, said the Brazilian, had forestalled the least display of discord.[58]

The Third International Conference of the American States held its last session on 27 August. To give the delegates a Brazilian farewell, the Baron of Rio Branco returned to the rostrum. But the foreign minister left to the popular Nabuco the real summation of the conference achievements. "The political observer who interprets these events," he asserted,

> ... will see the inception of a new spirit, on the formation of which the real worth of these conferences depends, as well as the creation of American solidarity. ... The Pan American Union came of age in this Third Congress. ... The general aspiration of the entire continent is to form one sole community in all matters of international law and for all the common interests of our civilization.[59]

By their gestures at these final ceremonies Buchanan's Latin American colleagues recognized the central role he had played throughout the meetings. At the outset President Nabuco appointed him to a committee of four to welcome the foreign minister. The Uruguayan delegate who responded to Rio Branco's remarks paid special tribute to the United States and the conduct of its delegation. And all the delegates united in selecting the American to prepare and present their effusive resolution of thanks to Brazil and its government officials.[60]

At this point at least the Buffalo diplomat could feel reasonably confident that he and his colleagues had justified Secretary Root's faith in them. Nothing in their actions had violated his admonition that they should not "sit in judgment upon the conduct of any State" or seek "to accomplish any striking or spectacular final results." Scrupulously they had complied with his counsel that they work "toward the acceptance of ideals the full realization of which may be postponed to a distant future."[61] Under Buchanan's leadership they had minimized showdown debate over sensitive political issues and successfully secured transfer to The Hague of the two most potentially explosive bones of contention. At the outset of the conference Root's soothing assurances had helped to allay the recent surge of Latin American suspicion and mistrust and smooth the way for the American delegation, but in the debates it was Buchanan who had served as overseer of the secretary's new design for restoring Latin American good will.

With his long experience in dealing with their leaders and his knowledge of Latin American character, Buchanan must have realized that much of the oratory at Rio was no more than conference rhetoric or restatement of faded dreams. At the same time, a number of conference actions had revealed the growth of a genuine community of interest, a developing trend toward inter-American cooperation, and an increasing realization of the need to safeguard continental security. Essential steps had been taken to strengthen the Bureau of the American Republics and to enhance its authority. And there had also been considerable ploughing of new soil, particularly in plans to codify international law, to improve Hemisphere sanitary arrangements, and to clarify the status of naturalized citizens.[62]

If Buchanan chose to analyze his own role in the conference, he must have found abundant personal satisfaction in the recognition accorded him by the Latin American delegates. Clearly they had looked to him as a veteran of inter-American diplomacy. He had lived among them, learned to appreciate their problems, and tried to understand the issues that faced them. They trusted his judgment and conciliatory skills. For them he represented a continuity in Hemisphere relations unmatched by any other delegate.

While awaiting their ship's departure for Buenos Aires, the Buchanans found time to relax from their strenuous official and social duties. They said farewell to the other American delegates and reluctantly watched Donald board ship to return for the fall semester of his American school.[63] Will used the opportunity to write letters of appreciation to the clerks and telephone operators who had served the delegates at the Monroe Palace and to the officials of Brazilian postal, telegraph, and railway services.[64]

The Buchanans' visit to Buenos Aires in early September was not the occasion of unmixed satisfaction they had anticipated. The two-week stay did provide pleasant moments with old friends and fresh views of familiar scenes, but former President Roca, in whose inauguration Will had shared, was out of the country, and two of his predecessors in office, Bartolomé Mitre and Carlos Pellegrini, had died only months before.[65] Other officials with whom Will had worked closely—former Foreign Minister Alcorta and former Minister to the United States García Mérou—were no longer living. An even darker cloud, however, was cast over their visit by an unexpected news story from the Brazilian capital they had just left: the Rio government had signed contracts with British shipyards for the construction of three modern battleships.[66] This direct threat to long-cherished Argentine naval supremacy in the South Atlantic provoked immediate alarm among government officials and porteño newspapers.[67] In view of the harmonious spirit which had prevailed at the Rio meeting, the announcement came as a shock to Buchanan as to the Argentines.

Though now without official portfolio, Buchanan discussed the problem with a porteño businessman and confidant of ranking government officials, Ernesto Tornquist. And, as he promised he would do, immediately upon his return to Rio in late September the American conferred with Foreign Minister Rio Branco and other influential Brazilian leaders. As a result of these conversations and his own observations, he prepared for Tornquist a lengthy hand-written analysis of the escalating situation.[68] Certain pressure groups in Argentina, Buchanan wrote, including elements of the press, scented a hidden objective in Brazil's naval rearmanent plans. In response, Rio's leaders resented Argentina's attempts to discredit Brazil's sincerity. Each side suspected the other of expansionist ambitions, especially toward the buffer states of Uruguay and Paraguay. Each imagined the other to be seeking dominance in South American affairs. But Brazil, in Buchanan's view, was in no position to undertake imperialist adventures. Its sprawling expanse, its extensive coast line, and its small and unintegrated population "furnish now, and will for years to come, a task for her public men to accomplish that will tax their abilities and resources to the utmost." Brazil needs complete peace, Buchanan reassured Tornquist, and its rearmanent program is only an attempt to rebuild the naval strength destroyed in its civil war.[69]

Several weeks later Tornquist cabled Buchanan in New York that he had submitted copies of this analysis to the president, foreign minister, and a dozen other Argentine officials. "YOUR COMMUNICATIONS HAVE CAUSED AN *EXCELLENT IMPRESSION* HERE AND I CAN ASSURE YOU THAT A VERY FAVORABLE CHANGE HAS COME ABOUT WITH REGARD TO THE FEELING TOWARD BRAZIL."[70] In Rio, on the other hand, however well-intentioned Buchanan's initiative, his interposition met with a cool reception. In analyzing press reaction, the American ambassador reported to Washington that "Brazil would not welcome any suggestion, however friendly on our part, which would tend to discourage the increase of her naval armament." Labelled "officious" by a journalist, Buchanan's unofficial overtures went for naught.[71] The Argentine-Brazilian naval rivalry would continue.[72]

Soon after the Buchanans returned from Rio in late October, Will went to Washington to fulfill a debriefing appointment with Secretary Root, who had himself returned only a month before from his South American tour. Root immediately made clear that his plans for Buchanan did not stop with his work at the Rio Conference. New developments in the Caribbean area were demanding attention. Buchanan would soon find himself involved again in the still unsettled relationship between Panama and Colombia.[73]

But before he could take up this new assignment, the Buffalonian became enmeshed in another Caribbean trouble spot, Cuba. Within three weeks of his return from Rio, he went off to Havana, ostensibly on a private mission for Cuban-American banking interests.[74] His arrival coincided with an uncertain, even precarious, phase in the island's status as a self-governing nation. Three months before, civil strife had forced the resignation of President Estrada Palma. Two months earlier Secretary of War William Howard Taft and Assistant Secretary of State Robert Bacon had arrived to assess the situation. Two thousand United States Marines had soon followed. Now, at the time of Buchanan's visit, 6,000 American troops patrolled the streets of Havana and other cities. Charles E. Magoon had become provisional governor.[75]

Journalists in Havana, however, refused to accept at face value Buchanan's stated purpose for his visit. Convinced that his banker's role was a mere cover, they saw him as the envoy of Roosevelt and Root, commissioned by them to investigate the entire Cuban situation and recommend an American policy on Cuba's future status. Indeed, they noted that "the movement for a protectorate is slowly growing and would sweep the country if Mr. Buchanan should even whisper the opinion that an emphatic demand that the Americans remain might make it possible of realization."[76]

Interviewed by inquiring reporters when he returned to New York in late November, Buchanan refused to discuss the Cuban situation. Beyond the view that general elections should be postponed, he would give no opinion on Cuban politics nor would he speculate on how long American occupation should continue.[77] That same day, however, in advising Root of an anticipated trip to Washington, he wrote, "I will be ready to take up the Colombian matter then if that is your wish and I shall be especially glad to have an opportunity to give you my impressions of the Cuban mess."[78]

Early in December, as he had promised, Buchanan agreed to undertake preliminary negotiations on the Colombian problem. Since 1903 Bogotá's bitter resentment over the Panamanian revolt and American acquisition of the Canal Zone seemed gradually to have abated. Rafael Reyes, Buchanan's correspondent of 1904, now president, and other leaders seemed ready to consider a fresh approach. After conversations with Colombian and Panamanian representatives at Rio, Panama, and Cartagena, Root had determined to reopen discussions on the long-stalemated problems. His design for resolving the lingering impasse consisted of a tripartite system of treaties. If ratified, they would restore friendship between the United States and Colombia, institute amicable relations between Colombia and Panama, and clarify the American position in Panama.[79]

During the next six months, while commuting between Buffalo and Washington, Buchanan conferred frequently with the Colombian and Panamanian ministers, Enrique Cortés and J. Domingo de Obaldía—usually with one, sometimes with both. Occasionally all met with Root. The American representative promptly recognized revised versions of issues he had confronted as minister to Panama in 1903-1904: Colombian recognition of Panamanian independence, Panamanian payments on Colombia's foreign debt, determination of boundary limits, and adjustment of reciprocal tariffs.[80] Gradually, through "a great number of interviews," he was able to narrow the gulf separating their resolute national positions.[81]

Capitalizing on Buchanan's conciliatory preliminaries, Root by April 1907 prepared to suggest specific treaty terms.[82] Even before this time, however, he had selected his veteran envoy for another sensitive mission—delegate to the Hague Conference. After accepting this appointment, Buchanan gradually withdrew from his second round of efforts to resolve the administration's Colombian problem and left its settlement in the hands of other negotiators.[83]

While pursuing these protracted negotiations in Washington, Buchanan was able to interpolate a variety of personal activities. In early December he was pleased when Roosevelt devoted more than two thousand words in his state-of-the-union message to summarizing and applauding the work of the Rio Conference.[84] In mid-January he addressed a national convention called by the New York Board of Trade and Transportation to consider the expansion of foreign commerce. Before a gathering of some eight hundred delegates in Washington he shared the rostrum with Root, former Secretary of State John W. Foster, former New York City Mayor Seth Low, and other national figures.[85] Back home in Buffalo in mid-February he entertained Joaquim Nabuco, when the Brazilian ambassador come to address a local gathering on the "Lessons and Prophecies of the Recent Pan American Conference."[86] Later in the month he could rejoice in the formal appearance of his delegation report on the Rio meeting, upon which he and his colleagues had worked intermittently since October.[87] In April he served as member of the general committee for the National Arbitration and Peace Congress in New York. Andrew Carnegie was its president, William H. Taft and Charles Evans Hughes among its several vice-presidents, and a long list of national leaders among its sponsors.[88] Some weeks later, as a professional consultant to its sponsors, he spent three days at the Jamestown Tercentennial Exposition, then in its final stages of preparation.[89] And when time permitted, he carried on his part-time duties for the New York Life Insurance Company.

But, personally satisfying as were these diverse activities, Buchanan was looking forward to the larger challenge offered by the Hague Conference and the opportunities it presented to renew his efforts on behalf of Root's new Latin American policy. The secretary, too, saw the Hague assembly as an essential corollary to the "good neighbor" proposition he had initiated by his visit to Rio and his South American tour.

Though Latin America was by no means the sole focus of Root's interests in the Hague meeting, he had overlooked no step to assure its active participation. By securing postponement of the world assembly he had made possible the attendance of Latin American representatives and their adherence to the 1899 Convention for Pacific Settlement of International Disputes. In fulfillment of specific American commitment at Rio he had reserved the right to introduce at The Hague the unresolved question of forcible collection of public debts. To avoid exacerbation of Argentine-Brazilian rivalry he had urged American delegates to work for distribution of conference posts to Portuguese Americans as well as to Spanish Americans. And, as if to cap these deferential measures, he appointed Buchanan to the American delegation and charged him with "the special duty of doing all he can to help the Latin Americans in this appearance on their part as members of the world family."[90]

But, indispensable as his role might become for the nations of the Western Hemisphere, Buchanan obviously would not be the dominant figure in the American delegation. Headed by Joseph H. Choate, former ambassador to London, it comprised three commissioners plenipotentiary with the rank of ambassador and four, including Buchanan, with the rank of minister plenipotentiary. Among these were a former ambassador to France, the current minister to the Netherlands, the judge advocate general of the United States Army, and a former president of the Naval War College.[91]

Moreover, Buchanan's special competencies in international affairs did not extend to such Hague agenda items as limitation of armaments, rules of maritime warfare, laws and customs of war on land, and rights and duties of neutrals.[92] When, therefore, the delegates met with Root on 20 April, Buchanan took little part in the discussions. In the main he restricted his commentary to the two issues that most troubled the Latin Americans: forcible collection of public debts, including the Drago Doctrine, and arbitration of international disputes.[93] In any case, his role at The Hague would be that of liaison between the Latin American representatives and the leaders of his own delegation, not that of floor tactician which he had filled at Rio.

Because of his involvement in the negotiations with Colombia and his commitment to the Jamestown Exposition, Buchanan did not sail for Europe until 5 June—later than all other American delegates—and only ten days before the conference opening. His belated departure enabled him to accept Root's invitation to convey the official delegation instructions of 21 May to Joseph Choate.[94]

As they had on similar occasions at Mexico City and Rio, the

Buchanans enjoyed the pomp and ceremony of the opening conference festivities at The Hague. Gathered in the great banqueting room of the historic Hall of Knights in the ancient Binnenhof, a distinguished group of world leaders received the welcome of their Dutch hosts.[95] Among the delegates were fifteen current or past ministers of state, sixteen ambassadors, forty-seven ministers, more than fifty military and naval experts, and nearly as many jurists and professors.[96] Of the forty-four nations represented, Buchanan found satisfaction in noting, seventeen were Latin American, and their spokesmen included such veteran statesmen as Drago and Saenz Peña of Argentina, Ruy Barbosa of Brazil, and José Batlle y Ordóñez of Uruguay.

In a personal note to Root ten days later, Buchanan was able to report that "the Conference is in working order. . . . The impression I receive from the machine is that it is a very large town meeting with all of the latent possibilities of such a gathering for doing matured or immatured things."[97] By that time the conference leaders had organized and staffed four commissions, each to deal with several agenda topics. To facilitate Buchanan's access to the Latin Americans with whom he would be working, the American delegation had succeeded in securing his appointment to each of the four commissions.[98]

The official proceedings of the conference record no speeches by Buchanan, either in committee or plenary sessions, no casting of delegation votes.[99] His work, rather, was behind the scenes—rounding up the opinions and probable votes of the Latin American delegates, relaying their views and intentions to Chairman Choate, interpreting the American position on key issues, offering counsel or discussing alternatives.

As to the conference agenda itself, Buchanan's Western Hemisphere orientation in world affairs obviously focused his attention on the three issues which most concerned the Latin Americans—forcible collection of public debts, a general arbitration treaty, and the proposal for a permanent Court of Arbitral Justice. The first and second of these had been transferred to The Hague largely through his efforts at Rio;[100] the third involved Root's special instruction to his own delegation.[101] Buchanan must have been pleased, therefore, when the Latin Americans entered actively into floor debates on all three items.

On the public-debt question, for example, the Argentine Drago wasted no time in introducing his controversial doctrine. Resolutely and eloquently he argued that, in the Western Hemisphere at least, forceful intervention should be unconditionally proscribed.[102] Whatever Buchanan's personal feelings on the matter, he had no choice but to support the American position that the use of force is permissible if a nation should refuse to arbitrate or abide by an arbitral decision. In the end, all but one of the Latin American nations voted for the American proposition, but Argentina and others did so only with reservations supporting the integrity of the Drago arguments.[103]

When the question of a general arbitration convention came to the floor, the Latin Americans introduced the arguments with which Buchanan had long been familiar. Though the convention adopted fell short of their expectations, at least they had made the most of their first opportunity to lay their views before a world tribunal.[104]

Root's plan for a world court proved Buchanan's most vexing lobbying assignment. It proposed selection of judges on some population or other statistical base. Led by Ruy Barbosa and the Brazilians, the Latin Americans remained steadfast to their traditional belief in the equality of sovereign states. Each nation, large or small, must be permitted to name a permanent member of the proposed court. Repeated soundings of their delegations convinced Buchanan of their obduracy. They would go no further than to support in principle the secretary's court proposal.[105] On most of the other conference actions, especially those related to limitation of armaments and rules of warfare, Buchanan found the Latin American delegations willing to support the United States.[106]

After four busy months filled with innumerable committee meetings and a dozen plenary sessions, Buchanan saw the Hague Conference come to an end on 18 October.[107] For him the assembly had been a logical consummation of actions he had initiated at Rio. As Root's special representative, he had identified himself with Washington's new attitude of neighborliness and established himself indispensably as a trouble-shooting envoy for the Roosevelt administration. By assisting the Latin American nations to move from Hemisphere stage to world arena, he had played an unobtrusive but integral part in opening the doors of world councils to their statesmen; they would soon be invited to sit on the Permanent Court of Arbitration and later would serve with distinction on various international bodies.

Together with his Latin American colleagues Buchanan would soon receive a special tribute for the Western Hemisphere's role at the Conference. In emphasizing the contributions of the Latin American republics and, even more specifically the services of Buchanan and the other Americans, a French representative, the Baron d'Estournelles, saw "America" as a hemisphere, not as a single nation. "America . . . has, beyond any doubt, saved the Conference," he wrote, "but for America the Conference was lost, cut in two, or, rather would never have existed."[108]

For both the Buchanans summer and autumn in the Netherlands had not been all high international politics. Like the wives of other delegates, Mrs. Buchanan, whenever invited, had enjoyed the social and entertainment accompaniments she had come to expect at international assemblies. Queen Wilhelmina gave a reception for all delegates at the Royal Palace in The Hague. Eager to show off Rotterdam's new waterway to the North Sea, the Netherlands government provided an extended excursion through its main channels and tributary canals. The city of The Hague honored its guests at an artistic festival featuring national dances and typical provincial dress. To reciprocate the hospitality of their Dutch hosts visiting delegations tried to outdo each other in the lavishness or originality of their entertainment. With distinctive galas and fetes, for the first time at a world conference, the Latin American nations competed with Old World states on the social plane. Fulfilling American custom at its diplomatic posts round the world, the United States minister to the Netherlands gave a reception on the Fourth of July.

With many delegates and distinguished guests, the Buchanans also joined in the most significant extracurricular event of the Second Hague Conference. This was the cornerstone-laying for the new building of the Permanent Court of Arbitration. As he had already done for the Pan American Union Building and as he would soon do for the Central American Court of Justice, Andrew Carnegie had donated funds for the edifice to be known as the "Palace of Peace."[109]

On 20 October the Buchanans left The Hague on their homeward journey. Since early July 1906 they had spent nine months in transoceanic travel and foreign residence. They had visited Brazil, Argentina, and the Netherlands and relished the joys while enduring the travail of two memorable international conferences. Now they would be happy to return to familiar scenes in Buffalo.

For Buchanan, the Hague Conference had served as a significant sequel to the Rio assembly. There would, however, be another. Early in February 1908 Root would invite him to join a national committee whose duties included essential follow-up to the resolutions enacted at Rio.[110] Each member nation was expected to create a similar watchdog committee. But even before this development Washington found a new and far more pressing assignment for the Buffalonian. Scarcely had Buchanan unpacked his luggage at home when he received Roosevelt's invitation to represent the United States in the Central American Peace Conference scheduled to open in Washington in early November.[111] In a setting quite different from the Hague Conference he would now have new opportunity to promote Root's design for good neighborliness with the Latin Americans.

Chapter 15
PROMOTING STABILITY IN UNSTABLE NATIONS
Central America, 1907-1909

By the time he returned from The Hague in late October 1907, Buchanan had rounded out more than thirteen years as an emissary-on-call for State Department missions involving Latin America. Dovetailed between commitments to the Columbian and Pan-American Expositions and the New York Life Insurance and Westinghouse Companies, his official assignments had taken him to Argentina, Mexico, Panama, and Brazil. He had visited Paraguay, vacationed in Uruguay, and done business in Cuba. From time to time he had negotiated with representatives of Chile, Venezuela, and Colombia. Through either first-hand observation or close appraisal of their aspirations he had come to know all of these nations.

With the remaining Hemisphere republics, on the other hand, the peripatetic Buffalonian had had few direct contacts. Though he had mingled with their envoys at two inter-American conferences and two world expositions, he had neither visited their lands nor dealt with their peculiar problems. This was particularly true of the five Central American states. Within a few days of his return from Europe, however, the Roosevelt administration prepared to close this gap in his Latin American experience. Without prior warning, the State Department involved him in the maze of Central America's political turmoil.

Rarely since gaining independence from Spain in 1821 had

the peoples of Central America enjoyed stable government or the tranquillity it might have produced. Annexed briefly to their aggressive northern neighbor, Mexico, the people of the ancient Spanish Captaincy General of Guatemala had soon seceded to form their own nation, the United Provinces of Central America. But this initial attempt to shape a viable federal union had lasted only until 1838, when each of the component states determined to follow its own path. Succeeding decades would bring new efforts to restore the federation, but in the end the proponents of separatism would overcome the ambitions of the unionists.

Though the five small nations shared a common land, a common history, and a common coffee-bananas economy, each developed during the nineteenth century its own distinctive nationality. To some degree their cultivated individuality grew out of their ethnic diversity. The majority of the Guatemalans were descendants of Maya Indians, the majority of Costa Ricans of white Spanish stock. In the nations between—Honduras, Nicaragua, and El Salvador—the blood of Indians, Spaniards, and Negroes mixed in varying proportions.[1]

These were some of the obvious Central American realities Buchanan would have to contemplate as he took up his new assignment for Secretary Root. But there were subtler obstacles to the attainment of human welfare and freedom from political strife. Central America presented the same yawning gaps he had observed in Mexico, Panama, and South America: between rich and poor, landowners and peasants, conservatives and liberals, authoritarians and democrats, militarists and *civilistas,* xenophobes and internationalists. Military dictators frequently intervened in neighboring nations. Guerrilla *emigrados* sometimes operated across international boundaries. And recurrently there was the menace of foreign intervention to satisfy bondholder nationals who sought renewal of service on defaulted securities. As Washington's appointed agent, Buchanan would not be called upon to moderate these disharmonies or resolve the problems. He would, however, need to recognize them as the nuances or substantive issues that motivated the Central American leaders with whom he would confer.

After 1903 the potential for instability in the nations adjacent to Panama had taken on far more importance for Washington policymakers. By their projection of the Platt Amendment and the Roosevelt Corollary Roosevelt and Hay had sought to safeguard the Caribbean sealanes to the future Panama Canal. But in the republics of the Isthmus itself turbulence of whatever form would confront Washington with an even more imminent threat to the security of the waterway now under construction.

In seeking ways to allay Central America's chronic unrest, Secretary Root was guided by his early determination to treat the Latin Americans like gentlemen while infusing a new spirit into Washington's policies. His decision to adopt the posture of the good neighbor forbade his resort to marine landings or unilateral interventions. Rather, in late 1905 when new tremors threatened Isthmian peace, Root solicited the advice and cooperation of Central America's closest neighbor, Mexico. Through a series of conferences with its ambassador to the United States, Enrique Creel, he enlisted the support of Presidents Roosevelt and Díaz for a policy of joint good offices.[2]

During the next three years, as ferment in Central America increased, Root repeatedly fell back upon this two-nation collaboration. In July 1906, when border incidents presaged hostilities among Guatemala, Honduras, and El Salvador, the two presidents interposed their influence to produce a truce. This was the diplomatic success that had stimulated such enthusiastic approval at Rio de Janeiro when Buchanan announced it to the delegates of the Third Inter-American Conference. Later all the Central American states except Nicaragua agreed to submit future differences to Presidents Roosevelt and Díaz.[3]

Within a few months, however, renewed disturbances upset Root's hopes for stabilizing relations among Panama's neighbors. As the only nonsignatory to the 1906 agreement, Nicaragua committed aggressions that threatened a general Central American war. Guerrilla raids, frontier violations, and political machinations exacerbated the situation. With conditions rapidly deteriorating, Roosevelt and Díaz determined once again to inject their influence. By mid-September they had persuaded the five nations to accept a new truce and to reopen discussions.⁴ Agreeing with unexpected promptness to confer in Washington in November, they invited representatives of Mexico and the United States to join them "in a friendly capacity."⁵ Thus was the door opened for Buchanan's entry into the labyrinth of Central American politics.⁶ Appropriately, his Mexican colleague would be Ambassador Creel.

Throughout seven weeks of almost daily sessions the two diplomats fulfilled their functions as friendly observers of the Central American Peace Conference. Though the American and Mexican presidents had provided the original impetus for the meeting, the Central Americans themselves planned all its working arrangements. They framed the protocol convening the assembly, drafted the rules that would govern its deliberations, and decreed that all sessions except the opening and closing ceremonies should be held behind closed doors.⁷ The designated role of the two outsiders, therefore, was essentially nonparticipatory, though at several critical junctures their conciliatory skills would assist the delegates around potential roadblocks.

To inaugurate the conference with appropriate ceremony, the delegates invited high officials of the State Department and the Bureau of American Republics as well as the personnel of the Central American legations in Washington. At this opening session Buchanan's interest focused on the inaugural remarks of Secretary Root and Ambassador Creel, spokesman for Mexico's Foreign Minister Ignacio Mariscal. As representatives of the sponsoring nations and the American republics most concerned with Central America's welfare, the two men enjoined the delegates to find harmonious means for calming their continuing ferment. But Creel went even further. Voicing a strategic consideration that Root may have deliberately avoided, he stressed the indispensability of Central American peace to the successful completion and operation of the Panama Canal.⁸

In the official protocol delineating conference ground rules, the Central Americans had limited their agenda to two items that effectively epitomized their problems. First, to clear the air, they would discuss "the steps to be taken and the measures to be adopted for the purpose of adjusting any differences which exist between said Republics." At the opening business session, however, the chairman of each delegation announced that his country had no claim against any of the other republics. Unexpectedly, even unabashedly, the five nations seemed willing to drop the contentions that had produced their recent discord. Like most of the delegates to this point, Buchanan and Creel believed the way cleared for conference action on the second agenda item—conclusion of "a treaty which shall define their general relations."[9]

But, in a parliamentary action of questionable intent, the Honduran delegation brought forward a surprise project that threatened for a time to disrupt the conference. Representing the nation sometimes called the geographic and strategic keystone of Central America, the Hondurans sought to revive the oft-frustrated scheme for a federated union of the five republics. The Nicaraguans gave their immediate support. Inflexible in opposition, the Costa Ricans termed the Honduran overture unauthorized by the conference protocol and the Guatemalans countered with a proposal of their own. They recommended that the conference proceed with the drafting of a general treaty of peace while considering creation of a court of international justice. The Salvadorans were at first noncommittal.[10]

Unable to reconcile these two propositions a special five-nation study committee confronted the plenary session with two reports. Though not opposed to immediate negotiation of a general peace treaty, the Hondurans and Nicaraguans adhered to their position that the surest road to peace was through reestablishment of the old confederation. Recommendation of this proposition to the five legislatures would place the final decision in the hands of popularly elected representatives. However desirable a federal union, delegates of the other three nations argued, circumstances were not yet propitious for its revival. Let the nations first agree to strengthen and stabilize their relationships through a series of evolutionary harmonizing experiments. Railroad construction, modernized communications, promotion of trade, frequent conferences, and creation of an international court should precede any new attempt to federalize. Only through these and complementary preliminaries could union be made "durable and solid."[11] As stalemate threatened to impede conference proceedings, Buchanan ventured to interpose his capacity as friendly observer. He recommended a simple but effective parliamentary expedient to ease the situation. Supported by Ambassador Creel, he persuaded the delegates to postpone consideration of the two reports and proceed with the drafting of specific projects.[12]

With this vexing issue safely by-passed, Buchanan and Creel followed closely the progress of deliberations on a variety of salutary proposals. By 20 December they had seen the delegates conclude a complex of treaties and conventions that seemed prophetic of improved relationships.[13] In three of the conventions the delegates took steps to prepare the Central American people for eventual union. They agreed to create a permanent bureau for the study and encouragement of uniform laws, monetary standards, and commercial regulations for the five nations. They authorized the holding of annual conferences to consider the implementation of economic measures affecting mutual interests. To encourage the development of a common system of schools and education they determined to establish a Central American pedagogical institute. In two other conventions—on extradition and on construction and improvement of international railway connections—the delegates looked to the tightening of relations among the republics.[14]

But, helpful as these steps might be for long-range purposes, they did not reach the heart of Central America's problems. From his contacts with Root, Buchanan realized that the secretary's hopes would be completely satisfied only if the delegates could agree on a broad treaty of peace and amity and a convention creating an international court of justice. To the satisfaction of all concerned they achieved both these actions.

By obligating the five nations to submit all disputes to adjudication, the general treaty of peace and amity was made interdependent with the convention creating the Central American Court of Justice. Each pact would run for ten years. The treaty also provided neutralization of Honduras, as Root had desired, and incorporated various articles designed to inhibit revolutionary movements across international borders.[15] All of these treaty provisions originated with the Central Americans themselves, but Buchanan may have influenced the insertion of the key article in a corollary convention.[16] This was the novel doctrine, later adopted by the United States, that governments created by coup d'etat or revolutionary action which failed to receive the endorsement of popularly elected representatives would not be recognized.[17]

The court convention prescribed a tribunal of five judges, one appointed by each republic. It would sit in Cartago, Costa Rica, and would have wide jurisdiction over the kinds of international disputes that had long disrupted Central American concord.[18] Of all the conference actions none involved Buchanan so intimately. In microcosm it suggested Root's conception of a world tribunal for which the Buffalonian had sought, with such frustration, to recruit Latin American support at the recent Hague Conference.[19] Later Buchanan would serve as President Roosevelt's representative at the inauguration of the court in May 1908.

Though this network of agreements did not bring Central America the permanent peace and stability that Roosevelt and Root had desired, the conference delegates for a time at least had demonstrated their eagerness and ability to reconcile national goals. In further demonstration of this new found harmony, a number of representatives met privately during the last days of the conference to form an extracurricular, semisocial group they chose to call the "Central American Fraternity." Proud of their success in creating the world's first permanent court of international justice, they were determined

> to promote the peace, harmony and progress of Central America; to render still closer its relations with Mexico, the United States of America and other countries; and generally to carry out the propaganda of the principles embodied in the conventions of the Central American Peace Conference of Washington.[20]

As a manifestation of the confidence they placed in their official observers, the Central American delegates named Creel their permanent president and Buchanan a member of the fraternity's permanent committee in Washington. They elected Secretary Root and Foreign Minister Mariscal as honorary presidents and voted honorary memberships to Assistant

Secretary of State Robert Bacon, John Barrett, director of the Bureau of American Republics, and Andrew Carnegie, who would soon donate funds for the court's headquarters in Costa Rica.[21]

With Secretary Root presiding, as he had at the opening session, the conference held its official closing ceremonies on 20 December. Earlier that day Buchanan and Creel had joined the delegates in paying courtesy farewell calls on President Roosevelt and the secretary of state.[22]

The United States and Mexico were not signatories to any of the agreements of the Central American Conference, but patently Buchanan's "profound understanding of Latin American affairs"[23] and Creel's prudence and geniality had augmented their countries' influence in Central American politics. Again and again in the closing sessions and in the days that followed both men received effusive expressions of Central American appreciation. None of these tributes, however, quite equalled that paid Buchanan by the Costa Rican delegate, who expressed gratitude to Secretary Root for "the eminent services lent to the five republics of Central America by the able and distinguished diplomat, Mr. Buchanan, to whose exquisite tact and untiring perseverance is owed in so great a measure the success of the delicate and difficult labors of the conference."[24]

The adjournment of the Washington Conference did not mark the end of Buchanan's obligations as the American representative nor terminate his connections with the Central American situation. He would require several months to assemble official documents and prepare his report of the conference for the State Department.[25] And soon Root would suggest the possibility of the good will mission to Costa Rica for the inauguration of the Court of Justice. At the same time, the secretary was considering still another assignment for his envoy—appointment to the special Pan American Committee recommended by the Rio Conference.[26]

While awaiting these developments, Buchanan for the first time in many months was able to give his full attention to the New York Life Insurance Company. Since mid-1906 his State Department duties in Rio, The Hague, and Washington had severely restricted his field activities for the company. Yet his intimate association with Root and other State Department officials had placed him in an advantageous position to continue his advisory functions for NYLIC. Relying upon the assistance of his diplomatic colleagues, he had become a kind of company watchdog, delegated to monitor insurance developments round the world wherever regulatory actions seemed to threaten alien companies—Japan, Austria, Portugal, Spain, Denmark, and Mexico.

Numerous documents in the case files of the State Department testify to the assistance given Buchanan as he sought to protect NYLIC's overseas interests. Marginal notations by ranking staff officers on incoming despatches—"This may go to Mr. Buchanan"; "Show to Mr. Buchanan"; "Telephoned to Mr. Buchanan"; "Mr. Buchanan would like to have a copy"—suggest their willingness to assist the NYLIC representative. He frequently wrote to Root to report impending overseas developments in insurance regulations and to request official action; the secretary often responded with directives to foreign service agents in the field. Ambassadors and ministers occasionally by-passed regular channels to report their findings directly to Buchanan.[27] Clearly during these years he had evolved a pattern of personal conduct in which he was able to coordinate his free-lance activities for NYLIC with his free-lance diplomacy for the State Department.

No foreign insurance situation in the late months of 1907 gave Buchanan more concern than Spain's proposed new restrictions on nonnational companies. Even while serving the State Department at The Hague he had kept in close touch with Spanish developments and had asked Root to suggest the interposition of the American minister in Madrid.[28] Failing to secure desired relief through diplomatic channels, NYLIC determined in early January that Buchanan himself should go to Spain. Accompanied by Mrs. Buchanan, the Buffalo diplomat again sailed for Europe on a business mission. Engaging a car in The Hague, they motored by easy stages across Belgium and France to the Spanish capital.[29]

In Madrid the American minister carefully arranged their introductions to the capital's official society. At a gala legation banquet they met prominent Spanish cabinet ministers and their wives as well as the resident envoys of Austria-Hungary, Italy, Mexico, and other countries. They visited the Prado Museum and Madrid's historic sites. They motored to Toledo and through the countryside of Andalucía. They found themselves portrayed in a Spanish newspaper as the "distinguished and *simpático* North American diplomat" and his "*amable señora*."[30]

Buchanan's travels and observations in central Spain led him to form enthusiastic judgments of the young King Alfonso and his country's industrial and agricultural progress.[31] On the other hand, though he extended his visit several weeks, he had no success in tempering the effects of the new insurance regulations. In the end, he accomplished no more than Root's authorization for continued "friendly representations" by the American legation. Advised of new State Department assignments awaiting him in Washington, on 2 March he and Mrs. Buchanan departed from Spain by way of Gibraltar.[32]

Within hours of his return from Spain Buchanan was briefed on his new diplomatic assignments. The first of these involved membership on the newly instituted Pan American Committee—an interim American body of the type recommended for each Hemisphere nation by the Rio Conference of 1906.[33] As chairman of the American delegation at Rio Buchanan had assumed continuing custodial responsibilities for assuring Washington's compliance with the conference conventions and resolutions. When the State Department had failed to move with despatch, he had reminded Root of its obligations. Now, in mid-March 1908, Buchanan found himself a member of the committee the secretary had belatedly established.[34]

The first meeting of the committee brought together a group of distinguished American leaders: Andrew Carnegie, Senator Stephen B. Elkins of West Virginia, several congressmen, a United States Army major general, university presidents and professors, and ranking officials of the State Department and Bureau of American Republics. When the committee failed to persuade either Root or Carnegie to accept the permanent chairmanship, it turned to Buchanan as the logical choice. Since the group would meet only on call of the chairman, its procedural functions would be performed by an executive committee, directed at the outset by two of Buchanan's former associates, Leo S. Rowe and John Barrett.[35]

In reporting these initial deliberations Buchanan assured Root of the committee's eagerness to work closely with counterpart agencies in the other American Republics. Their mutual interests, he emphasized, lay not only in assuring implementation of the Rio resolutions but also in laying plans for the next inter-American conference, scheduled to meet in Buenos Aires.[36] With these preliminaries tidied up, Buchanan could leave matters in the hands of his executive committee while he took up the new overseas assignment to which Root had already alerted him.[37]

Since the close of the Washington Conference the administration had been contemplating a good will mission to Central America that would reinforce the region's newly pledged stability while perpetuating the Mexican-American collaboration that had promoted it. According to this plan, special representatives of the two nations would visit each of the five capitals en route to Costa Rica for the inauguration of the Court of Justice.[38]

Buchanan was happy to broaden his background as the Roosevelt administration's special envoy, but Mrs. Buchanan, who had accompanied her husband on each of his previous diplomatic missions, did not relish a 13,000-mile trip of arduous land and sea travel, with many changes and stopovers. Instead, already seasoned as his father's travelling companion, Donald would resume his services as personal secretary. Will, in a sketchy date book faithfully maintained, would record the joys and ordeals of their journey "round Central America in eighty days."[39]

On 2 April the two Buchanans left Buffalo on their 5,000-mile rail journey to Mexico City. With half-a-dozen stopovers to conduct business or visit friends and relatives, they spent three full weeks in completing the first leg of their extended pilgrimage.[40] Their most important stopover was at Chihuahua, home of Ambassador Creel, where Buchanan delivered Root's urgent plea that he join the special mission as Mexico's envoy. Here, however, the American learned that his presumed colleague had not yet been appointed and that President Díaz was showing great reluctance to cooperate with Root's plans.[41] Not until he reached the capital would Buchanan appreciate the gravity of Mexico's unexpected disinclination.

Meanwhile, however, in the Chihuahua countryside, Creel introduced the city-dwelling father and son to a genuine Mexican *hacienda*. "The largest land holder in the world," Buchanan wrote of its owner, the ambassador's father-in-law, "6,000,000 acres in practically one block—has 300,000 cattle, 200,000 sheep, 30,000 horses and owns 1/2 Chihuahua." The guests attended a family baptismal service, enjoyed an ice cream social, and shared a meal at which "the whole tribe sat down to dinner at once 100 strong."[42]

Buchanan's arrival in Mexico City on 22 April coincided with burgeoning rumors and reports about Mexico's coolness toward Root's good will mission. Even an English-language newspaper was caustic in its criticism of Washington's purposes. The Central Americans had already thanked Presidents Roosevelt and Díaz for their conciliatory efforts and "the first general handshake all around was enough . . . but it seems that the administration at Washington, which at this time is the Uncle Sam of the world, wants some more palavering and maybe something else." "What's the use?" asked the writer. "Why send two men down there to splurge and to impress upon Central Americans the all powerfulness of their two sister nations to the north?"[43]

But from American Ambassador D. E. Thompson Buchanan quickly learned that Mexico's feelings ran much deeper. Its officials were offended that the Central Americans had made no direct approach to them on the mission's acceptability and that Washington had assumed complete responsibility in the matter. In addition, border tensions with Guatemala and its dictator's disinterest in the Court of Justice sharpened Mexico's reluctance to send an uninvited emissary.[44] Only "TO PLEASE THE AMERICAN GOVERNMENT, AND FOR NO OTHER REASON," Thompson cabled Root, would Díaz consent to send Ambassador Creel.[45]

Mexico's obduracy at this point placed the entire problem in Buchanan's hands. Unless he could find some formula for compromise, the mission itself might be aborted. Within twenty-four hours of his arrival he had wired Washington his proposed solution and received Root's approval to proceed. If Mexico originated the suggestion, he might agree to eliminate the good will stops and restrict the trip to attendance at the court's inauguration in Costa Rica. During the next eight days the American envoy conferred with President Díaz on five occasions, several times in the presence of Foreign Minister Mariscal and Ambassador Creel. When the president volunteered the solution Buchanan had envisioned, they quickly effected arrangements for fulfillment of the mission. An American cruiser from San Diego would convey the two commissioners to Costa Rica; it would even stop at Pacific ports to pick up the judges from the other Central American states.[46]

With the cruiser *Albany* unavailable until 14 May, however, Buchanan and son found they had two weeks of leisure. They enjoyed Xochimilco and nearby villages; they went to a circus and to the country club for Donald's golf; they were entertained at breakfasts, luncheons, and dinners—and supplied a special train for trips into the countryside. Between sightseeing trips, always alert for NYLIC interests, Will discussed a proposed new insurance law with the finance minister.[47]

With proper invitations at last in hand for both Buchanan and Creel, their party could depart Mexico City on the fourteen-day trip by rail and ship to Costa Rica.[48] Enjoying the pleasures of President Díaz's special train, complete with cooks and servants, they travelled southward by easy stages to the Pacific port of Salina Cruz. On 14 May they boarded the United States cruiser *Albany*.[49] During the next week, like a tramp freighter picking up cargo at every port, the *Albany* sailed from one Central American country to the next. At each stop Buchanan and Creel welcomed the judge-appointee as he joined their party for the remainder of the trip. And at each port the ship offered appropriate cannon salutes to the welcoming commission of dignitaries who came aboard. In one instance it required ninety-six rounds to pay suitable honor to nation, cabinet ministers, military officers, judges, and diplomats.[50]

At San José, Guatemala, where Creel had presidential instructions not to land, Buchanan felt constrained to contrive an explanation for his own inability to attend the proffered banquet. In his place he sent Donald on his first diplomatic errand. Early the next morning the visiting commissioners welcomed President Estrada Cabrera's delegation of "cabinet ministers and big party [of] Generals." During subsequent calls at Acajutla, El Salvador, and Amapala, Honduras, hosts and guests exchanged similar civilities.[51]

The commissioners originally planned to enter Costa Rica through its Pacific port of Puntarenas, but reports of yellow fever in the coastal city forced a last-minute change in itinerary. Instead they would sail directly from Amapala to Panama, cross the Isthmus by rail to Colón, and there board the United States cruiser *Des Moines* for the short trip to the Caribbean port of Limón.[52] In Panama City Buchanan renewed acquaintance with President Amador and conferred with his friend, Foreign Minister Ricardo Arias, currently a strong candidate to succeed Amador. Then accompanied by Arias and Canal Zone Governor Joseph C. S. Blackburn, the commissioners prepared to view canal construction from their trans-Isthmian train. As they travelled from famous Culebra Cut to dockside at Colón, they enjoyed explanations of the massive operations by the canal's chief engineer, Colonel George W. Goethals.[53]

The decision of the Central American Conference to locate its new Court of Justice in the Republic of Costa Rica was a marked tribute to the small nation's tradition of peace and order. Recognized as the most stable and least aggressive of the five republics, it had normally stood on the periphery of Central America's turmoil. Installation of the international court on the soil of their homeland, therefore, gave the Costa Rican people an unparalleled opportunity to celebrate their enviable position.[54] The arrival at Puerto Limón of an American warship carrying the visiting commissioners and the newly elected judges touched off twelve days of jubilation unique in the nation's history.

Even before the *Des Moines* fired its national salute of twenty-one guns, the porteños of Limón were ready with their city's welcome—reception committee, gaily decorated landing stage, and military band playing the Mexican and United States anthems.[55] On the following morning all the guests and their hosts boarded a special Costa Rica Railway train for the spectacular trip to the more salubrious Central Mesa cities of Cartago and San José. As they travelled past banana plantations, through jungles, and over mountains, Buchanan must have given thought to his fellow New Yorker, Minor C. Keith, who only a few years before had promoted completion of the railway and contributed to the founding of the United Fruit Company.[56] At Cartago, officially designated as the court's permanent seat, the visitors were met by cabinet members from San José, other members of the reception committee, and special aides-de-camp named by President Cleto González Víquez to serve Buchanan and Creel.[57]

At the end of their rail journey in San José the commissioners and judges enjoyed a still more colorful welcome. In carriages assigned them for the duration of their stay they rode through flag-festooned streets lined on both sides by more than 3,500 school children. Showered along the way with bunches of flowers, Buchanan and Creel were driven to furnished houses assigned to their exclusive use. On the following day, introduced by the foreign minister, both commissioners presented their official credentials to the president and promptly received his protocol return visits. Not overlooked in these ceremonies, Donald was delighted at the president's order appointing him honorary captain in the Costa Rican artillery.[58]

By 25 May the Costa Ricans had completed their arrangements for the inauguration of the international Court of Justice. As Buchanan noted in his jottings for the day, "all San José" moved by train to Cartago to participate in the celebration. From the railroad station to the assembly hall the American and Mexican Commissioners joined President González Víquez and an eighty-piece band in leading the procession between walls of applauding Costa Ricans.[59]

In the small city of Cartago only a public school building was large enough to accommodate all invited guests. Here, seating protocol placed the president of the republic and the five judges in the center of the rostrum. Scheduled to speak during the ceremonies, the visiting commissioners occupied nearby seats with cabinet members and former presidents and vice-presidents. Lesser positions of honor were accorded the diplomatic corps, members of the Costa Rican supreme court and congress, and church dignitaries.[60] The citizens admitted to the hall viewed what Buchanan described as "one of the most distinguished and representative assemblages that had ever convened in Costa Rica."[61]

One after another the Latin American orators spoke with idealistic eloquence. Costa Rica's Foreign Minister Luis Anderson thought it "a glorious thing for Central America to have purified its past by throwing to the winds this new banner. . . . The present moment presents signs of a happy awakening for these countries agitated by disunion and revolution." He paid lengthy tribute to Presidents Roosevelt and Díaz, "initiators of the conference of peace," to Root and Mariscal as their "indefatigable apostles," and to Buchanan and Creel as "prudent and fraternal councilors," who contributed "their vast fund of intelligence."[62]

In response Ambassador Creel acknowledged the "serious moral responsibility" assumed by Mexico and the United States. "The court of justice for Central America," he continued,

> is neither an occurrence of the moment nor without antecedents. It is in the New World the seed sown by Simon Bolivar, . . . It is the result of the forces which for a great time past have been moving on the road toward international justice and toward the frank, cordial, and friendly unity of the Republics of the American Continent. It is the result of the labor of the Pan-American conferences; it is a consequence of the deliberations of The Hague; it is the national soul which palpitates in the Mexican people, always disposed to glorify justice; it is the fruit of the voyage of the distinguished Secretary of State, Mr. Elihu Root, that sincere friend of Latin America.[63]

When his turn arrived, Buchanan made no attempt to match the perorations of the Latin American spokesmen. Instead, in less dramatic prose, he elected to sound a realistic note. "While applauding this new movement toward the quiet, orderly, and judicial adjustment of international questions," he suggested,

> the world still confidently expect that success will follow, and will not be satisfied with less than that.
> To reach this splendid ideal it is necessary, however, that the conclusions of this court shall be of so high and of so impartial a character,

and the acquiescence therein on the part of the Governments of Central America so full and prompt, that together they shall be morally recognized as an expression of the national conscience of Central America.[64]

Then, shifting easily from English to Spanish, Buchanan made the dramatic announcement just cabled to him by Secretary Root. Andrew Carnegie had pledged $100,000 toward the construction in Cartago of a "temple of peace" for the new court's exclusive use.[65]

For still another week the ceremony and pageantry surrounding the court's installation kept Buchanan and Creel in Costa Rica. By day they visited schools, colleges, government buildings, and business establishments and enjoyed railroad excursions through the green countryside. By night they were honored at official galas and even sponsored one of their own. At a presidential ball for fifteen hundred guests Buchanan escorted the wife of the congressional president during the grand march. At the presidential banquet Donald wore his honorary captain's uniform for the first time.[66]

On 2 June the social whirl that followed the court's installation came to an end. Appropriately on that day, as a token of their appreciation to the government and people of Costa Rica, the Americans entertained at a farewell reception aboard the *Des Moines*. Seconded by the American chargé d'affaires and the cruiser's officers, Buchanan had invited all notables involved in the ten days of ceremony. They travelled from San José to Puerto Limón by special train and all boarded the warship for the unique levee. Given the peaceful purpose of the *Des Moines's* presence in Costa Rican waters, the Central American guests were apparently pleased at this manifestation of "gunboat diplomacy" in reverse.[67]

In renewing its good will voyage northward the *Des Moines* sailed first to Vera Cruz to return Ambassador Creel to his homeland and to permit the commissioners to make their firsthand reports to President Díaz. Enjoying again the luxury of the presidential train, the itinerant diplomats reached Mexico City on 8 June to find the capital's newspapers filled with complimentary notices of their mission.[68] Besieged upon arrival by eager journalists, the two men revealed their restrained hopes for Central America's future as well as the respect they had gained for each other. Creel referred to Buchanan's "friendship for Mexico and the other Latin American countries, his desire to serve them, his eagerness to tighten their relations, and his ample spirit, always open to conciliation and harmony."[69] In their reports to President Díaz and during the subsequent banquet with which he honored them at Chapultepec Castle, the emissaries continued to toast each other as well as their superiors in Mexico City and Washington. At what he described as "the most splendid dinner" he had ever attended, Buchanan heard the president express his satisfaction over Mexican-American collaboration in Central American affairs.[70]

The Buchanans now faced another ten days of land and sea travel to complete their journey to Washington and Buffalo. Slowed by frequent transfers en route—presidential train to Vera Cruz, the *Des Moines* to Havana, smaller ship to Key West, then by rail to Washington—they made their meandering way homeward. In Havana they enjoyed the hospitality of the American governor, Charles E. Magoon, and said their farewells to the *Des Moines* as it prepared to return to its base at Guantánamo.[71]

Back in Buffalo, however, Buchanan soon realized that his mission to Costa Rica had not terminated his involvement in Central America's turbulent affairs. At once he began preparation of his high commissioner's report and situation estimate for Secretary Root. When completed on 21 July, the none-too-sanguine prognosis did not sound the bright note Roosevelt and Root had hoped to hear. "It will be no doubt difficult, on the part of the five Republics," he wrote, "for a time to harmonize that unity of purpose that must form the underlying necessary stratum upon which the success of the court depends, with the national individualism that has been the rule in Central America." He expressed special concern about the continuing threat of "internal outbreaks." On this point he ventured "the belief that if the excellent work represented in the organization of this court is not to be jeopardized as to its future usefulness, the greatest prudence, tact, and statesmanship must be shown by each of the five Republics in everything even remotely likely to reach the court."[72]

During the following months, as the Court of Justice began to effect its organization, Buchanan became a convenient repository of the Central Americans' problems. Trusted by all concerned parties, he received confidences from all sides. When, for example, Costa Rican Foreign Minister Anderson initiated specific planning for the construction and financing of the new court building in Cartago, he placed in Buchanan's hands the essential dealings with Andrew Carnegie and the Department of State.[73] When in July Honduran neutrality was threatened by revolution from within and concomitant border crossings from without, Buchanan again became the pivot of Mexican-American conciliation efforts. The incident involved two festering problems he felt had been inadequately covered by the 1907 Washington treaties—the continuing threat of "internal outbreaks" and the plottings of "*políticos emigrados*."

For a time it appeared that guerrilla forays from Guatemala and El Salvador might precipitate a general war with Honduras and Nicaragua. Eager to prevent escalation of the conflict, Costa Rica suggested interposition by the new Central American court. When the court indicated its readiness to arbitrate the dispute, Honduras and Nicaragua placed formal charges against their two neighbors for violation of the 1907 treaties. Supported by the State Department and Ambassador Creel, the court promptly demanded that the four nations withdraw all troops from frontier areas.[74] Once the withdrawal was accomplished, Buchanan could find satisfaction in the applauding commentary of a Washington newspaper, which hailed the case as "the first dispute between nations ever submitted to a permanent standing court [and] the first time that any court ever intervened to prevent preparations for war."[75]

Though kept informed from time to time of these developments, Buchanan became personally involved only with the court's consideration of the Honduran charges. By this time he had reassumed his responsibilities for the New York Life Insurance Company. In early September he had undertaken a hasty three-week trip to London, Berlin, and Paris.[76] Ten days after his return from Europe he suddenly departed for Mexico, ostensibly to confer with government officials about a proposed new insurance law.[77] Because of his conferences with

President Díaz, ranking cabinet ministers, and Ambassador Creel, however, the Mexican press assumed his NYLIC business to be a façade cloaking his official mission on the Central American situation. Though decidedly scanty on the subject, State Department files reveal the accuracy of the journalistic surmise.[78]

Secretary Root appears to have authorized his agent to approach President Díaz about the possibility of a new joint Mexican-American interposition on two scores: to suggest that Honduras withdraw its charges and to recommend general Central American amnesty for all political exiles. The first proposal came from the American minister to El Salvador; the second originated with Buchanan after his arrival in Mexico City. As he envisioned it, "complete joint amnesty for all present emigrados politicos [would] guarantee that they can return home in safety both as to their personal liberty and as to their property."[79] While granting the efficacy of both approaches, the Mexican authorities questioned the propriety of the initiative coming from outside.[80] His overtures thus rebuffed, the American diplomat returned to Washington empty-handed, a rare experience in his diplomatic career. By mid-December, when the Court of Justice ruled against Honduras's claims,[81] he was en route to Venezuela on another special assignment.

In the meantime, however, Buchanan continued to receive pleas from Central American friends for his personal assistance in the solution of their nations' problems. In September the Nicaraguan judge on the Court of Justice requested his aid in procuring printed materials on the United States Supreme Court and the Hague Tribunal.[82] In October the president of the International Central American Bureau advised him of the inauguration of that agency as mandated by the Washington Conference and requested "the valued assistance of his personal influence."[83]

Soon after, as the Honduran situation continued to cloud the Central American horizon, Costa Rican Foreign Minister Anderson besought Buchanan's aid in persuading the State Department to call a new conference to review and broaden the treaties of Washington. "Would to God," he wrote in near supplicatory terms, "that you should be pleased to take into consideration this idea, that I submit absolutely to your sense of justice; and if you should agree with my way of thinking, perhaps you could procure some powerful influence that would move the governments to hold the Conference forthwith, and to give it all the importance it deserves." If he would consent to lend his presence, Anderson assured Buchanan, "with the same interest and the same efficiency with which you did last year," the conference could be held in Tegucigalpa, Washington, "or at another place convenient for you."[84] Attentive as he was to the Costa Rican's entreaty, however, the part-time diplomat could do no more at this time than transmit it to his superiors in the State Department.[85]

Even in later months Buchanan continued to receive appeals with which he could sympathize but not comply. On several occasions Anderson solicited the Buffalonian's aid in persuading the State Department to mediate Costa Rica's still unresolved boundary dispute with Panama.[86] Later he requested assistance in plans to refund his country's foreign debt. From time to time other Central American diplomats sought to exploit his influence with Washington officials.[87]

By the early months of 1909 such optimism as Buchanan had about the future stability of Central America had sharply declined. His year of association with its recurrent turbulence had not been the most satisfying nor most productive of his diplomatic career. His hopes for the Court of Justice withered markedly when its judges rendered their first decision strictly on the bases of national partisanship.[88] From his intimate contacts with Central American leaders he sensed that their feeling of futility and frustration was growing. From first-hand experience he knew that Mexican suspicion of Washington's aims was increasing and its eagerness to cooperate ebbing. Since collaboration with Mexico had been the cornerstone of Root's Central American policy, this shift in President Díaz's attitude seemed to dictate Washington's turn to unilateral action.[89] Moreover, Root resigned in January and Buchanan's relationship with the new secretary was still undefined.

But, even in his growing disillusionment, Buchanan was unwilling to forsake the basic goal of Root's diplomacy. He still believed in "the great desirability of having all of the territory north of the canal brought within the field of quiet, of stability, and of such progress as will render it possible for all of us to look with satisfaction upon the work we have done." In this vein, on the last day of Roosevelt's presidency, he addressed a long, self-revealing letter to the former secretary of state.[90]

Foreign Minister Anderson's earlier proposal for a new Central American conference, Buchanan now suggested, should be revived. Its primary purpose should be to enhance the legal authority and moral status of the Court of Justice. This could be done, he submitted, by tightening controls over political exiles and strengthening the guarantees of Honduran neutrality. However difficult the task might be, Mexico must be persuaded to renew its former spirit of cooperation. Above all, it would "be necessary to have the whole subject worked out and carried through by some one in the Department, or connected with it, who will hang on the thing until it is successfully worked out in every way." Was the time appropriate, Buchanan inquired of Root, to bring these views to the attention of the incoming secretary of state, Philander C. Knox?[91]

Though only recently installed as United States senator from New York, Root responded promptly to Buchanan's inquiry. Like his envoy, the former secretary had grown somewhat disenchanted about Washington's ability to promote Central American concord.[92] He confessed his long-time objective of a joint Mexican-American guarantee of Honduran neutrality, but "in such form that the President could use our naval force to prevent violation of that neutrality without himself over-stepping the constitutional limitation upon his power." Such a guarantee, even without the necessity of its exercise, would forestall the "atrocious and repulsive" domination of Central American affairs by dictators like José Zelaya in Nicaragua and Manuel Estrada Cabrera in Guatemala. But this objective could only be attained, he insisted, upon the initiative of the Central Americans themselves. He invited Buchanan to join him in presenting their views to Secretary Knox.[93]

However, three months before this exchange of letters Roosevelt and Root had tapped their perennial agent for quite a different assignment. This was the onerous task of reestablishing diplomatic relations with the government of Venezuela.

It would be Buchanan's last official mission for the Roosevelt administration and his final opportunity to foster Root's good-neighborly hopes for Latin America.

Chapter 16
CLAIMS, COUNTER CLAIMS, AND ARBITRATION
Venezuela, 1908-1909

T hings are evidently on the verge of a complete upsetting in Venezuela. Surely this is the time to send a first-class man down there in order to be in on the ground floor before the trouble takes place."[1] With this premonitory message on 17 December 1908, President Roosevelt forswore his own inclination to settle the Venezuelan problem by forceful intervention and acknowledged Secretary Root's commitment to neighborly relations with Latin America. In recommending Buchanan as the "first-class man" for the president's assignment, the secretary confidently anticipated early solution of the difficulties that had shadowed Venezuelan-American friendship for half a decade. In accepting the commission Buchanan fully understood that his mission to Caracas could help to determine the future course of Root's general Latin American policy.[2]

Since 1903 security of the sealanes to the Panama Canal had been the focus of the Roosevelt administration's Caribbean policy. Like the islands of the Antilles and the nations of Middle America, Venezuela occupied a strategic location along those approaches. It also possessed vast unexploited natural resources attractive to American and European investors. Moreover, like other independent states of the American Mediterranean, Venezuela had incurred overseas financial obligations that recurrently raised the specter of foreign intervention. And like the Central American governments Root and Buchanan had worked to stabilize, Venezuela perpetually endured a corrupt and capricious dictatorship with which it was possible to have only fitful diplomatic intercourse.

The nation's current dictator, Cipriano Castro, represented the climax of a century of misgovernment and abortive attempts to establish democratic institutions. Its people had lived through more than fifty revolts or coups d'état, while their leaders repeatedly drafted and discarded constitutions. Characterized by ineptitude and truculence, internal maladministration had impaired the management of foreign policy. Even after the Anglo-German-Italo blockade of 1902-1903 and the resulting arbitrations, the Castro regime had not satisfactorily adjudicated new claims of foreign investors or normalized its relations with their governments.[3]

In planning the future security of the canal, the Roosevelt administration had grown increasingly apprehensive about Castro's continuing intransigence toward foreign investors. By early 1906 it had agreed to support the contentions of five American claimants for redress of alleged wrongs. When a variety of approaches failed to bring the Venezuelan dictator to the negotiators' table or the arbiter's bench, Roosevelt and Root in June 1908 had determined to break diplomatic relations.[4] Six months later, however, they eagerly responded to Venezuelan overtures to restore normal intercourse.[5]

This abrupt shift in the long-strained relationship resulted from a sudden change of circumstances. Like the United States, other nations had for several years pressured Venezuela for satisfaction of claims. With Washington's approval, France and the Netherlands had intimated the use of force. At one point Colombia had suggested American intervention. Still showing no disposition to bow to these pressures, Castro in late November had suddenly sailed for Europe to seek medical assistance. In his absence Vice-President Juan Vicente Gómez had waited only a few days to elevate himself to the presidency and initiate steps to restore Venezuela's international posture.[6]

Official notification of Gómez's more tractable attitude had reached the White House from the Brazilian minister in Caracas, who since the diplomatic rupture in June had been representing American interests. Immediately following

Gómez's coup d'état the Venezuelan foreign minister had advised the Brazilian of the new administration's decision to resolve the nation's international problems. Surprisingly, he had also suggested that the visit of an American warship to Venezuelan waters would be looked upon as "convenient."[7] In this situation Roosevelt and Root had called upon Buchanan and the United States Navy.

Just four days after the president had first alerted Root to the probability of imminent change in Caracas, Buchanan arrived in Washington to accept his appointment as high commissioner. Signed by both the president and the secretary of state, the envoy's commission gave him "full power to confer with the Government of Venezuela in all matters relating to the re-establishment of diplomatic relations."[8] His instructions bade him depart at once for Hampton Roads, where the cruiser *North Carolina* was already coaling up to speed him to Venezuelan shores.[9]

Buchanan's five-day trip to La Guaira on a warship plowing winter seas at full steam was not the most pleasant of his many ocean crossings. No sooner had the 17,000-ton *North Carolina* moved out of Chesapeake Bay than it encountered high winds blowing rain and hail. For the envoy, as for most of the eight hundred officers and men aboard, the next thirty-six hours were "a sea sick blank." Moreover, as "the only passenger on a big cruiser hauling you like mad on special orders," he was appalled to learn that "we are burning 282 tons of coal a day to get me down Caracas way at an early moment." And to add to his disquiet, the trip forced him to miss Mrs. Buchanan's birthday and, for the first time, to spend Christmas at sea. Even bunches of cedar and sprigs of holly "tied to the top of every blessed rod and pole and door" could not make the warship seem like the family hearth.[10]

As the *North Carolina* sped southward, however, smoother seas gave Buchanan opportunity to prepare himself for the delicate negotiations that awaited him. Before his arrival he would need to scrutinize the claims cases he was expected to resolve, assess the record of past American policies and the nature of Venezuelan reactions, and review the details of Root's lengthy instructions. Lacking prior orientation or briefing, he faced an arduous assignment of hasty self-instruction.

In examining the official materials provided him, Buchanan discovered that between 1904 and 1906 Washington had promised diplomatic assistance to four American companies and an individual American citizen. Two of the corporations alleged government violation of their contractual rights to develop asphalt concessions. The New York and Bermúdez Asphalt Company had refused to accept the adverse verdict of the Venezuelan courts that it had surrendered its rights by participating in local politics. Officials of the United States and Venezuela Company had suspended operations when the government levied what they regarded as illegal taxes and assessments.[11]

Two of the other claims entailed efforts to appeal from the decisions of the arbitral commissions of 1903. The Orinoco Steamship Company contended that the arbiter had favored Venezuela by violating the letter of his instructions. The Orinoco Corporation, owning a lease to develop the delta of the Orinoco River, alleged Venezuelan efforts to annul its concession. In each case the referee had invoked the so-called Calvo Clause—still unrecognized by the United States—that required contractual disputes involving foreign companies to be resolved by national courts in accord with national laws and not by appeal to international adjudication.[12]

The fifth case supported by the United States embraced the grievances of an American citizen, Albert Felix Jaurett. Expelled from the country after alleged illegal participation in domestic politics, he sought indemnity for personal financial losses.[13] Because of the distinctive features of the grievances in the five cases, Buchanan concluded from his reading of the evidence that the process of negotiation might be protracted.

In reviewing the five-year record of diplomatic stalemate, the commissioner must have been impressed by both the variety of Washington's approaches and the inflexibility of Castro's resistance. On at least four occasions Secretaries Hay and Root had proposed resolution of the claims by negotiation or arbitration. Once Hay had cloaked his proposal with a virtual ultimatum; subsequently, Root had drafted an ultimatum only to have second thoughts about despatching it. Urged by resident envoys to send a gunboat or to make some show of force, President Roosevelt had recurrently considered forceful action. Once he consulted the War Department's General Staff about its readiness for a tropical campaign. Later, without results, he had joined Root in consulting the United States Senate about possible action. When confronted with the possibility of intervention by France or the Netherlands, he had encouraged them with assurances that only their permanent occupation of Venezuelan territory would be regarded as a violation of the Monroe Doctrine. Presidential election campaigns at home and crisis situations abroad had sometimes inhibited Roosevelt's own contemplation of forceful action.[14] More often, Buchanan knew, it was Root's restraining hand that had curbed the president's zeal for action to break down Castro's obstinacy.

Besides explaining the government's position on the claims controversy, Root's letter of instructions delineated the specific nature of Buchanan's mission. He should assume President Gómez's acceptance of the American proposal for "the arbitration of the pending claims and the disavowal of the discourtesies" implicit in "the tone and character of the communications received from the Venezuelan Government." While not expected to "complete definitively the signing and submission to arbitration" of each claim, he should endeavor at least to secure a general protocol in which the Gómez government explicitly committed itself to arbitration. This accomplished, normal diplomatic intercourse could be restored.[15]

On 28 December the *North Carolina* entered the Venezuelan port of La Guaira to rendezvous with two other American men-of-war, the *Maine* and the *Dolphin*. As instructed, Buchanan transferred at once to the *Dolphin*.[16] This was his first visit to the storied Spanish Main. In repeated voyages across the Caribbean Sea he had sailed along its peripheral islands, visited Cuba, and travelled to the lands of Middle America, but he had not touched the northern shores of South America. Unfortunately, however, this last of his many missions for Secretary Root would leave him little time for sightseeing. Instead, to deal expeditiously with his disquieting assignment, he would spend most of his days in conference at the Ministry of Foreign Affairs and in composing despatches at his hotel room desk.

Before setting foot on Venezuelan soil, however, protocol required the American commissioner to call upon the Brazilian Legation to establish his first contact with government officials in Caracas. Through the agency of the Brazilian minister, Luis R. de Lorena Ferreira, Buchanan informed President Gómez of his arrival and set forth the purpose of his mission. Upon receiving a cordial reply, he debarked from the *Dolphin* and undertook at once the short train trip up the mountains to the capital.[17] At the railroad station, he was greeted warmly by the Brazilian minister and a representative of the Venezuelan Foreign Office and, to his astonishment, welcomed by some five thousand citizens.[18] Equally surprising was the state coach which awaited him. Lined with brocaded yellow satin and presided over by coachman and footman in gay livery, it was hardly the form of transportation he had anticipated. Through the narrow streets of central Caracas, the equipage conveyed him to his hotel on the Plaza Bolívar. Here he could look out over the government palace and the cathedral and, only a block away, the capitol.[19] At the heart of the plaza the equestrian statue of Simón Bolívar would remind him each day of the great South American liberator.

Before settling in to a regimen of negotiating sessions, Buchanan spent five days in an exacting round of diplomatic ceremony, formal visits, and year-end festivities. On 29 December, in the company of the Brazilian minister, he called on Foreign Minister Francisco González Guinán to present a copy of his commission and a special communication from Secretary Root.[20] On the following evening, joined by Rear Admiral C. H. Arnold and ranking officers from United States warships at La Guaira, he enjoyed dinner at the Brazilian Legation. The next afternoon, after their formal presentation to President Gómez, Buchanan and the naval officers paid visits to all cabinet members and to the diplomatic representatives of half a dozen nations.[21] From his hotel room window later that evening he watched Venezuelan crowds gather in the brightly illuminated plaza to say farewell to 1908.[22] The new year began as the old had ended—with receptions and dinners. Following President Gómez's New Year's Day reception at the government palace, the Americans entertained the diplomatic corps at their legation. And on 2 January the German minister, as dean of the diplomatic corps, gave a dinner for Buchanan, the American naval officers, and a number of European envoys.[23]

Even amid this round of festivities the commissioner utilized odd moments to work at the memorandum he would present to the foreign minister.[24] Then, as the social and protocol activities tapered off, Buchanan plunged into a steady round of almost daily negotiating sessions with Foreign Minister González Guinán. After his initial conference the envoy cabled Root that he had found the Venezuelan eager for an amicable solution. He believed that he could resolve one, possibly more, of the claims and arrange satisfactorily for the arbitration of the remaining cases. Ensuing discussions seemed to proceed smoothly.[25]

Within a week the conferees had arrived at bases of settlement for three cases and two days later had "agreed on nearly all questions." By 12 January, satisfied that "all has turned out right," Buchanan was hopeful that he could conclude his mission in another week or ten days. The only remaining item seemed to be the framing of an inclusive protocol. To speed this task he drew up a Spanish-language draft and referred it to the foreign minister for review and editing. Quickly they agreed on its phraseology and submitted it to the approval of President Gómez and his cabinet.[26] At this point the commissioner had no hesitation in advising González Guinán that, once the protocol was signed, the United States would take essential steps to restore normal diplomatic relations.[27]

But Buchanan had allowed himself to become oversanguine. In the even tenor of his conversations with the foreign minister he had overlooked the possibility of presidential or cabinet refusal to ratify the agreements. When their approval was not forthcoming, Buchanan postponed his planned departure. "My patience is becoming exhausted with all the delay," he commented after leaving his eighteenth bargaining conference on the 26th.[28] Four days later, his disillusionment mounting after five more conferences with the foreign minister and a long session with the president, he sent Secretary Root a comprehensive review of the situation. "I AM GREATLY DISAPPOINTED," he concluded, "AT SEEMINGLY UNSATISFACTORY ENDING MY EFFORTS AND *BELIEF*. I AM CABLING AT THIS LENGTH SO THAT YOU MAY SEE THAT I HAVE DONE ALL I COULD MEET VENEZUELA ON A FAIR BASIS IN EVERYTHING."[29]

All the vexing issues of fact and principle which Buchanan thought he had resolved with the foreign minister now seemed to be revived. At root was the issue of arbitration itself versus Gómez's recurring resort to the Calvo Clause. From the beginning Root had tied his envoy to the broad doctrine that "THE ESSENTIAL QUALITY OF ARBITRATION IS THE SUBSTITUTION OF A TRIBUNAL, WHICH IS INTERNATIONAL AND THEREFORE UNPREJUDICED FOR A TRIBUNAL WHICH IS NATIONAL AND THEREFORE PARTIAL."[30] To Venezuela's "DISINCLINATION . . . TO ADMIT PRINCIPLE AND REVISION JUDICIAL DECISIONS," Buchanan could only refuse "TO TREAT DECISIONS OF COURTS OF VENEZUELA AS FINALITY."[31]

There were other points of contention. When Venezuela argued that the United States case before international arbiters must show denial of justice in Venezuelan courts, Buchanan held to the position that the claims should be adjudicated purely on their merits. Any other action would only cast aspersions on Castro's government, a course Root had ruled the United States would refuse to take. The Venezuelans also contended that both governments should describe to the arbiters all the diplomatic exchanges that had taken place. In their view the facts would then emerge. Buchanan held that the referees should first examine the facts, then render just and equitable decisions without reference to past diplomatic contentions. By the end of January the negotiations were deadlocked.[32]

At the same time Buchanan was harassed by other circumstances. Frequently he was forced to await the results of conferences between Venezuelan legal counsel and company representatives in Caracas. At times he required several cable exchanges with Washington while the State Department consulted the American claimants on proposed terms of settlement.[33] The imminence of pressure on Caracas by the Italians and French gave Buchanan concern about a possible log jam of claimants against the still untested Gómez government.[34] Moreover rumors began to circulate: he was demanding $50,000,000 plus concessions impossible to grant; the United States was planning to "arrange" the 1911 Venezuelan elections.[35]

The deadlock which Buchanan had deplored on 30 January persisted for another two weeks. Yet though no instruments of settlement had yet been signed, the margin of disagreement between the two protagonists seemed gradually to narrow. On the Jaurett claim Venezuela had agreed to award an indemnity of $3,000. Because in three cases (Orinoco Steamship Company, Orinoco Corporation, and United States and Venezuela Company) the views of the two governments were so "diametrically opposed," the conferees had concurred in the advisability of arbitration.[36] It was the fifth case—the claim of the New York and Bermúdez Asphalt Company—that impeded closing of the other suits, forestalled signature of the general protocol, and threatened to send Buchanan home empty-handed. Here Venezuela sought to stand fast on the Calvo doctrine; the American clung to his contention that the case must be decided on its merits. "IF THEY INSIST ON THEIR STAND," Buchanan cabled Root on 7 February, "I WOULD FAVOR IMMEDIATELY STOPPING NEGOTIATIONS WITHOUT CLOSING ANY OF FIVE CASES. . . . CONSIDER FURTHER DISCUSSION USELESS AND DESIRE SAIL NEXT SUNDAY WITH OR WITHOUT PROTOCOL."[37]

Buchanan's despairing cablegram to Washington marked the low point of his mission to Caracas. Yet screening his pessimism from the Venezuelan foreign minister, he accelerated his efforts to wrest a settlement. Ten more times during the next four days he conferred with his opposite. On several occasions, in the hope of effecting an out-of-court settlement, he served as mediator between government lawyers and Bermúdez representatives in Caracas.[38] On the 11th, with unanticipated suddenness, the two parties signed a new contract that effectively terminated reciprocal contentions and restored the company's property and operating rights.[39] Two days later, in the presence of President Gómez and his entire cabinet, Buchanan and González Guinán signed all essential documents pertaining to the American claims.[40]

During the preceding forty-five days the American commissioner had held thirty-nine conferences with the Venezuelan foreign minister. He had discussed basic issues and principles with President Gómez. He had composed and despatched to Washington some fifty cablegrams, several of extraordinary length. From the State Department he had received almost as many messages of instruction.[41] In addition, without missing a day, he had faithfully maintained his Date Book entries of activities and reactions. On 14 February, with evident joy, he wrote: "Valentine day. The first peaceful day I have had since reaching here."[42]

Buchanan's mission ended with a series of social affairs. To mark the successful termination of the protracted negotiations and to symbolize Venezuela's return to more cordial relations with other nations, President Gómez offered a state dinner for the departing commissioner and all members of the diplomatic corps. On behalf of the president the foreign minister thanked Buchanan for his "conciliatory spirit" and the diplomats for their "sympathy and moral support." Speaking for the diplomatic corps, its acting dean, Brazilian Minister Lorena, congratulated both Venezuelan and American negotiators on the reestablishment of harmonious relations. To close the program of toasts Buchanan responded with effusive thanks and expansive good wishes to his Venezuelan hosts. This pattern of toasts was repeated the following morning when the American envoy entertained at breakfast the cabinet ministers, several high court judges, and the Brazilian diplomats who had aided him. And there were still more toasts that evening when Minister Lorena gave Buchanan a farewell dinner. In his journal that evening, his fifty-second in Venezuela, the tired diplomat could write with feeling, "This is my last night in Caracas and I go with the things I came for and everyone happy and newspapers satisfied as well so I am happy."[43]

After seven weeks of strenuous negotiating sessions in Caracas Buchanan found quite "like home" the familiar decks of the USS *Des Moines*. The cruiser which had carried him from Costa Rica to Vera Cruz only a few months before now bore him northward from La Guaira to Guantánamo Bay. Scheduled to change ships at the navy's Cuban base, he found the 1000-ton *Marietta* coaled up and ready for the five-day passage to Washington. Aboard the less commodious vessel, his guest cabin "about 6 × 6 × 6 and not an inch more," the envoy immediately began to hope for calm seas and storm-free entry into Chesapeake Bay.[44]

Reaching Washington on 26 February, prepared to submit the final accounting of his Venezuelan mission, Buchanan confronted a changed situation in the Department of State. His friend and counsellor, Elihu Root, who had entrusted him with the Venezuelan assignment, had left the secretaryship just a month before. Robert Bacon was entering the final week of his stopgap incumbency. On 5 March Philander C. Knox would assume direction of President Taft's foreign policy.

Buchanan's final report to the Department consisted of a series of brief communications, all dated 26 February. In submitting English and Spanish copies of the protocol he had negotiated, he delineated his resolution of the five long-standing claims: settlement of the Jaurett and New York and Bermúdez Company cases and eventual arbitration of the other three. He detailed his efforts to persuade the Venezuelan government and the authorities of two of the three companies (Orinoco Corporation and United States and Venezuela Company) to seek direct settlement of their claims before the arbiters took over. With appropriate covering memoranda he submitted a copy of the Jaurett agreement and his considerable accumulation of evidential documents for the other cases. Finally, he explained carefully the conditions he had presented to the Venezuelan authorities as prerequisites for resumption of diplomatic intercourse.[45]

Once finished with these official communications to the Department of State, Buchanan composed a brief personal note to Root. Here, in less formal language, he revealed his innermost thoughts about the former secretary's hopes for

Venezuela and his own efforts in Caracas: "Hope to see you soon to tell you of my Venezuela experience. That much scribbled old slate is clear and best of all every one down there is satisfied and happy. We have all we ever wanted and more too with the settlement worked out in the Bermúdez case. While it was hard work it was great fun."[46] Upon his return to Buffalo Buchanan elaborated his views to an inquiring journalist: "The situation in Venezuela is very much improved since Castro left, . . . There is no evidence of disaffection, and the government is doing the very best it can to untangle and reform the difficulties that brought about the unhappy conditions that existed."[47]

From his Buffalo home then Buchanan became the official instrumentality through which the estranged nations renewed formal relations. Acting under authorization of Secretary Knox on his first day in office, Buchanan cabled Foreign Minister González Guinán that the American minister was prepared to return to Caracas. When the secretary learned the identity of Venezuela's minister-designate, he immediately enlisted Buchanan's assistance: "If you think the selection a good one, the Department would be glad if you would telegraph to Caracas expressing the pleasure it would give to the President to receive him." By 13 March both ministers were en route to their posts.[48]

Relaxing for a time before resuming his New York Life duties, Buchanan could ponder both the past and future of his diplomatic career. He must have reflected on the considerate note Secretary Root had found time to compose on his last day in office. After reviewing Buchanan's connections with the Central American Peace Conference, the Central American Court of Justice, the lengthy negotiations with Panama and Colombia, and the dispute with Venezuela, he praised his envoy's "patience and tact," his "skill and sagacity." "For all these services," he acknowledged, "I feel grateful to you, and in addition to that my work in the State Department has been made much more agreeable and easy by the pleasant intimacy and friendship which has existed between us."[49] Root's 26 January letter did not come to Buchanan's attention until his return from Caracas. At once he acknowledged the former secretary's encomium. "I find your simpatica letter here and it goes among the few things that will always remain bright and treasured in connection with my Latin American work. The chief thing however is your friendship and regard which I shall always hold higher than all else."[50]

But even this exchange was not the last of their mutual expressions of admiration and appreciation. To Buchanan's note of 26 February the new senator replied, "I have received your kind telegram upon your return from Venezuela and I want to tell you how much I rejoice in the great success that you made there. There is no other man in America who could have accomplished it but yourself. I met some of the Bermuda Asphalt lawyers in New York the other day and they were very jubilant and think you are the greatest man who ever was." Root was especially pleased that his appointee had concluded the vexing Venezuelan controversy "by means of a peaceful and dignified course of treatment, as contrasted with the bullying and threatening method, and the effect of the whole proceeding upon our relations with the Latin-American countries."[51]

Neither Root nor Buchanan could have known, of course, that only a few days before President Roosevelt had written to Andrew Carnegie in praise of his secretary's Latin American policies: "During the last three years the bulk of the most important work we have done has been in connection with the South and Central American States. We have done more as regards these States than ever before in the history of the State Department. This work has been entirely Root's."[52] Throughout these three years, as Root sought to develop his neighborly attitude toward Western Hemisphere nations, he had chosen Buchanan to carry his torch in every face-to-face confrontation with the Latin Americans. He had made the Buffalonian his right-hand man in "smoothing away obstacles" that interfered with inter-American comity.[53]

From Caracas, too, Buchanan received tokens of consideration for his conduct of the claims negotiations. In a continuing series of communications apprising him of Venezuela's improving international status, Foreign Minister González Guinán assured the former commissioner of the firm place he had won in the estimate of President Gómez and other Venezuelan leaders.⁵⁴ As tangible evidence of their appreciation, they conferred upon him the decoration, with diploma, of the Order of the Bust of Bolívar.⁵⁵

But however rewarding he may have regarded these expressions of government and business satisfaction with his performance, Buchanan knew they pertained to his affiliation with a past administration in Washington. Now William Howard Taft and Philander C. Knox had replaced Theodore Roosevelt and Elihu Root. Until the new leaders committed themselves, he had no way of knowing what their attitude would be toward him. From his own experience in Mexico City, Panama, Rio, and Central America, however, he could conclude that successful execution of a special diplomatic assignment usually produced its consequent responsibility. Through these March days, therefore, though still committed to the New York Life Insurance Company, he must have wondered if Secretary Knox would invite his assistance in handling the Venezuelan claims arbitration at The Hague. His answer was soon forthcoming.

The new administration waited barely a month to develop its plans for implementing Buchanan's 13 February arbitration protocol. Initiating a practice he would continue to follow toward Latin American affairs, Knox placed these arrangements largely in the hands of Assistant Secretary Huntington Wilson. The department would appoint an agent for the arbitration, a solicitor to advise him, and a special representative to collect essential documents in Caracas. It would insist upon screening and approving judges assigned to hear the cases and would invite the three companies to nominate the attorneys who would represent them at The Hague. Essential court expenses, including $10,000 for the agent, would be paid by the department, though these might later be deducted from any awards granted the companies.⁵⁶

In Wilson's view, "an ideal Agent [for the arbitration] should be a pretty good lawyer, a pretty good diplomatist and a man who speaks French, and he should have a good knowledge of the cases." He seriously considered the appointment of Robert C. Morris, who had served as the American agent for the United States-Venezuelan Claims Commission of 1903, and

John Bassett Moore, distinguished legal authority and former assistant secretary of state.[57] In the end, however, like Hay and Root before him, Wilson turned to Buchanan.[58]

But the veteran of special missions was already planning overseas trips for NYLIC to Mexico and Europe, possibly also to Brazil and Argentina. He expected to be in Mexico in late May and early June and in Europe during most of July. Assured that his absence of three or four months would not interfere with the assignment, he eagerly accepted the opportunity to complete the Venezuelan work he had started. At once he briefed W. T. Sherman Doyle, appointed special representative for the Caracas mission, and conferred with William C. Dennis, who would serve as his solicitor.[59]

During the following months, while travelling abroad or commuting between Buffalo and New York or Washington, Buchanan managed to interweave his State Department duties with his NYLIC responsibilities. To keep him abreast of current developments Washington officials forwarded to his Buffalo home copies of every essential document relating to the arbitration cases.[60] Occasionally they cabled him at the American embassies in Mexico City, London, Berlin, or Paris. His files on the cases assumed formidable proportions.

This steady flow of communications from the State Department provided Buchanan several kinds of documentary materials. He received copies of all cabled exchanges between the department and its representatives in Caracas, the United States minister and the special representative for the arbitration. He reviewed the extensive correspondence between the department and the two American companies he had urged to reconcile differences with Venezuela before the Hague Court assumed jurisdiction. These communications included documents on claims and counter claims, on depositions taken in Caracas and elsewhere, and on the department's role as intermediary. And, finally, he received notification of official efforts to evaluate the fitness of various members of the Permanent Court of Arbitration to serve as arbiters for the claims cases.

By the time Buchanan returned from Mexico in mid-June he felt the need to review this accumulating evidence with Assistant Secretary Wilson and Solicitor Dennis and to begin preparation of the case he would present before the Hague Tribunal. The three men readily reached tentative agreement upon a number of tactical procedures. In accord with Buchanan's proposal, they determined that the United States case should involve no attack on the Dictator Castro "as essentially lawless and tyrannical." Rather, it should "show that his control of the Government was such that the claimants had a right to rely upon his representations." They agreed to adhere to the department's traditional reservations on the Calvo Clause. They adopted priorities for selection of judges to hear the cases. To contribute from the first-hand background he had acquired in Caracas, Doyle would accompany Buchanan and Dennis to The Hague.[61]

With these matters satisfactorily arranged in Washington, Buchanan could return to his planned program of overseas missions for NYLIC. From late June to early August, as he moved from his usual base at Claridge's in London to Berlin and Paris, he received little news of the developments on the claims cases. Though an occasional cablegram from Washington required his immediate attention, the bulk of routine State Department communications continued to flow to his Buffalo home. Back again in the United States, Buchanan returned to the pattern of activity that had now become almost a way of life. Between brief intervals with his frequently neglected family, he commuted to New York and Washington to meet his dual professional responsibilities. And even while at home he faced the necessity of absorbing a new profusion of despatches on the Venezuelan claims.

Before his next planned departure for Europe, however, two developments greatly eased preparations for his presentation at The Hague. On 21 August the United States and Venezuela Company agreed to accept Venezuela's offer of $475,000 to settle the original claim of $1,500,000. On 9 September the Orinoco Corporation accepted a similar offer of $385,000 to satisfy its claim of $1,750,000.[62] For both of these prearbitration protocols Buchanan had laid the bases during his mission to Caracas and repeatedly during the following months had urged company representatives to push for settlement by direct negotiation. Now he regarded as "very fair" the definitive terms the companies had finally accepted.[63] At the same time, he could find satisfaction in knowing that his work at The Hague would be reduced by two-thirds.

Harassed as he was by his almost constant travels, Buchanan still found time to attend to his other Latin American interests. Though the work of his Pan American Committee had necessarily devolved on its executive committee, he continued to serve as its nominal chairman.[64] Committee concerns now consisted chiefly of delegation membership and agenda preparations for the Fourth Conference of the American States scheduled for Buenos Aires in mid-1910. Through communications with both Senator Root and Assistant Secretary Wilson, Buchanan urged appointment of the American delegates "at the earliest date."[65]

Though it was ten years since he had resigned as minister to Argentina, the Buffalonian had steadfastly maintained his interest in the country of his first diplomatic assignment. And Argentina leaders still remembered him. When they began preparations for an elaborate agricultural exhibition to honor their nation's centennial celebration in 1910, they made the former minister an honorary commissioner.[66] In accepting this position he saw a new opportunity to foster the Argentine-American trade he had with such frustration sought to encourage in the 1890s. To assure a Department of Agriculture exhibit of representative dimensions he secured the enthusiastic assistance of Senator Root. The former secretary's corollary observation that American entrepreneurs should establish a bank in Buenos Aires and inaugurate a direct line of steamships aroused warm response in Buchanan.[67] He had been urging these developments for more than a decade.

On 15 September, with dates for his presentation at The Hague still not fixed, Buchanan sailed again for Europe—his fourth foreign trip in nine months. Though his primary purpose was to revisit London, Berlin, and Paris for NYLIC, his family letters suggest that he also planned to perform services for J. P. Morgan and Company.[68] In addition, to keep abreast of the forthcoming arbitration, he included in his portfolio essential papers on the Orinoco Steamship Company case.[69]

Accustomed in recent months to ocean travel aboard austere American men-of-war, Buchanan was now able to enjoy all the amenities of the Cunard luxury liner *Mauretania*.[70] Following his normal shipboard pattern when travelling alone, Buchanan devoted his time to reading, conversing with fellow passengers, and writing daily notes to Mrs. Buchanan. Long a prodigious reader, his interests now seemed to emphasize biography, as he explored such widely disparate lives as those of St. Francis, Thomas Jefferson, Robert Fulton, and Lady Hamilton. Among interesting ship companions he found the director of a vaudeville chimpanzee act and the world's largest manufacturer of roller skates—the latter, he observed, "not a very uplifting occupation."[71] Beyond relating these routine shipboard activities, his daily additions to Mrs. Buchanan's letter reflected a deepening solicitude for the welfare and serenity of his family. "We will have good times yet," he assured her, "free from the cares and worries of this year and enjoy each other and the sunshine that all are entitled to have as the years close in."[72]

Just as he had done only two months before, Buchanan followed his arrival at Claridge's, London, with shuttle trips to Paris and Berlin. In each of the capitals he met with NYLIC representatives to iron out the problems that continued to beset the company's gradually diminishing foreign operations. From time to time he held conferences with officials of the Morgan interests.[73]

Though State Department responsibilities were not the focus of his trip, Buchanan did not permit Latin American matters to escape his vigilance. Through the cable services of American embassies he kept in touch with developments on the Venezuelan claims case and the Pan American Committee's planning for the Buenos Aires Conference. He continued to give advice on the State Department's selection of a judge for the Hague arbitration and followed closely the changing timetable for the presentation of case and countercase.[74]

With a view to briefing himself on the developing situation in Buenos Aires, he sought out Argentine diplomats in each of the European capitals. From Luis María Drago in London he learned that Argentina had already named its delegation to the forthcoming inter-American conference—five former ministers of foreign affairs and the nation's probable president-elect, Roque Saenz Peña. In a long despatch to Knox, Buchanan promptly relayed his findings on the strength of Argentina's delegation to the conference it would host. In Paris he renewed his friendship with Saenz Peña himself, recently named as Venezuela's choice for the Hague hearings. In Berlin he conferred with Argentine Minister Indalecio Gómez.[75]

By the early days of October, already anticipating his return to Buffalo, Buchanan was beginning to feel the pressure of his hurried journeys, frequent conferences, and multiple responsibilities. During the previous two years he had spent more than half his time in foreign assignments and the ship or train travel to fulfill them. Moreover in every journey since he and Mrs. Buchanan had returned from Spain in March 1908, he had travelled alone. He missed the joys he had known in earlier years when members of his family had accompanied him to Buenos Aires, Mexico, Panama, Rio, The Hague, and Central America. Never in his decade or more of traveling had his correspondence revealed so deeply his fatigue, his loneliness, his concern for family problems, or his eagerness to find a more settled way of life. Repeatedly in his letters to Mrs. Buchanan he expressed his anxieties about their son's personal plans, their daughter's happiness, and their son-in-law's health and financial cares.[76]

Always resourceful in composing tender messages to his wife, he seemed now to search for ever fresher ways of expressing his feelings toward her. "This world could never give you," he wrote in late September, "what it owes you in happiness and in sweetness of all things touching you."[77] Three weeks later, in more unpretending vein, he disclosed a deepening passion to return to a more simple life: "Laurie, your picture of being at home quiet and comfy marketing and putting up fruit jams and jellies and of your being taken back to Sioux City days, made me frightfully jealous of your surroundings and wild to be with you." Even more to betray the ennui that seemed to be growing within him, he added, "The difference between that sane and healthful atmosphere and the Americanized unrest and fashionable Restaurant way of living over here . . . really gives one a pain in the plexis solaris."[78]

But, however tired and concerned, the fifty-seven-year-old diplomat was not dispirited. He still had professional obligations to meet. Soon he would return to Buffalo to prepare for another train trip to Mexico on behalf of NYLIC. Early in 1910 he would meet his scheduled State Department appointment at The Hague to present the American case for the Orinoco Steamship Company.[79] And between these assignments he faced visits to New York and Washington to report to his superiors. Solicitously he urged Mrs. Buchanan to accompany him and, in the hope that she would select new gowns for the occasions, sent her three fashion books from Paris.[80]

But none of these plans would come to fruition. In the early evening of 15 October, comfortable in his hotel room at Claridge's, Will wrote his last letter to Lulu: "The wind is howling this evening. . .," he reminded her, "Thank heaven I do not have to cross the channel. . . . Now if only you were here honey because it is simply too lonely."[81] Twenty-four hours later, while returning to his hotel after dinner with a business associate, William Buchanan died.[82]

At memorial services in Buffalo two weeks later colleagues from his varied careers paid their respects. Fellow officials of the Pan-American Exposition served as honorary bearers. The Department of State and the Bureau of American Republics sent special representatives. George Westinghouse arrived from Pittsburgh in his private railroad car.[83] The New York Life Insurance Company and various other business and civic organizations presented appropriate resolutions or floral tributes.[84] Diplomats of Great Britain, Argentina, Venezuela, Costa Rica, Guatemala, and other Latin American nations sent expressions of condolence. In formal memorial to the Department of State the Central American Court of Justice remembered Buchanan for his "contemporaneous work of international pacification . . . [among] the Spanish American peoples."[85]

Chapter 17
PIONEER GOOD NEIGHBOR
Epilogue

William Buchanan spent most of his last thirty years in some form of public service. During these three decades he intermittenly pursued three careers, two of them sometimes running concurrently. In the 1880s he was at once a commercial salesman and an entrepreneur of public entertainment. In the 1890s he was both an exposition chief and a regularly appointed envoy for the Department of State. In the 1900s he was an overseas representative for American corporations, entrusted with tasks of a semidiplomatic nature, while serving on call as a roving United States diplomat.

Of all these career endeavors, however, none seemed quite to satisfy Buchanan's longing for a settled way of life. Each of his experiences with theater management and exposition direction was of short duration. His employment by companies selling cigars, chinaware, electrical equipment, and insurance led to no permanent full-time affiliation. In spite of his numerous missions for the Department of State, he never became a true career diplomat. As he occasionally mused about his frequent shifts in activity, each change seemed to him a deviation from the main purpose of his life—a digression, usually at the expense of unity and continuity. To the historian, however, Buchanan's career of diverse endeavors appears more episodic than digressive. At first glance, perhaps, each business connection or diplomatic mission seems incidental, separable from any personal design he might have had. Yet on closer analysis, each episode seems to flow naturally from the mainstream of his life pattern and to form an essential part of its development. Sometimes through good planning, sometimes, good fortune, he used each position or each activity as a stepping stone to the next.

Management of Sioux City's theaters led to supervision of its Corn Palace festivals. Success with Corn Palaces and a personal background of farm life brought appointment as the Columbian Exposition's agricultural chief. Contacts in Chicago with American industrialists and farm leaders and with Latin American exhibitors suggested to President Cleveland Buchanan's availability for diplomatic service in Argentina. His experiences in both Chicago and Buenos Aires made him the natural choice to direct Buffalo's Pan-American Exposition. His varied, but progressively intimate, relations with President McKinley brought appointment to the Mexico Conference of American States.

On a different tack, assistance to the New York Life Insurance Company in Buenos Aires opened the door to permanent affiliation with its overseas operations. Repeated conferences with Theodore Roosevelt and John Hay in Buffalo and Washington placed Buchanan in their minds as the ideal envoy for the sensitive assignment to Panama in 1903. And, most significantly, consultation with Secretary of War Root prior to the Panama mission contributed significantly to Buchanan's success as a trouble-shooting diplomat. When two years later Root became secretary of state, he promptly made Buchanan the principal field agent for promotion of his good-neighbor attitude toward the Latin Americans.

How then does one evaluate Buchanan's episodic career? What is the measure of his achievement? How did a son of the Midwestern prairies, however full-blooded and abounding in vitality, become a faithful exponent of Washington's new Latin American policy, a skilled negotiator known and respected throughout the Hemisphere? What amalgam of inherited and acquired characteristics produced in him the "ability to enter into the peculiar mental processes of the Latin American people"?[1]

During his lifetime Buchanan received no honorary degrees, no official citations from his government, only a single decoration from a foreign nation. Yet, at the time of his death, testimonials flowed abundantly from journalists, Washington officials, and Latin American statesmen. Of these, perhaps the most discerning, if not the most eloquent, was the commentary of Assistant Secretary of State Alvey A. Adee. As its highest ranking permanent officer in 1909, Adee had served the Department of State for thirty years; he would hold office another twenty. Secretaries and assistant secretaries moved in and out, but through one administration after another he retained his post. Even presidents relied upon his mastery of protocol, international law, and the traditions of American foreign policy.[2] In the view of this veteran diplomat, Buchanan possessed to a greater degree than any other man he had known the "instinct of diplomacy."[3]

To the modern behavioral scientist or psychohistorian this characterization may not pass the tests of scientific validity. Yet to Adee and many of his contemporaries, Buchanan in several ways did seem to reveal "a natural aptitude" for the conduct of human relations and for the diplomatic processes of mediation and conciliation. In any case, without attempting to demonstrate cause-and-effect relationships, one may seek connections between Buchanan's early experiences and his later diplomatic successes.

In the first place, he was essentially a grass-roots diplomat, one who operated largely behind the scenes while avoiding undue emphasis upon personal or national self-interest. Successful foreign policy, as he repeatedly demonstrated, is based upon good will, proper regard for the rights and customs of other peoples, and the desire to know and understand. The greater the cultural differences between nations, the longer and more difficult the process of comprehension.

Early in his careers as commercial salesman and entertainment manager Buchanan learned the indispensability of knowing his territory and the people who comprised it. If he hoped to sell cheap stogies or Havana perfectos, butter crocks or Haviland china, he needed to understand his prospective clients. In managing theaters and directing Corn Palace celebrations, he learned that only perfection of detail and insistence upon the innovative would attract patrons. Similarly, in his exposition work he constantly reminded his superiors and his staffs of the opportunities at hand to raise the aesthetic and educational horizons of patrons. Here, too, he first came to know the Latin Americans and to sense their needs and desires. Without the necessity of demanding something in return, he found himself in a position to render them the assistance of a good neighbor.

After fifteen years of commercial travelling to the whistle stops and cities of the American West and varied experiences with the exhibition of farm animals and produce, Buchanan in 1894 suddenly found himself transposed to the grasslands and grain fields of Argentina. Nothing came more naturally to the former farm boy-drummer than to seek to understand the people and countryside of the Argentine pampas as he had come to know the people and countryside of his own Middle West. Through his observations, conversations, and travels he gradually cultivated his ability to exercise "proper regard for the rights and customs of the people with whom he dealt."[4] As time permitted on later missions, this became the pattern of his conduct in half a dozen other Latin American nations.

Just as fundamentally, successful foreign policy consists of more than a grand design or statements of salutary purpose. It involves more than the eloquently posed doctrines of presidents or the carefully phrased instructions of secretaries of state. It is also the mundane work of the envoy in the field, the slow, day-to-day confrontation of problems and unraveling of details. Throughout his decade as theater manager, Corn Palace overseer, and exposition chief, Buchanan faced precisely these kinds of assignments, usually without the kudos that went to his superiors. Well planned and diversified theater seasons redounded to the credit of the owners, not the manager. Successful Corn Palace festivals brought plaudits for Sioux City's mayor and city fathers. Well-rounded exhibits of livestock and farm produce at the Columbian Exposition merely increased acclaim for the Chicago citizens who had pioneered and produced the project.

Well before he undertook his first diplomatic assignment

in Argentina, therefore, he had mastered the practice that later government and military bureaucrats would call "completed staff work." Again and again during his later careers as State Department envoy and as diplomat of business he called upon this ability. Through many difficult situations "he never failed to know his own case in its completeness and the case of the other side as well."[5]

Closely allied to Buchanan's appetite for knowledge and his mastery of details—so often called into play in his grass-roots operations—was his capacity to cope with crisis situations. In diplomacy, clearly, as in labor-management relations and other human activities, crisis situations demand special handling by a special kind of negotiator. Unlike the resident envoy, primarily concerned with day-to-day conduct of routine relations, the special emissary can operate with a specific limited objective. His singleness of purpose gives him a fresher outlook, a different perspective, one that enables him to analyze a crucial situation more sharply against the background of a nation's character or mood.

Through his managerial assignments in Sioux City, Chicago, and Buffalo, Buchanan demonstrated that, whether by innate ability or predilection, he was the trouble-shooting type. At Sioux City he developed the calm and poise essential to stimulate and coordinate the volunteer work of citizen committees. At Chicago, in directing the recruitment, emplacement, and dismantling of hundreds of exhibits for four exposition departments, his "Anglo-Saxon vigor of manner" won the confidence of Latin Americans as well as of his own countrymen.[6] At Buffalo, to keep the exposition on even keel, he overcame the deleterious effects of freakish weather, civic apathy, labor unrest, financial problems, and a presidential assassination. Out of these diverse experiences, Buchanan distilled the qualities and abilities that would make him an effective envoy for both government and business. He had taught himself how to focus on the immediate problem, to sense its keys, sort out its essentials, and, without injecting his own self-image, find a compromise solution. He came to appreciate the restricted objectives and limited utility of crisis actions.

During his extended residence in Argentina at the outset

of his diplomatic career, he called upon these skills to establish his place among people of a different culture. By his persistent efforts to improve Argentine-American relations and his success in settling the Andean boundary dispute, he convinced Latin American leaders of his honesty, sagacity, and genuine concern for the welfare of their nations. He became more deeply aware of the impact of his own government's policies on the Latin Americans and increasingly concerned with the promotion of Hemisphere good will and understanding.

This background of Buchanan's attracted the confidence of Secretaries Hay and Root and businessmen Perkins and Westinghouse. Testing both his skills and his stamina during the next decade, they plied him with one critical assignment after another: to clarify American treaty rights in Panama and to assist the young nation in framing its first constitution; to compromise arbitration and other accords at two inter-American conferences; to assist the Latin Americans at the Second Hague Peace Conference; to promote peace and stability in Central America; to facilitate rapprochement between Panama and Colombia; to effect renewal of relations with Venezuela; and to cope with overseas problems of two American corporations.

In still a third way Buchanan may be said to have possessed what Adee regarded as the "instinct of diplomacy." This involved his intimate association in the years after 1890 with the country's growing confidence in its own material progress and its deepening belief in the exportability of its democratic and free-enterprise ideas. Not always unreservedly, he became an essential cog in the wheel of American efforts to spread its system to other parts of the world, especially to less developed regions.

As early as 1888, when Sioux City welcomed its Latin American visitors, Buchanan became aware of Washington's eagerness to demonstrate the nation's growing economic power. In his exposition work in Chicago and Buffalo he shared in urban efforts to spread the doctrine of progress through display of the products of American and Hemisphere farms and factories. After Chicago, he fully realized that his appointment to improve commercial relations with Argentina stemmed from the concerted support of American farm organizations, manufacturers, and exporters. Once at his post, while struggling interminably to conclude a new trade agreement, he initiated an inspection visit of American industrialists to the Atlantic nations of South America.

At the Mexico and Rio Conferences of the American States, though concentrating his efforts on arbitration agreements, Buchanan supported varied proposals to improve inter-American commerce and to strengthen the Bureau of American Republics. Each of his later missions to Panama, Central America, and Venezuela involved Washington's hopes for political stability in the vicinity of the Panama Canal or along the sealanes approaching it. And throughout the decade of his free-lance activities for the New York Life Insurance Company he personified the intimate partnership that was developing between the American government and American business.

Buchanan, of course, was not alone in his promotion of the new commercial expansionism. He was but one in a new breed of American diplomats who helped to spread in foreign fields the new doctrines of Presidents McKinley and Roosevelt and their secretaries of state. Better known among these was his friend and occasional colleague, John Barrett. After an early diplomatic assignment in the Far East, Barrett had joined Buchanan on the United States delegation to the Mexico Conference, followed him as minister to Panama and Argentina, and, as director general of the Pan American Union after 1907, assisted Buchanan's committee planning for the Buenos Aires Conference of 1910. In a recent perceptive study of Barrett's career as commercial publicist and expansionist, Salvatore Prisco III characterizes him as a zealot "in the cause of industrial, commercial, and scientific progress" and "a missionary for world progress according to the gospel of the American business civilization."[7] But spreading the doctrines of America's Progressive Era required spokesmen and activists of varied molds. Buchanan, clearly, was not a zealot, nor the missionary type. He was more the educator than preacher or publicist, more the conciliator than politician or propagandist. Above all, he was the pragmatist, not the theorist.

Perhaps the salient feature of his unsung career was the element of continuity he contributed to his country's developing goals in the Western Hemisphere. Once he entered the arena of diplomacy, he could not escape it; government and business executives alike repeatedly commanded his involvement. For fifteen years (1894-1909) he represented a degree of consistency in inter-American affairs—understanding the issues, learning to know the Latin American leaders, being known and trusted by them, appreciating their problems, assuaging their concerns, yet always feeling that the honor of his country was entrusted to his hands. In promoting "true Pan-American good will and friendship," as John Barrett wrote of him, William Buchanan was a pioneer good neighbor.

NOTES

(With few exceptions, authors and titles of printed books are identified in accordance with entries in the National Union Catalog.)

ABBREVIATIONS

BECHS—Buffalo and Erie County Historical Society
BECPL—Buffalo and Erie County Public Library
BP—Buchanan Papers
CHS—Chicago Historical Society
Cong. Rec.—*Congressional Record*
Cont.—Container
Corres. of State Dept.—Correspondence of State Department
DAB—*Dictionary of American Biography*
Desp. Arg.)   (Argentina
Desp. Chile)   Despatches   (Chile
Desp. Mex.)   from Ministers   (Mexico
Desp. Pan.)   (Panama
For. Rel.—*Papers relating to the Foreign Relations of the United States*
Gen. Corres.—General Correspondence
H. Rep.—*House Report*
IAC—International American Conference
Inst. Arg.)   Instructions   (Argentina
Inst. Pan.)   to Ministers   (Panama
LC, MD—Library of Congress, Manuscript Division
Letters from DG—Letters from Director General (Pan-American Exposition)
Letters from Ex. Com.—Letters from Executive Committee (Pan-American Exposition)
Memoria—Argentine Republic, Ministerio de Relaciones Exteriores y Culto, *Memoria de relaciones exteriores presentada al Congreso Nacional*
Mrs. WIB—Mrs. William I. Buchanan
NA, DS—National Archives, Department of State
Notes from Arg.—Notes from Argentina
Num. File—Numerical File
RC, AN—Republic of Chile, Archivo Nacional
Report of DG—Report of Director General (Pan-American Exposition)
SCJ—*Sioux City* (Iowa) *Journal*
Sen. Doc.—*Senate Document*
WCE—World's Columbian Exposition
WIB—William I. Buchanan

Chapter 1
DIPLOMAT OF THE AMERICAS

1. Pan American Union, *Bulletin* 29 (Nov. 1909): 821. Uppercase letters as in original.
2. The director general was John Barrett, former United States Foreign Service officer (see pp. 195, 258, 313, 352-353).
3. Richard Williams Leopold, *Elihu Root and the Conservative Tradition,* p. 62.
4. See ch. 14 and pp. 298, 312-313, 342.
5. See ch. 15.
6. See pp. 256-258, 269, 296.
7. See ch. 16.
8. See chs. 5-7.
9. See ch. 4.
10. See chs. 8-9.
11. Later he served as official consultant for St. Louis's Louisiana Purchase Exposition (1904) and Jamestown's Tercentenary Exposition (1907), each in its way recalling a significant Western Hemisphere development (see pp. 190-191, 197, 207, 208, 222, 232, 236, 268, 297).
12. See ch. 10.
13. See ch. 12.
14. *Washington Times,* 14 May 1907.
15. See ch. 11 and Index entry. Buchanan managed to weave still another business affiliation among his recurring State Department assignments. From a London base in 1904-1906 he served as managing director of George Westinghouse's diversified manufacturing interests in Europe (see ch. 13). This was his only major activity after 1891 not connected, directly or indirectly, with Latin America.
16. Root to William I. Buchanan (henceforth WIB), National Archives, Department of State (henceforth NA, DS), Numerical File (henceforth Num. File.), Case 16180/4a.
17. Enrique Creel, quoted in unidentified newspaper clipping, 12 June 1908, Buffalo and Erie County Historical Society (henceforth BECHS), Buchanan Papers (henceforth BP).
18. Alfredo Jiménez to William L. Merry, US minister to Costa Rica, 26 Oct. 1909, Num. File, Case 16180/130.
19. Martin Garcia Mérou to Hay, 15 Dec. 1898, US Department of State, *Papers relating to the Foreign Relations of the United States* (henceforth *For. Rel.*), 1898, pp. 2-3.
20. Julio Roca to WIB, 26 Jan. 1900, BP.
21. *Washington Times,* 14 May 1907.
22. Expression used by anonymous writer in Pan American Union, *Bulletin,* 29 (Nov. 1909): 835.
23. NA, DS, Appointment Cards.

Chapter 2
BEGINNINGS OF CAREER AND FAMILY

1. WIB to Mrs. Buchanan (henceforth Mrs. WIB), [10 Sep.], 1879, BP.

2. Leonard U. Hill, *John Johnston and the Indians in the Land of the Three Miamis: The History of Miami County, Ohio,* pp. 433-435; Writers' Program, Ohio, *The Ohio Guide,* p. 484.

3. Belle C. Buchanan, *The Buchanan Clans,* pp. 31, 39-45; *The History of Miami County,* pp. 461-462; *Memoirs of the Miami Valley,* John C. Hover, et al (eds.), I, 559.

4. Robert E. Chaddock, *Ohio Before 1850,* pp. 30-35.

5. *A Genealogical and Biographical Record of Miami County, Ohio* (henceforth *Genealogical Record*), pp. 242-243; Buchanan, *Buchanan Clans,* pp. 30-32. Eight of their twelve children grew to maturity.

6. The Ohio Buchanans traced their ancestry to King Hugh Capet, Alfred the Great, and Robert Bruce. According to a family tradition, George Buchanan's father, James, was one of three brothers who emigrated from Scotland in mideighteenth century (Buchanan, *Buchanan Clans,* pp. 46-50; *Genealogical Record,* pp. 240-241). However, another tradition says that James was born in Rockingham County, Virginia (Letter to author from A. E. Buchanan, Piqua, Ohio, 15 Oct. 1974).

7. Chaddock, *Ohio Before 1850,* pp. 19-21; Thomas Chalmers Harbaugh (ed. and comp.), *Centennial History. Troy, Piqua and Miami County, Ohio,* pp. 69-72.

8. Harbaugh, *Centennial History,* pp. 72-78; Chaddock, *Ohio Before 1850,* pp. 23-24.

9. *Genealogical Record,* p. 243; Buchanan, *Buchanan Clans,* p. 31.

10. *The History of Miami County,* pp. 436-437; Harbaugh, *Centennial History,* pp. 131-147 *passim; The Ohio Guide,* p. 485.

11. *Genealogical Record,* pp. 243-244; Buchanan, *Buchanan Clans,* pp. 33-36.

12. Unidentified newspaper clipping, BP, confirmed by deed on record, according to letter, A. E. Buchanan to author, 15 Oct. 1974.

13. *Dictionary of American Biography* (henceforth *DAB*), III, 219; letter to author from A. E. Buchanan, 14 July 1969.

14. Buchanan, *Buchanan Clans,* p. 37; unidentified newspaper clipping, BP.

15. Draft of speech delivered at Cooper Union (henceforth Cooper Union speech), New York, 20 Jan. 1894, and unidentified newspaper clipping [1893], BP.

16. Cooper Union speech, BP.

17. As quoted in *ibid.*

18. At the opening of the Congress on Agriculture, World's Columbian Exposition (unidentified newspaper clipping, [1893?], BP).

19. Cooper Union speech, BP.
20. *Ibid.*
21. WIB to Mrs. WIB and children, 10 June 1898, BP.
22. Unidentified newspaper clipping, BP; Buchanan, *Buchanan Clans,* p. 37.
23. Entry in "The Log of the 'Royston Grange,' " compiled by Buchanan en route to Buenos Aires, Argentina, 22 May 1898, BP.
24. *Buffalo Express,* 19 July 1901; WIB to family, 11 Dec. 1881, and unidentified newspaper clipping, [1893?], BP.
25. *DAB,* III. 219; Pan American Union, *Bulletin* 29 (Nov. 1909): 835; unidentified newspaper clipping, 4 Feb. 1904, BP.
26. *The History of Montgomery County, Ohio,* pp. 604-637, 758-760.
27. Augustus Waldo Drury, *History of the City of Dayton and Montgomery County, Ohio,* I, 1058; *Williams' Dayton City Directory for 1880-81,* p. 81.
28. *History of Dayton, Ohio,* p. 564.
29. *Ibid.,* pp. 564-565.
30. *Dayton Daily Journal,* 17 April 1878.
31. WIB to Mrs. WIB, 3, 6-8 Sep. 1879, 17 Aug. 1880, BP. In the following notes of this chapter, unless otherwise specified, all dates refer to Buchanan's letters to his wife (all filed in BP). He evidently wrote many of these letters in haste, while riding in trains, waiting in railroad stations, or trying to keep warm in cold hotel rooms, often with more thought to substance than form. In reproducing excerpts I have sometimes inserted punctuation marks or corrected capitalization. Unless indicated, I have neither added nor deleted words. A number of the letters are undated.
32. 23 Mar. 1879, 3 Aug., 14 Nov. 1880, and undated letters.
33. 9 Dec. 18[80?].
34. 28 June 1880, Thanksgiving eve, 18[81?].
35. [7 Sep. 1879?], 18 Jan., 20, 28, 30 June, 2 July, 1 Dec. 1880, 11 Dec. 1881, and undated letters.
36. 23 Mar., 30 Oct. 1879, 21 Jan., 7 Apr., 28 Oct., 7-12 Dec. 1880.
37. 20, 23 Sep. 1880, 17 Sep., 11 Dec. 1881, and undated letters.
38. 8, 24, 27 June 1880.
39. 27 June, 31 Oct., 1, 3 Nov. 1880.
40. 3, 5 Nov. 1880.
41. 5 Dec. 1880.
42. 20 Mar., 3, 4, 11 Nov. 1879.
43. 14 Jan. 1880, 25 Jan. 1881.
44. 31 Jan. 1881.
45. 25 Sep. 1879.
46. 10 Aug. 18[80?].
47. 4 Apr., 17, 20, 27 June, 11 Aug. 1880.
48. 4, 7 Apr., 28 Oct., 1 Dec. 1880.
49. 14 Sept. 1879, 27 June 1880, and undated letters.
50. 28 June 1880.
51. *Ibid.*

52. 25 Sep., 11 Oct. 1879, 1, 29 July 1880.
53. 5, 7 Dec. 1880, 20 Mar., 5 Sep. 1881.
54. 23 Mar., 12 Oct. 1879.
55. 5 Dec. 188[1?].
56. 5 Sep. 188[1?]. Just after their wedding in 1878 the Buchanans had visited the Prughs in Ottumwa (*Dayton Daily Journal,* 17 Apr. 1878).
57. *History of the Counties of Woodbury and Plymouth, Iowa,* pp. 808-809; *Sioux City Journal* (henceforth *SCJ*), 11, 14 Jan., 31 Mar. 1881.
58. 28 June 1880, 16 Mar., 12 Oct. 1881.
59. 28 June 1880, and undated letter.

Chapter 3
CROCKS, CHORUSES, AND CORN PALACES

1. Unless otherwise noted, the following account of early Sioux City and northwestern Iowa is based upon *History of the Counties of Woodbury and Plymouth, Iowa,* especially, pp. 11-116; *History of Sioux City, Iowa, from Earliest Settlement to January, 1892;* Writers' Program, Iowa, "Woodbury County History, Iowa"; *Sioux City Sunday Journal* (henceforth *SCJ*), centennial ed., 25 July 1954.

2. *SCJ,* 25 July 1954.

3. *History of the Counties of Woodbury and Plymouth, Iowa,* pp. 122-130, 214; *SCJ,* 25 July 1954.

4. WIB to Mrs. WIB, 23 Feb. 188[2], BP; *SCJ,* 22 May 1882.

5. In a continuing flow of letters to Mrs. Buchanan from February until her departure from Dayton, WIB reported his reactions to Sioux City. Though all are undated, internal evidence reveals approximate times.

6. *SCJ,* 6, 8, 9 Mar., 5, 6 May 1882.

7. Lloyd Lewis and Henry Justin Smith, *Oscar Wilde Discovers America (1882),* pp. 6-7, 226-227.

8. *SCJ,* 21 Mar. 1882.

9. WIB to family, 20 Mar. 1882 [?], BP.

10. WIB to Mrs. WIB, undated letters, BP; *SCJ,* 21 May 1882.

11. *SCJ,* 25 Mar., 23 Sep. 1883, 2, 6 Mar., 14 Sep. 1884, 5 Apr., 28 July, 9 Aug., 25 Dec. 1885, 25 Apr., 10 June 1886, 9 Apr. 1887.

12. Buchanan's sellings trips continued until 1890. Occasionally he undertook buying trips to Chicago, Pittsburgh, and Wheeling. Regularly in his travels he renewed his old habit of writing frequent, but undated, letters to his family (see BP). His comings and goings were often noted in the "personal items" of the *Sioux City Journal.*

13. WIB to family, 8 Mar. 1885, BP.

14. *Ibid.*

15. *SCJ,* 24 May 1883.

16. *Ibid.,* 3 May 1884; *La Mars Daily Sentinel,* 10 May 1884.

17. Except as indicated, this description of Sioux City's boom in the 1880s relies on *History of the Counties of Woodbury and Plymouth, Iowa,* especially pp. 180-236.

18. *SCJ,* 25 July 1954.

19. *Ibid.*

20. *Ibid.*

21. *Ibid.*

22. *Ibid.,* 7 Dec. 1884, 25 July 1954; *Sioux City Times,* 26 May [1891?].

23. *SCJ,* 4 July 1884, 20, 27 Dec. 1885, 24 Jan. 1886, 11 Nov. 1887.

24. Justin Brooks Atkinson, *Broadway,* p. 89; *SCJ,* 30 Mar., 5 Apr. 1887.

25. For brief histories of the Sioux City Corn Palaces, see *History of the Counties of Woodbury and Plymouth,* pp. 249-253; *Sioux City's Corn Palaces, 1890, 1889, 1888, 1887;* John E. Briggs, "The Sioux City Corn Palaces," *The Palimpsest* 44, no. 12 (Dec. 1963):549-572; *SCJ,* 25 July 1954.

26. *SCJ,* 21 Aug. 1887, 23 Sep. 1888. Interesting reminiscences of the first palace are contained in a letter, dated 22 Nov. 1913, from E. D. Allen, in charge of decorations, to T. A. Black, president, Commercial Club, Sioux City (Sioux City Public Library Collections).

27. *SCJ,* 21 Aug. 1887.

28. *Ibid.,* 21, 24-27 Aug. 1887.

29. *Ibid.,* 7-15, 27 Sep. 1887, 1 Jan. 1888; letter, Allen to Black, 22 Nov. 1913.

30. *SCJ,* 28 Sep. 1887.

31. *Ibid.,* 24, 27 Sep., 1 Oct. 1887, 25 July 1954; Writers' Program, Iowa, "Woodbury County History," p. 89.

32. *SCJ,* 27 Sep. 1887.

33. *Ibid.,* 4 Oct. 1887, 25 July 1954; Writers' Program Iowa, "Woodbury County History," p. 90. See photograph in Illustration Section.

34. *SCJ,* 2, 5, 7 Oct. 1887.

35. *Ibid.,* 2 Oct. 1887.

36. *Ibid.,* 12 Oct. 1887, 1 Jan. 1888.

37. Grover Cleveland to Wilson S. Bissell, member of Cleveland's former Buffalo law firm, 27 Aug. 1887, *Letters of Grover Cleveland, 1850-1908,* Allan Nevins (ed.), p. 150; Nevins, *Grover Cleveland: A Study in Courage,* pp. 317-319.

38. *SCJ,* 4, 6 Sep., 12 Oct. 1887.

39. *Ibid.,* 12, 13, 15 Oct. 1887.

40. *Ibid.,* 18 Sep. 1887.

41. Quoted in *ibid.,* 26 Oct. 1887.

42. *Ibid.,* 23 Sep. 1888.

43. *Ibid.,* 14, 15, 18, 20 Mar., 25 Apr., 11 May, 8 June 1888.

44. *Ibid.,* 17, 19, 20, 26 June 1888.

45. *Sioux City's Corn Palaces; SCJ.* 7, 22, 23, 26-30 Sep. 1888. See photograph in Illustration Section.

46. *SCJ,* 9 Aug., 13 Sep. 1888.

47. *Ibid.,* 9, 25 Sep. 1888; 25 July 1954. A copy of the invitation is preserved in BP.

48. *SCJ,* 19, 24 July, 5ff Aug. 1884.

49. *Ibid.,* 9 Aug. 1888, 28 Apr. 1889; Atkinson, *Broadway,* p. 12.

50. *SCJ,* 28 Apr. 1889; *Sioux City Times,* 26 May 1891; Writers' Program, Iowa, "Woodbury County History," pp. 103-104.

51. Writers' Program, Iowa, pp. 103-104; *SCJ,* 23 Jan., 9 June, 7, 14 July 1889.

52. *SCJ,* 1 Jan. 1890. Members and kin of the Buchanan family were among those who made use of the Peavey stage. In one evening program of home-talent performances nine-year old Florence Buchanan danced a minuet. As a featured part of a memorial service to mark the twenty-fourth anniversary of Lincoln's death, Mrs. Buchanan exhibited a life-like portrait of the martyred president. An original New York cast appeared in a comedy success, "An American Princess," written by Mrs. Buchanan's sister, Mrs. Eva Best (*ibid.,* 26 Feb., 21 Apr., 24 Nov. 1889).

53. *Ibid.,* 22 Nov., 5 Dec. 1889, 25 Apr., 24 May 1890.

54. *Ibid.,* 16, 18 June., 17 Aug., 22 Sep. 1889, 1 Jan. 1890, 25 July 1954; *Sioux City's Corn Palaces.* See photograph in Illustration Section.

55. *SCJ,* 10 July 1888.

56. James G. Blaine to WIB, 26 Nov. 1890, BP.

57. International American Conference, 1889-1890, *Reports of Committees and Discussions Thereon,* Vol. III, *Excursions Appendix* (henceforth IAC, 1889-1890).

58. *Ibid.,* pp. 3-261.

59. *SCJ,* 10 July, 4 Sep. 1889.

60. *Ibid.,* 18, 25-27 Oct. 1889; IAC, 1889-1890, pp. 165-170.

61. *SCJ,* 26 Oct. 1889.

62. See chs. 10 and 14.

63. *SCJ,* 27 Oct. 1889. On Curtis and Buchanan's later associations with him, see below, pp. 62-63, 69-70, 130, 146, 149, 159, 193.

64. *SCJ,* 25 Apr., 4 May 1890.

65. *Ibid.,* 11, 19, 20 June, 14 Sep., 4 Oct. 1890.

66. *Ibid.,* 9, 28, 30 Sep., 1, 8 Oct. 1890. See BP for copy of invitation to Blaine.

67. *SCJ,* 11, 19 June, 16 July, 15 Aug. 1890; *Sioux City's Corn Palaces.* See photograph in Illustration Section.

68. Sioux City businessmen built their fifth and last Corn Palace in 1891. Inclement weather brought financial failure and the end of the festival (*SCJ,* 25 July 1954). In 1892 Mitchell, South Dakota, adopted the idea and in a permanent building has perpetuated it to the present day.

69. *SCJ,* 15, 21 May 1890. See below, pp. 48-51.

Chapter 4
HOMAGE TO AMERICA'S DISCOVERER

1. Unless otherwise indicated, the following account of Chicago's growth between 1871 and 1893 is based upon Bessie Louise Pierce, *A History of Chicago,* III, and Harold Melvin Mayer and Richard C. Wade, *Chicago: Growth of a Metropolis,* pp. 117-192.

2. Thomas S. Hines, *Burnham of Chicago: Architect and Planner,* pp. 44-72.

3. Pierce, *Chicago,* III, 500-503. The earliest suggestion for a Columbian quadricentennial apparently came from a Mexican citizen, Dr. T. Zaremba, who in 1882 submitted to diplomatic representatives in Washington a plan for an exposition to be held in Mexico City. (NA, DS, Records relating to the World's Columbian Exposition at Chicago, 1893. Final Report of the President of the Exposition [henceforth Final Report of the President]), Pt. I, pp. 1-2.

4. US Congress, *Congressional Record* (henceforth *Cong. Rec.*), 51 Cong., 1 sess., XXI, pt. 2, pp. 1664-1665, pt. 4, p. 3615; US Laws, etc., *The Statutes at Large of the United States of America* (henceforth *U. S. Stat. at L.*), XXVI, 62-66.

5. Under the statute President Harrison received authority to appoint two commissioners (one from each of the two leading political parties) from each state and territory and from the District of Columbia—as well as eight commissioners-at-large. Governors were authorized to nominate candidates (*U. S. Stat. at L.,* XXVI, 62-63; Final Report of the President, Pt. I, p. 105).

6. *Sioux City Tribune,* 8 Apr. 1890; *SCJ,* 15 May 1890; NA, DS. Records relating to the World's Columbian Exposition, Final Report of the Secretary of the Exposition (henceforth Final Report of the Secretary), Pt. I, 126.

7. *SCJ,* 10 June 1890.

8. Final Report of the Secretary, Pt. II, 1-20.

9. *SCJ,* 5, 28 July 1890.

10. 24 Sep. 1890.

11. Final Report of the Secretary, Pt. II, 3-9; *SCJ,* 24 Sep., 17 Oct., 9 Nov. 1890; George R. Davis, Director General of the Exposition, to WIB, 9 Oct. 1890, BP.

12. *Commercial Advertiser* (Buffalo), 23 Oct. 1890.

13. Final Report of the President, Pt. I, 33-36.

14. Davis to WIB, 6, 8 Dec. and WIB to Davis, 9, 11 Dec. 1890, BP; Chicago Historical Society (henceforth CHS), World's Columbian Exposition (henceforth WCE), Board of Directors, Minutes, 12 Dec. 1890.

15. Boies to WIB, 18 Dec. 1890, and unidentified newspaper clippings, BP.

16. WIB to Davis, 11 Dec. 1890, BP.

17. *U. S. Stat. at L.,* XXVI, 62.

18. WIB to Rusk, 17 Dec., and Rusk to WIB, 22 Dec. 1890, BP.

19. See copies of correspondence in BP.

20. WCE, Department of Forestry, Official Report, 20 Jan. 1894, copy filed in BP; Rossiter Johnson (ed.), *A History of the World's Columbian Exposition held in Chicago in 1893,* II, 79-84.

21. *SCJ,* 13 Jan., 1, 15, 22 Feb., 5, 23 Mar., 2, 26 May 1891.

22. WIB to A. G. Veith, [n. d.], and unidentified newspaper clipping, BP.

23. WIB to Davis, 31 Jan., 11 Feb. 1891, BP; *SCJ,* 6 Feb. 1891.

24. *SCJ,* 5 Apr., 3 May, 7 June 1891.

25. Pierce, *Chicago,* 504-508; Mayer and Wade, *Chicago,* pp. 193-200.

26. Mayer and Wade, *Chicago,* pp. 194-195; Pierce, *Chicago,* pp. 506-508. More detailed descriptions are to be found in Final Report of the President. See ground plan in Illustration Section.

27. 13, 27 June 1891.

28. *Chicago Daily Tribune,* 15 July 1891, 14 Jan. 1892; *Chicago Inter-Ocean,* 25 Feb. 1893.

29. His plea before the Iowa legislature was an eloquent justification of world expositions (see BP).

30. *Chicago Times,* 29 Jan. 1893.

31. *Sioux City Tribune,* 31 Dec. 1892.

32. WIB to Davis, 31 Jan. 1891; BP; William Evelyn Cameron (ed.), *History of the World's Columbian Exposition,* p. 66.

33. WCE, Letters from Director General to WIB, filed in BP.

34. WCE, Department of Agriculture, Official Report, 26 Mar. 1894, filed in BP.

35. *Capitol* (Albany), 14 Feb. 1893.

36. *Chicago Daily Tribune,* 24 Mar., 30 Apr. 1893; Department of Agriculture, Official Report.

37. Final Report of the President, Pt. II, 135-136.

38. *Ibid.,* pp. 126-136.

39. *SCJ,* 9 Nov. 1892.

40. Final Report of the President, Pt. II, 117-119.

41. Department of Forestry, Official Report, and Department of Agriculture, Official Report.

42. Hubert Howe Bancroft, *The Book of the Fair,* II, 617.

43. *Ibid.,* II, 953-954; unidentified clipping, BP.

44. *Report of the Iowa Columbian Commission,* pp. 78, 84-86; Buffalo and Erie County Public Library (henceforth BECPL), Buchanan Papers.

45. Scrapbooks, BP; *Chicago Daily Tribune,* 10 Feb., 7, 16 Apr., 28 June, 24 Sep., 12 Oct. 1893.

46. Undated clipping from *Davenport Democrat,* BP.

47. Scrapbooks, BP; *Chicago Daily Tribune,* 22 July 1893; *The World's Columbian Exposition Illustrated,* pp. 182-183.

48. *The World's Columbian Exposition Illustrated,* p. 183.

49. CHS, WCE, Executive Committee, Minutes, 19 Aug. 1891. Curtis has been called "a self-appointed, one-man lobby for Pan Americanism" (see Thomas Francis McGann, *Argentina, the United States, and the Inter-American System, 1880-1914,* p. 122).

50; *The Capitals of Spanish America* (1887) and *Trade and Transportation between the United States and Spanish America* (1889).

51. See p. 43.

52. WCE, Executive Committee, Minutes, 23 July, 17 Dec. 1891.

53. *Ibid.,* 7 Jan. 1801; WCE, Board of Directors, Minutes, 31 Dec. 1890.

54. Curtis, *The Relics of Columbus,* pp. 3, 5.

55. Final Report of the Secretary, Pt. I, 115; *Cong. Rec.,* 52 Cong., 1 sess. pp. 7239, 7445.

56. *Cong. Rec.,* 52 Cong., 1 sess., p. 7125.

57. Final Report of the President, Pt. II, 150-161; *Chicago Inter-Ocean,* 4 May 1893.

58. Lt. W. McCarty Little to Curtis, 24 Nov. 1892, CHS, WCE, Little Correspondence.

59. His file of correspondence covers the period 6 Sep. 1892-27 Mar. 1893.

60. The following account of the voyage of the caravels and their reception in Chicago is based on Final Report of the President, Pt. II, 191-193, and *Chicago Daily Tribune,* 8 July 1893. A brief narrative of the episode is "The Columbus Caravels," *Chicago History* 8 (Fall 1968): 257-269.

61. *Chicago Daily Tribune,* 8 July 1893.

62. *Ibid.*

63. *Ibid.*; Philip Sheldon Foner, *The Life and Writings of Frederick Douglass,* IV, 128-139.

64. Davis to Chiefs of Departments, 18 Sep. 1890, and to WIB, 11 Dec. 1893, BP; Final Report of the Secretary, Pt. II, 227-229, 299-302, 398-399.

65. Copies of the report are filed in BP.

66. Texts of both papers are filed in BP.

67. Donald was born in December 1887.

68. Evidence of these suggestions is contained in letters and many news stories from different parts of the country (BP).

69. *The World's Columbian Exposition Illustrated,* p. 182; F. Howard Annes to WIB, and enclosure, 10 Oct. 1893, BP.

70. WIB to J. J. Richardson, 7 Nov. 1893, Library of Congress, Manuscript Division (henceforth LC, MD), Cleveland Papers, Ser. 2, Vol. 282.

71. Richardson to Cleveland, 9 Sep. 1893, NA, DS, Applications and Recommendations for Office, 1893-1897 (henceforth Applications for Office).

72. Undated clipping, BP.

73. Richardson to Cleveland, 13, 28 Oct., 7, 17, 18 Nov., 19, 21 Dec. 1893, Cleveland Papers, Ser. 2, Vols. 279, 281, 282, 283, 287.

74. Applications for Office.

75. Many newspapers reflected the views of these industrial and agricultural interests (see clippings in BP).

76. 25 Oct. 1893, Applications for Office.

77. WIB to Richardson, 19 Dec. 1893, enclosure in Richardson to Cleveland, 21 Dec. 1893, Cleveland Papers, Ser. 2, Vol. 287.

78. *SCJ,* 18 Jan. 1894; Edwin F. Uhl, acting secretary of state, to WIB, 30 Jan. 1894; NA, DS, Instructions to Ministers, Argentina (henceforth Inst.

Arg.), XVII, 71. A shower of congratulatory messages greeted Buchanan on his appointment (see BP).

79. WIB to Cleveland, (n.d.), Cleveland Papers, Ser. 2, Vol. 291; WIB to Walter Q. Gresham, secretary of state, 15 Feb. 1894, NA, DS, Despatches from Ministers, Argentina (henceforth Desp. Arg.), XXI.

80. *SCJ,* 7 Feb. 1894; *Sioux City Times,* 8, 27 Feb. 1894.

81. Buchanan Diary, 1894-1897, BP.

Chapter 5
DIPLOMAT IN THE MAKING

1. For a geographic description of the pampas see Preston Everett James, *Latin America,* pp. 324-359; for a historian's interpretation, James R. Scobie, *Revolution on the Pampas: A Social History of Argentine Wheat, 1860-1910,* pp. 3-26.

2. Buchanan Diary, 1894-1897, 6 May 1894, BP.

3. *Ibid.*

4. *Ibid.,* 21-30 Mar. 1894. The invitation to serve as shipboard master of ceremonies was the first of many that would come his way in future Atlantic crossings.

5. *Ibid.,* 30 Mar.-5 Apr. 1894.

6. *Ibid.,* 6-16 Apr. 1894.

7. *Ibid.,* 17 Apr.-1 May 1894.

8. *Ibid.,* 2-6 May 1894.

9. *Ibid.,* 7 May 1894; WIB to Gresham, 7 May 1894, Desp. Arg., XXXI.

10. WIB to Gresham, 21 May 1894, Desp. Arg., XXXI; Buchanan Diary, 19 May 1894, BP.

11. *Buenos Aires Herald,* 21 May 1894.

12. Buchanan Diary, 21 May 1894.

13. WIB to Gresham, 10, 11 May, 4 June, 1 Aug. 1894, Desp. Arg., XXXI. The documents included *American State Papers, Annals of Congress, Congressional Directories,* and *Registers of the Department of State.*

14. WIB to Gresham, 11, 27 May, 4 June, 1 Aug. 1894, *ibid.;* Gresham to WIB, 7 July 1894, Inst. Arg., XVII, 82-83.

15. WIB to Gresham, 17 May, 4, 7 June, 12 July 1894, Desp. Arg., XXXI; Alvey A. Adee, asst. sec. of state, to WIB, 27 July 1894, Inst. Arg., XVII, 86.

16. WIB to Gresham, 6 July 1894, Desp. Arg., XXXI.

17. *Buenos Ayres Standard,* 5, 6 July 1894; *Buenos Aires Herald,* 5 July 1894.

18. Only a few months before, Brazil had joined Argentina in submitting their boundary dispute to Cleveland's arbitration (see note 34, p. 371).

19. WIB to Gresham, 10 July 1894, Desp. Arg., XXXI. There are copies of many invitations in NA, DS, Records of Diplomatic Posts, Argentina, 1813-1935 (henceforth Post Records, Argentina), Notes from Foreign Office.

20. *Sioux City Times,* 20 Apr. 1898.
21. Programs filed in BP.
22. Scobie, "Buenos Aires as a Commercial-Bureaucratic City, 1880-1910; Characteristics of a City's Orientation," *The American Historical Review* 77 (Oct. 1972): 1035-1073; Curtis, *The Capitals of Spanish America,* pp. 549-556, 577-590; McGann, *Argentina,* pp. 1-19, *passim,* 62-65.
23. José Luis Romero, *A History of Argentine Political Thought,* pp. 174-182.
24. Harold F. Peterson, *Argentina and the United States, 1810-1960,* p. 526.
25. Cf. McGann, *Argentina,* pp. 61-62.
26. WIB to Gresham, 17 July 1894, Desp. Arg., XXXI.
27. 3 Aug. 1894.
28. This account of Buchanan's trip is based on WIB to Gresham, 20 Sep. 1894, Desp. Arg., XXXI, and unidentified newspaper clippings in BP.
29. *La Nación,* 3 Sep. 1894; *El Diario,* 8 Sep. 1894; *La Prensa,* 9 Sep. 1894.
30. See BP.
31. WIB to Gresham, 8 Apr. 1895, and to Richard Olney, secretary of state, 19 Aug. 1895, Desp. Arg., XXXII; Post Records, Argentina, Register of Correspondence, II, 47-48. Though he later travelled to the foot of Mt. Aconcagua, he was never able to make his proposed visit to Chile.
32. *Buenos Aires Herald,* 28 Oct. 1898; *Chicago Record,* 14 July 1898.
33. Buchanan Diary, 7, 15 May 1894, BP.
34. Undated speech manuscript, BP.
35. *Buenos Aires Herald,* 17 June 1896.
36. *Ibid.*
37. Speech at meeting of 30 Nov. 1895, BP.
38. Remarks at meeting of 30 Nov. 1896., *ibid.*
39. Speech of 30 Nov. 1895, *ibid.*
40. Undated notes, *ibid.*
41. Undated draft of lectures, *ibid.*
42. The following discussion is based upon Buchanan's lecture manuscript, filed in *ibid.*

Chapter 6
DIPLOMAT IN ACTION

1. For fuller discussion of these factors, see Arthur Preston Whitaker, *The United States and Argentina,* pp. 85-89, and Peterson, *Argentina and the United States,* pp. 211-215, 220-221. In this chapter I have borrowed extensively from my earlier work.
2. See pp. 119-124.
3. The United States had sent the *Lexington* to retaliate for alleged illegal seizure of American sealing vessels in Falkland waters. Following the *Lexington*'s raid, the British moved in to reestablish a claim they had ostensibly

abandoned in 1774 (see Peterson, *Argentina and the United States,* pp. 101-120).

4. See pp. 130-131.

5. Buchanan was the third American appointed to the rank. Not until 1914 did the two nations raise their missions to embassies.

6. Peterson, *Argentina and the United States,* pp. 525-526.

7. These topics are discussed in this and the following chapters.

8. US Treasury Department, *American Commerce: Commerce of South America, Central America, Mexico, and West Indies, . . . 1821-1898,* pp. 3300-3301.

9. *Ibid.*; Peterson, *Argentina and the United States,* pp. 149, 222.

10. Peterson, *Argentina and the United States,* pp. 224-226.

11. Luis L. Domínguez to F. T. Frelinghuysen, secretary of state, 29 Sep. 1883, and to Thomas F. Bayard, secretary of state, 15 Aug. 1885, NA, DS, Notes from Argentine Legation (henceforth Notes from Arg.), II, III.

12. See pp. 98, 138.

13. Peterson, *Argentina and the United States,* pp. 226-228.

14. *Chicago Times,* 13 June 1894.

15. *Ibid.*

16. *Buffalo Courier,* 25 Jan. 1900.

17. Zeballos to Gresham, 30 Jan. 1894, *For. Rel.,* 1894, pp. 3-4.

18. WIB to Gresham, 20 June, Gresham to WIB, 7 Aug. 1894, *ibid.,* pp. 4-7.

19. US Congress, *House Report* (henceforth *H. Rep.*), No. 2263, 54 Cong., 1 sess., pp. 79-82; Peterson, *Argentina and the United States,* pp. 227-228.

20. WIB to Gresham, 1 Oct. 1894, *For. Rel.,* 1894, pp. 12-13.

21. WIB to Gresham, 13 Aug., 1 Oct. 1894, *ibid.,* pp. 7-8, 12-13.

22. WIB to Gresham, 1, 5 Oct. 1894, *ibid.,* pp. 12-14; 19 Nov. 1894, 10 Jan. 1895, *ibid.,* 1895, pp. 3-4.

23. WIB to Olney, 17 Nov. 1896, Desp. Arg., XXXIV.

24. 30 Oct. 1895, *ibid.,* XXXII.

25. WIB to Alcorta, 29 Aug., Alcorta to WIB, 31 Aug. 1895, enclosure in WIB to Olney, 30 Oct. 1895, *ibid.*

26. Fishback to Olney, 16, 23 Apr., 16 June 1896, *ibid.,* XXXIII; Olney to Fishback, 21 Apr., 18 June 1896, Inst. Arg., XVII, 182-183, 190-191.

27. WIB to Olney, 22 Aug. 1896, and enclosures, Desp. Arg., XXXIII; Martín García Mérou, minister to US, to Olney, 22 Sep., 1896, Notes from Arg., IV.

28. Fishback to Olney, 6 Oct. 1896, Desp. Arg., XXXIII.

29. Vicente J. Domínguez, chargé d'affaires to US, to Alcorta, 16 Mar. 1896, Argentine Republic, Ministerio de Relaciones Exteriores y Culto, *Memoria de relaciones exteriores presentada al Congreso Nacional* (henceforth *Memoria*), 1896, p. 60, and García Mérou to Alcorta, 10 Oct. 1896, *ibid.,* 1897, pp. 251-330; Alcorta to García Mérou, 16 Feb. 1897, *ibid.,* 1898, 48-49.

30. *Buenos Aires Herald,* 10 Nov. 1896; WIB to Olney, 12 Dec. 1896, Desp. Arg., XXXIV; Olney to WIB, 22 Jan. 1897, Inst. Arg., XVII, 224-225.

31. *Buenos Ayres Standard,* 19 Feb. 1897.
32. To McKinley, Desp. Arg., XXXIV.
33. WIB to John Sherman, secretary of state, Desp. Arg., XXXIV; William R. Day, act. secretary of state, to WIB, 10 June 1897, Inst. Arg., XVII, 253-254. Buchanan's request for leave, dated 5 March, had still not been granted.
34. WIB to Sherman, 20 Mar., 1 Apr., 15 Sep. 1897, Desp. Arg.,XXXIV, XXXV.
35. García Mérou to Alcorta, 29 Mar. 1897, *Memoria,* 1898, pp. 49-50; to Sherman, 1 May 1897, Notes from Arg., IV; WIB to Sherman, 3, 30 June 1897, Desp. Arg., XXXIV.
36. 8 Nov. 1897, Inst. Arg., XVII, 285-287.
37. WIB to Sherman, 9 Sep., 16 Nov. 1897, 8 Jan. 1898, Desp. Arg., XXXV.
38. 8 Jan. 1898, *ibid.*
39. See pp. 125-129.
40. 8 Jan. 1898, Desp. Arg., XXXV.
41. WIB to Sherman, 6 Dec. 1897, *ibid.,* XXXV; Sherman to WIB, 7 Dec. 1897, Inst. Arg., XVII, 298.
42. *SCJ,* 19 Mar. 1898.
43. Inst. Arg., XVII, 305.
44. *Times of Argentina,* 28 Jan. 1898; *SCJ,* 19 Mar. 1898.
45. To Sherman, 27 Jan. 1898, Desp. Arg., XXXV.
46. *Buenos Ayres Standard,* (?) Jan. 1898.
47. *New York Sun,* 3 Mar. 1898; *SCJ,* 19 Mar. 1898.
48. Sherman to Jones, 18 Mar. 1898, Desp. Arg., XXXV.
49. *Chicago Times-Herald,* 11 Apr. 1898.
50. 13 Apr. 1898, Desp. Arg., XXXVI.
51. *Sioux City Times,* 20 Apr. 1898; *St. Louis Globe-Democrat,* 21 Apr. 1898; WIB to family, 10 June 1898, BP.
52. WIB to family, 21, 22 Apr. 1898, *ibid.*
53. WIB to family, 21 Apr. 1898, *ibid.*
54. WIB to family, 22 Apr. 1898, *ibid.* Buchanan suggested that Woodford's delay in presenting the note may have been the result of the State Department's procrastination.
55. WIB to family, 22 Apr. 1898, *ibid.* The question mark is Buchanan's.
56. WIB to family, 24, 25 Apr. 1898, *ibid.*
57. 25 Apr., 4 May 1898, *ibid.*
58. WIB to family, 22 Apr., 5 May 1898, *ibid.*; WIB to Day, 7 May 1898, Desp. Arg., XXXVI.
59. WIB to Day, 3 May 1898, *ibid.;* to family, 5 May 1898, BP.
60. WIB to family, 5, 11, 13, 18 May 1898, BP.
61. 5, 18, 19, 20, 21 May 1898, *ibid.*
62. 22 May to 15 June 1898, *ibid.*
63. 10 June 1898, *ibid.*
64. WIB to Day, 16 June 1898, Desp. Arg., XXXVI; WIB to family, 16, 23 June 1898, BP.

65. WIB to Mrs. WIB, 1 July 1898, *ibid.; Buenos Ayres Standard,* 5 July 1898.
66. WIB to family, 18 July 1898, BP; Buchanan to Day, 13 Oct. 1898, Desp. Arg., XXXVII.
67. WIB to family, 19, 20 May 1898, BP.
68. See pp. 125-130.

Chapter 7
DIPLOMAT'S ROUTINE

1. Ismael Bucich Escobar, *Historia de los presidentes argentinos,* p. 334.
2. Useful for summary and interpretation of Argentina's development in the 1880s and 1890s are *ibid.,* pp. 201-352; McGann, *Argentina,* pp. 9-34, 165-187; Ysabel (Fisk) Rennie, *The Argentine Republic,* pp. 136-201; and Scobie, *Argentina, A City and a Nation,* pp. 189-201.
3. For an analysis, incorporating extensive quotations from official newspaper sources, of Buchanan's relationship to President Roca and his administration, see Courtney Letts de Espil, *La segunda presidencia Roca vista por los diplomáticos norteamericanos,* pp. 15-115, *passim.*
4. François S. Jones, chargé d'affaires, *ad interim,* to Sherman, 28 Mar., 20, 22, 27 Apr., 5, 13 May 1898, Desp. Arg., XXXV-XXXVI.
5. WIB to Olney, 19, 26 Dec. 1895, and enclosures, *ibid.,* XXXII.
6. WIB to family, 23 June 1898, BP; James M. Ayres, US consul in Rosario, to asst. secretary of state, 15 Aug. 1898, NA, DS, Consular Letters, Rosario, II; WIB to Sherman, 14 July 1898, Desp. Arg., XXXVI.
7. WIB to Sherman, 14 July 1898, Desp. Arg., XXXVI.
8. *Ibid.*
9. WIB to family, 24 June 1898, BP.
10. *Ibid.*
11. WIB to Mrs. WIB, 7 July 1898, *ibid.*
12. WIB to Day, 25 Aug. 1898, Desp. Arg., XXXVI.
13. WIB to family, 18, 24 Aug. 1898, BP.
14. WIB to Mrs. WIB, 14, 22 July, 16 Sep., 11 Oct., and WIB to Florence, 1 Sep., 6 Dec. 1898, *ibid.*
15. WIB to Mrs. WIB, 14, 31 July, 18 Aug., 10 Sep., 28 Oct., 11 Nov. 1898, *ibid.*
16. The following discussion of Buchanan's mediation is adapted from Peterson, *Argentina and the United States,* pp. 240-246, 250-255. See also Letts de Espil, *La segunda presidencia Roca,* pp. 33-55, 65-68, 71-73, 79-84.
17. Peterson, *Argentina and the United States,* pp. 240-245.
18. WIB to Gresham, 24 May 1895, Desp. Arg., XXXII.
19. Argentine Republic, *Tratados, convenciones, protocolos, actos y acuerdos internacionales,* VII, 144-150, 151-156, 182-183.
20. *Ibid.,* pp. 184-186.

21. Sir Thomas Hungerford Holdich, *The Countries of the King's Award*, pp. 22-24.

22. Chile, *Chilo-Argentine Boundary. The Puna de Atacama. Memorandum presented by the Government of Chile to the Government of the United States of America*, pp. 3-4, 23-24.

23. Norberto Piñero, Argentine minister to Chile, to Latorre, 20 June, 11 July 1898; Latorre to Piñero, 21 June, 12 July 1898, Republic of Chile, Archivo Nacional (henceforth RC, AN), Gobierno y legación de la República Arjentina en Chile, 1898 a 1899.

24. Eliodoro Infante, Chilean minister to US, to Latorre, 9 Aug. 1898, RC, AN, Legación de Chile en los Estados Unidos de Norte América, 1898, II.

25. *Ibid.*

26. *For. Rel.,* 1898, p. 1.

27. Wilson to Latorre, 1, 6 Aug. 1898, RC, AN, Gobierno y legación de los Estados Unidos en Chile, 1898; WIB to Day, 5 Aug. 1898, Desp. Arg., XXXVI; Wilson to Day, 8 Aug. 1898, NA, DS, Despatches from Ministers, Chile (henceforth Desp. Chile), XLVI.

28. Wilson to Day, 31 Oct. 1898, Desp. Chile, XLVI; WIB to family, 25 Sep. 1898, BP.

29. 26 Oct. 1898; BECPL, Buchanan Papers. Chilian-Argentine Boundary Arbitration: Private Papers, W. I. Buchanan, Deciding Member of the Commission, 1899 (henceforth Chilian-Argentine Boundary Arbitration).

30. WIB to Day, 22 Sep. 1898, Desp. Arg., XXXVII.

31. Argentine Republic, *Frontera argentino-chilena. Memoria presentada al tribunal nombrada por el gobierno de Su Majestad Británica,* I, viii, II, 1121.

32. 28 Oct., 2 Nov. 1898, BP.

33. *For. Rel.,* 1898, pp. 179-181.

34. In addition, President Cleveland had arbitrated an Argentine boundary dispute with Brazil in 1895. Except to report Argentine reaction to the Cleveland award, Buchanan had played no part in that case.

35. Hay to WIB, Inst. Arg., XVII, 403.

36. García Mérou to Hay, 15 Dec. 1898, *For. Rel.,* 1898, pp. 2-3.

37. US President, *A Compilation of the Messages and Papers of the Presidents,* James Daniel Richardson (ed.) (henceforth Richardson, *Messages and Papers*), X, 98.

38. WIB to Hay, 7 Apr. 1899, and encl., Desp. Arg., XXXIX.

39. The original minutes are filed in RC, AN, Legación de Chile en la Arjentina, 1893-1907. Together with other official documents of the episode, Buchanan's original pencilled memorandum on the voting is bound in a letter book now filed in the collection of the BECPL as Chilian-Argentine Boundary Arbitration.

40. See note 38, ch. 7.

41. 28 Mar., 3 Apr. 1899, BP.

42. WIB to Florence, 3 Apr. 1899, *ibid.*

43. See note 38, ch. 7.

44. WIB to family, 27 Apr. 1899, BP.
45. Wilson to WIB, 7 July 1899, Chilian-Argentine Boundary Arbitration; Wilson to Hay, 9 Aug. 1899, Desp. Chile, XLII; David J. Hill, act. secretary of state, to Wilson, 9 Oct. 1899, NA, DS, Instructions to Ministers, Chile, XVIII, 14-15.
46. 13 June 1899, BP.
47. Jones to Sherman, 8 Apr. 1898, Desp. Arg., XXXVI; Day to WIB, 7 May 1898, Inst. Arg., XVII, 357-359.
48. WIB to Day, 1 July 1898, Desp. Arg., XXXVI.
49. WIB to Day, 13 May 1898, *ibid.;* Letts de Espil, *La segunda presidencia Roca,* pp. 68-71, 95-102.
50. Day to WIB, 7 May 1898, Inst. Arg., XVII, 357-359.
51. WIB to Day, 12 Aug. 1898, Desp. Arg., XXXVI.
52. *Ibid.*
53. *Ibid.*
54. Hay to WIB, 9 Dec. 1898, Inst. Arg., XVII, 409.
55. 12 Dec. 1898, BP.
56. WIB to Hay, 20 Jan., 4 May, 5 June 1899, Desp. Arg., XXXVII, XXXVIII; Hay to WIB, 28 Mar. 1899, Inst. Arg., XVII, 448-449.
57. Hay to WIB, 9 Dec. 1898, 28 Mar., 1 Apr. 1899, Inst. Arg., XVII, 409, 448-451.
58. WIB to Hay, 17 June, 10 July 1899, Desp. Arg., XXXVIII; Hay to WIB, 28 June 1899, Inst. Arg., XVII, 476.
59. 20 June 1899, BP.
60. Tyler Dennett, *John Hay: From Poetry to Politics,* pp. 416-420.
61. Hay to William P. Lord, minister to Argentina, 26 Mar. 1900, Inst. Arg., XVII, 504.
62. John W. Foster, secretary of state, to Pitkin, 6 Jan. 1893, Inst. Arg., XVII, 36, 39; WIB to Gresham, 21 July 1894, Lord to Hay, 12 June 1900, Desp. Arg., XXXI, XXXIX.
63. Edwin A. Uhl, acting secretary of state, to WIB, 1 Sep. 1894, 1 May 1895, Inst. Arg., XVII, 94-95, 118-119; WIB to Olney, 26 Sep. 1896, Desp. Arg., XXXIII.
64. 1 June 1898, Inst. Arg., XVII, 365-367.
65. Lord to Hay, 12 June 1900, Desp. Arg., XXXIX; US Treaties, etc., *Treaties, Conventions, International Acts, Protocols, and Agreements between the United States of America and Other Powers, 1776-1909,* William M. Malloy (comp.), (henceforth Malloy, *Treaties*), I, 25-28.
66. WIB to William H. Michael, chief clerk, Dept. of State, 5 Mar. 1901, NA, DS, Records relating to the Pan American Exposition, 1901, Correspondence of the State Department with the Board of Management (henceforth Corres. of State Dept.).
67. WIB to Uhl, 18 June 1895; and to Olney, 6 Sep., 1 Oct. 1895, Desp. Arg., XXXII.
68. WIB to Olney, 10 Oct. 1896, Desp. Arg., XXXIII.
69. WIB to Olney, 9 Nov. 1895, 16 Oct. 1896, 9 Jan. 1897; to Sherman, 11

Mar. 1897; and to Day, 26 Aug. 1898, *ibid.,* XXXIII, XXXIV, XXXVI.

70. Gresham to WIB, 21 Sep. 1894, Inst. Arg., XVII, 96-97.

71. WIB to Olney, 2 Sep. 1896, and encl., Desp. Arg., XXXIII.

72. WIB to Sherman, 28 May 1897, *ibid.,* XXXIV.

73. WIB to Olney, 14 Mar. 1896, *ibid.,* XXXIII.

74. Hay to WIB, 7 Nov., 17 Dec. 1898, 28 Jan. 1899, Inst. Arg., XVII, 401-402, 413, 428-430; WIB to Hay, 17, 19 Dec. 1898, Desp. Arg., XXXVII. Also see Letts de Espil, *Le segunda presidencia Roca,* pp. 57-64.

75. 23 May 1899, BP.

76. WIB to family, 10 Sep. 1898, *ibid.*

77. See files of "Miscellaneous Correspondence," Post Records, Argentina; WIB to Olney, 23 Dec. 1895, 10 Mar. 1896, and to Hay, 15 May, 7 July 1899, Desp. Arg., XXXII, XXXVIII.

78. WIB to Mrs. WIB, 4 Oct. 1898, BP.

79. Thomas J. Page to WIB, 19 Nov. 1895, Post Records, Argentina.

80. 18 Jan. 1896, Inst. Arg., XVII, 154-155.

81. 4 Oct. 1898, BP.

82. Richardson, *Messages and Papers,* X, 99.

83. Day to WIB, 31 May 1898, Inst. Arg., XVIII, 363-364; WIB to family, 15 Jan. 1899, BP.

84. WIB to family, 15 Jan. 1899, BP; WIB to Hay, 23 Jan. 1899, Desp. Arg., XXXVII.

85. Hay to WIB, 8 Apr. 1899, Inst. Arg., XVII, 455-461.

86. For fuller discussion of this case and Buchanan's later association with the New York Life Insurance Company, see ch. 11.

87. WIB to Hay, 31 Jan. 1899, Desp. Arg., XXXVII; Hay to WIB, 13 Mar. 1899, Inst. Arg., XVII, 445.

88. WIB to family, 20 Apr. 1899, BP; to Hay, 11 July 1899, Desp. Arg., XXXVIII.

89. Edwin Fleming, secretary Pan-American Exposition, to WIB, 9 June 1899, and WIB to Fleming, 11 June 1899, BP. See p. 147.

90. WIB to family, 13 June 1899, BP.

91. *La Prensa,* 28 June 1899; *La Nación,* 8 July 1899; WIB to family, 27 June, 6 July 1899, BP.

92. Jones to Hay, 12 July 1899, Desp. Arg., XXXVIII.

93. *La Prensa,* 12 July 1899, *Buenos Ayres Standard,* 22 June 1899.

94. *New York Daily News,* 4 Sep. 1899.

95. WIB to family, 9 Jan 1899, BP.

96. See Bibliography for specific titles and references.

97. See Bibliography.

98. 36 (13 Dec. 1899), 745-748.

99. Undated draft of speech, BP.

100. WIB to family, 13 June 1899, *ibid.*

Chapter 8
BUILDING A WORLD EXPOSITION

1. Though current usage omits the hyphen in Pan American, I have retained it, as was customary in 1899-1901, in referring to the Pan-American Company, the Pan-American Exposition, or the Pan-American [Exposition].

2. For general background on Buffalo in the nineties I have utilized Walter S. Dunn (ed.), *History of Erie County, 1870-1970;* Henry Wayland Hill (ed.), *Municipality of Buffalo, New York: A History, 1720-1923,* II; John Theodore Horton, *History of Northwestern New York* . . . , I; Josephus Nelson Larned, *A History of Buffalo* . . . , I; Merton Merriman Wilner, *Niagara Frontier: A Narrative and Documentary History,* I.

3. *Greater Buffalo* 1 (15 Apr. 1897): 6-8; Dunn, *History Erie County,* p. 31.

4. *Greater Buffalo* 3 (Jan. 1900): 13; Selig Adler and Thomas E. Connolly, *From Ararat to Suburbia; The History of the Jewish Community of Buffalo,* pp. 167-168.

5. *Greater Buffalo* 1 (15 Apr. 1897): 7-8; 3 (Jan. 1900): 13; Hill, *Municipality of Buffalo,* II, 747.

6. *Greater Buffalo* 1 (15 Apr. 1897): 7-8.

7. Horton, *History of Northwestern New York,* I, 334-335.

8. Hill, *Municipality of Buffalo,* II, 789, 794-795.

9. Edward Dean Adams, *Niagara Power: History of the Niagara Falls Power Company, 1886-1918,* pp. 269-276; Wilner, *Niagara Frontier,* I, 490-491.

10. Lloyd Graham and Frank H. Severance, *The First Hundred Years of the Buffalo Chamber of Commerce,* p. 125; *Greater Buffalo* 1 (15 Apr. 1897): 8.

11. Frank Presbrey, *The City of Buffalo* (unpaged pamphlet).

12. Larned, *History Buffalo,* I. 94.

13. Horton, *History of Northwestern New York,* I, 318-319, 359; Wilner, *Niagara Frontier,* I, 516.

14. Horton, *History of Northwestern New York,* I, 62; Adler and Connolly, *From Ararat to Suburbia,* p. 124.

15. *Greater Buffalo* 1 (15 Apr. 1897): 8; Presbrey, *City of Buffalo.*

16. Horton, *History of Northwestern New York,* I, 335; Floyd Miller, *Statler, America's Extraordinary Hotelman,* pp. 48-55.

17. BECHS, Pan-American Exposition Papers, Report of Director General (henceforth Report of DG), I, 8-9.

18. *Report of the Board of General Managers of the Exhibit of New York at the Pan-American Exposition* (henceforth *Report of Board of Managers*), p. 10.

19. *Ibid.,* pp. 10-12; Hill, *Municipality of Buffalo,* II, 851; *The Pan-American* I (Oct. 1899): 4. The president had come to Buffalo to participate in the 31st Encampment of the GAR.

20. Pan American Union, *Bulletin* 5 (Apr. 1898): 1704-1705.

21. 1 (9 Mar. 1899): 10.
22. *Report of Board of Managers,* p. 13.
23. *Ibid.,* pp. 13-14; *Buffalo Express,* 5-6, 18, 20 Jan., 1-2 Feb., 2-4 Mar. 1899; *U. S. Stat. at L.,* XXX, 1022-1024.
24. Report of DG, I, 56-57; *Report of Board of Managers,* pp. 13-14; BECHS, Pan-American Exposition Papers, Board of Directors, Minutes, (henceforth Directors, Minutes), I, 7-19, 78-79, 1266.
25. Directors, Minutes, I, 1-5; *Buffalo Courier-Express,* 12 Aug. 1930; *The Pan-American* 1 (Oct. 1899): 26.
26. H. I. Higinbotham to Milburn, 22 May, Curtis to Fleming, 7 June 1899, BP; Directors, Minutes, I, 76; *Buffalo Express,* 4 Aug., 9 Sep. 1899.
27. "William I. Buchanan," *Illustrated Industrial and Architectural Review* 4 (Aug. 1900): 2; *The Pan-American Herald* 1 (1 Sep. 1899): 8-9. The *Herald* was founded in July as a competitor to *The Pan-American.*
28. See pp. 165-167.
29. [Fleming] to WIB, 9 June 1899, BP.
30. See p. 136.
31. WIB to Fleming, 19 June, and Fleming to WIB, 19 June 1899, BP.
32. *The Pan-American Herald* 1 (15 Aug. 1899): 7.
33. WIB to Fleming, 3 Sep. 1899; BP; *Buffalo Express,* 9, 11 Sep. 1899.
34. *Buffalo Express,* 11 Sep. 1899. The park system was designed by Frederick Law Olmsted.
35. WIB to Scatcherd, 30 Sep., 12 Oct., and Scatcherd to WIB, 9 Oct. 1899, BP. His later immersion in the exposition's management precluded his visiting any country except Canada.
36. WIB to Scatcherd, 12, 18 Oct., and Scatcherd to WIB, 13 Oct. 1899, BP.
37. *Buffalo Express,* 2 Nov. 1899.
38. *Ibid.,* 18 May, 9, 18 June, 30 July, 5, 26 Sep. 1899; Directors, Minutes, I, 7-19; Charles Dudley Arnold, *et al., Photographs Showing the Building of the Pan-American Exposition.*
39. *Buffalo Express,* 2 Nov. 1899.
40. Report of DG, I, Annex no. 15, pp. 144-146.
41. *Buffalo Express,* 7 May 1899; BECHS, Pan-American Exposition Papers, Letters from Executive Committee to Director General (henceforth Letters from Ex. Com.), I-IV, *passim.* See Illustration Section.
42. Directors, Minutes, I, 159-160, 167; WIB to Scatcherd, 30 Sep. 1899, BP; *Buffalo Express,* 2 Nov. 1899.
43. *Commercial Advertiser,* 10 Nov. 1899; Directors, Minutes, I, 166ff.
44. *Buffalo Express,* 10, 28 Dec. 1899.
45. Letters from Ex. Com., I, *passim.*
46. BECHS, Pan-American Exposition Papers, Letters from Director General to Executive Committee (henceforth Letters from DG) II, no. 87; Letters from Ex. Com., I, 4, 70; *Commercial Advertiser,* 11 May 1900.
47. Letters from Ex. Com., I, 112; *The Pan-American* I (Apr. 1900): 17.
48. Report of DG, I, 7-8.

49. *The Pan-American* 1 (Apr. 1900): 17.

50. Henry Adams, *The Education of Henry Adams,* pp. 465, 467. Adams spent many days at the World's Columbian and Louisiana Purchase Expositions.

51. *Collier's Weekly* 26 (1 Dec. 1900): 5.

52. Report of DG, I, 8-9.

53. Letters from DG, III, 107, and nos. 122, 157; Kenneth W. Luckhurst, *The Story of Expositions,* p. 193. The collaboration of artists with architects and contractors was not easily achieved. "Had we not personally supervised the work," Turner wrote in his final report, "hundreds of times stood in the snow and slush actually teaching the painters to do their work, it would never have been done. . . . I submitted because I wished to keep the procession moving" (Report of DG, I, Annex, no. 17, p. 169).

54. Report of DG, I, 13-14. On the construction of electric power lines to Buffalo, see Frank Leroy Blanchard, "Niagara Power at Buffalo," *Harper's Weekly* 41 (5 June 1897): 569-570, and John Joseph O'Neill, *Prodigal Genius: The Life of Nikola Tesla,* pp. 104-107.

55. Letters from Ex. Com., I, 6; Letters from DG, II, no. 87.

56. Report of DG, I, 46-47.

57. Letters from Ex. Com., I, 4, 26, 29, 39; Directors, Minutes, II, 200, 213, 285; Letters from DG, II, no. 48.

58. Letters from DG, III, no. 135; Directors, Minutes, II, 192; Letters from Ex. Com., I, 4, 14, 158.

59. Letters from Ex. Com., I, 51; Letters from DG, II, no. 110; *The Pan-American* 1 (Dec. 1899): 9.

60. Directors, Minutes, II, 212ff.

61. *Ibid.,* II, 197; Letters from DG, IV, no. 98; Report of DG, I, 74, 76, 102.

62. Report of DG, I, 25-29.

63. *Ibid.,* I, 27-29.

64. Letters from DG, II, no. 64, IV, no. 210 1/2.

65. BECHS, Pan-American Exposition Papers, Board of Women Managers, Minutes, *passim.*

66. Letters from DG, II, no. 47, IV, no. 136.

67. Report of DG, I, 13.

68. Letters from DG, V, no. 83.

69. Report of DG, I, 8-12.

70. Letters from Ex. Com., I, 52.

71. Letters from DG, IV, 225.

72. 2 (Apr. 1900): 5-6.

73. Letters from DG, IV, 225, V, no. 83.

74. Letters from Ex. Com., I, II, *passim.*

75. Letters from DG, VI, no. 40.

76. *Ibid.,* V, nos. 148, 158, VII, no. 34, XI, no. 166; Letters from Ex. Com., II, 69.

77. Report of DG, I, 8-9. The state and national governments, however, provided funds for their exhibit buildings. The New York State building

eventually became the permanent home of the Buffalo and Erie County Historical Society.

78. Directors, Minutes, II, 265-266.

79. Report of DG, I, 9-12.

80. *Ibid.*; BECHS, Pan-American Exposition Papers, Estimates and Budgets Made by the Director General, 1900-1901.

81. See pp. 166-167.

82. Report of DG, I, 33-36, 38-41, 47-48; Letters from DG, V, nos. 140, 196, 210.

83. Report of DG, I, 48-49.

84. *Ibid.*, Exhibit B, 298, 303-307, 315-316. Three of these scrapbooks are preserved in NA, DS, Records relating to the Pan-American Exposition at Buffalo, 1901, Scrapbooks of Newspaper Clippings regarding the Exposition, 1899-1901.

85. Report of DG, Exhibit B, pp. 315-316.

86. Letters from DG, V, no 193; *Buffalo Enquirer,* 23 Nov. 1900; 2 Feb. 1901; *Rochester Herald,* 5 Feb. 1901; *Brooklyn Life,* 24 Nov. 1900.

87. 26 (1 Dec. 1900): 5.

88. Report of DG, I, *passim;* Letters from DG, *passim;* Letters from Ex. Com., *passim.*

89. Letters from Ex. Com., pp. 61-63.

90. *Buffalo Express,* 13, 23 Sep., 3-5 Oct., 14, 30 Nov. 1900; *Buffalo Courier,* 3, 5, 22 Nov. 1900.

91. Report of DG, I, 14-15, Exhibit I, pp. 421-422.

92. *Ibid.,* pp. 70, 551.

93. *Ibid.,* pp. 66ff.

94. *Ibid.,* Exhibit K, pp. 448-450. The Albright Art Gallery was not strictly intended to be part of the Pan-American Exposition.

95. *Ibid., passim;* Directors, Minutes, IV, *passim;* Letters from DG, IV, no. 113, VII, no. 38, X, no. 218, XII, no. 191.

96. These included E. M. Statler's first hotel, the Pan-American, erected near an exposition entrance and capable of accommodating 5,000 guests (Miller, *Statler,* pp. 56-68).

97. Letters from DG, XII, no. 135; Report of DG, I, 30-32. In his final report Buchanan noted that "arrangements were so perfected that all [blacks] who came were made welcome and properly cared for" (Exhibit D, p. 334).

98. Report of DG, I, p. 9.

Chapter 9
HOMAGE TO A HEMISPHERE

1. *Collier's Weekly* 26 (1 Dec. 1900): 5.

2. Report of DG, I, 8-9. Portions of the report were printed under the title *Pan-American Exposition: Report of William I. Buchanan, Director General.*

3. See Arthur Preston Whitaker, *The Western Hemisphere Idea: Its Rise and Decline,* pp. 1-6.

4. *Collier's Weekly* 26: 5.

5. Report of DG, I, 8-9.

6. *Collier's Weekly* 26: 5.

7. *Ibid.; Rochester Herald,* 5 Feb. 1901.

8. *Collier's Weekly* 26: 5.

9. *Ibid.*

10. See relevant correspondence in Letters from DG, *passim,* and NA, DS, Records relating to the Pan American Exposition at Buffalo, 1901, Correspondence of the State Department with the Board of Management, 1900-1901 (henceforth Corres. of State Dept.).

11. J. W. Weber, commissioner general, to William H. Michael, chief clerk, Dept. of State, 16, 21 Aug. 1899, Corres. of State Dept.

12. WIB to Michael, 12, 13 Feb., to Hay, 26 Mar. 1900, *ibid.;* Letters from DG, II, nos. 7, 27, V, no. 193; *Buffalo Courier,* 16 Sep.; *Buffalo Express,* 3 Aug.; *Buffalo Evening News,* 21 June 1900.

13. 20 Nov. 1899, BP. In reviewing troops at his inaugural on 12 October 1898, Roca had invited Buchanan, as dean of the diplomatic corps, to stand at his side (Letts de Espil, *La segunda presidencia Roca,* p. 19).

14. Letters from DG, VI, no. 148.

15. See Corres. of State Dept.

16. These were Canada, Chile, Cuba, the Dominican Republic, Ecuador, Guatemala, Honduras, and Mexico (Report of DG, I, 33-37; Pan American Union *Bulletin,* 10 [May 1901]: 919-923).

17. Letters from DG, VII, no. 53, XII, no. 126; Report of DG, I, 33-36, 47-54.

18. Letters from DG, III, no. 137, IV, no. 73.

19. *Buffalo Times,* 27 Nov. 1899.

20. *Buffalo Courier,* 25 July 1900; WIB to Michael, 25 Oct. 1900, Corres. of State Dept.

21. Letters from DG., VI, no. 46.

22. WIB to Michael, 14 May, 18 June 1900, 22 Feb. 1901, Corres. of State Dept.

23. *Collier's Weekly* 26: 5; Report of DG, I, 7-8, 13-14, 58-63.

24. Christian Brinton, "Art at the Pan-American Exposition," *The Critic* 38 (June 1901): 512-513.

25. Report of DG, I, 58ff, and Annex 17, p. 170; Brinton, "Art at the Pan-American Exposition."

26. Brinton, "Art at the Pan-American Exposition." The Buffalo and Erie County Historical Society possesses various reproductions of the ground plan. For example, see ground plan in Illustration Section.

27. Richard Watson Gilder, *Poems and Inscriptions,* pp. 88-89.

28. Brinton, "Art at the Pan-American Exposition."

29. Report of DG, I, Annex 18, pp. 183ff.

30. *Ibid.,* pp. 15-16; Letters from Ex. Com. II, 135-140.

31. Report of DG, I, 16-17.
32. *Buffalo Express,* 2 May 1901; Letters from DG, XII, no. 75.
33. *Buffalo Express,* 21 May 1901.
34. LC, MD, McKinley Papers, Ser. I, Vol. 80.
35. The *Buffalo Express,* 21 May 1901, carried full texts of the addresses.
36. Peterson, *Argentina and the United States,* p. 283.
37. *Buffalo Express,* 21 May 1901.
38. Report of DG, I, Exhibit F, pp. 367-368.
39. *Ibid.,* I, 9, 16-17.
40. *Ibid.,* I, 81-82.
41. *Ibid.,* I, 17.
42. *Ibid.,* I, 55-60; Letters from DG, XIII, nos. 55, 218, 355.
43. Letters from DG, XIII, nos. 83, 89, 325; Letters from Ex. Com., IV, 1.
44. Directors, Minutes, IV, 711-712.
45. *Ibid.,* 708, 711-712.
46. Report of the DG, I, 96-98. Also see copies of the *Official Daily Program* in the Pan-American collection of the Buffalo and Erie County Historical Society.
47. *Official Daily Program.*
48. *Buffalo Courier,* 11 Aug. 1901.
49. Pan-American Exposition, *Official Catalog and Guide Book,* pp. 65-69.
50. Report of DG, I, 81-82, 237-239.
51. Letters from DG, VII, no. 53; Report of DG, Annex no. 7, pp. 47-54, Annex no. 14, p. 139.
52. Report of DG, I, 90-94; Letters from Ex. Com., II, 73-74; Letters from DG, X, no. 2.
53. Report of DG, I, 84-89.
54. *Ibid.,* I, Exhibit I, p. 279.
55. See pertinent letters in Corres. of State Dept., especially WIB to Hay, 17 June 1901, and Hay to William L. Marcy, president, Japanese Village, 24 June 1901.
56. Letters from Ex. Com., II, 156; *Official Daily Program, passim.*
57. Report of DG, I, 99-101; Letters from DG, XIII, no. 252.
58. Official archives of the company abound in records of day-to-day administration (see the Report of DG, Letters from DG, XII, XIII, XV, and Directors, Minutes, IV, V).
59. Like Buchanan, he had already been appointed as delegate to the Second International Conference of the American States, scheduled for Mexico in December, 1901 (see ch. 10).
60. *Buffalo Express,* 21 Aug. 1901.
61. *Buffalo Express,* 8, 9, 17 Oct. 1899, 1 May 1900; George B. Cortelyou, secretary to Pres. McKinley, to WIB, 19 May, 1900, McKinley Papers, Ser. II, Vol. 159, p. 306; WIB to McKinley, 28 June 1900, *ibid.,* Ser. III, Vol. 266; WIB to Cortelyou, 13 Apr. 1901, *ibid.,* Vol. 294.
62. *Buffalo Courier,* 6 May 1900; *Buffalo Times,* 7 May, 22 Nov. 1900; WIB to Cortelyou, 10 Jan. 1901, McKinley Papers, Ser. III, Vol. 282.

63. *Buffalo Express,* 8 Oct. 1899; WIB to Cortelyou, 10 Jan., and Cortelyou to WIB, 19 Jan. 1901, McKinley Papers, Ser. III, Vol. 282, and Ser. II, Vol. 175, p. 126.

64. Cortelyou to WIB, 19 May, and WIB to Cortelyou, 22 May 1901, McKinley Papers, Ser. II, Vol. 182, p. 107, and Ser. III, Vol. 303.

65. *The Pan-American Herald* 1 (Dec. 1899): 15.

66. Richardson, *Messages and Papers,* X, 157-158, 211.

67. WIB to Cortelyou, 3 July, 9 Aug. 1901, McKinley Papers, Ser. III, Vols. 307, 309.

68. *Buffalo Express,* 10 Aug. 1901.

69. *Ibid..*

70. WIB to Michael, 31 Aug., 1 Sep. 1901, McKinley Papers, Ser. I, Vol. 85, and 3 Sep., Corres. of State Dept.

71. Cortelyou to WIB, 2 Sep., and WIB to Cortelyou, 3 Sep. 1901, McKinley Papers, Ser. III, Vol. 310; Report of DG, I, 102.

72. WIB to Cortelyou, 24, 31 Aug. and Cortelyou to WIB, 29 Aug. 1901, McKinley Papers, Ser. III, Vol. 310.

73. Cortelyou to WIB, 27 Aug., 2 Sep., and WIB to Cortelyou, 31 Aug. 1901, *ibid.*

74. Letters from DG, XV, nos. 22, 55.

75. See especially, Margaret Leech, *In the Days of McKinley,* pp. 582-603; Walter Lord, *The Good Years: From 1900 to the First World War,* pp. 38-61; Charles Sumner Olcott, *The Life of William McKinley,* II, 313-327; Selig Adler, "The Operation on President McKinley," *Scientific American* 208 (Mar. 1963): 118-120.

76. Unless otherwise noted, the following account of McKinley's visit to Buffalo and Buchanan's share in it is based on *Official Daily Program,* II, 5-6 Sep. 1901, and the detailed coverage in the *Buffalo Express,* 4-15 Sep. 1901.

77. See pp. 106-107, 112, 115-118, 125-129, 165.

78. See ch. 10.

79. Richardson, *Messages and Papers,* X, 393-397.

80. See the eye-witness account (though written thirty years after) of the grand marshal of the exposition, Louis L. Babcock, "The Assassination of President William McKinley," Robert W. Bingham (ed.), *Niagara Frontier Miscellany,* pp. 11-30.

81. Lord, *The Good Years,* p. 47.

82. *Buffalo Express,* 7 Sep. 1901.

83. Letters from DG, XV, no. 98.

84. WIB to Cortelyou, 10 Sep. 1901, McKinley Papers, Ser. III, Vol. 311.

85. Directors, Minutes, V, 789, 791-892.

86. *Ibid.,* pp. 794-795; Letters from DG, XV, No. 169.

87. *Buffalo Illustrated Express,* 15 Sep. 1901.

88. Directors, Minutes, V, 869-882, *passim;* Letters from DG, XVI, no. 11.

89. Report of DG, I, 82, and Exhibit A, pp. 237-239.

90. Letters from Ex. Com., II, pp. 147-150; Letters from DG, XV, no. 87; Directors, Minutes, V, 883-886.

91. Report of DG, Exhibit A, pp. 237-239.
92. Letters from DG, XV, nos. 313, 323, XVI, nos. 1, 26, 27, 29, 46, 47, 56; Directors, Minutes, V, 885, 886, 895, 925, 927.
93. Directors, Minutes, XV, no. 318.
94. *Buffalo Express,* 17 Feb., 6 May 1902; WIB to J. C. Williams, secretary, US Delegation to Mexico, 6 Mar. 1902, NA, DS, Records of the US Delegation to the Second International Conference of the American States, 1901-02 (henceforth Records of US Delegation), Letters and Telegrams Received.
95. *Buffalo Express,* 6 May 1902.
96. WIB to Milburn, 7 Feb. 1902, BP.
97. Report of DG, I, 107.
98. *Ibid.,* p. 1.
99. *Ibid.,* p. 106.
100. *Ibid.,* pp. 106-107.
101. *Buffalo Express,* 17 Feb. 1902.
102. James Brown Scott (ed.), *The International Conferences of American States, 1889-1928,* pp. 106-107.
103. See p. 124.
104. *Philadelphia Enquirer,* 23 July 1901; *St. Louis Globe-Democrat,* 27 Apr., 12 June 1901; *St. Louis Star,* 21 July 1901; *Sioux City Tribune,* 18 June 1901; *Syracuse Journal,* 12 June 1901.
105. *Buffalo Express,* 27 Feb., 16 Dec. 1902; *St. Louis Globe-Democrat,* 29 Aug. 1901; *St. Louis Star,* 21, 22 July 1901; *St. Louis Republic,* 29 Aug. 1901. For one of these occasions (26 Oct. 1901), he prepared a formal manuscript on "Expositions as Educational Factors" (see copy in BP).
106. *Buffalo Evening News,* 6 July 1901.
107. He submitted his formal resignation on 26 April 1902 (Directors, Minutes, V, 937-938).

Chapter 10
PROMOTING THE PAN AMERICAN SPIRIT

1. US Congress, *Senate Document* (henceforth *Sen. Doc.*), No. 330, 57 Cong., 1 sess., p. 5. Document is called "Second International Conference of the American States. Message from the President of the United States, transmitting . . . the Report . . . of the Delegates."
2. The United States had seized the *Itata* while transporting arms to Chilean revolutionaries and demanded indemnity from Chile for injuries committed against sailors on shore leave in Valparaiso from the Cruiser *Baltimore.*
3. John Bassett Moore, *A Digest of International Law,* VI, 553.
4. See pp. 115-118.
5. *Collier's Weekly* 26 (1 Dec. 1900): 5.
6. Richardson, *Messages and Papers,* X, 157.

7. 2 (March 1900): 9.
8. Letters from DG, II, no. 76.
9. LC, MD, Hay Papers, General Correspondence (henceforth Gen. Corres.), 1900 (Cont. 5).
10. *DAB*, V, 117-118, XXII, 253; John Vavasour Noel, *History of the Second Pan-American Conference*, pp. 31-53. See delegation photograph in Illustration Section.
11. WIB to Hay, 5 Aug. 1901, NA, DS, Records of the United States Delegation to the Second International Conference of the American States, 1901-02 (henceforth Records of U. S. Delegation), Letters Sent, pp. 1-2, and WIB to William C. Fox, Bureau of American Republics, 2 Aug. 1901, *ibid.*, Letters Received.
12. WIB to Hay, 1 Oct. 1901, Records of U. S. Delegation, Letters Sent, pp. 3-6.
13. Roosevelt to Hay, 8 Oct. 1901, *Sen. Doc.*, No. 330, pp. 31-36.
14. *Ibid.*, pp. 31, 32, 36.
15. WIB to Hay, 1 Oct. 1901, Records of U. S. Delegation, Letters Sent; Noel, *History Second Pan-American Conference*, pp. 54-64.
16. Letters from DG, XV, no. 318.
17. 5 Nov. 1901, LC, MD, Barrett Papers, Gen. Corres., 1900-Aug., 1904 (Cont. 7).
18. To his mother, 28 Oct. 1901, *ibid.*
19. *Ibid.*
20. Stanley Robert Ross, *Francisco I. Madero, Apostle of Mexican Democracy*, p. 21.
21. Powell Clayton, ambassador to Mexico, to Hay, 8 Jan. 1902, NA, DS, Despatches from Ministers, Mexico (henceforth Desp. Mex.), Vol. 153.
22. Charles C. Cumberland, *Mexico, the Struggle for Modernity*, pp. 211-240, *passim*.
23. Ross, *Madero*, pp. 46ff.
24. Davis to Hay, 29 Oct., 4 Nov. 1901, Records of U. S. Delegation, Letters Sent, pp. 19-23, 32-34; Noel, *History Second Pan-American Conference*, pp. 105-106.
25. *Sen. Doc.*, No. 330, pp. 4-6; Charles Melville Pepper, *The Life and Times of Henry Gassaway Davis, 1823-1916*, pp. 110-120.
26. See p. 125.
27. P. 301.
28. Davis to Hay, 29 Oct. 1901, and committee memo, 30 Oct. 1901, Records of U. S. Delegation, Letters Sent, pp. 19-23, 26-27; International American Conference, Mexico, 1901-1902, *Organization of the Conference, Projects, Reports, Motions, Debates, and Resolutions*, pp. 77-78.
29. IAC, Mexico, 1901-1902, *Organization*, pp. 77-78.
30. A. Curtis Wilgus, "The Second International Conference at Mexico City," *The Hispanic American Historical Review* 11 (Feb. 1931): 59; Buchanan, "Latin America and the Mexican Conference," *Annals of the American Academy of Political and Social Science* 22 (July 1903): 52-53.

31. *Sen. Doc.*, No. 330, p. 35.

32. Wilgus, *The Hispanic American Historical Review* 11 (Feb. 1931): 32-39, 59.

33. Hay to Davis, 21 Oct., 18 Dec. 1901, Records of U. S. Delegation, Letters Received, and Davis to Hay, 24 Oct., 20 Dec. *ibid.*, Letters Sent, pp. 17-18, 144.

34. Davis to Hay, 8 Nov. 1901, WIB to Hay, 16, 29 [?] Nov. 1901, *ibid.*, pp. 39-42, 56, 76-77.

35. WIB to Hay, Records of U. S. Delegation, Letters Sent, pp. 76-77. The subcommittee consisted of Argentina, Brazil, Chile, Guatemala, Mexico, Peru, and the United States.

36. Davis to Hay, 30 Nov., 12, 26 Dec. 1901, *ibid.*, pp. 84-93, 118-119, 151-154.

37. WIB memorandum of 3 Dec., enclosure in Davis to Hay, 3 Dec. 1901, *ibid.*, pp. 96-97; Hay to Davis, 9, 12 Dec. 1901, *ibid.*, Letters Received; *Sen. Doc.*, No. 330, pp. 36-39.

38. *Sen. Doc.*, No. 330, pp. 40-47; Davis to Hay, 26 Dec. 1901, 4 Jan. 1902, Records of U. S. Delegation, Letters Sent, pp. 155, 202-203.

39. WIB to Hay, 17 Jan. 1901, Records of U. S. Delegation, Letters Sent, pp. 231-232; *Sen. Doc.*, No. 330, pp. 83, 94-96.

40. Davis to Hay, 26 Dec. 1901, WIB to Hay, 11 Jan. 1902, Records of U. S. Delegation, Letters Sent, pp. 174-175, 220.

41. *Sen. Doc.*, No. 330, p. 35.

42. Hay to Barrett, 19 Dec. 1901, Records of U. S. Delegation, Letters Received.

43. WIB to Hay, 18 Jan. 1902, Records of U. S. Delegation, Letters Sent, pp. 247, 276-279; Noel, *History of Second Pan-American Conference*, pp. 137-138.

44. Hay to Davis, 9 Dec. 1901, Records of U. S. Delegation, Letters Received; Davis to Hay and enclosure, 28 Dec. 1901, *ibid.*, Letters Sent, pp. 179-184.

45. WIB to Hay, 25 Jan. 1902, Hay Papers, Gen. Corres., 1902 (Cont. 9).

46. *Sen. Doc.*, No. 330, pp. 230-232.

47. *Ibid.*, pp. 170-172, 178; Davis to Hay, 17 Dec. 1901, Records of U. S. Delegation, Letters Sent, pp. 137-139.

48. *Sen. Doc.*, No. 330, pp. 143-155, 160-164, 173.

49. Davis to Hay, 27 Nov. 1901, 7 Jan. 1902, Records of U. S. Delegation, Letters Sent, pp. 74-75, 217-218.

50. Davis to Hay, 19 Nov., 10 Dec. 1901, *ibid.*, pp. 57, 115-116; invitations to the Buchanans, 29 Dec. 1901, 6 Jan. 1902, BP.

51. Davis to Hay, 19 Nov. 1901, Records of U. S. Delegation, Letters Sent; Barrett to his mother, 23 Nov., Barrett Papers, Gen. Corres., 1900-Aug., 1904 (Cont. 7). Copies of the invitations and menus, many of them autographed, are filed in BP.

52. Barrett to his mother, 30 Nov. 1901, Barrett Papers.

53. Unidentified newspaper clippings, 31 Dec. 1901, BP.

54. WIB to Hay, 27, 31 Jan. 1902, Records of U. S. Delegation, Letters Sent, pp. 282, 295-296; Hay to WIB, 31 Jan. 1902, *ibid.,* Letters Received; Noel, *History Second Pan-American Conference,* pp. 271-272.
55. Williams to Davis, 30 Jan. 1902, Records of U. S. Delegation, Letters Sent, p. 283.
56. *Sen. Doc.,* No. 330, pp. 36-232.
57. *Ibid.,* p. 32.
58. Cf. McGann, *Argentina,* p. 217.
59. Buchanan, *The Mexican International American Conference and Arbitration* (pamphlet).
60. *Annals of the American Academy* 22 (July 1903): 54.
61. *Mexican Herald,* 23 Mar. 1902.
62. *Buffalo Express,* 17 Feb. 1902.
63. See pp. 188-189.
64. Williams's Minutes, 25 Feb. 1902, Williams to Hay, 26 Feb. 1902, Records of U. S. Delegation, Letters Sent, pp. 298-307.
65. WIB to Williams, 6, 17 Mar., 2 Apr. 1902, *ibid.,* Letters Received; Williams to WIB, 11, 26 Mar., 8 Apr. 1902, *ibid.,* Letters Sent, pp. 309, 321-323, 330.
66. WIB to Williams, 9 Apr. 1902, Records of U. S. Delegation, Letters Received; *Sen. Doc.,* No. 330, pp. 26-27. The report also included the initial publication of the official instructions (*ibid.,* pp. 31-36).
67. WIB to Williams, 6 Mar. 1902, Records of U. S. Delegation, Letters Received.
68. *Buffalo Evening News,* 8 Apr. 1902.
69. Buchanan also referred to two million French-speaking Latin Americans.
70. See pp. 207-208 and notes 59 and 60 above, as well as *Advocate of Peace* 64 (May 1902): 93-100, and *Boston Herald,* 16 Apr. 1902.
71. *Buffalo Express,* 3 Jan., 17 Feb., 6 May 1902.
72. WIB to Executive Committee, BECHS, Pan-American Exposition Papers, Directors, Minutes, V, 937-938.
73. *Ibid.,* Report of DG. See this volume, pp. 189-190.

Chapter 11
DIPLOMAT OF AMERICAN BUSINESS

1. Morton Keller, *The Life Insurance Enterprise, 1885-1910: A Study in the Limits of Corporate Power,* p. 13.
2. Letter to author from V. DeKamel, public relations associate, New York Life Insurance Company, 13 Feb. 1969.
3. Keller, *Life Insurance,* pp. 13, 243, 265, 284.
4. Shepard Bancroft Clough, *A Century of American Life Insurance; A*

History of the Mutual Life Insurance Company of New York, 1843-1943, pp. 12-15.

5. *Ibid.,* pp. 130-134; Keller, *Life Insurance,* pp. 12-13.

6. Keller, *Life Insurance,* pp. 13, 20; Clough, *Century American Life Insurance,* p. 176; John Arthur Garraty, *Right-Hand Man: The Life of George W. Perkins,* p. 48.

7. Keller, *Life Insurance,* pp. 79, 81-82, 87, 90, 94.

8. Lawrence Fraser Abbott, *The Story of NYLIC; A History of the Origin and Development of the New York Life Insurance Company from 1845 to 1929,* p. 130.

9. Keller, *Life Insurance,* pp. 95-97, 276ff.

10. *The Story of NYLIC,* pp. 130-131.

11. *Grover Cleveland: A Study in Courage,* p. 758.

12. *Life Insurance,* p. 1.

13. *Ibid.,* pp. 16, 42, 268; Garraty, *Right-Hand Man,* p. 57.

14. Garraty, *Right-Hand Man,* pp. 81-146, *passim;* Keller, *Life Insurance,* pp. 24-25.

15. See pp. 310-311.

16. See pp. 135-136.

17. Inst. Arg., XVII, 418; WIB to Hay, 11 Jan. 1899, Desp. Arg., XXXVII.

18. 7 Jan. 1899, Desp. Arg., XXXVII.

19. 10 Jan. 1899, Inst. Arg., XVII, 420.

20. 8 Apr. 1899, *ibid.,* XVII, 455-461.

21. 13 Feb. 1899, Desp. Arg., XXXVII. (Italics mine.)

22. Hay to WIB, 8 Apr. 1899, Inst. Arg., XVII, 455-461; WIB to Hay, 13 Feb., 3 July 1899, Desp. Arg., XXXVII, XXXVIII.

23. WIB to Hay, 11 Jan., 6, 9 Feb. 1899, Desp. Arg., XXXVII.

24. 8 Apr. 1899, Inst. Arg., XVII, 455-461.

25. 3 July 1899, Desp. Arg., XXXVIII.

26. WIB to John A. McCall, president, NYLIC, 7 Oct. 1899, BP.

27. *Ibid.;* WIB to Alcorta, 14 Oct. 1899, BP.

28. WIB to McCall, 7 Oct. 1899, *ibid.*

29. WIB to Alcorta, 14 Oct. 1899, and to García Mérou, 14 Nov., *ibid.*

30. Darwin P. Kingsley, third vice-president, NYLIC, to WIB, 1 Nov. 1899, and Hay to WIB. 11 Nov. 1899, *ibid.*

31. 14 Nov. 1899, *ibid.*

32. 20 Nov. 1899, *ibid.*

33. 16 Jan. 1900, *ibid.*

34. 26 Jan. 1900, *ibid.*

35. Form letters, NYLIC to WIB, 29 Oct., 29 Nov. 1900, *ibid.*

36. Maitland S. Edye, NYLIC agent in Buenos Aires, to vice-president, NYLIC, 24 Jan. 1900, *ibid.*

37. WIB to Argentine finance minister, 26 Feb. 1900, and finance minister to WIB, 5 May 1900, *ibid.*

38. WIB to Argentine finance minister, 26 Oct. 1900, and finance minister to WIB, 6 Mar. 1901, *ibid.*

39. WIB to Perkins, 16 Apr. 1901, *ibid.*
40. *Buffalo Evening News,* 6 July 1901.
41. Francis to McCall, 15 Mar. 1901, and McCall to Francis, 18 Mar., BP.
42. WIB to "My Dear Uncle," 23 Apr. 1902, *ibid.; Sioux City Daily Tribune,* 8 Mar. 1902.
43. WIB to family, 10 May 1902, BP.
44. WIB to Perkins, 12 Mar. 1902, and Buckner to NYLIC, Rio, 29 Apr. 1902, *ibid.*
45. Unsigned memo, 21 Feb. 1902, *ibid.*; Keller, *Life Insurance,* p. 104; Garraty, *Right-Hand Man,* p. 36.
46. WIB to Bryan, 22 May 1902, BP.
47. *Ibid.*
48. Buckner to WIB, 9 May 1902, and WIB to Juan Cuestas, 15 May, *ibid.*
49. WIB to family, 25 May 1902, and WIB account book of trip to Brazil, *ibid.; La Tribuna* (Buenos Aires), 25 Aug. 1902.
50. *A Epoca* (Lisbon), 5 July 1902.
51. WIB to Buckner, 5 July 1902, BP.
52. WIB to Perkins, 26 July 1902, *ibid.*; Lawrence Francis Hill, *Diplomatic Relations between the United States and Brazil,* pp. 285-287; *La Nación* (Buenos Aires), 5 Aug. 1902; *Buenos Ayres Standard,* 2 Aug. 1902; *New York Herald,* 14 Dec. 1902.
53. *New York Herald,* 14 Dec. 1902.
54. WIB to NYLIC, 26 Sep., 5 Nov. 1902, and to Perkins, 28 Oct., BP.
55. WIB to Buckner, 9 Aug. 1902, and to Perkins, 24 Sep., *ibid.*
56. WIB to Perkins, 26 July 1902, *ibid.*
57. WIB to Buckner, 9 Aug. 1902, *ibid.*
58. WIB to Buckner and to NYLIC, Paris, 9 Aug. 1902, *ibid.*
59. WIB to Buckner, 9, 13 Aug. 1902, *ibid.*
60. WIB to Perkins, 20 Sep. 1902, *ibid.*
61. 25 Aug. 1902.
62. 25 Aug. 1902.
63. 26 Aug. 1902.
64. *La Tribuna,* 25 Aug. 1902.
65. To review troops following his investiture, Roca had invited Buchanan to stand at his side (Letts de Epsil, *La segunda presidencia Roca,* p. 19).
66. 8 Sep. 1902, BP.
67. WIB to Perkins, 24 Sep., 18 Nov. 1902, and to W. E. Ingersoll, NYLIC manager for Europe, 14 Nov. 1902, *ibid.*
68. WIB to Perkins, 24 Sep. 1902, *ibid.*
69. WIB to NYLIC, 10 Oct. 1902, and to Perkins, 13 Oct., *ibid.*
70. WIB to Perkins, 13 Oct. 1902, *ibid.*
71. WIB to Perkins, 7, 13 Oct. 1902, and Perkins to WIB, 9, 12 Oct., *ibid.*
72. 1 Oct. 1902, *ibid.*
73. 2 Nov. 1902, *ibid.*
74. WIB to NYLIC, 5, 8 Nov. 1902, to Ingersoll, 14 Nov., and to Perkins, 18 Nov., *ibid.*

75. Ingersoll to WIB, 19 Sep. 1902, WIB to Perkins, 25 Sep., and to Ingersoll, 26 Sep., *ibid.*

76. WIB to Perkins, 20 Sep. 1902, *ibid.*

77. WIB to Perkins, 26 July 1902, *ibid.; New York Herald,* 14 Dec. 1902. While still in Europe, Buchanan had received a request from the New York attorneys for the Bolivian Syndicate that he urge the Brazilian government "to take a more reasonable view of the matter" (Frederick W. Whitbridge to WIB, 17 June 1902, BP). Perkins had advised Buchanan to avoid involvement (2 July 1902, *ibid.*).

78. See WIB's translation, filed in BP, from *Diario Oficial. Estados Unidos do Brasil,* XLI, no. 268, 15 Nov. 1902; and WIB to Perkins, 18 Nov. 1902, BP.

79. WIB to Ingersoll, 14 Nov. 1902, BP.

80. Brandão to WIB, 20, 22, 28 Nov. 1902, *ibid.* Bahía and Pernambuco are known today as São Salvador and Recife.

81. Cf. Keller, *Life Insurance,* p. 79.

82. *Ibid.*, pp. 86-102, *passim.*

83. *Buffalo Express,* 16 Dec. 1902; WIB account book of trip to Brazil, BP.

84. WIB to Buckner, 30 Dec. 1902, 13 Jan. 1903, and to Christie, 19, 21 Feb. 1902, BP.

85. WIB to Christie, 9 Mar. 1903, *ibid.*

86. WIB to Brandão, 17 Jan. 1903, and to Perkins, 26 Mar. 1903, *ibid.* Also see Keller, *Life Insurance,* pp. 102-103.

87. Perkins by this time, while retaining his NYLIC vice-presidency, had become a partner in J. P. Morgan and Company (Garraty, *Right-Hand Man,* p. 87).

88. The reference is not to the "mayor of Columbus" but to Charles R. Mayers, an officer of the First National Bank of Columbus.

89. BP.

90. WIB to Charles Rohl, Venezuelan agent, 22 Apr. 1901, *ibid.; Commercial Advertiser,* 15 Dec. 1902.

91. Mayers to WIB, 20, 22, 24 Dec. 1902, and WIB to Mayers, 21, 22, 26 Dec., BP.

92. *Commercial Advertiser,* 15 Dec. 1902; *Buffalo Express,* 16 Dec. 1902. Buchanan's statements to the press antedated by several weeks the celebrated dictum of Argentine Foreign Minister Luis M. Drago regarding the proscription of armed intervention to collect public debts (see pp. 281-283, 289-290, 298, 300).

93. WIB to A.B. Loomis, 16 Jan. 1903, BP.

94. Mayers to WIB, 22, 24 Dec. 1902, WIB to Mayers, 21 Dec., and to Cortelyou, 25 Dec., *ibid.*

95. Cortelyou to WIB, 23 Dec. 1902, and WIB to Cortelyou, [25 Dec. 1902?], *ibid.*

96. 26 Dec. 1902, and Goiticoa to WIB, 30 Dec., *ibid.*

97. 26 Jan. 1903, *ibid.*

98. 26 Jan. 1903, *ibid.*

99. 14 Feb. 1903, Hay Papers, Gen. Corres., 1903 (Cont. 11).

100. WIB to Hay, 12 May 1903, *ibid.*
101. *Buffalo Evening News,* 10 Feb. 1903.
102. *Annals of the American Academy* 22 (July 1903): 47-55. The diplomats included Matías Romero, former Mexican ambassador to Washington, and Francis B. Loomis, assistant secretary of state; the professors, John Bassett Moore, of Columbia University, John H. Latané, Washington and Lee, and Leo S. Rowe, University of Pennsylvania.
103. 28 Apr. 1903, BECPL, Buchanan Papers, and Hay Papers, Letterbook II, 1900 to 1903, p. 430 (Cont. 26).
104. 28 Apr. 1903, BECPL, Buchanan Papers; WIB to Hay, 12 May 1903, Hay Papers, Gen. Corres., 1903, (Cont. 11).
105. WIB to Hay, 7 Dec. 1903, *ibid.*
106. Hay to WIB, 5 Dec. 1903, Hay Papers, Letterbook III, 9 July 1903, to 24 May 1905, p. 56. See ch. 12.
107. See ch. 13 and pp. 310-312, 315, 321-322, 339-343, *passim.*

Chapter 12
NURSEMAID TO AN INFANT NATION

1. See pp. 236-237.
2. Dwight Carroll Miner, *The Fight for the Panama Route: The Story of the Spooner Act and the Hay-Herrán Treaty,* especially chs. V-XI.
3. Dennett, *John Hay,* pp. 264-265.
4. See pp. 165, 182, 183.
5. WIB to Hay, 22 Jan. 1902, NA, DS, Records of U. S. Delegation, Letters Sent, p. 258.
6. 26 Nov. 1901, Hay Papers, Gen. Corres., 1901 (Cont. 7).
7. *Epitomist,* 16 Mar. 1899.
8. 5 Dec. 1903, LC, MD, Theodore Roosevelt Papers, Ser. 1, Letters Received (Cont. 64).
9. 5 Dec. 1903, Hay Papers, Letterbook III, 9 July 1903-24 May 1905, p. 26.
10. 7 Dec. 1903, Hay Papers, Gen. Corres., 1903 (Cont.11).
11. *New York Times,* 13 Dec. 1903.
12. Roosevelt to Hay, 12 Dec. 1903, Roosevelt Papers, Ser. 2, Vol. 44, p. 89 (microfilm reel 332): Philip Caryl Jessup, *Elihu Root,* I, 406-407.
13. Francis B. Loomis, asst. secretary of state, to WIB, 12 Dec. 1903, NA, DS, Instructions to Ministers, Panama (henceforth Inst. Pan.), I, 1; WIB to Hay, 14 Dec. 1903, NA, DS, Despatches from Ministers, Panama (henceforth Desp. Pan.), I.
14. *New York Times,* 13 Dec. 1903.
15. See letters and newspaper clippings, BP.
16. *Cong. Rec.,* 58th Cong., 2 sess., XXXVIII, Pt. 1, pp. 339, 399-402.
17. *Ibid.*, pp. 65-924, *passim.*

18. 23 Dec. 1903, Desp. Pan., I.
19. *Buffalo Express*, 16 Dec. 1903.
20. 21 [?] Dec. 1903, BP.
21. WIB to Binnie, [n.d.] Dec. 1903, BP.
22. *Buffalo Express,* 23 Dec. 1903.
23. Lawrence O. Ealy, *The Republic of Panama in World Politics, 1903-1950,* p. 16.
24. G. A. Mellander, *The United States in Panamanian Politics: The Intriguing Formative Years,* pp. 29-33.
25. WIB to Hay, 22 Dec. 1903, Desp. Pan., I; Loomis to WIB, 4 Jan. 1904, Inst. Pan., I, 2-3.
26. WIB to Colonel José A. Arango, 23 Dec. 1903, NA, DS, Records of Diplomatic Posts, Panama (henceforth Post Records, Panama), Despatches between American Legation and Foreign Office.
27. WIB to Hay, 25 Dec. 1903, and encl., Desp. Pan., I.
28. *Ibid.*
29. Mellander, *United States in Panamanian Politics,* pp. 48-54.
30. Mrs. WIB to Binnie, 3, 11 Jan. 1903, BP.
31. Donald to Binnie, 28 Dec. 1903, 3 Jan. 1904, *ibid.*
32. WIB to Hay, 28 Dec. 1903, Desp. Pan., I.
33. WIB to Hay, 4 Jan. 1904, *ibid.*
34. WIB to Hay, 31 Dec. 1903, 4 Jan. 1904, *ibid.* Cf. Mellander, *United States in Panamanian Politics,* p. 49.
35. WIB to Hay, 7, 21 Jan. 1904, Desp. Pan., I.
36. WIB to Hay, 30 Jan. 1904, *ibid.*
37. WIB to Hay, 21, 23 Jan. 1904, *ibid.*
38. WIB to Hay, 4 Jan. 1904, *ibid.*
39. *Ibid.*
40. WIB to Hay, 5, 30 Jan. 1904, *ibid.*
41. 6 Jan. 1904, Inst. Pan., I, 4.
42. 19 Jan. 1904, *ibid.*, pp. 9-10. Assistant Secretary Adee regarded Buchanan's proposal as "unwise and short sighted" (memo to Hay, 18 Jan. 1904, Desp. Pan., I).
43. Ricardo Arias to WIB, 8 Feb. 1904, Num. File, Case 1502/overflow.
44. *For. Rel.,* 1904, p. 578; WIB to Hay, 30 Jan. 1904, Desp. Pan., I.
45. WIB to William W. Russell, chargé d'affaires *ad interim* to Panama, 1 Feb. 1904, Desp. Pan., I.
46. 30 Jan. 1904, *ibid.*
47. Cf. William David McCain, *The United States and the Republic of Panama,* pp. 62-63.
48. WIB to Hay, 28 Dec. 1903, Desp. Pan., I.
49. WIB to Hay, 28 Dec. 1903, 2, 18 Jan. 1904, *ibid.*; Hay to WIB, 11 Jan. 1904, Hay Papers, Letterbook III, pp. 78-79.
50. WIB to Hay, 18 Jan. 1904, Desp. Pan., I.
51. WIB to Hay, 18, 22 Jan. 1904, *ibid.*.
52. Bunau-Varilla to Hay, 31 Dec. 1903, *For. Rel.,* 1903, pp. 281-283.

53. WIB to Hay, 2, 22 Jan. 1904, Desp. Pan., I.
54. Hay Papers, Diaries, 18 Jan. 1904 (Cont. 27).
55. Malloy, *Treaties,* I, p. 1349.
56. WIB to Hay, 2, 4, 15, 18 Jan. 1904, Desp. Pan., I.
57. Bunau-Varilla to Hay, 31 Dec. 1903, *For. Rel.,* 1904, pp. 282-283; WIB to Hay, 1 Jan. 1904, Desp. Pan., I.
58. WIB to Russell, 1 Feb. 1904, Desp. Pan., I; Arias to WIB, 8 Feb. 1904, Num. File. Case 1502/overflow.
59. WIB to Charles and Binnie, 4 Jan. 1904, BP.
60. WIB to Hay, 8, 9, 16 Jan. 1904, and encl., *For Rel.,* 1904, pp. 552-553, 555-556.
61. WIB to Dr. Reed, and to Hay, 16 Jan. 1904, Desp. Pan., I.
62. 7 Jan. 1904, *ibid.*
63. WIB and Mrs. WIB to Charles and Binnie, 17 Jan. 1904, BP; Dept. of State to WIB, 21 Jan. 1904, Inst. Pan., I, 11.
64. Dept. of State to WIB, 29 Jan. 1904, *ibid.*
65. 1 Feb. 1904, Desp. Pan., I.
66. WIB to Hay, 11 Feb. 1904, *ibid.*
67. *New York Evening Post,* 9 Feb. 1904; *Buffalo Express,* 11 Feb. 1904.
68. *Buffalo Express,* 12 Feb. 1904.
69. *Ibid.,* 10 Feb. 1904; *Buffalo Evening News,* 12, 13 Feb. 1904.
70. WIB to Hay, 11 Mar. 1904, and encl., Hay Papers, Gen. Corres., 1904 (Cont. 14).
71. Hay Papers, Letterbook III, p. 124.
72. WIB to Hay, 12 Feb. 1904, Desp. Pan., I; Hay to WIB, 15 Feb., Inst. Pan., I, 20.
73. Arias to WIB, 27 Apr. 1904, and WIB to Amador, 20 July, 29 Sep. 1904, Num. File, Case 1502/overflow.
74. This was the kind of scheme for which he had been criticized in February, although the ratio of 5 to 1 was far removed from the earlier 20 to 1 alleged.
75. WIB to Amador, 30 Apr., 20 July 1904, WIB to Arias, 12 May 1904, Num. File, Case 1502/overflow.
76. WIB to Amador, 29 Sep. 1904, and Amador to WIB, 17 Oct. 1904, *ibid.*
77. Amador to WIB, 21 June, 30 Aug. 1904, and WIB to Amador, 20 July, 29 Sep. 1904, *ibid.*
78. WIB to Hay, 11 Mar. 1904, Hay Papers, Gen. Corres., 1904, (Cont. 14). En route to Paris in late 1903, Reyes had visited Washington to confer with Secretary Hay on Colombian-American relations in connection with the Panama crisis (see *For. Rel.,* 1903, pp. 283-314, and Charles D. Ameringer, "Philippe Bunau-Varilla: New Light on the Panama Canal Treaty," *The Hispanic American Historical Review* 46 [Feb. 1966]: 39-51.). At this time Buchanan had advised Hay that he would be glad to go to Washington if he could be "of any further service in connection with General Reyes' visit" (5 Dec. 1903, Roosevelt Papers, Ser. 1, Letters Received [Cont. 64]).
79. Reyes to WIB, 2 Mar. 1904, encl. in WIB to Hay, 11 Mar. 1904, Hay

Papers, Gen. Corres., 1904 (Cont. 14).

80. 31 Mar. 1904, *ibid.*

81. WIB to Hay, 11, 31 Mar. 1904, and encls. Reyes to WIB, 2, 27 Mar. 1904, *ibid.*

82. See pp. 295-296. On Reyes's later attempts to conciliate the dispute, see E. Taylor Parks, *Colombia and the United States, 1765-1934,* pp. 429-437.

83. 30 Apr. 1904, Roosevelt Papers, Ser. 1, Letters Received, (Cont. 73).

84. 8 Nov. 1904, Hay Papers, Gen. Corres., 1904 (Cont. 14).

85. Barrett to Nicholas Murray Butler, 27 Apr. 1904, and to his mother, 8 June 1904, Barrett Papers, Gen. Corres., 1900-1904 (Cont. 7); WIB to Arias, 12 May 1904, Num. File, Case 1502/overflow.

86. Cf. Mellander, *United States in Panamanian Politics,* p. 192.

Chapter 13
BACK TO THE WORLD OF BUSINESS

1. Henry Gosler Prout, *A Life of George Westinghouse,* p. 21; *DAB,* XX, 18.

2. *DAB,* pp. 16-17; Prout, *George Westinghouse,* pp. 212-213.

3. Prout, *George Westinghouse,* pp. 12, 134-136, 141-154; *DAB,* XX, 17-18.

4. Prout, *George Westinghouse,* pp. 35, 62-65.

5. Westinghouse Electric Corporation, Central Library, E. H. Heinrichs in Charles F. Scott (ed.), unpublished manuscript, "Anecdotes and Reminiscences of George Westinghouse, 1846-1914. Contributed by his Former Associates," p. 22. (Heinrichs was Westinghouse's personal press representative from 1889 to 1914.)

6. Prout, *George Westinghouse,* pp. 12, 262-263.

7. *Financial Times* (London), 6 Feb. 1904.

8. John Dummelow, *1889-1949,* pp. 4-22; Francis Ellington Leupp, *George Westinghouse: His Life and Achievements,* pp. 188-193; Heinrichs, "Anecdotes and Reminiscences," pp. 27-29.

9. Heinrichs, "Anecdotes and Reminiscences," pp. 20-25.

10. *Ibid.,* p. 26; Prout, *George Westinghouse,* pp. 264-266.

11. WIB to Hay, 7 Dec. 1902, Hay Papers, Gen. Corres., 1903 (Cont. 11); WIB to Colonel Clarence R. Edwards, US Army, 14 Dec. 1903, NA, DS, Post Records, Panama, Miscellaneous Correspondence.

12. *Buffalo Enquirer,* 7 Jan. 1904; unidentified newspaper clipping, 18 Feb. 1904, BP.

13. *Financial Times,* 6 Feb. 1904; Companies Registration Office, London, Certificate no. 39, Company File 62919, 5 Feb. 1904; WIB to Mrs. WIB, 15 Mar. 1904, BP.

14. WIB to family, 17-24 Feb. 1904, *ibid.*

15. 26, 28 Feb. 1904, *ibid.*

16. WIB to Mrs. WIB, 2, 11, 14, 17 Mar., 12, 18 Apr., 1, 2 May 1904, and to Florence, 9 Mar. 1904, *ibid.*

17. WIB to Mrs. WIB, 11 Mar. 1904, *ibid.*
18. WIB to Mrs. WIB, 28 Feb., 11, 17 Mar., 12 Apr. 1904, and to family, 25 Mar. 1904, *ibid.*
19. WIB to Mrs. WIB, 26, 29 Mar. 1904, *ibid.* In the following notes of this chapter all entries of dates without source citations refer to Buchanan's letters to Mrs. Buchanan (all filed in BP).
20. 14 Mar. 1904.
21. 3, 10, 26 Apr. 1904.
22. 24 Apr. 1904.
23. 3, 22 Apr. 1904.
24. 3 Apr. 1904.
25. 26 Mar., 22 Apr. 1904.
26. 11, 14, 16, 26 Mar. 1904.
27. WIB to Mrs. WIB, 14, 22, 23, 26, 29 Mar., 3, 10, 18 Apr. 1904, to Donald, 7 Mar. 1904, and to Florence, 9 Apr. 1904, *ibid.* The property was located at Gates Circle on Buffalo's fashionable Delaware Avenue. Later, when the house was finished, the Buchanans made their home for a time with their daughter and son-in-law, Mr. and Mrs. Charles Hoyt Williams.
28. 14, 15 Mar. 1904.
29. 1 May 1904.
30. See pp. 256-258.
31. 3 Apr. 1904.
32. 11, 16, 22 May, 8, 23, 30 June 1904.
33. 10 [?], 15 [?] June 1904.
34. 23 June 1904.
35. 22 June, 1, 26 July 1904.
36. 23 June, 1, 30 July 1904.
37. 23-26 June 1904.
38. 7, 20 May, 13 June, 3 July 1904.
39. 23, 29 May, 8 June, 14, 24 July 1904.
40. WIB to Donald, 12 Oct. 1904, BP.
41. See pp. 256-258, 269.
42. See printed notice of the meeting, BP.
43. *Financial Times,* 7 Dec. 1904; *Manchester Courier,* 7 Dec. 1904; *The Electrical Review* 55 (Dec. 1904): 969-970; Dummelow, *1889-1949,* p. 29.
44. Dummelow, *1889-1949,* p. 29.
45. WIB to Perkins, 23 Nov. 1904, Columbia University, Butler Library, The George Walbridge Perkins Papers (henceforth Perkins Papers), Gen. File, 1904 (Cont. 13).
46. Garraty, *Right-Hand Man,* pp. 64-68; Keller, *Life Insurance,* p. 119.
47. WIB to Perkins, 5 Jan. 1905, Perkins Papers, Gen. File, 1905 (Cont. 14).
48. WIB to Perkins, 3 Jan. 1905, *ibid.*
49. WIB to Perkins, 5 Jan. 1905, *ibid.*
50. WIB to Perkins, 3, 5 (two reports) Jan. 1905, *ibid.*
51. Sidney Harcave, *Russia, A History,* pp. 369-372.
52. WIB to Perkins, 5 Jan. 1905, Perkins Papers, Gen. File, 1905 (Cont. 14).

53. Source materials on Buchanan's Westinghouse years are almost nonexistent. The Central Library of the Westinghouse Electric Corporation, East Pittsburgh, contains few company records for the period (letter to author from Miss Fern L. Gass, Librarian, 13 Jan. 1969). On the British Westinghouse Electric & Manufacturing Company, neither the British Museum nor seven other English archives consulted could turn up more than a few documents. Buchanan's personal papers, while helpful for 1904, are singularly lacking on his Westinghouse association during 1905.

54. Dummelow, *1889-1949*, p. 29.

55. *Manchester Courier*, 19 Dec. 1905.

56. Dummelow, *1889-1949*, p. 29.

57. See below, ch. 14.

58. Dummelow, *1889-1949*, p. 29. Though Buchanan's name continued to be carried on the official company rosters with the English Registrar of Companies until May 1907, he actually discontinued his duties in early 1906 (Companies Registration Office, London, Certificate no. 56, Company File 62919, 31 May 1907).

59. When the financial panic of 1907 pushed several Westinghouse companies into the hands of receivers, it marked the beginning of Westinghouse's loss of control of the vast empire he had created. Even friends and adulatory biographers could later write: "The British Westinghouse Company proved a losing venture from its very beginning, in the maintenance of which the profits of the home company were largely sunk," (Heinrichs, "Anecdotes and Reminiscences," p. 26), or "I presume that most men would look upon the British Westinghouse enterprise as one of Mr. Westinghouse's failures" (Prout, *George Westinghouse*, p. 265). At the end of World War I, however, the British Westinghouse Electric & Manufacturing Company was absorbed by Metropolitan-Vickers Electrical Company (Registry of Business Names, London, Certificate no. 40986, dated 20 July 1920), which proceeded to implement plans for the electrification of British railroads much as Westinghouse had envisioned them twenty years before (Prout, *George Westinghouse*, pp. 265-266).

60. See pp. 213-214.

61. Garraty, *Right-Hand Man*, pp. 182-186; "Insco" (WIB) to "Obelisk" (Perkins), 14 Dec. 1905, Perkins Papers, Gen. File, 1905 (Cont. 14).

62. WIB to "Obelisk," 26 May 1906, *ibid.*, Gen. File, 1906, Jan.-June (Cont. 16).

63. WIB to Perkins, 17, 29 June 1906, to Milburn, 29 June, and to Francis, 30 June 1906, *ibid.*

64. See ch. 14.

65. 29 June 1906, Perkins Papers, Gen. File, 1906, Jan.-June (Cont. 16).

66. Garraty, *Right-Hand Man*, p. 271.

Chapter 14
FROM HEMISPHERE STAGE TO WORLD ARENA

1. Dennett, *John Hay,* pp. 264-265.
2. Jessup, *Elihu Root,* I, 285-288, 310-311.
3. *For. Rel.,* 1903, pp. 1-5. See also Whitaker, *The Western Hemisphere Idea,* pp. 86-89, 95-99, and Peterson, *Argentina and the United States,* pp. 258-261.
4. See pp. 115-118, 232.
5. Dennett, *John Hay,* p. 264; Henry Fowles Pringle, *Theodore Roosevelt, A Biography,* p. 206.
6. Quoted in Jessup, *Elihu Root,* p. 469.
7. Leopold, *Elihu Root,* pp. 65-66.
8. See pp. 337-338.
9. Leopold, *Elihu Root,* pp. 62-69.
10. See many letters WIB to Root and to C. R. Dean, secretary to delegation, NA, DS, Records of the United States Delegation to the Third International Conference of American States, 1906, (henceforth Records of U. S. Delegation), Box 6, unnumbered folder "Transportation, etc."
11. 7 Apr. 1906, *ibid.*
12. WIB to Robert Bacon, asst. secretary of state, 11 Apr., and to Root, 15 May 1906, *ibid.*
13. *Ibid.,* Box 6; *New York Commercial,* 9 Mar. 1906. See delegation photograph in Illustration Section.
14. Copy filed in Records of U. S. Delegation.
15. Minutes of meeting of 8 June 1906, *ibid.,* Box 4, folder 16.
16. *Ibid.*
17. WIB, *Report of the Delegates of the United States to the Third International Conference of the American States* (henceforth *Report of Delegates*), pp. 39-40.
18. *Ibid.,* pp. 40-41.
19. *Ibid.,* pp. 41-42.
20. WIB to Dean, 21 June 1906, Records of U. S. Delegation, Box 6, unnumbered folder "Papers Relative to Personnel"; *New York Tribune,* 1 July 1906; *The Outlook,* 8 Sep. 1906, pp. 69-73.
21. *The Outlook,* 8 Sep. 1906, pp. 69-73.
22. *Report of Delegates,* p. 26; George Agnew Chamberlain, "Secretary Root's Diplomatic Triumph in South America," *Harper's Weekly* 50 (8 Sep. 1906): 1272-1274.
23. *Harper's Weekly* 50: 1272-1274; *Report of Delegates,* pp. 3-4.
24. Carolina Nabuco, *The Life of Joaquim Nabuco,* pp. 305, 309, 317.
25. *Ibid.,* 253ff, 308, 310, 318.
26. Jessup, *Elihu Root,* I, 471-472.
27. Nabuco, *Joaquim Nabuco,* p. 317.
28. *Report of Delegates,* pp. 4, 55-58.

29. Third International American Conference, *Minutes, Resolutions, Documents* (henceforth Third IAC, *Minutes*), pp. 45-46, 49, 77, 100, 371.
30. Paul S. Reinsch, "The Third International Conference of American States," *The American Political Science Review* 1 (Feb. 1907): 196.
31. WIB to Nabuco, 24 July 1906, Records of U. S. Delegation, Box 6, unnumbered folder "Correspondence While in Rio"; *Report of Delegates,* pp. 5, 58-60.
32. Jessup, *Elihu Root,* I, 478; Lloyd C. Griscom, US ambassador, to Root, 31 Aug. 1906, Num. File, Case 194/46.
33. Griscom to Root, 31 Aug. 1906, Num. File, Case 194/46. Jessup, *Elihu Root,* I, 478-479; *New York Times,* 27 July 1906; *Buffalo Express,* 3 Aug. 1906.
34. *Buffalo Express,* 3 Aug. 1906.
35. Griscom to Root, 31 Aug. 1906, Num. File, Case 194/46; *Washington Post,* 29 July 1906.
36. Nabuco, *Joaquim Nabuco,* pp. 325-326.
37. *Report of Delegates,* pp. 61-65.
38. Nabuco, *Joaquim Nabuco,* pp. 325, 328; *Report of Delegates,* pp. 61-62.
39. Elihu Root, *Latin America and the United States; Addresses by Elihu Root,* Robert Bacon and James Brown Scott (eds.), pp. 6-11.
40. *Ibid.,* pp. 9-11.
41. Quoted in Jessup, *Elihu Root,* I, 483.
42. See pp. 200-203.
43. WIB to Root, 6 Aug. 1906, Records of U. S. Delegation, Box 6, unnumbered folder "Correspondence While in Rio"; *Report of Delegates,* pp. 9-11, 97; Third IAC, *Minutes,* pp. 132-138.
44. *Report of Delegates,* pp. 71-74.
45. WIB to Root, 7 Aug. 1906, Num. File, Case 249/17.
46. Nabuco, *Joaquim Nabuco,* p. 328.
47. Cf. Whitaker, *United States and Argentina,* pp. 86-102, *passim,* and Peterson, *Argentina and the United States,* pp. 257-263.
48. *Report of Delegates,* pp. 12-14.
49. Peterson, *Argentina and the United States,* p. 290.
50. *Report of Delegates,* pp. 12-14; Third IAC, *Minutes,* pp. 216-226.
51. This activity involved four conventions, fourteen resolutions, and three motions (Curtis A. Wilgus, "The Third International American Conference at Rio de Janeiro, 1906," *The Hispanic American Historical Review* 12 [Nov. 1932]: 443).
52. *Report of Delegates,* pp. 6-7; Third IAC, *Minutes,* pp. 573-581, 611-613.
53. Third IAC, *Minutes,* pp. 77-79, 118-120.
54. WIB to Hay, 12 Feb. 1904, Desp. Pan., I; Third IAC, *Minutes,* pp. 141-143.
55. Third IAC, *Minutes,* pp. 213-214; WIB to minister of interior, Chile, 28 Aug. 1906, Records of U. S. Delegation, Box 6, unnumbered folder "Correspondence While in Rio."
56. WIB to Root, 24 Aug. 1906, Num. File, Case 249/19-21.

57. See invitations and other papers in Records of U. S. Delegation, Box 6, unnumbered folder "Correspondence While in Rio."
58. *Boston Globe,* 24 Aug. 1906.
59. Nabuco, *Joaquim Nabuco,* pp. 326-329.
60. Third IAC, *Minutes,* pp. 353-354, 402; WIB to Root, 28 Aug. 1906, Num. File, Case 249/13.
61. *Report of Delegates,* pp. 39-40.
62. Cf. McGann, *Argentina,* pp. 246-251, and Reinsch, *The American Political Science Review* 1 (Feb. 1907): 197-199.
63. WIB to Root, 24 Aug. 1906, Num. File, Case 249/18.
64. See Records of U. S. Delegation, Box 6, unnumbered folder "Miscellaneous Correspondence."
65. Third IAC, *Minutes,* pp. 58-63. At an appropriate moment in the proceedings at Rio Buchanan had paid special tribute to Mitre.
66. Griscom to Root, 17, 20 Sep. 1906, Num. File, Case 1070/1-3.
67. Peterson, *Argentina and the United States,* pp. 291-292.
68. WIB to Tornquist, 5 Oct. 1906, Records of U. S. Delegation, Box 6, unnumbered folder "Miscellaneous Correspondence."
69. *Ibid.*
70. Tornquist to WIB, 26 Oct., 17 Dec. 1906, *ibid.*
71. Griscom to Root, 13 Oct. 1906, Num. File, Case 1070/5-7.
72. Peterson, *Argentina and the United States,* pp. 292-297.
73. See p. 296.
74. WIB to Root, 6 Nov. 1906, LC, MD, Root Papers, Gen. Corres., 1906 (Cont. 44); *Havana Post,* 15 Nov. 1906.
75. Dana Gardner Munro, *Intervention and Dollar Diplomacy in the Caribbean, 1900-1921,* pp. 125-140.
76. *Havana Post,* 15 Nov. 1906; unidentified newspaper clipping in BP.
77. *Springfield* (Mass.) *Republican,* 28 Nov. 1906. Other newspaper reports suggested that Buchanan was being considered as a successor to Provisional Governor Magoon (*Buffalo Evening News,* 3 Jan. 1907).
78. WIB to Root, 28 Nov. 1906, NA, DS, Minor File, 1906-1910, Vol. 9.
79. Jessup, *Elihu Root,* I, 521-523; James Brown Scott, *Robert Bacon, Life and Letters,* p. 126.
80. Buchanan's extensive correspondence and pertinent papers are found in Num. File, Cases 1502, 4181, 9271. See also Minor File, 1906-1910, Vol. 9, and Root Papers, Gen. Corres., 1907 (Cont. 49).
81. Root to Obaldía, 24 Apr. 1907, Num. File, Case 1502/10a.
82. *Ibid.*
83. Secretary of War William H. Taft and Attorney W. Nelson Cromwell, who had for many years been associated with the canal question. At one point Cromwell charged the delays to Buchanan's earlier proposals that Panama discharge its debt obligations by purchasing Colombia's bonds at their depreciated price (Cromwell to Taft, 4 June 1907, Num. File, Case 1502/21, 22. Also see pp. 256-258.). Though not again associated with the negotiations, Buchanan in August 1908 proposed that he "endeavor to pull

the thing into shape" (Root Papers, Gen. Corres., 1908 [Cont. 54]). The matter dragged on for many months (Jessup, *Elihu Root,* I, 523). Though eventually signed in January 1909, all three treaties failed to become operative when Colombia refused to ratify (*For. Rel.,* 1909, pp. 223-233, and 1910, pp. 261-408).

84. *For. Rel.,* 1906, I, xliv-1.
85. See convention program in BP.
86. *Buffalo Express,* 21 Feb. 1907.
87. Correspondence in Records of U. S. Delegation, Box 6, unnumbered folder "Miscellaneous Correspondence."
88. See letterhead dated 10 Apr. 1907, Barrett Papers, Cont. 10.
89. *Sun* (Baltimore), 27 May 1907.
90. Root to Joseph H. Choate, chairman U. S. delegation to Second Hague Conference, 31 May 1907, Num. File, Case 40/288.
91. *Ibid.,* Case 40/152.
92. *For. Rel.,* 1907, II, 1128-1139.
93. Minutes, meeting of the Commission, 20 Apr. 1907, Num. File, Case 40/210 1/2.
94. Root to Choate, 6 June 1907, *ibid.,* Case 40/297.
95. James Brown Scott, solicitor, Department of State, to Root, 26 June 1906, *ibid.,* Case 40/368-379; William Isaac Hull, *The Two Hague Conferences and Their Contributions to International Law,* pp. 8-9.
96. General George B. Davis, delegate, to Bacon, 25 June 1906, Num. File, Case 40/491.
97. 25 June 1907, Root Papers, Gen. Corres., 1907 (Cont. 49).
98. *The Proceedings of the Hague Peace Conference. The Conference of 1907,* James Brown Scott (ed.), (henceforth *Proceedings*), I, 3-32, *passim.*
99. *Ibid.,* I-IV.
100. See pp. 288, 289.
101. *For. Rel.,* 1907, II, 1135.
102. *Proceedings,* I, 549, 553-555, II, 251.
103. *Ibid.,* I, 332, 558-559; Joseph Hodges Choate, *The Two Hague Conferences,* pp. 59-65.
104. Hull, *The Two Hague Conferences,* pp. 314-323; *Proceedings,* II.
105. Choate to Root, 23 Aug., and Root to Choate, 28 Aug. 1906, Num. File, Case 40/430, 623; Jessup, *Elihu Root,* II, 75-79.
106. Hull, "The United States and Latin America at The Hague," *International Conciliation* 44 (July 1911): 12-13.
107. Its final act comprised thirteen conventions, two resolutions, one declaration, and five recommendations.
108. Baron d'Estournelles de Constant, *The Results of the Second Hague Conference,* p. 15.
109. Hull, *The Two Hague Conferences,* pp. 18-20.
110. Root to WIB, 11 Feb. 1908, BP.
111. WIB to Bacon, 7 Nov. 1907, Num. File, Case 775/201.

Chapter 15
PROMOTING STABILITY IN UNSTABLE NATIONS

1. This background in based in large part on Munro, *Intervention and Dollar Diplomacy,* pp. 141-144.
2. *Ibid.,* pp. 144-151; Jessup, *Elihu Root,* I, 500-502.
3. *For. Rel.,* 1906, I, 834-866. See p. 285.
4. *For. Rel.,* 1907, II, 606-665.
5. WIB, "Report of the Central American Peace Conference held at Washington, D. C., 1907," *For. Rel.,* 1907, II, 665. (The complete report is pp. 665-727.) See conference photograph in Illustration Section.
6. WIB to Robert Bacon, asst. secretary of state, 7 Nov. 1907, Num. File, Case 6775/201.
7. *For. Rel.,* 1907, II, 665-667.
8. *Ibid.,* pp. 667, 687-691.
9. *Ibid.,* p. 668.
10. *Ibid.,* pp. 669-671.
11. *Ibid.,* pp. 669, 671-673.
12. *Ibid.,* p. 673. As Buchanan had foreseen, pressure for union gradually diminished.
13. *Ibid.,* pp. 673-674.
14. *Ibid.,* pp. 676-678, 702-711.
15. *Ibid.,* pp. 674-675, 692-696.
16. Jessup, *Elihu Root,* I, 511.
17. *For. Rel.,* 1907, II, 696.
18. *Ibid.,* pp. 675-676, 697-701.
19. See p. 300.
20. *Charter Act and By-Laws of the Central American Fraternity,* p. 9; "Constitutional Act of the Central American Fraternity," Pan American Union *Bulletin* 26 (Feb. 1908): 301-310; Num. File, Case 6775/335.
21. *Charter Act,* pp. 7-9.
22. *For. Rel.,* 1907, II, 678-680.
23. Angel Ugarte, Honduran minister to US, to Root, 12 Nov. 1907, Num. File, Case 6775/215.
24. J. B. Calvo, Costa Rican minister to US, to Root, 27 Dec. 1907, *For. Rel.,* 1907, II, 664-665.
25. Num. File, Case 6775/411-412.
26. See pp. 312-313, 342, 343.
27. See, for example, various documents in Num. File, Cases 3442, 4434, 5450, 7152, 8014.
28. WIB to Root, 3 Aug. 1907, and W. M. Collier, minister to Spain, to Root, 30 Aug. 1907, Num. File, Case 8014/1.
29. *Daily Mail* (London), 3 Feb. 1908.
30. Unidentified newspaper clipping, BP.
31. *Washington Post,* 20 Mar. 1908.

32. Root to American Legation, Madrid, 10 Feb. 1908, and WIB to Root, 2 Mar. 1908, Num. File, Case 8014/9, 12. The case continued to plague Buchanan for many months (*ibid.,* Case 8014/16).

33. *Report of the Delegates to the Third International Conference of the American States,* pp. 110-111.

34. WIB to Root, 8 Dec. 1907, Num. File, Case 249/210; Root to WIB, 11 Feb., 21 Mar. 1908, BP.

35. Root proclamation, 21 Feb. 1908, and WIB to Root, 19 Mar. 1908, Num. File, Case 12372/1, 2. Barrett had been a member of the US delegation to the Mexico Conference and Rowe to that at Rio.

36. *Ibid.; Washington Post,* 8 Apr. 1908.

37. Because of other commitments, Buchanan met with the committee only rarely. Rowe and Barrett performed most of its functions.

38. Root to American Embassy, Mexico, 18, 20 Mar. 1908, Num. File, Case 6775/361A, 362.

39. "Date Book for 1908," BP (henceforth Date Book).

40. Date Book, pp. 93-113.

41. WIB to Creel, 7 Apr. 1908, Root to Creel, 9 Apr., and Root to D. E. Thompson, ambassador to Mexico, 11 Apr., Num. File, Case 6775/407B, 408, 413A.

42. Date Book, pp. 109-112. The *hacendado* was General Terrazas, longtime governor of the state of Chihuahua.

43. *Daily Record* (Mexico City), 21 Apr. 1908.

44. See Num. File, Case 5316.

45. 9, 16 Apr. 1908, Num. File, Case 6775/408, 426.

46. WIB to Root, 22, 27, 28, 30 Apr. 1908, and Root to WIB 23, 29 Apr., *ibid.,* Case 6775/430, 433, 438, 441, 445, 450; Date Book, pp. 114-130.

47. Date Book, pp. 122-130.

48. Root to American Legation, Costa Rica, 5 May 1908, and to Luis Anderson, Costa Rican foreign minister, 7 May, Num. File, Case 6775/454, 459.

49. Date Book, pp. 131-135; "Report of William I. Buchanan, High Commissioner Representing the President of the United States to Attend to Inauguration of the Court of Justice for Central America," *For. Rel.,* 1908, p. 217. (The complete report is pp. 217-247.)

50. *For. Rel.,* 1908, pp. 217-218; Date Book, pp. 135-141.

51. Date Book, pp. 136-139; *For. Rel.,* 1908, pp. 217-219.

52. WIB to Root, 9 May 1908, Num. File, Case 6775/469.

53. *For. Rel.,* 1908, pp. 219-220; Date Book, p. 142.

54. *For. Rel.,* 1908, p. 247.

55. *Ibid.,* pp. 220-221.

56. Watt Stewart, *Keith and Costa Rica, passim.*

57. *For. Rel.,* 1908, p. 221; Date Book, p. 144.

58. Date Book, pp. 144-145; *For. Rel.,* 1908, p. 222.

59. *For. Rel.,* 1908, pp. 222-223; Date Book, p. 146.

60. WIB to Bacon, 21 July 1908, Num. File, Case 6775/569-570.

61. *For. Rel.,* 1908, p. 223. See photograph in Illustration Section.
62. *Ibid.,* pp. 224-225.
63. *Ibid.,* p. 227.
64. *Ibid.,* p. 228.
65. *Ibid.,* pp. 229, 233-236; Root to WIB, 23 May, and WIB to Root, 25 May 1908, Num. File, Case 6775/501A, 503.
66. Date Book, pp. 146-153.
67. G. T. Weitzel, chargé d'affaires in Costa Rica, to Root, 4 June 1908, Num. File, Case 6775/537-538; *For. Rel.,* 1908, pp. 244-245.
68. Clippings from *El Imparcial, El Heraldo,* and *El Diario,* 8-10 June 1908, filed in BP.
69. Unidentified newspaper clipping, 12 June 1908, BP.
70. Date Book, pp. 161-162; *For. Rel.,* 1908, pp. 245-246.
71. *Havana Post,* 15 June 1908.
72. *For. Rel.,* 1908, pp. 245-246.
73. Bacon to Root, 28 Oct. 1908, Root Papers, Gen. Corres., 1908 (Cont. 54). Also see correspondence in Num. File, Case 6775/564, 565, 598-603, 612, 613.
74. Munro, *Intervention and Dollar Diplomacy,* pp. 156-158.
75. *Sunday Star* (Washington), 13 Dec. 1908.
76. WIB to Mrs. WIB, 29 Aug., 5, 7, 14 Sep. 1908, BP.
77. The proposal stipulated that foreign companies must invest in Mexican securities sums equivalent to the reserves they carried on Mexican policies.
78. Date Book, pp. 275-295; W. F. Sands, of US Embassy in Mexico, to Root, 16, 22, 25 Oct. 1908, and enclosures, Num. File, Case 16180/1-3, Case 15545/4-7.
79. William Heinke, US minister to Guatemala, to Root, 14 Sep. 1908, Num. File, Case 5316/93; WIB's rough draft memo, [?] Oct. 1908, BP.
80. See correspondence in Num. File, Case 7357/440, 441, 457, 458, 515.
81. W. L. Merry, US minister to Costa Rica, to Root, 20 Dec. 1908, *ibid.,* Case 7357/566.
82. José Madriz to WIB, 5 Sep. 1908, BP.
83. R. J. Echeverria to WIB, 1 Oct. 1908, *ibid.*
84. Num. File, Case 6775/598-600.
85. WIB to Bacon, 2 Nov. 1908, *ibid.*
86. WIB to Root, 30 Sep., and to Bacon, 7 Dec. 1908, *ibid.,* Case 2491/35, 46; Anderson to WIB, 16 July 1909, *ibid.,* Case 2755/27.
87. WIB to Root, 4 Mar. 1909, Root Papers, Gen. Corres., 1909 (Cont. 58); WIB to Philander C. Knox, secretary of state, 24 Apr. 1909, Num. File, Case 19216.
88. This was the Honduran case (see pp. 321-323).
89. Cf. Jessup, *Elihu Root,* I, 514.
90. 4 Mar. 1909, Root Papers, Gen. Corres., 1909 (Cont. 58).
91. *Ibid.*
92. Root to Policarpo Bonilla, former Honduran minister to Mexico, 16 Dec. 1908, Num. File, Case 6775/611.
93. 20 Mar. 1909, Root Papers, Gen. Corres., 1909 (Cont. 58).

Chapter 16
CLAIMS, COUNTER CLAIMS, AND ARBITRATION

1. Theodore Roosevelt, *Letters,* selected and edited by Elting E. Morison (henceforth Roosevelt, *Letters*), VI, 1427-1428.

2. Root to WIB, 21 Dec. 1908, *For. Rel.,* 1909, pp. 609-612; BECPL, Buchanan Papers, "Documents Relating to the Re-Establishment of Diplomatic Relations between the United States and Venezuela" (henceforth BECPL, Buchanan Papers, Documents Relating to Venezuela), p. 9. This is Buchanan's personal file of correspondence related to the Venezuelan mission.

3. For summaries of these developments, see Howard K. Beale, *Theodore Roosevelt and the Rise of America to World Power,* pp. 339-370, 405-406; Jessup, *Elihu Root,* I, 493-499; and Munro, *Intervention and Dollar Diplomacy,* pp. 67-77.

4. Root to Jacob Sleeper, United States chargé d'affaires in Caracas, 13 June 1908, Num. File, Case 4832/9A. For background details, see *For. Rel.,* 1908, pp. 774-830, and Num. File, Case 5082. For analysis of the 1903-1908 circumstances and negotiations leading to Buchanan's mission of December 1908, see Embert J. Hendrickson, "Roosevelt's Second Venezuelan Controversy," *The Hispanic American Historical Review* 50 (Aug. 1970): 483-498, and "Root's Watchful Waiting and the Venezuelan Controversy," *The Americas* 23 (Oct. 1966): 115-129.

5. Root to J. de J. Paúl, Venezuelan foreign minister, 12 Dec. 1908, Num. File, Case 4832/68.

6. Cf. Hendrickson, *The Hispanic American Historical Review* 50: 497.

7. Root to Paúl, 21 Dec. 1908, Num. File, Case 4832/68.

8. *For. Rel.,* 1909, p. 609.

9. Root to WIB, 21 Dec. 1908, *For. Rel.,* 1909, pp. 609-612. For the detailed instructions, see below, pp. 329-330.

10. WIB, "Date Book for 1908" (henceforth Date Book), pp. 357-362; WIB to Mrs. WIB, 27 Dec. 1908, BP.

11. US Congress, *Sen. Doc.,* No. 413, 60 Cong., 1 sess., pp. 91-157.

12. *Ibid.,* pp. 37-90.

13. *Ibid.,* pp. 9-36. Secretary Root summarized the five cases in notes to Minister W. W. Russell, 28 Feb., 21 June 1907 (*For. Rel.,* 1908, pp. 774-796, 800-805).

14. Details are recorded in Num. File, Cases 4832 and 5082, and *Sen. Doc.,* No. 413, 60 Cong., 1 sess., pp. 273-644.

15. 21 Dec. 1908, *For. Rel.,* 1909, pp. 609-612; Root to Sleeper, 13 June 1908, Num. File, Case 4832/9A.

16. Date Book, p. 362; Root to WIB, 21 Dec. 1908, *For. Rel.,* 1909, pp. 609-612.

17. Lorena to WIB, 28 Dec. 1908, Num. File, Case 5082; WIB to Root, 31 Dec., *For. Rel.,* 1909, p. 612.

18. Date Book, p. 363.
19. *Ibid.*
20. WIB to Root, 31 Dec. 1908, Num. File, Case 4832/76; Root to Paúl, 21 Dec. 1908, Num. File, Case 4832/68.
21. Arnold to secretary of navy, 5 Jan. 1909, Num. File, Case 4832/84. Admiral Arnold was commander of the 3rd Squadron, US Atlantic Fleet.
22. Date Book, pp. 364-366.
23. *Ibid.,* pp. 18-19; Arnold to secretary of navy, 5 Jan. 1909, Num. File, Case 4832/84.
24. Date Book, pp. 18-19.
25. *Ibid.,* pp. 20-25; WIB to Root, 2 Jan. 1909, Num. File, Case 5082/66.
26. Date Book, pp. 26-30.
27. 18 Jan. 1909, Num. File, Case 5082.
28. Date Book, p. 42.
29. Num. File, Case 5082/98.
30. 5 Jan. 1909, *ibid.,* no. 68.
31. WIB to Root, 17 Jan. 1909, and Root to WIB, 5 Jan., *ibid.,* nos. 68, 88.
32. WIB to Root, 2, 17 Jan. 1909, and Root to WIB, 5, 13 Jan., *ibid.,* nos. 66, 68, 69, 88.
33. WIB to Root, 2, 10 Jan., 2, 3, 4 Feb. 1909, and Root to WIB, 5, 6 Jan., *ibid.,* nos. 66, 68, 69, 76, 99, 100.
34. WIB to Root, 10, 17 Jan. 1909, *ibid.,* nos. 76, 88. Also see Num. File, Case 15363.
35. Date Book, pp. 47, 51.
36. *For. Rel.,* 1909, pp. 617-624, 629-630.
37. Num. File, Case 5082/116.
38. Date Book, pp. 54-60.
39. WIB to Root, *For. Rel.,* 1909, p. 613.
40. *Ibid.,* pp. 617-624.
41. BECPL, Buchanan Papers, Documents Relating to Venezuela. In addition to his primary mission, Buchanan had received additional assignments from Secretary Root: to lay bases for a general treaty of arbitration (Num. File, Case 17408); to seek Venezuela's permission to attach health officers to US Consulates in La Guaira and other ports (Case 5173/75, 81, 91-93); and to utilize his good offices for restoring Venezuela's relations with Colombia (Case 5435/13-19, 21, 32).
42. Date Book, p. 61.
43. *Ibid.,* pp. 62-63. Accounts of these affairs are filed in Num. File, Case 5082.
44. Date Book, pp. 64-72.
45. WIB to secretary of state, Num. File, Case 5082/127-138, Case 4832/89-91.
46. Num. File, Case 16180.
47. *Buffalo Express,* 1 Mar. 1909.
48. WIB to Knox, 5, 12, 13 Mar. 1909, and Knox to WIB, 10 Mar., Num. File, Case 2143/28, Case 6035/7-9.

49. 26 Jan. 1909, *ibid.,* Case 16180/4a. Also see p. 338.
50. Num. File, Case 16180/no no.
51. 20 Mar. 1909, Root Papers, Gen. Corres., 1909 (Cont. 58).
52. 26 Feb. 1909, Roosevelt, *Letters,* VI, 1539.
53. Root to WIB, 26 Jan. 1909, Num. File, Case 16180/4a.
54. 13, 20 Mar., 6 May 1909, Num. File, Case 6890/27-29, and Case 5082/140-141, 146-147.
55. *Ibid.,* Case 18788/no no.
56. Wilson to Knox, 5 Apr. 1909, and to Diplomatic Bureau, 8 Apr., Num. File, Case 18944/no nos.
57. Wilson to Knox, 5 Apr. 1909, *ibid.*
58. Wilson to WIB, 8 Apr. 1909, Num. File, Case 18944/ no no.
59. WIB to Wilson, 12, 16 Apr. 1909, and Wilson to WIB, 13 Apr., 1 May, *ibid.,* Case 18944/2, 3.
60. See pertinent documents in Num. File, Cases 1537, 1948, 5082, 18944, 19420, and 20434.
61. Notes as to a conversation, 16 June 1909, *ibid.,* Case 18944/23-24.
62. *For. Rel.,* 1909, pp. 624-629.
63. WIB to Solicitor's Office, 13 Aug. 1909, Num. File, Case 1537/159.
64. See pp. 312-313.
65. WIB to Root, 30 Aug. 1909, Root Papers, Gen. Corres., 1909 (Cont. 58).
66. WIB to Root, 26 Aug. 1909, *ibid.* The Argentines also appointed Leo Rowe and John Barrett as honorary commissioners.
67. WIB to Root, 26, 30 Aug. 1909, and Root to WIB, 28 Aug., *ibid.*
68. WIB to Mrs. WIB, 27, 28 Sep. 1909, BP.
69. Subsequently the papers were included in US Department of State, *The Case of the United States of America on Behalf of the Orinoco Steamship Company against the United States of Venezuela,* Washington, 1910.
70. WIB to Mrs. WIB, 15-20 Sep. 1909, BP.
71. *Ibid.*
72. *Ibid.*
73. WIB to Mrs. WIB, 27, 28 Sep., 12 Oct. 1909, *ibid.*
74. WIB to Knox, 28 Sep. 1909, Num. File, Case 11302/54. Also see *ibid.,* Case 18944/48-52, 54.
75. WIB to Knox, 28 Sep. 1909, Num. File, Case 11302/54; WIB to Mrs. WIB, 12 Oct. 1909, BP.
76. 23, 27, 28 Sep., 12 Oct. 1909, *ibid.*
77. 23 Sep. 1909, *ibid.*
78. 14 Oct. 1909, *ibid.*
79. However, the case was not settled until 26 Oct. 1910 (*For Rel.,* 1911, pp. 749-753).
80. 14 Oct. 1909, BP.
81. 15 Oct. 1909, *ibid.*
82. Whitelaw Reid, ambassador to London, to secretary of state, 18 Oct. 1909, Num. File, Case 16180/8; *The Times* (London), 18 Oct. 1909; *Buffalo*

Courier, 18 Oct. 1909; *Buffalo Express,* 18 Oct. 1909. An inquest two days later revealed the cause of death as heart failure (*Commercial Advertiser,* 20 Oct. 1909).

83. *Commercial Advertiser,* 30 Oct., 1 Nov. 1909; *Buffalo Express,* 1 Nov. 1909; *Buffalo Courier,* 1 Nov. 1909.

84. *DAB,* III, 219-220; Pan-American Exposition, Directors, Minutes, V, 2[9?]47-2[9?]48; *Buffalo Courier,* 1 Nov. 1909.

85. Num. File, Case 16180/ 9, 10, 12, 32, 130.

Chapter 17
PIONEER GOOD NEIGHBOR

1. *Commercial Advertiser,* 18 Oct. 1909.
2. William Roscoe Thayer, *The Life and Letters of John Hay,* II, 187.
3. *Evening Star* (Washington), 18 Oct. 1909.
4. *DAB,* III, 220.
5. *Buffalo Evening News,* 18 Oct. 1909.
6. *The Outlook* 93 (30 Oct. 1909): 497.
7. *John Barrett, Progressive Era Diplomat: A Study of a Commercial Expansionist, 1887-1920,* p. 105. See also pp. viii-xi, 99-100, 104-105.

BIBLIOGRAPHY

BIBLIOGRAPHY

1. Manuscripts

A. Buffalo and Erie County Historical Society

William I. Buchanan Papers. (These comprise personal letters, diaries, and date books, together with drafts of speeches, scrapbooks, newspaper clippings, and memorabilia.)
Pan-American Exposition Company Papers:
    Board of Directors, Minutes. 5 vols.
    Board of Women Managers, Minutes.
    Director General, Report. 2 vols.
    Estimates and Budgets Made by the Director General, 1900-1901.
    Letters from Director-General to Executive Committee. 16 vols.
    Letters from Executive Committee to Director-General. 5 vols.
World's Columbian Exposition Papers:
    Department of Agriculture, Official Report, 26 Mar. 1894, filed in Buchanan Papers.
    Department of Forestry, Official Report, 20 Jan. 1894, filed in Buchanan Papers.
    Letters from Director-General [to William I. Buchanan], filed in Buchanan Papers.

B. Buffalo and Erie County Public Library

William I. Buchanan Papers:
    Chilian-Argentine Boundary Arbitration: Private Papers, W. I. Buchanan, Deciding Member of the Commission, 1899.
    Documents relating to the Re-Establishment of Diplomatic Relations between the United States and Venezuela. William I. Buchanan, High Commissioner representing the President of the United States.
    Portfolio of Miscellaneous Papers.

C. Chicago Historical Society

Little, William McCarty, Spain, Letterpress Copies of Correspondence and Other Papers of Lt. Little, US Naval Attaché, Relative to the Outfitting of Reproductions of Columbus' Caravelles. . . .
World's Columbian Exposition (1893) Papers:
    Board of Directors, Minutes. 2 vols.
    Executive Committee, Minutes. 2 vols. and miscellaneous items.

D. Chile, Archivo Nacional:
Archives of the Ministry of Foreign Relations

Gobierno y legación de la República Arjentina en Chile. 1898 a 1899.
Gobierno y legación de los Estados Unidos en Chile. 1898; 1899.
Legación de Chile en la Arjentina. 1898-1899.
Legación de Chile en los Estados Unidos de Norte América. 1898, Vol. II; 1899.

E. Columbia University, Butler Library

The George Walbridge Perkins Papers:
    General File, 1904 (Cont. 13), 1905 (Cont. 14), Jan.-Sep. 1906 (Cont. 16), Jan.-June 1906, July-Dec. 1906 (Cont. 17).
    Letterbooks, No. 8, 16 Oct. 1901-2 Nov. 1902.

F. Library of Congress, Manuscript Division

John Barrett Papers:
    General Correspondence, 1900-04 (Cont. 7), 1906-07 (Cont. 10).
Grover Cleveland Papers:
    Series 2, Vol. 282.
John Hay Papers:
    Diaries, 1904-1905 (Cont. 27).
    General Correspondence, 1900, 1901, 1902, 1903, 1904 (Conts. 5, 7, 9, 11, 14).
    Letterbooks, II (1900, 22 Aug.-1903, 26 June), and III (1903, 9 July-1905, 24 May), (Cont. 26).
William McKinley Papers:
    Series 1, Vols. 80, 85; Series 2, Vols. 159, 175, 182; Series 3, Vols. 266, 282, 294, 303, 307, 310, 311.
Theodore Roosevelt Papers:
    Series 1, Letters Received (Conts. 64, 73); Series 2, Vols. 29, 44 (microfilm reels 326, 332).
Elihu Root Papers:
    General Correspondence, 1906, 1907, 1908, 1909 (Conts. 44, 49, 54, 58).
    Letterbooks, 1905-06 (Cont. 186).

G. National Archives:
Records of the Department of State

Applications and Recommendations for Office, 1893-1897.
Appointment Cards.
Consular Letters (Despatches from Consuls):

Córdoba, Argentina, Vol. I: Rosario, Argentina, Vol. II.
Despatches from Ministers:
  Argentina, Vols. XXXI-XXXVIII.
  Chile, Vol. XLII.
  Mexico, Vols. CLI-CLIV.
  Panama, Vols. I-II.
Instructions to Ministers:
  Argentina, Vol. XVII.
  Chile, Vol. XVIII.
  Panama, Vol. I.
Minor File, 1906-1910. Vol. IX.
Notes from Argentine Legation. Vol. IV.
Numerical File, 1906-1910. (See footnotes for individual case numbers.)
Post Records. See Records of Diplomatic Posts.
Records of Diplomatic Posts, Argentina, 1813-1935:
  Notes from the Argentine Foreign Office, 1894-1900.
Records of Diplomatic Posts, Panama, 1903-1927:
  Despatches between American Legation and Foreign Office, Panama, from 23 Dec. 1903 to 2 Feb. 1904.
  Miscellaneous Correspondence, 13 Nov. 1903 to 31 Aug. 1904.
Records of the United States Delegation to the Second International Conference of American States, 1901-2:
  Letters and Telegrams Received, Feb. 1901-Jan. 1902.
  Letters Sent, Aug. 1901-May 1902.
Records of the United States Delegation to the Third International Conference of the American States, 1906.
Records relating to the Pan American Exposition at Buffalo, 1901:
  Correspondence of the State Department with the Board of Management, 1900-1901.
  Scrapbooks of Newspaper Clippings Regarding the Exposition, 1899-1901. 3 vols.
Records relating to the World's Columbian Exposition at Chicago, 1893:
  Final Report of the President of the Exposition, 1896.
  Final Report of the Secretary of the Exposition, 1896. 2 vols.

H. Miscellaneous

Buchanan, A. E., Letters to author, 13 Mar., 14 July 1969, 15 Oct. 1974.
Companies Registration Office, London: Company File 62,919, certificates no. 39, dated 5 Feb. 1904, and no. 56, dated 31 May 1907.
The New York Life Insurance Company: Letter to author from V. deKamel, public relations associate, 13 Feb. 1969.
Registry of Business Names, London: Certificate no. 40986, dated 20 July 1920.
Sioux City Public Library, Sioux City, Iowa: Letter from E. D. Allen to T. S. Black, president, Commercial Club, Sioux City, 22 Nov. 1913.

Westinghouse Electric Corporation, Central Library, East Pittsburgh, Pennsylvania:
Heinrichs, E. H. See Scott, Charles F.
Letter to author from Miss Fern L. Gass, librarian, 13 Jan. 1969.
Scott, Charles F. (ed.), "Anecdotes and Reminiscenses of George Westinghouse, 1846-1914. Contributed by his Former Associates."

2. Buchanan's Official Reports and Unofficial Writings

"Argentine Tariff Changes," *US Consular Reports,* No. 225 (June 1899): 345-347.
"Census of the Argentine Republic," *US Consular Reports* 52 (Nov. 1896), no. 194, pp. 438-439.
"Export Bounties in Foreign Countries: Argentine Republic," *US Consular Reports* 58 (Dec. 1898), no. 219, p. 584.
"Immigration into the Argentine Republic," *US Consular Reports* 56 (Jan. 1898), no. 208, pp. 32-34.
"Latin America and the Mexican Conference," *The Annals of the American Academy of Political and Social Science* 22 (July 1903): 47-55.
"Life on the Estancias of Argentina, South America," *The Breeder's Gazette* 36 (13 Dec. 1899): 745-748.
"Los fletes marítimos y el comercio argentino-americano," *Revista de Derecho, Historia y Letras,* year I, 3 (June 1899): 491-494.
"The Mexican Conference and Arbitration," *The Advocate of Peace* 64 (May 1902): 94-100.
The Mexican International American Conference and Arbitration. Boston, 1902.
"Mines of the Argentine Republic," *US Consular Reports* 52 (Dec. 1896), no. 195, p. 624.
"Moneda y la vida en la República Argentina,"*Revista de Derecho, Historia y Letras,* year I, 2 (Dec. 1898): 197-221.
"Ocean Freight Rates and Argentine Trade," *US Consular Reports,* No. 224 (May 1899): 141-143.
"The Organization of an Exposition," *The Cosmopolitan* 31 (Sep. 1901): 517-522.
Pan-American Exposition. Report of William I. Buchanan, Director General. Buffalo, 1902.
"The Pan-American Exposition at Buffalo," *Collier's Weekly* 26 (1 Dec. 1900): 5-7.
"Powers of Attorney in Argentina," *US Consular Reports* 53 (Mar. 1897), no. 198, pp. 393-395.
"Production of Sugar in the Argentine Republic," *US Consular Reports* 51 (July 1896), no. 190, pp. 369-370.
"Proposed Argentine Tariff," in *US Consular Reports,* No. 228 (Sep. 1899): 58-59.

"Report on the Central American Peace Conference held at Washington, D.C., 1907," *Papers relating to the Foreign Relations of the United States,* 1907, II, 665-727.

Report of the Delegates of the United States to the Third International Conference of the American States, Held at Rio de Janeiro, Brazil, July 21 to August 26, 1906. Washington, 1907. Also published as *Senate Document,* No. 365, 59 Cong., 2 sess.

"Report of William I. Buchanan, High Commissioner Representing the President of the United States to Attend the Inauguration of the Court of Justice for Central America," *Papers relating to the Foreign Relations of the United States,* 1908, pp. 217-247.

"Tariff Changes in the Argentine Republic," *US Consular Reports* 58 (Nov. 1898), no. 218, p. 470.

"Trade in the Argentine Republic; Imports from United States," *US Consular Reports,* No. 228 (Sep. 1899): 21-26.

"United States Trade in the Argentine Republic," *US Consular Reports* 53 (Apr. 1897), no. 199, pp. 559-571.

"Wool in the Argentine Republic," *US Consular Reports,* No. 206 (Nov. 1897): 411-419.

3. *Government and Other Official Publications*

Argentine Republic, *Frontera argentino-chilena. Memoria presentada al tribunal nombrada por el gobierno de Su Majestad Británica "para considerar é informar sobre las diferencias suscitados respecto á la frontera entre las Repúblicas Argentina y Chilena.* London, 1902. 2 vols.

———. Ministerio de Relaciones Exteriores y Culto, *Memoria de relaciones exteriores presentada al Congreso Nacional.* Buenos Aires, 1860-.

———. Treaties, etc., *Tratados, convenciones, protocoles, actos y acuerdos internacionales.* Buenos Aires, 1911-1912. 11 vols.

Central American Fraternity, *Charter Act and By-Laws of the Central American Fraternity.* Washington, 1908.

Chile, *Chilo-Argentine Boundary. The Puna de Atacama. Memorandum presented by the Government of Chile to the Government of the United States of America.* Washington, [1898?].

International American Conference, 1st, Washington, D. C., 1889-1890, *Reports of Committees and Discussions Thereon.* Washington, 1890. 4 vols.

———. 2nd, Mexico, 1901-1902, *Organization of the Conference, Projects, Reports, Motions, Debates and Resolutions.* Mexico City, 1902.

———. 3d, Rio de Janeiro, 1906, *Minutes. Resolutions, Documents.* Rio de Janeiro, 1907.

Iowa Columbian Commission, *Report of the Iowa Columbian Commission, containing a Full Statement of Its Proceedings.* Cedar Rapids, 1895.

Malloy, William M. See United States, Treaties.

Pan-American Exposition Company, *Official Catalogue and Guide Book.*

Buffalo, 1901.

———. *Official Daily Program of the Pan-American Exposition.* Buffalo, 1901. 2 vols.

Report of the Board of General Managers of the Exhibit of the State of New York at the Pan-American Exposition. Albany, 1902.

United States. Congress, *Congressional Record.* Washington, 1873-.

———. Congressional Documents (figures in parentheses represent the Congress and session).

House Report, No. 2263 (54.1).

Senate Documents, No. 330 (57.1), No. 413 (60.1).

United States. Department of State, *The Case of the United States of America on Behalf of the Orinoco Steamship Company against the United States of Venezuela.* Washington, 1910.

———. *Papers relating to the Foreign Relations of the United States.* Washington, [1862]-.

United States. Laws, Statutes, etc. *The Statutes at Large of the United States of America.* Washington, 1845-.

United States. Treasury Department, *American Commerce: Commerce of South America, Central America, Mexico, and West Indies. . . . 1821-1898.* [Washington, 1899.]

United States. Treaties, etc. *Treaties, Conventions, International Acts, Protocols, and Agreements between the United States of America and Other Powers, 1776-1909,* William M. Malloy (comp.). Washington, 1910. 2 vols.

World's Columbian Exposition, *Report of the President to the Board of Directors of the World's Columbian Exposition, 1892-1893.* [Chicago, 1898.]

4. Unofficial Publications

A. Documents, Correspondence, Speeches, and Memoirs

Adams, Henry, *The Education of Henry Adams, an Autobiography.* Boston, 1961.

Cleveland, Grover, *Letters of Grover Cleveland, 1850-1908,* Allan Nevins (ed.). Boston and New York, 1933.

Estournelles de Constant, Paul Henry Benjamin, Baron d', *The Results of the Second Hague Conference.* New York, 1907.

Foner, Philip Sheldon, *The Life and Writings of Frederick Douglass.* New York, [1950-1955]. 4 vols.

García Mérou, Martín, *Estudios americanos.* Buenos Aires, 1900.

Hague International Peace Conference, *The Proceedings of the Hague Peace Conference. The Conference of 1907.* James Brown Scott (ed.), New York, 1920-1921.

Memoirs of the Miami Valley, John C. Hover, et al. (eds.). Chicago, 1919. 3 vols.

Moore, John Bassett, *A Digest of International Law,* . . . Washington, 1906. 8 vols.

Nevins, Allan. See Cleveland, Grover.

Proceedings. See Hague International Peace Conference.

Richardson, James Daniel. See United States. President.

Roosevelt, Theodore, *Letters,* selected and edited by Elting E. Morison. Cambridge, Mass., 1951-1954. 8 vols.

Root, Elihu, *Latin America and the United States; Addresses by Elihu Root,* Robert Bacon and James Brown Scott (eds.). Cambridge, Mass., 1917.

Scott, James Brown (ed.), *The International Conferences of American States, 1889-1928.* New York, 1931.

———. *Robert Bacon, Life and Letters.* Garden City, N.Y., 1923.

Thayer, William Roscoe, *The Life and Letters of John Hay.* Boston and New York, 1915. 2 vols.

United States. President. *A Compilation of the Messages and Papers of the Presidents, 1789-1902,* James Daniel Richardson (ed.). New York, 1903. 10 vols.

B. Other Books and Pamphlets

Abbott, Lawrence Fraser, *The Story of NYLIC; A History of the Origin and Development of the New York Life Insurance Company from 1845 to 1929.* New York, 1930.

Adams, Edward Dean, *Niagara Power; History of the Niagara Falls Power Company, 1886-1918.* Niagara Falls, 1927. 2 vols.

Adler, Selig and Thomas E. Connally, *From Ararat to Suburbia; The History of the Jewish Community of Buffalo.* Philadelphia, 1960.

Arnold, Charles Dudley, et al., *Photographs Showing the Building of the Pan-American Exposition* [n. p., n.d.] 3 vols.

Atkinson, Justin Brooks, *Broadway.* New York, 1970.

Bancroft, Hubert Howe, *The Book of the Fair; An Historical and Descriptive Presentation of the World's Science, Art, and Industry,* . . . Chicago and San Francisco, 1895. 2 vols.

Beale, Howard Kennedy, *Theodore Roosevelt and the Rise of America to World Power.* Baltimore, 1956.

Buchanan, Belle C., *The Buchanan Clans.* Piqua, Ohio, 1893.

Bucich Escobar, Ismael, *Historia de los presidentes argentinos.* Buenos Aires. [n. d.].

Cameron, William Evelyn (ed.), *History of the World's Columbian Exposition.* Chicago, 1893.

Chaddock, Robert Emmet, *Ohio Before 1850. A Study of the Early Influence of Pennsylvania and Southern Populations in Ohio.* New York, 1967.

Choate, Joseph Hodges, *The Two Hague Conferences.* Princeton, 1913.

Clough, Shepard Bancroft, *A Century of American Life Insurance: A His-*

tory of the Mutual Life Insurance Company of New York, 1843-1943. Westport, Conn., 1946.

Cumberland, Charles C., *Mexico, The Struggle for Modernity.* New York, 1968.

Curtis, William Eleroy, *The Capitals of Spanish America.* New York, 1888.

———. *The Relics of Columbus: An Illustrated Description of the Historical Collection in the Monastery of La Rabida.* Washington, [1893].

———. *Trade and Transportation between the United States and Spanish America.* Washington, 1889.

Dennett, Tyler, *John Hay: From Poetry to Politics.* New York, 1933.

Dictionary of American Biography. New York, 1928-1936. 20 vols.

Drury, Augustus Waldo, *History of the City of Dayton and Montgomery County, Ohio.* Chicago and Dayton, 1909. 2 vols.

Dummelow, John, *1889-1949.* Manchester, England, 1949.

Dunn, Walter S. (ed.), *History of Erie County, 1870-1970.* Buffalo, [1972].

Ealy, Lawrence O., *The Republic of Panama in World Affairs, 1903-1950.* Philadelphia, 1951.

Garraty, John Arthur, *Right-Hand Man. The Life of George W. Perkins.* New York, 1957.

A Genealogical and Biographical Record of Miami County, Ohio. Chicago, 1900.

Gilder, Richard Watson, *Poems and Inscriptions.* New York, 1901.

Graham, Lloyd and Frank H. Severance, *The First Hundred Years of the Buffalo Chamber of Commerce.* Buffalo, [1945].

Harbaugh, Thomas C. (ed. and comp.), *Centennial History. Troy, Piqua and Miami County, Ohio, and Representative Citizens.* Chicago, [1909].

Harcave, Sidney, *Russia, A History.* New York, [1953].

Hill, Henry Wayland (ed.), *Municipality of Buffalo, New York; A History, 1720-1923.* New York, 1923. 4 vols.

Hill, Lawrence Francis, *Diplomatic Relations Between the United States and Brazil.* Durham, N. C., 1932.

Hill, Leonard, *John Johnston and the Indians in the Land of the Three Miamis.* Piqua, Ohio, 1957.

Hines, Thomas S., *Burnham of Chicago: Architect and Planner.* New York, 1974.

History of the Counties of Woodbury and Plymouth, Iowa, including an Extended Sketch of Sioux City. Chicago, 1890-1891.

History of Dayton, Ohio, with Portraits and Biographical Sketches of Some of Its Pioneer and Prominent Citizens. Dayton, 1889.

The History of Miami County, Ohio, containing a History of the County, . . . Chicago, 1880.

The History of Montgomery County, Ohio, containing a History of the County, . . . Chicago, 1882.

History of Sioux City, Iowa, from Earliest Settlement to January, 1892. Boston, 1892.

Holdich, Sir Thomas Hungerford, *The Countries of the King's Award.* London, 1904.

Horton, John Theodore, *History of Northwestern New York; Erie, Niagara, Wyoming, Genesee and Orleans Counties.* New York, [1947]. 3 vols.

Hull, William Isaac, *The Two Hague Conferences and their Contributions to International Law.* Boston, 1908.

Ins and Outs of Buffalo, The Queen City of the Lakes; A Thoroughly Authentic and Profusely Illustrated Guide. Buffalo, 1899.

James, Preston Everett, *Latin America.* New York, [1942].

Jessup, Philip Caryl, *Elihu Root.* New York, 1938. 2 vols.

Johnson, Rossiter (ed.), *A History of the World's Columbian Exposition held in Chicago in 1893.* New York, 1898. 4 vols.

Keller, Morton, *The Life Insurance Enterprise, 1885-1910: A Study in the Limits of Corporate Power.* Cambridge, Mass., 1963.

Larned, Josephus Nelson, *A History of Buffalo, Delineating the Evolution of the City.* New York, 1911. 2 vols.

Leech, Margaret, *In the Days of McKinley.* New York, 1959.

Leopold, Richard William, *Elihu Root and the Conservative Tradition.* Boston, [1954].

Letts de Espil, Courtney, *La segunda presidencia Roca vista por los diplomáticos noteamericanos.* Buenos Aires, 1972.

Leupp, Francis Ellington, *George Westinghouse; His Life and Achievements.* Boston, 1918.

Lewis, Lloyd and Henry Justin Smith, *Oscar Wilde Discovers America (1882).* New York, [1936].

Lord, Walter, *The Good Years: From 1900 to the First World War.* New York, 1960.

Luckhurst, Kenneth W., *The Story of Exhibitions.* London and New York, 1951.

McCain, William David, *The United States and the Republic of Panama.* Durham, N.C., 1937.

McGann, Thomas Francis, *Argentina, the United States, and the Inter-American System, 1880-1914.* Cambridge, Mass., 1957.

Mayer, Harold Melvin and Richard C. Wade, *Chicago: Growth of a Metropolis.* Chicago, [1969].

Mellander, G. A., *The United States in Panamanian Politics: The Intriguing Formative Years.* Danville, Ill., 1971.

Miller, Floyd, *Statler, America's Extraordinary Hotelman.* New York, 1968.

Miner, Dwight Carroll, *The Fight for the Panama Route: The Story of the Spooner Act and the Hay-Herrán Treaty.* New York, 1940.

Munro, Dana Gardner, *Intervention and Dollar Diplomacy in the Caribbean, 1900-1921.* Princeton, N. J., 1964.

Nabuco, Carolina, *The Life of Joaquim Nabuco.* Palo Alto, Cal., [1950].

Nevins, Allan, *Grover Cleveland: A Study in Courage.* New York, 1932.

Noel, John Vavasour, *History of the Second Pan-American Conference,* Baltimore, 1902.

The Ohio Guide. See Writers' Program, Ohio.

Olcott, Charles Sumner, *The Life of William McKinley.* Boston, 1916. 2 vols.
O'Neill, John Joseph, *Prodigal Genius: The Life of Nikola Tesla.* Binghamton, New York, [1944].
Parks, E. Taylor, *Colombia and the United States, 1765-1934.* Durham, N. C., 1935.
Pepper, Charles Melville, *The Life and Times of Henry Gassaway Davis, 1823-1916.* New York, 1920.
Peterson, Harold F., *Argentina and the United States, 1810-1960.* Albany, New York, 1964.
Pierce, Bessie Louise, *A History of Chicago.* New York, 1937-1957. 3 vols.
Presbrey, Frank, *The City of Buffalo.* [New York, 1895.] (Pamphlet reprinted from *The Forum,* Mar. 1895.)
Pringle, Henry Fowles, *Theodore Roosevelt, A Biography.* New York, [1931].
Prisco III, Salvatore, *John Barrett, Progressive Era Diplomat: A Study of a Commercial Expansionist, 1887-1920.* University, Ala., 1973.
Prout, Henry Gosler, *A Life of George Westinghouse.* New York, 1922.
Rennie, Ysabel (Fisk), *The Argentine Republic.* New York, 1945.
Romero, José Luis, *A History of Argentine Political Thought.* Stanford, Cal., 1963.
Ross, Stanley Robert, *Francisco I. Madero, Apostle of Mexican Democracy.* New York, 1955.
Scobie, James R., *Argentina, A City and a Nation.* New York, 1964.
―――. *Revolution on the Pampas: A Social History of Argentine Wheat, 1860-1910.* Austin, Tex., [1964].
Sioux City's Corn Palaces, 1890, 1889, 1888, 1887. [Sioux City], 1890.
Stewart, Watt, *Keith and Costa Rica. A Biographical Study of Minor Cooper Keith.* Albuquerque, New Mex., [1964].
Whitaker, Arthur Preston, *The United States and Argentina.* Cambridge, Mass., 1954.
―――. *The Western Hemisphere Idea: Its Rise and Decline.* Ithaca, N.Y., [1954].
Williams' Dayton City Directory for 1875-1876. Dayton, Ohio, 1875.
Wilner, Merton Merriman, *Niagara Frontier; A Narrative and Documentary History.* Chicago, 1931. 4 vols.
The World's Columbian Exposition Illustrated. . . . 1891-March 1894. Chicago, 1892-1894. 3 vols.
Writers' Program, Iowa of WPA, "Woodbury County History, Iowa." Sioux City, Iowa, 1942.
Writers' Program, Ohio, *The Ohio Guide.* New York, [1940].

5. Articles in Serial Publications

Adler, Selig, "The Operation on President McKinley," *Scientific American* 208 (Mar. 1963): 118-130.
Ameringer, Charles D., "Philippe Bunau-Varilla: New Light on the Panama

Canal Treaty," *The Hispanic American Historical Review* 46 (Feb. 1966): 28-52.
Babcock, Louis L., "The Assassination of President William McKinley," in Robert W. Bingham (ed.), *Niagara Frontier Miscellany* 34: 11-30.
Blanchard, Frank Leroy, "Niagara Power at Buffalo," *Harper's Weekly* 41 (5 June 1897): 569-570.
Briggs, John Ely, "The Sioux City Corn Palaces," *The Palimpsest* 44, no. 12 (Dec. 1963): 549-572.
Brinton, Christian, "Art at the Pan-American Exposition," *The Critic* 38 (June 1901): 513-528.
Chamberlain, George Agnew, "Secretary Root's Diplomatic Triumph in South America," *Harper's Weekly* 50 (8 Sep. 1906): 1272-1274.
"The Columbus Caravels," *Chicago History* 8 (Fall 1968): 257-269.
"Constitutional Act of the Central American Fraternity," Pan American Union, *Bulletin* 26 (Feb. 1908): 301-310.
The Electrical Review 55 (Dec. 1904): 969-970.
Hendrickson, Embert J., "Roosevelt's Second Venezuelan Controversy," *The Hispanic American Historical Review* 50 (Aug. 1970): 482-498.
―――. "Root's Watchful Waiting and the Venezuelan Controversy," *The Americas* 23 (Oct. 1966): 115-129.
Hull, William Isaac, "The United States and Latin America at the Hague," *International Conciliation*, no. 44 (July 1911).
Reinsch, Paul S., "The Third International Conference of American States," *The American Political Science Review* 1 (Feb. 1907): 187-199.
Scobie, James R., "Buenos Aires as a Commercial-Bureaucratic City, 1880-1910: Characteristics of a City's Orientation," *The American Historical Review* 77 (Oct. 1972): 1035-1073.
Wilgus, A. Curtis, "The Second International American Conference at Mexico City," *The Hispanic American Historical Review* 11 (Feb. 1931): 27-68.
―――. "The Third International American Conference at Rio de Janeiro, 1906," *The Hispanic American Historical Review* 12 (Nov. 1932): 420-456.
"William I. Buchanan," *Illustrated Industrial and Architectural Review* 4 (Aug. 1900): 2.
"William I. Buchanan: Pan-American Diplomat," Pan American Union, *Bulletin* 29 (Nov. 1909): 835-837.

6. Newspapers and Serial Publications

(For the periods of Buchanan's residence in Sioux City, Chicago, and Buffalo, I have surveyed for extended periods the files or microfilms of the *Sioux City Journal,* the *Chicago Daily Tribune,* and several Buffalo newspapers. Most of the other papers listed below I have seen only through clippings mounted in scrapbooks in the Buchanan Papers (Buffalo and Erie County Historical Society) and in Records Relating to the Pan Ameri-

can Exposition at Buffalo, 1901 (National Archives, Department of State Records) or through enclosures to diplomatic messages in Despatches from Ministers (Department of State Records).
Boston Globe.
Boston Herald.
Brooklyn Life.
Buenos Aires Herald.
Buenos Ayres Standard.
Buffalo Courier.
Buffalo Courier-Express. (Title varies.)
Buffalo Enquirer.
Buffalo Evening News.
Buffalo Times.
Capitol (Albany, N. Y.).
Chicago Daily Tribune.
Chicago Inter-Ocean.
Chicago Record.
Chicago Times.
Chicago Times-Herald.
Commercial Advertiser (Buffalo). (Title varies.)
Daily Mail (London, England).
Daily Record (Mexico City).
Davenport (Iowa) *Democrat.*
Dayton Daily Journal.
El Diario (Buenos Aires, Argentina).
El Diario (Mexico City).
Epitomist.
A Epoca (Lisbon, Portugal).
Evening Star (Washington).
Financial Times (London, England).
Greater Buffalo.
Havana Post.
El Heraldo (Mexico City).
El Imparcial (Mexico City).
La Mars (Iowa) *Daily Sentinel.*
Manchester (England) *Courier.*
Mexican Herald (Mexico City).
La Nación (Buenos Aires, Argentina).
New York Commercial.
New York Daily News.
New York Evening Post.
New York Herald.
New York Sun.
New York Times.
New York Tribune.
Northwest Lumberman.

The Outlook.
(The) Pan-American (Buffalo).
(The) Pan-American Herald (Buffalo).
Pan American Union, *Bulletin.* (Title varies.)
Philadelphia Enquirer.
Piqua (Ohio) *Daily Call.*
La Prensa (Buenos Aires, Argentina).
Rochester (New York) *Herald.*
Sioux City (Iowa) *Journal.* (Title varies).
Sioux City Times.
Sioux City Tribune.
St. Louis Globe-Democrat.
St. Louis Republic.
St. Louis Star.
Springfield (Massachusetts) *Republican.*
Standard (Buenos Aires, Argentina).
Sun (Baltimore).
Syracuse (New York) *Journal.*
(The) Times (London, England)
Times of Argentina (Buenos Aires).
La Tribuna (Buenos Aires).
Washington Post.
Washington Times.

INDEX

INDEX

(The initials WIB are used to denote William I. Buchanan and NYLIC, the New York Life Insurance Company)

Abbott, Lawrence F., quoted on NYLIC, 213-214
Academy of Music, Sioux City, features touring attractions, 25-26, 31-32; WIB's management of, 31-32
Acajutla, El Salvador, 316
Acre territory, WIB and Brazil-Bolivia dispute over, 225, 226, 230; Hay proposes WIB as U.S. representative to conference on, 237, 238
Adams, Henry, quoted on expositions as educational, 152
Addams, Jane, 271
Adee, Alvey A., assistant secretary of state, briefs U. S. delegation to Mexico Conference of American States, 195; comments on WIB's diplomatic skills, 348, 351
Aforo rates, as Argentine system of customs valuation, 127
Agriculture, WIB's early contacts with, 10-11; promoted by WIB through Corn Palaces, 32-44; as key feature of Columbian Exposition, 50, 51-53, 54-56, 57, 59, 67-68; WIB delineates problems of, 67-68; WIB's interest in Argentina's, 71, 73, 82-83

Agriculture, Department of, World's Columbian Exposition, WIB directs, 51, 53, 54, 56, 57, 59, 67
Albany, U. S. cruiser, conveys WIB, Creel, and Central American judges to Panama, 315-316
Albright, John J., *see* Albright Art Gallery
Albright Art Gallery, Buffalo, built on grounds adjacent to Pan-American Exposition, 162 and note 94
Alcorta, Amancio, Argentine minister for foreign affairs, approves WIB's plan for visit of U. S. manufacturers, 100; welcomes WIB's return, 111; retained as Roca's foreign minister, 114; negotiates commercial and extradition treaties with WIB, 125-128, 129-130; explains Argentine views of inter-American movement, 130-131; assists WIB's work with NYLIC, 217, 218-220
Alfonso, King, of Spain, WIB comments on, 312
Allen, Charles H., governor of Puerto Rico, 167
Allison, William B., U. S. senator from Iowa, arranges Sioux City visit for

delegates to Washington Conference of American States, 41; encourages WIB's return to Argentina in 1898, 106, 108; assists WIB on Pan-American Exposition, 167; and WIB's Venezuelan loan project, 235; defends administration's position on Panama, 241

Amador Guerrero, Dr. Manuel, president of Panama, WIB discusses constitutional and treaty problems with, 245-251; WIB characterizes, 253; shifts position on Panama's share of Colombia's foreign debt, 256-257; WIB confers with, 316

Amapala, Honduras, 316

American Academy of Political and Social Science, addressed by WIB on Mexico Conference, 236

American Exhibitors Association, assists Pan-American Exposition Company, 144

American Peace Society, Boston, arranges WIB lecture on Mexico Conference of American States, 209-210

Andean boundary dispute, 119-124

Anderson, Luis, Costa Rican foreign minister, welcomes guests at installation of Central American Court of Justice, 318; beseeches WIB's aid on Central American problems, 321, 322-323, 324

Andes, 74, 82, 83

Anglo-German intervention in Venezuela, 327; WIB's involvement in, 233-236; and the Drago Doctrine, 279, 287, 289, 300

Anglo-Venezuelan boundary dispute, arouses anti-Americanism in Argentina, 115; Latin Americans resent Olney statement on, 193

Anti-Americanism, WIB reports on, 107, 112, 115-118, 162, 165, 193-194, 217, 232; aroused in Argentina by Anglo-Venezuelan dispute of 1895, 115, 193; by Spanish-American War, 115-118, 163, 193, 217, 232; and Mexico Conference of American States, 196; aroused by U. S. Caribbean policy, 279

Arango, Colonel José Agustín, recognizes WIB as minister to Panama, 244

Arbitration, debated at Mexico Conference of American States, 196, 200-204; at Rio Conference of American States, 281, 282, 288; at Second Hague Conference, 298, 300

Argentina, 192, 217; and boundary dispute with Chile, 4, 93; WIB appointed minister to, 70-72; national aspirations of, 73, 82, 93-94; 19th century growth of, 73-75; national extent of, 74; class structure in, 81; constitutional democracy in, 81; WIB travels hinterland in, 82-84, 119, 122, 124; sensitive to popular feelings in, 86, 107, 112, 115-118; factors influencing relations of U. S. with, 92-95; sets goals of foreign policy, 93-95; disdains multilateral diplomacy, 94, 193; forms low opinion of U. S. diplomatic representatives, 94-95; barriers to U. S. trade with, 94-105; reveals reluctance to sign commercial treaty with U. S., 95-99, 102-105, 112; presidential election of 1898 in, 113; party conflict in national government of, 114; immigration to, 116; submits Chilean boundary dispute to WIB's mediation, 119-124; negotiates commercial and extradition agreements with U.S., 125-130; reactivates participation in Bureau of American Republics, 130-131; resists claims of NYLIC, 135-136, 215-222; at the Pan-American Exposition, 175; exerts leadership at Mexico Conference of

American States, 199-204; supports obligatory arbitration, 201-204; admits reentry of NYLIC, 220-222; WIB revisits, 1902, 227-228, and 1906, 293-294; participates in Rio Conference of American States, 289; WIB seeks to conciliate Brazilian naval rivalry with, 293-294; in Second Hague Conference, 298-300; names WIB honorary commissioner for centennial, 342
Argentine-American trade, 95-105, 125-128, 138
Arias, Ricardo, assists WIB on Panama's Colombian debt problem, 251, 256-257; WIB characterizes, 253; WIB confers with, 316
Arias, Tomás, foreign minister of Panama, WIB discusses new constitution with, 247; WIB characterizes, 253
Armstrong Committee, investigates life insurance business in New York State, 212, 213, 214; precipitates Perkins's withdrawal from NYLIC management, 275-276
Arnold, Rear Admiral C. H., commands U. S. warships at La Guaira, 331-332
Asiatics, in Chicago, 47
de Aspiroz, Manuel, ambassador of Mexico to U.S., 185
Association of American Agricultural Colleges and Experiment Stations, endorses WIB's appointment as minister to Argentina, 70
Asunción, Paraguay, WIB visits, 83
Atherton, Gertrude, WIB attends London dinner for, 270
Authors, *see* Writers
Aztecs, 35, 41

Bacon, Robert, assistant secretary of state, 336; appraises Cuban situation, 295

Bahía (São Salvador), Brazil, Buchanans sail to, 76
Bahía, Brazil, state of, WIB advises NYLIC purchase of bonds of, 230
Bahía Blanca, Argentina, WIB visits, 124
Baker, Edward L., U. S. consul, Buenos Aires, welcomes Buchanans, 77
Balfour, Lord Arthur, Buchanans hear speech by, 75
Baltimore, Chileans resent incident over, 193
Bancroft, George, quoted by WIB, 85
Barbosa, Ruy, represents Brazil at Second Hague Conference, 299, 300
Barnum, P. T., plans street parade for 1890 Corn Palace celebration, 43
Barrados, Dr. J. da C., Brazilian jurist, assists WIB on NYLIC case, 229
Barrett, John, as director general of International Bureau of American Republics, 3, 310, 352; commends WIB, 3, 197, 353; serves as delegate to Mexico Conference of American States, 195, 203, 206; comments on Buchanan family, 197; appointed WIB's successor in Panama, 258; confers on Panama with WIB in London, 258; assists work of Pan American Committee, 313, 352; as exponent of U. S. business civilization, 352
Barrett, Lawrence, engaged by WIB for Sioux City performances, 32, 39
Barriers to trade, Argentine-American, 92-93, 96-105, 112
Batlle y Ordóñez, José, 227; represents Uruguay at Second Hague Conference, 299
Bayard, Thomas F., U. S. ambassador to London, WIB confers with, 75

Beck, W. H., assists WIB as Cleveland host in Sioux City, 36
"Beck design," as official emblem of Pan-American Exposition, 149
Beecher, Henry Ward, lectures in Sioux City, 32
Belgium, trades with Argentina, 96, 126
Berlin, WIB visits for Louisiana Purchase Exposition, 222, 224; visits for NYLIC, 1908, 1909, 321, 342-343
Bermejo, Antonio, Argentine delegate to Mexico Conference of American States, cooperates with WIB, 200
Best, Mrs. Eva, WIB's sister-in-law, 14; as composer, author, and artist, 14
Big Sioux River, near site of Sioux City, 22
"Binnie," *see* Buchanan, Florence
Bitter, Karl, director for sculpture at Pan-American Exposition, 152, 169
Blackburn, C. S., Canal Zone governor, escorts WIB and Creel across Canal Zone, 316
Black Hills, Sioux City as gateway to, 23
"Black Legend," 65
Blacks, WIB and Pan-American Exposition authorities find housing for, 162 and note 97
Blaine, James G., U. S. secretary of state, invited to 1890 Corn Palace, 43-44; Argentines defeat Hemisphere plans of, 94; and Pan American ideas, 145, 193
"Bloody Sunday," in St. Petersburg, 274
Board of Architects, Pan-American Exposition, 167
Board of Directors, Pan-American Exposition, 146, 148, 158, 162, 170, 173, 187
Board of Directors, World's Columbian Exposition Company, 58
Board of Women Managers, Pan-American Exposition, created by WIB, 153; attracts women's conventions and entertains visiting dignitaries, 156
Bogotá, Colombia, 238
The Bohemian Girl, booked by WIB for Sioux City, 39
Boies, Horace, governor of Iowa, appoints WIB as Iowa representative on National Commission for Columbian Exposition, 48; joins WIB in opening Iowa State Building at Columbian Exposition, 60; mentioned for renomination as governor, 69
Bolívar, Simón, 331, and the Panama Congress of 1826, 94
Bolivia, claims the Puna de Atacama, 120; cedes rights to Argentina, 120; Curtis promotes Pan-American Exposition in, 147; claims Acre, 225
Book of the Tartan, 110
Booth, Edwin, engaged by WIB for Sioux City performance, 39
Booth, General, and Salvation Army, WIB attends London meeting of, 270
Boundary disputes, 4, 95; *see* Puna de Atacama and "The Wire Treaty"
Brazil, 205; WIB promotes Pan-American Exposition in, 147; at the Pan-American Exposition, 175; prefers non-alignment with U. S., 193; supports voluntary arbitration at Mexico Conference of American States, 201; WIB's NYLIC activities in, 223-224, 225-227, 228-231; hosts Third Conference of American States, 283-291; WIB seeks to conciliate naval rivalry with Argentina, 293-294; represented at Hague Conference, 299, 300
The Breeder's Gazette, commends

WIB for diplomatic post, 70; publishes WIB article on Argentine estancias, 138
Britain, trades with Argentina, 93, 96; invests in Argentina, 97
British Westinghouse Electric & Manufacturing Company, organized in 1899, 263; builds huge plant near Manchester, 263-264; proves unprofitable, 264, 269-270, 271-272, 274-275; WIB confronts annual directors' meetings of, 271-272, 274-275; decline and receivership of, 275 and note 59; WIB concludes responsibilities for, 281; *see* Westinghouse, George
Bryan, Colonel Charles Page, U. S. minister to Brazil, assists WIB's NYLIC efforts in Brazil, 223-224, 226, 227, 229
Bryan, William Jennings, and election of 1900, 181
Buchanan, Donald, 344; birth of, 69, note 67; adjusts to life in Buenos Aires, 79, 80; returns to Chicago and Sioux City, 107; counselled by WIB *in absentia,* 108, 111, 118; moves to Buffalo, 150; accompanies WIB to Mexico, 1901, 188, 197, 206, 207; accompanies WIB to Panama, 242-243, 244, 245, 252; urges family purchase of Pierce, 268, 271; enters military academy, 271; joins WIB on mission to Rio, 283, 291, 293; serves as WIB's secretary on mission to Central American Court of Justice, 313, 316; commissioned honorary captain in Costa Rican artillery, 317, 319
Buchanan, Florence, 344; birth of, 18; as "Binnie" to parents, 19; appears on Sioux City stage, 40, note 52; influenced by Chicago experience, 69; adjusts to life in Buenos Aires, 79, 80; returns to Chicago and Sioux City, 107; receives counsel from father in Buenos Aires, 108, 110, 111, 119; attends school in Knoxville, Illinois, 118-119; moves to Buffalo, 150; accompanies parents to Mexico, 1901, 188, 197, 206, 207; marriage of, 242; contemplates new home, 268, 271
Buchanan, George, great grandfather of WIB, 8; as captain of volunteer company in Miami County, Ohio, 8; migrates from Natural Bridge, Virginia, to Miami County, Ohio, 8; founds Buchanan clan in Ohio, 8
Buchanan, George Preston, WIB's father, 9; marries Mary Eliza Gibson, 10
Buchanan, James Harvey, WIB's grandfather, birth, 8; settles in Miami County, Ohio, 9; provides home and early training for WIB 9-13
Buchanan, James Harvey, Mrs. (Joanna Hall), WIB's grandmother, 9, 10
Buchanan, William I.:
Synopsis of Career, 3-6
Youth and Early Manhood: birth and farm boyhood, 7, 9-13; orphaned at eight, 10; under tutelage of grandparents, 10-13; indoor and outdoor education, 10-13; early work experiences in Indiana, 13; settles in Dayton, Ohio, 13; marriage and family beginnings, 14, 18, 19
Personality and Personal Interests: estimates by others, 3, 5-6, 48, 51, 61, 70-71, 102, 136-137, 208, 227-228, 241, 255, 310, 318, 320, 335, 337-338, 345, 348, 353; contradictions in career of, 6; interest in outdoor life, 10-12; in literature, 12, 13, 15, 21, 28, 84-90, 110, 343; religion, 12, 16, 21, 24, 26-27; family life, 14, 18-21, 26, 31, 45, 53, 69,

71, 72, 75-77, 79-80, 107-108, 109-111, 118-119, 150, 177, 188, 190, 197, 206, 207, 222-223, 242, 244, 245, 252, 268, 271, 283, 293, 311-312, 313, 328, 343-345; history, 15, 16, 85, 267, 270, 312; music and drama, 15-16, 19, 24, 27-29, 31-32, 38-40, 119, 154, 176, 266, 270; politics, 16-17, 21, 58, 69; human relations, 20, 24, 27-28, 66, 73, 91, 111-112, 132, 279-280, 337-338; public speaking, 55, 59, 61-62, 67-68, 85-90, 160, 297; writing, 137-138, 160, 164-165

Career as Salesman, Theater Manager, and Exposition Director, 346, 347, 348, 349, 350, 351; sales representative for Dayton tobacco firm, 13-21; travels states of old Northwest Territory, 13-16, 18-20; enters china and glassware business in Sioux City, 20, 26, 27-28, 40, 44; travels Great Plains states, 27-28; assists amateur productions of Gilbert and Sullivan, 39-40, 42, 45; sponsors lecture series, 31-32; accepts managership of Academy of Music, 31-32; administers four Corn Palace celebrations, 32-45; entertains Clevelands and other notables, 36-37, 41-44; manages Peavey Grand Opera House, 39-40, 42, 45; serves as Iowa Democratic representative on National Commission for Columbian Exposition, 44, 45, 48-51; assists preliminary planning for Columbian, 49-50, 51; appointed chief of agriculture and other departments, 50-51; conceives and directs plan of operations for departments, 51-57, 59-61, 66-67; moves family to Chicago, 53; feted by exhibitors, 60-62; oversees exposition dismantlement, 66-67; prepares final reports, 67, 72; lectures on exposition, 67-68; offered directorship of Pan American commercial company, 69-70; appointed director general of Pan-American Exposition, 140, 146-148; oversees planning and construction of exposition, 148-162, 168-170; stresses promotional activities, 149, 153, 159-160, 172-175; emphasizes artistic, educational, and entertainment aspects, 152-154, 168-170, 175-177; copes with crises, 157-162, 165-167, 174; stresses Pan American theme, 163-165, 167; plans opening and dedication days, 170-172; welcomes distinguished guests, 171-172, 177, 179; extends repeated invitations to McKinleys, 179; plans and oversees arrangements for McKinleys' visit, 180-188; copes with emergency actions necessitated by assassination, 185-188; fulfills timetable for closing exposition, 188; renegotiates salary with Exposition Company, 188-190; prepares final report, 189-190, 209-210; evaluates exposition, 189-190; resigns exposition directorship, 210

Career as "Diplomat of the Americas," 3-6, 346, 347, 350-352; serves as State Department trouble-shooter, 6, 300-301, 346, 347, 350; boomed for appointment to diplomatic service, 70-71; appointed minister to Argentina, 71-72; serves diplomatic apprenticeship, 73, 76-80, 90-91; travels with family to Buenos Aires, 75-77; settles in to legation assignment, 77-80, 95; makes observation trips to hinterland, 82-84, 119, 122, 124; presents formal lectures on U. S. history and literature, 84-90; seeks improved relations, 95-105, 125-130, 138; arranges visit of U. S. manufacturers, 99-101; negotiates commercial treaty, 104, 125-128; resigns Argentine post and returns to U.S., 104-107; accepts McKinley's request to resume Argentine post, 106, 107-111, 113; receives welcome of Argentine officialdom, 111; becomes dean of diplomatic corps, 111, 132; negotiates extradition treaty, 112, 129-130; encounters anti-Americanism, 115-116; mediates Argentine-Chilean boundary dispute, 119-124, 190; seeks to modernize treaty relations, 129-130; revives Argentine interest in Bureau of American Republics, 130-131; resolves all pecuniary claims of American citizens, 133-136; reviews his 5-year mission to Argentina, 137-139; serves as delegate to Mexico Conference of American States, 182, 188, 192, 195-196, 199-205, 208-209; deals with arbitration, pecuniary claims, and other matters, 200-205; becomes acting delegation chief, 203; prepares official delegation report, 208-209; appointed first minister to Panama, 238-242; travels to Panama with family, 242-243; works to protect U. S. canal-building rights, 244, 246-248, 250, 259; advises on Panama's constitution-drafting, 245-248, 254, 259; advises Washington on ratifying Hay-Bunau-Varilla Treaty, 249, 250-251, 252; fingers sensitive issues in treaty, 249; suggests bases for settlement of Panama's problems with Colombia, 250-252, 256-258, 259, 296; urges attention to health and sanitation problems, 251-252; advises successors in office, 253-254, 258; resigns as minister, 255; serves as chairman U. S. delegation to Rio Conference of American States, 275, 277, 278, 280-293; becomes Root's right-hand man, 278, 280, 300-301, 326, 338; contributes to key committees, 288-291; prepares delegation report, 297; serves as delegate, Second Hague Peace Conference, 297-302; as chairman Pan American Committee, 302, 312-313, 342, 343-344; as U. S. representative to Central American Peace Conference, 1907, 302, 306-310; as member "Central American Fraternity," 309-310; prepares report on conference, 310; serves as U. S. high commissioner to installation Central American Court of Justice, 313-320; prepares commissioner's report, 320; becomes repository of Central American appeals, 321, 322-323; confers with Root on Central American problems, 324; appointed special agent to reestablish relations with Venezuela, 324-325, 326, 328-332; negotiates claims settlement and restores relations with, 332-335, 336-339, 341-342; appointed U. S. agent to handle claims arbitration at The Hague, 339-341, 342, 343, 345

Career as "Diplomat of Business," 346, 347, 351, 352; accepts appointment with NYLIC, 5, 136, 191, 210, 211; uses "good offices" for NYLIC case against Argentina, 135, 215-222; arranges NYLIC reentry to Brazilian market, 223-232; secures State Department assistance for NYLIC activities, 231-232, 310-311, 312; promotes loan project for Venezuela, 233-235; terminates full-time relationship with NYLIC, 237; accepts managerial position with Westinghouse in Europe, 237, 261, 264-265; receives personalized orientation from George Westinghouse, 266-269; supervises Westinghouse installations in England, 269-270, 274-275; reorganizes French Westinghouse company, 270; confronts annual directors' meetings in London, 271-272, 274-275; gathers wartime intelligence in Russia for Perkins and NYLIC, 272-274; gradually reduces Westinghouse responsibilities, 275; undertakes mission to Madrid for NYLIC, 1908, 311-312; travels to Europe and Mexico for NYLIC and J. P. Morgan, 322-323, 342-343, 345; promotes U. S. commercial expansion, 352

Attitudes and Perceptions: on the aesthetic in life, 10, 16, 25, 26, 152, 168; on farm life, 10-11; outdoor education, 10-12; presidential politics, 16, 17, 58; blacks and the Southern question, 17; self-examination and self-discipline, 19, 20-21, 28, 132, 267-268, 346; Oscar Wilde, 25-26; ethnic minorities, 27, 162 and note 97; fairs and expositions, 43, 67-68, 149-150, 152-156, 160-161, 165; Pan-Americanism, 66, 71, 130-131, 163-165, 182, 193-194, 207, 209-210, 239, 280, 290, 292, 293; foreign trade, 67-68, 97-98, 128, 163, 182, 205, 351-352; agriculture and agricultural education, 67-68, 73, 82, 83-84; candidacy for public office, 69, 209; travel, 82, 119, 122, 124, 242-243, 265; protective tariffs, 97-98, 205; anti-Americanism, 107, 112, 115-118, 162, 165, 193-194, 217, 232; Spanish-American War, 108, 109, 193-194; U. S. colonialism, 109, 116-117, 163, 182, 239; Monroe Doctrine, 117, 171, 204; mediation and arbitration, 119-124, 201-204, 259, 282, 286, 288-289; Latin American character, 112, 122, 146, 292, 293; conduct of diplomacy, 130-133; an interoceanic canal, 165, 182, 205, 239; big business, 267-268; U. S. commercial expansionism, 351-353

Relations with National and Hemisphere Leaders: Alcorta, 100, 111, 125-131, 219-220; Amador, 245-253, 256-257, 316; Cleveland, 4, 34-35, 36, 58, 69, 70-71, 347; Creel, 236, 308, 309-310, 313-320; Curtis, 43, 62-63, 69-70, 146; Díaz, 198, 206, 315, 320, 321-322; García Mérou, 5, 109, 125, 131, 219; Hay, 4, 109, 124, 126-128, 135, 159, 201, 202, 204, 207, 215-218, 236-237, 238-240, 248, 250, 254, 255, 347; McKinley, 4, 106, 108, 123, 128, 134, 136, 139, 146, 148, 347; Perkins, 214-215, 221-222, 228, 233, 272-274, 275-276; Roca, 5, 111, 119, 135, 220-221; Roosevelt, 186, 187, 195, 207, 237, 240, 252, 255, 278, 303, 324, 347; Root, 186, 215, 240, 244, 278, 279-283, 287-288, 295-296, 297-300, 302, 304, 308, 310-313, 322, 323, 324, 326, 328, 337-338, 347; Westinghouse, 237, 261, 266-269, 275, 277, 345

Death; Tributes; Estimate of Career, 345-353

Buchanan, William I., Mrs. (Lulu Williams), 265, 266, 328; early years of marriage of, 14, 15, 16, 18-21; artistic interests of, 14, 19, 24, 32, 33, 36, 44, 61, 150, 168; receives reports on Sioux City, 24-25, 26; shares Sioux City community life, 27, 28-29, 31, 32, 45; as "Laurie" to her husband, 28; participates in Corn Palace celebrations, 32, 33, 35, 36, 37, 38, 40-41, 44; abets husband's career, 45; moves with family to Chicago, 53; shares social life of Columbian Exposition, 60-61; weighs post-Columbian family prospects, 69; prepares for move to Buenos Aires, 71-72; travels to Argentina via England, 75-77; adjusts to life in Argentina, 79-81, 91; returns to Chicago and Sioux City, 107; receives counsel from WIB in Buenos Aires, 107-108, 110-111; receives WIB's ruminations on anti-Americanism and diplomatic career, 117, 132; interviewed by press in Buffalo, 150; and social calendar at Pan-American Exposition, 177; attends Mrs. McKinley, 180, 182; attends reception for McKinleys, 184; accompanies WIB to Mexico Conference, 188, 197, 206, 207; contemplates move to London, 223; accompanies WIB on Panama mission, 242, 244, 245, 252; manages home affairs, 268, 271; joins WIB on mission to Rio and Buenos Aires, 283, 291, 293, 294; accompanies WIB to The Hague, 299, 302; to Europe, 1908, 311-312; WIB's solicitude for, 343, 344, 345

Buchanan clan, prospers in Miami County, Ohio, 8-13

Buckner, Thomas A., vice-president, NYLIC, 214

Buenos Aires, Argentina, 163, 211, 217, 218, 245, 265; as exporter of surplus foodstuffs, 73, 140; as principal port and power base, 74-75; Buchanans arrive in, 75, 76-77; compared with Chicago, New York, Washington, 80-82; aspirations of, 82; WIB returns to, 1902, 227-228; Buchanans revisit, 1906, 293-294

Buenos Aires, Argentine province of, WIB travels through, 82

Buenos Aires Conference of the American States (1910), *see* International Conference of the American States, Fourth

Buffalo, New York, 232; aspirations of, 140-144; boasts advantages as "Queen City of the Lakes," 140-144; dreams of world exposition, 142, 144; population elements in, 142-143; labor situation in, 155-156; WIB encounters civic apathy in, 157; sends exposition invitations to Latin American presidents, 166; finds satisfaction in exposition opening, 172; turns out to welcome McKinleys, 181, 183; WIB appraises exposition benefits to, 189-190; *see* Pan-American Exposition

Bunau-Varilla, Philippe, negotiates canal treaty with Hay, 239; confers with WIB in New York, 242

Bureau of Information, Pan-American Exposition, finds housing for exposition guests, 162; gives special attention to housing for blacks, 162 and note 97

Burnham, Daniel H., as pioneer in development of skyscraper architecture, 47; as architectural supervisor for Columbian Exposition, 49; consults with WIB on exhibit facilities for exposition, 53; architect of Buffalo's Ellicott Square Building, 143; urges WIB's appointment as director general of Pan-American Exposition, 146

Byron, conveys Buchanans to Rio de Janeiro, 283

Calvo Clause, as basis of Venezuelan defense in U. S. claims cases, 329, 333, 341

Camp Millard Fillmore, Pan-American Exposition, as scene of varied military events, 176, 177

Campos Salles, Manoel de, president of Brazil, assists WIB's NYLIC efforts, 225, 226-227, 229, 230, 231

Canada, 164; as part of Buffalo's market region, 141; lack of manufacturing establishments in, 161,

175; WIB discusses continental importance of, 165; seeks exposition participation of, 165-166
Caracas, Venezuela, 253, 331, 333, 334, 336, 337, 338, 340
Carbo, Luis F., Ecuadorian minister to Washington, speaks at Ecuador Day, Pan-American Exposition, 174; at Mexico Conference of American States, 199
Caribbean policy, of McKinley and Roosevelt administrations, 326; WIB keeps abreast of, 182, 238-239; Hay and Root contribute to shaping of, 278-279, 305
Cariocas, 225, 283, 286, 288
Carlota, Empress, 198
Carlton, Newcomb, vice-president, Westinghouse Corporation, provides technical assistance to WIB in London, 274-275
Carnegie, Andrew, 338; WIB attends London dinner for, 270; as president, National Arbitration and Peace Congress, 297; provides funds for Pan American Union Building and Hague Palace of Peace, 302; becomes member Pan American Committee, 312; pledges funds for "temple of peace" in Costa Rica, 310, 319, 321
Carnot, Marie François Sadi, president of France, WIB attends memorial for, 79
Cartagena, Colombia, 296
Cartago, Costa Rica, welcomes WIB and guests for installation of Central American Court of Justice, 317-319
Casa Rosada, Buenos Aires, 77, 115
Casasús, Joaquín D., secretary general of Mexico Conference of American States, lauds WIB's appointment to Panama, 241
Castro, Cipriano, president of Venezuela, WIB involved in loan project for, 233-235; inept government of, 327; Roosevelt administration presses American claims against, 327-330, 333, 341
Cayuga Island, Niagara River, as initial site for Pan-American Exposition, 144
Centennial Exposition, Philadelphia, WIB attends, 19; compared with Columbian and Pan-American, 53, 169, 187
Centeotl, as Aztec goddess of Corn Palace celebrations, 35
Central American Court of Justice, 337; WIB serves as High Commissioner to inauguration of, 3, 309, 310, 313-320; Creel serves as Mexican High Commissioner to, 313-319; Costa Rica as scene of installation of, 317-319; pays tribute to WIB, 345
The Central American Fraternity, formed at Washington Conference of Central American States, 1907, 309-310
Central American Peace Conference, Washington, 1907, 3, 280, 305-306, 337; WIB and Creel invited to attend, 306; drafts complex of treaties and conventions, 306-309
Central American pedagogical institute, 308
Central Europeans, in Chicago, 47
Ceres, as deity of Corn Palace celebrations, 34
Chaco, in Argentina and Paraguay, WIB visits, 83
Champs Elysées, 267
Chapultepec Castle, 198, 206, 320
Charleston, U. S. S., conveys Root and party around South America, 286
Chautauqua, New York, 160, 173

Chesterfield, Lord, WIB quotes on politics, 17
Chicago, Illinois, its resurgence from 1871 fire, 46-48; becomes seat of economic empire, 46-47; as scene of Columbian Exposition, 46-67, 163
Chicago, Milwaukee, and St. Paul Railroad, 27
Chicago Tribune, quotes WIB on Columbian Exposition, 49
Chief Cornstalk, and Shawnee Indians in Miami County, Ohio, 7
Chihuahua, Mexico, WIB and Donald visit *hacienda* in, 314
Chile, and boundary dispute with Argentina, 4, 115, 120-123; submits dispute to WIB's mediation, 122-123; Curtis promotes Pan-American Exposition in, 147; represented at Pan-American Exposition by Carlos Morla Vicuña, 177; supports voluntary arbitration at Mexico Conference of American States, 201, 202, 203
Choate, Joseph H., chairman, U. S. delegation, Second Hague Peace Conference, 298
"Christ of the Andes," 119
Churches, in Sioux City, 24, 26-27, 28, 29; in Buenos Aires, 84
Cincinnati, Ohio, waterway to Piqua from, 8
City of Berlin, conveys Buchanans to Southampton, 1894, 72, 75
Claims, of American citizens against Argentina resolved by WIB, 133-134; against Venezuela settled by WIB, 326, 328-330, 332-336
Claridge's Hotel, London, 263, 270, 341, 343, 345
Clark, George Rogers, and campaigns against English, 7
Clay, Henry, 42
Clayton, Powell, U. S. ambassador to Mexico, 206

Cleveland, Grover, 214; appoints WIB minister to Argentina, 4, 69-71, 347; visits and comments on 1887 Corn Palace, 34-35; greeted by WIB in Sioux City, 36; serves as keynote speaker at Columbian Exposition inauguration, 57-58; lauded by Argentine president, 79; shows interest in Argentine market, 92, 95; evokes Monroe Doctrine, 1895, 115
Cleveland, Mrs. Grover, visits 1887 Corn Palace, 36-37
Cleveland administration, *see* Cleveland, Grover
Collier's Weekly, features WIB's article on Pan-American Exposition, 160; details his ideas on Pan Americanism, 164-165
Colombia, 185, 199, 239, 241, 246, 247; WIB considers Panama's relationships with, 250-252, 255, 256-258, 259, 269, 271, 296, 337; prefers league of Spanish-American states, 193; rejects Hay-Herrán Treaty, 238; suggests U. S. intervention in Venezuela, 327
Colón, Panama, 252, 253, 254; as a "free port," 249
Columbian Court of Honor, as thematic heart of Columbian Exposition, 54, 66
Columbian Exposition, *see* World's Columbian Exposition
Columbus, Christopher, as honoree of World's Columbian Exposition, 48, 62-66; his memorabilia displayed at Columbian, 63; replicas of his caravels sail from Spain to Chicago, 63-66
Columbus, Ohio, 233
El Comercio (Lima, Peru), praises WIB's appointment to Panama, 241
Commerce, *see* Trade
Commercial Bureau of the American Republics, *see* International Bur-

eau of the American Republics

Commercial Gazette (Cincinnati), reports alleged Cleveland comment on 1887 Corn Palace, 37

Committee on Agriculture, World's Columbian Exposition, WIB appointed to membership on, 50

Committee on Ceremonies, Pan-American Exposition, arranges visit of President McKinley to Pan-American Exposition, 179; meets with McKinley in Buffalo, 181

Committee on Fine Arts, World's Columbian Exposition, WIB appointed to membership on, 50

The Comte de Paris, invited to Corn Palace, 44

Concas, Captain Victor M., commands voyage to Columbian Exposition of replicas of Columbus's caravels, 64

Congress, declares war against Spain, 107; and official invitations to heads of state, 166

Consular Reports, U. S., WIB's official reports published in, 138

Cooper Union, New York, presents WIB lecture on benefits of Columbian Exposition, 67-68

Córdoba, Argentine province of, WIB travels through, 82; entertained in, 82-83

"The Corn Palace City of the World," Sioux Cityans' catchword for their city, 32, 140

Corn Palaces, conceived by Sioux Cityans as harvest celebration, 32-33; first (1887), 32-37; second (1888), 37-38; third (1889), 40-43; fourth (1890), 43-44; WIB's role in, 32-45, 146, 347, 349, 350; attract distinguished visitors, 36-37, 41-42, 43-44; simulated in Iowa State Building, Columbian Exposition, 53, 60

Cortelyou, George B., secretary to President McKinley, cooperates with WIB on McKinley visit to Buffalo, 179-180, 181, 184; at McKinley's side in Temple of Music, 184-185; summons Roosevelt and Cabinet to Buffalo, 185-186; improvises executive office in Buffalo, 186; and Venezuelan loan project, 235

Cortés, Enrique, Colombian minister to Washington, discusses Panamanian problem with WIB, 296

Costa, Eduardo, Argentine minister of foreign affairs, encourages WIB on tariff modifications, 98; WIB confers with, 99

Costa Rica, 185, 304, 313, 315; participates in Washington Conference, 307-310; designated seat of Central American Court of Justice, 309; as scene of installation of Court, 316-319; sends condolences on WIB's death, 345

Cotton States and International Exposition, Atlanta, whets Buffalo interest in sponsoring exposition, 144

Court of Honor, World's Columbian Exposition, 54, 66

Court of the Fountains, Pan-American Exposition, 168, 181

Covington, Ohio, early Buchanan settlement near, 9-10

Creel, Enrique C., Mexican ambassador to Washington, commends WIB, 5 and note 17, 320; entertained by WIB in Buffalo, 236; represents Mexico at Washington Conference, 306-309; entertains Buchanans at Chihuahua *hacienda*, 313-314; represents Mexico at installation of Central American Court, 313-315, 317-319; travels with WIB from Mexico to Costa Rica and return, 315-317, 319-320

Cuba, 239, 330; and the Spanish-

American War, 116-118, 145; WIB weighs Argentine indifference toward, 116; WIB explains U. S. policy toward, 116-118; its nationals in Argentina criticize U. S., 117; WIB views "professional revolutionists" in, 118; WIB rumored as U. S. agent to, 1900, 190, 209; and the Platt Amendment, 278; WIB visits, 295, 320

Culebra Cut, Panama Canal, 316

Cumberland Road, and westward migration of WIB's forbears, 8

Curtis, William E., 193; serves as State Department host for delegates to Washington Conference of American States, 1889, 43 and note 63; as enthusiast for Pan Americanism, 62; serves as chief, Latin American Bureau, Columbian Exposition, 62-63; offered editorial position with Pan American commercial company, 69-70; promotes Pan-American Exposition in Latin America, 146, 147, 149, 159; recommends WIB as director general of exposition, 146

Czolgosz, Leon F., and assassination of McKinley, 184-185, 186

Dairying, Department of, Columbian Exposition, WIB directs, 51, 53, 54-55, 57, 59, 67

Dakota Territory, as hinterland of Sioux City, 24, 26, 27, 28

Davenport (Iowa) *Democrat*, 70

Davis, George R., director general Columbian Exposition, appoints WIB chief, departments of Agriculture, Live Stock, Dairying, and Forestry, 51; consults with WIB on exhibit facilities, 53; supports WIB's appointment as minister to Argentina, 70

Davis, Henry Gassaway, 203, 290; appointed delegate to Mexico Conference of American States, 194-195; named chairman U. S. delegation, 195; promotes Pan American railway, 195, 290; declines conference presidency, 199; named chairman committee on committees, 200

Day, William, R., U. S. secretary of state, urges arbitration of Argentine-Chilean boundary dispute, 121

Dayton, Ohio, 268; waterway to Piqua from, 8; WIB settles in, 13-14, 18

Dedication Day, Pan-American Exposition, 170-171

Deere, Charles H., advises WIB on farm implement exhibits for Columbian Exposition, 52

Deerfield, Ohio, birthplace of WIB's grandfather, 8

Delaware Indians in Miami County, Ohio, 7

Delphi, Indiana, WIB works in , 13

Demeter, as deity of Corn Palace celebrations, 34

Democratic party, and election of 1880, 16-17; WIB schedules Iowa state convention of, 40; and trade negotiations with Argentina, 92, 98, 99, 128, 163; senators criticize Roosevelt's Panama policy, 241-242

Dennis, William C., appointed solicitor to WIB for Venezuelan claims case at The Hague, 340-341

Depew, Chauncey M., visits 1887 Corn Palace, 34; and loan project to Venezuela, 235

Des Moines, Iowa, WIB attracts GOP state convention from, 40

Des Moines, U. S. cruiser, conveys WIB, Creel, and Central American judges from Colón to Puerto Limón, 316; WIB gives reception aboard, 319; conveys WIB to Vera Cruz and Havana, 319-320; con-

veys WIB from La Guaira to Guantánamo, 336
El Diario (Buenos Aires), quoted on WIB, 228
Díaz, Porfirio, president of Mexico, 166; entertains delegates to Conference of American States, 1901, 197-198, 205, 207; promotes Mexican modernization while ignoring many problems, 198-199; cooperates with U. S. on Central American problems, 285, 305-306, 310, 313-315, 317-320, 322; *see* Mexico
Dickens, Charles, reaction of WIB to, 13
Diehl, Conrad, mayor of Buffalo, promotes Pan-American Exposition, 145; participates in Dedication Day, 171
Dingley Tariff Act, causes WIB problems in Argentina, 102-103; WIB seeks Argentine treaty under, 104, 109, 126-128
"Diplomat of the Americas," WIB as, 3-6, 346-352
Divortia aquarum, as principle considered in Puna de Atacama boundary dispute, 119, 120, 123; WIB wrestles with, 119-120, 123
Dole, Sanford B., governor of Hawaii, invited to Pan-American Exposition, 167
Dolphin, U. S. S., despatched to La Guaira, 330-331
Don Quijote (Buenos Aires), levels pro-Spanish attacks on U. S., 116
Douglass, Frederick, Haitian commissioner to Columbian Exposition, quiets tense situation during ceremonies, 65-66; quoted by WIB, 85
Doyle, W. T. Sherman, 340
D'Oyle Carte Company, presents Oscar Wilde in Sioux City, 25
Drago, Luis M., Argentine foreign minister, proposes "economic corollary" to Monroe Doctrine, 279, 287, 289; represents Argentina at Second Hague Conference, 299; opposes forcible collection of public debts at Hague, 300; confers with WIB in London, 343-344
Drago Doctrine, *see* Drago, Luis M.
Drews, the, engaged by WIB for Sioux City performance, 39
Dubois, François, French designer, plans street pageant for 1890 Corn Palace celebration, 43
Dupuy de Lôme, Enrique, Spanish ambassador in Washington, escorts Spanish dignitaries to Columbian Exposition, 63; welcomes replicas Columbus's caravels to Chicago, 64
Duse, Eleanora, 32

Ecuador, 199, 251; erects building at Pan-American Exposition, 174; threatens to bolt Mexico Conference of American States, 203
Elbe, conveys Buchanans to Buenos Aires, 75
"The Electric March," 172
Electric Power, first transmitted to Buffalo from Niagara Falls, 1896, 142; and illumination of Pan-American Exposition, 153; Westinghouse interest in production and transmission of, 261-264
Electric Tower, Pan-American Exposition, 168, 181
Elgin, Illinois, concert band, featured at 1887 Corn Palace celebration, 38
Elkins, Stephen B., U. S. senator from West Virginia, appointed member Pan American Committee, 312
English frontier posts in Ohio, 7
The English Literary Society, Buenos Aires, WIB delivers formal lecture to, 88-90
Entre Ríos, Argentine province of, 133-134

INDEX 437

Equitable Life Assurance Society, 212
Erie Canal, 141
Esplanade, Pan-American Exposition, 168, 181
Estancias, in Argentina, 74
Estancieros, Argentine, economic and political power of, 74
d'Estournelles, Baron, comments on Western Hemisphere delegations to Second Hague Peace Conference, 301
Estrada Cabrera, Manuel, dictator of Guatemala, 316, 324
Estrada Palma, Tomás, president of Cuba, 295
Estudios americanos, García Mérou writes favorably of WIB in, 200
Executive Committee, Pan-American Exposition, 146, 149, 151, 157, 162, 166, 167, 176, 177, 180, 187
"*Expedir,*" as feature of Panamanian constitution, 246
Extradition convention, negotiated by WIB with Argentina, 129-130

Falkland Islands, as factor in Argentine-U. S. relations, 93-94
"Farmer Buchanan," as title for WIB at Columbian Exposition, 55
Farmers' Alliances, WIB seeks their participation in Columbian Exposition, 51, 52
Faust, presented in Sioux City, 32
Fay Templeton Star Opera Company, appears in Sioux City, 25
Field, Eugene, quoted by WIB, 11
First Baptist Church, Sioux City, Buchanans join, 26
Fishback, George W., secretary U. S. legation, Buenos Aires, welcomes Buchanans to Buenos Aires, 76-77; assists WIB's orientation, 78, 79; as adviser to NAM delegation to Argentina, 100

Flambeau Club of Sioux City, 35
Fleming, Edwin, secretary, Pan-American Exposition Company, 146; offers WIB director generalship of exposition, 136, 147
Flour, as factor in Argentine-American relations, 93
Floyd River, near site of Sioux City, 22
Foraker, Senator Joseph B., 234
Foreign Bond-holders Committee, London, approached by WIB on Panama's proposal to share Colombia's foreign debt, 251, 256-257, 269
Foreign Office, Argentine, 78; WIB's notes to, 138; *see* Alcorta and García Mérou
Forestry, Department of, Columbian Exposition, WIB directs, 51, 53, 54-55, 59, 67
Fort Buchanan, Ohio, as headquarters of George Buchanan's militia company, 8
Fort Recovery, Ohio, and General St. Clair's defeat by Indians, 7
Foster, John, secretary of state, 297
Foster, Volney, appointed U. S. delegate to Mexico Conference of American States, 195
Fox Indians, expelled beyond Missouri River, 22
France, trades with Argentina, 96, 126; invests in Argentina, 97; Westinghouse operates in, 262; WIB reorganizes Westinghouse company in, 270; presses Venezuela for satisfaction of claims, 327, 330
Francesca da Rimini, presented in Sioux City, 32
Francis, David R., president of Louisiana Purchase Exposition, engages WIB to promote exposition in Europe, 222, 224, 232; suggested by WIB as NYLIC trustee, 276; *see* Louisiana Purchase Exposition

French, Daniel Chester, executes statue for Columbian Exposition, 54
French frontier posts in Ohio, 7
French Westinghouse Company, WIB reorganizes, 270; concludes responsibilities for, 281

G. A. R., Sioux City, enlists WIB's services, 27
García Mérou, Martín, Argentine minister to Washington, commends WIB, 5 and note 19; confers with WIB in London, 1898, 109; as minister to Washington, 125, 131; encourages Argentina's support of inter-American organization, 131; writes of WIB in *Estudios americanos,* 200; and WIB at Mexico Conference of American States, 199-200, 201; assists WIB on NYLIC case, 219; death of, 293
Garfield, James, WIB criticizes candidacy of, 16-17
Germans, migration of, to Ohio, 8; in Chicago, 47
Germany, trades with Argentina, 96, 126; gives financial aid to Argentina, 97; Westinghouse operates in, 262
Gibson, Mary Eliza, WIB's mother, marries George Preston Buchanan, 9
Gilbert and Sullivan, WIB enjoys operettas of, 16; manages productions of, 28-29
Gladstone, William, 109
Glasgow, as site of Westinghouse plants, 267
Goethals, Colonel George W., chief engineer, Panama Canal, orients WIB, Creel, and Central American judges, 316
Goiticoa, N. Veloz, and WIB's Venezuelan loan project, 235
Gómez, Indalecio, Argentine minister to Germany, confers with WIB, 344
Gómez, Juan Vicente, president of Venezuela, seeks to restore Venezuela's international posture, 327-328; moves to restore relations with U. S., 327-328, 330, 331; delays WIB's settlement of claims cases, 332-335; agrees to settlement of claims cases, 335
Gompers, Samuel, 271
González Guinán, Francisco, Venezuelan foreign minister, WIB negotiates settlement of U. S. claims cases with, 331-335; confers decoration upon WIB, 336-337; WIB arranges recognition with, 337
González Víquez, Cleto, president of Costa Rica, hosts visit of WIB, Creel, and Central American judges, 317
Grant, Ulysses S., WIB participates in memorial services for, 27
Greater Buffalo, as public relations medium for city's aspirations, 141
Great Miami River, Buchanan clan grows in valley of, 7-9
Great Plains, Sioux City as gateway to, 23
Greeley, Horace, quoted by WIB, 85
Gresham, Walter Q., U. S. secretary of state, 71; confers with Argentine minister in Washington, 98
Guanabara Bay, Rio de Janeiro, 284
Guantánamo Bay, Cuba, 320, 336
Guatemala, 304; involved in border incidents with Central American neighbors, 285, 305, 321; participates in Washington Conference, 307-310; opposes revival of Central American federation, 307; joins Central American Court of Justice, 309, 315-316, 317-319
Guatemala, Captaincy General of, 304

INDEX 439

El Guerrillero Español (Buenos Aires), levels pro-Spanish attacks on U.S., 116
The Gypsy Baron, performed at opening of Peavey Grand Opera House, 38-39

The Hague, 303; as seat of Second Peace Conference, 288, 289, 292, 297-300; *see* Hay, Root, Hague Convention, Hague Peace Conference, and Hague Tribunal
Hague Convention on Pacific Settlement of Disputes, as basis for arbitration convention at Mexico Conference of American States, 201-203; Root and WIB seek Latin American adherence to, 282; Latin American views of, 300
Hague Peace Conference, First, 182, 201
Hague Peace Conference, Second, WIB as U. S. delegate to, 3, 297-300; Hay secures Latin American invitations to, 280; considers questions transferred from Rio Conference, 288, 289, 292, 297-300
Hague Tribunal, 322; WIB invited to represent Latin American interests at, 235-236; WIB named to present Venezuelan claims case before, 339-341, 343, 345
Hancock, General Winfield S., WIB approves candidacy of, 16-17
Hanna, Mark, U. S. senator, 142, 179, 186
Harper's Weekly, mentioned, 32
Harrison, Benjamin, invited to 1890 Corn Palace, 44; appoints WIB as Iowa representative on National Commission for World's Columbian Exposition, 44, 45, 48
Harrison, Carter, mayor of Chicago, criticizes Spanish Indian policy in the Americas, 65

Harrison, General William Henry, establishes headquarters near Piqua, Ohio, 8
Havana, WIB visits, 295, 320
Hawaiian Islands, 165
Hay, John, secretary of state, 193, 195; names WIB delegate to Mexico Conference of American States, 4; as ambassador to London, confers with WIB, 109; receives reports on WIB's mediation of Puna de Atacama question, 124; directs WIB's negotiations of commercial treaty with Argentina, 126-128; directs WIB's efforts on behalf of NYLIC against Argentina, 135, 215-218; assists WIB and Pan-American Exposition, 159, 166, 173; speaks at exposition, 182; urges Mexico as site for Conference of American States, 194; briefs U. S. delegation to conference, 196; instructs WIB on arbitration, pecuniary claims, and Monroe Doctrine, 201, 202, 203, 204; instructs WIB on Panama mission, 239-241, 248, 250, 253, 347; helps shape U. S. Caribbean policy, 278, 305
Hay-Bunau-Varilla Treaty, 239; ratified by Panama, 238; WIB discusses terms of, 249-250, 253-254, 259; advises against Senate amendment of, 249, 250-251; urges speedy ratification of, 249, 250-251, 252
Hay-Herrán Treaty, rejected by Colombia, 238
Heinrich Conried English Opera Company, inaugurates Peavey Grand Opera House, 38-39
Herbert, Hilary H., secretary of the navy, welcomes Spanish guests at Columbian Exposition, 64
Herbert, Victor, and his orchestra, at Pan-American Exposition, 176
Hiawatha, 34

Holman English Opera Company; appears in Sioux City, 25
Honduras, 304; involved in border incidents with neighbors, 285, 321-322; participates in Washington Conference, 307-310; proposes revival of Central American union, 307; joins Central American Court of Justice, 309, 316-319
House of Commons, 75
Hughes, Charles Evans, as vice-president, National Arbitration and Peace Congress, 297
Hungarians, in Buffalo, 143

Incas, 41
Indiana, WIB's youthful experiences in, 13
Indians, in western Ohio, 7; in western Iowa, 22
Ingersoll, Robert, WIB attends lecture of, 16; appears in Sioux City, 32
Inter-American conferences, *see* International Conference of the American States
International Bureau of the American Republics, 3, 192; John Barrett as director general of, 3 and note 2, 352; William E. Curtis as first director of, 62, 130; WIB seeks to invigorate Argentina's involvement in, 130-131, 163, 192-193; enjoys little success in 1890's, 193; prepares agenda for Rio Conference of American States, 281
International Central American Bureau, WIB notified of founding of, 322
International Conference of the American States, First, Washington (1889-1890), 193, 200; its delegates tour country and visit 1889 Corn Palace, 41-42; Argentina opposes Blaine's hopes for, 94; Saenz Peña speaks at, 171
International Conference of American States, Second, Mexico (1901-1902), 182, 192-208, 352; WIB serves as U. S. delegate to, 4, 43, 182, 188, 192-208, 347; Roosevelt briefs U. S. delegation to, 195-196; debates key Hemisphere issues, 200-205; *see* Buchanan, William I., and Hay
International Conference of American States, Third, Rio de Janeiro (1906), 305, 352; WIB serves as chairman, U. S. delegation to, 3, 41, 275, 277, 278-283, 285-293; Root briefs U. S. delegation to, 281-283; Root attends, 286-288; debates key Hemisphere issues, 288-290; *see* Buchanan, William I., and Root
International Conference of the American States, Fourth, Buenos Aires (1910), WIB chairs committee to prepare plans for, 3, 302, 342, 343-344, 352
International Harvester Corporation, 215
International Peace Congress, Thirteenth, WIB addresses, 271
Interoceanic canal, *see* Panama Canal
Intervention, as U. S. treaty right in Panama considered by WIB, 247-248, 259-260
Iolanthe, WIB director of and soloist in, 29
Iowa, in mid-nineteenth century, 22; represented on National Commission for the Columbian Exposition, 44, 48; adopts Corn Palace motif for state building at Columbian, 49, 60; celebrates "Iowa Day," 60
"Iowa day," arranged by WIB at Columbian Exposition, 60
Irish, in Chicago, 47
Irving, Washington, as subject of WIB's readings to Argentine audience, 87

Isthmian canal, *see* Panama Canal
Isthmian Canal Commission, 253
Italy, invests in Argentina, 97; trades with Argentina, 126
Itata, Chile resents incident over, 193

Jackson Park, Chicago, as site for Columbian Exposition, 49-50
Jamestown Tercentennial Exposition, WIB serves as consultant for, 297, 298
Japan, 185
Jaurett, Albert Felix, secures diplomatic assistance in claims case against Venezuela, 329, 332-334; WIB settles claim of, 334, 336
Jefferson, Joseph, engaged by WIB for Sioux City performance, 39
Jenny, William LeBaron, as pioneer in development of skyscraper architecture, 47
Jews, in Buffalo, 143
Jiménez, Alfredo, Costa Rican foreign minister, commends WIB, 5 and note 18
João, Dom, 286
John Deere and Company, endorses WIB's appointment as minister to Argentina, 70
Jones, François S., secretary of legation in Buenos Aires, 103; as chargé d'affaires *ad interim,* 105-106; reports porteño regret at WIB's departure, 106
Journal do Commercio (Rio de Janeiro), 226
J. P. Morgan and Company, 215; floats loans to Panama, 249, 256; and Perkins seek Russian wartime market, 273; utilizes WIB's services in Europe, 342, 343
Juárez Celman, Miguel, president of Argentina, collapse of government under, 114

Keith, Minor C., 317

Keller, Morton, quoted on life insurance business, 214
Kelvin, Lord, English scientist, as friend of Westinghouse, 263, 266
King's Award on Andean boundary, 119
Kingsley, David P., vice-president, NYLIC, 214; and the Argentine case, 219
Klaw, Marc, and Abraham Erlanger, as WIB's booking agents in New York, 39
Knights Templar, Sioux City, enlist WIB's services, 27
Knox, Philander C., secretary of state, 336; Root and WIB consider interview on Central America with, 324; WIB arranges recognition of Venezuela for, 337; authorizes WIB's handling of Venezuela claims case at The Hague, 339-340
Knoxville, Illinois, 118, 150
Kokovsoff, Russian finance minister, WIB confers with, 273

Labor Bureau, Pan-American Exposition, expedites construction, 155-156
Lackawanna Iron and Steel Company, moves from Scranton to western New York, 142
Ladies Corn Palace Decorating Association, Mrs. Buchanan chosen president of, 40-41
Lake Erie, waterway to Piqua from, 8; advantages to Buffalo of, 141
La Plata, Argentina, 119
Larrinaga, Tulio, as U. S. delegate to Rio Conference of American States, 281
Las Casas, Bartolomé de, given salute at Columbian Exposition, 64-65
Latorre, J. J., Chilean minister of foreign affairs, and Andean boundary dispute, 121
Latzina, Dr. Francisco, Argentine

minister of finance, assists visit of U. S. manufacturers, 100
"Laurie," *see* Buchanan, Mrs. William I.
Le Havre, France, as site of Westinghouse plant, 267
Lexington, U. S. S., disarms the Falkland Islands, 93-94
Life insurance business, grows in U. S., 211-214; investigated by N. Y. State's Armstrong Committee, 212, 213; becomes world wide, 213-214; *see* Buchanan, William I., and NYLIC
Limantour, José Ives, Mexican minister of hacienda, WIB consults, 202
Lincoln, Abraham, subject of WIB address in Buenos Aires, 85
Lincoln Parkway gate, Pan-American Exposition, 181
Lisbon, Portugal, 269; WIB visits, 224, 229
Literature, American, as subject of WIB lectures to Argentine audiences, 87-90
Little, Lt. W. McCarty, supervises construction of replicas of Columbus's caravels for Columbian Exposition, 63-64
Liverpool, England, as site of Westinghouse operations, 266; WIB inspects Westinghouse operations, 269
Live Stock, Department of, Columbian Exposition, WIB directs, 51, 53, 54-55, 57, 59, 67
Lodge, Henry Cabot, U. S. senator, speaks on Monroe Doctrine at Pan-American Exposition, 171, 182; defends administration's position on Panama, 241
"The Log of the 'Royston Grange' — England to Buenos Aires," as title of WIB's journal, 1898, 110
London, Buchanans visit parks and historic sites in, 75, 266, 270; WIB revisits in 1898, 109-110; in 1902, 222-224; WIB takes up Westinghouse duties in, 255, 260, 265-266; visits for, NYLIC, 1908 and 1909, 321, 342, 343
Loomis, Francis P., assistant secretary of state, advises WIB on Panamanian constitution, 247-248
Lorena Ferreira, Luis R. de, Brazilian minister to Venezuela, represents U. S. interests in Caracas, 327-328, 331, 335
Louisiana Purchase Exposition, St. Louis, WIB engaged as consultant to, 190-191; WIB consults with promoters of, 197, 207, 208, 209, 222, 232, 236, 268; Mexico Conference endorses plans for, 205; WIB tours European capitals on behalf of, 222-223, 224, 232
Low, Seth, mayor of New York City, 297

McCall, John A., president, NYLIC, 214; and the Argentine case, 219
McCormick, Cyrus H., pays tribute to WIB, 61; supports his appointment as minister to Argentina, 70; commends his belief in Pan Americanism, 71
Maceio, Brazil, Buchanans sail to, 76
MacIver, Enrique, Chilean commissioner to settle Puna de Atacama boundary dispute, 123
McKim, Meade & White, awarded contract for agriculture building at Columbian Exposition, 52
McKinley, William, 192; retains WIB as minister to Argentina, 4, 106, 107, 108; appoints WIB delegate to Mexico Conference of American States, 4, 194, 347; and tariff controversy with Argentina, 96, 98, 101, 102, 103-105; calls for war against Spain, 107; advises Congress of WIB's selection as media-

tor of Puna de Atacama boundary dispute, 123; submits Argentine commercial treaty to Senate, 128; mentions Page claim in annual message, 134; WIB as last Democratic appointee to serve as chief of mission for, 136; as consultant to WIB on Pan-American Exposition appointment, 136, 139, 147, 148; and election of 1896, 142; takes personal interest in Pan-American Exposition, 144, 145, 146, 180; sends greetings for Dedication Day, 171; receives repeated invitations to attend, 178-179; WIB and Cortelyou arrange security for, 180; at the exposition, 180-185; addresses crowd on foreign policy, 182-183; visits Niagara Falls, 184; assassination and death of, 185-187; WIB's loyalty and responsibility toward, 186; seeks to rejuvenate inter-American movement, 194; and U.S. commercial expansionism, 352

McKinley, William, Mrs., 178, 179, 180, 181, 182, 183, 184, 185

McKinley administration, *see* McKinley, William

McKinley Tariff Act, creates problems for WIB in Argentina, 96-98

McLaughlin, Reverend W. P., pastor, Methodist Episcopal Church in Buenos Aires, assists Buchanans' orientation, 84-85; sponsors WIB's addresses, 85

MacMonnies, Frederick, designs fountain for Columbian Exposition, 54

Madrid, WIB visits, 224, 311-312

Magoon, Charles E., provisional governor of Cuba, 295, 320

Maine, U. S. S., its explosion affects WIB's plans, 106-107; changes date for opening Pan-American Exposition, 145; despatched to Venezuelan waters, 330

Manchester, England, as site of British Westinghouse plant, 264; WIB inspects Westinghouse operations in, 269

Marietta, Ohio, 8

Marietta, U. S. S., conveys WIB from Guantánamo to Washington, 336

Marine Health Office, Panama, 253

Marines, United States, its band invited to attend McKinley at Pan-American Exposition, 179, 183; landed in Cuba, 1906, 295

Mariscal, Ignacio, Mexican foreign minister, 197, 199, 306, 315, 318

Martínez Silva, Carlos, Colombian delegate to Washington Conference of the American States, speaks at 1889 Corn Palace celebration, 42

Maumee River, and Ohio's canal system, 8

Mauretania, conveys WIB to Europe, 343

Maximilian, Emperor, 198

Maya Indians, 304

Mayers, Charles R., involves WIB in Venezuelan loan project, 233-235

Medical Bureau, Pan-American Exposition, created at WIB's behest, 155; McKinley attended at hospital of, 185

Mendoza, Argentina, WIB travels in presidential car to, 119

Mersey River, England, WIB reports on Westinghouse railway under, 270

Mesabi Range, contributes to Buffalo's growth, 142

Methodist Episcopal Church, Sioux City, assisted by Mrs. Buchanan, 27; in Buenos Aires, 81

Mexico, Argentina ignores inter-American plans of, 94; Curtis promotes Pan-American Exposition in, 147; sends Artillery Band to exposition, 167, 176; its ambassador to Washington visits exposition, 185; hosts Conference of American States, 1901, 192, 194-209; plays key role in debate on arbitration, 202-203; cooperates with U. S. on Central American problems, 285, 305-306, 310, 313-315, 317-320

Mexico City, 245; Díaz modernizes, 198; as seat of Second Conference of American States, 198-199; WIB revisits, 314-315, 319-320, 321-322; fulfills NYLIC mission to, 340

Mexico Conference of the American States (1901-1902), *see* International Conference of the American States, Second, Mexico

Miami County, Ohio, early settlement of Buchanan clan in, 7-13; birth and youth of WIB in, 7-13

Miami Indians in Miami County, Ohio, 7

Michael, Colonel William H., provides State Department aid to WIB, 166

Midway, at Columbian Exposition, 54; at Pan-American Exposition, 154, 176

Midway Plaisance, as part of Columbian Exposition grounds, 50, 54

Milan Grand Opera Company, presents *Faust* in Sioux City, 32

Milburn, John G., president, Pan-American Exposition Company, 146, 147, 171, 174; McKinleys entertained at home of, 181, 182, 184, 185, 186; introduces McKinley at exposition, 183; joins Cortelyou and WIB in vigil for McKinley, 185; WIB renegotiates salary with, 185; suggested by WIB for NYLIC trustee, 276

Miller Brothers, tobacco firm, employs WIB as traveling salesman, 13-20

Missouri River, as Iowa's western boundary, 22-23

Mitcherlich, E. T., Russian judge of awards, Columbian Exposition, commends WIB and Russo-American relations, 61

Mitre, Bartolomé, president of Argentina, quoted by WIB, 85; death of, 293

Mondamin, as deity of Corn Palace celebrations, 34, 44

Monroe Doctrine, 330; Cleveland evokes in 1895, 115; Argentines claim U. S. violation of, 116-117; eulogized at Pan-American Exposition, 171; discussion of forestalled by WIB at Mexico Conference of American States, 204; Roosevelt administration debates infringement of, 233; clashes with Argentina's Drago Doctrine, 282, 289-290

Monroe Palace, in Rio de Janeiro, 284, 285, 287

Montague, Andrew J., as U. S. delegate to Rio Conference of American States, 281, 287

Montevideo, Uruguay, Buchanans sail to, 76; WIB visits, 119

Moore, John Bassett, 339-340

Morla Vicuña, Carlos, Chilean minister to Washington, dies in Buffalo, 177-178; WIB represents State Department at memorial services for, 178

Morris, Robert C., 339

Morton, J. Sterling, secretary of agriculture, engaged by WIB as speaker for Columbian Exposition, 59

Morton, Levi, U. S. vice-president, seeks State Department aid on behalf of bondholders' claims against

Argentina, 134-135
Morton, Rose & Company, WIB gives assistance to its claims against Argentine government, 134-135
Mt. Aconcagua, WIB travels to, 83-84
Mutual Life Insurance Company of New York, 212

Nabuco, Joaquim, Brazilian ambassador to U. S., as author of Brazilian-American friendship, 284-285; as president, Rio Conference of American States, 285-286, 287, 291-292
La Nación (Buenos Aires), shifts attitude on U. S. intervention in Cuba, 116; comments on Puna de Atacama boundary settlement, 124
Nast, Thomas, lectures in Sioux City, 32
National Arbitration and Peace Congress, WIB as member of committee for, 297
National Association of Manufacturers, sends committee to visit Argentina, 100-101
National Commission for World's Columbian Exposition, President Harrison appoints WIB as Iowa representative on, 44, 45, 48; WIB shares in planning sessions of, 49-50; reorganizes its functions and jurisdiction, 50; WIB resigns from, 51
National Grange, WIB seeks its participation in Columbian Exposition, 51, 52
National Palace, Mexico City, 197, 198
National Railway Board of Commissioners, Buenos Aires, 82
Natural Bridge, Virginia, birthplace of George Buchanan, 8

Nebraska, as hinterland of Sioux City, 24, 27
Netherlands, presses Venezuela for satisfaction of claims, 327, 330
Nevins, Allan, quoted on life insurance business, 214
Newcastle-upon-Tyne, England, as site of Westinghouse installations, 267
New Jersey State Agricultural Society, presents WIB lecture on benefits of Columbian Exposition, 67-68
New Jersey State Board of Agriculture, endorses WIB's appointment as minister to Argentina, 70
New West, as region of WIB's crockery selling, 20
New York and Bermúdez Asphalt Company, secures diplomatic assistance in claims case against Venezuela, 329, 332-334; WIB mediates and settles case for, 334-335, 336, 337, 338
New York Commissioner of Insurance, 223
New York Life Insurance Company (NYLIC), engages WIB's services, 5, 134-136, 191, 192, 210, 256, 268, 297, 347, 352; WIB exerts "good offices" for, in Argentina, 135-136, 215-222; WIB plans trip to Brazil for, 208, 222-223; becomes largest U. S. life insurance company, 211-213; destroys records of foreign agencies, 211; administration of, 214-215; uses WIB and other State Department officials to aid overseas operations, 135-136, 215-221, 310-311; seeks to reenter Brazilian market, 223-232; involved in loan project for Venezuela, 233-235; WIB gathers wartime intelligence in Russia for, 272-274; WIB makes final trips to Europe and Mexico for, 340-345;

see Buchanan, William I., and Perkins, George A.

New York Regiment Band, 71st, performs at 1888 Corn Palace celebration, 40

New York State, *see* New York State Government

New York State Government, and Pan-American Exposition, 145, 158 and note 77, 164, 175, 184

New York Times, features special edition on Pan-American Exposition, 154

Niagara Falls, provides hydroelectric power for Buffalo, 142, 152; McKinleys and other exposition guests visit, 184

Niagara Frontier, as region of Buffalo's influence, 141, 144

Niagara River, as setting for world exposition, 144, 146

Nicaragua, 304; WIB favors canal route through, 239; participates in Washington Conference, 307-310; favors revival of Central American union, 307; joins Central American Court of Justice, 309, 316-319; involved in border incidents with neighbors, 321

North Carolina, U. S. S., conveys WIB to Venezuela, 328

Northwest Lumberman, characterizes "Farmer Buchanan," 55

Obaldía, J. Domingo de, Panamanian minister to Washington, discusses Colombian relations with WIB, 296

Ohio, western, and early settlement of Buchanan clan, 7-13

Ohio River, George Buchanan crosses, 8

Old West, as region of WIB's tobacco selling, 14-16, 20

Olmsted, Frederick Law, as landscape artist for Columbian Exposition, 49; for Buffalo park near Pan-American, 147 and note 34

Olney, Richard, U. S. secretary of state, 99-100; and the Page claim against Argentina, 134; arouses Latin American resentment over statement on Venezuelan boundary dispute, 193

Oporto, Portugal, Buchanans sail to, 76

Order of the Bust of Bolívar, conferred upon WIB by Venezuela, 339

Organization of American States, 41; *see* International Bureau of the American Republics

Orinoco Corporation, secures diplomatic assistance in claims case against Venezuela, 329, 332-334; agrees to arbitration of its case, 334; WIB arranges prearbitration settlement of case of, 336, 341-342

Orinoco River, 329

Orinoco Steamship Company, secures diplomatic assistance in claims case against Venezuela, 329, 332-334; agrees to arbitration of case, 334; WIB named as agent to handle its case before the Hague Tribunal, 339-341, 342 and note 69, 343, 345 and note 79

Ottawa Indians in Miami County, Ohio, 7

Oxford and Cambridge Club, London, WIB dines with lord mayor at, 75

Pabst Brewing Company, endorses WIB's appointment as minister to Argentina, 70

Page, Thomas Jefferson, his claims against Argentina resolved by WIB, 133-134

Page, Thomas Nelson, assists claims of T. J. Page against Argentina, 134

"Palace of Peace," dedicated at Second Hague Peace Conference, 301-302

Palmer, Potter, endorses WIB's appointment as minister to Argentina, 70

Palmer, Thomas W., president, World's Columbian Exposition board, welcomes replicas of Columbus's caravels to Chicago, 64; pays tribute to Spanish Indian policy and Bartolomé de las Casas, 64-65

Pampas, as Argentina's heartland, 74, 82; WIB visits, 124

Panama, WIB consults with leaders on constitutional and international problems of, 3, 244-251, 259, 269, 271, 296, 337; sent as first minister to, 4, 237, 238-242, 280; seeks to protect U. S. canal-building rights in, 244, 246-248, 250, 259; considers questions of public health and sanitation in, 251-252; negotiates with English bondholders on behalf of, 256-257

Panama, Isthmus of, see Panama Canal

Panama Canal, WIB advocates construction of, 165, 182, 205, 239; observes developing U. S. policy toward, 238; accepts mission to safeguard U. S. interests in, 244, 246-248, 250, 259, 347; security of, 305, 306, 323-324, 326; WIB, Creel, and Central American judges examine construction of, 316

Panama Congress, 94

Panama Railroad Company, 242

The Pan-American (Buffalo), promotes Pan American idea, 145

Pan American Committee, created by Root for Rio Conference follow-up, 302; Root appoints WIB to, 302; WIB assists its planning for Buenos Aires Conference of American States, 342, 343-344, 352

Pan American conferences, see International Conferences of the American States

Pan-American Exposition, 211, 222, 262, 264, 303; WIB selected as director general of, 4, 136, 138-139, 146-148, 347; genesis of, 144-145; adopts Pan American theme, 144, 145, 146, 149, 161, 162, 167-168; Buffalo promoters form company to produce, 144-146; promotional activities for, 149, 153, 159-160, 172-175; construction of, 151, 155, 158, 161-162, 168-169; features artistic and educational aspects, 152-154, 168, 175-176; offers diversified program, 154, 160-161, 175-177; plans security measures, 155, 180; copes with labor problems, 155-156, 158; attracts state and national conventions, 156, 173-175; encounters problems and crises, 157-159, 165-167, 350; handicapped by foul weather, 161, 169-170, 172, 175; deals with housing problems, 162; dedication and opening days of, 170-172; entertains distinguished guests, 171-172, 177-178; celebrates special "days," 173-174; features two-day visit of McKinleys, 179-184; shocked by McKinley's assassination and death, 184-187; closes gates, 188; WIB appraises benefits of, 189-190; see Buchanan, William I., and Pan-American Exposition Company

Pan-American Exposition Company, organized, 145-148; engages WIB as director general, 148; encounters financing problems, 151, 152, 158-159, 162, 172, 175, 187, 189;

sets opening date, 161, 170; invites foreign countries and distinguished guests, 166-167; emphasizes Pan American theme, 167-169; Dedication Day planned by, 170-171; WIB shares details with officers of, 177; extends repeated invitations to McKinley, 178-180; makes special plans for McKinley visit, 180; and the McKinley assassination, 185-187; WIB's final report and recommendations to, 189-190, 210; pays tribute to WIB, 345; *see* Buchanan, William I., and Pan-American Exposition

The Pan-American Herald, scores Buffalo apathy toward Pan-American Exposition, 157; promotes Buffalo for inter-American conference, 194

Pan Americanism, WIB revives Argentine interest in, 130-131; Buffalo's interest in theme of, 144, 145, 146, 161, 162, 164, 167, 175, 190, 192, 353; WIB relates goals of Pan-American Exposition to, 161, 162, 163-165; WIB explains his views of, 163-165; exemplified by WIB at Mexico Conference of American States, 192-210; at Rio Conference of American States, 280, 290, 292, 293; reflected in Pan American Committee, 312-313; expressed by Creel, 318; expressed in Root's Latin American policy, 278, 280, 300-301, 326, 337-338

Pan American Medical Congress, WIB recommends Panama City for meeting of, 251-252

Pan American Railway, 195, 290

Pan American Railway Committee, WIB appointed member of, 290

Pan American Union, 41; *see* International Bureau of the American Republics

Paraguay, Buchanans visit, 83; as buffer state between Argentina and Brazil, 93

Paraná, Argentina, 83

Paris, WIB enjoys parks and historic sights in, 266, 270; visits for Westinghouse, 267, 268, 269, 270; visits for NYLIC, 1908 and 1909, 321, 342, 343

Paris Exposition of 1889, compared with Columbian Exposition, 54

Park, Dr. Roswell, medical director, Pan-American Exposition, attends President McKinley, 186

Paseo de la Reforma, Mexico City, 198

Patagonia, 74; WIB visits, 83, 124

Peace and Amity, General Treaty of, Central American, signed at Washington Conference, 308

Pearson, Henry W., British superintendent of agriculture, chairs banquet to honor WIB at Columbian Exposition, 61

Peavey Grand Opera House, WIB as first manager of, 38-40; as important stopover for road companies, 39; as Sioux City's principal assembly hall, 40; WIB concludes services for, 48, 53

Pecuniary claims, as agenda item at Mexico Conference of American States, 196; conference endorses convention on, 203-204; at Rio Conference of American States, 281, 282, 289

"Peerless Princess of the Plains," Sioux Cityans' catchword for their city, 23, 140

Pellegrini, Carlos, president of Argentina, death of, 293

Pennsylvania Railroad, provides tour for delegates to International Conference of American States, 1889, 41

Pepper, Charles M., appointed U. S. delegate to Mexico Conference of American States, 195
Perkins, George A., vice-president, NYLIC, as WIB's respondent and counsellor, 214-215, 221, 351; and NYLIC's Argentine case, 221-222; and NYLIC's Brazilian program, 228-229, 231; and WIB's Venezuelan loan project, 233-235; and WIB's financial proposals for Panama, 256; WIB collects intelligence on wartime Russia for, 272-274; resigns NYLIC vice-presidency, 275-276; WIB retains confidence in, 276; assists Roosevelt's 1912 presidential campaign, 276; see New York Life Insurance Company
Permanent Court of Arbitration, 301-302; see Hague Tribunal
Pernambuco (Recife), Brazil, Buchanans sail to, 76
Peru, 185, 251; Argentina ignores inter-American plans of, 94; Pan-American Exposition promoted in, 147; prefers league of Spanish-American states, 193; seeks return of Tacna and Arica at Mexico Conference of American States, 201; supports obligatory arbitration at Mexico Conference, 201, 202
Philadelphia's Centennial Exposition, WIB visits, 19; compared with Columbian Exposition, 53, 54; compared with Pan-American, 169
Philippine Islands, 165; WIB views U. S. policy toward, 117
Pinchot, Gifford, commended by WIB, 68
Piqua, Ohio, and headquarters of Gen. William Henry Harrison in War of 1812, 8; early development of, 8-9

The Pirates of Penzance, 16; WIB directs and performs in, 29
Pires Brandão, Dr. José, NYLIC attorney in Rio de Janeiro, assists WIB's NYLIC case, 226
Pitkin, John R. G., U. S. minister to Argentina, presses Argentina for trade treaty, 96-97
Pittsburgh, 264, 269
Platt Amendment, 190, 239, 278; and security of Panama Canal, 305
Poinsett, Joel Roberts, first American diplomat to Argentina, 75
Poles, in Buffalo and Chicago, 143
Políticos emigrados, as factor in Central American unrest, 304, 321, 322
Polk, Van Leer, as U. S. delegate to Rio Conference of American States, 281
Porteños, residents of Buenos Aires, Argentina, 75
La Prensa (Buenos Aires), comments on WIB's travels in Argentina, 82; shifts attitude on U. S. intervention in Cuba, 116; reports porteño farewell to WIB, 136-137
Presidential campaigns and elections: 1880, 16-17; 1892, 58; 1896, 102; 1912, 276
"President's Day," Pan-American Exposition, 178, 181-184; see McKinley, William
Press Department, Pan-American Exposition, 160
Prisco, Salvatore, III, characterizes John Barrett, 352
Progressive Era, John Barrett as spokesman of, 352
Progressive National Committee, Roosevelt appoints Perkins chairman of Executive Committee of, 276
Propylaea, Pan-American Exposition, designed to symbolize Pan American theme, 169

Providencia Islands, Rafael Reyes proposes U. S. purchase of, 257-258
Prugh, J. K., WIB's brother-in-law, moves from Cincinnati to Sioux City, Iowa, 20; sets up dealership in crockery and glassware, 20; offers position to WIB, 20
Prugh, J. K., Mrs. (Mamie Williams), sister of Mrs. W. I. Buchanan, 20, 32
Prugh, J. K., and Company, WIB accepts position with, 20; WIB's diverse assignments with, 26, 27-28, 40, 44
Public debts, forcible collection of, Roosevelt and U. S. policy on, 282-283; delegates to Rio Conference of American States debate issue of, 289-290; debated at Second Hague Conference, 298, 300
Publicity Bureau, Pan-American Exposition, oversees broad public relations campaign, 149, 153-154, 159-160
Puerto Limón, Costa Rica, welcomes WIB, Creel, and Central American judges, 316-317, 319
Puerto Rico, 278; focuses U. S. attention on Latin America, 145; invited to participate in Pan-American Exposition, 165, 167; annexed by U. S., 239
Puna de Atacama, physical characteristics of, 120; Argentine-Chilean dispute over boundaries of, 119-124; WIB mediates boundary of, 119, 122-124
Puntarenas, Costa Rica, 316

"Queen City of the Lakes," as Buffalonians' catchword for their city, 140, 141, 142, 143, 179

La Rábida, Convent of, Columbian Exposition features replica of, 63

Radicals, popular name for *Unión Cívica Radical* in Argentina, 114
Raigosa, Genaro, president, Mexico International Conference of American States, 202, 207
Railroads, Sioux City enjoys services of, 23, 30; serve the Columbian Exposition, 47, 49; advocated by WIB for Latin America, 165; offer bargain rates to Pan-American Exposition, 173; WIB collects data on Russian system of, 273
Reinsch, Paul S., as U. S. delegate to Rio Conference of American States, 281
"The Republic," Daniel Chester French statue at Columbian Exposition, 54
Republican National Committee, Perkins contributes to presidential campaign of, 275-276
Republican party, and election of 1880, 16-17; WIB schedules Iowa state convention of, 40; and trade negotiations with Argentina, 102, 103, 128, 163; senators support Roosevelt's Panama policy, 241-242
La Revista de Derecho, Historia y Letras (Buenos Aires), reprints WIB's official reports, 138
Reyes, General Rafael, discusses Panama Canal route with WIB, 239; as candidate for president of Colombia, 257; offers to sell Providencia Islands to U. S., 257; considers Colombia's Panamanian problems with WIB, 257-258, 259, 269, 296
Reyes, Nestor and Enrique, Colombian jungle explorers, 290
Richardson, J. J., publisher of *Davenport* (Iowa) *Democrat,* heads drive for WIB's appointment as minister to Argentina, 70
Rio Branco, Baron of, Brazilian for-

eign minister, 285; and Rio Conference of American States, 287, 291

Rio Conference of the American States (1906), *see* International Conference of the American States, Third, Rio de Janeiro

Rio de Janeiro, 223, 224, 225, 227, 228, 265; Buchanans sail to, 1898, 75-76; WIB visits, 1902, 137; WIB fulfills NYLIC mission to, 223-224, 225-227, 228-231; hosts Third Conference of American States, 283-285

Rio de Janeiro, state of, WIB advises NYLIC on bonds of, 230

Río de la Plata, 74; reminds Buchanans of the Missouri, 76-77; Argentina insists on control of, 93; *Water Witch* explores tributaries of, 133

Río Paraná, WIB travels through valley of, 82; Buchanans sail to Paraguay by way of, 83

River Plate, *see* Río de la Plata

Rixey, Dr. P. M., physician to President McKinley, 180, 183, 185

Roca, Julio A., president of Argentina, 194; commends WIB, 5 and note 20; welcomes WIB's return to Buenos Aires, 1898, 111; elected president of Argentina, 113-114; as stabilizing force in Argentine politics, 114; assists WIB's travels, 119; responds to WIB appeal on Morton claim, 135; invited by WIB to Pan-American Exposition, 166, 220; assists WIB's work for NYLIC, 217-221; acknowledges *recuerdos* from WIB, 220

Rodrígues, Dr. Carlos, editor, *Jornal do Commercio* (Rio de Janeiro), assists WIB's NYLIC efforts, 226, 229

Rodrígues Alves, Francisco de Paula, president of Brazil, WIB appeals NYLIC case to, 227

Roosevelt, Theodore, 192; WIB as roving envoy for, 3-5; supports Pan-American Exposition, 145, 168; lauds Monroe Doctrine on Dedication Day, 171-172; reaches Buffalo after McKinley's assassination, 186; confers with WIB on Czolgosz's confession, 186; holds confidential conference with WIB, 187; briefs U. S. delegation to Mexico Conference of American States, 195-196, 201, 203, 207; considers Anglo-German intervention in Venezuela, 233; names WIB minister to Panama, 237, 252, 255, 259, 347; speaks of Perkins to WIB, 276; and 1912 presidential campaign, 276; appoints WIB as chairman of U. S. delegation to Rio Conference of American States, 278; addresses Congress on Rio Conference, 296-297; appoints WIB as U. S. representative to Central American Peace Conference, 302; cooperates with Díaz on Central American problems, 305, 314, 318, 323; appoints WIB as high commissioner to installation Central American Court of Justice, 313; and Venezuelan claims cases, 326, 327-328; lauds Root's Latin American policy, 338; and U. S. commercial expansionism, 352

Roosevelt administration, *see* Roosevelt, Theodore

Roosevelt Corollary to Monroe Doctrine, WIB statement on Cuban intervention seems to anticipate, 117; and U. S. police power in Latin America, 279; and Drago Doctrine at Rio Conference of American States, 289-290; and security of Panama Canal, 305

Root, Elihu, 215; as the "first good neighbor," 3, 279, 280; WIB fulfills special assignments for, 3, 278, 280, 347; commends WIB, 5, 337-338; reaches Buffalo during McKinley crisis, 186; confers with WIB on handling of Czolgosz's confession, 186; instructs WIB on Panama mission, 240, 244, 245, 347, 351; becomes secretary of state, 278; courts Latin American friendship, 279-280, 284-285, 305; instructs U. S. delegation to Rio Conference of American States, 281-283; attends Rio Conference, 286-287; sails round South America, 288, 296; names WIB to conciliate Colombia-Panama stalemate, 296, 351; and Second Hague Conference, 297-301; appoints WIB to assist Latin Americans at Hague Conference, 298, 299, 300, 351; proposes international court, 300; appoints WIB to Pan American Committee, 302, 310, 312, 342; names WIB as U. S. representative to Washington Conference, 1908, 304; cooperates with Mexico on Central American affairs, 305, 314, 322; addresses Washington Conference, 306; assists WIB's NYLIC activities, 311; appoints WIB high commissioner to installation Central American Court of Justice, 313; resigns secretaryship of state, 323, 326; corresponds with WIB on Central American problems, 324; names WIB to settle claims and renew relations with Venezuela, 326, 328-330, 351; exchanges compliments with WIB, 337-338; assists WIB on Argentine relations, 342

Root, John W., as pioneer in development of skyscraper architecture, 47

Rosario, Argentina, 83; Spanish partisans attack U. S. Consulate in, 115-116

Rothschild, Baron, 267

Rowe, Leo S., as U. S. delegate to Rio Conference of American States, 281; assists work of Pan American Committee, 313

Royston Grange, see "the Log of the 'Royston Grange'"

Ruppert, Jacob, advises on brewery exhibits for Columbian Exposition, 52

Rusk, Jeremiah H., secretary of agriculture, invited to 1890 Corn Palace, 44; WIB seeks his assistance for Columbian Exposition, 52

Russell, William W., WIB's sucessor in Panama, WIB prepares letter of instructions for, 253-254

Russia, WIB visits, 1904-1905, 273-274; gathers intelligence on wartime economy of, 273-274

Russo-Japanese War, Perkins authorizes WIB to collect intelligence on Russia during, 272-274

Sacs, expelled beyond the Missouri River, 22

Saenz Peña, Luis, president of Argentina, accepts WIB's letter of credence, 77; expresses admiration for Cleveland and the U. S., 79

Saenz Peña, Roque, speaks at First Conference of the American States, 171; confers with WIB in Paris, 344

The St. Andrew's Society of the River Plate, invites WIB's remarks at annual meetings, 85-87

St. Clair, General, defeated by Indians, 7

Saint-Gaudens, Augustus, consults WIB on Columbian Exposition plans, 52

St. Louis, *see* Louisiana Purchase Exposition
St. Mary's Catholic Church, Sioux City, WIB becomes music consultant for, 27
St. Mary's Episcopal School for Girls, Knoxville, Illinois, attended by Florence Buchanan, 118, 150
St. Petersburg, Russia, 224; Westinghouse interests in, 262
St. Thomas Episcopal Church, Sioux City, presents *The Pirates of Penzance* under WIB's direction, 29
SALIC, *see* Sul América Insurance Company
Salina Cruz, Mexico, 315
El Salvador, 304; involved in border incidents with Central American neighbors, 285, 321; participates in Washington Conference, 307-310; joins Central American Court of Justice, 309, 316-319
Samoan Islands, 165
Sánchez, Joaquín, heads NYLIC's Spanish-American department, 223; affiliates with Sul América Insurance Company (SALIC) in Brazil, 223; resists WIB's NYLIC efforts, 223, 226, 228, 230
San Francisco, WIB recalls earthquake in, 290
San José, Costa Rica, welcomes WIB and guests for installation of Central American Court of Justice, 317-319
San José, Guatemala, 315-316
San Luis, Argentine province of, WIB travels through, 82
San Martín, General José de, WIB eulogizes, 85; recalls military campaigns of, 116
San Salvador island, 242
Santa Fé, Argentina, 83; WIB entertained in, 82-83
Santa Fé, Argentine province of, WIB travels through, 82

Santa María, Pinta, Niña, see Columbus
Santiago del Estero, Argentine province of, WIB travels through, 82
Scandinavians, in Chicago, 47
Scatcherd, John N., chairman, executive committee, Pan-American Exposition Company, 146, 180
Scotch-Irish, migration of, to Ohio, 8
Scotland Home Rule question, Buchanans hear Balfour speak on, 75
Scott, Sir Walter, reaction of WIB to novels of, 13
Senate, U. S., fails to ratify Argentine commercial treaty, 128, 165; ratifies extradition treaty with Argentina, 129; delays ratification of Hay-Bunau-Varilla Treaty, 248-250; consulted by Root on Venezuelan claims, 330
Shaler, Colonel J. R., superintendent, Panama Railroad, recommended by WIB, 253
Shawnee Indians in Miami County, Ohio, 7
Sherman, John, senator from Ohio, welcomes Spanish guests at Columbian Exposition, 64; WIB's relations with, as secretary of state, 103-104, 105, 106, 107
Siouan Indians, expelled from northwestern Iowa, 22
Sioux City, Iowa, 46, 50, 51, 52, 55, 60, 62, 69, 72, 148, 150, 152, 157, 158, 210, 347, 351; as first important settlement in northwestern Iowa, 22; choice location of, 22-23; dubbed "Peerless Princess of the Plains," 23, 140; experiences slow growth at midcentury, 23; designated county seat for Woodbury County, 23; enjoys boom times in 1880's, 23-24, 29-31; as railroad center, 23, 30; population of, 23, 29; ethnic diversity in, 23-24; WIB cites first impressions of,

24-25; as frontier community, 24, 31; Buchanans move to, 26; specializes in wholesaling, meat-packing, and small manufacturing, 30; emphasizes growth of civic and cultural institutions, 30-31; develops public transit system, 30; dubbed "The Corn Palace City of the World," 32; conceives and produces annual Corn Palaces, 32-45; entertains distinguished guests, 36-37, 41-42, 43-44; contributes Corn Palace idea to Columbian Exposition, 49, 53, 60; Buchanans return from Argentina to, 107

The Sioux City Corn Palace Exposition Company, formed to sponsor 1888 Corn Palace, 37

Sioux City Journal, criticizes Oscar Wilde, 25; reviews WIB's productions of Gilbert and Sullivan, 29; quotes Longfellow's *Hiawatha* on Corn Palace celebrations, 34; endorses Pan American idea, 42; lauds WIB's work for Columbian Exposition, 50

Sociedad Rural Argentina, criticizes U. S. wool tariff, 103

Sousa, John Philip, performs at Pan-American Exposition, 154, 176

Southampton, England, Buchanans sail to Argentina via, 75, 76

Southern question, WIB comments on, 17

Spanish-American War, WIB oversees American interests in Argentina during, 95, 107; causes anti-American feeling in Argentina, 107, 115-118, 163; forces postponement of Pan-American Exposition, 145; brings changes in Hemisphere relations, 165

Spanish language, WIB's use of, 6, 80, 84, 87, 91; children's competence in, 80; WIB advocates study of, 165

Spanish Renaissance architectural style, adopted for Pan-American Exposition, 167; viewed by critics, 167-168, 169

"The Spirit of Niagara," Pan-American Exposition posters feature reproductions of painting called, 160

The Standard (Buenos Aires), quoted on WIB, 228

State, Department of, 91, 135, 212, 250, 261, 303, 346, 347; receives letters urging WIB's appointment as minister to Argentina, 70; briefs WIB on Argentina, 72, 78, 92; provides inadequate legation quarters in Buenos Aires, 78; approves WIB's travel plans in Argentina, 83; slowly improves representation in Argentina, 94-95; oversees WIB's tariff negotiations with Argentina, 96-99, 102-105, 125-128; receives WIB's rationalizations of U. S. policy toward Cuba, 116-117; authorizes WIB's mediation of Argentine-Chilean boundary dispute, 121-123, 124; delays exchange of ratifications on extradition treaty with Argentina, 129; assists NYLIC claims against Argentina, 134-135; WIB and Pan-American Exposition make use of his contacts at, 144-145, 159, 166; WIB reports on Argentina to, 147; WIB fulfills mission to Mexico Conference for, 208; assists WIB's NYLIC work in South America, 135, 215-218, 231-232; recognizes Panama, 238, 242, 243; briefs WIB on Rio Conference, 275, 276; introduces WIB to Central America's problems, 303, 306, 310, 322, 323, 324; and Venezuelan claims cases, 335, 336, 339, 340; *see* Hay, John, and Root, Elihu

Statler, E. M., opens his first restaurant, in Buffalo, 144; builds his first hotel (to accommodate 5,000

INDEX 455

guests) near exposition grounds, 162, note 96
Stillwater River, Ohio, site of Fort Buchanan near, 8
Studebaker, J. M., joins visit of U. S. manufacturers to Argentina, 101
Studebaker Brothers, endorse WIB's appointment as minister to Argentina, 70
Suez Canal, compared with Erie, 141
Sul América Insurance Company, resists WIB's NYLIC efforts in Brazil, 223, 226, 228, 230; WIB recommends NYLIC's purchase of, 230
Sullivan, Louis, as pioneer in development of skyscraper architecture, 47
Swift and Company, endorses WIB's appointment as minister to Argentina, 70

Tacna and Arica, Peru seeks return of, 201
Taft, William Howard, as secretary of war, assesses Cuban situation, 295; as vice-president, National Arbitration and Peace Congress, 297; and foreign policy, 336, 339
Tariffs and tariff laws; in Argentine-American relations, 96-99, 101-105, 125-128; McKinley Tariff Act, 96-98; Wilson-Gorman Tariff Act, 98-99; Argentina's, 98-99, 103-104; Dingley Tariff Act, 102-104
Teller, Henry M., senator from Colorado, criticizes WIB's proposal on Colombian debt, 255
Temple of Music, planned as feature of Pan-American Exposition, 154, 168, 176; opening ceremonies in, 171-172; as site of McKinley's assassination, 184, 187
Tesla, Nikola, hails Buffalo's access to Niagara power, 142; engaged by Westinghouse, 262

Theater, WIB's early interest in, 15-16, 19, 25, 28-29, 31
Thompson, D. E., U. S. ambassador to Mexico, advises WIB on Central American mission, 314
Thoreau, Henry, as subject of WIB's readings to Argentine audience, 87
Toledo, Ohio, waterway to Piqua from, 8
Tornquist, Ernesto, discusses Argentine-Brazilian naval rivalry with WIB, 293-294
Trade, Argentine-American, grows slowly in 19th century, 95-96; affected by U. S. wool tariffs, 96, 98, 99, 103; efforts of WIB to improve, 95-105, 125-128
Trafalgar Square, 75
Trans-Siberian Railroad, WIB reports to Perkins and NYLIC on, 273
Treaties: Argentine-American Treaty of 1853, 96, 129; WIB negotiates commercial agreement and extradition convention with Argentina, 125-128, 129-130; WIB recommends conventions with Argentina on protection of copyrights, etc., and on parcel post regulations, 130; WIB and agreements concerning Argentine-Chilean boundary, 119-123; Hague Convention on Pacific Settlement of Disputes, 201-203, 288, 300; WIB and inter-American conventions on arbitration and pecuniary claims, 201-204, 288-289; Colombia rejects Hay-Herrán, 238; WIB and Hay-Bunau-Varilla, 238, 239, 248-249, 260; Central American Treaty of Peace and Amity, 308; convention creating Central American Court of Justice, 308-309
Treaty of 1853, Argentine-American, provides equitable treatment for

U. S. traders, 96; WIB seeks updating of, 129
Trevelyan, George Otto, WIB attends dinner for, 270
La Tribuna (Buenos Aires), quoted on WIB, 227-228
Triumphal Bridge, Pan-American Exposition, 168, 181, 182
Trotter's Creek, site of J. H. Buchanan homestead, 9-12; as playground for WIB, 10, 11
Tucumán, Argentine province of, WIB visits, 82
Turner, C. Y., director for color, Pan-American Exposition, 152 and note 53

Unión Azucarera, criticizes U. S. wool tariff, 103
Unión Cívica Radical, as opposition party in Argentina, 114
Union Switch & Signal Company, 262; *see* Westinghouse, George
United Provinces of Central America, 304
United States, 73, 74; hosts First International Conference of American States, 41; designates Chicago as site of World's Columbian Exposition, 48; authorizes exposition invitation to Spanish notables, 63; authorizes visit of replicas of Columbus's caravels, 63; factors influencing relations of Argentina with, 92-95; assigns unimpressive envoys to Argentina, 94; barriers to Argentine trade with, 95-105; seeks commercial treaty with Argentina, 95-99, 102-105, 112; declares war against Spain, 107; Argentines attack Cuban policy of, 116-117; moves toward world power status, 163, 182; participates in Mexico Conference of American States, 192-210; assists Panama's birth as a nation, 238-254, 259-260; participates in Rio Conference of American States, 278, 280-293; participates in Second Hague Peace Conference, 298-302; cooperates with Mexico on Central American problems, 295, 305-306, 308, 313-315, 317-320; restores diplomatic relations with Venezuela, 326, 329-330, 332, 337; *see* State, Department of, and United States government
United States and Venezuela Company, secures diplomatic assistance in claims case against Venezuela, 329, 332-334; agrees to arbitration of its case, 334; WIB arranges prearbitration settlement of case of, 336, 341-342
United States Government, at Columbian Exposition, 54; at Pan-American Exposition, 145, 158 and note 77, 168, 175, 184; creates executive office in Buffalo after McKinley's assassination, 186; *see* State, Department of, and United States
United States Navy, in Panamanian waters, 245, 250; invited to Venezuelan waters, 328
United States Steel Corporation, 215; and Perkins seek Russian wartime market, 273
Uriburu, José E., president of Argentina, serves as commissioner to settle Puna de Atacama boundary dispute, 123
Uruguay, as buffer state between Argentina and Brazil, 93; WIB promotes Pan-American Exposition in, 147; WIB's NYLIC activities in, 223, 224, 227, 233

Valparaíso, Chile, WIB sponsors condolence resolution over earthquake in, 290

INDEX 457

Vanderbilt, Cornelius, visits 1887 Corn Palace, 36
Velarde, Juan F., Ecuadorian delegate to Washington Conference of the American States, speaks at 1889 Corn Palace celebration, 42
Venezuela, 251, 352; WIB resolves claims against, 4, 326, 341; WIB involved in loan project for, 233-235; and Anglo-German intervention, 279, 287, 289, 300; Roosevelt and Root support pecuniary claims against, 326-330; Gómez replaces Castro as president of, 327; offers warm reception to WIB, 331-332, 335; settles U. S. claims cases, 332-335, 336-339, 341-342
Vera Cruz, Mexico, 205
Viceroyalty of the Río de la Plata, Argentina claims boundaries of, 74
Victoria, Queen, 75, 109
Vigo, Spain, Buchanans sail to, 76

War Department General Staff, consulted by Roosevelt on Venezuelan situation, 330
War of the Pacific, 120
Washington, D. C., compared with Buenos Aires, 81-82
Washington Conference, 1907, see Central American Peace Conference
Washington Conference of the American States (1889-1890), see International Conference of the American States, First, Washington
Washington Times, commends WIB, 5 and note 14
Water Witch, U. S. S., explores Argentine waters, 133
Wayne, General Anthony, and military campaigns in Miami County, Ohio, 7-8
Ways and Means Committee, House of Representatives, and Wilson-Gorman Tariff Act, 98
Western Hemisphere, U. S. ambitions in, 163; WIB describes potentialities and needs of, 164-165
Western Hemisphere idea, WIB explains his understanding of, 164
Westinghouse, George, 351; offers WIB position in Europe, 237, 261, 264-265; as inventor and promoter in U. S. and Europe, 261-264; introduces WIB to his European responsibilities, 264-269, 271; provides technical assistance for WIB's operations in England, 274-275; attends WIB's funeral, 345; see British Westinghouse
Westinghouse, Mrs. George, and *bon voyage* to WIB, 265
Westinghouse Air Brake Company, see Westinghouse Company and Westinghouse, George
Westinghouse Brake Company, Ltd., 262; see Westinghouse, George, and British Westinghouse
Westinghouse Company, 278; WIB offered position with, 237, 240; assumes London duties with, 255, 260, 261, 264-266; see British Westinghouse and Westinghouse, George
"White City," catchword for Chicago's Columbian Exposition, 59, 60, 140, 169
White House, 196, 215; Buchanans call on President Cleveland at, 72; WIB confers with President McKinley and Iowa senators at, 106; Pan-American Exposition promoters send delegations to, 145, 179; advised of presidential change in Venezuela, 327-328; see Cleveland, McKinley, Roosevelt
Wilde, Oscar, enjoys the Iowa countryside, 25; criticized by *Sioux City Journal,* 25; enjoyed

by WIB, 25-26
Wilhelmina, Queen, 301
Williams, George L., treasurer, Pan-American Exposition Company, 146
Williams, John C., secretary, U. S. delegation to Second International Conference of the American States, assists WIB on report of delegation, 208-209
Williams, John Insco, WIB's father-in-law, 14
Williams, Lulu, *see* Buchanan, Mrs. William I.
Williams, Mamie, *see* Prugh, Mrs. J. K.
Williams, Mrs. John Insco, WIB's mother-in-law, 14
Wilson, Henry R., U. S. minister to Chile, corresponds with WIB on Puna de Atacama boundary dispute, 121-122, 124
Wilson, Huntington, assistant secretary of state, names WIB as U. S. agent to present Venezuelan claims case at The Hague, 339-340
Wilson-Gorman Tariff Act, WIB seeks Argentine treaty under, 98-102
Windsor Castle, 75, 109
Winifreda, conveys WIB to England, 1898, 108
"The Wire Treaty," U. S. diplomats assist in negotiation of, 119-120
Witte, Sergei, Russian finance minister, Perkins and NYLIC arrange bond deals with, 272-273
Wood, Governor General Leonard, approached by WIB on Cuban participation in Pan-American Exposition, 167
Woodbury County, Iowa, Sioux City designated county seat of, 23
Woodford, Stewart L., U. S. minister to Spain, criticized by WIB, 108

Woodruff, Timothy L., lieutenant governor of New York, 171
Wool, as factor in Argentine-American relations, 93, 96-97, 98-103, 126-128; Argentine pressure groups attack tariffs on, 103
Wordsworth, conveys WIB Buenos Aires to New York, 137
World's Columbian Exposition, 262, 264, 280, 303; WIB as department chief of, 4, 163; WIB appointed as Iowa representative on National Commission for, 44; Washington gives official approval to, 48; Congress creates National Commission for, 48-51; clarifies its administrative organization, 50-51; WIB's activities and responsibilities for, 48-53, 54-57, 59-62, 66-67, 347, 349, 350; offers diversified program, 58-59; stimulates WIB to recommendations for future expositions, 67, 138, 146
Writers, favored by WIB for personal reading, 13, 15, 21, 87-90, 110, 343
Wyandot Indians in Miami County, Ohio, 7

Yucatán, conveys Buchanans to Panama, 242

Zeballos, Estanislao S., Argentine minister to Washington, entertains Buchanans in Washington, 72; as foreign minister, refuses to sign commercial treaty with U. S., 96-97; as minister, confers with Secretary Gresham in Washington, 97, 98, 99; reprints WIB's articles, 138; WIB renews friendship with, 228
Zelaya, José, dictator of Nicaragua, 324
Zemstvo Congress (Nov., 1904), 274
Zócalo, Mexico City, 197